N INDOLOGY

MOTILAL BANARSIDASS PUBLISHERS
DELHI

2003

ANARSIDASS

SHERS

BUDDHACARITA

AŚVAGHOṢA'S

BUDDHACARITA

or Acts of the Buddha

Complete Sanskrit Text with English Translation

Cantos I to XIV translated from the Original Sanskrit supplemented by the Tibetan Version together with an introduction and notes by

E.H. JOHNSTON

Part I	:	Sanskrit Text, Sargas I-XIV, pp. i-xxii+1-165
Part II	:	English Translation, Cantos I - XIV, pp. i - xcviii + 1- 232
Part III	:	English Translation of Cantos XV-XXVIII from Tibetan and Chinese Versions, pp. 1-130

MOTILAL BANARSIDASS PUBLISHERS
PRIVATE LIMITED • DELHI

First Published: Lahore, 1936
Reprint: Delhi, 1972, 1978
New Enlarged Edition: Delhi, 1984
Reprint: Delhi, 1992, 1995, 1998, 2004

ISBN: 81-208-1029-5 (Cloth)
ISBN: 81-208-1279-4 (Paper)

Also available at:
MOTILAL BANARSIDASS
41 U.A. Bungalow Road, Jawahar Nagar, Delhi 110 007
8 Mahalaxmi Chamber, 22 Bhulabhai Desai Road, Mumbai 400 026
236, 9th Main III Block, Jayanagar, Bangalore 560 011
120 Royapettah High Road, Mylapore, Chennai 600 004
Sanas Plaza, 1302 Baji Rao Road, Pune 411 002
8 Camac Street, Kolkata 700 017
Ashok Rajpath, Patna 800 004
Chowk, Varanasi 221 001

Printed in India
BY JAINENDRA PRAKASH JAIN AT SHRI JAINENDRA PRESS,
A-45 NARAINA, PHASE-I, NEW DELHI 110 028
AND PUBLISHED BY NARENDRA PRAKASH JAIN FOR
MOTILAL BANARSIDASS PUBLISHERS PRIVATE LIMITED,
BUNGALOW ROAD, DELHI 110 007

THE BUDDHACARITA:

Or,

ACTS OF THE BUDDHA

PART I—Sanskrit Text

NIRVĀṆA : the passing of the sage.

Enlightenment has come : after the pain
Of countless births endured throughout the lapse
Of immemorial time, I have at length
Crossed to the farther shore of mundane life.
Henceforth sorrow and joy touch me no more,
Now love and hate are meaningless to me :
My mind is tranquil like the forest pool
Unruffled by the breeze. The potter's wheel,
After the bowl is made, revolves awhile
Without effect ; so for a space have I
Lived on, freed from the grip of Karma's bonds.
For me the fruit of former deeds has ceased
To ripen, nor can the acts now done by me
Produce new fruit. The goal, for many an age
So infinitely far, is reached at last.
Slowly the gathering shades of night descend
Upon mine eyes. The vital flame burns low
And flickers out as I begin to sink
Into the limitless eternal void,
Enwrapped for ever in forgetfulness.

A. A. M.

SANCHI,
At sunset,
March 21, 1908.

PREFACE.

Over forty years have passed since the late Professor E. B. Cowell brought out the *editio princeps* of Aśvaghoṣa's *Buddhacarita*, followed by a translation in volume XLVI of the *Sacred Books of the East.* Though scholars in Europe were quick to accord it a high place among Sanskrit *kāvya* works and to appreciate the excellence of the editing, they did not fail to see that the materials from which the text was prepared were extremely faulty, and that much correction would be required to bring the poem approximately to the state in which it left its author's hands. Accordingly at the suggestion of the veteran von Böhtlingk, who himself led the way with a list of amendments, many of which undoubtedly hit the mark, a number of scholars set to work on improving the text by conjecture. The process has continued to the present time, but, though the alterations put forward were in general distinguished by knowledge and acumen, there is no such thing as a certain conjecture, and, if in the easier passages the right alternative was often found, no measure of agreement was possible in the more substantial difficulties. A new edition, talked of more than once, has however never appeared, presumably because a text, whose differences from that of Professor Cowell would be merely subjective, must necessarily be of too speculative a character to have real value. Of recent years the position has changed. Early in the century a MS., much older than those used for the first edition but covering only the same portion of the text, was acquired by the Nepal Durbar and described by MM. H. P. Sastri in *JASB*, 1909, 47. Since the beginning of the century the use of Tibetan translations for the correction of faulty Sanskrit originals has also come to be much better understood, and lately the translation of the *Buddhacarita* has been made accessible to students in an edition by Dr. Friedrich Weller, constant use of which has convinced me of the high standard of excellence it attains. Further the Chinese translations have now been made easier to consult for those who are not Chinese scholars by the appearance of the Taishō Issaikyō edition. And finally the publication of many Buddhist texts and of Sanskrit works, not far removed in date from Aśvaghoṣa, not to speak of a long and important work by the poet himself, the *Saundarananda*, has provided us with further means for the critical examination of his language and ideas.

The availability of so much fresh material makes a new edition both possible and highly desirable, but its very mass has as a consequence that much time and labour must be devoted to its collection and sifting, so that it is now more than ten years since, at the suggestion of the late Professor A. A. Macdonell, the present editor set his hand to the task. While well aware of the many respects in which my attainments fall short of those of the ideal editor of the *Buddhacarita*, I have endeavoured to cover the ground, both by reading with one eye on Aśvaghoṣa's works everything published in Sanskrit or Pali that might throw any light on obscure passages and by acquiring that smattering of Tibetan and Chinese which is requisite for comparing the translations in those languages with the Sanskrit original. The fruit of this labour I now present to Orientalists, with the earnest hope that they may find, not finality it is true, but at least a substantial advance in the restitution and interpretation of the extant fragments of a famous poem.

This edition consists of two volumes; the first contains the Sanskrit text and the apparatus criticus, and the second the translation of the first fourteen cantos, filling up the lacunæ in the Sanskrit from the Tibetan, together with an introduction dealing with various aspects of the poet's works, with notes which discuss the many difficulties of text and translation, and with an index. The arrangement is such that with the two volumes open before him at the same point the reader can see at a glance what help I can give him.

The chief authority for the text is the old MS. in the Kathmandu Library, which I call A. It was sent over to England by the Nepal Durbar in 1924 at the request of the late

Professor Macdonell to be rotographed and the reproduction, unfortunately far from perfect, belongs to the Trustees of the Max Müller Fund and is described in Mr. Gambier Parry's catalogue of the collection. The MS. consisted originally of 55 palm leaves, of which numbers one, three, seven, and eight are no longer in existence, covering verses i, 1 to 8*b*, i, 24*d* to 40*c*, and ii, 1 to 35. It ends abruptly in the middle of the second line of leaf 55*b* at verse xiv, 31, of this edition, and has no colophon, repeating simply the last line of the last verse in a late Newari hand. The handwriting is an early form of Bengali, having the Bengali *pa* and tending to write *ga* and *śa* in accordance with that alphabet. To judge from the dated MSS. in the Cambridge University Library, particularly Addl. MSS. no. 1699 of 1199 A.D. and 1364 of 1446 A.D., the margin of error should not exceed 50 years on one side or the other, if the date of 1300 A.D. is assigned to it. While the handwriting is good, mistakes abound and a number of passages are so rubbed as to be barely legible. Palæographically it is important to note that *ba* and *va* are written alike, though distinguished by me for clearness' sake in the variants, and that as the second members of compound characters these two letters are indistinguishable from *dha*, that *ca* and *va* are often so much alike that the reading can only be settled by examining the pen strokes under a magnifying glass (the loop of *ca* is written with two strokes, of *va* with one), that *ra* often resembles *ca* and *va*, that *rṇṇa* and *lla* are practically identical in shape, that *rtha*, *vva* and *cca* are liable to confusion, and that *ta* and *bha*, *tu* and *tta*, *sa* and *ma*, *pa* and *ya*, *su* and *sva*, are hard to separate. Occasionally *ṣa* and *ya* are much alike. In countless places I suspected *anusvāra* of having been added by a later hand,[1] and *avagraha* is inserted 20 times in all, at times marking not an elision but the fusion of *ā* and *ă*. The collation of the MS. therefore demanded unusual care to determine with precision the intention of the copyist.

[1] On the leaves which have been cleaned, as mentioned below, it is probable that many *anusvāras* were omitted in reinking and added later.

The relationship of A to the three MSS. used by Cowell is easily deduced. For subject to the loss of leaves 7 and 8 in A and to its containing two passages in cantos ix and xii which are missing in the *editio princeps*, it gives all the verses in Cowell's MSS. which are shown by the Chinese and Tibetan translations to be either part of the original or old interpolations and it ends at the same point, xiv. 31 here, xiv. 32 in Cowell's edition. The three MSS. used by the latter constantly repeat A's minor errors and are almost invariably faulty where A is corrupt or difficult to read. Finally four lines of A's leaf 37 are eaten away at one end and the gaps in it (ix. 26 to 37) coincide exactly with the hiatuses in Cowell's MSS. at this point. Evidently therefore the three modern MSS. in Europe descend from A. Greater precision is however possible. For these MSS. give the text as copied out by Amṛtānanda, the Residency pandit in Hodgson's days, with the additions he made, and were clearly taken from his transcript of A.[1] For instance, certain letters in i. 15*b*, and i. 83*d*, are so rubbed as to be almost illegible; the solution I finally arrived at after prolonged scrutiny proved on comparison with the Tibetan to be correct, but Cowell's MSS. all agree in the same misreadings, so that they must have been made from one and the same copy of A. It was in fact treated in a peculiar way by the pandit. The earlier leaves are all much rubbed and often hard to read, and the margins are covered with trivial glosses in a late hand. For the first canto and apparently for leaves 7 and 8 in the second canto Amṛtānanda filled up the lacunæ with his own words and guessed at the readings where he had not the patience to decipher them. Once at least he altered a word he did not understand, *avāpya* in i. 56*b*, to *apāsya*. He did not continue this process throughout, but was content later on to leave gaps for illegible or torn places, giving the reading he understood the MS. to have. Leaf 55 is torn at one

---

[1] Another copy of his transcript exists in Tokyo; see the frontispiece to T. Kimura and T. Byōdō's *Butsden bungaku no kenkyo*.

end, so as to lose one or two characters in each line, but apparently it was intact in his time, as the Tibetan shows that the letters now missing were correctly supplied in his copies. In one much rubbed passage, ix. 17*d*, I found it quite impossible to fix A's reading, but to my surprise Cowell's text corresponded exactly to the Tibetan. It seems that Amṛtānanda wetted the leaf in order to read it and, though he succeeded in this, he so spoilt the characters as to make them illegible for his successors. I have mentioned that the earlier leaves are much rubbed and covered with marginal glosses, but from the verso of leaf 9 onwards the majority of leaves are extraordinarily clean and clear, showing in places very faint traces of marginal glosses; such leaves usually have also a number of minor errors which do not occur in Cowell's MSS., as may be seen by comparing the variants for iii. 6–60, on the clean leaves 10, 11, 12, and 13*a*, as against verses 61–65 on 13*b*, which is in its original state and much rubbed. I infer that, after Amṛtānanda had made his transcript with additions and alterations of his own, many of the leaves were cleaned and reinked, a process which would naturally lead to mistakes and which may perhaps have been responsible for the loss of leaves 7 and 8. This would also account for a fact which puzzled me not a little, the remarkable fluctuations in the forms of certain letters, notably *ga*, *la*, *ha*, and *pha*, the alternative shapes often appearing on the same page, so that the hypothesis of several copyists having been at work or of dilapidated leaves having been replaced by new ones did not afford an adequate explanation. The loss of the marginal glosses on the leaves so treated is of small account, but, to judge from the later copies, we have also lost a few marginal corrections, supplying omitted characters or correcting wrong ones. While the general procedure is clear to me, I cannot determine in all cases whether reinking has taken place or not, but it is typical of the vicissitudes the MS. has been through that the numbering of the cantos should be in far more modern figures than that of the pages. Enough at least has been said to show how fortunate it is that A has been recovered and that, in view of its existence, Cowell's MSS. have no subsisting value for settling the text except for verses ii. 1–35, where A is now wanting, and occasionally perhaps for those cases where it has been wrongly reinked.

Next in importance comes the Tibetan translation, here styled T. My transcript was prepared from the India Office copy, but scholars now have available Dr. Weller's admirable edition, which has progressed to the end of the seventeenth canto, that is, beyond the point where A and this edition stop. For a few troublesome passages I have consulted the Peking edition in the Bibliothèque Nationale, not used by Dr. Weller, and which sometimes has better readings. As a rule I would accept Dr. Weller's text, but have not thought it necessary to indicate those passages where I would not follow his conjectural amendments, except when the divergence of my view has some bearing on the Sanskrit original. These differences in the main either are based on the Peking edition or restore the original reading in place of suggested amendments. Besides the liability to confusion of certain letters, notably *da* and *ṅa*, and *pa*, *pha*, and *ba*, the monosyllabic nature of the Tibetan language not merely makes the entrance of corruptions easy but also renders their correction a matter of far greater uncertainty than in Sanskrit. There is curiously little variance between the different editions and all of them have the same lacunæ. The translator clearly had at his command a MS. that belonged to the same textual tradition as A but in general was superior, despite a certain proportion of inferior readings.[1] As usual he made a word for word rendering, paying the greatest respect to his text and never wilfully altering it, when it did not give a good sense. Thus in xii. 113*d*, he found the word *śaśākārṇavadvayor*, but, instead of making the trivial and obvious correction to *śaśāṅkā°*, he

[1] It may be surmised from the fact that the spurious verse in canto ix appears in different places in A and T, that their common ancestor had this verse added in the margin and that subsequent copyists incorporated it at different points in the text.

translates *śaśāka-arṇavadvayor.* But his command of Sanskrit was peculiar, at times showing a knowledge of the meaning of rare words, at times making a hash of simple phrases, e.g. translating *mṛgāś calākṣā* in vii. 5*d*, as *mṛgāś ca lākṣā*, and dividing *tatrāsa* at xiii. 1, into *tatra-āsa.* We may be sure then that, if we can be certain of the equivalents for the Tibetan, we know what stood in his MS. and it is precisely here that the difficulty lies.

The method I have used must therefore be exactly described. Of recent years the use of Tibetan translations has grown greatly and it is often supposed to be a perfectly simple matter to turn them back into Sanskrit. This delusion has given rise to some work of doubtful value and students, who do not know Tibetan, should be chary of accepting amendments to Sanskrit texts on this basis, till they are quite satisfied that those who propose them have followed critical and scholarly methods. The Tibetan translations cover a considerable period of time and different translators naturally differ in their ways, so that each text should be carefully studied by itself as a whole to grasp the peculiarities of its author's style, instead of relying on dictionaries which often fail to give the right word. For the present work I indexed the equivalent in the Sanskrit text of every Tibetan word ; when a passage occurs in which A is faulty or A and T disagree, the various possible equivalents of the Tibetan have to be considered, and, in order to select the right one, weight must be given to metrical and palæographical requirements, to the characteristics of Aśvaghoṣa's language and style, and to the possibility that a small correction in T may bring it and A into accord. In the majority of cases this leads to conclusions that I would hold to be certain about the reading of T's original, but in some passages certainty is not possible and my inability to reach a definite result is indicated in the critical apparatus dealing with those places. T is not entirely word for word in fact ; in particular it often omits particles and conjunctions (except *api*) or alters their arrangement, and it sometimes gives and sometimes leaves out prepositions.[1] It often uses the same word for more than one Sanskrit preposition and has more than one equivalent for some of them. Further the rules of Tibetan metre do not allow sufficient space for the accurate reproduction of the case-endings in all cases, and in addition the text frequently confuses the endings in *-s* with the similar ones without *s* (e.g. *kyis* and *kyi*, *las* and *la*). Subject to these limitations T is an invaluable authority, without which it would not have been possible to give a satisfying text.

In the apparatus criticus I have borne in mind that many readers of this volume will be ignorant of the elements of Tibetan. When the text reproduces T exactly and disagrees with A or the Chinese, I give the Tibetan without comment, but, where T's reading has not been adopted or is doubtful, I give the Tibetan with the Sanskrit equivalent if I can determine it, or else with a literal Sanskrit translation in brackets. The appearance therefore of the Sanskrit equivalent of T in any passage shows that it has not been followed there or only followed in part. For the English translation T is of less use and, as Dr. Weller's version shows, is frequently misleading, when construed literally in accordance with the principles of Tibetan style. For many terms purely mechanical equivalents are given and the construction of the Sanskrit often cannot be deduced from it. For this reason any attempt to restore Aśvaghoṣa's text from a translation of T, instead of from the original Tibetan, can only lead to the darkening of counsel.

The third authority for the text, the Chinese translation, which I denote by the letter C, is far less useful. It was made early in the fifth century A.D. by an Indian monk, the first portion of whose name was Dharma, the second half containing the letter *kṣ*; the forms favoured at various times have been

[1] It may for instance be noted that the *Nyāyabindu* uses *pratibhāsa* and *ābhāsa* to render different conceptions, but that the Tibetan confounds the two by translating both alike with *snaṅ-ba*.

Dharmarakṣa, Dharmakṣema and Dharmākṣara.[1] An English translation was made by Beal for volume XIX of the *Sacred Books of the East*, before the Sanskrit text was published; while it gives some idea of the original and is of use to any one working on the Chinese, it misses the sense so frequently that it cannot be relied on by itself. A much better rendering, despite a few mistakes, is to be found in Else Wohlgemuth's translation of the first two cantos into German in 1915. I have used the version printed in the Taishō Issaikyō edition of the Chinese Tripiṭaka, which, though not critical, is pleasant to read and has useful variants. In some cases a better reading is relegated to the latter and occasionally two words of the same pronunciation have been confused, as at ix. 52*a*, where, if we replace *shên*, 'deep', by *shên*, = *ātman*, we get the exact reproduction of the Sanskrit. The author had no doubt an excellent text at his disposal, but, in addition to some misunderstandings of the original, he has paraphrased rather than translated the poem. All passages of real *kāvya* style are either abridged or omitted altogether, and other verses are cut down or expanded according as they appealed to the translator, who was evidently a pious Buddhist, keen on matters of legend or moral, but with little taste for literature. In legendary details he sometimes makes additions to the text, and, as he evades textual niceties, contenting himself with giving the general sense, his work has to be used with caution. Only very rarely have I thought the Sanskrit equivalent of his text sufficiently certain to justify me in following it against the indications of A and T. Two of these cases (vi. 36, and xi. 31) are proper names, where it undoubtedly offers an improved reading. For the English translation I have often found it helpful. As so few Sanskrit scholars can read Chinese and as the reproduction of the Chinese characters would add greatly to the cost of this book, I have thought it better only to give

---

1 See P. C. Bagchi, *Le Canon bouddhique en Chine* (Paris, 1927), 212ff., for his life and works. The author supports the form Dharmakṣema; *Hobogirin, fasicule annexe*, gives Dharmarakṣa at one place and Dharmakṣema at another.

in the apparatus criticus a fairly literal English translation of those passages, which I conceive to have any bearing on the constitution of the Sanskrit text. Unlike T, it is the meaning, not the actual wording, which is of value, and C is easily available to those who, knowing Chinese better than I do, might hope to extract more from it than I have been able to find there.

In addition to C, I have also examined another work, only extant in Chinese, the *Fo pen hsing chi ching*, quoted in the footnotes under the letters FP. This is a verbose life of the Buddha, attempting, as the name implies, to give all the legends in full detail and quoting liberally from other works. It has been translated in an abridgement by Beal under the name of the *Romantic Legend of Śākya Buddha*, where the effect of the original (except for proper names) is given far more accurately than in his translation of C, the fact being that it is written in better Chinese.[1] It consists of prose interspersed with *gāthās*, the latter being mainly quotations, and the author has borrowed largely from the *Buddhacarita* for details, especially from cantos iv to ix inclusive and canto xi. The prose part at times follows Aśvaghoṣa, but so diffusely as never to be of any help, as far as I could see, for the constitution or understanding of the original, but it also quotes as *gāthās* over 90 verses from the poem, a list of which with references will be found in the appendix to this volume. Though it follows the original more closely than C, it equally shirks difficulties and is seldom of much assistance. The author was possibly not competent to deal with *kāvya*, to judge from his gross misunderstanding of xiii. 63*c*. Like C, I quote it only in my own English translation.

Such are the materials at my disposal and the textual problem of the *Buddhacarita* thereby differs *toto caelo* from that set by the *Saundarananda*, for which my only authorities were

---

[1] This work is also the chief source for H. Doré's *Vie illustrée du Bouddha Çakyamouni* (Shanghai, 1929), but the passages in question are so abbreviated in translation, that I have derived no help from it.

two MSS.[1] One was much damaged and covered only about two-thirds of the text, but was so good that it was not to be departed from without the strongest of reasons; the other which contained the whole poem was so full of corruptions and mistakes that by nothing but extensive amendment could one reach a readable text for those parts which depended on it alone. As editor, I had to admit many conjectures to the text, whether I liked it or no, but the proceeding is deprived of half its objectionableness when the MSS. variants are fully given, and I would claim that my edition of it should be judged, not by the number of conjectures accepted, but by the skill or the reverse with which I selected them from among the possible alternatives. For the *Buddhacarita* we have three independent text traditions, and for ten per cent. of the poem four, none of them adequate in themselves to providing a good text, but between them affording reasonable solutions of most cruces. To proceed by way of conjecture in these circumstances would be improper, and I have only amended the text against my authorities, when I saw no other way out, my reasons in such cases being given in the notes. A naturally forms the basis of the text, but, where T differs from it, I have as a rule chosen that reading which C suggests or appears to favour. Where C denies help, I have exercised my own judgement, which has, I hope, been sharpened by so many years devoted to one author's works. In a few cases I have accepted the indications of C against A and T, but only when I was fully satisfied of its reading. In some cases I have not accepted either A or T entirely, but have combined the two. In other words I have followed no fixed rule but have been guided by the circumstances of each case.

Certain special points require a few words. For canto ii. 1–35, I have had to take Cowell's text as my basis, but, as it is clear that the two leaves of A concerned were much rubbed

---

1 Excellent reproductions of these MSS. are now in the India Office Library, where they may be consulted by scholars who wish to check my collation of them.

and had lacunæ of several characters in verses 24*b*, 25*d*, and 27*a*, I have introduced T's readings with greater readiness than in the rest of the text. Where verses are incomplete in A, such as i. 8, 24 and 40, and in ix. 26–37, I have filled in the gaps from T, so far as I was certain of the original. Verse xii. 91, which is missing in A, I have been able to restore in part only. In iv. 87, where A's second line is shown by C and T to be a late falsification, I have given instead the probable restoration of T.

In two passages C raises the question whether our text is in the right order. In canto ix it transposes verses 19–22 to the order 22, 20, 19, 21; this is hardly an improvement in the sequence of the argument. In canto viii its rearrangement is more drastic. As A's and T's text stands, the order is open to the charge of being disjointed. Śuddhodana is mentioned in verse 15 and ignored thereafter till verse 72. Yaśodharā's lamentations, 61–69, would follow more suitably on Chandaka's defence of himself, and Mahāprajāpati Gautamī's speech, 52–58, would come better after the description of her fall on the ground in verse 24, thus giving her the prominence which a Buddhist would feel was due to her. According to C the order after verse 14 is 16–24, 51–59, 25–50, 60–71, 15, 72–end, and FP, which is unhappily not authoritative on such a point, follows the same order. I should have preferred to reconstruct the canto on these lines, but have felt that so great a change might fail to win general approval, as well as being harassing to those brought up on the *editio princeps*.

The way in which obviously or probably interpolated verses should be dealt with has also caused me much anxious thought. Finally I have decided to exclude from the text only a spurious verse in the passage at canto ix, which was wanting in Cowell's MSS., the verse at the end of canto xiii, which, though its lack of authenticity was detected long ago by Lüders, has been quoted of recent years as typical of Aśvaghoṣa's style in a standard history of Sanskrit literature, and the verse numbered xiv. 21, in Cowell's edition; not one of these can possibly be genuine. For other doubtful verses I regard C as peculiarly deserving of attention ; while omitting much descriptive matter, it never fails to take up anything of legendary or moral interest and any such verse omitted from it is on that score alone subject to grave suspicion. The following verses I regard for the reasons given in the notes on the translation of each as meriting consideration in this connexion, some being almost certain interpolations, others merely doubtful, viz., i. 81, ii. 15, iii. 21 and 65, iv. 17 and 48, v. 65, viii. 47, 48 and 54, xi. 57, and xiii. 23.

The text, as constituted by me, differs in the numbering of certain cantos from Cowell's and it may be found useful to give here a table of the variations :—

Present edition.	*Cowell's edition.*
Omitted.	i. 1–24.
i. 8.	Omitted.
i. 9.	i. 25.
Omitted.	i. 26–28.
i. 10–24.	i. 29–43.
Omitted.	i. 44-45.
i. 40.	Omitted.
i. 41–89.	i. 46–94.
ix. 1–41.	ix. 1–41.
ix. 42–51.	Omitted.
ix. 52–82.	ix. 42–72.
xi. 29.	xi. 30.
xi. 30.	xi. 29.
xii. 1–71*ab*.	xii. 1–71*ab*.
xii. 71*cd*–73*ab*.	Omitted.
xii. 73*cd*–90.	xii. 71*cd*–88.
xii. 91.	Omitted.
xii. 92–121.	xii. 89–118.
Omitted.	xiii. 73.
xiv. 1–20.	xiv. 1–20.
Omitted.	xiv. 21.

Present edition.	*Cowell's edition.*
xiv. 21–28.	xiv. 22–29.
xiv. 29.	xiv. 31.
xiv. 30.	xiv. 30.
xiv. 31.	xiv. 32.

The manner in which T and C have been dealt with in the apparatus criticus has already been stated. A complete collation of A is also given, and I have normalised the spelling in the text, but not in the apparatus. The question whether to include all conjectures by other scholars had also to be considered and I finally decided to mention them only in the few cases where I have accepted them without authority from A, T or C, and in certain passages where the text I give remains doubtful and the attempts of others to find the correct reading might prove of help to future workers. It was not only the bulk of the additional matter that weighed with me. A conjecture remains a conjecture, however good, and in the many cases where my text coincides with previous conjectures the conclusive evidence for such readings is to be found in A, T or C, not in the fact that such and such scholars, however eminent, have put them forward, while very few of the remainder have any subsisting interest in the light of the material given here. Those who wish to ascertain quickly what conjectures have been made regarding particular verses will find all the earlier ones discussed in the notes to Formichi's translation, while I have mentioned those which A and T confirmed in two articles in the *JRAS* (1927, 209ff., and 1929, 537ff.)[1] and others are referred to in the notes to Weller's translation of T. In brief I do not think that mention of *all* the conjectures would have been of any value towards the constitution and interpretation of the text. The same reasoning applies still more strongly to the four Indian editions of the first five cantos, published for the use of students at Bombay Universịty in 1911. Some of these

---

[1] These articles, quite apart from one or two mistakes, do not give my final views, but only a preliminary account of the material to be found in A and T for settling the text.

claim to be based on independent MSS., but internal evidence showed that, if such MSS. were not veritable *khapuṣpas*, they were merely copies of Cowell's text with such alterations as modern taste would suggest. One editor professed to find in his MS. the verses missing in Cowell's canto ix, but in printing them in an appendix he reproduced the seven mistakes which MM. H. P. Sastri had made in his version of A's text of them, published a couple of years earlier. Could any two persons make exactly the same mistakes in copying a passage independently of each other? Any variants found in these editions are in fact nothing more than conjectures. While their notes have been found useful at times for the translation, textually they are devoid of all authority.

A list of all the editions, translations and special articles of which the *Buddhacarita* is the main subject, so far as known to me, will be found at the beginning of the second volume, and I reserve for the foreword to it the few remarks that are necessary to explain my methods of translation and annotation.

For a task that has been spread out over many years it is but in accordance with the kindly ways of Sanskrit scholars that I should have received help on special points from many quarters, only a portion of which can be acknowledged here. The work owes its inception to the generous and enlightened policy of the Nepal Durbar, which, by sending the MS. A to the Bodleian Library, enabled me to appreciate its importance and exploit its contents; and by the publication of these volumes the University of the Panjab, and its Vice-Chancellor, Professor A. C. Woolner, C.I.E., have earned my heart-felt gratitude, all the more so in that, having no claim to the funds at their disposal, I am entitled to feel assured that they have been actuated solely by a desire to advance Sanskrit learning. Among those who have helped me with answers to queries the Librarians of the India Office, particularly Dr. H. N. Randle, take the first place, and of other scholars I would tender special thanks, in England, to Professor Soothill and Mr. C. E. A. W. Oldham, and, on the Continent, to Dr. J. Ph. Vogel, Professor P.

Demiéville, Mr. Lin Li-Kouang, who undertook a particularly troublesome piece of work at my request, M. Jean Buhot, and Mademoiselle M. Lalou, who collated part of canto xiv for me in the Peking edition of the Tanjore, while correspondence with others, such as Professors de la Vallée Poussin, Konow and Charpentier, has influenced me for good in ways that are not always obvious from the text. To the late Professor Macdonell's daughters I am indebted for permission to publish the lines placed at the beginning of this volume; any virtues my work may possess are ultimately due to the ideals and exact methods of scholarship which that great teacher never wearied of impressing on his pupils.

ADDERBURY, E. H. JOHNSTON.
December, 1934.

ABBREVIATIONS.

A .. .. MS. of the *Buddhacarita* in the Library of the Nepal Durbar at Kathmandu.

C .. .. Chinese translation of the *Buddhacarita*, ed. Taishō Issaikyō, volume IV, no. 192; translated by S. Beal, *Sacred Books of the East*, volume XIX.

Co. .. .. *The Buddhakarita of Asvaghosha*, edited by E. B. Cowell, Anecdota Oxoniensia, Oxford, 1893.

e.c. .. .. ex conjectura.

FP .. .. *Fo pen hsing chi ching*, ed. Taishō Issaikyō, volume III, no. 190. Abridged translation by S. Beal, *The Romantic Legend of Śākya Buddha*, London, 1875.

T .. .. Tibetan translation of the *Buddhacarita*, edited and translated by Friedrich Weller, *Das Leben des Buddha von Aśvaghoṣa*, Leipzig; Part I, 1926; Part II, 1928.

CONTENTS.

THE BUDDHACARITA

CANTO I

*   *   *   *   *   *   *

तस्मिन्वने श्रीमति राजपत्नी प्रसूतिकालं समवेक्षमाणा ।
शय्यां वितानोपहितां प्रपेदे नारीसहस्रैरभिनन्द्यमाना ॥ ८ ॥

ततः प्रसन्नश्च बभूव पुष्यस्तस्याश्च देव्या व्रतसंस्कृतायाः ।
पार्श्वात्सुतो लोकहिताय जज्ञे निर्वेदनं चैव निरामयं च ॥ ९ ॥

ऊरोर्यथौर्वस्य पृथोश्च हस्तान्मान्धातुरिन्द्रप्रतिमस्य मूर्ध्नः ।
कक्षीवतश्चैव भुजांसदेशात्तथाविधं तस्य बभूव जन्म ॥ १० ॥

क्रमेण गर्भादभिनिःसृतः सन् बभौ च्युतः खादिव योन्यजातः ।
कल्पेष्वनेकेषु च भावितात्मा यः संप्रजानन्सुषुवे न मूढः ॥ ११ ॥

8. ab. Fol. 2 of A begins with the last syllables māṇā ; dpal-daṅ-ldan-paḥi nags der rgyal-poḥi bdag-ldan-ma rab-tu-bltams-paḥi dus ni yaṅ-dag mṅon-gzigs-śiṅ, T ; ‘ in that grove then the queen of herself knew that the time of delivery had come ’, C.

9. a. rab-ldan-par (prasannaś ?), T.

10. a. yathorvvasya, A. c. lag-paḥi cha-śas gsaṅ-ba-nas (bhujāṁśa-guhyāt), T ; ‘ armpit ’, C.

11. a. gzugs mdzes-te (rūpeṇa babhau), T ; ‘ gradually ’, C. ab. °sṛtasya (?ssa?) babhau (all rewritten), A. c. anekeṣv iva, A ; T omits iva ; ‘ having practised virtue for countless ages ’, C.

दीप्त्या च धैर्येण च यो रराज बालो रविर्भूमिमिवावतीर्णः ।
तथातिदीप्तोऽपि निरीक्ष्यमाणो जहार चक्षूंषि यथा शशाङ्कः॥१२॥
स हि स्वगात्रप्रभयोज्ज्वलन्त्या दीपप्रभां भास्करवन्मुमोष ।
महार्हजाम्बूनदचारुवर्णो विद्योतयामास दिशश्च सर्वाः ॥ १३ ॥
अनाकुलान्युब्जसमुद्गतानि निष्पेषवद्व्यायतविक्रमाणि ।
तथैव धीराणि पदानि सप्त सप्तर्षितारासदृशो जगाम ॥ १४ ॥
बोधाय जातोऽस्मि जगद्धितार्थमन्त्या भवोत्पत्तिरियं ममेति ।
चतुर्दिशं सिंहगतिर्विलोक्य वाणीं च भव्यार्थकरीमुवाच ॥ १५ ॥
खात्प्रसृते चन्द्रमरीचिशुभ्रे द्वे वारिधारे शिशिरोष्णवीर्ये ।
शरीरसंस्पर्शसुखान्तराय निपेततुर्मूर्धनि तस्य सौम्ये ॥ १६ ॥
श्रीमद्विताने कनकोज्ज्वलाङ्गे वैडूर्यपादे शयने शयानम् ।
यद्गौरवात्काञ्चनपद्महस्ता यक्षाधिपाः संपरिवार्य तस्थुः ॥ १७ ॥
* * श्च दिवौकसः खे यस्य प्रभावात्प्रणतैः शिरोभिः ।
आधारयन् पाण्डरमातपत्रं बोधाय जेपुः परमाशिषश्च ॥ १८ ॥

12. a. dhairyeṇa * (character defaced) yā, A ; brtan-pas gaṅ-zhig, T.

13. a. °prabhayā jvalantyā, A ; ḥod rab-ḥbar-ba-yis, T.

14. a. °nyubja° (corrected to °ny abja°), A ; yon-poḥi skyon-dag rab-bsal-zhiṅ (= ?), T. b. niṣpeṣavanty āyata°, A ; śin-tu-brtan-pa rnam-par-yaṅs-paḥi ḥgros, T. c. de-ltar mi-gyo rab-tu-brtan-paḥi gom-pa (=tathācalāny atidhīrāṇi padāni), T.

16. c. śarīra (four characters torn and illegible) khantarāya, A ; lus-la yaṅ-dag reg-pas bde-ba bskyed-paḥi phyir, T ; 'caused his body pleasure', C.

17. a. gser-kyis ḥbar-zhiṅ mtshan (kanakojjvalāṅke), T. c. yaṁ gauravāt, Lüders.

18. a. First eight syllables illegible in A ; mi-mṅon gyur-paḥi lha-rnams-kyis (=adṛśyabhāvāś ca divaukasaḥ), T. c. adhārayan, Böhtlingk.

महोरगा धर्मविशेषतर्षाद्बुद्धेष्वतीतेषु कृताधिकाराः ।
यमव्यजन् भक्तिविशिष्टनेत्रा मन्दारपुष्पैः समवाकिरंश्च ॥ १९ ॥

तथागतोत्पादगुणेन तुष्टाः शुद्धाधिवासाश्च विशुद्धसत्त्वाः ।
देवा ननन्दुर्विगतेऽपि रागे मग्नस्य दुःखे जगतो हिताय ॥ २० ॥

यस्य प्रसूतौ गिरिराजकीला वाताहता नौरिव भूश्चचाल ।
सचन्दना चोत्पलपद्मगर्भा पपात वृष्टिर्गगनादनभ्रात् ॥ २१ ॥

वाता ववुः स्पर्शसुखा मनोज्ञा
दिव्यानि वासांस्यवपातयन्तः ।
सूर्यः स एवाभ्यधिकं चकाशे
जज्वाल सौम्यार्चिरनीरितोऽग्निः ॥ २२ ॥

प्रागुत्तरे चावसथप्रदेशे कूपः स्वयं प्रादुरभूत्सिताम्बुः ।
अन्तःपुराण्यागतविस्मयानि यस्मिन् क्रियास्तीर्थ इव प्रचक्रुः ॥२३॥

धर्मार्थिभिर्भूतगणैश्च दिव्यैस्तद्दर्शनार्थं वनमापुपूरे ।
कौतूहलेनैव च पादपेभ्यः पुष्पाण्यकालेऽपि * * * * ॥ २४ ॥

* * * * * * * * * *

* * * * निदर्शनान्यत्र च नो निबोध ॥ ४० ॥

20. b. śuddhāddhivāsāś, A. d. hitoya, A'; phan-paḥi phyir, T.

21. a. yasya prasūto, A ; gaṅ-gi rab-tu-bltams tshe, T.

22. c. sūrya, A.

23. b. bsil-baḥi chu-yi (śītāmbuḥ), T.

24. a. dharmmārthibhi bhūta°, A. b. vanam āprapūrai, A ; nags-tsha rab-gaṅ-ste, T. cd. Fol. 2 of A ends with the tenth syllable of *c* ; śiṅ-las kyaṅ me-tog-rnams ni dus-ma-yin-par ṅes-par-brul, T.

40. d. Fol. 4 of A begins traiva ca no nibodha ; ḥdir yaṅ bdag-gis dper-brjod-dag ni mkhyen-par-mdzod, T ; 'now I should mention the examples ; let the king now too investigate and listen ', C.

यद्राजशास्त्रं भृगुरङ्गिरा वा न चक्रतुर्वंशकरावृषी तौ ।
तयोः सुतौ सौम्य ससर्जतुस्तत्कालेन शुक्रश्च बृहस्पतिश्च ॥ ४१ ॥
सारस्वतश्चापि जगाद नष्टं वेदं पुनर्यं ददृशुर्न पूर्वे ।
व्यासस्तथैनं बहुधा चकार न यं वसिष्ठः कृतवानशक्तिः ॥ ४२ ॥
वाल्मीकिरादौ च ससर्ज पद्यं जग्रन्थ यन्न च्यवनो महर्षिः ।
चिकित्सितं यच्च चकार नात्रिः पश्चात्तदात्रेय ऋषिर्जगाद ॥ ४३ ॥
यच्च द्विजत्वं कुशिको न लेभे तद्गाधिनः सूनुरवाप राजन् ।
वेलां समुद्रे सगरश्च दध्रे नेक्ष्वाकवो यां प्रथमं बबन्धुः ॥ ४४ ॥
आचार्यकं योगविधौ द्विजानामप्राप्तमन्यैर्जनको जगाम ।
ख्यातानि कर्माणि च यानि शौरेः शूरादयस्तेष्वबला बभूवुः ॥४५॥
तस्मात्प्रमाणं न वयो न वंशः कश्चित्क्वचिच्छ्रैष्ठ्यमुपैति लोके ।
राज्ञामृषीणां च हि तानि तानि कृतानि पुत्रैरकृतानि पूर्वैः ॥४६॥
एवं नृपः प्रत्ययितैर्द्विजैस्तैराश्वासितश्चाप्यभिनन्दितश्च ।
शङ्कामनिष्टां विजहौ मनस्तः प्रहर्षमेवाधिकमारुरोह ॥ ४७ ॥

42. a. Sāraśvataś, A. b. cedam, A; rig-byed, T. d. vaśiṣṭhaḥ, A. kṛtavān śaktiḥ (virāma under n a later addition ?), A; nus-med . . . byas-gyur-pa, T.

43. c. nātri, A. mthoṅ-ba (dadarśa), T. d. byas (cakāra), T.

44. b. rājaṁ, A; rgyal-po-la (rājñe ?), T; 'king Gādhina' (?), C.

45. c. saureḥ, A; khyab-ḥjug-gi (=viṣṇoḥ), T.

46. a. na vayo na kālaḥ, A; laṅ-tsho daṅ ni rigs-dag, T; 'in the case of imperial kings and divine ṛṣis one certainly does not hold family to be the basis', C. b. upeti, A.

47. a. pratyayitai(?to?), A; gñis-skyes de-rnams-kyis ni yid-ches-te (=pratyāyito dvijais taiḥ), T. c. saṅkām, A.

प्रीतश्च तेभ्यो द्विजसत्तमेभ्यः सत्कारपूर्वं प्रददौ धनानि ।
भूयादयं भूमिपतिर्यथोक्तो यायाज्जरामेत्य वनानि चेति ॥ ४८ ॥
अथो निमित्तैश्च तपोबलाच्च तज्जन्म जन्मान्तकरस्य बुद्ध्वा ।
शाक्येश्वरस्यालयमाजगाम सद्धर्मतर्षादसितो महर्षिः ॥ ४९ ॥
तं ब्रह्मविद्ब्रह्मविदं ज्वलन्तं ब्राह्म्या श्रिया चैव तपःश्रिया च ।
राज्ञो गुरुर्गौरवसत्क्रियाभ्यां प्रवेशयामास नरेन्द्रसद्म ॥ ५० ॥
स पार्थिवान्तःपुरसंनिकर्षं कुमारजन्मागतहर्षवेगः ।
विवेश धीरो वनसंज्ञयेव तपःप्रकर्षाच्च जराश्रयाच्च ॥ ५१ ॥
ततो नृपस्तं मुनिमासनस्थं पाद्यार्घ्यपूर्वं प्रतिपूज्य सम्यक् ।
निमन्त्रयामास यथोपचारं पुरा वसिष्ठं स इवान्तिदेवः ॥ ५२ ॥
धन्योऽस्म्यनुग्राह्यमिदं कुलं मे
यन्मां दिदृक्षुर्भगवानुपेतः ।
आज्ञाप्यतां किं करवाणि सौम्य
शिष्योऽस्मि विश्रम्भितुमर्हसीति ॥ ५३ ॥

48. c. yathoktau, A.

49. b. tajjanya, A; bltams-pa de ni, T. cd. dam-paḥi chos-la gus-paḥi (?pas?) śākyaḥi dbaṅ-phyug-gi (Śākyeśvarasya . . . saddharmabhaktasya, or °bhakter?), T.

50. a. brahmavidbrahmavidāṁ, A; ḥbar-baḥi tshaṅs-rig-rnams-kyi tshaṅs-rig de-la ni (i.e. brahmavidbrahmavidaṁ as a compound), T. c. °śatkriyābhyāṁ, A.

51. c. °saṁjñayaiva, A; ḥdu-śes-kyis ltar, T; ' despite all the women as if he were in an empty fenced grove ', C. d. jara(?corrected to rā?)śrayāc ca, A.

52. d. vaśiṣṭhaṁ, A.

एवं नृपेणोपमन्त्रितः सन्सर्वेण भावेन मुनिर्यथावत् ।
स विस्मयोत्फुल्लविशालदृष्टिर्गम्भीरधीराणि वचांस्युवाच ॥ ५४ ॥

महात्मनि त्वय्युपपन्नमेत-
त्प्रियातिथौ त्यागिनि धर्मकामे ।
सत्त्वान्वयज्ञानवयोऽनुरूपा
स्निग्धा यदेवं मयि ते मतिः स्यात् ॥ ५५ ॥

एतच्च तद्येन नृपर्षयस्ते धर्मेण सूक्ष्मेण धनान्यवाप्य ।
नित्यं त्यजन्तो विधिवद्बभूवुस्तपोभिराढ्या विभवैर्दरिद्राः ॥ ५६ ॥

प्रयोजनं यत्तु ममोपयाने तन्मे शृणु प्रीतिमुपेहि च त्वम् ।
दिव्या मयादित्यपथे श्रुता वाग्बोधाय जातस्तनयस्तवेति ॥ ५७ ॥

श्रुत्वा वचस्तच्च मनश्च युक्त्वा ज्ञात्वा निमित्तैश्च ततोऽस्म्युपेतः ।
दिदृक्षया शाक्यकुलध्वजस्य शक्रध्वजस्येव समुच्छ्रितस्य ॥ ५८ ॥

इत्येतदेवं वचनं निशम्य प्रहर्षसंभ्रान्तगतिर्नरेन्द्रः ।
आदाय धात्र्यङ्कगतं कुमारं संदर्शयामास तपोधनाय ॥ ५९ ॥

चक्राङ्कपादं स ततो महर्षिर्जालावनद्धाङ्गुलिपाणिपादम् ।
सोर्णभ्रुवं वारणवस्तिकोशं सविस्मयं राजसुतं ददर्श ॥ ६० ॥

54. a. nṛpenopa°, A.

56. b. sūkṣmāṇi, A; phra-moḥi chos-kyis, T. c. mchod-sbyin-byas (yajanto), T. d. tapobhir ādyā, A; dkaḥ-thub-rnams-kyis phyug-ciṅ, T.

57. b. upaihi, A. c. mayā divyapathe, A; bdag-gis ñi-maḥi lam-du, T; 'I came, following the path of the sun', C.

59. a. etad aivam, A. c. yum-gyi paṅ-du (mātryaṅke), T.

60. a. tathā, A; de-nas, T. b. jālāvanaddhāvaṅguli°, A. c. svarṇṇa-bhuvaṁ, A; smin-ma mdzod-spur-bcas, T.

धात्र्यङ्कसंविष्टमवेक्ष्य चैनं देव्यङ्कसंविष्टमिवाग्निसूनुम् ।
बभूव पक्ष्मान्तविचञ्चिताश्रुर्निश्वस्य चैव त्रिदिवोन्मुखोऽभूत् ॥ ६१ ॥

दृष्ट्वासितं त्वश्रुपरिप्लुताक्षं स्नेहात्तनूजस्य नृपश्चकम्पे ।
सगद्गदं बाष्पकषायकण्ठः पप्रच्छ स प्राञ्जलिरानताङ्गः ॥ ६२ ॥

अल्पान्तरं यस्य वपुः सुरेभ्यो बह्वद्भुतं यस्य च जन्म दीप्तम् ।
यस्योत्तमं भाविनमात्थ चार्थं तं प्रेक्ष्य कस्मात्तव धीर बाष्पः ॥६३॥

अपि स्थिरायुर्भगवन् कुमारः कच्चिन्न शोकाय मम प्रसूतः ।
लब्धा कथंचित्सलिलाञ्जलिर्मे न खल्विमं पातुमुपैति कालः ॥६४॥

अप्यक्षयं मे यशसो निधानं कच्चिद्ध्रुवो मे कुलहस्तसारः ।
अपि प्रयास्यामि सुखं परत्र सुप्तोऽपि पुत्रेऽनिमिषैकचक्षुः ॥ ६५ ॥

कच्चिन्न मे जातमफुल्लमेव
कुलप्रवालं परिशोषभागि ।
क्षिप्रं विभो ब्रूहि न मेऽस्ति शान्तिः
स्नेहं सुते वेत्सि हि बान्धवानाम् ॥ ६६ ॥

इत्यागतावेगमनिष्टबुद्ध्या बुद्ध्वा नरेन्द्रं स मुनिर्बभाषे ।
मा भून्मतिस्ते नृप काचिदन्या निःसंशयं तद्यदवोचमस्मि ॥ ६७ ॥

61. d. e.c. Böhtlingk; caivaṁ, A; T omits. dbugs-med gyur-nas (= niḥśvāso bhūtvā, for niḥśvasya ?), T.

62. a. tv asru°, A. d. prāñjali c(?)ānatāṅgaḥ, A.

63. b. ṅo-mtshar maṅ-poḥi sgron-ma-ste (bahvadbhuto . . . dīpo), T. d. prekṣa, A.

64. b. kaścin, A; nam-ci, T. d. yātum upeti, A; ḥthuṅ-phyir ñe-bar-ḥoṅs, T (omitting khalu).

65. d. e.c. Lévi and Formichi; supto pi putro, A; gñid-par-gyur kyaṅ bu ni (supto 'pi putro ?), T; for C see note in translation.

66. c. me stiḥ (mark over visarga to show error), A.

67. b. budhvā, A.

नास्यान्यथात्वं प्रति विक्रिया मे
स्वां वञ्चनां तु प्रति विक्लवोऽस्मि ।
कालो हि मे यातुमयं च जातो
जातिक्षयस्यासुलभस्य बोद्धा ॥ ६८ ॥

विहाय राज्यं विषयेष्वनास्थस्तीव्रैः प्रयत्नैरधिगम्य तत्त्वम् ।
जगत्ययं मोहतमो निहन्तुं ज्वलिष्यति ज्ञानमयो हि सूर्यः ॥ ६९ ॥

दुःखार्णवाद्व्याधिविकीर्णफेनाज्जरातरङ्गान्मरणोग्रवेगात् ।
उत्तारयिष्यत्ययमुह्यमानमार्तं जगज्ज्ञानमहाप्लवेन ॥ ७० ॥

प्रज्ञाम्बुवेगां स्थिरशीलवप्रां समाधिशीतां व्रतचक्रवाकाम् ।
अस्योत्तमां धर्मनदीं प्रवृत्तां तृष्णार्दितः पास्यति जीवलोकः ॥७१॥

दुःखार्दितेभ्यो विषयावृतेभ्यः संसारकान्तारपथस्थितेभ्यः ।
आख्यास्यति ह्येष विमोक्षमार्गं मार्गप्रनष्टेभ्य इवाध्वगेभ्यः ॥ ७२ ॥

विदह्यमानाय जनाय लोके रागाग्निनायं विषयेन्धनेन ।
प्रह्लादमाधास्यति धर्मवृष्ट्या वृष्ट्या महामेघ इवातपान्ते ॥ ७३ ॥

तृष्णार्गलं मोहतमःकपाटं द्वारं प्रजानामपयानहेतोः ।
विपाटयिष्यत्ययमुत्तमेन सद्धर्मताडेन दुरासदेन ॥ ७४ ॥

68. b. vā(?va?)ñcanān tu, A.

69. c. mun-pa rnam-ḥjoms-phyir (°tamo vihantum), T.

70. b. °taraṅgāt, A. d. jagata jñāna°, A.

71. a. °vaprā, A. c. rab-bskor-la (pravṛtāṁ), T.

72. a. viṣayāvṛttebhyaḥ, A; yul-gyis bsgribs-rnams, T. b. ḥbrog-dgon ḥjigs-par gnas-pa-rnams-la (°kāntārabhayasthitebhyaḥ), T.

73. c. prahlāyam (glossed sukha), A; rab-tu-sim, T.

74. a. tṛṣṇārggaḍam, A; sred-paḥi sgo-gtan ma-rig mun-paḥi sgo-glegs-can (=tṛṣṇārgalāvidyātamaḥkapāṭaṁ), T. d. dam-paḥi chos-kyi sgras (=saddharmaśabdena), T.

स्वैर्मोहपाशैः परिवेष्टितस्य दुःखाभिभूतस्य निराश्रयस्य ।
लोकस्य संबुध्य च धर्मराजः करिष्यते बन्धनमोक्षमेषः ॥ ७५ ॥

तन्मा कृथाः शोकमिमं प्रति त्व-
मस्मिन्स शोच्योऽस्ति मनुष्यलोके ।
मोहेन वा कामसुखैर्मदाद्वा
यो नैष्ठिकं श्रोष्यति नास्य धर्मम् ॥ ७६ ॥

भ्रष्टस्य तस्माच्च गुणादतो मे
ध्यानानि लब्ध्वाप्यकृतार्थतैव ।
धर्मस्य तस्याश्रवणादहं हि
मन्ये विपत्तिं त्रिदिवेऽपि वासम् ॥ ७७ ॥

इति श्रुतार्थःससुहृत्सदार-
स्त्यक्त्वा विषादं मुमुदे नरेन्द्रः ।
एवंविधोऽयं तनयो ममेति
मेने स हि स्वामपि सारवत्ताम् ॥ ७८ ॥

आर्षेण मार्गेण तु यास्यतीति चिन्ताविधेयं हृदयं चकार ।
न खल्वसौ न प्रियधर्मपक्षः संताननाशात्तु भयं ददर्श ॥ ७९ ॥

75. a. raṅ-gi las-kyi zhags-pa-rnams-kyis (svakarmapāśaiḥ), T ; 'self-entangled in the nets of *moha*', C.

76. b. tat saumya śocya (corrected to cye) ha (written over a double letter) manuṣyaloke, A ; mi-yi ḥjig-rten ḥdir de mya-ṅan bya-baḥi gnas, T ; 'you ought to grieve over all those beings', C. d. neṣṭhikaṁ, A.

77. a. yon-tan rgya-mtsho ḥdi-las ḥkhrul-gyur bdag-gi ni (asmāc ca bhraṣṭasya guṇārṇavān me), T. b. ladhvāpy, A.

78. d. e.c. Böhtlingk ; sāramattāṁ, A.

79. a. āryeṇa mārggeṇa, A ; ḥphags-paḥi chos-rnams-kyis (=āryair dharmaiḥ), T ; 'cultivating the path of the ṛṣis', C.

अथ मुनिरसितो निवेद्य तत्त्वं सुतनियतं सुतविक्लवाय राज्ञे ।
सबहुमतमुदीक्ष्यमाणरूपः पवनपथेन यथागतं जगाम ॥ ८० ॥

कृतमितिरनुजासुतं च दृष्ट्वा
मुनिवचनश्रवणे च तन्मतौ च ।
बहुविधमनुकम्पया स साधुः
प्रियसुतवद्विनियोजयांचकार ॥ ८१ ॥

नरपतिरपि पुत्रजन्मतुष्टो विषयगतानि विमुच्य बन्धनानि ।
कुलसदृशमचीकरद्यथावत्प्रियतनयस्तनयस्य जातकर्म ॥ ८२ ॥

दशसु परिणतेष्वहःसु चैव प्रयतमनाः परया मुदा परीतः ।
अकुरुत जपहोममङ्गलाद्याः परमभवाय सुतस्य देवतेज्याः ॥ ८३ ॥

अपि च शतसहस्रपूर्णसंख्याः स्थिरबलवत्तनयाः सहेमशृङ्गीः ।
अनुपगतजराः पयस्विनीर्गाः स्वयमददात्सुतवृद्धये द्विजेभ्यः ॥ ८४ ॥

बहुविधविषयास्ततो यतात्मा स्वहृदयतोषकरीः क्रिया विधाय ।
गुणवति नियते शिवे मुहूर्ते मतिमकरोन्मुदितः पुरप्रवेशे ॥ ८५ ॥

द्विरदरदमयीमथो महार्हां
सितसितपुष्पभृतां मणिप्रदीपाम् ।
अभजत शिविकां शिवाय देवी
तनयवती प्रणिपत्य देवताभ्यः ॥ ८६ ॥

80. c. udīkṣamāṇa°, A.

81. C omits this verse. a. blo-gros byas-paḥi sriṅ-moḥi bu (kṛtamatim anujāsutaṁ), T.

82. b. bandhavāni A ; ḥchiṅ-ba-rnams, T. c. kulaśadṛśam, A.

84. a. satasahasra°, A.

85. c. guṇavati divase, A ; yon-tan-ldan-śiṅ (for zhiṅ) dge-baḥi yud-tsam ṅes-pa-na, T ; 'by divination selecting a favourable time', C.

86. a. marhārhāṁ, A.

पुरमथ पुरतः प्रवेश्य पत्नीं स्थविरजनानुगतामपत्यनाथाम् ।
नृपतिरपि जगाम पौरसंघैर्दिवममरैर्मघवानिवार्च्यमानः ॥ ८७ ॥

भवनमथ विगाह्य शाक्यराजो भव इव षण्मुखजन्मना प्रतीतः ।
इदमिदमिति हर्षपूर्णवक्त्रो बहुविधपुष्टियशस्करं व्यधत्त ॥ ८८ ॥

इति नरपतिपुत्रजन्मवृद्धा
सजनपदं कपिलाह्वयं पुरं तत् ।
धनदपुरमिवाप्सरसोऽवकीर्णं
मुदितमभून्नलकूबरप्रसूतौ ॥ ८९ ॥

इति बुद्धचरिते महाकाव्ये भगवत्प्रसूतिर्नाम प्रथमः सर्गः ॥ १ ॥

89. a. de-nas (atha), T.

CANTO II

आ जन्मनो जन्मजरान्तगस्य तस्यात्मजस्यात्मजितः स राजा ।
अहन्यहन्यर्थगजाश्वमित्रैर्वृद्धिं ययौ सिन्धुरिवाम्बुवेगैः ॥ १ ॥
धनस्य रत्नस्य च तस्य तस्य कृताकृतस्यैव च काञ्चनस्य ।
तदा हि नैकान्स निधीनवाप मनोरथस्याप्यतिभारभूतान् ॥ २ ॥
ये पद्मकल्पैरपि च द्विपेन्द्रैर्न मण्डलं शक्यमिहाभिनेतुम् ।
मदोत्कटा हैमवता गजास्ते विनापि यत्नादुपतस्थुरेनम् ॥ ३ ॥
नानाङ्कचिह्नैर्नवहेमभाण्डैर्विभूषितैर्लम्बसटैस्तथान्यैः ।
संचुक्षुभे चास्य पुरं तुरङ्गैर्बलेन मैत्र्या च धनेन चाप्तैः ॥ ४ ॥
पुष्टाश्च तुष्टाश्च तथास्य राज्ये साध्व्योऽरजस्का गुणवत्पयस्काः ।
उदग्रवत्सैः सहिता बभूवुर्बह्व्यो बहुक्षीरदुहश्च गावः ॥ ५ ॥
मध्यस्थतां तस्य रिपुर्जगाम मध्यस्थभावः प्रययौ सुहृत्त्वम् ।
विशेषतो दार्ढ्यमियाय मित्रं द्वावस्य पक्षावपरस्तु नास ॥ ६ ॥

1. a. ā janme, A; fol. 6 of A ends here. °jarāntakasya, Co; rga-ba mthar soṅ, T.

2. b. kṛtasyākṛtasyeva, Co.'s MSS.; byas daṅ ma-byas-pa ñid, T. c. e.c. Kern; tadā hi naikātmanidhīn avāpi, Co.; de-la gcig-tu phan-paḥi cha-śas gter rñed-gyur (tadā hitaikāṁśanidhīn avāpa), T.

3. b. ñe-bar-ḥoṅ-bar (upanetuṁ?), T.

4. b. abhūṣitair, Co.; ābhūṣitair, Kern; brgyan-byas (=bhūṣitair), T. d. cāptiḥ, Co.'s MSS.; thob-pa-yi . . . mgyogs-ḥgro-rnams, T.

5. a. tadāsya, Co.; de-bzhin ḥdi-yi, T. c. udagravatsāsahitā, Co.'s MSS.; rab-mchog beḥu-rnams-daṅ-bcas, T.

6. b. madhyasvabhāvaḥ, Co.; dbus-gnas gyur-pa, T. d. aparas tu nāśam, Co.; dgra yaṅ yod-ma-yin, T.

तथास्य मन्दानिलमेघशब्दः सौदामिनीकुण्डलमण्डिताभ्रः ।
विनाश्मवर्षाशनिपातदोषैः काले च देशे प्रववर्ष देवः ॥ ७ ॥
रुरोह सस्यं फलवद्यथर्तु तदाकृतेनापि कृषिश्रमेण ।
ता एव चास्यौषधयो रसेन सारेण चैवाभ्यधिका बभूवुः ॥ ८ ॥
शरीरसंदेहकरेऽपि काले संग्रामसंमर्द इव प्रवृत्ते ।
स्वस्थाः सुखं चैव निरामयं च प्रजज्ञिरे कालवशेन नार्यः ॥ ९ ॥
पृथग्व्रतिभ्यो विभवेऽपि गर्ह्ये न प्रार्थयन्ति स्म नराः परेभ्यः ।
अभ्यर्थितः सूक्ष्मधनोऽपि चार्यस्तदा न कश्चिद्विमुखो बभूव ॥ १० ॥
नागौरवो बन्धुषु नाप्यदाता नैवाव्रतो नानृतिको न हिंस्रः ।
आसीत्तदा कश्चन तस्य राज्ये राज्ञो ययातेरिव नाहुषस्य ॥ ११ ॥
उद्यानदेवायतनाश्रमाणां कूपप्रपापुष्करिणीवनानाम् ।
चक्रुः क्रियास्तत्र च धर्मकामाः प्रत्यक्षतः स्वर्गमिवोपलभ्य ॥ १२ ॥
मुक्तश्च दुर्भिक्षभयामयेभ्यो हृष्टो जनः स्वर्ग इवाभिरेमे ।
पत्नीं पतिर्वा महिषी पतिं वा परस्परं न व्यभिचेरतुश्च ॥ १३ ॥
कश्चित्सिषेवे रतये न कामं कामार्थमर्थं न जुगोप कश्चित् ।
कश्चिद्धनार्थं न चचार धर्मं धर्माय कश्चिन्न चकार हिंसाम् ॥ १४ ॥

7. b. °maṇḍitāṅgaḥ, Co. ; brgyan-paḥi sprin, T.

8. a. ruroha samyak, Co. ; ḥbru . . . skyes-te, T. b. zhiṅ-gi las-kyi ṅal-dub byed-pa ñuṅ-ṅus kyaṅ (svalpaṁ kṛtenāpi kṛṣiśramena ?), T. c. tā eva caivauṣadhayo, Co ; de-rnams ñid kyaṅ ḥdi-yi sman-du byuṅ-gyur-la, T.

9. d. garbhadharāś ca, Co. ; dus-kyi dbaṅ-gyis, T.

10. a. yac ca pratibhvo(bhyo, MSS.) vibhave 'pi śakye, Co. ; brtul-zhugs-ldan-rnams ma-gtogs nor-rdzas dman-na yaṅ, T. c. 'pi cāyaṁ, Co. ; ḥphags-pa . . . yaṅ, T.

11. a. nāśo vadho, Co. ; gñen-la zhe-sa med min, T.

12. c. rab-tu-mdzad (=pracakruḥ), T.

स्तैयादिभिश्चाप्यरिभिश्च नष्टं स्वस्थं स्वचक्रं परचक्रमुक्तम् ।
क्षेमं सुभिक्षं च बभूव तस्य पुरानरण्यस्य यथैव राष्ट्रे ॥ १५ ॥
तदा हि तज्जन्मनि तस्य राज्ञो मनोरिवादित्यसुतस्य राज्ये ।
चचार हर्षः प्रणनाश पाप्मा जज्वाल धर्मः कलुषः शशाम ॥ १६ ॥
एवंविधा राजकुलस्य संपत्सर्वार्थसिद्धिश्च यतो बभूव ।
ततो नृपस्तस्य सुतस्य नाम सर्वार्थसिद्धोऽयमिति प्रचक्रे ॥ १७ ॥
देवी तु माया विबुधर्षिकल्पं दृष्ट्वा विशालं तनयप्रभावम् ।
जातं प्रहर्षं न शशाक सोढुं ततो निवासाय दिवं जगाम ॥ १८ ॥
ततः कुमारं सुरगर्भकल्पं स्नेहेन भावेन च निर्विशेषम् ।
मातृष्वसा मातृसमप्रभावा संवर्धयामात्मजवद्बभूव ॥ १९ ॥
ततः स बालार्क इवोदयस्थः समीरितो वह्निरिवानिलेन ।
क्रमेण सम्यग्ववृधे कुमारस्ताराधिपः पक्ष इवातमस्के ॥ २० ॥
ततो महार्हाणि च चन्दनानि रत्नावलीश्चौषधिभिः सगर्भाः ।
मृगप्रयुक्तान्रथकांश्च हैमानाचक्रिरेऽस्मै सुहृदालयेभ्यः ॥ २१ ॥
वयोऽनुरूपाणि च भूषणानि हिरण्मयान् हस्तिमृगाश्वकांश्च ।
रथांश्च गोपुत्रकसंप्रयुक्तान् पुत्रीश्च चामीकररूप्यचित्राः ॥ २२ ॥

15. a. cāpy abhitaś ca naṣṭaṁ, Co. ; daṅ dgra yaṅ ñams-par, T. d. e.c. Gawroński and Sovani ; purāṇy araṇyāni, Co. ; purāṇy araṇyasya, Co.'s MS. C ; phya-rol mya-ṅan med-pa ji-lta-ba ñid bzhin . . . rgyal-po de-la (=tasya parasyāśokasya yathaiva rājñaḥ?), T.

17. a. evaṁvidhā rājasutasya tasya, Co. ; rgyal-poḥi rigs-kyi phun-sum-tshogs-pa byuṅ-gyur-te, T ; ' thus in the king's palace all things were exceedingly prosperous ', FP.

18. d. tato 'vināśāya, Co. ; de-nas gnas-paḥi phyed-du, T.

22. b. hiraṇmayā hastimṛgāśvakāś ca, Co. cd. rathāś ca gāvo vasanaprayuktā gantrīś ca, Co. ; tantrīś ca, Co.'s MSS. D and P ; mi chuṅ gzugs-rnams daṅ śiṅ-rta ba-glaṅ phyuṅ-ṅus (byuṅ dus, Weller) yaṅ-dag sbyar-rnams, T.

एवं स तैस्तैर्विषयोपचारैर्वयोऽनुरूपैरुपचर्यमाणः ।
बालोऽप्यबालप्रतिमो बभूव धृत्या च शौचेन धिया श्रिया च ॥२३॥
वयश्च कौमारमतीत्य सम्यक् संप्राप्य काले प्रतिपत्तिकर्म ।
अल्पैरहोभिर्बहुवर्षगम्या जग्राह विद्याः स्वकुलानुरूपाः ॥ २४ ॥
नैःश्रेयसं तस्य तु भव्यमर्थं श्रुत्वा पुरस्तादसितान्महर्षेः ।
कामेषु सङ्गं जनयांबभूव वनानि यायादिति शाक्यराजः ॥ २५ ॥
कुलात्ततोऽस्मै स्थिरशीलयुक्तात्साध्वीं वपुर्ह्रीविनयोपपन्नाम् ।
यशोधरां नाम यशोविशालां वामाभिधानां श्रियमाजुहाव ॥२६॥
विद्योतमानो वपुषा परेण सनत्कुमारप्रतिमः कुमारः ।
सार्धं तया शाक्यनरेन्द्रवध्वा शच्या सहस्राक्ष इवाभिरेमे ॥ २७ ॥
किंचिन्मनःक्षोभकरं प्रतीपं कथं न पश्येदिति सोऽनुचिन्त्य ।
वासं नृपो व्यादिशति स्म तस्मै हर्म्योदरेष्वेव न भूप्रचारम् ॥ २८ ॥
ततः शरत्तोयदपाण्डरेषु भूमौ विमानेष्विव रञ्जितेषु ।
हर्म्येषु सर्वर्तुसुखाश्रयेषु स्त्रीणामुदारैर्विजहार तूर्यैः ॥ २९ ॥

24. ab. madhyaṁ samprāpya bālaḥ sa hi rājasūnuḥ (two MSS. omit *b*), Co.; yaṅ-dag-par ḥdu-byed las ni rab-tu-thob-nas dus-su ni, T.

25. ab. don-gyi skal-ba thos-nas (bhāgyam arthaṁ śrutvā), T. d. vṛddhir bhavac chākyakulasya rājñaḥ (two MSS. omit *d*), Co.; nags-su gśegs-par ḥgyur zhes śākyaḥi rgyal-po-yis, T.

26. a. °śīlasaṁyutāt, Co.; tshul-khrims spyod-pa spyan-gyi (read sbyar-gyi ?), T. d. tulyābhidhānāṁ (tāmābhidhānāṁ, two MSS.), Co.; btsun-mor mṅon-par-brjod-paḥi, T.

27. a. athāparaṁ bhūmipateḥ priyo yaṁ (one MS. only in margin, all MSS. have in text pūyāpareṇa, six syllables short), Co.; mchog-gi lus-kyis sṅan-zhiṅ gsal-ba, T. b. de ñid (sa eva for kumāraḥ), T.

28. b. kathaṁ ca paśyed, Co.; gaṅ-gis mthoṅ mi-ḥgyur, T. c. hy ādiśati, Co.; rnam-par-bstan, T.

कलैर्हि चामीकरबद्धकक्षैर्नारीकराग्राभिहतैर्मृदङ्गैः ।
वराप्सरोनृत्यसमैश्च नृत्यैः कैलासवत्तद्भवनं रराज ॥ ३० ॥
वाग्भिः कलाभिर्ललितैश्च हावैर्मदैः सखेलैर्मधुरैश्च हासैः ।
तं तत्र नार्यो रमयांबभूवुर्भ्रूवञ्चितैरर्धनिरीक्षितैश्च ॥ ३१ ॥
ततः स कामाश्रयपण्डिताभिः स्त्रीभिर्गृहीतो रतिकर्कशाभिः ।
विमानपृष्ठान्न महीं जगाम विमानपृष्ठादिव पुण्यकर्मा ॥ ३२ ॥
नृपस्तु तस्यैव विवृद्धिहेतोस्तद्भाविनार्थेन च चोद्यमानः ।
शमेऽभिरेमे विरराम पापाद्भेजे दमं संविबभाज साधून् ॥ ३३ ॥
नाधीरवत्कामसुखे ससञ्जे न संररञ्जे विषमं जनन्याम् ।
धृत्येन्द्रियाश्वांश्चपलान्विजिग्ये बन्धूंश्च पौरांश्च गुणैर्जिगाय ॥ ३४ ॥
नाध्यैष्ट दुःखाय परस्य विद्यां ज्ञानं शिवं यत्तु तदध्यगीष्ट ।
स्वाभ्यः प्रजाभ्यो हि यथा तथैव सर्वप्रजाभ्यः शिवमाशशंसे ॥ ३५ ॥
भं भासुरं चाङ्गिरसाधिदेवं यथावदानर्च तदायुषे सः ।
जुहाव हव्यान्यकृशे कृशानौ ददौ द्विजेभ्यः कृशनं च गाश्च ॥ ३६ ॥
सस्नौ शरीरं पवितुं मनश्च तीर्थाम्बुभिश्चैव गुणाम्बुभिश्च ।
वेदोपदिष्टं सममात्मजं च सोमं पपौ शान्तिसुखं च हार्दम् ॥ ३७ ॥
सान्त्वं बभाषे न च नार्थवद्यज्जजल्प तत्त्वं न च विप्रियं यत् ।
सान्त्वं ह्यतत्त्वं परुषं च तत्त्वं ह्रियाशकन्नात्मन एव वक्तुम् ॥ ३८ ॥

31. a. hārair (corrected in one MS. to hāvair), Co. ; T uncertain.

32. a. tataś ca, Co. ; de-nas de ni, T.

36. Fol. 9 of A begins with this verse. a. bhāṣ(?)ura cāṅgir(?)asādhidai-(?de?)vaṁ, A (much rubbed). d. kṛṣanañ ca, A.

37. c. ātmañjañ ca, A ; zhi-ba bdag-skyes (śamam ātmajaṁ), T.

38. c. atatva, A. d. hriyāsakan, A.

इष्टेष्वनिष्टेषु च कार्यवत्सु न रागदोषाश्रयतां प्रपेदे ।
शिवं सिषेवे व्यवहारशुद्धं यज्ञं हि मेने न तथा यथा तत् ॥ ३९ ॥

आशावते चाभिगताय सद्यो देयाम्बुभिस्तर्षमचेच्छिदिष्ट ।
युद्धादृते वृत्तपरश्वधेन द्विड्दर्पमुद्वृत्तमबेभिदिष्ट ॥ ४० ॥

एकं विनिन्ये स जुगोप सप्त सप्तैव तत्याज ररक्ष पञ्च ।
प्राप त्रिवर्गं बुबुधे त्रिवर्गं जज्ञे द्विवर्गं प्रजहौ द्विवर्गम् ॥ ४१ ॥

कृतागसोऽपि प्रतिपाद्य वध्यान्नाजीघनन्नापि रुषा ददर्श ।
बबन्ध सान्त्वेन फलेन चैतांस्त्यागोऽपि तेषां ह्यनयाय दृष्टः ॥ ४२ ॥

आर्षाण्यचारीत्परमव्रतानि वैराण्यहासीच्चिरसंभृतानि ।
यशांसि चापद्गुणगन्धवन्ति रजांस्यहार्षीन्मलिनीकराणि ॥ ४३ ॥

न चाजिहीर्षीद्बलिमप्रवृत्तं न चाचिकीर्षीत्परवस्त्वभिध्याम् ।
न चाविवक्षीद्द्विषतामधर्मं न चाविवक्षीद्धृदयेन मन्युम् ॥ ४४ ॥

तस्मिंस्तथा भूमिपतौ प्रवृत्ते भृत्याश्च पौराश्च तथैव चेरुः ।
शमात्मके चेतसि विप्रसन्ने प्रयुक्तयोगस्य यथेन्द्रियाणि ॥ ४५ ॥

39. c. vyavahāralabdhaṁ, A; dge-baḥi tha-sñad gtsaṅ-ma-la, T. d. e.c. Formichi; yathāvat, A; ji-ltar bzhin (yathāvat, yatheva?), T; for C see note in translation.

40. c. °paraśvavena, A; ye-śes-kyi ni sta-re-yis (jñānaparaśvadhena ?), T. d. dvidarppam, A; dgra-bo-rnams-kyi ṅa-rgyal, T.

41. c. bubudhe t(?)ivarggaṁ, A.

42. a. rab-tu-bskyabs-nas (pratipālya), T. b. nājīghanat nāpi, A. cd. caitāṁ tyāgo, A.

43. b. vairāṇy ahāsīṁś cira°, A. c. guṇavāndhavanti, A. d. rajāṁsv, A. rnam-par-dor (vyahāsīn, vyahārṣīn?), T.

44. b. na cācikīṣīt, A. d. e.c. Finot; na cāvidhakṣīd, A; bzuṅ-ba ma-yin-no (from dhṛ or grah), T; na cādidhakṣīd, Co.; na cābibhakṣīd, Kielhorn.

45. b. byas (cakruḥ), T. c. samātmake, A; zhi-baḥi bdag-ñid, T.

काले ततश्चारुपयोधरायां यशोधरायां स्वयशोधरायाम् ।
शौद्धोदने राहुसपत्नवक्त्रो जज्ञे सुतो राहुल एव नाम्ना ॥ ४६ ॥

अथेष्टपुत्रः परमप्रतीतः कुलस्य वृद्धिं प्रति भूमिपालः ।
यथैव पुत्रप्रसवे ननन्द तथैव पौत्रप्रसवे ननन्द ॥ ४७ ॥

पुत्रस्य मे पुत्रगतो ममेव स्नेहः कथं स्यादिति जातहर्षः ।
काले स तं तं विधिमाललम्बे पुत्रप्रियः स्वर्गमिवारुरुक्षन् ॥ ४८ ॥

स्थित्वा पथि प्राथमकल्पिकानां राजर्षभाणां यशसान्वितानाम् ।
शुक्लान्यमुक्त्वापि तपांस्यतप्त यज्ञैश्च हिंसारहितैरयष्ट ॥ ४९ ॥

अजाज्वलिष्टाथ स पुण्यकर्मा नृपश्रिया चैव तपःश्रिया च ।
कुलेन वृत्तेन धिया च दीप्तस्तेजः सहस्रांशुरिवोत्सिसृक्षुः ॥ ५० ॥

स्वायंभुवं चार्चिकमर्चयित्वा
जजाप पुत्रस्थितये स्थितश्रीः ।
चकार कर्माणि च दुष्कराणि
प्रजाः सिसृक्षुः क इवादिकाले ॥ ५१ ॥

तत्याज शस्त्रं विममर्श शास्त्रं शमं सिषेवे नियमं विषेहे ।
वशीव कंचिद्विषयं न भेजे पितेव सर्वान्विषयान्ददर्श ॥ ५२ ॥

46. b. yaśodharāyā, A. c. sauddhodane, A.

47. a. athentaputraḥ, A ; de-nas ḥdod-paḥi bu-mṅaḥ, T.

48. a. puta(?tra?)sya, A ; bu-yi, T. mamaiva, A ; bdag bzhin, T. d. ḥdzegs-par-gyur (āruroha?), T.

49. b. rājarṣabhānāṁ, A. yasasānvitānāṁ, A ; grags daṅ sñan-pas mtshan-rnams-kyi (yaśasāṅkitānām), T. d. ayaṣṭaḥ, A.

50. a. ajajvaliṣṭātha, A.

51. b. jajāya putraḥsthitaye (mark over visarga to show error), A. brtan-paḥi dpal-gyis (sthiraśrīḥ?), T.

52. a. vimamarṣa, A. b. samaṁ, A ; ñe-bar zhi-la, T.

बभार राज्यं स हि पुत्रहेतोः पुत्रं कुलार्थं यशसे कुलं तु ।
स्वर्गाय शब्दं दिवमात्महेतोर्धर्मार्थमात्मस्थितिमाचकाङ्क्ष ॥ ५३ ॥

एवं स धर्मं विविधं चकार सद्भिर्निपातं श्रुतितश्च सिद्धम् ।
दृष्ट्वा कथं पुत्रमुखं सुतो मे वनं न यायादिति नाथमानः ॥ ५४ ॥

रिरक्षिषन्तः श्रियमात्मसंस्थां रक्षन्ति पुत्रान् भुवि भूमिपालाः ।
पुत्रं नरेन्द्रः स तु धर्मकामो ररक्ष धर्माद्विषयेषु मुञ्चन् ॥ ५५ ॥

वनमनुपमसत्त्वा बोधिसत्त्वास्तु सर्वे
विषयसुखरसज्ञा जग्मुरुत्पन्नपुत्राः ।
अत उपचितकर्मा रूढमूलेऽपि हेतौ
स रतिमुपसिषेवे बोधिमापन्न यावत् ॥ ५६ ॥

इति बुद्धचरिते महाकाव्येऽन्तःपुरविहारो नाम द्वितीयः सर्गः ॥ २ ॥

53. d. ācakāṁksaṁ, A.

54. b. niyātāṁ, A ; ṅes-thob-paḥi, T. c. katha, A.

55. a. ātmasaṁsthā, A ; bdag-la yaṅ-dag gnas-paḥi dpal, T. d. viṣayeṣv amuñcan, A ; yul-rnams ḥdor-pa med-par (=A), T ; viṣayeṣv amuñcat, Co. ; 'the king now, having begotten a son, in accordance with his feelings let him throw off all bounds in the five passions ; he only wished him to take pleasure in worldly glory ', C.

56. c. de-phyir (tata?), T. d. zhi-ba ma-thob (śāntim āpan na ?), T.

CANTO III

ततः कदाचिन्मृदुशाद्वलानि पुंस्कोकिलोन्नादितपादपानि ।
शुश्राव पद्माकरमण्डितानि गीतैर्निबद्धानि स काननानि ॥ १ ॥

श्रुत्वा ततः स्त्रीजनवल्लभानां मनोज्ञभावं पुरकाननानाम् ।
बहिःप्रयाणाय चकार बुद्धिमन्तर्गृहे नाग इवावरुद्धः ॥ २ ॥

ततो नृपस्तस्य निशम्य भावं पुत्राभिधानस्य मनोरथस्य ।
स्नेहस्य लक्ष्म्या वयसश्च योग्यामाज्ञापयामास विहारयात्राम् ॥ ३ ॥

निवर्तयामास च राजमार्गे संपातमार्तस्य पृथग्जनस्य ।
मा भूत्कुमारः सुकुमारचित्तः संविग्नचेता इति मन्यमानः ॥ ४ ॥

प्रत्यङ्गहीनान्विकलेन्द्रियांश्च जीर्णातुरादीन् कृपणांश्च दिक्षु ।
ततः समुत्सार्य परेण साम्ना शोभां परां राजपथस्य चक्रुः ॥ ५ ॥

ततः कृते श्रीमति राजमार्गे श्रीमान्विनीतानुचरः कुमारः ।
प्रासादपृष्ठादवतीर्य काले कृताभ्यनुज्ञो नृपमभ्यगच्छत् ॥ ६ ॥

अथो नरेन्द्रः सुतमागताश्रुः शिरस्युपाघ्राय चिरं निरीक्ष्य ।
गच्छेति चाज्ञापयति स्म वाचा स्नेहान्न चैनं मनसा मुमोच ॥ ७ ॥

1. b. puskokilonnāditapādapāṇi, A. d. śīte nibaddhāni, A ; glu-rnams daṅ ni ṅes-ldan, T. kānanī (corrected marginally to kānanāni), A.

2. d. antagṛhe nāgam ivāvaruddhaḥ, A.

3. a. nṛpaṁ tasya, A.

4. d. iva manyamānaḥ, A ; zhes sems-śiṅ, T.

5. b. dikṣuḥ, A ; phyogs-rnams-su, T.

7. b. nirīkṣyaḥ, A ; rnam-gzigs-nas (vilokya ?), T. d. snehān(?) nu(?) cainaṁ, A.

ततः स जाम्बूनदभाण्डभृद्भिर्युक्तं चतुर्भिर्निभृतैस्तुरङ्गैः ।
अक्लीबविद्वच्छुचिरश्मिधारं हिरण्मयं स्यन्दनमारुरोह ॥ ८ ॥

ततः प्रकीर्णोज्ज्वलपुष्पजालं विषक्तमाल्यं प्रचलत्पताकम् ।
मार्गं प्रपेदे सदृशानुयात्रश्चन्द्रः सनक्षत्र इवान्तरीक्षम् ॥ ९ ॥

कौतूहलात्स्फीततरैश्च नेत्रैर्नीलोत्पलार्धैरिव कीर्यमाणम् ।
शनैः शनै राजपथं जगाहे पौरैः समन्तादभिवीक्ष्यमाणः ॥ १० ॥

तं तुष्टुवुः सौम्यगुणेन केचिद्ववन्दिरे दीप्ततया तथान्ये ।
सौमुख्यतस्तु श्रियमस्य केचिद्वैपुल्यमाशंसिषुरायुषश्च ॥ ११ ॥

निःसृत्य कुब्जाश्च महाकुलेभ्यो व्यूहाश्च कैरातकवामनानाम् ।
नार्यः कृशेभ्यश्च निवेशनेभ्यो देवानुयानध्वजवत्प्रणेमुः ॥ १२ ॥

ततः कुमारः खलु गच्छतीति श्रुत्वा स्त्रियः प्रेष्यजनात्प्रवृत्तिम् ।
दिदृक्षया हर्म्यतलानि जग्मुर्जनेन मान्येन कृताभ्यनुज्ञाः ॥ १३ ॥

ताः स्रस्तकाञ्चीगुणविघ्निताश्च सुप्तप्रबुद्धाकुललोचनाश्च ।
वृत्तान्तविन्यस्तविभूषणाश्च कौतूहलेनानिभृताः परीयुः ॥ १४ ॥

प्रासादसोपानतलप्रणादैः काञ्चीरवैर्नूपुरनिस्वनैश्च ।
वित्रासयन्त्यो गृहपक्षिसङ्घानन्योन्यवेगांश्च समाक्षिपन्त्यः ॥ १५ ॥

8. c. °rasmidhāraṁ, A.

9. a. ḥbras-spos (Peking ed., sbos) me-tog (°puṣpalājaṁ?), T. b. visakta°, A.

10. b. e.c.; kiryamāṇaḥ, A. c. jagāhai, A. d. abhivīkṣamānaḥ, A; mṅon-par-dgaḥ (abhinandyamānaḥ), T.

11. d. āsasiṣur, A.

14. a. śrastakāñcīguṇavighnatāś, A.

15. a. °sopāṇa°, A. d. °vegāś ca (on margin °vegāc ca), A; śugs-rnams-las kyaṅ (°vegaiś ca ?), T.

कासांचिदासां तु वराङ्गनानां जातत्वराणामपि सोत्सुकानाम् ।
गतिं गुरुत्वाज्जगृहुर्विशालाः श्रोणीरथाः पीनपयोधराश्च ॥ १६ ॥
शीघ्रं समर्थापि तु गन्तुमन्या गतिं निजग्राह ययौ न तूर्णम् ।
ह्रियाप्रगल्भा विनिगूहमाना रहःप्रयुक्तानि विभूषणानि ॥ १७ ॥
परस्परोत्पीडनपिण्डितानां संमर्दसंक्षोभितकुण्डलानाम् ।
तासां तदा सस्वनभूषणानां वातायनेष्वप्रशमो बभूव ॥ १८ ॥
वातायनेभ्यस्तु विनिःसृतानि परस्परायासितकुण्डलानि ।
स्त्रीणां विरेजुर्मुखपङ्कजानि सक्तानि हर्म्येष्विव पङ्कजानि ॥ १९ ॥
ततो विमानैर्युवतीकरालैः कौतूहलोद्घाटितवातयानैः ।
श्रीमत्समन्तान्नगरं बभासे वियद्विमानैरिव साप्सरोभिः ॥ २० ॥
वातायनानामविशालभावादन्योन्यगण्डार्पितकुण्डलानाम् ।
मुखानि रेजुः प्रमदोत्तमानां बद्धाः कलापा इव पङ्कजानाम् ॥२१॥
तं ताः कुमारं पथि वीक्षमाणाः स्त्रियो बभुर्गामिव गन्तुकामाः ।
ऊर्ध्वोन्मुखाश्चैनमुदीक्षमाणा नरा बभुर्द्यामिव गन्तुकामाः ॥ २२ ॥

16. c. garutvāj jagṛhur viśālā, A.

17. b. nijajagrāha, A. c. ninigūhamānā, A ; rnam-par-sbas-pa, T.

18. b. saṅkhobhita°, A ; bskyod-gyur, T. d. aprasamo, A ; rab-tu-zhi-bar (vātāyaneṣu praśamo), T.

19. d. sakt{i/a}ni, A.

20. a. vimāmo yu° (corrected to vimānau yu°), A. b. vātapānaiḥ, Kern. c. babhāṣe, A ; mdzes-par-gyur, T.

21. b. °kuṇḍo(?a?)lānāṁ, A. c. pamadottamānāṁ, A. d. kapālā (corrected to kalāpā), A.

22. a. tebhyaḥ kumāraṁ pithi, A ; gzhon-nu de-la lam-du . . . de-rnams, T. c. ūrdhonmukhāś cenam, A.

दृष्ट्वा च तं राजसुतं स्त्रियस्ता
जाज्वल्यमानं वपुषा श्रिया च ।
धन्यास्य भार्येति शनैरवोच-
ञ्शुद्धैर्मनोभिः खलु नान्यभावात् ॥ २३ ॥

अयं किल व्यायतपीनबाहू
रूपेण साक्षादिव पुष्पकेतुः ।
त्यक्त्वा श्रियं धर्ममुपैष्यतीति
तस्मिन् हि ता गौरवमेव चक्रुः ॥ २४ ॥

कीर्णं तथा राजपथं कुमारः पौरैर्विनीतैः शुचिधीरवेषैः ।
तत्पूर्वमालोक्य जहर्ष किंचिन्मेने पुनर्भावमिवात्मनश्च ॥ २५ ॥

पुरं तु तत्स्वर्गमिव प्रहृष्टं शुद्धाधिवासाः समवेक्ष्य देवाः ।
जीर्णं नरं निर्ममिरे प्रयातुं संचोदनार्थं क्षितिपात्मजस्य ॥ २६ ॥

ततः कुमारो जरयाभिभूतं दृष्ट्वा नरेभ्यः पृथगाकृतिं तम् ।
उवाच संग्राहकमागतास्थस्तत्रैव निष्कम्पनिविष्टदृष्टिः ॥ २७ ॥

क एष भोः सूत नरोऽभ्युपेतः केशैः सितैर्यष्टिविषक्तहस्तः ।
भ्रूसंवृताक्षः शिथिलानताङ्गः किं विक्रियैषा प्रकृतिर्यदृच्छा ॥ २८ ॥

23. c. sanair avocan, A.

24. d. sauravam (reinked), A.

25. ab. kirṇnan taṁthā rājapathāṁ kumāraḥ pauraiḥ vinītaiḥ śucidhīraceṣiḥ (corrected to °ṣaiḥ), A. d. punabhāvam, A.

26. a. suarggam iva prahṛṣṭa, A. b. samavekṣyā vevāḥ (written over devāḥ apparently), A.

27. a. jarayā vibhūtaṁ, A ; rga-bas zil-non-zhiṅ, T.

28. b. sitai yaṣṭiviśakta°, A. d. vikriyeṣā, A.

इत्येवमुक्तः स रथप्रणेता निवेदयामास नृपात्मजाय ।
संरक्ष्यमप्यर्थमदोषदर्शी तैरेव देवैः कृतबुद्धिमोहः ॥ २९ ॥

रूपस्य हन्त्री व्यसनं बलस्य शोकस्य योनिर्निधनं रतीनाम् ।
नाशः स्मृतीनां रिपुरिन्द्रियाणामेषा जरा नाम ययैष भग्नः ॥३०॥

पीतं ह्यनेनापि पयः शिशुत्वे कालेन भूयः परिसृप्तमुर्व्याम् ।
क्रमेण भूत्वा च युवा वपुष्मान् क्रमेण तेनैव जरामुपेतः ॥ ३१ ॥

इत्येवमुक्ते चलितः स किंचिद्राजात्मजः सूतमिदं बभाषे ।
किमेष दोषो भविता ममापीत्यस्मै ततः सारथिरभ्युवाच ॥ ३२ ॥

आयुष्मतोऽप्येष वयःप्रकर्षो निःसंशयं कालवशेन भावी ।
एवं जरां रूपविनाशयित्रीं जानाति चैवेच्छति चैव लोकः ॥ ३३ ॥

ततः स पूर्वाशयशुद्धबुद्धि-
र्विस्तीर्णकल्पाचितपुण्यकर्मा ।
श्रुत्वा जरां संविविजे महात्मा
महाशनेर्घोषमिवान्तिके गौः ॥ ३४ ॥

29. b. sa-skyoṅ bdag-ñid skyes-la (bhūpātmajāya ?), T. d. tair aiva, A.

30. d. jarā ṇama (corrected to nāma in margin), A.

31. b. e.c. Böhtlingk ; parisṛṣṭam, A ; dus-kyis sa-la gñid-log gyur-pa-ste (kālena bhūmau parisuptabhūtaṃ, or bhūyaḥ misunderstood), T. bālena, Gawroński. c. vayuṣmān, A ; lus rab-ldan-paḥi, T.

32. a. evam uktaś, Cappeller ; de skad ces smras (ambiguous), T. cakitaḥ, Speyer ; ḥdar zhiṅ (ambiguous), T. d. de-bzhin ḥdi-la (asmai tathā), T.

33. c. °vināsayitrīṁ, A. d. daṅ mthoṅ-ba ñid (caivekṣati ?), T ; 'the whole world knows this and seeks it ', C.

34. a. tataḥ śa, A. c. gzhon-nu (kumāraḥ), T. d. mahāśane ghoṣam ivāntike śauḥ, A ; ba-laṅ bzhin, T.

निःश्वस्य दीर्घं स्वशिरः प्रकम्प्य तस्मिंश्च जीर्णे विनिवेश्य चक्षुः ।
तां चैव दृष्ट्वा जनतां सहर्षां वाक्यं स संविग्न इदं जगाद ॥ ३५ ॥

एवं जरा हन्ति च निर्विशेषं स्मृतिं च रूपं च पराक्रमं च ।
न चैव संवेगमुपैति लोकः प्रत्यक्षतोऽपीदृशमीक्षमाणः ॥ ३६ ॥

एवं गते सूत निवर्तयाश्वान् शीघ्रं गृहाण्येव भवान्प्रयातु ।
उद्यानभूमौ हि कुतो रतिर्मे जराभये चेतसि वर्तमाने ॥ ३७ ॥

अथाज्ञया भर्तृसुतस्य तस्य निवर्तयामास रथं नियन्ता ।
ततः कुमारो भवनं तदेव चिन्तावशः शून्यमिव प्रपेदे ॥ ३८ ॥

यदा तु तत्रैव न शर्म लेभे जरा जरेति प्रपरीक्षमाणः ।
ततो नरेन्द्रानुमतः स भूयः क्रमेण तेनैव बहिर्जगाम ॥ ३९ ॥

अथापरं व्याधिपरीतदेहं त एव देवाः ससृजुर्मनुष्यम् ।
दृष्ट्वा च तं सारथिमाबभाषे शौद्धोदनिस्तद्गतदृष्टिरेव ॥ ४० ॥

स्थूलोदरः श्वासचलच्छरीरः स्रस्तांसबाहुः कृशपाण्डुगात्रः ।
अम्बेति वाचं करुणं ब्रुवाणः परं समाश्रित्य नरः क एषः ॥ ४१ ॥

35. a. sa śiraḥ prakampya, A ; raṅ-gi mgo bsgul-zhiṅ, T. b. jīrṇṇo, A. d. samaṁ vignam idaṁ, A ; sems ni khoṅ-du chud-pa de-yis tshig ḥdi smras, T.

36. c. upeti, A.

37. b. śīghra, A. bhavāt prayātu, A. c. kho-bo-la . . . bde-ba (sukhaṁ me ?), T. d. jarābhave, A ; rgas-paḥi ḥjigs-pa, T.

38. a. bhṛ(corrected to bha)rtṛsutasya, A ; rgyal-poḥi sras-po (rājasutasya), T.

39. d. bahi jagāma, A.

40. b. manuṣya, A.

41. b. e.c. Cowell ; śrastāṁśabāhuḥ, A ; lag-pa cha-śas zha-zhiṅ (srastāṁśabāhuḥ), T. c. kuruṇaṁ, A. d. samāsṛtya, A ; rten (for brten)-nas, T.

ततोऽब्रवीत्सारथिरस्य सौम्य धातुप्रकोपप्रभवः प्रवृद्धः ।
रोगाभिधानः सुमहाननर्थः शक्तोऽपि येनैष कृतोऽस्वतन्त्रः ॥ ४२ ॥
इत्यूचिवान् राजसुतः स भूयस्तं सानुकम्पो नरमीक्षमाणः ।
अस्यैव जातो पृथगेष दोषः सामान्यतो रोगभयं प्रजानाम् ॥ ४३ ॥
ततो बभाषे स रथप्रणेता कुमार साधारण एष दोषः ।
एवं हि रोगैः परिपीड्यमानो रुजातुरो हर्षमुपैति लोकः ॥ ४४ ॥
इति श्रुतार्थः स विषण्णचेताः प्रावेपताम्बूर्मिगतः शशीव ।
इदं च वाक्यं करुणायमानः प्रोवाच किंचिन्मृदुना स्वरेण ॥ ४५ ॥
इदं च रोगव्यसनं प्रजानां पश्यंश्च विश्रम्भमुपैति लोकः ।
विस्तीर्णमज्ञानमहो नराणां हसन्ति ये रोगभयैरमुक्ताः ॥ ४६ ॥
निवर्त्यतां सूत बहिःप्रयाणान्नरेन्द्रसद्मैव रथः प्रयातु ।
श्रुत्वा च मे रोगभयं रतिभ्यः प्रत्याहतं संकुचतीव चेतः ॥ ४७ ॥
ततो निवृत्तः स निवृत्तहर्षः प्रध्यानयुक्तः प्रविवेश वेश्म ।
तं द्विस्तथा प्रेक्ष्य च संनिवृत्तं पर्येषणं भूमिपतिश्चकार ॥ ४८ ॥
श्रुत्वा निमित्तं तु निवर्तनस्य संत्यक्तमात्मानमनेन मेने ।
मार्गस्य शौचाधिकृताय चैव चुक्रोश रुष्टोऽपि च नोग्रदण्डः ॥ ४९ ॥

42. a. śaumya, A. c. romā(originally gā)bhidhānaḥ, A.

43. d. prajāṇāṁ, A.

44. c. rāgaiḥ, A. d. nad thar phyin-na (rujāntago ?), T. upeti, A.

45. a. śrutārtha, A. c. karuṇāyamāṇaḥ, A. d. kiñcit mṛdunā, A; cuṅ-zhig dṅar-baḥi dbyaṅs-kyis (kiṁcin madhunā svareṇa ?), T.

46. a. vyasana, A. b. raṅ-bzhin gnas-śiṅ (svasthaś ca), T. visrambham upeti, A. d. nad-las rnam-par grol-rnams (=rogād vimuktāḥ), T.

47. ab. bahiḥprayāṇāṁ narendrasadmeva, A. d. saṁkurativa, A.

48. c. prekṣa, A. d. pury āgamam, A; yoṅs-su-gros, T; 'the king asked what was the cause', C.

49. b. sa tyaktam, A; yaṅ-dag ḥdor, T.

भूयश्च तस्मै विदधे सुताय
    विशेषयुक्तं विषयप्रचारम् ।
चलेन्द्रियत्वादपि नाम सक्तो
    नास्मान्विजह्यादिति नाथमानः ॥ ५० ॥

यदा च शब्दादिभिरिन्द्रियार्थै-
    रन्तःपुरे नैव सुतोऽस्य रेमे ।
ततो बहिर्व्यादिशति स्म यात्रां
    रसान्तरं स्यादिति मन्यमानः ॥ ५१ ॥

स्नेहाच्च भावं तनयस्य बुद्ध्वा स रागदोषानविचिन्त्य कांश्चित् ।
योग्याः समाज्ञापयति स्म तत्र कलास्वभिज्ञा इति वारमुख्याः ॥५२॥

ततो विशेषेण नरेन्द्रमार्गे स्वलंकृते चैव परीक्षिते च ।
व्यत्यस्य सूतं च रथं च राजा प्रस्थापयामास बहिः कुमारम् ॥५३॥

ततस्तथा गच्छति राजपुत्रे तैरेव देवैर्विहितो गतासुः ।
तं चैव मार्गे मृतमुह्यमानं सूतः कुमारश्च ददर्श नान्यः ॥ ५४ ॥

अथाब्रवीद्राजसुतः स सूतं नरैश्चतुर्भिर्ह्रियते क एषः ।
दीनैर्मनुष्यैरनुगम्यमानो * भूषितश्चाप्यवरुद्यते च ॥ ५५ ॥

50. b. viṣayaprakāraṁ, A ; yul-la rab-tu-spyod-pa, T. c. śakto, A ; chags-bsñams-te, T ; 'rejoicing in worldly things', C.

51. d. mānyamānaḥ, A ; sems-śiṅ, T.

52. b. e.c ; saṁvegadōṣān, A ; de-la chags-paḥi skyon-rnams (tadrāgadoṣān), T.

53. b. parikṣyate, A ; yoṅs-su-brtags-pa-la, T.

55. a. atha bravīd, A. b. caturbhi hriyate, A. d. yo bhūṣitoś cāpy, A ; rgyan-gyis brgyan-pa-yin yaṅ (=bhūṣaṇena bhūṣitaś ca), T ; 'magnificently adorned with streamers and all sorts of flowers', C ; FP omits the phrase.

ततः स शुद्धात्मभिरेव देवैः शुद्धाधिवासैरभिभूतचेताः ।
अवाच्यमप्यर्थमिमं नियन्ता प्रव्याजहारार्थवदीश्वराय ॥ ५६ ॥

बुद्धीन्द्रियप्राणगुणैर्वियुक्तः सुप्तो विसंज्ञस्तृणकाष्ठभूतः ।
संवर्ध्य संरक्ष्य च यत्नवद्भिः प्रियप्रियैस्त्यज्यत एष कोऽपि ॥ ५७ ॥

इति प्रणेतुः स निशम्य वाक्यं संचुक्षुभे किंचिदुवाच चैनम् ।
किं केवलोऽस्यैव जनस्य धर्मः सर्वप्रजानामयमीदृशोऽन्तः ॥ ५८ ॥

ततः प्रणेता वदति स्म तस्मै
सर्वप्रजानामिदमन्तकर्म ।
हीनस्य मध्यस्य महात्मनो वा
सर्वस्य लोके नियतो विनाशः ॥ ५९ ॥

ततः स धीरोऽपि नरेन्द्रसूनुः श्रुत्वैव मृत्युं विषसाद सद्यः ।
अंसेन संश्लिष्य च कूबराग्रं प्रोवाच निह्रादवता स्वरेण ॥ ६० ॥

इयं च निष्ठा नियता प्रजानां
प्रमाद्यति त्यक्तभयश्च लोकः ।
मनांसि शङ्के कठिनानि नृणां
स्वस्थास्तथा ह्यध्वनि वर्तमानाः ॥ ६१ ॥

56. a. tataḥ sya, A.

57. d. priyas tyajyate (two syllables short), A ; sdug-pa sdug-pa-rnams-kyis (Weller amends to sdug ma-sdug-pa-rnams-kyis, =priyāpriyais), T.

58. a. niśāmya, A ; thos-nas, T. c. chos ḥdi ñid ni skye-ba ḥdi ñid kyaṅ gi ḥam (kim eṣa cāsyaiva janasya dharmaḥ?), T. d. mthar-gyur ḥdi-ḥdra . . . yin-nam-ci (athavedṛśo 'ntaḥ?), T.

59. b. antakarmaḥ, A.

60. b. śrutveva, A. c. aṁśena, A ; dpuṅ-pas, T.

61. b. pamādyati, A.

तस्माद्रथः सूत निवर्त्यतां नो विहारभूमेर्न हि देशकालः ।
जानन्विनाशं कथमार्तिकाले सचेतनः स्यादिह हि प्रमत्तः ॥ ६२ ॥

इति ब्रुवाणेऽपि नराधिपात्मजे निवर्तयामास स नैव तं रथम् ।
विशेषयुक्तं तु नरेन्द्रशासनात्स पद्मषण्डं वनमेव निर्ययौ ॥ ६३ ॥

ततः शिवं कुसुमितबालपादपं
परिभ्रमत्प्रमुदितमत्तकोकिलम् ।
विमानवत्स कमलचारुदीर्घिकं
ददर्श तद्वनमिव नन्दनं वनम् ॥ ६४ ॥

वराङ्गनागणकलिलं नृपात्मज-
स्ततो बलाद्वनमतिनीयते स्म तत् ।
वराप्सरोवृतमलकाधिपालयं
नवव्रतो मुनिरिव विघ्नकातरः ॥ ६५ ॥

इति बुद्धचरिते महाकाव्ये संवेगोत्पत्तिर्नाम तृतीयः सर्गः ॥ ३ ॥

62. a. rathaṁ, A. b. vihārabhumir nna, A; bdag-cag sa-la rnam-par rgyu-baḥi yul dus min, (=text or A), T. c. śes-nas (jñātvā), T. vināśaṁ kaṁ rttikāle (two syllables short), A; ñam-thag dus-su rnam-par ñams-pa . . . gaṅ ḥdra, T.

63. c. khyad-par ldan-pa-yin yaṅ mi-dbaṅ bstan-pa-las (viśeṣayuktāt tu narendraśāsanāt?), T.

64. c. padma daṅ bcas (sakamala°), T.

65. c. varāpsarovṛttam, A; lha mchog-mas bskor, T.

CANTO IV

ततस्तस्मात्पुरोद्यानात्कौतूहलचलेक्षणाः ।
प्रत्युज्जग्मुर्नृपसुतं प्राप्तं वरमिव स्त्रियः ॥ १ ॥

अभिगम्य च तास्तस्मै विस्मयोत्फुल्ललोचनाः ।
चक्रिरे समुदाचारं पद्मकोशनिभैः करैः ॥ २ ॥

तस्थुश्च परिवार्यैनं मन्मथाक्षिप्तचेतसः ।
निश्चलैः प्रीतिविकचैः पिबन्त्य इव लोचनैः ॥ ३ ॥

तं हि ता मेनिरे नार्यः कामो विग्रहवानिति ।
शोभितं लक्षणैर्दीप्तैः सहजैर्भूषणैरिव ॥ ४ ॥

सौम्यत्वाच्चैव धैर्याच्च काश्चिदेनं प्रजज्ञिरे ।
अवतीर्णो महीं साक्षाद्गूढांशुश्चन्द्रमा इति ॥ ५ ॥

तस्य ता वपुषाक्षिप्ता निगृहीतं जजृम्भिरे ।
अन्योन्यं दृष्टिभिर्हत्वा शनैश्च विनिशश्वसुः ॥ ६ ॥

1. c. nṛpasuta, A.

2. c. cak(?kr?)ire, A.

3. a. parivāryeṇam, A.

5. a. naumyatvāc, A; zhi-ba-ñid phyir, T. b. kaścid ainaṁ, A. d. candramā iva, A; zla-ba . . . bzhin (=A), T; 'saying the Moon-god had come', C.

6. c. anyonyān dṛṣṭibhir ggatvā, A; phan-tshun mig-rnams-kyis bsnun-nas, T.

एवं ता दृष्टिमात्रेण नार्यो ददृशुरेव तम् ।
न व्याजह्रुर्न जहसुः प्रभावेणास्य यन्त्रिताः ॥ ७ ॥
तास्तथा तु निरारम्भा दृष्ट्वा प्रणयविक्लवाः ।
पुरोहितसुतो धीमानुदायी वाक्यमब्रवीत् ॥ ८ ॥
सर्वाः सर्वकलाज्ञाः स्थ भावग्रहणपण्डिताः ।
रूपचातुर्यसंपन्नाः स्वगुणैर्मुख्यतां गताः ॥ ९ ॥
शोभयेत गुणैरेभिरपि तानुत्तरान् कुरून् ।
कुवेरस्यापि चाक्रीडं प्रागेव वसुधामिमाम् ॥ १० ॥
शक्ताश्चालयितुं यूयं वीतरागानृषीनपि ।
अप्सरोभिश्च कलितान् ग्रहीतुं विबुधानपि ॥ ११ ॥
भावज्ञानेन हावेन रूपचातुर्यसंपदा ।
स्त्रीणामेव च शक्ताः स्थ संरागे किं पुनर्नृणाम् ॥ १२ ॥
तासामेवंविधानां वो वियुक्तानां स्वगोचरे ।
इयमेवंविधा चेष्टा न तुष्टोऽस्म्यार्जवेन वः ॥ १३ ॥

7. b. dadṛsur, A. c. dgaḥ-med-par (na jahṛṣuḥ), T. d. prabhāvenāsya, A.

9. a. sarvvakalājñā, A. d. mukhyataṅ gatāḥ, A.

10. a. e.c. Kern ; śobhayata, A ; mdzes-te (śobhayatha ?), T. c. ca krīḍam, A ; skyed-tshal daṅ, T.

11. cd. apsarobhi kalitā gṛhītum (one syllable short), A ; lha-mo-rnams-kyis śes-pa-yi . . . len-par-ro, T.

12. b. e.c. ; cāturyārūpa°, A ; mdzaṅs daṅ gzugs ni phun-tshogs-pas, T. c. strīṇam, A. śaktā, A.

13. b. rab-sbyar-ba (prayuktānāṁ), T ; niyuktānāṁ, Co. c. coṣṭā, A. d. āryavena, A.

इदं नववधूनां वो ह्रीनिकुञ्चितचक्षुषाम् ।
सदृशं चेष्टितं हि स्यादपि वा गोपयोषिताम् ॥ १४ ॥
यदपि स्यादयं धीरः श्रीप्रभावान्महानिति ।
स्त्रीणामपि महत्तेज इतः कार्योऽत्र निश्चयः ॥ १५ ॥
पुरा हि काशिसुन्दर्या वेशवध्वा महानृषिः ।
ताडितोऽभूत्पदा व्यासो दुर्धर्षो देवतैरपि ॥ १६ ॥
मन्थालगौतमो भिक्षुर्जङ्घया वारमुख्यया ।
पिप्रीषुश्च तदर्थार्थं व्यसून्निरहरत्पुरा ॥ १७ ॥
गौतमं दीर्घतपसं महर्षिं दीर्घजीविनम् ।
योषित्संतोषयामास वर्णस्थानावरा सती ॥ १८ ॥
ऋष्यशृङ्गं मुनिसुतं तथैव स्त्रीष्वपण्डितम् ।
उपायैर्विविधैः शान्ता जग्राह च जहार च ॥ १९ ॥
विश्वामित्रो महर्षिश्च विगाढोऽपि महत्तपः ।
दश वर्षाण्यहर्मेने घृताच्याप्सरसा हृतः ॥ २० ॥

14. b. hrīvikuñcita°, Böhtlingk.

15. a. yady api, A; gaṅ-yaṅ, T. dpaḥ-ba (vīraḥ), T. d. iti kāryo, A; de-phyir . . . bya, T.

16. a. puro hi, A. c. padā bhyā (?vyā?)so, A; draṅ-sroṅ rgyas-pa rkaṅ-pas, T.

17. a. mānthala°, T. °gotamo, A. b. bhikṣu jaṅghayā, A.

18. a. gotamaṁ, A. mun riṅ-miṅ (dīrghatamasaṁ), T; 'practising long penance', C. b. maharṣaṁ, A.

19. a. ṛṣyaśṛṅga, A. thub-pa mchog (munivaram), T; 'the muni's son', C.

20. b. e.c.; mahattapāḥ, A; brtul-zhugs chen-po bstan-pa yaṅ (vigāḍho 'pi mahāvratam, or °vrataḥ), T. c. aha mene, A; ñi-mar śes, T.

एवमादीनृषींस्तांस्ताननयन्विक्रियां स्त्रियः ।
ललितं पूर्ववयसं किं पुनर्नृपतेः सुतम् ॥ २१ ॥
तदेवं सति विश्रब्धं प्रयतध्वं तथा यथा ।
इयं नृपस्य वंशश्रीरितो न स्यात्पराङ्मुखी ॥ २२ ॥
या हि काश्चिद्युवतयो हरन्ति सदृशं जनम् ।
निकृष्टोत्कृष्टयोर्भावं या गृह्णन्ति ता तु स्त्रियः ॥ २३ ॥
इत्युदायिवचः श्रुत्वा ता विद्धा इव योषितः ।
समारुरुहुरात्मानं कुमारग्रहणं प्रति ॥ २४ ॥
ता भ्रूभिः प्रेक्षितैर्हावैर्हसितैर्लडितैर्गतैः ।
चक्रुराक्षेपिकाश्चेष्टा भीतभीता इवाङ्गनाः ॥ २५ ॥
राज्ञस्तु विनियोगेन कुमारस्य च मार्दवात् ।
जहुः क्षिप्रमविश्रम्भं मदेन मदनेन च ॥ २६ ॥
अथ नारीजनवृतः कुमारो व्यचरद्वनम् ।
वासितायूथसहितः करीव हिमवद्वनम् ॥ २७ ॥
स तस्मिन् कानने रम्ये जज्वाल स्त्रीपुरःसरः ।
आक्रीड इव विभ्राजे विवस्वानप्सरोवृतः ॥ २८ ॥

21. a. evam mayādīn (one syllable in excess), A; T omits evam. b. vikriyān(?yā?) striyaḥ, A. d. puna nṛpateḥ, A.

23. a. yuvataye, A. b. śadṛśañ, A.

25. a. prekṣate hāvair, A; lta daṅ sgeg, T. b. rol (lalitair), T.

27. b. vyavacarad, A. c. vāsitayūtha°, A; gliṅ-moḥi tshogs, T.

28. c. vaibhrāje, Kern. d. 'Just as Śakra, the king of the gods' (=Marutvān?), C.

मदेनावर्जिता नाम तं काश्चित्तत्र योषितः ।
कठिनैः पस्पृशुः पीनैः संहतैर्वल्गुभिः स्तनैः ॥ २९ ॥

स्रस्तांसकोमलालम्बमृदुबाहुलताबला ।
अनृतं स्खलितं काचित्कृत्वैनं सस्वजे बलात् ॥ ३० ॥

काचित्ताम्राधरोष्ठेन मुखेनासवगन्धिना ।
विनिशश्वास कर्णेऽस्य रहस्यं श्रूयतामिति ॥ ३१ ॥

काचिदाज्ञापयन्तीव प्रोवाचार्द्रानुलेपना ।
इह भक्तिं कुरुष्वेति हस्तसंश्लेषलिप्सया ॥ ३२ ॥

मुहुर्मुहुर्मदव्याजस्रस्तनीलांशुकापरा ।
आलक्ष्यरशना रेजे स्फुरद्विद्युदिव क्षपा ॥ ३३ ॥

काश्चित्कनककाञ्चीभिर्मुखराभिरितस्ततः ।
बभ्रमुर्दर्शयन्त्योऽस्य श्रोणीस्तन्वंशुकावृताः ॥ ३४ ॥

चूतशाखां कुसुमितां प्रगृह्यान्या ललम्बिरे ।
सुवर्णकलशप्रख्यान्दर्शयन्त्यः पयोधरान् ॥ ३५ ॥

29. ab. rnam-par sgeg-bcas gzhon-nu-ma rgyags-pas ma-yaṅs (ma-gyeṅs, Weller e.c.) de-rnams ḥgaḥ (=savilāsā yoṣito madenānāyatās tāḥ kāścit), T. c. kaṭhinai, A. d. e.c.; saṁghatair, A ; lhan-cig-paḥi (sahitair), T.

30. a. śrastāṁśa°, A ; dpuṅ-pa-las brul, T. c. khalitaṅ, A. d. kṛtvenaṁ, A.

31. b. āśavagandhinā, A. d. rahasya; A. stod-cig ces(stūyatām iti), T.

32. d. e.c. ; hastasaṁśliṣyalipsayā, A ; rgod daṅ ḥkhyud daṅ ḥdod-pas ni (hāsasaṁśleṣalipsayā), T.

33. b. °śrasta°, A. c. °rasanā, A ; ska-rags phan-tshun sdud-pa ni (raśanā . . .), T.

34. a. °kāñcibhi, A.

35. d. darśayantya, A.

काचित्पद्मवनादेत्य सपद्मा पद्मलोचना ।
पद्मवक्त्रस्य पार्श्वेऽस्य पद्मश्रीरिव तस्थुषी ॥ ३६ ॥

मधुरं गीतमन्वर्थं काचित्साभिनयं जगौ ।
तं स्वस्थं चोदयन्तीव वञ्चितोऽसीत्यवेक्षितैः ॥ ३७ ॥

शुभेन वदनेनान्या भ्रूकार्मुकविकर्षिणा ।
प्रावृत्यानुचकारास्य चेष्टितं धीरलीलया ॥ ३८ ॥

पीनवल्गुस्तनी काचिद्धासाघूर्णितकुण्डला ।
उच्चैरवजहासैनं समाप्नोतु भवानिति ॥ ३९ ॥

अपयान्तं तथैवान्या बबन्धुर्माल्यदामभिः ।
काश्चित्साक्षेपमधुरैर्जगृहुर्वचनाङ्कुशैः ॥ ४० ॥

प्रतियोगार्थिनी काचिद्गृहीत्वा चूतवल्लरीम् ।
इदं पुष्पं तु कस्येति पप्रच्छ मदविक्लवा ॥ ४१ ॥

काचित्पुरुषवत्कृत्वा गतिं संस्थानमेव च ।
उवाचैनं जितः स्त्रीभिर्जय भो पृथिवीमिमाम् ॥ ४२ ॥

अथ लोलेक्षणा काचिज्जिघ्रन्ती नीलमुत्पलम् ।
किंचिन्मदकलैर्वाक्यैर्नृपात्मजमभाषत ॥ ४३ ॥

38. c. bskor-nas . . . rjes-ḥdoṅ (?ḥdod?) byas (*vṛtyānucacāra?), T; prākṛtyā°, Böhtlingk; pranṛtyā°, Formichi; ākṛtyā°, Speyer; vyāvṛtyā°, Cappeller.

39. c. avajahāsenaṁ, A.

40. a. tāthaivānyā, A.

41. c. puṣpaṁ nu, Cappeller.

42. c. uvācenaṁ, A.

43. b. kācid jighrantī, A.

पश्य भर्तश्चितं चूतं कुसुमैर्मधुगन्धिभिः ।
हेमपञ्जररुद्धो वा कोकिलो यत्र कूजति ॥ ४४ ॥

अशोको दृश्यतामेष कामिशोकविवर्धनः ।
रुवन्ति भ्रमरा यत्र दह्यमाना इवाग्निना ॥ ४५ ॥

चूतयष्ट्या समाश्लिष्टो दृश्यतां तिलकद्रुमः ।
शुक्लवासा इव नरः स्त्रिया पीताङ्गरागया ॥ ४६ ॥

फुल्लं कुरुबकं पश्य निर्भुक्तालक्तकप्रभम् ।
यो नखप्रभया स्त्रीणां निर्भर्त्सित इवानतः ॥ ४७ ॥

बालाशोकश्च निचितो दृश्यतामेष पल्लवैः ।
योऽस्माकं हस्तशोभाभिर्लज्जमान इव स्थितः ॥ ४८ ॥

दीर्घिकां प्रावृतां पश्य तीरजैः सिन्दुवारकैः ।
पाण्डुरांशुकसंवीतां शयानां प्रमदामिव ॥ ४९ ॥

दृश्यतां स्त्रीषु माहात्म्यं चक्रवाको ह्यसौ जले ।
पृष्ठतः प्रेष्यवद्भार्यामनुवर्त्यनुगच्छति ॥ ५० ॥

मत्तस्य परपुष्टस्य रुवतः श्रूयतां ध्वनिः ।
अपरः कोकिलोऽन्वक्षं प्रतिश्रुत्केव कूजति ॥ ५१ ॥

44. a. bhattaś citaṁ, A.

45. b. °vivaddhanah, A. d. dahyamānām ivā°, A.

46. a. samāśiṣṭo, A ; yaṅ-dag ḥkhyed, T.

47. d. nirbhatsita ivānabhaḥ, A ; rma-phab-gyur-te dud-pa ḥdra, T.

48. d. sthitiḥ, A.

49. b. e.c. Cowell ; sinduvārajaiḥ, A.

50. b. cakravākā, A. d. anuvṛrttyānu°, A ; rjes-ḥjug, T ; anuvṛtyānu°, Co.

51. b. ruvata, A. dhaniḥ, A. c. kokilo nutkaḥ, A ; khu-byug mṅon-sum-du, T. d. kūjita, A.

अपि नाम विहङ्गानां वसन्तेनाहृतो मदः ।
न तु चिन्तयतोऽचिन्त्यं जनस्य प्राज्ञमानिनः ॥ ५२ ॥

इत्येवं ता युवतयो मन्मथोद्दामचेतसः ।
कुमारं विविधैस्तैस्तैरुपचक्रमिरे नयैः ॥ ५३ ॥

एवमाक्षिप्यमाणोऽपि स तु धैर्यावृतेन्द्रियः ।
मर्तव्यमिति सोद्वेगो न जहर्ष न विव्यथे ॥ ५४ ॥

तासां तत्त्वेऽनवस्थानं दृष्ट्वा स पुरुषोत्तमः ।
समं विग्नेन धीरेण चिन्तयामास चेतसा ॥ ५५ ॥

किं विमा नावगच्छन्ति चपलं यौवनं स्त्रियः ।
यतो रूपेण संमत्तं जरा यन्नाशयिष्यति ॥ ५६ ॥

नूनमेता न पश्यन्ति कस्यचिद्रोगसंप्लवम् ।
तथा हृष्टा भयं त्यक्त्वा जगति व्याधिधर्मिणि ॥ ५७ ॥

अनभिज्ञाश्च सुव्यक्तं मृत्योः सर्वापहारिणः ।
ततः स्वस्था निरुद्विग्नाः क्रीडन्ति च हसन्ति च ॥ ५८ ॥

जरां व्याधिं च मृत्युं च को हि जानन्सचेतनः ।
स्वस्थस्तिष्ठेन्निषीदेद्वा शयेद्वा किं पुनर्हसेत् ॥ ५९ ॥

52. c. cintayataś cittaṁ, A ; bsams-pa-min sems, T.

54. a. ākṣipyamāno, A. d. na jaharṣa na sismiye, A ; dgaḥ daṅ ḥjigs-pa med-par-gyur, T ; ‘ neither grieved nor rejoiced ’, C.

55. a. bh(?)āsān tatve'nava°, A. c. sasaṁvignena, A ; mñam-la skyo, T.

56. c. rūpeṇa sampannaṁ, A ; gzugs-kyis myos-pa ni, T. d. jareyan nāśa°, A ; gaṅ-zhig rga-bas, T.

57. d. °dharmmiṇiḥ, A.

59. a. jarā, A. c. svastha, A. d. suped vā, A ; ñal-byed, T.

यस्तु दृष्ट्वा परं जीर्णं व्याधितं मृतमेव च ।
स्वस्थो भवति नोद्विग्नो यथाचेतास्तथैव सः ॥ ६० ॥
वियुज्यमाने हि तरौ पुष्पैरपि फलैरपि ।
पतति च्छिद्यमाने वा तरुरन्यो न शोचते ॥ ६१ ॥
इति ध्यानपरं दृष्ट्वा विषयेभ्यो गतस्पृहम् ।
उदायी नीतिशास्त्रज्ञस्तमुवाच सुहृत्तया ॥ ६२ ॥
अहं नृपतिना दत्तः सखा तुभ्यं क्षमः किल ।
यस्मात्त्वयि विवक्षा मे तया प्रणयवत्तया ॥ ६३ ॥
अहितात्प्रतिषेधश्च हिते चानुप्रवर्तनम् ।
व्यसने चापरित्यागस्त्रिविधं मित्रलक्षणम् ॥ ६४ ॥
सोऽहं मैत्रीं प्रतिज्ञाय पुरुषार्थात्पराङ्मुखः ।
यदि त्वा समुपेक्षेय न भवेन्मित्रता मयि ॥ ६५ ॥
तद्ब्रवीमि सुहृद्भूत्वा तरुणस्य वपुष्मतः ।
इदं न प्रतिरूपं ते स्त्रीष्वदाक्षिण्यमीदृशम् ॥ ६६ ॥
अनृतेनापि नारीणां युक्तं समनुवर्तनम् ।
तद्व्रीडापरिहारार्थमात्मरत्यर्थमेव च ॥ ६७ ॥

61. a. e.c. Gawroński ; viyujyamāne pi, A ; T omits api. d. mdzes-pa byed-ma-yin (na śobhate), T ; ' does not know fear ', C.

63. b. tubhyaṁ ksaḥ kilaḥ (one syllable short), A ; khyod-la . . . nus-pa lo (amended by Weller to ḥo, unnecessarily), T.

64. c. vyasane vāpari°, A ; sdug-pa-na yaṅ, T. d. yoṅs-rdzogs śes-kyi mtshan ñid-do (paryāptamitralakṣaṇam), T ; ' a friend has three characteristics', C.

65. a. maitrī, A. b. parāṅmukhaṁ, A ; T ambiguous ; ' if I should renounce the duty of a *puruṣa* ', C. d. na bhave mitratā, A ; grogs-po-ñid kyaṅ ma-yin-no (na bhaven mitratām api !), T.

67. b. yukta, A. c. de-yi ṅo-tshaḥi rgod don (tadvrīḍāparihāsārtham), T. d. °ratyandham (or °anvam), A ; dgaḥ-baḥi don-ñid-du, T.

संनतिश्चानुवृत्तिश्च स्त्रीणां हृदयबन्धनम् ।
स्नेहस्य हि गुणा योनिर्मानकामाश्च योषितः ॥ ६८ ॥

तदर्हसि विशालाक्ष हृदयेऽपि पराङ्मुखे ।
रूपस्यास्यानुरूपेण दाक्षिण्येनानुवर्तितुम् ॥ ६९ ॥

दाक्षिण्यमौषधं स्त्रीणां दाक्षिण्यं भूषणं परम् ।
दाक्षिण्यरहितं रूपं निष्पुष्पमिव काननम् ॥ ७० ॥

किं वा दाक्षिण्यमात्रेण भावेनास्तु परिग्रहः ।
विषयान्दुर्लभाँल्लब्ध्वा न ह्यवज्ञातुमर्हसि ॥ ७१ ॥

कामं परमिति ज्ञात्वा देवोऽपि हि पुरंदरः ।
गौतमस्य मुनेः पत्नीमहल्यां चकमे पुरा ॥ ७२ ॥

अगस्त्यः प्रार्थयामास सोमभार्यां च रोहिणीम् ।
तस्मात्तत्सदृशीं लेभे लोपामुद्रामिति श्रुतिः ॥ ७३ ॥

उतथ्यस्य च भार्यायां ममतायां महातपः ।
मारुत्यां जनयामास भरद्वाजं बृहस्पतिः ॥ ७४ ॥

बृहस्पतेर्महिष्यां च जुह्वत्यां जुह्वतां वरः ।
बुधं विबुधकर्माणं जनयामास चन्द्रमाः ॥ ७५ ॥

68. b. strīṇā, A.

70. a. oṣadhaṁ, A.

71. a. mkhas-paḥi raṅ-bzhin-gyis (dākṣiṇyabhāvena, or °mayena?), T. c. durllabhāl, A.

72. a. param ita, A ; mchog ces, T. c. gotamasya mune, A.

74. a. ūtasthyasya, A ; ubhathya-yi, T. b. e.c. Cowell ; samatāyām, A ; mthun-ma-la (saṁmatāyāṁ), T.

75. c. vibudhadharmmāṇaṁ, A ; lha-yi las-byed, T.

कालीं चैव पुरा कन्यां जलप्रभवसंभवाम् ।
जगाम यमुनातीरे जातरागः पराशरः ॥ ७६ ॥

मातङ्गामक्षमालायां गर्हितायां रिरंसया ।
कपिञ्जलादं तनयं वसिष्ठोऽजनयन्मुनिः ॥ ७७ ॥

ययातिश्चैव राजर्षिर्वयस्यपि विनिर्गते ।
विश्वाच्याप्सरसा सार्धं रेमे चैत्ररथे वने ॥ ७८ ॥

स्त्रीसंसर्गं विनाशान्तं पाण्डुर्ज्ञात्वापि कौरवः ।
माद्रीरूपगुणाक्षिप्तः सिषेवे कामजं सुखम् ॥ ७९ ॥

करालजनकश्चैव हृत्वा ब्राह्मणकन्यकाम् ।
अवाप भ्रंशमप्येवं न तु सेजे न मन्मथम् ॥ ८० ॥

एवमाद्या महात्मानो विषयान् गर्हितानपि ।
रतिहेतोर्बुभुजिरे प्रागेव गुणसंहितान् ॥ ८१ ॥

त्वं पुनर्न्यायतः प्राप्तान् बलवान्रूपवान्युवा ।
विषयानवजानासि यत्र सक्तमिदं जगत् ॥ ८२ ॥

इति श्रुत्वा वचस्तस्य श्लक्ष्णमागमसंहितम् ।
मेघस्तनितनिर्घोषः कुमारः प्रत्यभाषत ॥ ८३ ॥

76. c. yamunaḥi gliṅ-du (yamunādvīpe?), T.

77. a. gnod-sbyin ḥphreṅ-ma (yakṣamālāyāṁ), T. b. garhitāyā, A.

79. a. °saṁsargga, A.

80. c. bhraṁsam, A. ñid . . . kyaṅ (apy eva), T.

81. a. evamādīn, A ; de-la sogs-pa bdag-ñid chen, T ; 'thus all these many persons', C. b. marhitān api, A.

82. a. puna, A. d. ida, A.

83. b. °sahitaṁ, A ; bcas (=A), T. d. pratyabhāṣataḥ, A.

उपपन्नमिदं वाक्यं सौहार्दव्यञ्जकं त्वयि ।
अत्र च त्वानुनेष्यामि यत्र मा दुष्टु मन्यसे ॥ ८४ ॥
नावजानामि विषयान् जाने लोकं तदात्मकम् ।
अनित्यं तु जगन्मत्वा नात्र मे रमते मनः ॥ ८५ ॥
जरा व्याधिश्च मृत्युश्च यदि न स्यादिदं त्रयम् ।
ममापि हि मनोज्ञेषु विषयेषु रतिर्भवेत् ॥ ८६ ॥
नित्यं यद्यपि हि स्त्रीणामेतदेव वपुर्भवेत् ।
दोषवत्स्वपि कामेषु कामं रज्येत मे मनः ॥ ८७ ॥
यदा तु जरयापीतं रूपमासां भविष्यति ।
आत्मनोऽप्यनभिप्रेतं मोहात्तत्र रतिर्भवेत् ॥ ८८ ॥
मृत्युव्याधिजराधर्मा मृत्युव्याधिजरात्मभिः ।
रममाणो ह्यसंविग्नः समानो मृगपक्षिभिः ॥ ८९ ॥
यदप्यात्थ महात्मानस्तेऽपि कामात्मका इति ।
संवेगोऽत्रैव कर्तव्यो यदा तेषामपि क्षयः ॥ ९० ॥
माहात्म्यं न च तन्मन्ये यत्र सामान्यतः क्षयः ।
विषयेषु प्रसक्तिर्वा युक्तिर्वा नात्मवत्तया ॥ ९१ ॥

86. d. rati bhavet, A.

87. cd. sasamvitkasya kāmeṣu tathāpi na ratiḥ kṣamā, A; skyon-ldan ḥdod-pa-rnams-la yaṅ kho-boḥi sems ni ḥdod-la phyogs, T; 'though the lusts have their faults, still they might hold the feelings of man', C.

88. d. mohā tatra, A.

89. a. e.c. Cowell; °dharmmo, A. c. e.c. Lüders; ramamāno py, A; T omits api.

90. c. saṁvego tra karttavyo (one syllable short), A; ḥdir ni skyo-bar bya-ba-ste, T; 'that also can cause *saṁvega*', C.

91. a. na ca tan madhye, A; mi-sems-te (omitting ca tat), T. b. sāmanyataḥ, A; ci-las (=kutaścit?), T. c. praśaktir, A; chags-pa, T.

यदप्यात्थानृतेनापि स्त्रीजने वर्त्यतामिति ।
अनृतं नावगच्छामि दाक्षिण्येनापि किंचन ॥ ९२ ॥
न चानुवर्तनं तन्मे रुचितं यत्र नार्जवम् ।
सर्वभावेन संपर्को यदि नास्ति धिगस्तु तत् ॥ ९३ ॥
अधृतेः श्रद्दधानस्य सक्तस्यादोषदर्शिनः ।
किं हि वञ्चयितव्यं स्याज्जातरागस्य चेतसः ॥ ९४ ॥
वञ्चयन्ति च यद्येवं जातरागाः परस्परम् ।
ननु नैव क्षमं द्रष्टुं नराः स्त्रीणां नृणां स्त्रियः ॥ ९५ ।
तदेवं सति दुःखार्तं जरामरणभागिनम् ।
न मां कामेष्वनार्येषु प्रतारयितुमर्हसि ॥ ९६ ॥

अहोऽतिधीरं बलवच्च ते मन-
श्चलेषु कामेषु च सारदर्शिनः ।
भयेऽतितीव्रे विषयेषु सज्जसे
निरीक्षमाणो मरणाध्वनि प्रजाः ॥ ९७ ॥

अहं पुनर्भीरुरतीवविक्लवो
जराविपद्व्याधिभयं विचिन्तयन् ।
लभे न शान्तिं न धृतिं कुतो रतिं
निशामयन्दीप्तमिवाग्निना जगत् ॥ ९८ ॥

92. d. kiñcan, A. mkhas-pa-yis dpe-brjod ciṅ (=dākṣiṇyenāpy abhidadhat, udāharan), T.

94. a. anṛteḥ, A; mi-brtan-pa-yi, T. b. e.c. Cowell; śaktasyā°, A; skyon-du mthoṅ-baḥi nus-pa-yi (śaktasya doṣadarśinaḥ), T.

95. a. yady eva, A; gal-te de-ltar, T. c. neva, A; ñid ma-yin, T.

96. a. śati, A. c. kāmeṣu nāryeṣu, A; ḥphags-min ḥdod-pa-la, T.

97. c. bhaye pi tīvre, A; śin-tu rno-zhiṅ ḥjigs-paḥi, T.

98. a. puna bhīrur, A. d. niśāmayaṁ, A.

असंशयं मृत्युरिति प्रजानतो
नरस्य रागो हृदि यस्य जायते ।
अयोमयीं तस्य परैमि चेतनां
महाभये रज्यति यो न रोदिति ॥ ९९ ॥

अथो कुमारश्च विनिश्चयात्मिकां
चकार कामाश्रयघातिनीं कथाम् ।
जनस्य चक्षुर्गमनीयमण्डलो
महीधरं चास्तमियाय भास्करः ॥ १०० ॥

ततो वृथाधारितभूषणस्रजः
कलागुणैश्च प्रणयैश्च निष्फलैः ।
स्व एव भावे विनिगृह्य मन्मथं
पुरं ययुर्भग्नमनोरथाः स्त्रियः ॥ १०१ ॥

ततः पुरोद्यानगतां जनश्रियं
निरीक्ष्य सायं प्रतिसंहृतां पुनः ।
अनित्यतां सर्वगतां विचिन्तय-
न्विवेश धिष्ण्यं क्षितिपालकात्मजः ॥ १०२ ॥

99. c. paremi, A. d. mahābhaye rakṣati yo na r(?c?)odati, A ; ḥjigs-pa che-la chags-pa gaṅ-zhig ṅu-ba-med, T.

101. c. e.c. ; sa eva bhāve viniguhya manmathaṁ, A ; raṅ-gi sems-la yid-dkrugs ḥdod-pa rnam-smad-nas (=sve bhāve vigarhya manmathaṁ), T. d. yayu bhagna°, A.

102. a. janastriyaṁ, A ; skye-boḥi dpal, T. b. sāye(?), A. d. slar yaṅ mi-skyoṅ bdag-skyes (kṣitipātmajaḥ punaḥ), T.

ततः श्रुत्वा राजा विषयविमुखं तस्य तु मनो
न शिश्ये तां रात्रिं हृदयगतशल्यो गज इव ।
अथ श्रान्तो मन्त्रे बहुविविधमार्गे ससचिवो
न सोऽन्यत्कामेभ्यो नियमनमपश्यत्सुतमतेः ॥१०३॥

इति बुद्धचरिते महाकाव्ये स्त्रीविघातनो नाम चतुर्थः सर्गः ॥ ४ ॥

103. b. hṛdayaśatyo gaja (two syllables short), A; sñiṅ-la soṅ-baḥi zug-la glaṅ-chen, T. c. sṅags maṅ rnam-pa sna-tshogs lam-rnams-dag-gis (mantrair bahuvividhamārgaiḥ), T.

Colophon. Iti repeated at end of 103 and beginning of colophon.

CANTO V

स तथा विषयैर्विलोभ्यमानः परमार्हैरपि शाक्यराजसूनुः ।
न जगाम धृतिं न शर्म लेभे हृदये सिंह इवातिदिग्धविद्धः ॥ १ ॥
अथ मन्त्रिसुतैः क्षमैः कदाचित्सखिभिश्चित्रकथैः कृतानुयात्रः ।
वनभूमिदिदृक्षया शमेप्सुर्नरदेवानुमतो बहिः प्रतस्थे ॥ २ ॥
नवरुक्मखलीनकिङ्किणीकं प्रचलच्चामरचारुहेमभाण्डम् ।
अभिरुह्य स कन्थकं सदश्वं प्रययौ केतुमिव द्रुमाब्जकेतुः ॥ ३ ॥
स विकृष्टतरां वनान्तभूमिं वनलोभाच्च ययौ महीगुणाच्च ।
सलिलोर्मिविकारसीरमार्गां वसुधां चैव ददर्श कृष्यमाणाम् ॥ ४ ॥
हलभिन्नविकीर्णशष्पदर्भां हतसूक्ष्मक्रिमिकीटजन्तुकीर्णाम् ।
समवेक्ष्य रसां तथाविधां तां स्वजनस्येव वधे भृशं शुशोच ॥ ५ ॥

1. b. paramāhair, A ; dam-paḥi mchod-pa-rnams-kyis, T. c. na jagāma ratin (originally dhṛtin?), A ; brtan-par gśegs ma-gyur, T.

2. a. kṣamai, A. b. °kathai, A. cd. śamepsu nnara°, A ; nags-kyi sa-la ḥgro-ḥdod lta-bar ḥdod-pa-yis (vanabhūmiṁ didṛkṣayā gamepsur?), T. d. bahi, A.

3. ab. °kiṅkinīkaṁ pracalatcāmara°, A. c. stan-bcas (sakambalam?), T. sadaśva, A.

4. a. vikṛṣṇatarām, A ; rnam-par rgyaṅ-riṅ, T ; nikṛṣṭatarāṁ, Co. b. °guṇāccha(?cca?), A ; yon-tan-las, T. c. chu-gñer bzhin-du rnam-par-bkram-paḥi (salilormivikīrṇa°?), T. d. vasudhā, A.

5. c. samaveksa raśān tathavidhān tā, A.

कृषतः पुरुषांश्च वीक्षमाणः पवनार्कांशुरजोविभिन्नवर्णान् ।
वहनक्लमविक्लवांश्च धुर्यान् परमार्यः परमां कृपां चकार ॥ ६ ॥
अवतीर्य ततस्तुरङ्गपृष्ठाच्छनकैर्गां व्यचरच्छुचा परीतः ।
जगतो जननव्ययं विचिन्वन् कृपणं खल्विदमित्युवाच चार्तः ॥ ७ ॥
मनसा च विविक्ततामभीप्सुः सुहृदस्ताननुयायिनो निवार्य ।
अभितश्चलचारुपर्णवत्या विजने मूलमुपेयिवान् स जम्ब्वाः ॥ ८ ॥
निषसाद स यत्र शौचवत्यां भुवि वैडूर्यनिकाशशाद्वलायाम् ।
जगतः प्रभवव्ययौ विचिन्वन्मनसश्च स्थितिमार्गमाललम्बे ॥ ९ ॥
समवाप्तमनःस्थितिश्च सद्यो विषयेच्छादिभिराधिभिश्च मुक्तः ।
सवितर्कविचारमाप शान्तं प्रथमं ध्यानमनास्रवप्रकारम् ॥ १० ॥
अधिगम्य ततो विवेकजं तु परमप्रीतिसुखं मनःसमाधिम् ।
इदमेव ततः परं प्रदध्यौ मनसा लोकगतिं निशाम्य सम्यक् ॥११॥
कृपणं बत यज्जनः स्वयं सन्नवशो व्याधिजराविनाशधर्मा ।
जरयार्दितमातुरं मृतं वा परमज्ञो विजुगुप्सते मदान्धः ॥ १२ ॥

6. a. vīkṣyamāṇaḥ, A. b. rluṅ-gis gtor-baḥi rdul-gyis (pavanākṣiptarajo°), T.

7. b. vyacarat kṣudhā, A ; rnam-par-rgyu-zhiṅ mya-ṅan daṅ ldan-pa, T. c. e.c. Cowell ; vicintan, A ; rnam-sems-śiṅ (vicintayan?), T.

8. b. phyir-bzlogs-nas (nivartya), T. c. abhitacala°, A ; kun-nas mṅon-par gyo-zhiṅ, T. d. vijana, A. jamvāḥ, A.

9. a. niṣasāda ca yatra khocavatyāṁ, A ; gtsaṅ-mar ldan-paḥi sa-gzhi der de ni zhugs-te (niṣasāda sa tatra śaucavatyāṁ bhuvi), T.

10. b. viṣacchādibhir (one syllable short), A ; yul-la ḥdod sogs, T. d. zag-pa med-paḥi rab-bskyod-pa (anāsravaprakampam?), T.

11. c. e.c. Cowell ; imam eva, A. d. rab-brtags-nas (parikṣya?), T.

12. b. avaso vyādhijarāvināsadharmmaḥ, A ; dbaṅ ni yod-min . . . rnam-par-ñams-paḥi chos, T.

इह चेदहमीदृशः स्वयं सन्विजुगुप्सेय परं तथास्वभावम् ।
न भवेत्सदृशं हि तत्क्षमं वा परमं धर्ममिमं विजानतो मे ॥ १३ ॥
इति तस्य विपश्यतो यथावज्जगतो व्याधिजराविपत्तिदोषान् ।
बलयौवनजीवितप्रवृत्तो विजगामात्मगतो मदः क्षणेन ॥ १४ ॥
न जहर्ष न चापि चानुतेपे विचिकित्सां न ययौ न तन्द्रिनिद्रे ।
न च कामगुणेषु संररञ्जे न विदिद्वेष परं न चावमेने ॥ १५ ॥
इति बुद्धिरियं च नीरजस्का ववृधे तस्य महात्मनो विशुद्धा ।
पुरुषैरपरैरदृश्यमानः पुरुषश्चोपससर्प भिक्षुवेषः ॥ १६ ॥
नरदेवसुतस्तमभ्यपृच्छद्वद कोऽसीति शशंस सोऽथ तस्मै ।
नरपुंगव जन्ममृत्युभीतः श्रमणः प्रव्रजितोऽस्मि मोक्षहेतोः ॥ १७ ॥
जगति क्षयधर्मके मुमुक्षुर्मृगयेऽहं शिवमक्षयं पदं तत् ।
स्वजनेऽन्यजने च तुल्यबुद्धिर्विषयेभ्यो विनिवृत्तरागदोषः ॥ १८ ॥
निवसन् क्वचिदेव वृक्षमूले विजने वायतने गिरौ वने वा ।
विचराम्यपरिग्रहो निराशः परमार्थाय यथोपपन्नभैक्षः ॥ १९ ॥
इति पश्यत एव राजसूनोरिदमुक्त्वा स नभः समुत्पपात ।
स हि तद्वपुरन्यबुद्धदर्शी स्मृतये तस्य समेयिवान्दिवौकाः ॥ २० ॥

14. c. balayovanajīvitapravṛttau, A ; rab-zhugs-paḥi . . . rgyags-pa, T.

15. d. na vividveṣa, A ; rnam-par-sdaṅ-bar ma-gyur, T.

16. d. bhikṣuveśaḥ, A.

17. b. ko sī(written over ṣī)ti saśaṁsa, A. c. e.c. Cowell ; navapuṅgava, A ; mi-yi skyes-mchog (narapuṅgava?), T.

18. c. sujano (corrected to ajano) nyajane ca, A ; 'with mind that is equal towards relation and foe', C and FP ; T omits the *pāda*.

19. a. nivasat, A. d. yathepapannabhekṣaḥ (?bhikṣuḥ?), A ; ji-ltar ñer-ldan sloṅ-mo-ba, T ; °bhikṣaḥ, Kern.

20. c. anyabuddhidarśśī, A ; saṅs-rgyas gzhan gzigs-śiṅ, T ; 'the former Buddhas', C.

गगनं खगवद्गते च तस्मिन्नृवरः संजहृषे विसिस्मिये च ।
उपलभ्य ततश्च धर्मसंज्ञामभिनिर्याणविधौ मतिं चकार ॥ २१ ॥

तत इन्द्रसमो जितेन्द्रियाश्वः प्रविविक्षुः पुरमश्वमारुरोह ।
परिवारजनं त्ववेक्षमाणस्तत एवाभिमतं वनं न भेजे ॥ २२ ॥

स जरामरणक्षयं चिकीर्षुर्वनवासाय मतिं स्मृतौ निधाय ।
प्रविवेश पुनः पुरं न कामाद्वनभूमेरिव मण्डलं द्विपेन्द्रः ॥ २३ ॥

सुखिता बत निर्वृता च सा स्त्री पतिरीदृक्ष इहायताक्ष यस्याः ।
इति तं समुदीक्ष्य राजकन्या प्रविशन्तं पथि साञ्जलिर्जगाद ॥२४॥

अथ घोषमिमं महाभ्रघोषः परिशुश्राव शमं परं च लेभे ।
श्रुतवान्स हि निर्वृतेति शब्दं परिनिर्वाणविधौ मतिं चकार ॥२५॥

अथ काञ्चनशैलशृङ्गवर्ष्मा गजमेघर्षभबाहुनिस्वनाक्षः ।
क्षयमक्षयधर्मजातरागः शशिसिंहाननविक्रमः प्रपेदे ॥ २६ ॥

मृगराजगतिस्ततोऽभ्यगच्छन्नृपतिं मन्त्रिगणैरुपास्यमानम् ।
समितौ मरुतामिव ज्वलन्तं मघवन्तं त्रिदिवे सनत्कुमारः ॥ २७ ॥

21. c. dharmmasaṁjñam, A ; chos-kyi ḥdu-śes, T ; ‘ the idea of the good law ’, C. d. abhiniryāna°, A.

22. b. param aśvam, A ; groṅ-la . . . rta-la, T. c. parivartya janaṁ tv avekṣamanas, A ; ḥkhor-gyi skye-bo-dag kyaṅ mṅon-par ḥdod-pa-ste, T.

24. a. nivṛtā, A. b. īdṛk tvām ihāyatākṣa, A ; spyan-yaṅs . . . ḥdi-ḥdra ḥdir, T. c. samudīkṣa, A. śākyaḥi bu-mo zhig (śākyakanyā), T. d. rajñalir jjagāda, A ; thal-mo sbyar-ba daṅ bcas smras-so, T.

25. c. śrutavāṁś ca, A ; thos-pa daṅ ldan des, T. d. °vidho, A ; cho-gar, T.

26. d. śaśisihānanavikrama, A.

27. a. °gati tato, A. b. °ganair upāsyamāṇaṁ, A. c. śamitau, A ; ḥdun-sa-ru, T.

प्रणिपत्य च साञ्जलिर्बभाषे दिश मह्यं नरदेव साध्वनुज्ञाम् ।
परिविव्रजिषामि मोक्षहेतोर्नियतो ह्यस्य जनस्य विप्रयोगः ॥ २८ ॥
इति तस्य वचो निशम्य राजा करिणेवाभिहतो द्रुमश्चचाल ।
कमलप्रतिमेऽञ्जलौ गृहीत्वा वचनं चेदमुवाच बाष्पकण्ठः ॥ २९ ॥
प्रतिसंहर तात बुद्धिमेतां न हि कालस्तव धर्मसंश्रयस्य ।
वयसि प्रथमे मतौ चलायां बहुदोषां हि वदन्ति धर्मचर्याम् ॥ ३० ॥
विषयेषु कुतूहलेन्द्रियस्य व्रतखेदेष्वसमर्थनिश्चयस्य ।
तरुणस्य मनश्चलत्यरण्यादनभिज्ञस्य विशेषतो विवेके ॥ ३१ ॥
मम तु प्रियधर्म धर्मकालस्त्वयि लक्ष्मीमवसृज्य लक्षभूते ।
स्थिरविक्रम विक्रमेण धर्मस्तव हित्वा तु गुरुं भवेदधर्मः ॥ ३२ ॥
तदिमं व्यवसायमुत्सृज त्वं भव तावन्निरतो गृहस्थधर्मे ।
पुरुषस्य वयःसुखानि भुक्त्वा रमणीयो हि तपोवनप्रवेशः ॥ ३३ ॥
इति वाक्यमिदं निशम्य राज्ञः कलविङ्कस्वर उत्तरं बभाषे ।
यदि मे प्रतिभूश्चतुर्षु राजन् भवसि त्वं न तपोवनं श्रयिष्ये ॥ ३४ ॥
न भवेन्मरणाय जीवितं मे विहरेत्स्वास्थ्यमिदं च मे न रोगः ।
न च यौवनमाक्षिपेज्जरा मे न च संपत्तिमिमां हरेद्विपत्तिः ॥ ३५ ॥

28. c. yoṅs-su rnam-par gśegs-par bgyi (parivivrajiṣyāmi?), T.

29. a. nisamya, A.

30. a. pratisahara, A. d. chos-kyi spyod-pa gsuṅs-pa-rnams ni skyon maṅ-ṅo (=bahudoṣā vadanto dharmacaryā), T.

31. b. brtul-zhugs gyo-ba-rnams (equivalent uncertain), T. c. calaty araraṇyād, A.

32. ḅ. e.c.; lakṣabhūte (marginal gloss, sthānabhūte), A; mtshon-gyur, T; lakṣya°, Co.

33. b. tāvat nirato, A.

34. a. rnam-par gsan-nas (viśrutya, viśamya?), T.

35. d. haret vipattiḥ, A.

इति दुर्लभमर्थमूचिवांसं तनयं वाक्यमुवाच शाक्यराजः ।
त्यज बुद्धिमिमामतिप्रवृत्तामवहास्योऽतिमनोरथोऽक्रमश्च ॥ ३६ ॥

अथ मेरुगरुर्गुरुं बभाषे यदि नास्ति क्रम एष नास्मि वार्यः ।
शरणाज्ज्वलनेन दह्यमानान्न हि निश्चिक्रमिषुः क्षमं ग्रहीतुम् ॥३७॥

जगतश्च यदा ध्रुवो वियोगो ननु धर्माय वरं स्वयंवियोगः ।
अवशं ननु विप्रयोजयेन्मामकृतस्वार्थमतृप्तमेव मृत्युः ॥ ३८ ॥

इति भूमिपतिर्निशम्य तस्य
व्यवसायं तनयस्य निर्मुमुक्षोः ।
अभिधाय न यास्यतीति भूयो
विदधे रक्षणमुत्तमांश्च कामान् ॥ ३९ ॥

सचिवैस्तु निदर्शितो यथावद्
बहुमानात्प्रणयाच्च शास्त्रपूर्वम् ।
गुरुणा च निवारितोऽश्रुपातैः
प्रविवेशावसथं ततः स शोचन् ॥ ४० ॥

36. c. imāṅ gatipravṛttām (written over something else not legible), A ; śin-tu rab-tu-zhugs-paḥi blo ḥdi, T. d. e.c. Lüders ; °manorathaḥ(?tha?) kramaś ca, A ; yid-la re-ba . . . śa-thaṅ-ḥchad (°manorathaḥ śramaś ca), T ; °manorathakramaś ca, Co.

37. a. ga(?gu?)rūṁ, A. d. niścikramiṣuṁ, A ; phyi-rol ḥbyuṅ-bar ḥdod-pa . . . ma-yin (na bahiś cikramiṣuḥ ?), T.

38. For C and FP see note in translation. a. yathā, A ; gaṅ-gi tshe-na, T. b. e.c. Kielhorn ; na tu, A ; chos-phyir ma-yin ḥdi ni rnam-par-ḥbral-bar mchog (=dharmāya na varam ayaṁ viyogaḥ), T. c. na tu, Kielhorn.

39. a. niśāmya, A ; ṅes-par-thos-nas, T.

40. b. zhi-ba sṅon-ḥgro (śāntipūrvam), T ; ' instructed him fully in all the laws of propriety ', C.

चलकुण्डलचुम्बिताननाभिर्घननिश्वासविकम्पितस्तनीभिः ।
वनिताभिरधीरलोचनाभिर्मृगशावाभिरिवाभ्युदीक्ष्यमाणः ॥ ४१ ॥

स हि काञ्चनपर्वतावदातो हृदयोन्मादकरो वराङ्गनानाम् ।
श्रवणाङ्गविलोचनात्मभावान्वचनस्पर्शवपुर्गुणैर्जहार ॥ ४२ ॥

विगते दिवसे ततो विमानं वपुषा सूर्य इव प्रदीप्यमानः ।
तिमिरं विजिघांसुरात्मभासा रविरुद्यन्निव मेरुमारुरोह ॥ ४३ ॥

कनकोज्ज्वलदीप्तदीपवृक्षं वरकालागुरुधूपपूर्णगर्भम् ।
अधिरुह्य स वज्रभक्तिचित्रं प्रवरं काञ्चनमासनं सिषेवे ॥ ४४ ॥

तत उत्तममुत्तमाङ्गनास्तं निशि तूर्यैरुपतस्थुरिन्द्रकल्पम् ।
हिमवच्छिरसीव चन्द्रगौरे द्रविणेन्द्रात्मजमप्सरोगणौघाः ॥ ४५ ॥

परमैरपि दिव्यतूर्यकल्पैः स तु तैर्नैव रतिं ययौ न हर्षम् ।
परमार्थसुखाय तस्य साधोरभिनिश्चिक्रमिषा यतो न रेमे ॥ ४६ ॥

अथ तत्र सुरैस्तपोवरिष्ठैरकनिष्ठैर्व्यवसायमस्य बुद्ध्वा ।
युगपत्प्रमदाजनस्य निद्रा विहितासीद्विकृताश्च गात्रचेष्टाः ॥ ४७ ॥

अभवच्छयिता हि तत्र काचिद्विनिवेश्य प्रचले करे कपोलम् ।
दयितामपि रुक्मपत्त्रचित्रां कुपितेवाङ्कगतां विहाय वीणाम् ॥ ४८ ॥

41. d. udīkṣamāṇaḥ, A.

42. b. hṛdayotmāda°, A. c. śravanāṅga°, A. cd. °bhāvāṃ(?s?) vacana°, A.

43. a. divaśe, A. b. bzhin-du mṅon-par-gsal-ba (ivābhidīpyamānaḥ), T.

44. c. mṅon-par-ḥdzegs-nas (abhiruhya), T.

45. c. himavadśirasīva, A. d. °gaṇoghāḥ, A.

48. b. prabale, A; gyo-ba, T. c. gser-gyi snod ni sna-tshogs-paḥi (rukmapātracitrāṁ), T.

विबभौ करलग्नवेणुरन्या स्तनविस्रस्तसितांशुका शयाना ।
ऋजुषट्पदपङ्क्तिजुष्टपद्मा जलफेनप्रहसत्तटा नदीव ॥ ४९ ॥
नवपुष्करगर्भकोमलाभ्यां तपनीयोज्ज्वलसंगताङ्गदाभ्याम् ।
स्वपिति स्म तथापरा भुजाभ्यां परिरभ्य प्रियवन्मृदङ्गमेव ॥ ५० ॥
नवहाटकभूषणास्तथान्या वसनं पीतमनुत्तमं वसानाः ।
अवशा घननिद्रया निपेतुर्गजभग्ना इव कर्णिकारशाखाः ॥ ५१ ॥
अवलम्ब्य गवाक्षपार्श्वमन्या शयिता चापविभुग्नगात्रयष्टिः ।
विरराज विलम्बिचारुहारा रचिता तोरणशालभञ्जिकेव ॥ ५२ ॥
मणिकुण्डलदष्टपत्रलेखं मुखपद्मं विनतं तथापरस्याः ।
शतपत्रमिवार्धवक्रनाडं स्थितकारण्डवघट्टितं चकाशे ॥ ५३ ॥
अपराः शयिता यथोपविष्टाः स्तनभारैरवनम्यमानगात्राः ।
उपगुह्य परस्परं विरेजुर्भुजपाशैस्तपनीयपारिहार्यैः ॥ ५४ ॥
महतीं परिवादिनीं च काचिद्वनितालिङ्ग्य सखीमिव प्रसुप्ता ।
विजुघूर्ण चलत्सुवर्णसूत्रा वदनेनाकुलयोक्त्रकेण ॥ ५५ ॥

49. b. °viśrastaśitāṁśukā, A. c. sgra-sgrog padma (°ghuṣṭapadmā), T.

50. c. tathā purā, A ; de-bzhin gzhan-rnams (tathāparāḥ), T.

51. c. e.c. ; avaśā vata nidrayā, A ; dbaṅ-med-par ni sdug-ma (for stugs-ma or stugs-po) gñid-kyis (avaśā ghanā nidrayā, or ghananidrayā), T.

52. b. de-bzhin . . . ñal-bar gyur-paḥi lus-kyi mchod-sdoṅ rnam-ḥkhyog-pa (śayitaivaṁ pravibhugnagātrayaṣṭiḥ?), T ; ‘ with forms like a bow whose tips are bent together (or, suspended by the tips ?) ’, C. d. toranasāla°, A ; rta-babs-la śālabhanjika, T (which omits racitā).

53. a. daṣṭa*(?pe, ?ve, ?ne)tralekhaṁ, A ; ḥgram-paḥi logs-la . . . . rmugs-pa (°daṣṭagaṇḍalekhaṁ), T. b. rnam-rgyas-śiṅ (vitataṁ), T. d. gyos-par gyur (cakampe), T.

54. a. ji-ltar rnam-par-zhugs bzhin (for śiṅ?) (yathā vivṛttāḥ?), T. c. paraspara, A.

55. b. vanitāligya, A. d. °yoktrakena, A.

पणवं युवतिर्भुजांसदेशादवविस्रंसितचारुपाशमन्या ।
सविलासरतान्ततान्तमूर्वोर्विवरे कान्तमिवाभिनीय शिश्ये ॥ ५६ ॥

अपरा बभुर्निमीलिताक्ष्यो विपुलाक्ष्योऽपि शुभभ्रुवोऽपि सत्यः ।
प्रतिसंकुचितारविन्दकोशाः सवितर्यस्तमिते यथा नलिन्यः ॥ ५७ ॥

शिथिलाकुलमूर्धजा तथान्या जघनस्रस्तविभूषणांशुकान्ता ।
अशयिष्ट विकीर्णकण्ठसूत्रा गजभग्ना प्रतियातनाङ्गनेव ॥ ५८ ॥

अपरास्त्ववशा ह्रिया वियुक्ता
धृतिमत्योऽपि वपुर्गुणैरुपेताः ।
विनिशश्वसुरुल्बणं शयाना
विकृताः क्षिप्तभुजा जजृम्भिरे च ॥ ५९ ॥

व्यपविद्धविभूषणस्रजोऽन्या
विसृताग्रन्थनवाससो विसंज्ञाः ।
अनिमीलितशुक्लनिश्चलाक्ष्यो
न विरेजुः शयिता गतासुकल्पाः ॥ ६० ॥

विवृतास्यपुटा विवृद्धगात्री प्रपतद्वक्त्रजला प्रकाशगुह्या ।
अपरा मदघूर्णितेव शिश्ये न बभासे विकृतं वपुः पुपोष ॥ ६१ ॥

56. ab. bhujāṁśadeśād avaviśraṁsita°, A. b. mdzes-paḥi logs-can (°cārupārśvam), T.

58. b. °bhūṣaṇāśukā°, A; rgyan daṅ dar-rnams dpyi-la rnam-ñil de-rnams (jaghanavisrastabhūṣaṇāṁśukās tāḥ), T. d. patiyātāṅganeva (one syllable short), A; yan-lag-ma-yi gzugs-brñan . . . bzhin, T.

60. a. °śrajo ṇyā, A.

61. a. lus-po rab-brgyan-zhiṅ (=pratatagātrā), T; vivṛttagātrā, Gawroński. c. ḥkhrul-bar gyur-pa ñid (°ghūrṇitaiva), T. d. na babhāṣe, A; mdzes-ma-gyur, T.

इति सत्त्वकुलान्वयानुरूपं विविधं स प्रमदाजनः शयानः ।
सरसः सदृशं बभार रूपं पवनावर्जितरुग्णपुष्करस्य ॥ ६२ ॥

समवेक्ष्य तथा तथा शयाना विकृतास्ता युवतीरधीरचेष्टाः ।
गुणवद्वपुषोऽपि वल्गुभाषा नृपसूनुः स विगर्हयांबभूव ॥ ६३ ॥

अशुचिर्विकृतश्च जीवलोके वनितानामयमीदृशः स्वभावः ।
वसनाभरणैस्तु वञ्च्यमानः पुरुषः स्त्रीविषयेषु रागमेति ॥ ६४ ॥

विमृशेद्यदि योषितां मनुष्यः प्रकृतिं स्वप्नविकारमीदृशं च ।
ध्रुवमत्र न वर्धयेत्प्रमादं गुणसंकल्पहतस्तु रागमेति ॥ ६५ ॥

इति तस्य तदन्तरं विदित्वा निशि निश्चिक्रमिषा समुद्बभूव ।
अवगम्य मनस्ततोऽस्य देवैर्भवनद्वारमपावृतं बभूव ॥ ६६ ॥

अथ सोऽवततार हर्म्यपृष्ठाद्युवतीस्ताः शयिता विगर्हमाणः ।
अवतीर्य ततश्च निर्विशङ्को गृहकक्ष्यां प्रथमां विनिर्जगाम ॥ ६७ ॥

तुरगावचरं स बोधयित्वा जविनं छन्दकमित्थमित्युवाच ।
हयमानय कन्थकं त्वरावानमृतं प्राप्तुमितोऽद्य मे यियासा ॥ ६८ ॥

62. a. e.c. ; satvakulānvarūpam (two syllables short), A ; sems-pa daṅ ni rigs-kyi rjes-ḥgroḥi gzugs (sattvakulānvayarūpaṁ, one syllable short), T. c. mdzes-par gyur (babhāsa?), T. d. °puskarasya, A ; gser-gyi padma-yi (°rukmapuṣkarasya), T.

63. a. samavekṣya ta ta śayānā (two syllables short), A ; de-ltar . . . de-ltar ñal-baḥi . . . mthoṅ-nas, T.

64. a. hjig-rten-te (jīvaloko?), T.

65. Not in C. a. vimṛṣed, A ; rnam-dpyad-na, T. d. 'certainly he obtains the holy (*kung-te*=puṇya, guṇa) body of liberation ', FP.

67. d. prathamaṁ, A ; khaṅ-paḥi rim-pa daṅ-por, T.

68. b. abhyuvāca, Gawroński. d. bdag skom (so Peking edition) mo (me pipāsā), T.

हृदि या मम तुष्टिरद्य जाता
व्यवसायश्च यथा मतौ निविष्टः ।
विजनेऽपि च नाथवानिवास्मि
ध्रुवमर्थोऽभिमुखः समेत इष्टः ॥ ६९ ॥

ह्रियमेव च संनतिं च हित्वा
शयिता मत्प्रमुखे यथा युवत्यः ।
विवृते च यथा स्वयं कपाटे
नियतं यातुमतो ममाद्य कालः ॥ ७० ॥

प्रतिगृह्य ततः स भर्तुराज्ञां विदितार्थोऽपि नरेन्द्रशासनस्य ।
मनसीव परेण चोद्यमानस्तुरगस्यानयने मतिं चकार ॥ ७१ ॥

अथ हेमखलीनपूर्णवक्त्रं लघुशय्यास्तरणोपगूढपृष्ठम् ।
बलसत्त्वजवान्वयोपपन्नं स वराश्वं तमुपानिनाय भर्त्रे ॥ ७२ ॥

प्रततत्रिकपुच्छमूलपार्ष्णिं निभृतह्रस्वतनूजपुच्छकर्णम् ।
विनतोन्नतपृष्ठकुक्षिपार्श्वं विपुलप्रोथललाटकट्युरस्कम् ॥ ७३ ॥

69. a. T omits yā (i.e. reading hṛdaye?). b. dhṛtau, A ; blo-gros-la, T c. T omits iva ; yathāsmi, Gawroński. d. sa me ya iṣṭaḥ, A ; ḥdod-paḥi don ni mṅon-du phyogs ḥdu, T.

70. d. yātum anāmayāya kālaḥ, A ; bdag ni ḥdi-nas de-riṅ ḥgro-baḥi dus, T.

71. c. codyamāṇas, A.

72. cd. °javānvalopapanna sa varāṁśvan, A ; mgyogs daṅ rjes-ḥgro ñer-ldan-pa, T. d. der ni ñe-bar-hoṅs (upāninâya tatra), T.

73. For C see note in translation. a. sṅa-maḥi (for rṅa-maḥi?) rtsa-ba rtsib-log gsum-ga (°trikapucchamūlapārśvaṁ, or °trikapūrvamūlapārśvaṁ), T. b. e.c. ; nibhṛtaṁ hrasvatanūjapṛṣṭhakarṇṇaṁ, A ; rgyab daṅ rna-ba lus-skyes spu ni thuṅ-zhiṅ dul (=A), T ; nibhṛtahrasva°, Gawroński. c. rgyab-kyi rtsib-ma-dag ni dud-ciṅ rnam-rgyas-la (vitatonnatapṛṣṭhapārśvaṁ, or °pṛṣṭhakukṣipārśvaṁ?), T.

उपगुह्य स तं विशालवक्षाः कमलाभेन च सान्त्वयन् करेण ।
मधुराक्षरया गिरा शशास ध्वजिनीमध्यमिव प्रवेष्टुकामः ॥ ७४ ॥
बहुशः किल शत्रवो निरस्ताः समरे त्वामधिरुह्य पार्थिवेन ।
अहमप्यमृतं पदं यथावत्तुरगश्रेष्ठ लभेय तत्कुरुष्व ॥ ७५ ॥
सुलभाः खलु संयुगे सहाया विषयावाप्तसुखे धनार्जने वा ।
पुरुषस्य तु दुर्लभाः सहायाः पतितस्यापदि धर्मसंश्रये वा ॥ ७६ ॥

इह चैव भवन्ति ये सहायाः
कलुषे कर्मणि धर्मसंश्रये वा ।
अवगच्छति मे यथान्तरात्मा
नियतं तेऽपि जनास्तदंशभाजः ॥ ७७ ॥

तदिदं परिगम्य धर्मयुक्तं मम निर्याणमितो जगद्धिताय ।
तुरगोत्तम वेगविक्रमाभ्यां प्रयतस्वात्महिते जगद्धिते च ॥ ७८ ॥
इति सुहृदमिवानुशिष्य कृत्ये तुरगवरं नृवरो वनं यियासुः ।
सितमसितगतिद्युतिर्वपुष्मान् रविरिव शारदमभ्रमारुरोह ॥ ७९ ॥
अथ स परिहरन्निशीथचण्डं परिजनबोधकरं ध्वनिं सदश्वः ।
विगतहनुरवः प्रशान्तहेषश्चकितविमुक्तपदक्रमो जगाम ॥ ८० ॥

74. a. °vakṣyāḥ, A. b. śāntvayat, A. d. rgyal-mtshan sde-la dmag-dpon rab-tu-ḥjug-pa bzhin (=dhvajinīṁ mukhya iva praviśamānaḥ), T.

75. a. kila (corrected to kali), A ; T omits. nirastā, A. b. mṅon-par-zhon-nas (abhiruhya), T. c. paraṁ, A ; go-ḥphaṅ, T. d. de-ltar mdzod (= tathā kuruṣva), T.

79. a. T omits kṛtye.

80. d. °kramo (corrected to °krame), A ; ḥgros-kyis (°kramair or °kramo), T.

कनकवलयभूषितप्रकोष्ठैः
कमलनिभैः कमलानिव प्रविध्य ।
अवनततनवस्ततोऽस्य यक्षा-
श्चकितगतैर्दधिरे खुरान् कराग्रैः ॥ ८१ ॥

गुरुपरिघकपाटसंवृता या
न सुखमपि द्विरदैरपाव्रियन्ते ।
व्रजति नृपसुते गतस्वनास्ताः
स्वयमभवन्विवृताः पुरः प्रतोल्यः ॥ ८२ ॥

पितरमभिमुखं सुतं च बालं
जनमनुरक्तमनुत्तमां च लक्ष्मीम् ।
कृतमतिरपहाय निर्व्यपेक्षः
पितृनगरात्स ततो विनिर्जगाम ॥ ८३ ॥

अथ स विमलपङ्कजायताक्षः पुरमवलोक्य ननाद सिंहनादम् ।
जननमरणयोरदृष्टपारो न पुरमहं कपिलाह्वयं प्रवेष्टा ॥ ८४ ॥

इति वचनमिदं निशम्य तस्य द्रविणपतेः परिषद्गणा ननन्दुः ।
प्रमुदितमनसश्च देवसङ्घा व्यवसितपारणमाशशंसिरेऽस्मै ॥ ८५ ॥

81. b. pravidhyaḥ, A ; kamala-rnams rnam-byas-nas (=kamalān vikṛtya), T. d. cakitagater, A. ; tshim gyur lag-paḥi rtse-mos (cakitagatair . . . karāgraiḥ, or °gatāḥ), T.

82. a. °kavāṭa°, A. b. dviraḍhair ayādhri(?vri?)yante, A. c. gata-śvanās, A. d. abhavad, A.

84. a. vikajapaṅkajā°, A ; rnam-rgyas (vikaṭa°?), T ; 'with eyes like the pure lotus flower that springs from the mud', C ; vikaca°, Co. d. na punar ahaṁ, A ; groṅ-khyer, T.

85. a. niśāmya, A ; thos-nas, T.

हुतवहवपुषो दिवौकसोऽन्ये व्यवसितमस्य सुदुष्करं विदित्वा ।
अकृषत तुहिने पथि प्रकाशं घनविवरप्रसृता इवेन्दुपादाः ॥ ८६ ॥

हरितुरगतुरङ्गवत्तुरङ्गः
स तु विचरन्मनसीव चोद्यमानः ।
अरुणपरुषतारमन्तरिक्षं
स च सुबहूनि जगाम योजनानि ॥ ८७ ॥

इति बुद्धचरिते महाकाव्येऽभिनिष्क्रमणो नाम पञ्चमः सर्गः ॥ ५ ॥

86. a. divaukasau, A. b. asya ca duskaram, A; ḥdi-yi . . . śin-tu dkaḥ-ba, T. c. e.c. Joglekar; akuruta, A; byas, T; adadhata, Böhtlingk, Kern; vyadadhata, Sovani.

87. b. manaśīva, A; yid-kyis sprul-ba (amend to skul-ba?) bzhin-du rnam-par-rgyu bzhin-du (vicaran manaseva . . . ?), T.

CANTO VI

ततो मुहूर्ताभ्युदिते जगच्चक्षुषि भास्करे ।
भार्गवस्याश्रमपदं स ददर्श नृणां वरः ॥ १ ॥
सुप्तविश्वस्तहरिणं स्वस्थस्थितविहङ्गमम् ।
विश्रान्त इव यद्दृष्ट्वा कृतार्थ इव चाभवत् ॥ २ ॥
स विस्मयनिवृत्त्यर्थं तपःपूजार्थमेव च ।
स्वां चानुवर्तितां रक्षन्नश्वपृष्ठादवातरत् ॥ ३ ॥
अवतीर्य च पस्पर्श निस्तीर्णमिति वाजिनम् ।
छन्दकं चाब्रवीत्प्रीतः स्नापयन्निव चक्षुषा ॥ ४ ॥
इमं तार्क्ष्योपमजवं तुरङ्गमनुगच्छता ।
दर्शिता सौम्य मद्भक्तिर्विक्रमश्चायमात्मनः ॥ ५ ॥
सर्वथास्म्यन्यकार्योऽपि गृहीतो भवता हृदि ।
भर्तृस्नेहश्च यस्यायमीदृशः शक्तिरेव च ॥ ६ ॥
अस्निग्धोऽपि समर्थोऽस्ति निःसामर्थ्योऽपि भक्तिमान् ।
भक्तिमांश्चैव शक्तश्च दुर्लभस्त्वद्विधो भुवि ॥ ७ ॥

2. c. yat dṛṣṭvā, A.

6. a. thams-cad-nas . . . yin (sarvato 'smy?), T. c. bhatṛ°, A. d. e.c. ; īdṛśas sakta eva ca, A ; de-ḥdra-dag-la ñid (īdṛśeṣv eva?), T ; 'a devoted heart, a capable and diligent body, these two I now begin to see', C ; īdṛśī śaktir eva ca, Gawroński.

7. b. niḥsāmartho pi, A. c. bhaktimāś caiva, A.

तत्प्रीतोऽस्मि तवानेन महाभागेन कर्मणा ।
यस्य ते मयि भावोऽयं फलेभ्योऽपि पराङ्मुखः ॥ ८ ॥

को जनस्य फलस्थस्य न स्यादभिमुखो जनः ।
जनीभवति भूयिष्ठं स्वजनोऽपि विपर्यये ॥ ९ ॥

कुलार्थं धार्यते पुत्रः पोषार्थं सेव्यते पिता ।
आशयाच्छ्लिष्यति जगन्नास्ति निष्कारणा स्वता ॥ १० ॥

किमुक्त्वा बहु संक्षेपात्कृतं मे सुमहत्प्रियम् ।
निवर्तस्वाश्वमादाय संप्राप्तोऽस्मीप्सितं पदम् ॥ ११ ॥

इत्युक्त्वा स महाबाहुरनुशंसचिकीर्षया ।
भूषणान्यवमुच्यास्मै संतप्तमनसे ददौ ॥ १२ ॥

मुकुटाद्दीपकर्माणं मणिमादाय भास्वरम् ।
ब्रुवन्वाक्यमिदं तस्थौ सादित्य इव मन्दरः ॥ १३ ॥

अनेन मणिना छन्द प्रणम्य बहुशो नृपः ।
विज्ञाप्योऽमुक्तविश्रम्भं संतापविनिवृत्तये ॥ १४ ॥

जन्ममरणनाशार्थं प्रविष्टोऽस्मि तपोवनम् ।
न खलु स्वर्गतर्षेण नास्नेहेन न मन्युना ॥ १५ ॥

8. cd. dṛśyate mayi bhāvo yas phalebhyo pi parāṅmukhe, A ; gaṅ-zhig khyod-kyi bsam-pa ḥdi ḥbras-bu-las kyaṅ gzhan-du phyogs (=text, omitting mayi), T ; 'rejecting the profit of world glory, you come after me', and 'you alone follow me, turning your back on profit', C.

10. d. niṣkāraṇāsvatā, Co.

11. b. svamahat, A ; chen-legs, T. d. īpsitaṁ vanaṁ, A ; ḥdod-paḥi gnas, T ; 'I have now reached the place I sought', C.

12. b. ānṛśaṁsacikīrṣayā, A ; rjes-su-bsṅags-pa byed-ḥdod-pas, T.

13. d. ñi-ma ḥbigs-byed-la bzhin des (so 'ditya iva mandare!) T.

14. c. °visrambhaṁ, A.

15. a. jarāmaraṇa°, A ; skye daṅ ḥchi-ba, T ; 'birth, old age and death', C.

तद्देवमभिनिष्क्रान्तं न मां शोचितुमर्हसि ।
भूत्वापि हि चिरं श्लेषः कालेन न भविष्यति ॥ १६ ॥

ध्रुवो यस्माच्च विश्लेषस्तस्मान्मोक्षाय मे मतिः ।
विप्रयोगः कथं न स्याद्भूयोऽपि स्वजनादिति ॥ १७ ॥

शोकत्यागाय निष्क्रान्तं न मां शोचितुमर्हसि ।
शोकहेतुषु कामेषु सक्ताः शोच्यास्तु रागिणः ॥ १८ ॥

अयं च किल पूर्वेषामस्माकं निश्चयः स्थिरः ।
इति दायाद्यभूतेन न शोच्योऽस्मि पथा व्रजन् ॥ १९ ॥

भवन्ति ह्यर्थदायादाः पुरुषस्य विपर्यये ।
पृथिव्यां धर्मदायादाः दुर्लभास्तु न सन्ति वा ॥ २० ॥

यदपि स्यादसमये यातो वनमसाविति ।
अकालो नास्ति धर्मस्य जीविते चञ्चले सति ॥ २१ ॥

तस्माददैव मे श्रेयश्चेतव्यमिति निश्चयः ।
जीविते को हि विश्रम्भो मृत्यौ प्रत्यर्थिनि स्थिते ॥ २२ ॥

एवमादि त्वया सौम्य विज्ञाप्यो वसुधाधिपः ।
प्रयतेथास्तथा चैव यथा मां न स्मरेदपि ॥ २३ ॥

17. c. viprayoga, A. cd. syāt bhūyo, A. d. e.c.; svajanādibhiḥ, A; raṅ-gi skye-bo-las (svajanāt), T.

18. d. socyā'stu, A.

19. b. asmāka, A. ṅes-par gnas (niścayaḥ sthitaḥ), T; 'firmly resolved', C. c. dāyāda°, A; ster-byar, T; 'I now have inherited', C. d. yathā, A; lam-gyis, T.

20. c. chos-kyi bdag-po (dharmapatayo?), T.

21. b. vanasamāv iti, A. d. jivite, A.

22. d. ḥchi-baḥi dgra ni (mṛtyupratyarthini?), T.

अपि नैर्गुण्यमस्माकं वाच्यं नरपतौ त्वया ।
नैर्गुण्यात्त्यज्यते स्नेहः स्नेहत्यागान्न शोच्यते ॥ २४ ॥
इति वाक्यमिदं श्रुत्वा छन्दः संतापविक्लवः ।
बाष्पग्रथितया वाचा प्रत्युवाच कृताञ्जलिः ॥ २५ ॥
अनेन तव भावेन बान्धवायासदायिना ।
भर्तः सीदति मे चेतो नदीपङ्क इव द्विपः ॥ २६ ॥
कस्य नोत्पादयेद्बाष्पं निश्चयस्तेऽयमीदृशः ।
अयोमयेऽपि हृदये किं पुनः स्नेहविक्लवे ॥ २७ ॥
विमानशयनार्हं हि सौकुमार्यमिदं क्व च ।
खरदर्भाङ्कुरवती तपोवनमही क्व च ॥ २८ ॥
श्रुत्वा तु व्यवसायं ते यदश्वोऽयं मयाहृतः ।
बलात्कारेण तन्नाथ दैवेनैवास्मि कारितः ॥ २९ ॥
कथं ह्यात्मवशो जानन् व्यवसायमिमं तव ।
उपानयेयं तुरगं शोकं कपिलवास्तुनः ॥ ३० ॥
तन्नार्हसि महाबाहो विहातुं पुचलालसम् ।
स्निग्धं वृद्धं च राजानं सद्धर्ममिव नास्तिकः ॥ ३१ ॥
संवर्धनपरिश्रान्तां द्वितीयां तां च मातरम् ।
देवीं नार्हसि विस्मर्तुं कृतघ्न इव सत्क्रियाम् ॥ ३२ ॥

27. c. ayasmaye (corrected on margin to ayomaye), A.

28. a. gzhal-med khaṅ-gi lam ḥos-paḥi (vimānagamanārhaṁ?), T.

29. d. lha-yis . . . ḥdra (daiveneva), T; 'a heavenly spirit, appearing, compelled me', C.

30. a. katha, A. jānaṁ, A. d. sokaṅ, A.

31. b. puttra°, A. c. snigdha(?dhaṁ?), A.

32. b. dvitīyā, A. c. deva, A; ma de daṅ lha-mo, T.

बालपुत्रां गुणवतीं कुलश्लाघ्यां पतिव्रताम् ।
देवीमर्हसि न त्यक्तुं क्लीबः प्राप्तामिव श्रियम् ॥ ३३ ॥

पुत्रं याशोधरं श्लाघ्यं यशोधर्मभृतां वरम् ।
बालमर्हसि न त्यक्तुं व्यसनीवोत्तमं यशः ॥ ३४ ॥

अथ बन्धुं च राज्यं च त्यक्तुमेव कृता मतिः ।
मां नार्हसि विभो त्यक्तुं त्वत्पादौ हि गतिर्मम ॥ ३५ ॥

नास्मि यातुं पुरं शक्तो दह्यमानेन चेतसा ।
त्वामरण्ये परित्यज्य सुमन्त्र इव राघवम् ॥ ३६ ॥

किं हि वक्ष्यति मां राजा त्वदृते नगरं गतम् ।
वक्ष्याम्युचितदर्शित्वात्किं तवान्तःपुराणि वा ॥ ३७ ॥

यदप्यात्थापि नैर्गुण्यं वाच्यं नरपताविति ।
किं तद्वक्ष्याम्यभूतं ते निर्दोषस्य मुनेरिव ॥ ३८ ॥

हृदयेन सलज्जेन जिह्वया सज्जमानया ।
अहं यद्यपि वा ब्रूयां कस्तच्छ्रद्धातुमर्हति ॥ ३९ ॥

यो हि चन्द्रमसस्तैक्ष्ण्यं कथयेच्छ्रद्दधीत वा ।
स दोषांस्तव दोषज्ञ कथयेच्छ्रद्दधीत वा ॥ ४० ॥

33. d. klība, A.

34. b. varaḥ, A; T ambiguous; 'Yaśodharā's son . . . who bears the good law', C. d. yasaḥ, A.

35. c. tyaktu, A. d. khyod zhabs-na (tvatpāde ?), T.

36. c. tvām āraṇye, A. d. sumitra, A; bśes-bzaṅ (=A), T; 'Sumantra', C.

37. c. vakṣyāmy a(?u?)cita°, A.

39. a. salajyena, A. d. kas taṁ śrad°, A.

40. a. taikṣṇaṁ, A.

सानुक्रोशस्य सततं नित्यं करुणवेदिनः ।
स्निग्धत्यागो न सदृशो निवर्तस्व प्रसीद मे ॥ ४१ ॥
इति शोकाभिभूतस्य श्रुत्वा छन्दस्य भाषितम् ।
स्वस्थः परमया धृत्या जगाद वदतां वरः ॥ ४२ ॥
मद्वियोगं प्रति च्छन्द संतापस्त्यज्यतामयम् ।
नानाभावो हि नियतं पृथग्जातिषु देहिषु ॥ ४३ ॥
स्वजनं यद्यपि स्नेहान्न त्यजेयमहं स्वयम् ।
मृत्युरन्योन्यमवशानस्मान् संत्याजयिष्यति ॥ ४४ ॥
महत्या तृष्णया दुःखैर्गर्भेणास्मि यया धृतः ।
तस्या निष्फलयत्नायाः क्वाहं मातुः क्व सा मम ॥ ४५ ॥
वासवृक्षे समागम्य विगच्छन्ति यथाण्डजाः ।
नियतं विप्रयोगान्तस्तथा भूतसमागमः ॥ ४६ ॥
समेत्य च यथा भूयो व्यपयान्ति बलाहकाः ।
संयोगो विप्रयोगश्च तथा मे प्राणिनां मतः ॥ ४७ ॥
यस्माद्याति च लोकोऽयं विप्रलभ्य परंपरम् ।
ममत्वं न क्षमं तस्मात्स्वप्नभूते समागमे ॥ ४८ ॥
सहजेन वियुज्यन्ते पर्णरागेण पादपाः ।
अन्येनान्यस्य विश्लेषः किं पुनर्न भविष्यति ॥ ४९ ॥

43. c. ṅes-pa yin (niyataḥ?), T.

44. a. svajana, A. gaṅ yaṅ (yad api), T. b. tyajeyam mumukṣayā, A ; bdag-gis raṅ ni mi-ḥdor-te, T ; ‘ even if to-day I did not leave my relations ’, C. d. asmāt, A.

45. b. ggarbhenāsmi, A. c. nisphala°, A.

48. b. e.c. ; parasparaṁ, A ; gaṅ-phyir phyir-na (Weller), gaṅ-gis phyir-na (Peking edition), T (=yasmād . . . paraṁparam?).

तद्देवं सति संतापं मा कार्षीः सौम्य गम्यताम् ।
लम्बते यदि तु स्नेहो गत्वापि पुनराव्रज ॥ ५० ॥

ब्रूयाश्चास्मत्कृतापेक्षं जनं कपिलवास्तुनि ।
त्यज्यतां तद्गतः स्नेहः श्रूयतां चास्य निश्चयः ॥ ५१ ॥

क्षिप्रमेष्यति वा कृत्वा जन्ममृत्युक्षयं किल ।
अकृतार्थो निरारम्भो निधनं यास्यतीति वा ॥ ५२ ॥

इति तस्य वचः श्रुत्वा कन्थकस्तुरगोत्तमः ।
जिह्वया लिलिहे पादौ बाष्पमुष्णं मुमोच च ॥ ५३ ॥

जालिना स्वस्तिकाङ्केन चक्रमध्येन पाणिना ।
आममर्श कुमारस्तं बभाषे च वयस्यवत् ॥ ५४ ॥

मुञ्च कन्थक मा बाष्पं दर्शितेयं सदश्वता ।
मृष्यतां सफलः शीघ्रं श्रमस्तेऽयं भविष्यति ॥ ५५ ॥

मणित्सरुं छन्दकहस्तसंस्थं ततः स धीरो निशितं गृहीत्वा ।
कोशादसिं काञ्चनभक्तिचित्रं बिलादिवाशीविषमुद्बबर्ह ॥ ५६ ॥

निष्कास्य तं चोत्पलपत्त्रनीलं चिच्छेद चित्रं मुकुटं सकेशम् ।
विकीर्यमाणांशुकमन्तरीक्षे चिक्षेप चैनं सरसीव हंसम् ॥ ५७ ॥

51. a. brūyāc cāsmāsv anākṣepaṁ, A; kho-bo-cag-la ltos-byas-paḥi . . . smros, T; 'to those who think attentively on me, you should proclaim', C. b. °vastuni, A.

52. b. jarāmṛtyu°, A; rga daṅ ḥchi-ba (=A), T; 'if I pass over the ocean of birth and death', C. kilaḥ, A.

53. c. lilihe (corrected to lelihe), A.

54. a. jalinā, A.

55. b. darśiteya, A.

56. b. tataḥ kumāro, A; de-nas . . . brtan-pa des, T. d. āsīrviṣam udbabarhaḥ, A.

57. a. triṣkāsya, A. b. makuṭaṁ, A. c. atarīkṣe, A.

पूजाभिलाषेण च बाहुमान्याद्दिवौकसस्तं जगृहुः प्रविद्धम् ।
यथावदेनं दिवि देवसङ्घा दिव्यैर्विशेषैर्महयां च चक्रुः ॥ ५८ ॥

मुक्त्वा त्वलंकारकलत्रवत्तां श्रीविप्रवासं शिरसश्च कृत्वा ।
दृष्ट्वांशुकं काञ्चनहंसचिह्नं वन्यं स धीरोऽभिचकाङ्क्ष वासः ॥ ५९ ॥

ततो मृगव्याधवपुर्दिवौका भावं विदित्वास्य विशुद्धभावः ।
काषायवस्त्रोऽभिययौ समीपं तं शाक्यराजप्रभवोऽभ्युवाच ॥ ६० ॥

शिवं च काषायमृषिध्वजस्ते न युज्यते हिंस्रमिदं धनुश्च ।
तत्सौम्य यद्यस्ति न सक्तिरत्र मह्यं प्रयच्छेदमिदं गृहाण ॥ ६१ ॥

व्याधोऽब्रवीत्कामद काममारादनेन विश्वास्य मृगान्निहन्मि ।
अर्थस्तु शक्रोपम यद्यनेन हन्त प्रतीच्छानय शुक्लमेतत् ॥ ६२ ॥

परेण हर्षेण ततः स वन्यं जग्राह वासोंऽशुकमुत्ससर्ज ।
व्याधस्तु दिव्यं वपुरेव बिभ्रत्तच्छुक्लमादाय दिवं जगाम ॥ ६३ ॥

ततः कुमारश्च स चाश्वगोपस्तस्मिंस्तथा याति विसिस्मियाते ।
आरण्यके वाससि चैव भूयस्तस्मिन्नकार्ष्टां बहुमानमाशु ॥ ६४ ॥

छन्दं ततः साश्रुमुखं विसृज्य काषायसंभृद्धृतिकीर्तिभृत्सः ।
येनाश्रमस्तेन ययौ महात्मा संध्याभ्रसंवीत इवोडुराजः ॥ ६५ ॥

58. a. pūjābhilāṣena, A. d. viśerṣai mahayāñ, A.

59. c. dṛṣṭvāśukaṁ, A.

61. b. hiṁśram, A. c. śaktir, A ; chags, T. d. gṛhāṇaṁ, A.

62. a. ḥdod-pa sñiṅ-po-las (kāmasārāt), T. b. nihatya, A ; gsod-do, T.

63. a. mchog-tu rab-tu-dgaḥ-ba-yis (parapraharṣeṇa), T.

64. b. tasmin tathā, A. cd. bhūya tasminn, A.

65. a. chanda, A. b. e.c. ; kāṣāyasaṁvid dhṛti°, A ; brtan . . . . ṅur-smrig gyon-zhin (kāṣāya . . . dhṛti°), T ; ' he put on the *kāṣāya* robe ', C. d. ivoḍurājaḥ (corrected in later hand to ivādrirājaḥ), A ; skar-maḥi rgyal-po bzhin, T ; ' like the orb of the sun or moon surrounded by a dark-red cloud ', C.

ततस्तथा भर्तरि राज्यनिःस्पृहे
तपोवनं याति विवर्णवाससि ।
भुजौ समुत्क्षिप्य ततः स वाजिभृ-
द्भृशं विचुक्रोश पपात च क्षितौ ॥ ६६ ॥

विलोक्य भूयश्च रुरोद सस्वरं हयं भुजाभ्यामुपगुह्य कन्थकम् ।
ततो निराशो विलपन्मुहुर्मुहुर्ययौ शरीरेण पुरं न चेतसा ॥ ६७ ॥

क्वचित्प्रदध्यौ विललाप च क्वचित्
क्वचित्प्रचस्खाल पपात च क्वचित् ।
अतो व्रजन् भक्तिवशेन दुःखित-
श्चचार बह्वीरवश पथि क्रियाः ॥ ६८ ॥

इति बुद्धचरिते महाकाव्ये छन्दकनिवर्तनो नाम षष्ठः सर्गः ॥ ६ ॥

66. a. °nispṛhe, A. b. virṇṇavāsasi (one syllable short), A; mdog ñams snaṅ-ba-na (vivarṇabhāsasi?), T.

67. b. upagṛjya, A; ñer-ḥkhyud-nas, T; 'clasping the white horse's neck', C. c. nirāso, A. d. T omits puraṁ and adds kyaṅ (for punar?); 'he returned along the road', C.

68. c. vrajaṁ, A. d. byas-pa-ḥo (cakāra?), T.

CANTO VII

ततो विसृज्याश्रुमुखं रुदन्तं छन्दं वनच्छन्दतया निरास्थः ।
सर्वार्थसिद्धो वपुषाभिभूय तमाश्रमं सिद्ध इव प्रपेदे ॥ १ ॥

स राजसूनुर्मृगराजगामी मृगाजिरं तन्मृगवत्प्रविष्टः ।
लक्ष्मीवियुक्तोऽपि शरीरलक्ष्म्या चक्षूंषि सर्वाश्रमिणां जहार ॥ २ ॥

स्थिता हि हस्तस्थयुगास्तथैव कौतूहलाचक्रधराः सदाराः ।
तमिन्द्रकल्पं ददृशुर्न जग्मुर्धुर्या इवार्धावनतैः शिरोभिः ॥ ३ ॥

विप्राश्च गत्वा बहिरिध्महेतोः प्राप्ताः समित्पुष्पपवित्रहस्ताः ।
तपःप्रधानाः कृतबुद्धयोऽपि तं द्रष्टुमीयुर्न मठानभीयुः ॥ ४ ॥

हृष्टाश्च केका मुमुचुर्मयूरा दृष्ट्वाम्बुदं नीलमिवोन्नमन्तः ।
शष्पाणि हित्वाभिमुखाश्च तस्थुर्मृगाश्चलाक्षा मृगचारिणश्च ॥ ५ ॥

दृष्ट्वा तमिक्ष्वाकुकुलप्रदीपं ज्वलन्तमुद्यन्तमिवांशुमन्तम् ।
कृतेऽपि दोहे जनितप्रमोदाः प्रसुस्रुवुर्होमदुहश्च गावः ॥ ६ ॥

1. b. chanda vana°, A. nags-su ḥdun-paḥi dkaḥ-thub (vanacchandatapā, or °tapo), T.

3. a. lag-na gñaḥ-śiṅ bcas-par ḥgro-gyur (=gatāḥ sahastayugāḥ), T.

4. a. sbyin-sreg bud-śiṅ (haviridhma°), T. b. me-tog lo-ḥdab thob-paḥi lag-pa gtsaṅ-rnams (=prāptapuṣpaparṇapavitrahastāḥ), T.

5. b. unnamantaṁ, A; rma-bya-rnams . . . gyen-du dud-ciṅ, T; 'the peacocks . . . rose in the air', C. d. mṛgā calākṣā, A; rgya-skyegs . . . daṅ ni ri-dags-rnams (mṛgāś ca lākṣā !), T.

6. d. prasuśruvur, A.

कच्चिद्वसूनामयमष्टमः स्यात्स्यादश्विनोरन्यतरश्च्युतो वा ।
उच्चैरुरुच्चैरिति तत्र वाचस्तद्दर्शनाद्विस्मयजा मुनीनाम् ॥ ७ ॥

लेखर्षभस्येव वपुर्द्वितीयं धामेव लोकस्य चराचरस्य ।
स द्योतयामास वनं हि कृत्स्नं यदृच्छया सूर्य इवावतीर्णः ॥ ८ ॥

ततः स तैराश्रमिभिर्यथावदभ्यर्चितश्चोपनिमन्त्रितश्च ।
प्रत्यर्चयां धर्मभृतो बभूव स्वरेण साम्भोऽम्बुधरोपमेन ॥ ९ ॥

कीर्णं तथा पुण्यकृता जनेन स्वर्गाभिकामेन विमोक्षकामः ।
तमाश्रमं सोऽनुचचार धीरस्तपांसि चित्राणि निरीक्षमाणः ॥ १० ॥

तपोविकारांश्च निरीक्ष्य सौम्यस्तपोवने तत्र तपोधनानाम् ।
तपस्विनं कंचिदनुव्रजन्तं तत्त्वं विजिज्ञासुरिदं बभाषे ॥ ११ ॥

तत्पूर्वमद्याश्रमदर्शनं मे यस्मादिमं धर्मविधिं न जाने ।
तस्माद्भवानर्हति भाषितुं मे यो निश्चयो यत्प्रति वः प्रवृत्तः ॥ १२ ॥

ततो द्विजातिः स तपोविहारः शाक्यर्षभायर्षभविक्रमाय ।
क्रमेण तस्मै कथयांचकार तपोविशेषांस्तपसः फलं च ॥ १३ ॥

7. a. kaś (corrected to kac)cid vaśūnām, A ; yin-nam-ci, T. b. cyuto tra, A ; ḥphos-sam, T. c. uccairur, A.

8. a. leṣarṣabhasyeva, A ; lha-yi khyu-mchog, T. cd. kṛsnaṁ yadṛtsayā, A ; gaṅ ḥdod-pa-yis . . . mthaḥ-dag, T.

9. d. e.c. ; sāddhombudharo°, A ; chu-bcas chu-ḥdzin (sāmbho'-mbudharo°, or sāmbvambu°), T.

10. d. ṅes-par-rnam-gzigs-śiṅ (nivīkṣamāṇaḥ?), T.

11. ab. nirīkṣa saumya tapo°, A ; ṅes (des, Weller) gsan-nas (niśamya?), T.

12. d. ya (corrected in later hand to yaṁ) prati vaḥ pravṛrttiḥ (corrected to °vṛrttaḥ), A ; gaṅ-la rab-tu-ḥjug-pa-ḥo, T.

13. d. daṅ ni dkaḥ-thub ḥbras-bu daṅ bcas (satapaḥphalaṁ ca, or °phalāṁś ca?), T ; ' and together with the fruits of *tapas* ', C.

अग्राम्यमन्नं सलिले प्ररूढं पर्णानि तोयं फलमूलमेव ।
यथागमं वृत्तिरियं मुनीनां भिन्नास्तु ते ते तपसां विकल्पाः ॥ १४ ॥

उञ्छेन जीवन्ति खगा इवान्ये तृणानि केचिन्मृगवच्चरन्ति ।
केचिद्भुजङ्गैः सह वर्तयन्ति वल्मीकभूता वनमारुतेन ॥ १५ ॥

अश्मप्रयत्नार्जितवृत्तयोऽन्ये केचित्स्वदन्तापहतान्नभक्षाः ।
कृत्वा परार्थं श्रपणं तथान्ये कुर्वन्ति कार्यं यदि शेषमस्ति ॥ १६ ॥

केचिज्जलक्लिन्नजटाकलापा
द्विः पावकं जुह्वति मन्त्रपूर्वम् ।
मीनैः समं केचिदपो विगाह्य
वसन्ति कूर्मोल्लिखितैः शरीरैः ॥ १७ ॥

एवंविधैः कालचितैस्तपोभिः परैर्दिवं यान्त्यपरैर्नृलोकम् ।
दुःखेन मार्गेण सुखं ह्युपैति सुखं हि धर्मस्य वदन्ति मूलम् ॥ १८ ॥

इत्येवमादि द्विपेन्द्रवत्सः श्रुत्वा वचस्तस्य तपोधनस्य ।
अदृष्टतत्त्वोऽपि न संतुतोष शनैरिदं चात्मगतं बभाषे ॥ १९ ॥

14. a. e.c. Böhtlingk; salilaṁ prarūḍhaṁ, A; chu-la rab-skyes-paḥi, T; salilaprarūḍhaṁ, Co. b. prarṇṇāni, A.

15. a. uñcena jīvati, A. b. tṛnāni kecit mṛga°, A. d. °bhūtā iva mārutena, A; gyur-pa-rnams nags-na rluṅ-gis-so, T.

16. a. 'They do not eat what is husked with wood or stone', C. b. raṅ-gi so-yis ñe-bar-blaṅs (svadantopahṛta°), T. c. śrapaṇa, A.

17. d. kūrmmolikhitaiḥ, A; rus-sbal bzhin-du lus-rnams rab-tu-bskum-(skums, Weller)-pa-ḥo (hrasanti kūrmapratimaiḥ śarīraiḥ?), T.

18. a. evamvidhai, A. c. sukham upeti (corrected to sukhaṁ kṣu(?a?)-peti, A; bde-ba ñe-bar-thob phyir, T. d. dukhaṁ, A; bde-ba, T.

19. d. sanair, A.

दुःखात्मकं नैकविधं तपश्च
स्वर्गप्रधानं तपसः फलं च ।
लोकाश्च सर्वे परिणामवन्तः
स्वल्पे श्रमः खल्वयमाश्रमाणाम् ॥ २० ॥

प्रियांश्च बन्धून्विषयांश्च हित्वा ये स्वर्गहेतोर्नियमं चरन्ति ।
ते विप्रयुक्ताः खलु गन्तुकामा महत्तरं बन्धनमेव भूयः ॥ २१ ॥

कायक्लमैर्यश्च तपोऽभिधानैः प्रवृत्तिमाकाङ्क्षति कामहेतोः ।
संसारदोषानपरीक्षमाणो दुःखेन सोऽन्विच्छति दुःखमेव ॥ २२ ॥

त्रासश्च नित्यं मरणात्प्रजानां यत्नेन चेच्छन्ति पुनःप्रसूतिम् ।
सत्यां प्रवृत्तौ नियतश्च मृत्युस्तत्रैव मग्ना यत एव भीताः ॥ २३ ॥

इहार्थमेके प्रविशन्ति खेदं स्वर्गार्थमन्ये श्रममाप्नुवन्ति ।
सुखार्थमाशाकृपणोऽकृतार्थः पतत्यनर्थे खलु जीवलोकः ॥ २४ ॥

न खल्वयं गर्हित एव यत्नो यो हीनमुत्सृज्य विशेषगामी ।
प्राज्ञैः समानेन परिश्रमेण कार्यं तु तद्यत्र पुनर्न कार्यम् ॥ २५ ॥

शरीरपीडा तु यदीह धर्मः सुखं शरीरस्य भवत्यधर्मः ।
धर्मेण चाप्नोति सुखं परत्र तस्मादधर्मं फलतीह धर्मः ॥ २६ ॥

20. c. sarvvai, A.

21. a. śriyañ ca bandhūn, A; ḥphaṅs-pa-rnams daṅ gñen daṅ, T; 'quitting relations, giving up excellent *viṣayas*', C; 'you give up your loved relations and the joys of the world', FP. d. 'You do not see that in the future you return again to prison' (anāgate bandhanam eva bhūyaḥ?), FP.

22. a. kāyaklamai yaś ca, A. b. pravṛrttiṁ, A.

23. b. slar-yaṅ rab-tu-ḥjug-par (punaḥpravṛttiṁ), T; 'they seek to undergo birth', C. c. 'Having been born, then they must die' (satyāṁ prasūtau?), C. d. bhītaḥ, A; ḥjigs-pa-rnams, T.

24. c. āśākyapano, A; sred-paḥi bkren-pa, T.

25. d. de ḥdir (tad atra), T.

यतः शरीरं मनसो वशेन प्रवर्तते चापि निवर्तते च ।
युक्तो दमश्चेतस एव तस्माच्चित्तादृते काष्ठसमं शरीरम् ॥ २७ ॥

आहारशुद्ध्या यदि पुण्यमिष्टं
तस्मान्मृगाणामपि पुण्यमस्ति ।
ये चापि बाह्याः पुरुषाः फलेभ्यो
भाग्यापराधेन पराङ्मुखार्थाः ॥ २८ ॥

दुःखेऽभिसंधिस्त्वथ पुण्यहेतुः सुखेऽपि कार्यो ननु सोऽभिसंधिः ।
अथ प्रमाणं न सुखेऽभिसंधिर्दुःखे प्रमाणं ननु नाभिसंधिः ॥ २९ ॥

तथैव ये कर्मविशुद्धिहेतोः
स्पृशन्त्यपस्तीर्थमिति प्रवृत्ताः ।
तत्रापि तोषो हृदि केवलोऽयं
न पावयिष्यन्ति हि पापमापः ॥ ३० ॥

स्पृष्टं हि यद्यद्गुणवद्भिरम्भस्तत्तत्पृथिव्यां यदि तीर्थमिष्टम् ।
तस्माद्गुणानेव परैमि तीर्थमापस्तु निःसंशयमाप एव ॥ ३१ ॥

इति स्म तत्तद्बहुयुक्तियुक्तं जगाद चास्तं च ययौ विवस्वान् ।
ततो हविर्धूमविवर्णवृक्षं तपःप्रशान्तं स वनं विवेश ॥ ३२ ॥

27. a. vasena, A. b. pravartate vāpi nivartate vā, A; rab-tu-ḥjug-pa daṅ ni ldog-pa daṅ-no, T; 'the starting and extinction of bodily action are both', C.

28. b. tasmāt mṛgāṇām, A.

30. c. de-yi sñiṅ-la tshim-pa tsam yin-te (toṣo hṛdi kevalo 'sya), T.

31. c. guṇāṇ aiva paremi, A; yon-tan-ldan-rnams kho-na (=guṇina eva), T; 'one should honour this virtue', C.

32. b. vivaśvān, A. d. khrus-sar (savanaṁ), T.

अभ्युद्धृतप्रज्वलिताग्निहोत्रं कृताभिषेकर्षिजनावकीर्णम् ।
जाप्यस्वनाकूजितदेवकोष्ठं धर्मस्य कर्मान्तमिव प्रवृत्तम् ॥ ३३ ॥
काश्चिन्निशास्तत्र निशाकराभः परीक्षमाणश्च तपांस्युवास ।
सर्वं परिक्षेप्य तपश्च मत्वा तस्मात्तपःक्षेत्रतलाज्जगाम ॥ ३४ ॥
अन्वव्रजन्नाश्रमिणस्ततस्तं तद्रूपमाहात्म्यगतैर्मनोभिः ।
देशादनार्यैरभिभूयमानान्महर्षयो धर्ममिवापयान्तम् ॥ ३५ ॥
ततो जटावल्कलचीरखेलांस्तपोधनांश्चैव स तान्ददर्श ।
तपांसि चैषामनुरुध्यमानस्तस्थौ शिवे श्रीमति वृक्षमूले ॥ ३६ ॥
अथोपसृत्याश्रमवासिनस्तं मनुष्यवर्यं परिवार्य तस्थुः ।
वृद्धश्च तेषां बहुमानपूर्वं कलेन साम्ना गिरमित्युवाच ॥ ३७ ॥
त्वय्यागते पूर्ण इवाश्रमोऽभूत्संपद्यते शून्य इव प्रयाते ।
तस्मादिमं नार्हसि तात हातुं जिजीविषोर्देहमिवेष्टमायुः ॥ ३८ ॥
ब्रह्मर्षिराजर्षिसुरर्षिजुष्टः पुण्यः समीपे हिमवान् हि शैलः ।
तपांसि तान्येव तपोधनानां यत्संनिकर्षाद्बहुलीभवन्ति ॥ ३९ ॥

33. d. chos-kyi lam-gyi las-kyi mthaḥ (dharmādhvakarmāntam), T.

34. c. dkaḥ-thub thams-cad yoṅs-su-rtogs-śiṅ mkhyen-gyur-nas (sarvam pari . . . ya tapaś ca matvā), T; 'he did not see the real truth in them (i.e. the austerities)', C; parijñāya, or paricchidya, Böhtlingk; parīkṣyātha, Kern; matyā, Cappeller.

35. d. maharṣayau, A.

36. a. °ciracelāṁs, Hultzsch. d. śiṅ-gi rtsa-ba (vṛkṣamūle), T.

37. a. °vāśinas, A. d. dus-kyi (for kyis?) zhi-bas (kālasya sāmnā, or kālena), T.

39. b. himavāṁ, A. d. yatsaṁnikaṣād, A.

तीर्थानि पुण्यान्यभितस्तथैव सोपानभूतानि नभस्तलस्य ।
जुष्टानि धर्मात्मभिरात्मवद्भिर्देवर्षिभिश्चैव महर्षिभिश्च ॥ ४० ॥

इतश्च भूयः क्षममुत्तरैव दिक्सेवितुं धर्मविशेषहेतोः ।
न तु क्षमं दक्षिणतो बुधेन पदं भवेदेकमपि प्रयातुम् ॥ ४१ ॥

तपोवनेऽस्मिन्नथ निष्क्रियो वा संकीर्णधर्मापतितोऽशुचिर्वा ।
दृष्टस्त्वया येन न ते विवत्सा तद्ब्रूहि यावद्रुचितोऽस्तु वासः ॥ ४२ ॥

इमे हि वाञ्छन्ति तपःसहायं तपोनिधानप्रतिमं भवन्तम् ।
वासस्त्वया हीन्द्रसमेन सार्धं बृहस्पतेरभ्युदयावहः स्यात् ॥ ४३ ॥

इत्येवमुक्ते स तपस्विमध्ये तपस्विमुख्येन मनीषिमुख्यः ।
भवप्रणाशाय कृतप्रतिज्ञः स्वं भावमन्तर्गतमाचचक्षे ॥ ४४ ॥

ऋज्वात्मनां धर्मभृतां मुनीनामिष्टातिथित्वात्स्वजनोपमानाम् ।
एवंविधैर्मां प्रति भावजातैः प्रीतिः परा मे जनितश्च मानः ॥ ४५ ॥

40. cd. ātmavadbhi re(corrected to de?)varṣibhirś caiva nṛparṣibhiś ca, A; lha-yi draṅ-sroṅ-rnams daṅ draṅ-sroṅ chen-po ni . . . bdag-ñid chen-po-rnams-kyis (mahātmabhir devarṣibhiś caiva maharṣibhiś ca, or, amending to bdag-ñid ldan-pa, ātmavadbhir), T.

41. b. °viseṣa°, A. c. na ku(?) kṣaman (marginal comment, na tu yuktam), A; T omits tu.

42. b. °dharmā patito, Co.; °dharme patito, Gawroński. d. tad bru-(?ū?)hi, A. re-zhig (tāvad), T.

43. a. vācchanti, A. d. phur-bu-yi yaṅ mṅon-par-mtho-ba ḥdren-pa (bṛhaspater apy abhyudayāvahaḥ, one syllable in excess), T; bṛhaspater apy udayāvahaḥ, Lüders.

44. a. ukte (e marked as wrong), A; de-skad ces smras-te, T; uktaḥ, Böhtlingk. b. manīkhimukhyaḥ, A. d. raṅ-bzhin (svabhāvam?), T.

45. b. svajanopamānaṁ, A; raṅ-gi skye-bo daṅ mtshuṅs-paḥi . . . thub-pa-rnams, T. d. prītiḥ parā tma (corrected to me, or vice versa ?) janitaś ca mārggaḥ, A; bdag-gi dgaḥ-ba mchog daṅ bkur-ste skyes-par-gyur, T.

स्निग्धाभिराभिर्हृदयंगमाभिः समासतः स्नात इवास्मि वाग्भिः ।
रतिश्च मे धर्मनवग्रहस्य विस्पन्दिता संप्रति भूय एव ॥ ४६ ॥

एवं प्रवृत्तान् भवतः शरण्यानतीव संदर्शितपक्षपातान् ।
यास्यामि हित्वेति ममापि दुःखं यथैव बन्धूंस्त्यजतस्तथैव ॥ ४७ ॥

स्वर्गाय युष्माकमयं तु धर्मो ममाभिलाषस्त्वपुनर्भवाय ।
अस्मिन्वने येन न मे विवत्सा भिन्नः प्रवृत्त्या हि निवृत्तिधर्मः ॥४८॥

तन्नारतिर्मे न परापचारो वनादितो येन परिव्रजामि ।
धर्मे स्थिताः पूर्वयुगानुरूपे सर्वे भवन्तो हि महर्षिकल्पाः ॥ ४९ ॥

ततो वचः सूनृतमर्थवच्च सुश्लक्ष्णमोजस्वि च गर्वितं च ।
श्रुत्वा कुमारस्य तपस्विनस्ते विशेषयुक्तं बहुमानमीयुः ॥ ५० ॥

कश्चिद्द्विजस्तत्र तु भस्मशायी प्रांशुः शिखी दारवचीरवासाः ।
आपिङ्गलाक्षस्तनुदीर्घघोणः कुण्डैकहस्तो गिरमित्युवाच ॥ ५१ ॥

धीमन्नुदारः खलु निश्चयस्ते यस्त्वं युवा जन्मनि दृष्टदोषः ।
स्वर्गापवर्गौ हि विचार्य सम्यग्यस्यापवर्गे मतिरस्ति सोऽस्ति ॥ ५२ ॥

यज्ञैस्तपोभिर्नियमैश्च तैस्तैः स्वर्गं यियासन्ति हि रागवन्तः ।
रागेण सार्धं रिपुणेव युद्ध्वा मोक्षं परीप्सन्ति तु सत्त्ववन्तः ॥ ५३ ॥

46. a. ābhi hṛdayaṁ°, A. c. kun-nas ḥdzin-med chos-can (dharmānavagrahasya, against the metre), T.

47. d. bandhūs, A.

48. d. pravṛttyau, A.

50. a. sūnṛtram, A. b. sñiṅ-po daṅ ldan-pa (garbhitaṁ), T.

51. d. kuṇḍ · k(?v)ahasto girim, A (much rubbed) ; lag-gcig spyi-blugs ldan-pas, T.

52. a. rgya-chen blo-ldan-zhiṅ (dhīmān udāraḥ), T. niścayas tte, A. b. T omits yaḥ. c. °varggo, A.

53. b. yiyāsyaṁti, A.

तद्बुद्धिरेषा यदि निश्चिता ते तूर्णं भवान् गच्छतु विन्ध्यकोष्ठम् ।
असौ मुनिस्तत्र वसत्यराडो यो नैष्ठिके श्रेयसि लब्धचक्षुः ॥ ५४ ॥

तस्माद्भवाञ्छ्रोष्यति तत्त्वमार्गं सत्यां रुचौ संप्रतिपत्स्यते च ।
यथा तु पश्यामि मतिस्तथैषा तस्यापि यास्यत्यवधूय बुद्धिम् ॥५५॥

स्पष्टोच्चघोणं विपुलायताक्षं ताम्राधरौष्ठं सिततीक्ष्णदंष्ट्रम् ।
इदं हि वक्त्रं तनुरक्तजिह्वं ज्ञेयार्णवं पास्यति कृत्स्नमेव ॥ ५६ ॥

गम्भीरता या भवतस्त्वगाधा या दीप्तता यानि च लक्षणानि ।
आचार्यकं प्राप्स्यसि तत्पृथिव्यां यन्नर्षिभिः पूर्वयुगेऽप्यवाप्तम् ॥५७॥

परममिति ततो नृपात्मज-
स्तमृषिजनं प्रतिनन्द्य निर्ययौ ।
विधिवदनुविधाय तेऽपि तं
प्रविविशुराश्रमिणस्तपोवनम् ॥ ५८ ॥

इति बुद्धचरिते महाकाव्ये तपोवनप्रवेशो नाम सप्तमः सर्गः ॥ ७ ॥

54. d. yau neṣṭhike śreyasi, A.

55. c. e.c. ; matis tavaiṣā, A ; blo-gros de de-ltar (matis tathā sā), T. d. yāsyāty, A.

56. a. paṣṭoścaghoṇam, A ; gsal-zhiṅ mtho-baḥi śaṅs, T. b. tāmrādharauṣṭraṁ, A. d. ḥgro-ba (yāsyati), T ; 'you will drink up entirely the *jñeya*-water ', C. kṛtsṇam, A.

57. d. sṅon-gyi bskal-par draṅ-sroṅ-gis gaṅ ma-mthoṅ-baḥi (=yad ṛṣibhiḥ pūrvayuge na dṛṣṭam), T ; 'what was not obtained by the ṛṣis of old ', C.

CANTO VIII

ततस्तुरङ्गावचरः स दुर्मनास्तथा वनं भर्तरि निर्ममे गते ।
चकार यत्नं पथि शोकनिग्रहे तथापि चैवाश्रु न तस्य चिक्षिये ॥१॥

यमेकरात्रेण तु भर्तुराज्ञया जगाम मार्गं सह तेन वाजिना ।
इयाय भर्तुर्विरहं विचिन्तयंस्तमेव पन्थानमहोभिरष्टभिः ॥ २ ॥

हयश्च सौजा विचचार कन्थकस्तताम भावेन बभूव निर्मदः ।
अलंकृतश्चापि तथैव भूषणैरभूद्गतश्रीरिव तेन वर्जितः ॥ ३ ॥

निवृत्य चैवाभिमुखस्तपोवनं
भृशं जिह्रेषे करुणं मुहुर्मुहुः ।
क्षुधान्वितोऽप्यध्वनि शष्पमम्बु वा
यथा पुरा नाभिननन्द नाददे ॥ ४ ॥

ततो विहीनं कपिलाह्वयं पुरं महात्मना तेन जगद्धितात्मना ।
क्रमेण तौ शून्यमिवोपजग्मतुर्दिवाकरेणेव विनाकृतं नभः ॥ ५ ॥

1. a. durmmaṇās, A. d. cikṣipe, A ; khog (for khogs or bkog, Weller wrongly khob), T ; 'he kept on weeping', C.

3. a. e.c. ; hayaś ca saujasvi cacāra, A ; mgyogs-ḥgro ñid kyaṅ mdaṅs-med rgyu-ba-ste (hayo 'py anojasvi cacāra), T ; 'the good horse rushed on, naturally speedy and majestic in appearance', C ; saujā vicacāla, Böhtlingk. b. ḥthon-pa med-pas (=niḥsārābhāvena or niḥsṛtābhāvena), T.

4. d. purā bhinananda (one syllable short), A ; ji-ltar sṅon bzhin mṅon-par ma-dgaḥ, T.

5. a. pura, A. cd. °jagmatu divā°, A.

सपुण्डरीकैरपि शोभितं जलैरलंकृतं पुष्पधरैर्नगैरपि ।
तदेव तस्योपवनं वनोपमं गतप्रहर्षैर्न रराज नागरैः ॥ ६ ॥

ततो भ्रमद्भिर्दिशि दीनमानसैरनुज्ज्वलैर्बाष्पहतेक्षणैर्नरैः ।
निवार्यमाणाविव तावुभौ पुरं शनैरपस्नातमिवाभिजग्मतुः ॥ ७ ॥

निशाम्य च स्रस्तशरीरगामिनौ
विनागतौ शाक्यकुलर्षभेण तौ ।
मुमोच बाष्पं पथि नागरो जनः
पुरा रथे दाशरथेरिवागते ॥ ८ ॥

अथ ब्रुवन्तः समुपेतमन्यवो जनाः पथि च्छन्दकमागताश्रवः ।
क्व राजपुत्रः पुरराष्ट्रनन्दनो हृतस्त्वयासाविति पृष्ठतोऽन्वयुः ॥ ९ ॥

ततः स तान् भक्तिमतोऽब्रवीज्जनान्नरेन्द्रपुत्रं न परित्यजाम्यहम् ।
रुदन्नहं तेन तु निर्जने वने गृहस्थवेशश्च विसर्जिताविति ॥ १० ॥

इदं वचस्तस्य निशम्य ते जनाः सुदुष्करं खल्विति निश्चयं ययुः ।
पतद्धि जह्रुः सलिलं न नेत्रजं मनो निनिन्दुश्च फलोत्थमात्मनः ॥ ११ ॥

6. b. °dharai nnagair, A.

7. a. bhramadbhi diśi, A. b. hataikṣaṇair nnarai, A. c. nivāryamā* (?r,?n)āv iva, A. d. ayasnātam (corrected in later hand to aja°), A; log-paḥi khrus, T; 'as if at a funeral', C.

8. a. niśamya, A; mthoṅ-nas, T; 'seeing', C. b. śākyaḥi rigs-kyi draṅ-sroṅ (śākyakularṣiṇā), T; °arṣabhena, A.

9. b. āgatāsravaḥ, A. d. khyod-kyis gaṅ-du bor (kva. . . hitas (to hi, 'leave') tvayā), T; 'you stole and took him away', C. pṛṣṭhatau, A.

10. ab. bravīt janā narendra°, A.

11. a. niśāmya, A; thos-nas, T. b. vismayaṁ yayuḥ, Lüders; ṅes-par soṅ-gyur-la, T; 'were startled and considered it extraordinary', C; 'they exclaimed, "There are few who would do this",' FP. c. hgyel-zhiṅ mig-skyes chu ni rnam-par-ḥthor-ba-ste (patad vijahruḥ salilaṁ netrajam), T; 'they sobbed and they wailed, their tears joining flowed downwards', C. d. phalārtha(?)m ātmanaḥ, A; bdag-ñid-kyis (for kyi) ni ḥbras-bu loṅ, T.

अथोचुरद्यैव विशाम तद्वनं
गतः स यत्र द्विपराजविक्रमः ।
जिजीविषा नास्ति हि तेन नो विना
यथेन्द्रियाणां विगमे शरीरिणाम् ॥ १२ ॥

इदं पुरं तेन विवर्जितं वनं
वनं च तत्तेन समन्वितं पुरम् ।
न शोभते तेन हि नो विना पुरं
मरुत्वता वृत्रवधे यथा दिवम् ॥ १३ ॥

पुनः कुमारो विनिवृत्त इत्यथो
गवाक्षमालाः प्रतिपेदिरेऽङ्गनाः ।
विविक्तपृष्ठं च निशाम्य वाजिनं
पुनर्गवाक्षाणि पिधाय चुक्रुशुः ॥ १४ ॥

प्रविष्टदीक्षस्तु सुतोपलब्धये व्रतेन शोकेन च खिन्नमानसः ।
जजाप देवायतने नराधिपश्चकार तास्ताश्च यथाशयाः क्रियाः ॥ १५ ॥

ततः स बाष्पप्रतिपूर्णलोचनस्तुरङ्गमादाय तुरङ्गमानुगः ।
विवेश शोकाभिहतो नृपक्षयं युधापिनीते रिपुणेव भर्तरि ॥ १६ ॥

12. b. gñis-skyes rgyal-poḥi (dvijarāja°), T. d. lus-can dbaṅ-po ma-tshaṅ-rnams-kyi ji-lta-bar (=yathā śarīriṇāṁ vikalendriyāṇām), T.

13. a. vivarjita, A. b. yat tena, Ujjvaladatta on Uṇādisūtras, i, 156. c. tena vinādya no, Ujjvaladatta *ib.*

14. b. pratipedire ngavyaḥ, A. c. niśa (śa mutilated and next syllable lost by tear), A ; mthoṅ-gyur-nas, T. d. gavākṣān apidhāya, Prasāda.

15. a. sutopabdhaye (one syllable short), A ; sras-po ñer-thob-phyir, T. d. yathāśrayāḥ, A ; bsam-pa ji-ltar, T.

16. a. pratigh(?)ūrṇṇa°, A ; rab-tu-gaṅ-ba, T. b. turaṅgamānuṣ(?)aḥ, A ; mgyogs-ḥgro rjes-su-ḥgro-ba-ste, T. cd. nṛpakṣayaṁ dhāpinīte (one syllable short), A ; gyul-ḥgyed-pa-na . . . khyer-ba . . . mi-skyoṅ khaṅ-par, T.

विगाहमानश्च नरेन्द्रमन्दिरं विलोकयन्नश्रुवहेन चक्षुषा ।
स्वरेण पुष्टेन रुराव कन्थको जनाय दुःखं प्रतिवेदयन्निव ॥ १७ ॥
ततः खगाश्च क्षयमध्यगोचराः समीपबद्धास्तुरगाश्च सत्कृताः ।
हयस्य तस्य प्रतिसस्वनुः स्वनं नरेन्द्रसूनोरुपयानशङ्किनः ॥ १८ ॥
जनाश्च हर्षातिशयेन वञ्चिता जनाधिपान्तःपुरसंनिकर्षगाः ।
यथा हयः कन्थक एष हेषते ध्रुवं कुमारो विशतीति मेनिरे ॥१९॥
अतिप्रहर्षादथ शोकमूर्छिताः कुमारसंदर्शनलोललोचनाः ।
गृहाद्विनिश्चक्रमुराशया स्त्रियः शरत्पयोदादिव विद्युतश्चलाः ॥२०॥

विलम्बकेश्यो मलिनांशुकाम्बरा
निरञ्जनैर्बाष्पहतेक्षणैर्मुखैः ।
स्त्रियो न रेजुर्मृजया विनाकृता
दिवीव तारा रजनीक्षयारुणाः ॥ २१ ॥

अरक्तताम्रैश्चरणैरनूपुरैरकुण्डलैरार्जवकन्धरैर्मुखैः ।
स्वभावपीनैर्जघनैरमेखलैरहारयोक्त्रैर्मुषितैरिव स्तनैः ॥ २२ ॥
निरीक्ष्य ता बाष्पपरीतलोचना निराश्रयं छन्दकमश्वमेव च ।
विषण्णवक्त्रा रुरुदुर्वराङ्गना वनान्तरे गाव इवर्षभोज्झिताः ॥ २३ ॥

17. c. bsal-baḥi dbyaṅs-kyis (svareṇa dīptena?), T ; ' wailing terrifically " C. d. prativedayaṁti ca, A ; rab-tu-rtogs-ḥjug bzhin, T.

18. d. e.c. Kern ; °śaṅkitāḥ, A.

19. a. heṣātiśayena, Gawroński. cañcitā, A ; bslus-paḥi, T.

21. a. vilambaveśyo, A ; lan-bu rnam-par-ḥphyaṅ-zhiṅ, T. °kābarā, A. b. hataikṣaṇair mmuṣṭy(?ṣṇy?)aiḥ, A. c. kṛṣṇā vivarṇṇā majayā, A ; byi-dor daṅ bral bud-med rigs-rnams mdzes ma-gyur, T.

22. b. ārjavakarṇṇikair, A ; mgrin-pa draṅ-po-rnams, T. c. °pīnai jaghanair, A. d. T omits iva. stastaih, A ; nu-ma, T.

23. a. nirīkṣa tā bāṣpaparīritalocana, A ; mig ni mchi-ma ldan de-rnams-kyis mthoṅ-nas, T. d. nags-mthar (vanānte), T. ivārṣabhojitāḥ, A ; khyu-mchog daṅ bral-ba, T.

ततः सबाष्पा महिषी महीपतेः
प्रनष्टवत्सा महिषीव वत्सला ।
प्रगृह्य बाहू निपपात गौतमी
विलोलपर्णा कदलीव काञ्चनी ॥ २४ ॥

हतत्विषोऽन्याः शिथिलांसबाहवः
स्त्रियो विषादेन विचेतना इव ।
न चुक्रुशुर्नाश्रु जहुर्न शश्वसु-
र्न चेलुरासुर्लिखिता इव स्थिताः ॥ २५ ॥

अधीरमन्याः पतिशोकमूर्छिता
विलोचनप्रस्रवणैर्मुखैः स्त्रियः ।
सिषिञ्चिरे प्रोषितचन्दनान् स्तना-
न्धराधरः प्रस्रवणैरिवोपलान् ॥ २६ ॥

मुखैश्च तासां नयनाम्बुताडितै रराज तद्राजनिवेशनं तदा ।
नवाम्बुकालेऽम्बुदवृष्टिताडितैः स्रवज्जलैस्तामरसैर्यथा सरः ॥ २७ ॥

सुवृत्तपीनाङ्गुलिभिर्निरन्तरैरभूषणैर्गूढसिरैर्वराङ्गनाः ।
उरांसि जघ्नुः कमलोपमैः करैः स्वपल्लवैर्वातचला लता इव ॥२८॥

24. b. praṇaṣṭavatsā, A.

25. a. hataḥ(visarga marked as wrong)dviṣo nyāḥ śithilātmabāhavaḥ, A; dpuṅ-ba lag-pa sñoms-śiṅ gzi-brjid bcom-pa . . . gzhan-rnams, T. c. cukruśu nāśru, A. cd. śaśva nna celar āsu llikhitā (one syllable short), A; dbugs-med-par gyo-bral ri-mo bris-pa, T.

26. b. °praśravaṇair, A. c. siṣ(?s?)iñcire proṣitacandanā, A; tsan-dan rab-bskus (so Peking, bskud Weller) . . . rnam-par-ḥthor (vijahrire prokṣita-candanān, or vicakrire from kṝ), T. d. praśravaṇair, A.

28. b. varāṅgaṇāḥ (corrected to nāḥ), A.

करप्रहारप्रचलैश्च ता बभुस्तथापि नार्यः सहितोन्नतैः स्तनैः ।
वनानिलाघूर्णितपद्मकम्पितै रथाङ्गनाम्नां मिथुनैरिवापगाः ॥२९॥

यथा च वक्षांसि करैरपीडयंस्तथैव वक्षोभिरपीडयन् करान् ।
अकारयंस्तत्र परस्परं व्यथाः कराग्रवक्षांस्यबला दयालसाः ॥३०॥

ततस्तु रोषप्रविरक्तलोचना विषादसंबन्धिकषायगद्गदम् ।
उवाच निश्वासचलत्पयोधरा विगाढशोकाश्रुधरा यशोधरा ॥३१॥

निशि प्रसुप्तामवशां विहाय मां
गतः क्व स च्छन्दक मन्मनोरथः ।
उपागते च त्वयि कन्थके च मे
समं गतेषु त्रिषु कम्पते मनः ॥ ३२ ॥

अनार्यमस्निग्धममित्रकर्म मे नृशंस कृत्वा किमिहाद्य रोदिषि ।
नियच्छ बाष्पं भव तुष्टमानसो न संवदत्यश्रु च तच्च कर्म ते ॥३३॥

प्रियेण वश्येन हितेन साधुना
त्वया सहायेन यथार्थकारिणा ।
गतोऽर्यपुत्रो ह्यपुनर्निवृत्तये
रमस्व दिष्ट्या सफलः श्रमस्तव ॥ ३४ ॥

29. ab. babhur yathāpi, A; de-lta-na yaṅ . . . mdzes-par-gyur, T. d. rathāṅgaṇāmnā mithuner, A.

30. a. vakṣāsi karair apīḍayas, A.

31. b. e.c. Kern; viṣādasambandha°, A; sems-ḥkhral-gyis sbrel (viṣādasaṁnaddha°?), T; viṣādasaṁbaddha°, Böhtlingk.

32. a. avasāṁ, A. b. T omits man. c. tvāyi, A.

33. ab. kho-mo . . . phul-phyuṅ (=me 'tiśāyi?), T. c. So Cowell; nigaccha, A; ma-ḥdon (mā muñca ?), T. ḍ. aśru ru(?cu?) tac ca, A.

34. a. priyena, A. d. sems ni dgaḥ-bar gyis (ramasva citte or cittyāṁ), T.

वरं मनुष्यस्य विचक्षणो रिपुर्न मित्रमप्राज्ञमयोगपेशलम् ।
सुहृद्ब्रुवेण ह्यविपश्चिता त्वया कृतः कुलस्यास्य महानुपप्लवः ॥३५॥

इमा हि शोच्या व्यवमुक्तभूषणाः
प्रसक्तबाष्पाविलरक्तलोचनाः ।
स्थितेऽपि पत्यौ हिमवन्महीसमे
प्रनष्टशोभा विधवा इव स्त्रियः ॥ ३६ ॥

इमाश्च विक्षिप्तविटङ्कबाहवः प्रसक्तपारावतदीर्घनिस्वनाः ।
विनाकृतास्तेन सहावरोधनैर्भृशं रुदन्तीव विमानपङ्क्तयः ॥ ३७ ॥

अनर्थकामोऽस्य जनस्य सर्वथा
तुरङ्गमोऽपि ध्रुवमेष कन्थकः ।
जहार सर्वस्वमितस्तथा हि मे
जने प्रसुप्ते निशि रत्नचौरवत् ॥ ३८ ॥

यदा समर्थः खलु सोढुमागता-
निषुप्रहारानपि किं पुनः कशाः ।
गतः कशापातभयात्कथं न्वयं
श्रियं गृहीत्वा हृदयं च मे समम् ॥ ३९ ॥

35. c. neś-par mdzaḥ-bśes (suhṛddhruveṇa), T ; °bruveṇa or °dhruveṇa, A ; ‘ professing to be loyal ’, C.

36. b. praśaktaṣpāvila° (one syllable short), A ; rab-chags dri-mas (for mchi-mas ?) ḥdres-śiṅ, T. c. himavatmahī°, A.

37. b. praśakta°, A. c. sahaiva rodhanair, A ; pho-braṅ-ḥkhor daṅ bcas, T. d. °paktayaḥ, A.

39. a. mgyogs-ḥgro ḥdis ni. . . nus śes-grags-na (=ayaṁ hayaḥ samarthaḥ kila), T. c. kaśāyāta°, A. e.c. Kern ; kathat katha tv ayaṁ (two syllables in excess, mark against first two), A ; yin-nam-ci (kathaṁ nu ?), T.

अनार्यकर्मा भृशमद्य हेषते
नरेन्द्रधिष्ण्यं प्रतिपूरयन्निव ।
यदा तु निर्वाहयति स्म मे प्रियं
तदा हि मूकस्तुरगाधमोऽभवत् ॥ ४० ॥

यदि ह्यहेषिष्यत बोधयन् जनं
खुरैः क्षितौ वाप्यकरिष्यत ध्वनिम् ।
हनुस्वनं वाजनिष्यदुत्तमं
न चाभविष्यन्मम दुःखमीदृशम् ॥ ४१ ॥

इतीह देव्याः परिदेविताश्रयं निशम्य बाष्पग्रथिताक्षरं वचः ।
अधोमुखः सास्रुकलः कृताञ्जलिः शनैरिदं छन्दक उत्तरं जगौ ॥४२॥

विगर्हितुं नार्हसि देवि कन्थकं
न चापि रोषं मयि कर्तुमर्हसि ।
अनागसौ स्वः समवेहि सर्वशो
गतो नृदेवः स हि देवि देववत् ॥ ४३ ॥

अहं हि जानन्नपि राजशासनं बलात्कृतः कैरपि दैवतैरिव ।
उपानयं तूर्णमिमं तुरङ्गमं तथान्वगच्छं विगतश्रमोऽध्वनि ॥ ४४ ॥

40. b. yoṅs-su-gaṅ-ba (paripūrayann), T. d. mgyogs-ḥgro lkug-la thaṅ-chad gyur (mūkas turagaśramo 'bhavat ?), T.

41. b. khitau, A.

42. a. So Co.; paridevatāśrayan, A. b. niśāmya, A; thos-gyur-nas, T. °grathikṣaram (one syllable short), A. c. T omits kalaḥ; 'gathering his tears', C.

43. a. nāsi devi (one syllable short), A; lha-mo . . . ḥos min zhiṅ, T. c. bkra-śis kun-gyis (sarvāśiṣā for sarvaśo ?), T.

44. c. upānaya, A.

व्रजन्नयं वाजिवरोऽपि नास्पृश-
न्महीं खुराग्रैर्विधृतैरिवान्तरा ।
तथैव दैवादिव संयताननो
हनुस्वनं नाकृत नाप्यहेषत ॥ ४५ ॥

यतो बहिर्गच्छति पार्थिवात्मजे
तदाभवद्द्वारमपावृतं स्वयम् ।
तमश्च नैशं रविणेव पाटितं
ततोऽपि दैवो विधिरेष गृह्यताम् ॥ ४६ ॥

यदप्रमत्तोऽपि नरेन्द्रशासना-
द्गृहे पुरे चैव सहस्रशो जनः ।
तदा स नाबुध्यत निद्रया हृत-
स्ततोऽपि दैवो विधिरेष गृह्यताम् ॥ ४७ ॥

यतश्च वासो वनवाससंमतं
निसृष्टमस्मै समये दिवौकसा ।
दिवि प्रविद्धं मुकुटं च तद्धृतं
ततोऽपि दैवो विधिरेष गृह्यताम् ॥ ४८ ॥

तदेवमावां नरदेवि दोषतो
न तत्प्रयातं प्रति गन्तुमर्हसि ।
न कामकारो मम नास्य वाजिनः
कृतानुयात्रः स हि दैवतैर्गतः ॥ ४९ ॥

46. a. yadā bahir gacchati pārthivātmajas, A ; gaṅ-las sa-skyoṅ bdag-ñid skyes-pa gśegs-pa-na, T.

47. Not in C. b. gṛhai purai, A.

48. Not in C.

49. b. tatprayātemm, A.

इति प्रयाणं बहुदेवमद्भुतं निशम्य तास्तस्य महात्मनः स्त्रियः ।
प्रनष्टशोका इव विस्मयं ययुर्मनोज्वरं प्रव्रजनात्तु लेभिरे ॥ ५० ॥

विषादपारिप्लवलोचना ततः
प्रनष्टपोता कुररीव दुःखिता ।
विहाय धैर्यं विरुराव गौतमी
तताम चैवाश्रुमुखी जगाद च ॥ ५१ ॥

महोर्मिमन्तो मृदवोऽसिताः शुभाः
पृथक्पृथङ्मूलरुहाः समुद्गताः ।
प्रवेरितास्ते भुवि तस्य मूर्धजा
नरेन्द्रमौलीपरिवेष्टनक्षमाः ॥ ५२ ॥

प्रलम्बबाहुर्मृगराजविक्रमो महर्षभाक्षः कनकोज्ज्वलद्युतिः ।
विशालवक्षा घनदुन्दुभिस्वनस्तथाविधोऽप्याश्रमवासमर्हति ॥ ५३ ॥

अभागिनी नूनमियं वसुंधरा
तमार्यकर्माणमनुत्तमं पतिम् ।
गतस्ततोऽसौ गुणवान् हि तादृशो
नृपः प्रजाभाग्यगुणैः प्रसूयते ॥ ५४ ॥

50. a. bahudhevam adbhutaṁ, A; lha-yi mtshar maṅ, T. d. pravrajanārt tu, A. yid-la ḥbar-ba (manojvalaṁ), T.

51. b. pranapta(corrected to ṣṭa ?)potā, A. c. gotamī, A.

52. b. pṛthak mūla°, A. d. °pariveṣṭyamakṣamaḥ, A.

53. b. mahaṣabhākṣaḥ, A. c. °dundubhisvanās, A.

54. Not in T. a. abhāge(? gi ?)nī, A. c. tātas tato, A; gatas tato, Co.'s MSS. gunavā hi, A.

सुजातजालावतताङ्गुली मृदू
निगूढगुल्फौ बिसपुष्पकोमलौ ।
वनान्तभूमिं कठिनां कथं नु तौ
सचक्रमध्यौ चरणौ गमिष्यतः ॥ ५५ ॥

विमानपृष्ठे शयनासनोचितं
महार्हवस्त्रागुरुचन्दनार्चितम् ।
कथं नु शीतोष्णजलागमेषु त-
च्छरीरमोजस्वि वने भविष्यति ॥ ५६ ॥

कुलेन सत्त्वेन बलेन वर्चसा श्रुतेन लक्ष्म्या वयसा च गर्वितः ।
प्रदातुमेवाभ्युचितो न याचितुं कथं स भिक्षां परतश्चरिष्यति ॥५७॥

शुचौ शयित्वा शयने हिरण्मये प्रबोध्यमानो निशि तूर्यनिस्वनैः ।
कथं बत स्वप्स्यति सोऽद्य मे व्रती पटैकदेशान्तरिते महीतले ॥५८॥

इमं प्रलापं करुणं निशम्य ता
भुजैः परिष्वज्य परस्परं स्त्रियः ।
विलोचनेभ्यः सलिलानि तत्यजु-
र्मधूनि पुष्पेभ्य इवेरिता लताः ॥ ५९ ॥

55. b. e.c.; viṣapuṣpa°, A; padmaḥi rtsa-ba ltar ḥjam (bisapadmakomalau), T. c. draṅ-sroṅ-rnams-kyi nags-mthaḥi sa-la (vanāntabhūmiṁ vaninām̐?), T.

56. b. candanāccitaṁ, A; tsan-dan spras-śiṅ, T. c. °oṣṇajālā°, A. d. skor (bhramiṣyati), T.

57. c. e.c. Böhtlingk; abhyudito, A; mṅon-ḥoṅs-pa (=abhyudito, but read ḥos, abhyucito ?), T; 'he ought to give, there is nothing for him to ask for', C.

58. b. °niśvanaiḥ, A.

ततो धरायामपतद्यशोधरा विचक्रवाकेव रथाङ्गसाह्वया ।
शनैश्च तत्तद्विललाप विक्लवा मुहुर्मुहुर्गद्गदरुद्धया गिरा ॥ ६० ॥

स मामनाथां सहधर्मचारिणी-
मपास्य धर्मं यदि कर्तुमिच्छति ।
कुतोऽस्य धर्मः सहधर्मचारिणीं
विना तपो यः परिभोक्तुमिच्छति ॥ ६१ ॥

शृणोति नूनं स न पूर्वपार्थिवा-
न्महासुदर्शप्रभृतीन् पितामहान् ।
वनानि पत्नीसहितानुपेयुष-
स्तथा हि धर्मं मदृते चिकीर्षति ॥ ६२ ॥

मखेषु वा वेदविधानसंस्कृतौ
न दंपती पश्यति दीक्षितावुभौ ।
समं बुभुक्षू परतोऽपि तत्फलं
ततोऽस्य जातो मयि धर्ममत्सरः ॥ ६३ ॥

ध्रुवं स जानन्मम धर्मवल्लभो मनः प्रियेर्ष्याकलहं मुहुर्मिथः ।
सुखं विभीर्मामपहाय रोषणां महेन्द्रलोकेऽप्सरसो जिघृक्षति॥६४॥

60. c. T omits śanaiḥ. d. T omits ruddhayā. gadgaya(corrected to da ?)ruddhayā girāḥ, A.

61. a. anāthā, A. d. viṇā, A.

62. a. A omits na, leaving gap; ma-thos, T. d. e.c.; A omits hi; de-ltar ltos (tathā nu ?), T; tathā sa, Co.; tataḥ sa, Gawroński.

63. b. sa dampatī, Lüders. c. e.c. Cowell; parito pi, A; gzhan-du (paratra, omitting api), T; ‘in the hereafter’, C.

64. b. priyeṣyākalaham mahur, A; sdug daṅ phan-tshun phrag-dog-ciṅ yaṅ-yaṅ rtsod-par, T; priye ’py ākalahaṁ muhur, Co.

इयं तु चिन्ता मम कीदृशं नु ता
वपुर्गुणं बिभ्रति तत्र योषितः ।
वने यदर्थं स तपांसि तप्यते
श्रियं च हित्वा मम भक्तिमेव च ॥ ६५ ॥

न खल्वियं स्वर्गसुखाय मे स्पृहा
न तज्जनस्यात्मवतोऽपि दुर्लभम् ।
स तु प्रियो मामिह वा परत्र वा
कथं न जह्यादिति मे मनोरथः ॥ ६६ ॥

अभागिनी यद्यहमायतेक्षणं
शुचिस्मितं भर्तुरुदीक्षितुं मुखम् ।
न मन्दभाग्योऽर्हति राहुलोऽप्ययं
कदाचिदङ्के परिवर्तितुं पितुः ॥ ६७ ॥

अहो नृशंसं सुकुमारवर्चसः सुदारुणं तस्य मनस्विनो मनः ।
कलप्रलापं द्विषतोऽपि हर्षणं शिशुं सुतं यस्त्यजतीदृशं बत ॥६८॥

ममापि कामं हृदयं सुदारुणं शिलामयं वाप्ययसोऽपि वा कृतम् ।
अनाथवच्छ्रीरहिते सुखोचिते वनं गते भर्तरि यन्न दीर्यते ॥६९॥

65. b. vapugguṇam, A. d. bud-med (striyaṁ for śriyaṁ), T.

66. b. durllabhaṁḥ, A ; rñed-par dkaḥ-ba-min (na . . . 'sti durlabham ?), T ; hi durlabham, Kern ; 'tidurlabham, Böhtlingk. d. jakṣād iti, A ; spoṅ zhes, T.

67. a. abhāgiṇī, A. c. mandabhāgyo ḥati, A.

68. a. nṛsaṁsaṁ śukumāra°, A. d. °īdrśaṁ vataḥ, A ; ḥdi-ḥdra kye-ma, T.

69. a. samāpi, A ; bdag-gi ḥdod-paḥi sems yaṅ (mamāpi kāmahṛdayaṁ), T. b. ayasā (rewritten ?)pi, A ; lcags-las, T.

इतीह देवी पतिशोकमूर्छिता
रुरोद दध्यौ विललाप चासकृत्।
स्वभावधीरापि हि सा सती शुचा
धृतिं न सस्मार चकार नो ह्रियम् ॥ ७० ॥

ततस्तथा शोकविलापविक्लवां यशोधरां प्रेक्ष्य वसुंधरागताम्।
महारविन्दैरिव वृष्टिताडितैर्मुखैः सबाष्पैर्वनिता विचुक्रुशुः ॥७१॥

समाप्तजाप्यः कृतहोममङ्गलो नृपस्तु देवायतनाद्विनिर्ययौ।
जनस्य तेनार्तरवेण चाहतश्चचाल वज्रध्वनिनेव वारणः ॥ ७२ ॥

निशाम्य च च्छन्दककन्थकावुभौ
सुतस्य संश्रुत्य च निश्चयं स्थिरम्।
पपात शोकाभिहतो महीपतिः
शचीपतेर्वृत्त इवोत्सवे ध्वजः ॥ ७३ ॥

ततो मुहूर्तं सुतशोकमोहितो
जनेन तुल्याभिजनेन धारितः।
निरीक्ष्य दृष्ट्या जलपूर्णया हयं
महीतलस्थो विललाप पार्थिवः ॥ ७४ ॥

बहूनि कृत्वा समरे प्रियाणि मे
महत्त्वया कन्थक विप्रियं कृतम्।
गुणप्रियो येन वने स मे प्रियः
प्रियोऽपि सन्नप्रियवत्प्रवेरितः ॥ ७५ ॥

70. c. sucā, A.
71. cd. °tāḍitau mukhais m(?)abāṣpair, A.
72. c. jaṇasya, A. cd. cāhataḥ cacāla, A.
73. d. śacīpate vṛtta, A.
74. a. muhūrtta, A.

तदद्य मां वा नय तत्र यत्र स
व्रज द्रुतं वा पुनरेनमानय ।
ऋते हि तस्मान्मम नास्ति जीवितं
विगाढरोगस्य सदौषधादिव ॥ ७६ ॥

सुवर्णनिष्ठीविनि मृत्युना हृते
सुदुष्करं यन्न ममार संजयः ।
अहं पुनर्धर्मरतौ सुते गते
मुमुक्षुरात्मानमनात्मवानिव ॥ ७७ ॥

विभोर्दशक्षत्रकृतः प्रजापतेः
परापरज्ञस्य विवस्वदात्मनः ।
प्रियेण पुत्रेण सता विनाकृतं
कथं न मुह्येद्धि मनो मनोरपि ॥ ७८ ॥

अजस्य राज्ञस्तनयाय धीमते
नराधिपायेन्द्रसखाय मे स्पृहा ।
गते वनं यस्तनये दिवं गतो
न मोघबाष्पः कृपणं जिजीव ह ॥ ७९ ॥

76. b. vrajan drutaṁ, Lüders. punar evam, A ; der (for de ?) ni slar-yaṅ, T ; 'do you take me quickly and go to him ; if not (=or), go and come back with him', C ; punar enaṁ, Böhtlingk. d. vigāḍharogamya sadoṣadhād, A.

77. a. kṛte, A ; phrogs-par gyur-pa-na, T. b. sṛṁjayaḥ, Co. cd. gate 'mumukṣur, Co. ; bdag-ñid thar-ḥdod, T ; 'killing myself, will cause my body not to be', C.

78. d. yid mi-bde byas yid-kyi rmoṅs-pa gaṅ-las min (kṛtaṁ kathaṁ na muhyed vimano mano, omitting manor api), T.

79. a. rājñas punayāya, A ; rgyal-po ajaḥi sras-po, T. d. kṛpanaṁ, A.

प्रचक्ष्व मे भद्र तदाश्रमाजिरं हृतस्त्वया यत्र स मे जलाञ्जलिः ।
इमे परीप्सन्ति हि तं पिपासवो ममासवः प्रेतगतिं यियासवः ॥८०॥

इति तनयवियोगजातदुःखः
क्षितिसदृशं सहजं विहाय धैर्यम् ।
दशरथ इव रामशोकवश्यो
बहु विललाप नृपो विसंज्ञकल्पः ॥ ८१ ॥

श्रुतविनयगुणान्वितस्ततस्तं
मतिसचिवः प्रवयाः पुरोहितश्च ।
समधृतमिदमूचतुर्यथाव-
न्न च परितप्तमुखौ न चाप्यशोकौ ॥ ८२ ॥

त्यज नरवर शोकमेहि धैर्यं
कुधृतिरिवार्हसि धीर नास्रु मोक्तुम् ।
स्रजमिव मृदितामपास्य लक्ष्मीं
भुवि बहवो नृपा वनान्यतीयुः ॥ ८३ ॥

अपि च नियत एष तस्य भावः
स्मर वचनं तदृषेः पुरासितस्य ।
न हि स दिवि न चक्रवर्तिराज्ये
क्षणमपि वासयितुं सुखेन शक्यः ॥ ८४ ॥

80. a. °ājira, A. c. parīpsanti hi ta, A; de-la . . . yoṅs-ḥdod-de, T. d. pretagati, A.

81. a. °duḥkhaṁ, A; sdug-bsṅal skyes-gyur-te, T. b. dhaiyaṁ, A. d. visajñakalpaḥ, A.

82. b. pravayā, A. c. First two syllables uncertain, A; mñam-par bzhag, T; ‘without either slowness or urgency’, C; avadhṛta°, Co.

83. a. A omits vara; mi-mchog, T. c. śrajam, A. lakṣmī, A.

यदि तु नृवर कार्य एव यत्नस्त्वरितमुदाहर यावदत्र यावः ।
बहुविधमिह युद्धमस्तु तावत्तव तनयस्य विधेश्च तस्य तस्य ॥ ८५ ॥

नरपतिरथ तौ शशास तस्माद्द्रुतमित एव युवामभिप्रयातम् ।
न हि मम हृदयं प्रयाति शान्तिं वनशकुनेरिव पुत्रलालसस्य ॥८६॥

परममिति नरेन्द्रशासनात्तौ
ययतुरमात्यपुरोहितौ वनं तत् ।
कृतमिति सवधूजनः सदारो
नृपतिरपि प्रचकार शेषकार्यम् ॥ ८७ ॥

इति बुद्धचरिते महाकाव्येऽन्तःपुरविलापो नामाष्टमः सर्गः ॥ ८ ॥

85. a. kārya eṣa, Speyer.

86. a. narapatir api, A ; de-nas . . . mi-bdag-gis, T. b. ṅes-par ḥdi-nas (dhruvam ita), T. c. prāyānti, A ; dgaḥ-bar rab-tu-soṅ (prayāti harṣaṁ ?), T.

87. c. savadhūjanasyadāro, A.

CANTO IX

ततस्तदा मन्त्रिपुरोहितौ तौ बाष्पप्रतोदाभिहतौ नृपेण ।
विद्धौ सदश्वाविव सर्वयत्नात्सौहार्दशीघ्रं ययतुर्वनं तत् ॥ १ ॥
तमाश्रमं जातपरिश्रमौ तावुपेत्य काले सदृशानुयात्रौ ।
राजर्द्धिमुत्सृज्य विनीतचेष्टावुपेयतुर्भार्गवधिष्ण्यमेव ॥ २ ॥
तौ न्यायतस्तं प्रतिपूज्य विप्रं तेनार्चितौ तावपि चानुरूपम् ।
कृतासनौ भार्गवमासनस्थं छित्त्वा कथामूचतुरात्मकृत्यम् ॥ ३ ॥
शुद्धौजसः शुद्धविशालकीर्तेरिक्ष्वाकुवंशप्रभवस्य राज्ञः ।
इमं जनं वेत्तु भवानधीतं श्रुतग्रहे मन्त्रपरिग्रहे च ॥ ४ ॥
तस्येन्द्रकल्पस्य जयन्तकल्पः पुत्रो जरामृत्युभयं तितीर्षुः ।
इहाभ्युपेतः किल तस्य हेतोरावामुपेतौ भगवानवैतु ॥ ५ ॥
तौ सोऽब्रवीदस्ति स दीर्घबाहुः प्राप्तः कुमारो न तु नावबुद्धः ।
धर्मोऽयमावर्तक इत्यवेत्य यातस्त्वराडाभिमुखो मुमुक्षुः ॥ ६ ॥

1. a. manti°, A. b. nṛpena, A.

3. a. tshul bzhin (nyāyavat), T. vipra, A.

4. c. e.c.; adhīraṁ, A; nag-por (for bdag-por ?), T; adhīnaṁ, Kern. d. śruṣru(? sru ?)grahe, A; śruta rab-tu-ḥdzin, T.

5. c. kali, A; grags, T.

6. d. arājābhimukho, A; mṅon-par gdoṅ-phyogs ma-yin . . . skyen-par gśegs (yātas tvarānabhimukho), T; 'he has gone to Arāḍa', C.

तस्मात्ततस्तावुपलभ्य तत्त्वं तं विप्रमामन्त्र्य तदैव सद्यः ।
खिन्नावखिन्नाविव राजभक्त्या प्रसन्नतुस्तेन यतः स यातः ॥ ७ ॥

यान्तौ ततस्तौ मृजया विहीनमपश्यतां तं वपुषोज्ज्वलन्तम् ।
उपोपविष्टं पथि वृक्षमूले सूर्यं घनाभोगमिव प्रविष्टम् ॥ ८ ॥

यानं विहायोपययौ ततस्तं पुरोहितो मन्त्रधरेण सार्धम् ।
यथा वनस्थं सहवामदेवो रामं दिदृक्षुर्मुनिरौर्वशेयः ॥ ९ ॥

तावर्चयामासतुरर्हतस्तं दिवीव शुक्राङ्गिरसौ महेन्द्रम् ।
प्रत्यर्चयामास स चार्हतस्तौ दिवीव शुक्राङ्गिरसौ महेन्द्रः ॥ १० ॥

कृताभ्यनुज्ञावभितस्ततस्तौ निषेदतुः शाक्यकुलध्वजस्य ।
विरेजतुस्तस्य च संनिकर्षे पुनर्वसू योगगताविवेन्दोः ॥ ११ ॥

तं वृक्षमूलस्थमभिज्वलन्तं पुरोहितो राजसुतं बभाषे ।
यथोपविष्टं दिवि पारिजाते बृहस्पतिः शक्रसुतं जयन्तम् ॥ १२ ॥

त्वच्छोकशल्ये हृदयावगाढे मोहं गतो भूमितले मुहूर्तम् ।
कुमार राजा नयनाम्बुवर्षो यत्त्वामवोचत्तदिदं निबोध ॥ १३ ॥

7. b. āmatryaṁ, A. c. iva rājabha (gap for missing letter), A ; rgyal-po-la gus-pas, T. d. yattaḥ sa yātaḥ, A.

8. b. vapuṣā jvalantaṁ, A ; sku-lus rab-tu-ḥbar-ba, T. c. e.c. Windisch ; nṛpopaviṣṭaṁ, A ; ñe-bar-zhugs-pa, T. d. sūrya, A.

9. a. °opaye(corrected to ya)yo, A. d. aurvaseyaḥ, A.

10. b. śukrāṁgirisau, A. d. dīvīva śukrāṁgirisau, A.

11. a. kṛtābhyanujñav abhita tatas, A. b. niṣīdatuḥ, A.

12. a. ta vṛkṣa°, A. b. rājasuta, A. c. pārajātau, A ; yoṅs-ḥdus-dag, la, T.

13. b. rmoṅs-śiṅ brgyal-bar gyur-pa-ste (mohaṁ gato . . . . mumūrcha ?)-T ; ‘ bewildered and distracted, he lay on the dirty ground ’, C.

जानामि धर्मं प्रति निश्चयं ते परैमि ते भाविनमेतमर्थम् ।
अहं त्वकाले वनसंश्रयात्ते शोकाग्निनाग्निप्रतिमेन दह्ये ॥ १४ ॥
तदेहि धर्मप्रिय मत्प्रियार्थं धर्मार्थमेव त्यज बुद्धिमेताम् ।
अयं हि मा शोकरयः प्रवृद्धो नदीरयः कूलमिवाभिहन्ति ॥ १५ ॥
मेघाम्बुकक्षाद्रिषु या हि वृत्तिः समीरणार्काग्निमहाशनीनाम् ।
तां वृत्तिमस्मासु करोति शोको विकर्षणोच्छोषणदाहभेदैः ॥१६॥
तद्भुङ्क्ष्व तावद्वसुधाधिपत्यं काले वनं यास्यसि शास्त्रदृष्टे ।
अनिष्टबन्धौ कुरु मय्यपेक्षां सर्वेषु भूतेषु दया हि धर्मः ॥ १७ ॥
न चैष धर्मो वन एव सिद्धः पुरेऽपि सिद्धिर्नियता यतीनाम् ।
बुद्धिश्च यत्नश्च निमित्तमत्र वनं च लिङ्गं च हि भीरुचिह्नम् ॥१८॥
मौलीधरैरंसविषक्तहारैः केयूरविष्टब्धभुजैर्नरेन्द्रैः ।
लक्ष्म्यङ्कमध्ये परिवर्तमानैः प्राप्तो गृहस्थैरपि मोक्षधर्मः ॥ १९ ॥
ध्रुवानुजौ यौ बलिवज्रबाहू वैभ्राजमाषाढमथान्तिदेवम् ।
विदेहराजं जनकं तथैव * * द्रुमं सेनजितश्च राज्ञः ॥ २० ॥

14. b. te vāvinam etam, A; khyod-kyi ḥbyun-baḥi ḥgyur-baḥi don, T (omitting etam).

16. abc. only partially legible in A from vṛttiḥ to karoti; Co.'s text agrees with T.

17. ab. °patya kāme, A; dus-su, T. c. aniṣṭabandho kuru mapy apye-(? pyā ?)kṣāṁ, A; mi-ḥdod gñen-ḥdun kho-bo-la ni ltos-par mdzod, T. d. Illegible in A; Co.'s text agrees with T.

18. d. liṅga, A.

19. a. aṁśaviśaktahāraiḥ, A. c. phun-tshogs yan-lag dbus-na (lakṣmyaṅgamadhye), T. d. thar-paḥi lam (mokṣamārgaḥ), T.

20. For C and FP see notes in translation. a. dhruvājau (one syllable short), A; brtan-paḥi nu-bo, T. vadr(?)abāhū, A; rdo-rjeḥi lag-pa, T. d. yāṅge(?gi?)druma, A; ḥgro daṅ ljon-śiṅ can (. . . drumaṁ), T.

एतान् गृहस्थान्नृपतीनवेहि नैःश्रेयसे धर्मविधौ विनीतान् ।
उभौऽपि तस्माद्युगपद्भजस्व वित्ताधिपत्यं च नृपश्रियं च ॥ २१ ॥
इच्छामि हि त्वामुपगुह्य गाढं कृताभिषेकं सलिलार्द्रमेव ।
धृतातपत्रं समुदीक्षमाणस्तेनैव हर्षेण वनं प्रवेष्टुम् ॥ २२ ॥
इत्यब्रवीद्भूमिपतिर्भवन्तं वाक्येन बाष्पग्रथिताक्षरेण ।
श्रुत्वा भवानर्हति तत्प्रियार्थं स्नेहेन तत्स्नेहमनुप्रयातुम् ॥ २३ ॥

शोकाम्भसि त्वत्प्रभवे ह्यगाधे
दुःखार्णवे मज्जति शाक्यराजः ।
तस्मात्तमुत्तारय नाथहीनं
निराश्रयं मग्नमिवार्णवे नौः ॥ २४ ॥

भीष्मेण गङ्गोदरसंभवेन रामेण रामेण च भार्गवेण ।
श्रुत्वा कृतं कर्म पितुः प्रियार्थं पितुस्त्वमप्यर्हसि कर्तुमिष्टम् ॥२५॥
संवर्धयित्रीं समवेहि देवीमगस्त्यजुष्टां दिशमप्रयाताम् ।
प्रनष्टवत्सामिव वत्सलां गामजस्रमार्तां करुणं रुदन्तीम् ॥ २६ ॥
हंसेन हंसीमिव विप्रयुक्तां त्यक्तां गजेनेव वने करेणुम् ।
आर्तां सनाथामपि नाथहीनां त्रातुं वधूमर्हसि दर्शनेन ॥ २७ ॥

21. a. gṛhasthā nṛ°, A. c. ubho pi tasmāt yugapat bhajasva, A. d. cittādhipatyaṁ, Co.

23. a. bhūmipati bhavantam, A.

24. a. tvaṁ(?)prabhavai(?), A. c. T separates nātha hīnaṁ; 'without a saviour, with nothing to rely on', C. d. ivārṇṇave gauh, A; gru bzhin-du, T; 'you should be the captain of the ship', C.

25. a. gaṅgodac(?r?)abh(?nd?)āmbhavena, A; chu-bo gaṅgāḥi lto-nas byuṅ-ba, T. c. pitu, A.

26. a. ca samehi, A; mkhyen-par mdzod, T. d. ārttāṁ ka (rest torn out), A; ñam-thag sñiṅ-rjer ṅu-ba-mo, T.

27. a. First two syllables torn out in A; ṅaṅ-pa, T. b. vaṇe (marked above to show error) karenuṁ(?)ḥ, A.

एकं सुतं बालमनर्हदुःखं संतापमन्तर्गतमुद्वहन्तम् ।
तं राहुलं मोक्षय बन्धुशोकाद्राहूपसर्गादिव पूर्णचन्द्रम् ॥ २८ ॥
शोकाग्निना त्वद्विरहेन्धनेन निःश्वासधूमेन तमःशिखेन ।
त्वद्दर्शनाम्बिच्छति दह्यमानमन्तःपुरं चैव पुरं च कृत्स्नम् ॥ २९ ॥
स बोधिसत्त्वः परिपूर्णसत्त्वः श्रुत्वा वचस्तस्य पुरोहितस्य ।
ध्यात्वा मुहूर्तं गुणवद्गुणज्ञः प्रत्युत्तरं प्रश्रितमित्युवाच ॥ ३० ॥
अवैमि भावं तनये पितॄणां
विशेषतो यो मयि भूमिपस्य ।
जानन्नपि व्याधिजराविपद्भ्यो
भीतस्त्वगत्या स्वजनं त्यजामि ॥ ३१ ॥
द्रष्टुं प्रियं कः स्वजनं हि नेच्छेन्नान्ते यदि स्यात्प्रियविप्रयोगः ।
यदा तु भूत्वापि चिरं वियोगस्ततो गुरुं स्निग्धमपि त्यजामि ॥३२॥
मद्धेतुकं यत्तु नराधिपस्य शोकं भवानाह न तत्प्रियं मे ।
यत्स्वप्नभूतेषु समागमेषु संतप्यते भाविनि विप्रयोगे ॥ ३३ ॥

28. bc. saṁtāpas(?m?)antaḥ (tear covering seven syllables) rāhulam, A; kun-nas gduṅ-ba mthar-gyur-pa ni ḥdren-pa-ste . . . sgra-gcan ḥdzin de (=text, but antagatam for antar°), T.

29. cd. tvaddarśśanā (tear covering one syllable)cchati dahyamā (tear covering three syllables) puraṁ, A; pho-braṅ-btsun-moḥi ḥkhor. . . tshig-pa dag ni khyed-la lta-baḥi chu ḥdod-do, T. d. kṛsnaṁ, A.

30. c. yon-tan-ldan-zhiṅ yon-tan śes-pas (guṇavāṅ guṇajñaḥ), T; ‘answered properly and modestly’, C.

31. a. tanayaṁ (tear covering three syllables), A; pha-rnams-kyi ni bu-la, T. b. mapi bhūmipaśya, A. c. °jarāvidbhyo (one syllable short), A; rga daṅ rgud-pa-las, T. d. ḥjigs-te nags-su phyin-nas (=bhīto vanaṁ gatvā), T.

32. b. nāsti yadi syāt, A; mthar ni gal-te . . . yin-na, T. c. bhutvāpa (?pi?, then tear covering three syllables) yogas, A; yuṅ-riṅ gyur kyaṅ rnam-par-ḥbral-ba-ste (bhūto 'pi ciraṁ viyogas ?), T. d. guru, A.

33. b. bhavān āha na priyaṁ (one syllable short), A; khyod-kyis smras des bdag-la dgaḥ-ba med, T.

एवं च ते निश्चयमेतु बुद्धिर्दृष्ट्वा विचित्रं जगतः प्रचारम् ।
संतापहेतुर्न सुतो न बन्धुरज्ञाननैमित्तिक एष तापः ॥ ३४ ॥
यथाध्वगानामिह संगतानां काले वियोगो नियतः प्रजानाम् ।
प्राज्ञो जनः को नु भजेत शोकं बन्धुप्रतिज्ञातजनैर्विहीनः ॥ ३५ ॥
इहैति हित्वा स्वजनं परत्र प्रलभ्य चेहापि पुनः प्रयाति ।
गत्वापि तत्राप्यपरत्र गच्छत्येवं जने त्यागिनि कोऽनुरोधः ॥ ३६ ॥
यदा च गर्भात्प्रभृति प्रवृत्तः सर्वास्ववस्थासु वधाय मृत्युः ।
कस्मादकाले वनसंश्रयं मे पुत्रप्रियस्तत्रभवानवोचत् ॥ ३७ ॥
भवत्यकालो विषयाभिपत्तौ कालस्तथैवार्थविधौ प्रदिष्टः ।
कालो जगत्कर्षति सर्वकालान्निर्वाहके श्रेयसि नास्ति कालः ॥३८॥
राज्यं मुमुक्षुर्मयि यच्च राजा तदप्युदारं सदृशं पितुश्च ।
प्रतिग्रहीतुं मम न क्षमं तु लोभादपथ्यान्नमिवातुरस्य ॥ ३९ ॥

34. b. vici(tear covering three syllables)taḥ pracāraṁ, A; ḥgro-baḥi spyod-pa rnam-pa-sna-tshogs, T. c. °hetu na suto na bundhur, A. d. ḥchiṅ-ba de... mtshan-ma-ñid (°naimittika eṣa bandhaḥ ?), T; 'that which produces the grief of separation', C; eva tāpaḥ, Gawroński.

35. a. yadādhvagānām iva, A; lam-du ḥgro-rnams hdir ni ... ji-lta-baḥi, T. c. bhajetya (t added later to original ya), A. d. bandhu (tear covering seven syllables) hīnaḥ, A; gñen-ḥdun dam-ḥchaḥ skye-bos rnam-par-dman-pa-yi, T.

36. cd. gatvāpi tarāpy aparatra gacchety evaṁ jano yogini, A; der soṅ-nas kyaṅ pha-rol gzhan-du ḥgro-ḥgyur-la de-ltar ḥdor-ldan skye-la (=text, omitting one api), T.

37. ab. °prabhṛti pra (tear covering seven syllables) su vadhāya, A; gnas-skabs thams-cad-du ... rab-tu-gnas-pa-ste, T. c. akālaṁ, Cappeller; T ambiguous.

38. b. A omits la; de-bzhin nor-gyi cho-gar zhugs dus yin-no (kālas tathāsty arthavidhau praviṣṭaḥ ?), T. d. arcc(?vv?)āhake śreyasi sarvva-kālaḥ; A; dge-legs ṅes-par-thob-pa dus yod-ma-yin-no, T; 'in the *dharma* that takes away death there is no time', C.

39. a. yac ca rāgha, A; gaṅ yaṅ rgyal-po, T.

कथं नु मोहायतनं नृपत्वं क्षमं प्रपत्तुं विदुषा नरेण।
सोद्वेगता यत्र मदः श्रमश्च परापचारेण च धर्मपीडा ॥ ४० ॥

जाम्बूनदं हर्म्यमिव प्रदीप्तं विषेण संयुक्तमिवोत्तमान्नम्।
ग्राहाकुलं चाम्बिव सारविन्दं राज्यं हि रम्यं व्यसनाश्रयं च ॥४१॥

इत्थं च राज्यं न सुखं न धर्मः पूर्वे यथा जातघृणा नरेन्द्राः।
वयःप्रकर्षेऽपरिहार्यदुःखे राज्यानि मुक्त्वा वनमेव जग्मुः ॥ ४२ ॥

वरं हि भुक्तानि तृणान्यरण्ये तोषं परं रत्नमिवोपगुह्य।
सहोषितं श्रीसुलभैर्न चैव दोषैरदृश्यैरिव कृष्णसर्पैः ॥ ४३ ॥

श्लाघ्यं हि राज्यानि विहाय राज्ञां धर्माभिलाषेण वनं प्रवेष्टुम्।
भग्नप्रतिज्ञस्य न तूपपन्नं वनं परित्यज्य गृहं प्रवेष्टुम् ॥ ४४ ॥

जातः कुले को हि नरः ससत्त्वो धर्माभिलाषेण वनं प्रविष्टः।
काषायमुत्सृज्य विमुक्तलज्जः पुरन्दरस्यापि पुरं श्रयेत ॥ ४५ ॥

लोभाद्धि मोहादथवा भयेन यो वान्तमन्नं पुनराददीत।
लोभात्स मोहादथवा भयेन संत्यज्य कामान् पुनराददीत ॥४६॥

40. a. nṛpe(?a?)tvaṁ, A.

41. ab. pradīpta viṣe saṁyuktam (one syllable short), A. c. ca sthiv(?r?)a s(?m?)ārabindaṁ, A; padma-daṅ-bcas chu lta-bu, T. d. rgyal-srid daṅ ni gser-dag (rājyaṁ hiraṇyam ?), T; rammyaṁ, A; 'kingship is very pleasant', FP.

42. a. dharmma, A. b. tathā, A; ji-ltar, T. c. A reads avagraha and T omits it. d. rgyal-srid ṅes-par-dor-nas (rājyaṁ nimuktvā !), T.

43. b. toṣaṁ ka(corrected to va, dha or ga)rau ratnam, A; rin-chen bzhin-du tshim-pa mchog, T.

44. a. rāṣṭ(corrected to jñ)āṁ, A. b. vaṇaṁ, A. cd. e.c. Gawroński; nanūyapannaṁ vana, A; ḥthad-pa ma-yin-no (nāsty upapannam ?), T.

45. b. vaṇaṁ, A.

46. a. sred daṅ rnam-par-rmoṅs (lobhād vimohād), T. d. satyajya, A.

यश्च प्रदीप्ताच्छरणात्कथंचिन्निष्क्रम्य भूयः प्रविशेत्तदेव ।
गार्हस्थ्यमुत्सृज्य स दृष्टदोषो मोहेन भूयोऽभिलषेद्ग्रहीतुम् ॥ ४७ ॥
या च श्रुतिर्मोक्षमवाप्तवन्तो नृपा गृहस्था इति नैतदस्ति ।
शमप्रधानः क्व च मोक्षधर्मो दण्डप्रधानः क्व च राजधर्मः ॥ ४८ ॥

शमे रतिश्चेच्छिथिलं च राज्यं
राज्ये मतिश्चेच्छमविप्लवश्च ।
शमश्च तैक्ष्ण्यं च हि नोपपन्नं
शीतोष्णयोरैक्यमिवोदकाग्न्योः ॥ ४९ ॥

तन्निश्चयाद्वा वसुधाधिपास्ते राज्यानि मुक्त्वा शममाप्तवन्तः ।
राज्याङ्गिता वा निभृतेन्द्रियत्वादनैष्ठिके मोक्षकृताभिमानाः ॥५०॥
तेषां च राज्येऽस्तु शमो यथावत्प्राप्तो वनं नाहमनिश्चयेन ।
छित्त्वा हि पाशं गृहबन्धुसंज्ञं मुक्तः पुनर्न प्रविविक्षुरस्मि ॥ ५१ ॥
इत्यात्मविज्ञानगुणानुरूपं मुक्तस्पृहं हेतुमदूर्जितं च ।
श्रुत्वा नरेन्द्रात्मजमुक्तवन्तं प्रत्युत्तरं मन्त्रधरोऽप्युवाच ॥ ५२ ॥

47. c. gārhastham, A. A adds after this verse, T after verse 49, the following spurious verse, which is not in C :—

Vahneś ca toyasya ca nāsti saṁdhiḥ
śaṭhasya satyasya ca nāsti saṁdhiḥ |
Āryasya pāpasya ca nāsti saṁdhiḥ
śamasya daṇḍasya ca nāsti saṁdhiḥ ||

A reads śāmasya in d.

49. b. chamaviśiplavaś ca (mark against śi to cut it out), A. c. samaś ca, A.

50. b. samav āptavantaḥ, A ; zhi-ba thob-pa-can, T. c. e.c. ; rājyādmitā, A ; rgyal-srid-dag-la sñen-nas (=rajyāny āśritya, or rājyāśrayād), T. d. °kṛtābhidhānāḥ, A ; mṅon-paḥi ṅa-rgyal byas (so Peking edition), T.

51. b. vana moham (corrected in same hand to vanan nāham), A ; bdag ni nags-tshal (=text omitting na), T. c. °saṁjña, A.

52. c. uktavantas, A.

योे निश्चयो धर्मविधौ तवायं
नायं न युक्तो न तु कालयुक्तः ।
शोकाय दत्त्वा पितरं वयःस्थं
स्याद्धर्मकामस्य हि ते न धर्मः ॥ ५३ ॥

नूनं च बुद्धिस्तव नातिसूक्ष्मा धर्मार्थकामेष्वविचक्षणा वा ।
हेतोरदृष्टस्य फलस्य यस्त्वं प्रत्यक्षमर्थं परिभूय यासि ॥ ५४ ॥

पुनर्भवोऽस्तीति च केचिदाहुर्नास्तीति केचिन्नियतप्रतिज्ञाः ।
एवं यदा संशयितोऽयमर्थस्तस्मात्क्षमं भोक्तुमुपस्थिता श्रीः ॥ ५५ ॥

भूयः प्रवृत्तिर्यदि काचिदस्ति रंस्यामहे तत्र यथोपपत्तौ ।
अथ प्रवृत्तिः परतो न काचित्सिद्धोऽप्रयत्नाज्जगतोऽस्य मोक्षः ॥५६॥

अस्तीति केचित्परलोकमाहुर्मोक्षस्य योगं न तु वर्णयन्ति ।
अग्नेर्यथा ह्यौष्ण्यमपां द्रवत्वं तद्वत्प्रवृत्तौ प्रकृतिं वदन्ति ॥ ५७ ॥

केचित्स्वभावादिति वर्णयन्ति शुभाशुभं चैव भवाभवौ च ।
स्वाभाविकं सर्वमिदं च यस्मादतोऽपि मोघो भवति प्रयत्नः ॥ ५८ ॥

यदिन्द्रियाणां नियतः प्रचारः प्रियाप्रियत्वं विषयेषु चैव ।
संयुज्यते यज्जरयार्तिभिश्च कस्तत्र यत्नो ननु स स्वभावः ॥ ५९ ॥

53. a. mantradharo tavāyaṁ, A; chos-kyi cho-gar (so Peking edition cho-gas Weller) . . . khyod-kyi ḥdi, T. b. T omits na tu (but read min for yin ?).

54. a. buddhiḥ tava nātiśūkṣmā, A. cd. yas tva pratyakṣam artha, A,

55. a. kecid āhuḥ, A. b. °pratijñaḥ, A. c. śaṁsayito, A.

56. b. rasyāmahe, A. yathopapatti, Böhtlingk.

57. c. hy oṣṇām apā, A. d. prakṛttim vadanti, A; pravṛttiṁ prakṛter, Gawroński.

अग्निर्हुताशः शममभ्युपैति तेजांसि चापो गमयन्ति शोषम् ।
भिन्नानि भूतानि शरीरसंस्थान्यैक्यं च गत्वा जगदुद्वहन्ति ॥६०॥
यत्पाणिपादोदरपृष्ठमूर्ध्नां निर्वर्तते गर्भगतस्य भावः ।
यदात्मनस्तस्य च तेन योगः स्वाभाविकं तत्कथयन्ति तज्ज्ञाः ॥६१॥
कः कण्टकस्य प्रकरोति तैक्ष्ण्यं विचित्रभावं मृगपक्षिणां वा ।
स्वभावतः सर्वमिदं प्रवृत्तं न कामकारोऽस्ति कुतः प्रयत्नः ॥ ६२ ॥
सर्गं वदन्तीश्वरतस्तथान्ये तत्र प्रयत्ने पुरुषस्य कोऽर्थः ।
य एव हेतुर्जगतः प्रवृत्तौ हेतुर्निवृत्तौ नियतः स एव ॥ ६३ ॥
केचिद्वदन्त्यात्मनिमित्तमेव प्रादुर्भवं चैव भवक्षयं च ।
प्रादुर्भवं तु प्रवदन्त्ययत्नाद्यत्नेन मोक्षाधिगमं ब्रुवन्ति ॥ ६४ ॥

नरः पितॄणामनृणः प्रजाभि-
र्वेदैर्ऋषीणां क्रतुभिः सुराणाम् ।
उत्पद्यते सार्धमृणैस्त्रिभिस्तै-
र्यस्यास्ति मोक्षः किल तस्य मोक्षः ॥ ६५ ॥

60. b. tejāśi, A. e.c. Cowell ; śamayanti, A ; skems-par byed-pa-ste (=śoṣayanti), T ; ‘fire makes water dry up’, C. c. śarīrasasthāny, A. d. e.c. Gawroński ; aikyañ ca datvā, A ; gcig-ñid gyur-nas (=aikyaṁ bhūtvā), T ; ‘by their natures uniting, they make all creatures’, C.

61. a. °mūrddhnā, A and Co. ; mgo-rnams-kyi (=°mūrdhnāṁ, Weller amends to kyis=°mūrdhnā), T.

62. c. pravṛtta, A.

63. b. rab-tu-ḥjug-pa-la (pravṛttau), T ; ‘what room is there then for effort ?’, C.

64. b. ceva, A.

65. a. prajābhiḥ, A. b. surāṇā, A. d. yaktāsyāsti (ktā cut out by mark), A.

इत्येवमेतेन विधिक्रमेण मोक्षं सयत्नस्य वदन्ति तज्ज्ञाः ।
प्रयत्नवन्तोऽपि हि विक्रमेण मुमुक्षवः खेदमवाप्नुवन्ति ॥ ६६ ॥

तत्सौम्य मोक्षे यदि भक्तिरस्ति न्यायेन सेवस्व विधिं यथोक्तम् ।
एवं भविष्यत्युपपत्तिरस्य संतापनाशश्च नराधिपस्य ॥ ६७ ॥

या च प्रवृत्ता तव दोषबुद्धि-
स्तपोवनेभ्यो भवनं प्रवेष्टुम् ।
तत्रापि चिन्ता तव तात मा भूत्
पूर्वेऽपि जग्मुः स्वगृहान्वनेभ्यः ॥ ६८ ॥

तपोवनस्थोऽपि वृतः प्रजाभिर्जगाम राजा पुरमम्बरीषः ।
तथा महीं विप्रकृतामनार्यैस्तपोवनादेत्य ररक्ष रामः ॥ ६९ ॥

तथैव शाल्वाधिपतिर्द्रुमाख्यो वनात्ससूनुर्नगरं विवेश ।
ब्रह्मर्षिभूतश्च मुनेर्वसिष्ठाद्दध्रे श्रियं सांकृतिरन्तिदेवः ॥ ७० ॥

एवंविधा धर्मयशःप्रदीप्ता वनानि हित्वा भवनान्यतीयुः ।
तस्मान्न दोषोऽस्ति गृहं प्रयातुं तपोवनाद्धर्मनिमित्तमेव ॥ ७१ ॥

66. c. prayatnavanto 'nyavidhikramena, Speyer.

67. d. saṁtāpanāsaś, A.

68. a. bhava doṣa°, A; khyod-kyi skyon-gyi, T. d. svagṛhān (rubbed and barely legible) vanebhyaḥ, A; raṅ-gi khaṅ-par (svagṛhaṁ ?), T.

69. b. zhugs-gyur-la (viveśa), T. c. mahī, A.

70. a. sālvādhipati drumākṣe, A; ḍo-ba daṅ bcas bdag-poḥi ljon-śiṅ miṅ, T; 'the king of the Śālva country called Druma', C. b. sasunur gg(?)ag(?)ara viveśa (much rubbed), A; bu daṅ bcas-pa groṅ-du zhugs-pa-ste, T. d. sbyin-sreg daṅ bcas mthaḥ-can lha-yis (sāhutir antidevaḥ), T.

71. a. chos daṅ grags-par rab-zhugs-pa (dharmayaśaḥpraviṣṭā, or °pravṛttā), T; °pradīpā, Gawroński. b. bhavanāny an(?t?)tīyuḥ, A; khaṅ-khyim-rnams-su soṅ-ba-ste, T.

ततो वचस्तस्य निशम्य मन्त्रिणः
प्रियं हितं चैव नृपस्य चक्षुषः ।
अनूनमव्यस्तमसक्तमद्रुतं
धृतौ स्थितो राजसुतोऽब्रवीद्वचः ॥ ७२ ॥

इहास्ति नास्तीति य एष संशयः
परस्य वाक्यैर्न ममात्र निश्चयः ।
अवेत्य तत्त्वं तपसा शमेन च
स्वयं ग्रहीष्यामि यदत्र निश्चितम् ॥ ७३ ॥

न मे क्षमं संशयजं हि दर्शनं ग्रहीतुमव्यक्तपरस्पराहतम् ।
बुधः परप्रत्ययतो हि को व्रजेज्जनोऽन्धकारेऽन्ध इवान्धदेशिकः॥७४॥

अदृष्टतत्त्वस्य सतोऽपि किं तु मे
शुभाशुभे संशयिते शुभे मतिः ।
वृथापि खेदो हि वरं शुभात्मनः
सुखं न तत्त्वेऽपि विगर्हितात्मनः ॥ ७५ ॥

72. b. byas-paḥi (cakruṣaḥ for cakṣuṣaḥ), T. c. abhūnam, A; dman-min, T. aśaktam, A; chags-min, T. d. brtan daṅ gnas-pa-la (dhṛtaṁ sthitaṁ ?), T; 'words that were . . . resolute and peaceful' (dhṛtaṁ sthiraṁ ?), C.

73. c. śamena vā, A; daṅ ni zhi-bas, T.

74. a. kṣamaṁ saśataṁ hi (one syllable short), A; the-tshom skye-ba-yi lta-ba . . . nus, T. b. °paramparā°, A; phan-tshun gnod-cin mi-gsal, T; 'handed down over and over again (or, interchangeably)', C. c. buddhaḥ, A; mkhas-paḥi, T. parapratyayate, A.

75. b. sanśayite śu(gap for one character) matiḥ, A; the-tshom-na dge blo-gros gyur, T. c. e.c. Lüders; vṛthāpi khedo pi, A; ḥbras-bu-med byid(?, Weller reads byir and amends to byiṅ, Peking edition has phyir)-la yaṅ (=vṛthā khede'pi ?), T; 'it is better to follow the *dharma* of *śubha* by *tapas* than to take pleasure in the practice of *aśubha*', C.

इमं तु दृष्टागममव्यवस्थितं यदुक्तमाप्तैस्तदवेहि साध्विति ।
प्रहीणदोषत्वमवेहि चाप्ततां प्रहीणदोषो ह्यनृतं न वक्ष्यति ॥७६॥

गृहप्रवेशं प्रति यच्च मे भवानुवाच रामप्रभृतीन्निदर्शनम् ।
न ते प्रमाणं न हि धर्मनिश्चयेष्वलं प्रमाणाय परिक्षतव्रताः ॥७७॥

तदेवमप्येव रविर्महीं पते-
दपि स्थिरत्वं हिमवान् गिरिस्त्यजेत् ।
अदृष्टतत्त्वो विषयोन्मुखेन्द्रियः
श्रयेय न त्वेव गृहान् पृथग्जनः ॥ ७८ ॥

अहं विशेयं ज्वलितं हुताशनं
न चाकृतार्थः प्रविशेयमालयम् ।
इति प्रतिज्ञां स चकार गर्वितो
यथेष्टमुत्थाय च निर्ममो ययौ ॥ ७९ ॥

ततः सबाष्पौ सचिवद्विजावुभौ निशम्य तस्य स्थिरमेव निश्चयम् ।
विषण्णवक्त्रावनुगम्य दुःखितौ शनैरगत्या पुरमेव जग्मतुः ॥ ८० ॥

तत्स्नेहादथ नृपतेश्च भक्तितस्तौ
सापेक्षं प्रतिययतुश्च तस्थतुश्च ।
दुर्धर्षं रविमिव दीप्तमात्मभासा
तं द्रष्टुं न हि पथि शेकतुर्न मोक्तुम् ॥ ८१ ॥

76. b. avaihi, A. d. vakṣati, A.
77. c. pramāṇa, A. b. dper bstan-te (nidarśayan ?), T.
78. c. viṣayomukhe°, A ; yul-la kha-bltas dbaṅ-po, T.
79. cd. garvvitā yathaiṣṭam, A.
80. d. dal-bus soṅ-nas (=śanair gatvā, for śanair āgatya ?), T.
81. c. durddhaṣaṁ, A ; blta-bar dkaḥ-ba (durdarśam), T. d. draṣṭu, A. pathi śekar na (one syllable short), A.

तौ ज्ञातुं परमगतेर्गतिं तु तस्य
प्रच्छन्नांश्चरपुरुषाञ्छुचीन्विधाय ।
राजानं प्रियसुतलालसं नु गत्वा
द्रक्ष्यावः कथमिति जग्मतुः कथंचित् ॥ ८२ ॥

इति बुद्धचरिते महाकाव्ये कुमारान्वेषणो नाम नवमः सर्गः ॥ ९ ॥

CANTO X

स राजवत्सः पृथुपीनवक्षास्तौ हव्यमन्त्राधिकृतौ विहाय ।
उत्तीर्य गङ्गां प्रचलत्तरङ्गां श्रीमद्गृहं राजगृहं जगाम ॥ १ ॥
शैलैः सुगुप्तं च विभूषितं च धृतं च पूतं च शिवैस्तपोदैः ।
पञ्चाचलाङ्कं नगरं प्रपेदे शान्तः स्वयंभूरिव नाकपृष्ठम् ॥ २ ॥
गाम्भीर्यमोजश्च निशाम्य तस्य वपुश्च दीप्तं पुरुषानतीत्य ।
विसिस्मिये तत्र जनस्तदानीं स्थाणुव्रतस्येव वृषध्वजस्य ॥ ३ ॥
तं प्रेक्ष्य योऽन्येन ययौ स तस्थौ
यस्तत्र तस्थौ पथि सोऽन्वगच्छत् ।
द्रुतं ययौ यः स जगाम धीरं
यः कश्चिदास्ते स्म स चोत्पपात ॥ ४ ॥
कश्चित्तमानर्च जनः कराभ्यां सत्कृत्य कश्चिच्छिरसा ववन्दे ।
स्निग्धेन कश्चिद्वचसाभ्यनन्दन्नैवं जगामाप्रतिपूज्य कश्चित् ॥ ५ ॥

1. a. °vakṣyās, A. d. dpal daṅ ldan-paḥi rgyal-poḥi khyab-tu (=śrīmad rājagṛhaṁ, read dpal-ldan khaṅ-paḥi ?), T.

2. b. pūtaṁ va śivais, A. d. zhi-bar raṅ-byuṅ tshaṅs-pa (śāntaṁ svayaṁbhūr ?), T.

3. c. viśismiye, A. d. sthānuvratasyaiva, A ; de-yi brtul-zhugs brtan-pa bzhin (sthāṇuvrato 'syeva ?), T ; Co. as in text.

4. a. yo nyena yayo, A ; gzhan gaṅ ma soṅ (yo 'nyo na yayau), T. b. yaś cātra tasthau pathi yo nvagacchat, A ; der ni gaṅ-zhig lam-na gnas de rjes-ḥgro-zhiṅ, T.

5. a. kaści tam, A. d. naivaṁ, A ; kha-cig de-la rab-tu-mchod-nas soṅ-bar-gyur (=enaṁ jagāma pratipūjya kaścit), T. kaści, A.

तं जिह्रियुः प्रेक्ष्य विचित्रवेषाः प्रकीर्णवाचः पथि मौनमीयुः ।
धर्मस्य साक्षादिव संनिकर्षे न कश्चिदन्यायमतिर्बभूव ॥ ६ ॥
अन्यक्रियाणामपि राजमार्गे स्त्रीणां नृणां वा बहुमानपूर्वम् ।
तं देवकल्पं नरदेवसूनुं निरीक्षमाणा न ततर्प दृष्टिः ॥ ७ ॥
भ्रुवौ ललाटं मुखमीक्षणे वा वपुः करौ वा चरणौ गतिं वा ।
यदेव यस्तस्य ददर्श तत्र तदेव तस्याथ बबन्ध चक्षुः ॥ ८ ॥
दृष्ट्वा च सोर्णभ्रुवमायताक्षं ज्वलच्छरीरं शुभजालहस्तम् ।
तं भिक्षुवेषं क्षितिपालनार्हं संचुक्षुभे राजगृहस्य लक्ष्मीः ॥ ९ ॥
श्रेण्योऽथ भर्ता मगधाजिरस्य बाह्याद्विमानाद्विपुलं जनौघम् ।
ददर्श पप्रच्छ च तस्य हेतुं ततस्तमस्मै पुरुषः शशंस ॥ १० ॥
ज्ञानं परं वा पृथिवीश्रियं वा विप्रैर्य उक्तोऽधिगमिष्यतीति ।
स एष शाक्याधिपतेस्तनूजो निरीक्ष्यते प्रव्रजितो जनेन ॥ ११ ॥

6. a. °veśāḥ, A. b. maum īyuḥ (one syllable short), A ; smra-ba med-par soṅ, T. d. nna kaścid, A.

7. a. °kriyānām, A. c. e.c. Kielhorn and Kern ; ta devakalpaṁ naradevasūtraṁ, A ; lha daṅ mtshuṅs-paḥi mi-dbaṅ sras-po (=taṁ devakalpaṁ narendrasūnuṁ), T. d. na tarppa(?rmpa, ?rmya) dṛṣṭiḥ (one syllable short), A ; mthoṅ-nas . . . mig daṅ (? read dag ?) ṅom-par ma-gyur-to (=nirīkṣya na tatarpa dṛṣṭiḥ), T.

8. a. bhruvo, A. d. T omits atha.

9. a. e.c. ; dṛṣṭā svarṇṇabhruvam (one syllable short), A ; smin-ma mdzod-spu daṅ bcas mthoṅ-nas (=dṛṣṭvā sorṇabhruvam), T. b. śubhajala°, A. c. °veśaṁ, A. cd. °pālanārha saṁcakṣubhe, A.

10. d. sasaṁsa, A ; skyes-bu-rnams-kyis de smras-so (puruṣāḥ śaśaṁsuḥ), T.

11. b. vipre ya, A ; bram-ze-rnams-kyis gaṅ, T. c. sa eva śākṣyādhipates, A ; de ni ḥdi yin-no, T. d. nirāhyate (??, much rubbed), A ; ṅes-par-mthoṅ-ba-yi, T.

ततः श्रुतार्थो मनसागतास्थो राजा बभाषे पुरुषं तमेव ।
विज्ञायतां क्व प्रतिगच्छतीति तथेत्यथैनं पुरुषोऽन्वगच्छत् ॥ १२ ॥
अलोलचक्षुर्युगमात्रदर्शी निवृत्तवाग्यन्त्रितमन्दगामी ।
चचार भिक्षां स तु भिक्षुवर्यो निधाय गात्राणि चलं च चेतः ॥ १३ ॥
आदाय भैक्षं च यथोपपन्न ययौ गिरेः प्रस्रवणं विविक्तम् ।
न्यायेन तत्राभ्यवहृत्य चैनन्महीधरं पाण्डवमारुरोह ॥ १४ ॥
तस्मिन्नवौ लोध्रवनोपगूढे मयूरनादप्रतिपूर्णकुञ्जे ।
काषायवासाः स बभौ नृसूर्यो यथोदयस्योपरि बालसूर्यः ॥ १५ ॥
तत्रैनमालोक्य स राजभृत्यः श्रेण्याय राज्ञे कथयांचकार ।
संश्रुत्य राजा स च बाहुमान्यात्तत्र प्रतस्थे निभृतानुयात्रः ॥ १६ ॥
स पाण्डवं पाण्डवतुल्यवीर्यः शैलोत्तमं शैलसमानवर्ष्मा ।
मौलीधरः सिंहगतिर्नृसिंहश्चलत्सटः सिंह इवारुरोह ॥ १७ ॥
ततः स्म तस्योपरि शृङ्गभूतं शान्तेन्द्रियं पश्यति बोधिसत्त्वम् ।
पर्यङ्कमास्थाय विरोचमानं शशाङ्कमुद्यन्तमिवाभ्रकुञ्जात् ॥ १८ ॥

12. a. °gatārtho, A; yid-kyis chags-śiṅ zhen-gyur-paḥi, T. c. de ni gaṅ-du soṅ zhes (=sa kva gacchatīti), T. d. nvagacchan, A.

13. d. ṅes-bsdams-nas (nibadhya ?), T; nivārya, Windisch.

14. b. praśravaṇaṁ, A. cd. cainaṁ mahīdharaṁ, A.

15. a. tasmin vanau lodhravanopaga(?ṛ?)dhe, A; rodhraḥi nags-kyis ñe-bar-sbas-paḥi ri-bo der, T; 'on this mountain with its forest of luxuriant trees', FP.

16. a. tatraivam, A; der ni de ñid . . . mthoṅ-gyur-nas, T. b. śraiṇyāya, A.

17. a. °vīrya, A.

18. a. e.c.; tana sma tasyopari, A; de-nas de-yi steṅ-na (tatas tasyopari), T. c. virocamāna, A. d. śaśām udyantam (one syllable short), A; ri-boṅ-gi mtuhan . . . byuṅ-ba, T.

तं रूपलक्ष्म्या च शमेन चैव धर्मस्य निर्माणमिवोपविष्टम् ।
सविस्मयः प्रश्रयवान्नरेन्द्रः स्वयंभुवं शक्र इवोपतस्थे ॥ १९ ॥
तं न्यायतो न्यायविदां वरिष्ठं समेत्य पप्रच्छ च धातुसाम्यम् ।
स चाप्यवोचत्सदृशेन साम्ना नृपं मनःस्वास्थ्यमनामयं च ॥ २० ॥
ततः शुचौ वारणकर्णनीले शिलातले संनिषसाद राजा ।
उपोपविश्यानुमतश्च तस्य भावं विजिज्ञासुरिदं बभाषे ॥ २१ ॥
प्रीतिः परा मे भवतः कुलेन क्रमागता चैव परीक्षिता च ।
जाता विवक्षा स्ववयो यतो मे तस्मादिदं स्नेहवचो निबोध ॥ २२ ॥
आदित्यपूर्वं विपुलं कुलं ते नवं वयो दीप्तमिदं वपुश्च ।
कस्मादियं ते मतिरक्रमेण भैक्षाक एवाभिरता न राज्ये ॥ २३ ॥
गात्रं हि ते लोहितचन्दनार्हं काषायसंश्लेषमनर्हमेतत् ।
हस्तः प्रजापालनयोग्य एष भोक्तुं न चार्हः परदत्तमन्नम् ॥ २४ ॥

तत्सौम्य राज्यं यदि पैतृकं त्वं
स्नेहात्पितुर्नेच्छसि विक्रमेण ।
न च क्रमं मर्षयितुं मतिस्ते
भुङ्क्ष्वार्धमस्मद्विषयस्य शीघ्रम् ॥ २५ ॥

19. b. nirmānam ivopadiṣtaṁ, A ; sprul-ba bzhin-du ñe-bar-bzhugs, T.

20. b. dhātuśāmyaṁ, A ; khams mñam gyur-pa, T.

21. b. śilātale' (gap for missing syllable) niṣasāda, A ; rdo-baḥi log-la . . . yaṅ-dag-ṅes-gnas-śiṅ, T. c. nṛpopaviśyā°, A ; ñe-sar ñe-bar-bsdad-nas, T.

22. c. yātā vivakṣā sutayā yato me, A ; gaṅ-phyir bdag-la raṅ-gi na-tshod smra-ḥdod-pa skyes-te, T.

23. b. vanam vayo, A ; na-tshod gsar-pa, T. d. bhaikṣyāka, A.

24. ab. °arhaṁṅ kāṣāya°, A.

25. c. kṣamaṁ, A ; rim-par, T. d. bhuktvārddham, A ; phyed-la loṅs-spyod mdzod, T.

एवं हि न स्यात्स्वजनावमर्दः
कालक्रमेणापि शमश्रया श्रीः ।
तस्मात्कुरुष्व प्रणयं मयि त्वं
सद्भिः सहीया हि सतां समृद्धिः ॥ २६ ॥

अथ त्विदानीं कुलगर्वितत्वा-
दस्मासु विस्रम्भगुणो न तेऽस्ति ।
व्यूढान्यनीकानि विगाह्य बाणै-
र्मया सहायेन परान् जिगीष ॥ २७ ॥

तद्बुद्धिमचान्यतरां वृणीष्व धर्मार्थकामान्विधिवद्भजस्व ।
व्यत्यस्य रागादिह हि त्रिवर्गं प्रेत्येह च भ्रंशमवाप्नुवन्ति ॥ २८ ॥

यो ह्यर्थधर्मौ परिपीड्य कामः
स्याद्धर्मकामौ परिभूय चार्थः ।
कामार्थयोश्चोपरमेण धर्म-
स्त्याज्यः स कृत्स्नो यदि काङ्क्षितोऽर्थः ॥ २९ ॥

तस्मात्त्रिवर्गस्य निषेवणेन त्वं रूपमेतत्सफलं कुरुष्व ।
धर्मार्थकामाधिगमं ह्यनूनं नृणामनूनं पुरुषार्थमाहुः ॥ ३० ॥

26. b. śa(ma added in margin)śrayā śrīḥ, A ; dpal gaṅ bsṅags (bsdags, Peking edition)-pa-ste (equivalent uncertain), T ; śamāśrayā, Böhtlingk.

27. b. visrambha°, A. c. vyūhāny any(corrected to n)ekāvi vigāhya, A ; sde rgyas-rnams ni . . . rnam-par-dkrugs byas-nas, T. d. parā jigīṣa, A ; pha-rol-rnams ni pham-par mdzod, T.

28. a. atrānyataraṁ, A. d. bhraṁsam, A.

29. a. yo hy atra dharmmo, A ; gaṅ-zhig don daṅ chos-la, T. b. dharmmakāmye(?mpe?, corrected to mo), A. c. ñe-bar-zhi-bas (copaśamena ?), T.

30. a. nisevanena, A.

तन्निष्फलौ नार्हसि कर्तुमेतौ
पीनौ भुजौ चापविकर्षणार्हौ ।
मान्धातृवज्जेतुमिमौ हि योग्यौ
लोकानपि त्रीनिह किं पुनर्गाम् ॥ ३१ ॥

स्नेहेन खल्वेतदहं ब्रवीमि नैश्वर्यरागेण न विस्मयेन ।
इमं हि दृष्ट्वा तव भिक्षुवेषं जातानुकम्पोऽस्म्यपि चागताश्रुः ॥३२॥

यावत्स्ववंशप्रतिरूप रूपं
न ते जराभ्येत्यभिभूय भूयः ।
तद्भुङ्क्ष्व भिक्षाश्रमकाम कामान्
कालेऽसि कर्ता प्रियधर्म धर्मम् ॥ ३३ ॥

शक्नोति जीर्णः खलु धर्ममाप्तुं कामोपभोगेष्वगतिर्जरायाः ।
अतश्च यूनः कथयन्ति कामान्मध्यस्य वित्तं स्थविरस्य धर्मम् ॥३४॥

धर्मस्य चार्थस्य च जीवलोके प्रत्यर्थिभूतानि हि यौवनानि ।
संरक्ष्यमाणान्यपि दुर्ग्रहाणि कामा यतस्तेन पथा हरन्ति ॥ ३५ ॥

वयांसि जीर्णानि विमर्शवन्ति धीराण्यवस्थानपरायणानि ।
अल्पेन यत्नेन शमात्मकानि भवन्त्यगत्यैव च लज्जया च ॥ ३६ ॥

31. a. niṣphalo, A. cd. yogyo lokān ahi trīṇ ihi kiṁ pur (gap for missing syllable) ggāṁ, A ; ḥjig-rten gsum-rnams kyaṅ . . . ḥos-pa yin-na sa ḥdir smos-ci-dgos, T.

32. c. °veśaṁ, A.

33. A transposes the two lines ; T as in text. c. bhukṣva bhikṣyāśrama°, A. d. priyadharmma dharmma, A.

34. cd. kāmām madhyasya, A. d. dharmma, A.

35. d. tena yathā haranti, A ; lam de-las (read la ?) ḥphrogs-par-byed (tena pathā hriyante ?), T ; svena pathā, Windisch.

36. a. vimarṣayanti, A ; rnam-dpyod ldan-pa-ste, T. d. agatyeva, A ; soṅ-ba ma-yin phyir, T.

अतश्च लोलं विषयप्रधानं प्रमत्तमक्षान्तमदीर्घदर्शि ।
बहुच्छलं यौवनमभ्यतीत्य निस्तीर्य कान्तारमिवाश्वसन्ति ॥ ३७ ॥

तस्मादधीरं चपलप्रमादि नवं वयस्तावदिदं व्यपैतु ।
कामस्य पूर्वं हि वयः शरव्यं न शक्यते रक्षितुमिन्द्रियेभ्यः ॥ ३८ ॥

अथो चिकीर्षा तव धर्म एव यजस्व यज्ञं कुलधर्म एषः ।
यज्ञैरधिष्ठाय हि नाकपृष्ठं ययौ मरुत्वानपि नाकपृष्ठम् ॥ ३९ ॥

सुवर्णकेयूरविदष्टबाहवो मणिप्रदीपोज्ज्वलचित्रमौलयः ।
नृपर्षयस्तां हि गतिं गता मखैः श्रमेण यामेव महर्षयो ययुः ॥४०॥

इत्येवं मगधपतिर्वचो बभाषे
यः सम्यग्वलभिदिव ब्रुवन् बभासे ।
तच्छ्रुत्वा न स विचचाल राजसूनुः
कैलासो गिरिरिव नैकचित्रसानुः ॥ ४१ ॥

इति बुद्धचरिते महाकाव्येऽश्वघोषकृते श्रेण्याभिगमनो नाम दशमः सर्गः ॥ १० ॥

38. b. vyapetu, A.

39. c. yajñer, A. 'You should mount the back of the spiritual nāga' (nāgapṛṣṭhaṁ), C.

40. a. rnam-par-bciṅs-paḥi phyag-rnams (°vibaddhabāhavo ?), T.

41. a. A omits vaco; magadha-yi bdag-pos tshig smras-pa, T. b. dhruvam babhāṣe, A; smra-ba yaṅ-dag mdzes, T.

CANTO XI

अथैवमुक्तो मगधाधिपेन सुहृन्मुखेन प्रतिकूलमर्थम् ।
स्वस्थोऽविकारः कुलशौचशुद्धः शौद्धोदनिर्वाक्यमिदं जगाद ॥ १ ॥
नाश्चर्यमेतद्भवतो विधानं जातस्य हर्यङ्ककुले विशाले ।
यन्मित्रपक्षे तव मित्रकाम स्याद्वृत्तिरेषा परिशुद्धवृत्तेः ॥ २ ॥
असत्सु मैत्री स्वकुलानुवृत्ता न तिष्ठति श्रीरिव विक्लवेषु ।
पूर्वैः कृतां प्रीतिपरंपराभिस्तामेव सन्तस्तु विवर्धयन्ति ॥ ३ ॥

ये चार्थकृच्छ्रेषु भवन्ति लोके
समानकार्याः सुहृदां मनुष्याः ।
मित्राणि तानीति परैमि बुद्ध्या
स्वस्थस्य वृद्धिष्विह को हि न स्यात् ॥ ४ ॥

एवं च ये द्रव्यमवाप्य लोके मित्रेषु धर्मे च नियोजयन्ति ।
अवाप्तसाराणि धनानि तेषां भ्रष्टानि नान्ते जनयन्ति तापम् ॥५॥
सुहृत्तया चार्यतया च राजन् खल्वेष यो मां प्रति निश्चयस्ते ।
अत्रानुनेष्यामि सुहृत्तयैव ब्रूयामहं नोत्तरमन्यदत्र ॥ ६ ॥

1. b. sukṛnmukhena, A ; bśes-kyi sgo-nas, T. c. kulaśoca°, A.

2. a. bhavato bhidhātu, A ; khyod-kyi cho-ga, T ; bhavato 'bhidhānaṁ, Böhtlingk. d. pariśuddhavṛttaḥ, A ; yoṅs-su-dag-paḥi spyod-pas, T.

3. a. svakulānurūpā, A ; raṅ rigs rjes-su-spyod-pas, T.

5. c. aptasārāṇi (one syllable short), A ; sñiṅ-po thob-pa-ste, T.

6. b. e.c. ; vihāya prāg eva ti niścayas te, A ; khyod-kyi ṅes-pa gaṅ-zhig bdag-la dmigs-pa ḥdi (=text, omitting khalu), T.

अहं जरामृत्युभयं विदित्वा मुमुक्षया धर्ममिमं प्रपन्नः ।
बन्धून् प्रियानश्रुमुखान्विहाय प्रागेव कामानशुभस्य हेतून् ॥ ७ ॥
नाशीविषेभ्यो हि तथा बिभेमि नैवाशनिभ्यो गगनाच्च्युतेभ्यः ।
न पावकेभ्योऽनिलसंहितेभ्यो यथा भयं मे विषयेभ्य एव ॥ ८ ॥
कामा ह्यनित्याः कुशलार्थचौरा
रिक्ताश्च मायासदृशाश्च लोके ।
आशास्यमाना अपि मोहयन्ति
चित्तं नृणां किं पुनरात्मसंस्थाः ॥ ९ ॥
कामाभिभूता हि न यान्ति शर्म त्रिपिष्टपे किं बत मर्त्यलोके ।
कामैः सतृष्णस्य हि नास्ति तृप्तिर्यथेन्धनैर्वातसखस्य वह्नेः ॥ १० ॥
जगत्यनर्थो न समोऽस्ति कामैर्मोहाच्च तेष्वेव जनः प्रसक्तः ।
तत्त्वं विदित्वैवमनर्थभीरुः प्राज्ञः स्वयं कोऽभिलषेदनर्थम् ॥ ११ ॥
समुद्रवस्त्रामपि गामवाप्य पारं जिगीषन्ति महार्णवस्य ।
लोकस्य कामैर्न वितृप्तिरस्ति पतद्भिरम्भोभिरिवार्णवस्य ॥ १२ ॥
देवेन वृष्टेऽपि हिरण्यवर्षे द्वीपान्समग्रांश्चतुरोऽपि जित्वा ।
शक्रस्य चार्धासनमप्यवाप्य मान्धातुरासीद्विषयेष्वतृप्तिः ॥ १३ ॥
भुक्त्वापि राज्यं दिवि देवतानां शतक्रतौ वृत्रभयात्प्रनष्टे ।
दर्पान्महर्षीनपि वाहयित्वा कामेष्वतृप्तो नहुषः पपात ॥ १४ ॥

8. a. bibhaimi, A.
11. ab. kāmaiḥ mohāc, A. b. praśaktaḥ, A.
12. c. na hi tṛptir, Lüders ; T indeterminate.
13. b. loṅs-spyod-de (bhuñjan for jitvā ?), T. d. āśīd, A.
14. b. praṇaṣṭe, A. d. naghusaḥ prapāta, A.

ऐडश्च राजा त्रिदिवं विगाह्य नीत्वापि देवीं वशमुर्वशीं ताम् ।
लोभादृषिभ्यः कनकं जिहीर्षुर्जगाम नाशं विषयेष्वतृप्तः ॥ १५ ॥

बलेर्महेन्द्रं नहुषं महेन्द्रादिन्द्रं पुनर्ये नहुषादुपेयुः ।
स्वर्गे क्षितौ वा विषयेषु तेषु को विश्वसेद्भाग्यकुलाकुलेषु ॥ १६ ॥

चीराम्बरा मूलफलाम्बुभक्षा
जटा वहन्तोऽपि भुजङ्गदीर्घाः ।
यैर्नान्यकार्या मुनयोऽपि भग्नाः
कः कामसंज्ञान्मृगयेत शत्रून् ॥ १७ ॥

उग्रायुधश्चोग्रधृतायुधोऽपि येषां कृते मृत्युमवाप भीष्मात् ।
चिन्तापि तेषामशिवा वधाय सद्वृत्तिनां किं पुनरव्रतानाम् ॥१८॥

आस्वादमल्पं विषयेषु मत्वा संयोजनोत्कर्षमतृप्तिमेव ।
सद्भ्यश्च गर्हां नियतं च पापं कः कामसंज्ञं विषमाददीत ॥ १९ ॥

कृष्यादिभिः कर्मभिरर्दितानां कामात्मकानां च निशम्य दुःखम् ।
स्वास्थ्यं च कामेष्वकुतूहलानां कामान्विहातुं क्षममात्मवद्भिः ॥२०॥

15. a. eḍaś ca, A. cd. jihīrṣu jagāma, A.

16. a. naghuṣa, A. b. naghuṣād, A.

17. c. yair anyakāryā, A ; gaṅ-gis don gzhan ma-yin, T ; ' peaceful and seeking nothing ', C ; ' seeking for *mokṣa* by separation from the desires ', FP.

18. a. ugrāṣudhaś, A. b. bhīsmāt, A. d. e.c. ; tadvṛttināṁ kim pur avratānāṁ (one syllable short), A ; spyod-rnams-kyi ḥjoms-phyir de-phyir brtul-zhugs rnams-kyi smos-ci-dgos (=vṛttīnāṁ vadhāya tat kiṁ punar vratānām), T ; tadvṛttitā, Windisch.

19. a. āśvādam, A ; mya-ṅan (for myoṅ-ba ?), T. b. saṁyojanātkarṣam, A. c. garhā, A.

20. a. kṛṣyādibhir ddharmmabhir anvitānāṁ, A ; zhiṅ-gi las-la sogs-pa-rnams-kyis ñam-thag-ciṅ, T ; ' every difficult means of livelihood ', C.

ज्ञेया विपत्कामिनि कामसंपत्सिद्धेषु कामेषु मदं ह्युपैति ।
मदादकार्यं कुरुते न कार्यं येन क्षतो दुर्गतिमभ्युपैति ॥ २१ ॥
यत्नेन लब्धाः परिरक्षिताश्च ये विप्रलभ्य प्रतियान्ति भूयः ।
तेष्वात्मवान्याचितकोपमेषु कामेषु विद्वानिह को रमेत ॥ २२ ॥

अन्विष्य चादाय च जाततर्षा
यानत्यजन्तः परियान्ति दुःखम् ।
लोके तृणोल्कासदृशेषु तेषु
कामेषु कस्यात्मवतो रतिः स्यात् ॥ २३ ॥

अनात्मवन्तो हृदि यैर्विदष्टा
विनाशमर्छन्ति न यान्ति शर्म ।
क्रुद्धोग्रसर्पप्रतिमेषु तेषु
कामेषु कस्यात्मवतो रतिः स्यात् ॥ २४ ॥

अस्थि क्षुधार्ता इव सारमेया
भुक्त्वापि यान्नैव भवन्ति तृप्ताः ।
जीर्णास्थिकङ्कालसमेषु तेषु
कामेषु कस्यात्मवतो रतिः स्यात् ॥ २५ ॥

ये राजचौरोदकपावकेभ्यः
साधारणत्वाज्जनयन्ति दुःखम् ।
तेषु प्रविद्धामिषसंनिभेषु
कामेषु कस्यात्मवतो रतिः स्यात् ॥ २६ ॥

21. d. kṣate, A ; zad-ciṅ, T.

22. a. parirakṣitaś, A. d. vidvān ihi, A ; ḥdi-na mkhas-pa, T.

24. c. kruddhograśarppa°, A ; kun-nas ḥkhros-paḥi sbrul (saṁkruddha-sarpa°), T.

यच्च स्थितानामभितो विपत्तिः शत्रोः सकाशादपि बान्धवेभ्यः ।
हिंस्रेषु तेष्वायतनोपमेषु कामेषु कस्यात्मवतो रतिः स्यात् ॥ २७ ॥

गिरौ वने चाप्सु च सागरे च
यान् भ्रंशमर्छन्ति विलङ्घमानाः ।
तेषु द्रुमप्राग्रफलोपमेषु
कामेषु कस्यात्मवतो रतिः स्यात् ॥ २८ ॥

तीव्रैः प्रयत्नैर्विविधैरवाप्ताः क्षणेन ये नाशमिह प्रयान्ति ।
स्वप्नोपभोगप्रतिमेषु तेषु कामेषु कस्यात्मवतो रतिः स्यात् ॥ २९ ॥

यानर्जयित्वापि न यान्ति शर्म विवर्धयित्वा परिपालयित्वा ।
अङ्गारकर्षूप्रतिमेषु तेषु कामेषु कस्यात्मवतो रतिः स्यात् ॥ ३० ॥

विनाशमीयुः कुरवो यदर्थं वृष्ण्यन्धका मेखलदण्डकाश्च ।
सूनासिकाष्ठप्रतिमेषु तेषु कस्यात्मवतो रतिः स्यात् ॥ ३१ ॥

सुन्दोपसुन्दावसुरौ यदर्थमन्योन्यवैरप्रसृतौ विनष्टौ ।
सौहार्दविश्लेषकरेषु तेषु कामेषु कस्यात्मवतो रतिः स्यात् ॥ ३२ ॥

27. b. śakāśād api bāndhaveṣu (corrected in margin to °vebhyaḥ), A; gñer-ḥdun ḥbrel-pa-rnams-las kyaṅ, T.

28. b. yadbhraṁśam arcchanty abhilaṅghamānāḥ, A; gaṅ-la rnam-par-ḥphyo-ba-rnams ni lhuṅ ḥgyur-te, T. c. drumaprāgramalo°, A; ljon-śiṅ rtse-moḥi ḥbras-bu, T.

29. a. tīvvaiḥ, A; drag-po, T. c. svapnop(?g?)rabhoga°, A; rmi-lam ñe-bar-loṅs-spyod, T.

30. a. yān acc(??)ayitvāpi, A; gaṅ-rnams bsgrubs-nas, T. c. aṅgāra-karṣny(corrected to rṣ)apra°, A; lci-baḥi me-ma-mur, T; 'a firepit', C.

31. b. e.c.; maithiladaṇḍakāś ca, A; T omits the *pāda*; 'the Mekhali-Daṇḍa(ka)s', C. c. ro-bsregs śiṅ ('corpse-burning wood', śūnāśikāṣṭha° ?), T; sūnāsikāṣṭha°, C.

32. b. anyonyaveraprasṛto, A.

येषां कृते वारिणि पावके च क्रव्यात्सु चात्मानमिहोत्सृजन्ति ।
सपत्नभूतेष्वशिवेषु तेषु कामेषु कस्यात्मवतो रतिः स्यात् ॥ ३३ ॥
कामार्थमज्ञः कृपणं करोति प्राप्नोति दुःखं वधबन्धनादि ।
कामार्थमाशाकृपणस्तपस्वी मृत्युं श्रमं चार्छति जीवलोकः ॥३४॥
गीतैर्ह्रियन्ते हि मृगा वधाय रूपार्थमग्नौ शलभाः पतन्ति ।
मत्स्यो गिरत्यायसमामिषार्थी तस्मादनर्थं विषयाः फलन्ति ॥३५॥
कामास्तु भोगा इति यन्मतिः स्याद्भोगा न केचित्परिगण्यमानाः ।
वस्त्रादयो द्रव्यगुणा हि लोके दुःखप्रतीकार इति प्रधार्याः ॥३६॥
इष्टं हि तर्षप्रशमाय तोयं क्षुन्नाशहेतोरशनं तथैव ।
वातातपाम्ब्वावरणाय वेश्म कौपीनशीतावरणाय वासः ॥ ३७ ॥
निद्राविघाताय तथैव शय्या यानं तथाध्वश्रमनाशनाय ।
तथासनं स्थानविनोदनाय स्नानं मृजारोग्यबलाश्रयाय ॥ ३८ ॥

33. a. kāsāndh(?rth?)am ajñaḥ kṛpa pāvake ca, A; gaṅ-dag-rnams-kyi don-du chu daṅ me-la daṅ, T; ‘he may bind his body and throw himself into fire and water’, C.

34. a. kṛpanaṅ, A. c. tapaśvī, A. d. mṛtyu śramaṁ, A; ḥchiṅ-ba (for ḥchi-ba) daṅ ni ṅal-ba, T.

35. a. gītai hriyaṁte, A. b. śalabhā, A. cd. matsyo giranty āyasam āmiṣārthīn tasmād, A; śa-dag don gñer ña, T; ‘the pool fish longing for the baited hook’, C; ‘the fish in the water hangs on the hook on account of taking the bait’, FP.

36. ab. yan mataḥ syāt bhogā, A; ḥdod-paḥi loṅs-spyod yin zhes gaṅ-gi blo yin-la (kāmasya bhogā iti yanmatiḥ syād?), T; mataṁ, Co. b. kha-cig loṅs-spyod-rnams ni yoṅs-su-spyod-pa-ste (=kecid bhogāḥ paricaryamāṇāḥ, or parivartyamānāḥ), T; pariganyamāṇāḥ, A.

37. a. toya, A. c. vātātapāmvāvaraṇāya, A; rluṅ daṅ gduṅ-ba sgrib-pa ched-du (=vātātapāvaraṇāya), T. d. kopīna° (?kopane°?), A.

38. a. de-bzhin . . . gnas yin-la (tathāsti vāso?), T; ‘one sleeps to drive off drowsiness’, C. b. °śramaṇāśanāya, A. d. sṛjārogya°, A; gtsaṅ daṅ mad-med, T; ‘to remove dirt one bathes’, C.

दुःखप्रतीकारनिमित्तभूता-
स्तस्मात्प्रजानां विषया न भोगाः ।
अस्नामि भोगानिति कोऽभ्युपेया-
त्प्राज्ञः प्रतीकारविधौ प्रवृत्तः ॥ ३९ ॥

यः पित्तदाहेन विदह्यमानः शीतक्रियां भोग इति व्यवस्येत् ।
दुःखप्रतीकारविधौ प्रवृत्तः कामेषु कुर्यात्स हि भोगसंज्ञाम् ॥४०॥

कामेष्वनैकान्तिकता च यस्मा-
दतोऽपि मे तेषु न भोगसंज्ञा ।
य एव भावा हि सुखं दिशन्ति
त एव दुःखं पुनरावहन्ति ॥ ४१ ॥

गुरूणि वासांस्यगुरूणि चैव सुखाय शीते ह्यसुखाय घर्मे ।
चन्द्रांशवश्चन्दनमेव चोष्णे सुखाय दुःखाय भवन्ति शीते ॥ ४२ ॥

द्वन्द्वानि सर्वस्य यतः प्रसक्ता-
न्यलाभलाभप्रभृतीनि लोके ।
अतोऽपि नैकान्तसुखोऽस्ति कश्चि-
न्नैकान्तदुःखः पुरुषः पृथिव्याम् ॥ ४३ ॥

39. ab. °bhūtā tasmāt, A. b. de-bzhin skye-dgu-rnams (tathā prajānāṁ), T; 'therefore', C. c. annāni bhogā iti, Gawroński; loṅs-spyod-rnams ni bzaḥ zhes (indeterminate), T. d. e.c. Finot; pravṛttān, A; rab-tu-zhi-baḥi cho-gar rab-zhugs śes-rab-can (=text?), T.

40. a. pittadāhana, A; ḥgro-baḥi (for dro-baḥi?) gduṅ-bas (uncertain), T; 'a man who has got a burning fever', C. c. sdug-bsṅal zhi-baḥi bdag-ñid-la (duḥkhapratīkāratayā?), T. d. bhogasaṁjñaṁ, A.

41. a. yasyād, A. b. T omits api.

42. b. dharmme, A; dro-baḥi tshe-na, T. c. candrāṁśava candanam, A.

43. a. dvandāni, A. praśaktāny, A; rab-zhugs-te (pravṛttāny), T. d. paruṣaḥ pṛthivyāṁ, A; sa-la skyes-bu, T.

दृष्ट्वा विमिश्रां सुखदुःखतां मे
राज्यं च दास्यं च मतं समानम् ।
नित्यं हसत्येव हि नैव राजा
न चापि संतप्यत एव दासः ॥ ४४ ॥

आज्ञा नृपत्वेऽभ्यधिकेति यत्स्यान्महान्ति दुःखान्यत एव राज्ञः ।
आसङ्गकाष्ठप्रतिमो हि राजा लोकस्य हेतोः परिखेदमेति ॥४५॥

राज्ये नृपस्त्यागिनि बह्वमित्रे
विश्वासमागच्छति चेद्विपन्नः ।
अथापि विश्रम्भमुपैति नेह
किं नाम सौख्यं चकितस्य राज्ञः ॥ ४६ ॥

यदा च जित्वापि महीं समग्रां वासाय दृष्टं पुरमेकमेव ।
तत्रापि चैकं भवनं निषेव्यं श्रमः परार्थे ननु राजभावः ॥ ४७ ॥

राज्ञोऽपि वासोयुगमेकमेव क्षुत्संनिरोधाय तथान्नमात्रा ।
शय्या तथैकासनमेकमेव शेषा विशेषा नृपतेर्मदाय ॥ ४८ ॥

तुष्ट्यर्थमेतच्च फलं यदीष्टमृतेऽपि राज्यान्मम तुष्टिरस्ति ।
तुष्टौ च सत्यां पुरुषस्य लोके सर्वे विशेषा ननु निर्विशेषाः ॥४९॥

44. a. dṛṣṭvā ca miśrāṁ, A ; rnam-par-ḥdres mthoṅ-nas, T. b. rāṁjya (gap for missing character) dāsya ca, A ; rgyal-srid daṅ ni bran-ñid, T. d. hāsaḥ, A ; bran, T.

45. a. gaṅ-phyir . . . lhag-par gyur (abhyadhikāsti yasmān?), T ; 'if you say that the fact of a king giving orders makes him the best ', C.

46. a. vaṅkamitre, A ; bśes-min maṅ-por, T ; 'on account of the many enemies of kings ', C. c. visrambham upeti, A.

47. a. mahī, A.

48. Not in C. a. e.c. Böhtlingk ; rājye pi vāse yugam, A ; rgẏal-po sdod-paḥi gnas kyaṅ gñaḥ-śiṅ gcig ñid-de (rājño 'pi vāso yugam ekam eva), T. b. tathānamātrā, A ; de-bzhin . . . bzaḥ-ba tsam yin-la, T.

तन्नास्मि कामान् प्रति संप्रतार्यः
क्षेमं शिवं मार्गमनुप्रपन्नः ।
स्मृत्वा सुहृत्त्वं तु पुनः पुनर्मां
ब्रूहि प्रतिज्ञां खलु पालयेति ॥ ५० ॥

न ह्यस्म्यमर्षेण वनं प्रविष्टो न शत्रुबाणैरवधूतमौलिः ।
कृतस्पृहो नापि फलाधिकेभ्यो गृह्णामि नैतद्वचनं यतस्ते ॥ ५१ ॥

यो दन्दशूकं कुपितं भुजङ्गं
मुक्त्वा व्यवस्येद्धि पुनर्ग्रहीतुम् ।
दाहात्मिकां वा ज्वलितां तृणोल्कां
संत्यज्य कामान्स पुनर्भजेत ॥ ५२ ॥

अन्धाय यश्च स्पृहयेदनन्धो
बद्धाय मुक्तो विधनाय चाढ्यः ।
उन्मत्तचित्ताय च कल्यचित्तः
स्पृहां स कुर्याद्विषयात्मकाय ॥ ५३ ॥

भैक्षोपभोगीति च नानुकम्प्यः कृती जराम‍ृत्युभयं तितीर्षुः ।
इहोत्तमं शान्तिसुखं च यस्य परत्र दुःखानि च संवृतानि ॥ ५४ ॥

50. b. kṣema, A ; dge daṅ zhi-baḥi lam, T. d. smras-pa-ḥo (brūṣe or brūyāḥ?), T. pālayanti (corrected to °yeti), A ; skyoṅ zhes, T.

51. a. e.c. Böhtlingk ; vana praviṣto, A ; nags-su zhugs-pa, T. b. avadhūmauliḥ (one syllable short), A ; mgo-bo ḥdar-ba (avadhūtamūrdhā?), T ; 'I have cast off the royal diadem', C. c. kṛtaspṛhā, A. d. naid vacanaṁ (one syllable short), A ; tshig-de . . . ma-yin-no, T. de-phyir (tatas), T.

52. a. bhujagaṁ, A. b. puna grahītuṁ, A. c. tṛnolkāṁ, A. d. bhajet, A.

53. a. spṛhayed anartho, A ; ma-loṅ . . . ḥdod-pa-ste, T.

54. a. bhaiṣopabhogīti ca(?ra?), A ; sloṅs-mo ñe-bar-rgyu zhes (bhaikṣopacārīti?), T.

लक्ष्म्यां महत्यामपि वर्तमानस्तृष्णाभिभूतस्त्वनुकम्पितव्यः ।
प्राप्नोति यः शान्तिसुखं न चेह परत्र दुःखैः प्रतिगृह्यते च ॥५५॥
एवं तु वक्तुं भवतोऽनुरूपं सत्त्वस्य वृत्तस्य कुलस्य चैव ।
ममापि वोढुं सदृशं प्रतिज्ञां सत्त्वस्य वृत्तस्य कुलस्य चैव ॥ ५६ ॥
अहं हि संसारशरेण विद्धो विनिःसृतः शान्तिमवाप्तुकामः ।
नेच्छेयमाप्तुं त्रिदिवेऽपि राज्यं निरामयं किं बत मानुषेषु ॥५७॥

त्रिवर्गसेवां नृप यत्तु कृत्स्नतः
परो मनुष्यार्थ इति त्वमात्थ माम् ।
अनर्थ इत्येव ममात्र दर्शनं
क्षयी त्रिवर्गो हि न चापि तर्पकः ॥ ५८ ॥
पदे तु यस्मिन्न जरा न भीर्न रुङ्
न जन्म नैवोपरमो न चाधयः ।
तमेव मन्ये पुरुषार्थमुत्तमं
न विद्यते यत्र पुनः पुनः क्रिया ॥ ५९ ॥

यदप्यवोचः परिपाल्यतां जरा नवं वयो गच्छति विक्रियामिति ।
अनिश्चयोऽयं चपलं हि दृश्यते जराप्यधीरा धृतिमच्च यौवनम् ॥६०॥

57. Not in C. a. saṁsārarasena, A; ḥkhor-baḥi mdaḥ-yis, T; 'I who have been shot at by the arrow of the *saṁsāra*', FP. b. viniḥsṛtaḥ, A. cd. nad-med mtho-ris-na (tridive . . . nirāmaye?), T.

58. a. brten-pa ḥdi (=sevām imạm), T. yan tu kṛsnataḥ, A. b. tvam ārtha māṁ, A. c. e.c.; anartha ity eva mamārthadarśanaṁ, A; de-ltar don-med ces ni bdag-gi (so Peking edition) brtan-pa (so Peking edition, read bstan-pa) ḥdir (=anartha ity evaṁ mamātra darśanaṁ), T; 'this too is *anartha*', C. d. trivarge, A.

59. ab. na bhīrur nna janma (one syllable short), A; ḥjigs-min nad ma-yin skye-min, T.

60. a. pratipālyatāṁ, Gawroński. c. bahulaṁ hi, Kern.

स्वकर्मदक्षश्च यदान्तको जगद्
वयःसु सर्वेष्ववशं विकर्षति ।
विनाशकाले कथमव्यवस्थिते
जरा प्रतीक्ष्या विदुषा शमेप्सुना ॥ ६१ ॥

जरायुधो व्याधिविकीर्णसायको
यदान्तको व्याध इवाशिवः स्थितः ।
प्रजामृगान् भाग्यवनाश्रितांस्तुदन्
वयःप्रकर्षं प्रति को मनोरथः ॥ ६२ ॥

अतो युवा वा स्थविरोऽथवा शिशु-
स्तथा त्वरावानिह कर्तुमर्हति ।
यथा भवेद्धर्मवतः कृतात्मनः
प्रवृत्तिरिष्टा विनिवृत्तिरेव वा ॥ ६३ ॥

यदात्थ चापीष्टफलां कुलोचितां
कुरुष्व धर्माय मखक्रियामिति ।
नमो मखेभ्यो न हि कामये सुखं
परस्य दुःखक्रियया यदिष्यते ॥ ६४ ॥

61. b. vayassu sarvveṣu vasam vikarṣati, A ; na-tshod kun-la dbaṅ-med rnam-par-ḥgugs-pa-ste, T. d. samepsunā, A ; zhi-ḥdod, T.

62. b. ivāśritaḥ sthitaḥ, A ; dge-ba ma-yin . . . bzhin gnas-pas, T. c. °āśritān sudan, A ; rten-rnams gtor-te, T. d. priti ko, A.

63. a. suto (corrected to ato), A ; de-phyir, T. c. kṛpātmanaḥ, A ; bdag-ñid byas-pa, T.

64. a. e.c. ; yad āttha cādīptaphalāṁ, A ; yaṅ-na ḥdod-paḥi ḥbras-bu . . . gaṅ smras-pa (yad āttha vāpīṣṭaphalāṁ), T. d. pad iṣyate, A ; gaṅ-zhig . . . ḥdod-pa-ste, T.

परं हि हन्तुं विवशं फलेप्सया
न युक्तरूपं करुणात्मनः सतः ।
क्रतोः फलं यद्यपि शाश्वतं भवे-
त्तथापि कृत्वा किमु यत्क्षयात्मकम् ॥ ६५ ॥

भवेच्च धर्मो यदि नापरो विधि-
र्व्रतेन शीलेन मनःशमेन वा ।
तथापि नैवार्हति सेवितुं क्रतुं
विशस्य यस्मिन् परमुच्यते फलम् ॥ ६६ ॥

इहापि तावत्पुरुषस्य तिष्ठतः प्रवर्तते यत्परहिंसया सुखम् ।
तदप्यनिष्टं सघृणस्य धीमतो भवान्तरे किं बत यन्न दृश्यते ॥६७॥

न च प्रतार्योऽस्मि फलप्रवृत्तये
भवेषु राजन् रमते न मे मनः ।
लता इवाम्भोधरवृष्टिताडिताः
प्रवृत्तयः सर्वगता हि चञ्चलाः ॥ ६८ ॥

इहागतश्चाहमितो दिदृक्षया
मुनेरराडस्य विमोक्षवादिनः ।
प्रयामि चाद्यैव नृपास्तु ते शिवं
वचः क्षमेथा मम तत्त्वनिष्ठुरम् ॥ ६९ ॥

65. a. hantu, A. b. yuktarupa, A. c. krato, A. gaṅ yaṅ (yad api?), T. d. sñiṅ-rjeḥi bdag-ñid gaṅ-gi de-ltar byas-nas ci (=tathā kṛtvā kiṁ yat kṛpātmakam), T; 'how much more then in doing hurt to creatures in sacrifice, when seeking what is not permanent', C.

66. a. dharme, Böhtlingk. ab. vidhi vatena, A; brtul-zhugs-kyis ... cha-ga (for cho-ga), T. b. manaḥsamena va, A; sems zhi-ba-yis-sam, T.

69. a. de-yi phyir (ato?), T; 'therefore', C.

अथेन्द्रवद्दिव्यव शश्वदर्कवद्गुणैरव श्रेय इहाव गामव ।
अवायुरार्यैरव सत्सुतानव श्रियश्च राजन्नव धर्ममात्मनः ॥ ७० ॥

हिमारिकेतूद्भवसंभवान्तरे यथा द्विजो याति विमोक्षयंस्तनुम् ।
हिमारिशत्रुक्षयशत्रुघातने तथान्तरे याहि विमोक्षयन्मनः ॥ ७१ ॥

नृपोऽब्रवीत्साञ्जलिरागतस्पृहो
यथेष्टमाप्नोतु भवानविघ्नतः ।
अवाप्य काले कृतकृत्यतामिमां
ममापि कार्यो भवता त्वनुग्रहः ॥ ७२ ॥

स्थिरं प्रतिज्ञाय तथेति पार्थिवे
ततः स वैश्वंतरमाश्रमं ययौ ।
परिव्रजन्तं तमुदीक्ष्य विस्मितो
नृपोऽपि वव्राज पुरिं गिरिव्रजम् ॥ ७३ ॥

इति बुद्धचरिते महाकाव्ये कामविगर्हणो नामैकादशः सर्गः ॥ ११ ॥

70. a. athendravad, A; dbaṅ-po bzhin bsruṅs, T. b. iho ca gām acaḥ, A; sa bsruṅs ḥdir ni . . . bsruṅs, T. c. āyair ava śatsutān, A; ḥphags-pa-yis bsruṅs dam-paḥi bu-rnams, T.

71. c. e.c.; °kṣayaśatrughātinas, A; khyim-gyi dgra ḥjoms naṅ (probably=text, but uncertain), T. d. e.c. Cappeller; vimocayan, A.

72. b. avighnyataḥ, A. c. bya-ba byas-pa . . . dus-su ḥdir (kāle kṛtakṛtyatām iha, for ito?), T.

73. c. samudīkṣya, A; de mthoṅ-nas, T. d. vavrā puriṅ girivrajaṁ (one syllable short), A; ri-yi-tshogs-kyi groṅ-khyer-ñid-du soṅ, T.

CANTO XII

ततः शमविहारस्य मुनेरिक्ष्वाकुचन्द्रमाः ।
अराडस्याश्रमं भेजे वपुषा पूरयन्निव ॥ १ ॥

स कालामसगोत्रेण तेनालोक्यैव दूरतः ।
उच्चैः स्वागतमित्युक्तः समीपमुपजग्मिवान् ॥ २ ॥

तावुभौ न्यायतः पृष्ट्वा धातुसाम्यं परस्परम् ।
दारव्योर्मेध्ययोर्वृष्योः शुचौ देशे निषेदतुः ॥ ३ ॥

तमासीनं नृपसुतं सोऽब्रवीन्मुनिसत्तमः ।
बहुमानविशालाभ्यां दर्शनाभ्यां पिबन्निव ॥ ४ ॥

विदितं मे यथा सौम्य निष्क्रान्तो भवनादसि ।
छित्त्वा स्नेहमयं पाशं पाशं दृप्त इव द्विपः ॥ ५ ॥

सर्वथा धृतिमच्चैव प्राज्ञं चैव मनस्तव ।
यस्त्वं प्राप्तः श्रियं त्यक्त्वा लतां विषफलामिव ॥ ६ ॥

नाश्चर्यं जीर्णवयसो यज्जग्मुः पार्थिवा वनम् ।
अपत्येभ्यः श्रियं दत्त्वा भुक्तोच्छिष्टामिव स्रजम् ॥ ७ ॥

1. a. samavihārasya, A; zhi-bar gnas-paḥi, T. d. pūjayann, A; gaṅ-ba, T.

2. b. teṇā° (corrected to tenā°), A. d. samīpam ujagmivān (one syllable short), A; draṅ-du ñe-bar-gśegs-pa-ḥo, T.

3. a. pṛṣṭ(?ṇ?)yā, A; dris-nas, T. d. śuco (corrected to guro?), A; gtsaṅ-bar, T. niṣīdatuḥ, A.

7. b. vasaṁ (corrected to vanaṁ), A.

इदं मे मतमाश्चर्यं नवे वयसि यद्भवान् ।
अभुक्त्वैव श्रियं प्राप्तः स्थितो विषयगोचरे ॥ ८ ॥

तद्विज्ञातुमिमं धर्मं परमं भाजनं भवान् ।
ज्ञानप्लवमधिष्ठाय शीघ्रं दुःखार्णवं तर ॥ ९ ॥

शिष्ये यद्यपि विज्ञाते शास्त्रं कालेन वर्ण्यते ।
गाम्भीर्याद्व्यवसायाच्च न परीक्ष्यो भवान्मम ॥ १० ॥

इति वाक्यमराडस्य विज्ञाय स नरर्षभः ।
बभूव परमप्रीतः प्रोवाचोत्तरमेव च ॥ ११ ॥

विरक्तस्यापि यदिदं सौमुख्यं भवतः परम् ।
अकृतार्थोऽप्यनेनास्मि कृतार्थ इव संप्रति ॥ १२ ॥

दिदृक्षुरिव हि ज्योतिर्यियासुरिव दैशिकम् ।
त्वद्दर्शनमहं मन्ये तितीर्षुरिव च प्लवम् ॥ १३ ॥

तस्मादर्हसि तद्वक्तुं वक्तव्यं यदि मन्यसे ।
जरामरणरोगेभ्यो यथायं परिमुच्यते ॥ १४ ॥

8. c. abhukteva, A ; ñid loṅs-ma-spyad-nas (pas, Weller), T.

10. a. gaṅ yaṅ (yad api ?), T. b. ḥjug-ste (vartate or vartyate), T ; 'first one tests their abilities and thereafter one teaches them', C ; vartate, Co. d. e.c. ; su(?)parīkṣyo, A ; yoṅs-rtog khyod ma-yin (na parīkṣito bhavān ?), T ; 'I know already your good firm settled purpose, certainly you will be equal to learning and in the end nothing will be hid from you', C.

11. b. mi-yi draṅ-sroṅ des (sa nararṣiḥ), T.

13. a. didikṣur, A ; blta-bar ḥdod-pas, T. c. tvaddarśanāha (one syllable short), A ; khyed mthoṅ-ba-la bdag-gis, T.

14. c. rga daṅ ḥchi-baḥi ḥjigs-rnams-las (=jarāmaraṇabhayebhyo), T ; 'the troubles of birth (or, the troubles that produce), old age, disease and death', C.

इत्यराडः कुमारस्य माहात्म्यादेव चोदितः ।
संक्षिप्तं कथयांचक्रे स्वस्य शास्त्रस्य निश्चयम् ॥ १५ ॥

श्रूयतामयमस्माकं सिद्धान्तः शृण्वतां वर ।
यथा भवति संसारो यथा चैव निवर्तते ॥ १६ ॥

प्रकृतिश्च विकारश्च जन्म मृत्युर्जरैव च ।
तत्तावत्सत्त्वमित्युक्तं स्थिरसत्त्व परेहि तत् ॥ १७ ॥

तत्र तु प्रकृतिं नाम विद्धि प्रकृतिकोविद ।
पञ्च भूतान्यहंकारं बुद्धिमव्यक्तमेव च ॥ १८ ॥

विकार इति बुध्यस्व विषयानिन्द्रियाणि च ।
पाणिपादं च वादं च पायूपस्थं तथा मनः ॥ १९ ॥

अस्य क्षेत्रस्य विज्ञानात्क्षेत्रज्ञ इति संज्ञि च ।
क्षेत्रज्ञ इति चात्मानं कथयन्त्यात्मचिन्तकाः ॥ २० ॥

सशिष्यः कपिलश्चेह प्रतिबुद्धिरिति स्मृतिः ।
सपुत्रोऽप्रतिबुद्धस्तु प्रजापतिरिहोच्यते ॥ २१ ॥

15. d. śvasya, A.

16. d. yathā vai parivarttate, A; ji-ltar ṅes-par ldog-pa ñid (=text, omitting ca), T; 'the matter of the origin and destruction of the universe', C.

17. d. paraihi naḥ, A; de śes-mdzod, T.

18. a. e.c. Böhtlingk; prakṛtir nnāma (originally prakṛtin nāma ?), A.

19. c. vācaṁ, Böhtlingk.

20. d. kathayaty, A.

21. b. pratibuddhi, A; rab-tu-rtogs (pratibuddhir or °buddha), T; pratibuddha, Co. c. e.c.; saputraḥ pratibuddhas tu, A; bu daṅ bcas-paḥi rtogs-pa daṅ (=A, with ca for tu), T; 'Kapila, the ṛṣi, and his brothers, sons and dependants, on this important principle of the ego, practised learning and obtained salvation. This Kapila is now Prajāpati', C.

जायते जीर्यते चैव बाध्यते म्रियते च यत् ।
तद्व्यक्तमिति विज्ञेयमव्यक्तं तु विपर्ययात् ॥ २२ ॥
अज्ञानं कर्म तृष्णा च ज्ञेयाः संसारहेतवः ।
स्थितोऽस्मिंस्त्रितये जन्तुस्तत्सत्त्वं नातिवर्तते ॥ २३ ॥
विप्रत्ययादहंकारात्संदेहादभिसंप्लवात् ।
अविशेषानुपायाभ्यां सङ्गादभ्यवपाततः ॥ २४ ॥
तत्र विप्रत्ययो नाम विपरीतं प्रवर्तते ।
अन्यथा कुरुते कार्यं मन्तव्यं मन्यतेऽन्यथा ॥ २५ ॥
ब्रवीम्यहमहं वेद्मि गच्छाम्यहमहं स्थितः ।
इतीहैवमहंकारस्त्वनहंकार वर्तते ॥ २६ ॥
यस्तु भावानसंदिग्धानेकीभावेन पश्यति ।
मृत्पिण्डवदसंदेह संदेहः स इहोच्यते ॥ २७ ॥
य एवाहं स एवेदं मनो बुद्धिश्च कर्म च ।
यश्चैवैष गणः सोऽहमिति यः सोऽभिसंप्लवः ॥ २८ ॥

22. b. vadhyate, A ; na-ba, T ; C omits. d. avyaktañ ca, A ; mi-gsal-ba yaṅ-ṅo, T.

23. b. jñoyā, A. c. sthito smi tritaye yantus, A ; gsum-po ḥdir gnas ḥgro-ba, T.

24. a. log-pa-las (viparyayād ?), T ; 'not believing', C. b. sandehād apr(?bh?)isambhavā, A ; the-tshom-las daṅ mṅon-ḥphyo-las, T ; 'doubt, excess', C.

25. a. log-pa (viparyayo ?), T ; 'not believing', C. d. mantavya, A.

27. a. bhāvan asaṁdigdhān, A ; the-tshom-med dṅos-rnams, T. c. the-tshom-med-pas (asaṁdehaḥ), T.

28. c. e.c. ; yaś caiveśa, A ; gaṅ-zhig grans de de ñid ṅed (=yaḥ sa gaṇaḥ sa evāham), T.

अविशेषं विशेषज्ञ प्रतिबुद्धाप्रबुद्धयोः ।
प्रकृतीनां च यो वेद सोऽविशेष इति स्मृतः ॥ २९ ॥

नमस्कारवषट्कारौ प्रोक्षणाभ्युक्षणादयः ।
अनुपाय इति प्राज्ञैरुपायज्ञ प्रवेदितः ॥ ३० ॥

सज्जते येन दुर्मेधा मनोवाग्बुद्धिकर्मभिः ।
विषयेष्वनभिष्वङ्ग सोऽभिष्वङ्ग इति स्मृतः ॥ ३१ ॥

ममेदमहमस्येति यद्दुःखमभिमन्यते ।
विज्ञेयोऽभ्यवपातः स संसारे येन पात्यते ॥ ३२ ॥

इत्यविद्यां हि विद्वान्स पञ्चपर्वां समीहते ।
तमो मोहं महामोहं तामिस्रद्वयमेव च ॥ ३३ ॥

तत्रालस्यं तमो विद्धि मोहं मृत्युं च जन्म च ।
महामोहस्त्वसंमोह काम इत्येव गम्यताम् ॥ ३४ ॥

यस्मादत्र च भूतानि प्रमुह्यन्ति महान्त्यपि ।
तस्मादेष महाबाहो महामोह इति स्मृतः ॥ ३५ ॥

तामिस्रमिति चाक्रोध क्रोधमेवाधिकुर्वते ।
विषादं चान्धतामिस्रमविषाद प्रचक्षते ॥ ३६ ॥

29. b. rab-rgyas rab-rgyas ma-yin-paḥi (prativṛddhāpravṛddhayoḥ), T.

33. ab. pañcaparvvān, A : de-ltar mkhas-kyis ma-rig-pa gnas-skabs lṅa ni rab-thob-ste (=evam vidvān pañcaparvām avidyāṁ prāpnoti), T ; 'all the ignorant men in the world are united in five classes', C.

34. b. moha, A. d. T omits eva ; ity avagamyatām, Co.

35. b. chen-por yaṅ ni (mahaty api ?), T. c. eṣa mābāho (one syllable short), A ; phyag-chen ḥdi-dag ni, T.

36. c. viṣāda, A. mi-śes mun-las gyur-pa ni (ajñatāmisram), T.

अनयाविद्यया बालः संयुक्तः पञ्चपर्वया ।
संसारे दुःखभूयिष्ठे जन्मस्वभिनिषिच्यते ॥ ३७ ॥
द्रष्टा श्रोता च मन्ता च कार्यकरणमेव च ।
अहमित्येवमागम्य संसारे परिवर्तते ॥ ३८ ॥
इहैभिर्हेतुभिर्धीमन् जन्मस्रोतः प्रवर्तते ।
हेत्वभावात्फलाभाव इति विज्ञातुमर्हसि ॥ ३९ ॥
तत्र सम्यङ्मतिर्विद्यान्मोक्षकाम चतुष्टयम् ।
प्रतिबुद्धाप्रबुद्धौ च व्यक्तमव्यक्तमेव च ॥ ४० ॥
यथावदेतद्विज्ञाय क्षेत्रज्ञो हि चतुष्टयम् ।
आजवंजवतां हित्वा प्राप्नोति पदमक्षरम् ॥ ४१ ॥
इत्यर्थं ब्राह्मणा लोके परमब्रह्मवादिनः ।
ब्रह्मचर्यं चरन्तीह ब्राह्मणान्वासयन्ति च ॥ ४२ ॥
इति वाक्यमिदं श्रुत्वा मुनेस्तस्य नृपात्मजः ।
अभ्युपायं च पप्रच्छ पदमेव च नैष्ठिकम् ॥ ४३ ॥
ब्रह्मचर्यमिदं चर्यं यथा यावच्च यत्र च ।
धर्मस्यास्य च पर्यन्तं भवान्व्याख्यातुमर्हति ॥ ४४ ॥

37. c. sdug-bsṅal gyur-pa-yi (duḥkhabhūte ?), T. d. bab-par-byed (abhinipātyate ?), T.

38. a. srotā, A. b. bya-ba daṅ ni rgyu ñid dag (kāryaṁ kāraṇam eva ca), T; 'I am that which does', C.

39. ity ebhi hetubhir, A; rgyu ḥdi-rnams-kyis ḥdi (for ḥdir), T. b. jamasrotaḥ, A; skye-baḥi rgyun-la, T; 'the stream of birth and death', C. c. hetvabhāva phalābhāva, A; rgyu med-pa-las ḥbras-bu med, T; 'if this cause does not exist, the fruit also does not exist', C; hetvabhāve, Co. (e.c.).

40. a. yaṅ-dag ḥgro-ba (samyaggatir), T; 'call this the right opinion', C. c. rab-rgyas rab-rgyas-min (prativṛddhāpravṛddhau), T.

41. c. °javatā, A.

इत्यराडो यथाशास्त्रं विस्पष्टार्थं समासतः ।
तमेवान्येन कल्पेन धर्ममस्मै व्यभाषत ॥ ४५ ॥
अयमादौ गृहान्मुक्त्वा भैक्षाकं लिङ्गमाश्रितः ।
समुदाचारविस्तीर्णं शीलमादाय वर्तते ॥ ४६ ॥
संतोषं परमास्थाय येन तेन यतस्ततः ।
विविक्तं सेवते वासं निर्द्वन्द्वः शास्त्रवित्कृती ॥ ४७ ॥
ततो रागाद्भयं दृष्ट्वा वैराग्याच्च परं शिवम् ।
निगृह्णन्निन्द्रियग्रामं यतते मनसः शमे ॥ ४८ ॥
अथो विविक्तं कामेभ्यो व्यापादादिभ्य एव च ।
विवेकजमवाप्नोति पूर्वध्यानं वितर्कवत् ॥ ४९ ॥
तच्च ध्यानसुखं प्राप्य तत्तदेव वितर्कयन् ।
अपूर्वसुखलाभेन ह्रियते बालिशो जनः ॥ ५० ॥
शमेनैवंविधेनायं कामद्वेषविगर्हिणा ।
ब्रह्मलोकमवाप्नोति परितोषेण वञ्चितः ॥ ५१ ॥
ज्ञात्वा विद्वान्वितर्कांस्तु मनःसंक्षोभकारकान् ।
तद्वियुक्तमवाप्नोति ध्यानं प्रीतिसुखान्वितम् ॥ ५२ ॥
ह्रियमाणस्तया प्रीत्या यो विशेषं न पश्यति ।
स्थानं भास्वरमाप्नोति देवेष्वाभास्वरेषु सः ॥ ५३ ॥

45. a. ity arāḍe yathāśāstra, A ; de-ltar thub-pas bstan-bcos lta (evaṁ munir yathāśāstraṁ), T ; ‘ then that Arāḍa spoke according to the śāstras ’, C.

46. b. ligam, A.

50. a. °sukhāṁ, A.

51. d. gnas-pa-ḥo (vāsitaḥ), T.

53. a. hriyamās tapā prītyā (one syllable short), A ; dgaḥ-ba de-yis phrogs-pa, T.

यस्तु प्रीतिसुखात्तस्माद्विवेचयति मानसम् ।
तृतीयं लभते ध्यानं सुखं प्रीतिविवर्जितम् ॥ ५४ ॥
यस्तु तस्मिन्सुखे मग्नो न विशेषाय यत्नवान् ।
शुभकृत्स्नैः स सामान्यं सुखं प्राप्नोति दैवतैः ॥ ५५ ॥
तादृशं सुखमासाद्य यो न रज्यत्युपेक्षकः ।
चतुर्थं ध्यानमाप्नोति सुखदुःखविवर्जितम् ॥ ५६ ॥
तत्र केचिद्व्यवस्यन्ति मोक्ष इत्यभिमानिनः ।
सुखदुःखपरित्यागादव्यापाराच्च चेतसः ॥ ५७ ॥
अस्य ध्यानस्य तु फलं समं देवैर्बृहत्फलैः ।
कथयन्ति बृहत्कालं बृहत्प्रज्ञापरीक्षकाः ॥ ५८ ॥
समाधेर्व्युत्थितस्तस्माद्दृष्ट्वा दोषांश्छरीरिणाम् ।
ज्ञानमारोहति प्राज्ञः शरीरविनिवृत्तये ॥ ५९ ॥
ततस्तज्ज्ञानमुत्सृज्य विशेषे कृतनिश्चयः ।
कामेभ्य इव स प्राज्ञो रूपादपि विरज्यते ॥ ६० ॥

54. d. dgaḥ-baḥi bde daṅ bral-ba (sukhaprītivivarjitam), T.

55. Not in T. c. śubhakṛsnaiḥ, A.

56. b. e.c. ; yo na rajyaty upekṣate, A ; gaṅ-zhig chags-min btaṅ-sñoms-śiṅ (equivalent uncertain), T.

57. b. ity api (rewritten and marked to show error) māninaḥ, A ; zhes mṅon-paḥi ṅa-rgyal-gyis, T. c. sdug-bsṅal zhi-phyir (°duḥkhapraśamanād ?), T.

58. b. bṛhatphaleḥ, A. c. bṛhatphalaṁ, A ; chen-poḥi dus-su (ḥbras-bu, Weller e.c.), T ; ‘ because of life there being for a long time, it is called *bṛhatphala* ’, C.

59. b. doṣāc charīriṇāṁ, A ; lus-skyes skyon-rnams (doṣāṁś charīrajān ?), T ; ‘ he sees that to have a body makes faults ’, C. c. bsam-gtan-la (dhyānam), T ; ‘ advancing further, he practises *prajñā* and satiated separates himself from the fourth trance ’, C. d. °vinivarttaye, A.

60. c. satprājño, A ; śes-rab-ldan de, T.

शरीरे खानि यान्यस्मिन्तान्यादौ परिकल्पयन् ।
घनेष्वपि ततो द्रव्येष्वाकाशमधिमुच्यते ॥ ६१ ॥

आकाशगतमात्मानं संक्षिप्य त्वपरो बुधः ।
तदेवानन्ततः पश्यन्विशेषमधिगच्छति ॥ ६२ ॥

अध्यात्मकुशलस्त्वन्यो निवर्त्यात्मानमात्मना ।
किंचिन्नास्तीति संपश्यन्नाकिंचन्य इति स्मृतः ॥ ६३ ॥

ततो मुञ्जादिषीकेव शकुनिः पञ्जरादिव ।
क्षेत्रज्ञो निःसृतो देहान्मुक्त इत्यभिधीयते ॥ ६४ ॥

एतत्तत्परमं ब्रह्म निर्लिङ्गं ध्रुवमक्षरम् ।
यन्मोक्ष इति तत्त्वज्ञाः कथयन्ति मनीषिणः ॥ ६५ ॥

इत्युपायश्च मोक्षश्च मया संदर्शितस्तव ।
यदि ज्ञातं यदि रुचिर्यथावत्प्रतिपद्यताम् ॥ ६६ ॥

जैगीषव्योऽथ जनको वृद्धश्चैव पराशरः ।
इमं पन्थानमासाद्य मुक्ता ह्यन्ये च मोक्षिणः ॥ ६७ ॥

इति तस्य स तद्वाक्यं गृहीत्वा तु विचार्य च ।
पूर्वहेतुबलप्राप्तः प्रत्युत्तरमुवाच ह ॥ ६८ ॥

61. ab. yāny asya tāny, A; lus ḥdi-la ni kha gaṅ-du de-la yoṅs-su-rtog-pa-ste (=śarīre 'smin khāni yatra tatra parikalpayan), T.

62. a. ākāśag(?)atam, A; nam-mkhar soṅ-baḥi, T. b. gzhan-du blo-ldan-gyis (=paratra budhaḥ), T.

63. a. kuśale(corrected to la)svanyo, A; T omits tu. b. nivatyā°, A, d. ākiṁcinya, A.

64. a. iśīkeva, A. c. nisṛto, A; ḥthon-pa-las (for la), T.

66. c. e.c. Böhtlingk; ruci, A. d. rtogs-par mdzod (pratibudhyatām ?). T; 'he who deeply believes should learn', C.

68. a. de-yi dam-paḥi tshig ḥdi (idaṁ tasya ca sadvākyaṁ), T. b. e.c. Böhtlingk; gṛhītvā na vicārya ca, A; rnam-par dpyod-pa yaṅ bzuṅ-nas (equivalent uncertain), T. c. °prāpta, A.

श्रुतं ज्ञानमिदं सूक्ष्मं परतः परतः शिवम् ।
क्षेत्रज्ञस्यापरित्यागादवैम्येतदनैष्ठिकम् ॥ ६९ ॥

विकारप्रकृतिभ्यो हि क्षेत्रज्ञं मुक्तमप्यहम् ।
मन्ये प्रसवधर्माणं बीजधर्माणमेव च ॥ ७० ॥

विशुद्धो यद्यपि ह्यात्मा निर्मुक्त इति कल्प्यते ।
भूयः प्रत्ययसद्भावादमुक्तः स भविष्यति ॥ ७१ ॥

ऋतुभूम्यम्बुविरहाद्यथा बीजं न रोहति ।
रोहति प्रत्ययैस्तैस्तैस्तद्वत्सोऽपि मतो मम ॥ ७२ ॥

यत्कर्माज्ञानतृष्णानां त्यागान्मोक्षश्च कल्प्यते ।
अत्यन्तस्तत्परित्यागः सत्यात्मनि न विद्यते ॥ ७३ ॥

हित्वा हित्वा त्रयमिदं विशेषस्तूपलभ्यते ।
आत्मनस्तु स्थितिर्यत्र तत्र सूक्ष्ममिदं त्रयम् ॥ ७४ ॥

सूक्ष्मत्वाच्चैव दोषाणामव्यापाराच्च चेतसः ।
दीर्घत्वादायुषश्चैव मोक्षस्तु परिकल्प्यते ॥ ७५ ॥

अहंकारपरित्यागो यश्चैष परिकल्प्यते ।
सत्यात्मनि परित्यागो नाहंकारस्य विद्यते ॥ ७६ ॥

69. a. śūkṣma, A. c. kṣetrajya(?sya or sva rewritten)syāparityād (one syllable short), A ; śiṅ-śes yoṅs-su ma-btaṅ-phyir, T ; ‘ from non-abandonment of the cause-knower ’, C.

71. b. nimukta, A.

72. a. e.c. ; °ambuvihārād, A ; chu me-las (for med-pas), T ; ‘ when the season, soil, water, heat, wind are separated from it ’, C.

73. a. ṣat karmma°, A ; gaṅ-zhig . . . las, T.

74. c. ātmānas tu sthiti yatra, A.

75. a. śūkṣmatvāc, A. c. tshe ni . . . kyaṅ (āyuṣaś cāpi ?), T.

संख्यादिभिरमुक्तश्च निर्गुणो न भवत्ययम् ।
तस्मादसति नैर्गुण्ये नास्य मोक्षोऽभिधीयते ॥ ७७ ॥
गुणिनो हि गुणानां च व्यतिरेको न विद्यते ।
रूपोष्णाभ्यां विरहितो न ह्यग्निरुपलभ्यते ॥ ७८ ॥
प्राग्देहान्न भवेद्देही प्राग्गुणेभ्यस्तथा गुणी ।
तस्मादादौ विमुक्तः सन् शरीरी बध्यते पुनः ॥ ७९ ॥
क्षेत्रज्ञो विशरीरश्च ज्ञो वा स्यादज्ञ एव वा ।
यदि ज्ञो ज्ञेयमस्यास्ति ज्ञेये सति न मुच्यते ॥ ८० ॥
अथाज्ञ इति सिद्धो वः कल्पितेन किमात्मना ।
विनापि ह्यात्मनाज्ञानं प्रसिद्धं काष्ठकुड्यवत् ॥ ८१ ॥
परतः परतस्त्यागो यस्मात्तु गुणवान् स्मृतः ।
तस्मात्सर्वपरित्यागान्मन्ये कृत्स्नां कृतार्थताम् ॥ ८२ ॥
इति धर्ममराडस्य विदित्वा न तुतोष सः ।
अकृत्स्नमिति विज्ञाय ततः प्रतिजगाम ह ॥ ८३ ॥
विशेषमथ शुश्रूषुरुद्रकस्याश्रमं ययौ ।
आत्मग्राहाच्च तस्यापि जगृहे न स दर्शनम् ॥ ८४ ॥

77. c. nairgguṇyai, A; de-phyir yon-tan-med gyur-na (=tasmāt sati nairguṇye), T; ‘since this *guṇa* remains’, C.

79. c. kasmād, Co. (e.c.); de-phyir, T; ‘therefore’, C.

81. c. bdag daṅ bral yaṅ śes-pa ni (vināpy ātmanā jñānam), T; ‘to have knowledge without the *ātman*, the *ātman* then is the same as wood or stone’, C.

82. T omits b, c and d. d. kṛtsnāṁ kṛtāṁ (followed by faint traces of two characters, rthataṁ ?), A; ‘what one does is then finality’, C.

83. b. tutoṣa sa, A. c. akṛtsna iti, Hultzsch.

84. b. udrakasmā° (originally syā ?), A. c. ātmagrāhāt tu, Cappeller.

संज्ञासंज्ञित्वयोर्दोषं ज्ञात्वा हि मुनिरुद्रकः ।
आकिंचन्यात्परं लेभेऽसंज्ञासंज्ञात्मिकां गतिम् ॥ ८५ ॥
यस्माच्चालम्बने सूक्ष्मे संज्ञासंज्ञे ततः परम् ।
नासंज्ञी नैव संज्ञीति तस्मात्तत्रगतस्पृहः ॥ ८६ ॥
यतश्च बुद्धिस्तत्रैव स्थितान्यत्राप्रचारिणी ।
सूक्ष्मापट्वी ततस्तत्र नासंज्ञित्वं न संज्ञिता ॥ ८७ ॥
यस्माच्च तदपि प्राप्य पुनरावर्तते जगत् ।
बोधिसत्त्वः परं प्रेप्सुस्तस्मादुद्रकमत्यजत् ॥ ८८ ॥
ततो हित्वाश्रमं तस्य श्रेयोऽर्थी कृतनिश्चयः ।
भेजे गयस्य राजर्षेर्नगरीसंज्ञमाश्रमम् ॥ ८९ ॥
अथ नैरञ्जनातीरे शुचौ शुचिपराक्रमः ।
चकार वासमेकान्तविहाराभिरतिर्मुनिः ॥ ९० ॥

85. a. °tvayo ddoṣañ, A. cd. A omits avagraha ; ḥdu-śes ḥdu-śes-med bdag-min . . . thob, T ; 'separating himself from abiding in reflection and non-reflection ', C.

86. a. śūkṣme, A. b. ḥdu-śes ḥdu-śes-med-las gzhan (=saṁjñāsaṁjñitvayoḥ param, omitting tataḥ), T. c. T omits iti. d. der ni re-ḥdod-med (tatra gataspṛhaḥ), T ; Co. divides like T.

87. a. tatreva, A. c. e.c. ; sūkṣmā 'padvī, A ; phra-zhiṅ rno-ldan (sūkṣmā paṭvī), T.

88. a. de-phyir (tasmāc), T. e.c. Böhtlingk ; tam api, A. prāptya, A. c. bodhisatvaṁ, A.

89. cd. rājarṣe nagarī°, A.

90. d. °vihāṁ(corrected to ha ?)rā°, A.

* * * तत्पूर्वं पञ्चेन्द्रियवशोद्धतान् ।
तपः * * व्रतिनो भिक्षून् पञ्च निरैक्षत ॥ ९१ ॥

ते चोपतस्थुर्दृष्ट्वात्र भिक्षवस्तं मुमुक्षवः ।
पुण्यार्जितधनारोग्यमिन्द्रियार्था इवेश्वरम् ॥ ९२ ॥

संपूज्यमानस्तैः प्रह्वैर्विनयादनुवर्तिभिः ।
तद्वशस्थायिभिः शिष्यैर्लोलैर्मन इवेन्द्रियैः ॥ ९३ ॥

मृत्युजन्मान्तकरणे स्यादुपायोऽयमित्यथ ।
दुष्कराणि समारेभे तपांस्यनशनेन सः ॥ ९४ ॥

उपवासविधीन्नैकान् कुर्वन्नरदुराचरान् ।
वर्षाणि षट् शमप्रेप्सुरकरोत्कार्श्यमात्मनः ॥ ९५ ॥

अन्नकालेषु चैकैकैः स कोलतिलतण्डुलैः ।
अपारपारसंसारपारं प्रेप्सुरपारयत् ॥ ९६ ॥

91. A omits this verse and C puts it before verse 90. a. de-nas de ni sṅar brten-zhiṅ (=tatas tatpūrvam āśritān), T. b. dbaṅ-po lṅa-yi dbaṅ-las kheṅs, T. c. mun-pas bsñen-paḥi brtul-zhugs-can (=tamaḥsaṁśrayavratinaḥ), T. d. dge-sloṅ lṅa-rnams ṅes (so Peking edition, des Weller) gzigs-so, T. 'The five bhikṣus had gone there before him. He saw the five bhikṣus, virtuously restraining all the senses, holding to the prohibitions, practising *tapas*, dwelling in that penance grove', C.

92. a. pañcopatasthur, A; dge-sloṅ de-rnams . . . ñe-bar-gnas, T. b. T omits mumukṣavaḥ and adds api (kyaṅ); 'knowing him with diligent mind to be seeking *mokṣa*', C.

93. a. °māṇas, A. ab. prahvai vvinayānatapūrttibhiḥ, A; rab-tu (for rab-dud or rab-btud) de-rnams-kyis . . . rnam-par dul-las rjes-su-ḥjug, T; 'in all humility . . . never separating themselves', C. c. tadvaṁśa°, A; deḥi dbaṅ-gyi, T. d. ivaindriyaiḥ, A.

95. c. e.c.; vaṣāṇi ṣaṭ kamaprepsur, A; las ni thob-bzhed lo drug-tu (varṣāṇi ṣaṭ karmaprepsur), T; 'tranquil (*śānta*) and meditating in trance, so he passed six years', C.

देहादपचयस्तेन तपसा तस्य यः कृतः ।
स एवोपचयो भूयस्तेजसास्य कृतोऽभवत् ॥ ९७ ॥
कृशोऽप्यकृशकीर्तिश्रीर्ह्लादं चक्रेऽन्यचक्षुषाम् ।
कुमुदानामिव शरच्छुक्लपक्षादिचन्द्रमाः ॥ ९८ ॥
त्वगस्थिशेषो निःशेषैर्मेदःपिशितशोणितैः ।
क्षीणोऽप्यक्षीणगाम्भीर्यः समुद्र इव स व्यभात् ॥ ९९ ॥
अथ कष्टतपःस्पष्टव्यर्थक्लिष्टतनुर्मुनिः ।
भवभीरुरिमां चक्रे बुद्धिं बुद्धत्वकाङ्क्षया ॥ १०० ॥
नायं धर्मो विरागाय न बोधाय न मुक्तये ।
जम्बुमूले मया प्राप्तो यस्तदा स विधिर्ध्रुवः ॥ १०१ ॥
न चासौ दुर्बलेनाप्तुं शक्यमित्यागतादरः ।
शरीरबलवृद्ध्यर्थमिदं भूयोऽन्वचिन्तयत् ॥ १०२ ॥
क्षुत्पिपासाश्रमक्लान्तः श्रमादस्वस्थमानसः ।
प्राप्नुयान्मनसावाप्यं फलं कथमनिर्वृतः ॥ १०३ ॥
निर्वृतिः प्राप्यते सम्यक् सततेन्द्रियतर्पणात् ।
संतर्पितेन्द्रियतया मनःस्वास्थ्यमवाप्यते ॥ १०४ ॥

97. d. kṛto bhavet, A ; byas gyur, T.

98. ab. °śrī hlādaṁ, A.

99. Not in C. b. mmedapiśitaśonitaiḥ, A.

100. c. bhavabhīkar (very like rur) imāñ, A ; srid-las ḥjigs-pa, T.

101. d. sa vidhir ddhruvaṁḥ (anusvara added later), A ; de ṅes-pa yin (sa dhruvaḥ, omitting vidhir), T.

102. a. na cāso durbbalenāptaṁ, A. b. nus-pa med phyir gus ḥoṅs-śiṅ (=na . . . śakyaṁ hy āgatādaraḥ), T.

103. a. skom-pas yoṅs-bcer-zhiṅ (°pipāsāpariklāntaḥ), T. b. asvatth- (corrected to sth)amāsanaḥ, A ; raṅ-gnas med-paḥi sems, T. d. ldog-pa med-pa (=anivṛttaḥ), T.

104. a. gnas-pa ḥthob-pa-ste (saṁsthitiḥ prāpyate ?), T.

स्वस्थप्रसन्नमनसः समाधिरुपपद्यते ।
समाधियुक्तचित्तस्य ध्यानयोगः प्रवर्तते ॥ १०५ ॥
ध्यानप्रवर्तनाद्धर्माः प्राप्यन्ते यैरवाप्यते ।
दुर्लभं शान्तमजरं परं तदमृतं पदम् ॥ १०६ ॥
तस्मादाहारमूलोऽयमुपाय इतिनिश्चयः ।
आहारकरणे धीरः कृत्वामितमतिर्मतिम् ॥ १०७ ॥
स्नातो नैरञ्जनातीरादुत्ततार शनैः कृशः ।
भक्त्यावनतशाखाग्रैर्दत्तहस्तस्तटद्रुमैः ॥ १०८ ॥
अथ गोपाधिपसुता दैवतैरभिचोदिता ।
उद्भूतहृदयानन्दा तत्र नन्दबलागमत् ॥ १०९ ॥
सितशङ्खोज्ज्वलभुजा नीलकम्बलवासिनी ।
सफेनमालानीलाम्बुर्यमुनेव सरिद्वरा ॥ ११० ॥
सा श्रद्धावर्धितप्रीतिर्विकसल्लोचनोत्पला ।
शिरसा प्रणिपत्यैनं ग्राहयामास पायसम् ॥ १११ ॥
कृत्वा तदुपभोगेन प्राप्तजन्मफलां स ताम् ।
बोधिप्राप्तौ समर्थोऽभूत्संतर्पितषडिन्द्रियः ॥ ११२ ॥

107. ab. yam apā iti (one syllable short), A; ḥdi ni thabs zhes, T. c. āsu(? corrected to hā ?)rakaraṇe dhā(?ī?)raḥ, A; bzaḥ-ba byed-la brtan-pa ni, T.

108. a. nīrañjanā°, A. d. taṭaṁdramaiḥ, A; ḥgram-gyi ljon-śiṅ, T (see note in translation).

109. b. devatair, A.

110. ab. °śaṁkhojvalabhujā līla°, A; sṅon-po, T.

111. a. sā śrarddhā°, A. b. °locanātpalā, A. c. sirasā pratapaty enaṁ, A; de-la mgo-yis rab-btud-nas, T; 'she bowed her head at the Bodhisattva's feet', C.

112. c. bodhiprāpto, A.

पर्याप्ताप्यानमूर्तिश्च सार्धं स्वयशसा मुनिः ।
कान्तिधैर्ये बभारैकः शशाङ्कार्णवयोर्द्वयोः ॥ ११३ ॥

आवृत्त इति विज्ञाय तं जहुः पञ्च भिक्षवः ।
मनीषिणमिवात्मानं निर्मुक्तं पञ्च धातवः ॥ ११४ ॥

व्यवसायद्वितीयोऽथ शाद्वलास्तीर्णभूतलम् ।
सोऽश्वत्थमूलं प्रययौ बोधाय कृतनिश्चयः ॥ ११५ ॥

ततस्तदानीं गजराजविक्रमः
पदस्वनेनानुपमेन बोधितः ।
महामुनेरागतबोधिनिश्चयो
जगाद कालो भुजगोत्तमः स्तुतिम् ॥ ११६ ॥

यथा मुने त्वच्चरणावपीडिता
मुहुर्मुहुर्निष्टनतीव मेदिनी ।
यथा च ते राजति सूर्यवत्प्रभा
ध्रुवं त्वमिष्टं फलमद्य भोक्ष्यसे ॥ ११७ ॥

113. b. sārddha suyasasā, A ; raṅ-gi grags bcas, T. c. dhaiye kabhāraikaḥ, A ; brtan-pa gcig-pos bzuṅ, T. d. śaśāṁkārṇṇavadvardvayoḥ, A ; nus-gyur rgya-mtsho gñis-dag-gi (śaśākārṇavayor dvayoḥ), T.

114. b. jahruḥ, A ; dor, T. d. grol-ba-la (nirmuktau ?), T.

115. b. śāḍvalā°, A ; rtsva ḥjam bkram-paḥi (śādvalākīrṇa°), T.

116. a. tadīnā (corrected to tadānīṁ), A. ab. padasvamenā°, A ; ḥgros-mṅaḥ-baḥi dpe-med zabs-kyi sgra-yis (°vikramapadasvanenānupamena), T ; ' stepping like a lion (mṛgarāja°?), at every step the earth was shaken and moved ', C. d. bhujagottama, A.

117. b. mmuhu nistanatīva, A. c. rājani, A ; sṅan-ba-ste, T. d. dhruva, A. ḥdod-paḥi go-ḥphaṅ mkhyen-pa ñid (iṣṭaṁ padam eva bhotsyase, or bhakṣyase ?), T.

यथा भ्रमन्त्यो दिवि चाषपङ्क्तयः
प्रदक्षिणं त्वां कमलाक्ष कुर्वते ।
यथा च सौम्या दिवि वान्ति वायव-
स्त्वमद्य बुद्धो नियतं भविष्यसि ॥ ११८ ॥

ततो भुजङ्गप्रवरेण संस्तुत-
स्तृणान्युपादाय शुचीनि लावकात् ।
कृतप्रतिज्ञो निषसाद बोधये
महातरोर्मूलमुपाश्रितः शुचेः ॥ ११९ ॥

ततः स पर्यङ्कमकम्प्यमुत्तमं
बबन्ध सुप्तोरगभोगपिण्डितम् ।
भिनद्मि तावद्भुवि नैतदासनं
न यामि यावत्कृतकृत्यतामिति ॥ १२० ॥

ततो ययुर्मुदमतुलां दिवौकसो
ववाशिरे न मृगगणाः न पक्षिणः ।
न सस्वनुर्वनतरवोऽनिलाहताः
कृतासने भगवति निश्चितात्मनि ॥ १२१ ॥

इति बुद्धचरिते महाकाव्येऽराडदर्शनो नाम द्वादशः सर्गः ॥ १२ ॥

118. a. cāya(very like ṣa)paṅktayaḥ, A ; khug-rtaḥi phreṅ-ba-rnams, T ; 'five hundred blue kites in flocks', C. cd. vānta vāy(?v?)ayaḥ tvam, A ; rluṅ-rnams . . . ḥgro-ba-ste khyod-kyis (yānti vāyavas tvam), T.

119. a. sa stutas, A ; yaṅ-dag bstod-pa, T. b. lco-ga-las (lābakāt), T.

120. a. payaṅkanu(corrected to ma)kampyam, A. d. tāvat, A ; ji-srid, T.

121. a. divokaso, A. b. vavāsire ṇa (corrected on margin to na), A ; gnas-par ma-gyur (na vavāsire, to vas, 'dwell' !), T ; 'one and all the beasts and birds were quiet and uttered no sound at all', C. d. kṛtātmane, A ; gdan mdzad, T.

CANTO XIII

तस्मिन्विमोक्षाय कृतप्रतिज्ञे राजर्षिवंशप्रभवे महर्षौ ।
तत्रोपविष्टे प्रजहर्ष लोकस्तत्रास सद्धर्मरिपुस्तु मारः ॥ १ ॥

यं कामदेवं प्रवदन्ति लोके चित्रायुधं पुष्पशरं तथैव ।
कामप्रचाराधिपतिं तमेव मोक्षद्विषं मारमुदाहरन्ति ॥ २ ॥

तस्यात्मजा विभ्रमहर्षदर्पा-
स्तिस्रोऽरतिप्रीतितृषश्च कन्याः ।
पप्रच्छुरेनं मनसो विकारं
स तांश्च ताश्चैव वचोऽभ्युवाच ॥ ३ ॥

असौ मुनिर्निश्चयवर्म बिभ्रत्सत्त्वायुधं बुद्धिशरं विकृष्य ।
जिगीषुरास्ते विषयान्मदीयान्तस्मादयं मे मनसो विषादः ॥ ४ ॥

1. a. tasmāya kṛta° (three syllables short), A; der ni rnam-par-thar-phyir dam-bcaḥ mdzad-pa-na, T; 'established every firm vow that he would accomplish the path of liberation', C. b. rājarṣivaśa°, A. c. tratropa°, A. d. der ni . . . gyur-te (divides tatra=āsa), T.

2. a. ya kāma°, A. d. mokṣadviyam, A; thar-paḥi dgra-bo, T; 'hating those who strive for liberation', C.

3. b. e.c.; A, T and apparently C omit the avagraha. c. papracchur ena, A. d. vaco bhyuthāsa (meant for bhyuvāca ?), A; tshig mṅon-par-smras, T.

4. a. nniścayadharmma bibhrata, A; ṅes-paḥi go-cha-rnams gzuṅ-zhin T. b. bsdogs-byas-nas ('making ready', ? viṣajya), T; 'grasping', C. c. jigīṣuc āste, A. d. gaṅ-phyir . . rnam-par-ḥgyur (yasmād . . . vikāraḥ), T.

यदि ह्यसौ मामभिभूय याति लोकाय चाख्यात्यपवर्गमार्गम् ।
शून्यस्ततोऽयं विषयो ममाद्य वृत्ताच्च्युतस्येव विदेहभर्तुः ॥ ५ ॥

तद्यावदेवैष न लब्धचक्षुर्मद्गोचरे तिष्ठति यावदेव ।
यास्यामि तावद्व्रतमस्य भेत्तुं सेतुं नदीवेग इवातिवृद्धः ॥ ६ ॥

ततो धनुः पुष्पमयं गृहीत्वा शरान् जगन्मोहकरांश्च पञ्च ।
सोऽश्वत्थमूलं ससुतोऽभ्यगच्छदस्वास्थ्यकारी मनसः प्रजानाम् ॥ ७ ॥

अथ प्रशान्तं मुनिमासनस्थं पारं तितीर्षुं भवसागरस्य ।
विषज्य सव्यं करमायुधाग्रे क्रीडन् शरेणेदमुवाच मारः ॥ ८ ॥

उत्तिष्ठ भोः क्षत्रिय मृत्युभीत चर स्वधर्मं त्यज मोक्षधर्मम् ।
बाणैश्च यज्ञैश्च विनीय लोकं लोकात्पदं प्राप्नुहि वासवस्य ॥ ९ ॥

पन्था हि निर्यातुमयं यशस्यो
यो वाहितः पूर्वतमैर्नरेन्द्रैः ।
जातस्य राजर्षिकुले विशाले
भैक्षाकमश्लाघ्यमिदं प्रपत्तुम् ॥ १० ॥

5. a. yadi hṛ(?hya?)sau, A. c. śūnyas vato 'yam, A.

7. b. kun-tu rmoṅs-par byed-paḥi mdaḥ lṅa-rnams bzuṅ-nas (=saṁmohakarān śarān pañca gṛhītvā), T.

8. a. munim ātmasaṁtham, A ; thub-pa . . gdan-la bzhugs-pa-la, T. b. srid-pa ḥkhor-baḥi (=bhavasaṁsārasya), T. c. savya, A. brduṅs-nas (vihatya ?), T.

9. a. utiṣtha, A. c. bāṇeś ca (gap for three missing characters) vinīya lokān, A ; mdaḥ daṅ mchod-sbyin-rnams-kyis ḥjig-rten pham-byas-nas(=text, but vijitya for vinīya ?), T. d. lokān parān prāpnuhi, A ; ḥjig-rten-dag-nas . . . go-ḥphaṅ thob-par mdzod, T ; 'practise fighting, alms, happiness and power(?) ; moderating-subduing (vinīya) everything in the world, thereafter obtain the joys of a heavenly birth ', C.

10. a. yasasyo, A. d. bhaikṣyākam, A.

अथाद्य नोत्तिष्ठसि निश्चितात्मन्
भव स्थिरो मा विमुचः प्रतिज्ञाम् ।
मयोद्यतो ह्येष शरः स एव
यः शूर्पके मीनरिपौ विमुक्तः ॥ ११ ॥

स्पृष्टः स चानेन कथंचिदैडः सोमस्य नप्ताप्यभवद्विचित्तः ।
स चाभवच्छन्तनुरस्वतन्त्रः क्षीणे युगे किं बत दुर्बलोऽन्यः ॥ १२ ॥
तत्क्षिप्रमुत्तिष्ठ लभस्व संज्ञां बाणो ह्ययं तिष्ठति लेलिहानः ।
प्रियाविधेयेषु रतिप्रियेषु यं चक्रवाकेष्विव नोत्सृजामि ॥ १३ ॥
इत्येवमुक्तोऽपि यदा निरास्थो नैवासनं शाक्यमुनिर्बिभेद ।
शरं ततोऽस्मै विससर्ज मारः कन्याश्च कृत्वा पुरतः सुतांश्च ॥१४॥
तस्मिंस्तु बाणेऽपि स विप्रमुक्ते चकार नास्थां न धृतेश्चचाल ।
दृष्ट्वा तथैनं विषसाद मारश्चिन्तापरीतश्च शनैर्जगाद ॥ १५ ॥
शैलेन्द्रपुत्रीं प्रति येन विद्धो देवोऽपि शम्भुश्चलितो बभूव ।
न चिन्तयत्येष तमेव बाणं किं स्यादचित्तो न शरः स एषः ॥१६॥
तस्मादयं नार्हति पुष्पबाणं न हर्षणं नापि रतेर्नियोगम् ।
अर्हत्ययं भूतगणैरसौम्यैः संत्रासनातर्जनताडनानि ॥ १७ ॥

11. a. notiṣṭhasi, A. d. sūrpp(?yy?)ake, A ; sūrbaka-la, T.

12. a. pṛṣṭaḥ, A ; reg-pa, T ; 'just touched as by a breath of wind', C. c. chāntanur, A.

13. a. utiṣṭha, A. d. cakravākeṣv api, A ; ṅaṅ-pa-rnams-la bzhin-du, T.

15. c. viṣaśāda, A.

16. b. deyaśvi śambhuś, A ; bde-ḥbyuṅ lha yaṅ, T. d. śaraḥ sa eva, Gawroński.

17. a. ayaṁ nārhasi, A ; ḥdi ḥos-pa ma-yin-zhiṅ, T. b. rato niyogaṁ, A ; . . . sbyor-ba (two syllables short, niyogam), T ; 'it is not by means of . . . these three Devī daughters of mine', C. c. asyai(? for sau)myaiḥ, A ; zhi-ba ma-yin, T.

सस्मार मारश्च ततः स्वसैन्यं
विघ्नं शमे शाक्यमुनेश्चिकीर्षन् ।
नानाश्रयाश्चानुचराः परीयुः
शलद्रुमप्रासगदासिहस्ताः ॥ १८ ॥

वराहमीनाश्वखरोष्ट्रवक्त्रा व्याघ्रर्क्षसिंहद्विरदाननाश्च ।
एकेक्षणा नैकमुखास्त्रिशीर्षा लम्बोदराश्चैव पृषोदराश्च ॥ १९ ॥

अजानुसक्था घटजानवश्च दंष्ट्रायुधाश्चैव नखायुधाश्च ।
करङ्कवक्त्रा बहुमूर्तयश्च भग्नार्धवक्त्राश्च महामुखाश्च ॥ २० ॥

भस्मारुणा लोहितबिन्दुचित्राः खट्वाङ्गहस्ता हरिधूम्रकेशाः ।
लम्बस्रजो वारणलम्बकर्णाश्चर्माम्बराश्चैव निरम्बराश्च ॥ २१ ॥

श्वेतार्धवक्त्रा हरितार्धकायास्ताम्राश्च धूम्रा हरयोऽसिताश्च ।
व्यालोत्तरासङ्गभुजास्तथैव प्रघुष्टघण्टाकुलमेखलाश्च ॥ २२ ॥

18. b. e.c.; vighnaṁ same śākyamune cikīrṣan, A; śākya thub-pa-ḥ bgegs ni mñam-por byed ḥdod-po (vighnaṁ same, or samaṁ, śākyamuneś cikīrṣan), T. c. sna-tshogs bsam-pa (nānāśayāś ?), T. d. e.c.; (parīyuḥ) valadruma°, A; śiṅ-rtse ljon-śiṅ-rtse gsum-mdun (two syllables in excess, = ?), T; 'grasping lances, holding knives and swords, grasping trees', C; śara°, Co.

19. a. T omits aśva (reading varāhamīnāś ca ?). d. daṅ gsus-pa che-ba-rnams (mahodarāś ca ?), T; 'some with great bellies and long bodies', C; kṛśodarāś ca, Windisch.

20. a. e.c. Lüders and Kern; ajāmusakthā, A; brla-rnams pus-moḥi bar-du (ājānusakthā), T. b. draṣtrā°, A. c. kabandhahastā, A; keṅ-rus gdoṅ-can, T; 'some with faces that had neither heads nor eyes' (or 'without heads, eyes (var. breasts), or faces'), C.

21. a. tāmrāruṇā, A; thal-skya-rnams, T; 'some became ash-earth colour', C. c. ḥphoṅs ḥphyaṅ-rnams (=lambasphico, Weller amends to ḥphreṅ ḥphyaṅ-rnams=text), T; 'some with mountainous lumps on their backs', C. glaṅ-poḥi rna-baḥi rna-ba-rnams (vāraṇakarṇakarṇāś), T.

22. b. dhūmra, A. ljaṅ-khu dkar-po-rnams (harayaḥ sitāś ca), T. c. sbrul-gyi śam-thabs-rnams (vyālāntarāsaṅga° ?), T.

तालप्रमाणाश्च गृहीतशूला दंष्ट्राकरालाश्च शिशुप्रमाणाः ।
उरभ्रवक्त्राश्च विहंगमाक्षा मार्जारवक्त्राश्च मनुष्यकायाः ॥ २३ ॥
प्रकीर्णकेशाः शिखिनोऽर्धमुण्डा रक्ताम्बरा व्याकुलवेष्टनाश्च ।
प्रहृष्टवक्त्रा भृकुटीमुखाश्च तेजोहराश्चैव मनोहराश्च ॥ २४ ॥
केचिद्व्रजन्तो भृशमाववल्गुरन्योऽन्यमापुप्लुविरे तथान्ये ।
चिक्रीडुराकाशगताश्च केचित्केचिच्च चेरुस्तरुमस्तकेषु ॥ २५ ॥
ननर्त कश्चिद्भ्रमयंस्त्रिशूलं कश्चिद्विपुस्फूर्ज गदां विकर्षन् ।
हर्षेण कश्चिद्वृषवन्ननर्द कश्चित्प्रजज्वाल तनूरुहेभ्यः ॥ २६ ॥
एवंविधा भूतगणाः समन्तात्तद्बोधिमूलं परिवार्य तस्थुः ।
जिघृक्षवश्चैव जिघांसवश्च भर्तुर्नियोगं परिपालयन्तः ॥ २७ ॥
तं प्रेक्ष्य मारस्य च पूर्वरात्रे शाक्यर्षभस्यैव च युद्धकालम् ।
न द्यौश्चकाशे पृथिवी चकम्पे प्रजज्वलुश्चैव दिशः सशब्दाः ॥२८॥
विष्वग्ववौ वायुरुदीर्णवेगस्तारा न रेजुर्न बभौ शशाङ्कः ।
तमश्च भूयो विततान रात्रिः सर्वे च संचुक्षुभिरे समुद्राः ॥ २९ ॥

23. Not in C. b. daṁṣṭrā°, A. c. vihaṁgamāś ca, A ; bya-yi mig-can-rnams, T.

24. a. ral-pa daṅ byi-bo-rnams (śikhino 'tha muṇḍā ?), T. b. rajvambarā, A ; gos dmar-rnams, T. d. 'Some snatching men's lives' (vayoharāś ca ?), C.

25. b. e.c. Cowell ; āpuplutire, A ; C and T ambiguous.

26. a. bhramayan triśūlaṁ, A. b. e.c. Lüders ; kaścid va (or dha) pusphūrja, A ; T ambiguous.

27. b. e.c. Cowell ; tam bodhimulaṁ, A ; byaṅ-chub sems-dpaḥ de-la (taṁ bodhisattvaṁ), T ; 'surrounded the bodhi tree', C. c. 'Others again wished to eat him up' (jighatsavaś ca ?), C. d. bharttu nniyogam, A. rab-tu-skyoṅ-bar byed-pa-ste (pratipālayantaḥ ?), T.

28. a. prekṣyā, A. c. na dyo cakāśe, A ; na-mkhaḥ gsal-ba ma-yin, T.

29. a. viśvag, A. b. reju nna, A. c. e.c. Cappeller ; vitatāra rātri (or tre, top of letter cut off), A ; mtshan-mor . . . rgyas gyur-la (vitatāna rātrau ?), T.

महीभृतो धर्मपराश्च नागा महामुनेर्विघ्नममृष्यमाणाः ।
मारं प्रति क्रोधविवृत्तनेत्रा निःशश्वसुश्चैव जजृम्भिरे च ॥ ३० ॥

शुद्धाधिवासा विबुधर्षयस्तु सद्धर्मसिद्ध्यर्थमभिप्रवृत्ताः ।
मारेऽनुकम्पां मनसा प्रचक्रुर्विरागभावात्तु न रोषमीयुः ॥ ३१ ॥

तद्बोधिमूलं समवेक्ष्य कीर्णं हिंसात्मना मारबलेन तेन ।
धर्मात्मभिर्लोकविमोक्षकामैर्बभूव हाहाकृतमन्तरीक्षे ॥ ३२ ॥

उपप्लवं धर्मविधेस्तु तस्य दृष्ट्वा स्थितं मारबलं महर्षिः ।
न चुक्षुभे नापि ययौ विकारं मध्ये गवां सिंह इवोपविष्टः ॥३३॥

मारस्ततो भूतचमूमुदीर्णामाज्ञापयामास भयाय तस्य ।
स्वैः स्वैः प्रभावैरथ सास्य सेना तद्धैर्यभेदाय मतिं चकार ॥ ३४ ॥

केचिच्चलन्नैकविलम्बिजिह्वा-
स्तीक्ष्णाग्रदंष्ट्रा हरिमण्डलाक्षाः ।
विदारितास्याः स्थिरशङ्कुकर्णाः
संत्रासयन्तः किल नाम तस्थुः ॥ ३५ ॥

तेभ्यः स्थितेभ्यः स तथाविधेभ्यः रूपेण भावेन च दारुणेभ्यः ।
न विव्यथे नोद्विविजे महर्षिः क्रीडत्सुबालेभ्य इवोद्धतेभ्यः ॥३६॥

30. a. chos-dag ḥdzin-paḥi (dharmadharāś, or °bhṛtaś), T. b. mahāmunir, A. °mānāh, A.

31. a. śuddhāddhivāsā, A. b. °artham iva pravṛttāḥ, A ; don-du mṅon-par-zhugs-pa-rnams, T. c. °kampā, A.

32. c. dharmmātmabhi lloka°, A. d. antarikṣaṁ (anusvara added later), A ; na-mkhaḥ-dag-la, T.

33. a. dharmmavis tu (one syllable short), A ; chos-kyi cho-ga, T. d. gāvāṁ, A.

34. cd. senān taddhairya°, A.

35. a. calaṁnnaika°, A. ab. °jihvā tīkṣṇogradraṁṣṭrā, A ; mche-baḥi rtse-mo-rnams rno, T.

कश्चित्ततो रोषविवृत्तदृष्टिस्तस्मै गदामुद्यमयांचकार ।
तस्तम्भ बाहुः सगदस्ततोऽस्य पुरंदरस्येव पुरा सवज्रः ॥ ३७ ॥

केचित्समुद्यम्य शिलास्तरूंश्च
विषेहिरे नैव मुनौ विमोक्तुम् ।
पेतुः सवृक्षाः सशिलास्तथैव
वज्रावभग्ना इव विन्ध्यपादाः ॥ ३८ ॥

कैश्चित्समुत्पत्य नभो विमुक्ताः शिलाश्च वृक्षाश्च परश्वधाश्च ।
तस्थुर्नभस्येव न चावपेतुः संध्याभ्रपादा इव नैकवर्णाः ॥ ३९ ॥

चिक्षेप तस्योपरि दीप्तमन्यः कडङ्गरं पर्वतशृङ्गमात्रम् ।
यन्मुक्तमात्रं गगनस्थमेव तस्यानुभावाच्छतधा पफाल ॥ ४० ॥

कश्चिज्ज्वलन्नर्क इवोदितः खादङ्गारवर्षं महदुत्ससर्ज ।
चूर्णानि चामीकरकन्दराणां कल्पात्यये मेरुरिव प्रदीप्तः ॥ ४१ ॥

तद्बोधिमूले प्रविकीर्यमाणमङ्गारवर्षं तु सविस्फुलिङ्गम् ।
मैत्रीविहारादृषिसत्तमस्य बभूव रक्तोत्पलपत्त्रवर्षः ॥ ४२ ॥

शरीरचित्तव्यसनातपैस्तैरेवंविधैस्तैश्च निपात्यमानैः ।
नैवासनाच्छाक्यमुनिश्चचाल स्वनिश्चयं बन्धुमिवोपगुह्य ॥ ४३ ॥

37. a. rości(possibly corrected to dra)vivṛttadṛṣṭis, A; khros-pas lta-byed rnam-ḥgyur-zhiṅ, T. b. tasmai mudām, A; ḥdi-la dbyug-pa, T. d. purāṁdarasyaiva, A.

38. a. samuddamya, A; gyen-du ḥphyar-ba, T.

39. c. e.c. Cowell; ca nāvapetuḥ, A.

40. c. de ni ḥphaṅs-pa (tan mukta°), T.

41. c. °kandarāṇā, A. d. ḥjig-rten ḥjig-tshe (lokātyaye), T.

42. a. pratikīryamānam, A; rab-tu-rnam-ḥphaṅs-paḥi, T. d. °varṣam, Böhtlingk.

43. b. nipatyamānaiḥ, A; phab-pa, T.

अथापरे निर्जिगिलुर्मुखेभ्यः सर्पान्विजीर्णेभ्य इव द्रुमेभ्यः ।
ते मन्त्रबद्धा इव तत्समीपे न शश्वसुर्नोत्ससृपुर्न चेलुः ॥ ४४ ॥

भूत्वापरे वारिधरा बृहन्तः सविद्युतः साशनिचण्डघोषाः ।
तस्मिन्द्रुमे तत्यजुरश्मवर्षं तत्पुष्पवर्षं रुचिरं बभूव ॥ ४५ ॥

चापेऽथ बाणो निहितोऽपरेण जज्वाल तत्रैव न निष्पपात ।
अनीश्वरस्यात्मनि धूयमानो दुर्मर्षणस्येव नरस्य मन्युः ॥ ४६ ॥

पञ्चेषवोऽन्येन तु विप्रमुक्तास्तस्थुर्नभस्येव मुनौ न पेतुः ।
संसारभीरोर्विषयप्रवृत्तौ पञ्चेन्द्रियाणीव परीक्षकस्य ॥ ४७ ॥

जिघांसयान्यः प्रससार रुष्टो गदां गृहीत्वाभिमुखो महर्षेः ।
सोऽप्राप्तकामो विवशः पपात दोषेष्विवानर्थकरेषु लोकः ॥ ४८ ॥

स्त्री मेघकाली तु कपालहस्ता
कर्तुं महर्षेः किल चित्तमोहम् ।
बभ्राम तत्रानियतं न तस्थौ
चलात्मनो बुद्धिरिवागमेषु ॥ ४९ ॥

कश्चित्प्रदीप्तं प्रणिधाय चक्षुर्नेत्राग्निनाशीविषवद्दिधक्षुः ।
तत्रैव नासीनमृषिं ददर्श कामात्मकः श्रेय इवोपदिष्टम् ॥ ५० ॥

44. a. rnam-par-skyugs-pa-ste (=vijagaruḥ), T; nirjagaruḥ, Böhtlingk. d. na sasvasu nnotsasṛjur, A; soṅ-ba ma-yin dbugs-min, T.

45. a. vāridharān, A; chu-ḥdzin chen-po . . . gyur-nas, T.

46. a. vāpe, A; gzhu-la, T. nihato, A; bkod-pa, T. d. durmmarṣaṇasyaiva, A.

47. b. e.c. Kern and Böhtlingk; tasthau nayaty eva, A; nam-mkhar gnas-śiṅ (nabhasy, or viyaty), T.

48. c. so prāptakālo, A; des ni ḥdod-pa ma-thob, T.

49. b. kela mohacittaṁ, A; thugs ni rmoṅs-par byed ces grags, T.

50. b. °vad dhi (or vi) dhakṣuḥ, A; bzhin bsred ḥdod-pas, T. c. tatreva, A. d. ñer-gnas dpal bzhin-du (=śriyam ivopasthitām), T.

गुर्वीं शिलामुद्यमयंस्तथान्यः शश्राम मोघं विहतप्रयत्नः ।
निःश्रेयसं ज्ञानसमाधिगम्यं कायक्लमैर्धर्ममिवाप्तुकामः ॥ ५१ ॥

तरक्षुसिंहाकृतयस्तथान्ये प्रणेदुरुच्चैर्महतः प्रणादान् ।
सत्त्वानि यैः संचुकुचुः समन्ताद्वज्राहता द्यौः फलतीति मत्वा ॥५२॥

मृगा गजाश्चार्तरवान् सृजन्तो विदुद्रुवुश्चैव निलिल्यिरे च ।
रात्रौ च तस्यामहनीव दिग्भ्यः खगा रुवन्तः परिपेतुरार्ताः ॥५३॥

तेषां प्रणादैस्तु तथाविधैस्तैः सर्वेषु भूतेष्वपि कम्पितेषु ।
मुनिर्न तत्रास न संचुकोच रवैर्गरुत्मानिव वायसानाम् ॥ ५४ ॥

भयावहेभ्यः परिषद्गणेभ्यो यथा यथा नैव मुनिर्बिभाय ।
तथा तथा धर्मभृतां सपत्नः शोकाच्च रोषाच्च ससाद मारः ॥५५॥

भूतं ततः किंचिददृश्यरूपं विशिष्टभूतं गगनस्थमेव ।
दृष्ट्वर्षये द्रुग्धमवैररुष्टं मारं बभाषे महता स्वरेण ॥ ५६ ॥

मोघं श्रमं नार्हसि मार कर्तुं हिंस्रात्मतामुत्सृज गच्छ शर्म ।
नैष त्वया कम्पयितुं हि शक्यो महागिरिर्मेरुरिवानिलेन ॥ ५७ ॥

अप्युष्णभावं ज्वलनः प्रजह्यादापो द्रवत्वं पृथिवी स्थिरत्वम् ।
अनेककल्पाचितपुण्यकर्मा न त्वेव जह्याद्व्यवसायमेषः ॥ ५८ ॥

51. a. gurvvī, A. udyamayan tathā°, A.

52. a. tarakṣusihā°, A.

53. a. cāt(?bh?)uravān, A: ñam-thag skad, T. b. vidrudruvuś, A. ḥthig-pa ñid-du gyur-pa-ste (eva vililyire ?), T.

55. a. °ganebhyo, A. d. sasāra, A; bdud-rnams . . . byer-ba-ḥo (' the Māras dispersed ',=?), T; ' all the Māras were exceedingly dejected ', C; ' aroused in his mind (or, their minds), melancholy increased and he (or they) became angry ', FP; mamāra, Böhtlingk; śaśāra, Kern.

56. c. dṛṣṭvārṣaye, A.

58. a. jvalana, A. d. vyavasām eṣaḥ (one syllable short), A; ḥdis ni nan-tan, T.

यो निश्चयो ह्यस्य पराक्रमश्च तेजश्च यद्या च दया प्रजासु ।
अप्राप्य नोत्थास्यति तत्त्वमेष तमांस्यहत्वेव सहस्ररश्मिः ॥ ५९ ॥

काष्ठं हि मथ्नन् लभते हुताशं
भूमिं खनन्विन्दति चापि तोयम् ।
निर्बन्धिनः किंचन नास्त्यसाध्यं
न्यायेन युक्तं च कृतं च सर्वम् ॥ ६० ॥

तल्लोकमार्तं करुणायमानो रोगेषु रागादिषु वर्तमानम् ।
महाभिषङ् नार्हति विघ्नमेष ज्ञानौषधार्थं परिखिद्यमानः ॥ ६१ ॥

हृते च लोके बहुभिः कुमार्गैः सन्मार्गमन्विच्छति यः श्रमेण ।
स दैशिकः क्षोभयितुं न युक्तं सुदेशिकः सार्थ इव प्रनष्टे ॥ ६२ ॥

सत्त्वेषु नष्टेषु महान्धकारे ज्ञानप्रदीपः क्रियमाण एषः ।
आर्यस्य निर्वापयितुं न साधु प्रज्वाल्यमानस्तमसीव दीपः ॥ ६३ ॥

दृष्ट्वा च संसारमये महौघे मग्नं जगत्पारमविन्दमानम् ।
यश्चेदमुत्तारयितुं प्रवृत्तः कश्चिन्तयेत्तस्य तु पापमार्यः ॥ ६४ ॥

क्षमाशिफो धैर्यविगाढमूलश्चारित्रपुष्पः स्मृतिबुद्धिशाखः ।
ज्ञानद्रुमो धर्मफलप्रदाता नोत्पाटनं ह्यर्हति वर्धमानः ॥ ६५ ॥

59. b. yad yā va dayā, A. c. nocchāsyati, A; ldaṅ ma-yin, T. d. tamāsy, A. °rasmiḥ, A.

60. c. nāsya sādhyan (possibly meant for nāsty asādhyan), A; bsgrub-pa ma-yin . . . med, T.

62. b. śramena, A; zhi-bas (śamena), T. d. praṇaṣṭe, A.

64. a. mahoghe, A. c. pravattaḥ, A. d. kaś cinna(rewritten)yet, A; su-yi sems-pa byed, T. T omits tu; tasya nu, Kern.

65. a. veryavigāḍha°, A; brtan-paḥi . . . brtan-pa, T. c. dharmma-pradātā (two syllables short), A; chos-kyi ḥbras-bu ster-pa-po, T.

बद्धां दृढैश्चेतसि मोहपाशैर्यस्य प्रजां मोक्षयितुं मनीषा ।
तस्मिन् जिघांसा तव नोपपन्ना श्रान्ते जगद्बन्धनमोक्षहेतोः ॥६६॥

बोधाय कर्माणि हि यान्यनेन कृतानि तेषां नियतोऽद्य कालः ।
स्थाने तथास्मिन्नुपविष्ट एष यथैव पूर्वे मुनयस्तथैव ॥ ६७ ॥

एषा हि नाभिर्वसुधातलस्य कृत्स्नेन युक्ता परमेण धाम्ना ।
भूमेरतोऽन्योऽस्ति हि न प्रदेशो वेगं समाधेर्विषहेत योऽस्य ॥६८॥

तन्मा कृथाः शोकमुपेहि शान्तिं मा भून्महिम्ना तव मार मानः ।
विस्रम्भितुं न क्षममध्रुवा श्रीश्चले पदे विस्मयमभ्युपैषि ॥ ६९ ॥

ततः स संश्रुत्य च तस्य तद्वचो
महामुनेः प्रेक्ष्य च निष्प्रकम्पताम् ।
जगाम मारो विमनो हतोद्यमः
शरैर्जगच्चेतसि यैर्विहन्यते ॥ ७० ॥

गतप्रहर्षा विफलीकृतश्रमा प्रविद्धपाषाणकडङ्गरद्रुमा ।
दिशः प्रदुद्राव ततोऽस्य सा चमूर्हताश्रयेव द्विषता द्विषच्चमूः ॥७१॥

66. c. nopapannāṁ (anusvara added later), A.

68. a. nābhi vvasudhā°, A. b. paramena, A. d. veśaṁ samādhe vviṣa yo sya (gap for two missing characters), A ; gaṅ-zhig ḥdi-yi tiṅ-ṅe-ḥdzin-gyi śugs bzod-paḥi, T ; ' able entirely to bear the wonderful resolution ', C.

69. a. kṛthā (visarga added above line) sokam, A ; khro-bar (roṣam, krodham), T. c. visrambhituṁ, A. d. kiṁ padam at(?bh?)yupemi, A ; rgyags-par mṅon-par-ñer-ḥgro-zhiṅ (=text, Weller conjectures ḥgro ci=kiṁ madam), T.

70. b. prekṣa, A. c. matodyamaḥ, A ; ḥbad-pa bcom-zhiṅ, T. d. e.c. Böhtlingk ; vihanyase, A ; T ambiguous.

71. a. gatapaharṣā, A. d. dgrar-gyur dgra-boḥi dpuṅ (dviṣatī dviṣac-camūḥ, or amend to dgra-gyis dgra-boḥi dpuṅ=text), T.

द्रवति सपरिपक्षे निर्जिते पुष्पकेतौ
जयति जिततमस्के नीरजस्के महर्षौ ।
युवतिरिव सहासा द्यौश्चकाशे सचन्द्रा
सुरभि च जलगर्भं पुष्पवर्षं पपात ॥ ७२ ॥

इति बुद्धचरिते महाकाव्येऽश्वघोषकृते मारविजयो नाम त्रयोदशः सर्गः ॥ १३ ॥

72. c. cakāse, A. d. puṣpavarṣa, A. A and T add the following spurious verse :—

Tathāpi pāpīyase nirjite gate
diśaḥ praseduḥ prababhau niśākaraḥ |
Divo nipetur bhuvi puṣpavṛṣṭayo
rarāja yoṣeva vikalmaṣā niśā ||

b. praśeduḥ, A. c. °vṛṣṭaye, A.

Colophon : °kāvye aśva°, A.

CANTO XIV

ततो मारबलं जित्वा धैर्येण च शमेन च ।
परमार्थं विजिज्ञासुः स दध्यौ ध्यानकोविदः ॥ १ ॥
सर्वेषु ध्यानविधिषु प्राप्य चैश्वर्यमुत्तमम् ।
सस्मार प्रथमे यामे पूर्वजन्मपरंपराम् ॥ २ ॥
अमुत्राहमयं नाम च्युतस्तस्मादिहागतः ।
इति जन्मसहस्राणि सस्मारानुभवन्निव ॥ ३ ॥
स्मृत्वा जन्म च मृत्युं च तासु तासूपपत्तिषु ।
ततः सत्त्वेषु कारुण्यं चकार करुणात्मकः ॥ ४ ॥
कृत्वेह स्वजनोत्सर्गं पुनरन्यत्र च क्रियाः ।
अत्राणः खलु लोकोऽयं परिभ्रमति चक्रवत् ॥ ५ ॥
इत्येवं स्मरतस्तस्य बभूव नियतात्मनः ।
कदलीगर्भनिःसारः संसार इति निश्चयः ॥ ६ ॥

1. b. vairyena ca śamana ca, A; brtan daṅ zhi-ba-yis, T. c. paramārthaṁm vi°, A.

2. b. uttamaḥ (corrected to uttamaṁ), A.

3. ab. nāmā bhyutas, A; che-ge-mo bdag miṅ ḥdi ni . . . ḥphos-te (amuko(?) 'ham ayaṁ nāma cyutas), T. d. n(originally s?)asmarī(?ā?)nu°, A.

5. a. kṛtvehaṁ sujanotsarggaṁ, A; raṅ-gi skye-bo bor-nas ni (omitting iha, or read ḥdir for ni), T. b. kriyā, A; bya-ba-rnams, T. c. atrāṇa, A.

6. a. smāratas, A.

द्वितीये त्वागते यामे सोऽद्वितीयपराक्रमः ।
दिव्यं लेभे परं चक्षुः सर्वचक्षुष्मतां वरः ॥ ७ ॥
ततस्तेन स दिव्येन परिशुद्धेन चक्षुषा ।
ददर्श निखिलं लोकमादर्श इव निर्मले ॥ ८ ॥
सत्त्वानां पश्यतस्तस्य निकृष्टोत्कृष्टकर्मणाम् ।
प्रच्युतिं चोपपत्तिं च ववृधे करुणात्मता ॥ ९ ॥
इमे दुष्कृतकर्माणः प्राणिनो यान्ति दुर्गतिम् ।
इमेऽन्ये शुभकर्माणः प्रतिष्ठन्ते त्रिपिष्टपे ॥ १० ॥
उपपन्नाः प्रतिभये नरके भृशदारुणे ।
अमी दुःखैर्बहुविधैः पीड्यन्ते कृपणं बत ॥ ११ ॥
पाय्यन्ते क्वथितं केचिदग्निवर्णमयोरसम् ।
आरोप्यन्ते रुवन्तोऽन्ये निष्टप्तस्तम्भमायसम् ॥ १२ ॥
पच्यन्ते पिष्टवत्केचिदयस्कुम्भीष्ववाङ्मुखाः ।
दह्यन्ते करुणं केचिद्दीप्तेष्वङ्गारराशिषु ॥ १३ ॥
केचित्तीक्ष्णैरयोदंष्ट्रैर्भक्ष्यन्ते दारुणैः श्वभिः ।
केचिद्धृष्टैरयस्तुण्डैर्वायसैरायसैरिव ॥ १४ ॥
केचिद्दाहपरिश्रान्ताः शीतच्छायाभिकाङ्क्षिणः ।
असिपत्रवनं नीलं बद्धा इव विशन्त्यमी ॥ १५ ॥

7. a. dvitī tv āgate (one syllable short), A ; gñis-pa byuṅ-ba-na, T.

8. d. iva rmmale (one syllable short), A ; dri-ma med-pa, T.

10. a. duskṛtakarmmāṇi, A ; sdig-paḥi las-can-rnams, T ; 'the evil-livers', C. c. ime ṇye, A.

11. a. upapannā, A. c. duḥkhai bahuvidheḥ, A.

13. b. ayaṁkumbhīṣv, A. cd. keci dī(corrected to ddī ?)pteṣv, A.

14. ab. ayodraṁṣtrair bhakṣante dāruṇaiḥ svabhiḥ, A.

15. a. ked dāha° (one syllable short), A. c. aśipatravana, A.

पाट्यन्ते दारुवत्केचित्कुठारैर्बद्धबाहवः ।
दुःखेऽपि न विपद्यन्ते कर्मभिर्धारितासवः ॥ १६ ॥
सुखं स्यादिति यत्कर्म कृतं दुःखनिवृत्तये ।
फलं तस्येदमवशैर्दुःखमेवोपभुज्यते ॥ १७ ॥
सुखार्थमशुभं कृत्वा य एते भृशदुःखिताः ।
आस्वादः स किमेतेषां करोति सुखमण्वपि ॥ १८ ॥
हसद्भिर्यत्कृतं कर्म कलुषं कलुषात्मभिः ।
एतत्परिणते काले क्रोशद्भिरनुभूयते ॥ १९ ॥
यद्येवं पापकर्माणः पश्येयुः कर्मणां फलम् ।
वमेयुरुष्णं रुधिरं मर्मस्वभिहता इव ॥ २० ॥
इमेऽन्ये कर्मभिश्चित्रैश्चित्तविस्पन्दसंभवैः ।
तिर्यग्योनौ विचित्रायामुपपन्नास्तपस्विनः ॥ २१ ॥

16. c. duḥkhe nipipadya (one character torn off, and one syllable short), A ; sdug-bsṅal-na yaṅ rnam mi-smin (so Peking edition, smrin Weller), T. d. karmmabhim vā(corrected on margin to r ddhā)ritāśavaḥ, A.

17. b. duḥkhanivarttaye, A ; sdug-bsṅal bzlog-paḥi don-ched-du, T.

18. c. āśvādaḥ, A. karā (top of this character and all next one torn off) sukham anv api, A ; bde-ba phra-mo (ma Weller) yaṅ byed-dam, T.

19. b. kalāṣātmabhiḥ, A ; sdig-paḥi bdag-ñid, T.

20. a. yady eva, A ; gal-te de-ltar, T. c. skyen-par khrag ni skyug-pa ñid (vameyus tūrṇaṁ rudhiram ?), T. d. Half of syllable rmma torn off, A. A and T add the following spurious verse here :—

Śārīrebhyo 'pi duḥkhebhyo nārakebhyo manasvinaḥ |
Anāryaiḥ saha saṁvāso mama kṛcchratamo mataḥ ||

d. kṛcchu(?)tamo, A.

21. a. ime nyeḥ, A. b. °viṣy(or p)anda°, A ; rnam-gyo-las, T. c. viciträyam, A. d. tapaśvinaḥ, A.

मांसत्वग्बालदन्तार्थं वैरादपि मदादपि ।
हन्यन्ते कृपणं यत्र बन्धूनां पश्यतामपि ॥ २२ ॥

अशक्नुवन्तोऽप्यवशाः क्षुत्तर्षश्रमपीडिताः ।
गोऽश्वभूताश्च वाह्यन्ते प्रतोदक्षतमूर्तयः ॥ २३ ॥

वाह्यन्ते गजभूताश्च बलीयांसोऽपि दुर्बलैः ।
अङ्कुशक्लिष्टमूर्धानस्ताडिताः पादपार्ष्णिभिः ॥ २४ ॥

सत्स्वप्यन्येषु दुःखेषु दुःखं यत्र विशेषतः ।
परस्परविरोधाच्च पराधीनतयैव च ॥ २५ ॥

खस्थाः खस्थैर्हि बाध्यन्ते जलस्था जलचारिभिः ।
स्थलस्थाः स्थलसंस्थैश्च प्राप्य चैवेतरेतरैः ॥ २६ ॥

उपपन्नास्तथा चेमे मात्सर्याक्रान्तचेतसः ।
पितृलोके निरालोके कृपणं भुञ्जते फलम् ॥ २७ ॥

सूचीछिद्रोपममुखाः पर्वतोपमकुक्षयः ।
क्षुत्तर्षजनितैर्दुःखैः पीड्यन्ते दुःखभागिनः ॥ २८ ॥

22. a. °dantārtha, A. b. chags-pa-las-sam (rāgād api), T. c. kṛpa (gap for missing letter) yatra, A ; gaṅ-du sñiṅ-brje-bar, T.

24. d. °pāṣṇibhiḥ, A.

25. a. satsu py, A. b. vi(one character torn off)ṣataḥ, A ; khyad-par-ldan (viśeṣavat), T.

26. c. lalasaṁsthais, A ; skam-gnas-rnams-kyis, T. d. e.c. ; prāpya revai(these two characters marked for error)taretaraiḥ, A ; phan-tshun-du ni rab-phrad-nas (=itaretaraiḥ prāpya), T ; prāpyante cetaretaraih, Co. ; tāpyante, Cappeller.

27. ab. tathā ce(two characters torn off)tsaryā°, A ; ser-snas . . . ḥdi-rnams de-bzhin-du, T.

28. cd. °janitai duḥkhaiḥ pīḍyate, A.

आशया समतिक्रान्ता धार्यमाणाः स्वकर्मभिः ।
लभन्ते न ह्यमी भोक्तुं प्रविद्धान्यशुचीन्यपि ॥ २९ ॥

पुरुषो यदि जानीत मात्सर्यस्येदृशं फलम् ।
सर्वथा शिबिवद्दद्याच्छरीरावयवानपि ॥ ३० ॥

इमेऽन्ये नरकप्रख्ये गर्भसंज्ञेऽशुचिह्रदे ।
उपपन्ना मनुष्येषु दुःखमर्छन्ति जन्तवः ॥ ३१ ॥

* * * * * *

29. A and T transpose this and the next verse. b. sūkarmmabhiḥ, A ; raṅ-gi las-rnams-kyis, T. d. pravṛddhāni, A ; bor-baḥi, T ; 'impure food and thrown away', C.

30. ab. janī(two characters torn off)ātsarya(bottoms only of these letters preserved)sye°, A ; ser-snaḥi . . . śes-na, T.

31. ab. narakapakhye garbha(one character torn off)jñe, A ; dmyal-ba daṅ mtshuṅs-paḥi mṅal miṅ, T.

APPENDIX.

The *Buddhacarita* and the *Fo pen hsing chi ching.*

The following table gives the verses of the *Buddhacarita* which are quoted in the *Fo pen hsing chi ching,* with references to volume III of the Taishō Issaikyō edition of the Chinese Tripiṭaka and to Beal's translation in *The Romantic Legend of Śākya Buddha* :—

Buddhacarita.	Fo pen hsing chi ching.	Beal.	REMARKS.
i, 82, 83, 84, 85ab	701a, 12–19	62	
ii, 2	702a, 10-11	64	The following *gāthā* possibly reproduces ii, 5.
ii, 11ab	702b, 7-8	omitted.	
ii, 13ab	702b, 9-10	omitted.	
ii, 17	692c, 1-2	54	
ii, 26cd	712c, 13-14	92	Correspondence not quite certain.
ii, 27cd	712c, 15-16	92	
iii, 30	720b, 20-21	109	
iii, 55	723b, 4-5	118	
iii, 57	723b, 14-15	119	
iii, 59bcd	723b, 22-23	119	
iv, 9, 11, 12	726a, 24–29	omitted.	Correspondence incomplete and uncertain.
iv, 64	726c, 17-18	125	
iv, 70	727a, 1-2	125	
iv, 86	727a, 13-14	126	Correspondence probable, not certain.
iv, 89	727a, 19-20	126	
v, 18, 19	724b, 16–19	121	
v, 38	724c, 28-29	omitted.	
v, 64, 65	729a, 8–11	130	Different version of 65*d*.
v, 71	731a, 14-15	134-35	
vi, 10	733c, 25-26	140	Correspondence of second line not clear.
vi, 11	734a, 17-18	141	
vi, 16cd, 17ab	735a, 24-25	143	
vi, 27	735b, 26-27	omitted.	
vi, 46, 47, 48	736a, 7–12	omitted.	Different version of 48*cd*, and seven verses, not found in *Buddhacarita*, added.
vi, 54, 55	736c, 17–22	omitted.	
vi, 61	738a, 7-8	145	
vii, 2	745a, 18-19	153	*Pāda b* omitted.
vii, 7ab, 8cd	745b, 14-15	154	

Buddhacarita.	Fo pen hsing chi ching.	Beal.	REMARKS.
vii, 18	746b, 10-11	omitted.	
vii, 21	746b, 20-21	156	
vii, 27	746c, 9-10	157	
vii, 38	747c, 10-11	omitted.	
vii, 58	748a, 26-27	161	
viii, 2	738b, 22-23	146	
viii, 11ab	738c, 23	147	
viii, 13ab	738c, 24	147	
viii, 35	740c, 23-24	omitted.	
viii, 42cd, 43ab	741b, 11-12	150	
viii, 54	740b, 24-25	omitted.	
viii, 69	741c, 29 ; 742a, 1	omitted.	
viii, 71	742a, 22-23	omitted.	Correspondence probable, not certain.
viii, 72	743b, 22-23	omitted.	
viii, 76	744b, 16-17	151	
viii, 84	744c, 11-12	151	Last *pāda* differs.
ix, 6	748b, 24-25	162	
ix, 22	749b, 4-5	163	First line differs.
ix, 41	750a, 7-8	164	
ix, 47	750a, 28-29	165	
ix, 53	750b, 25-26	165-66	
ix, 62	750c, 18-19	166	
ix, 71	751a, 21-22	167-68	
ix, 82	751c, 3-4	168-69	
x, 15	760a, 18-19	181	
x, 24	760c, 6-7	182	
xi, 9	761c, 14-15	183	Correspondence exact for first *pāda* only.
xi, 10	761c, 16-17	omitted.	
xi, 12	761c, 20-21	omitted.	
xi, 13	761c, 18-19	omitted.	
xi, 17	762a, 11–14	omitted.	
xi, 32	762b, 15-16	omitted.	
xi, 34	762b, 21-22	omitted.	
xi, 35	753b, 3-4	omitted.	
xi, 57	763b, 12-13	183	
xi, 59abc	763b, 21	184	Following line in Chinese entirely different from xi, 59*d*.
xi, 67	763c, 19-20	184	
xi, 72	764b, 15-16	omitted.	Last *pāda* differs slightly.
xi, 73	764c, 4-5	185	
xii, 3	752a, 12-13	170	
xii, 15	753a, 23-24	omitted.	
xii, 65	754c, 25-26	omitted.	Last *pāda* differs slightly.
xii, 75	755b, 16-17	omitted.	
xii, 83	757b, 9-10	omitted.	

Buddhacarita.	Fo pen hsing chi ching.	Beal.	Remarks.
xii, 120	778b, 22-23	207	
xiii, 5, 6	779b, 9–14	omitted.	
xiii, 28cd, 29bcd	787b, 26-27	222	
xiii, 32	787c, 8-9	222	
xiii, 36	787c, 28-29	223	
xiii, 55	790c, 11-12	omitted.	
xiii, 58	788c, 5-7	224	
xiii, 61, 62, 63	788c, 8–14*a*	omitted.	
xiii, 64	788c, 19-20	omitted.	
xiii, 65, 66	788c, 14*b*–18	omitted.	
xiii, 67	788c, 21-22	omitted.	

THE BUDDHACARITA

Or,

ACTS OF THE BUDDHA

PART II :

Cantos i to xiv translated from the original Sanskrit supplemented by the Tibetan version

TOGETHER WITH AN INTRODUCTION AND NOTES

FOREWORD

In accordance with the intention expressed in the preface to the first part I give here an explanation of the contents of this part. The translation covers the whole of the first fourteen cantos, supplying the lacunæ of the Sanskrit text from the Tibetan translation, for whose correct interpretation I rely on the Chinese paraphrase. For the understanding of these passages missing in the Sanskrit I am heavily indebted to Dr. Weller's pioneer version and trust that in the few points where I differ from him my rendering is an improvement, not a darkening of counsel.[1] The result probably reproduces Aśvaghoṣa's meaning with a fair degree of accuracy, but would undoubtedly require modification in detail if the original were to come to light. My translation is a pedestrian affair, designed to be read with the text and to explain its meaning, not to transmute its spirit and literary quality into an alien tongue. Nor does it follow any rigid principles; where the constitution of the text or its exact significance are open to doubt, I have preferred a literal rendering, but allow myself a freer hand where the going is firmer. Despite innumerable divergencies in detail, the greatness of the debt I owe to the late Professor Cowell's translation, which still holds its own, will be apparent to anyone who cares to make the comparison. Of the other translations I have derived most help from that by Formichi; though an occasional tendency to let ingenuity degenerate into fantasy has led to its being judged at times with unmerited harshness, its criticism of earlier attempts to elucidate difficulties are usually acute and deserving of careful examination. Of the two German translations, Cappeller's is too free to be of much help in the task I set myself, and Schmidt's, though

---

[1] The numbering of the verses in Canto xiv differs from Dr. Weller, who includes the spurious verse after verse 20 and believes in the original existence of another verse between my verses 70 and 71.

scholarly, suffers from inadequate study of the material. The four Indian editions of the first five cantos have provided me with useful hints in places, especially in those points which often escape the eyes of European scholars.

In the notes I endeavour to mention all substantial difficulties of text and interpretation ; for, though regard for the expense involved in the printing of full discussions have often deterred me from dealing at the length I should have liked with many matters and have caused me to dispose summarily of the opinions of other scholars which were worthy of better treatment, it seemed to me that the best service I could render to future workers on the poem was by careful selection to focus attention on those points which really call for serious consideration. A number of references to parallel passages, drawn from all departments of Sanskrit and Pali literature, are given, partly because it is only by careful study of them that Aśvaghoṣa's exact place in the history of religion and literature can be determined, and partly because the translator must not only make sense of his text, but also give a sense which conforms with Indian ideas of the first century A.D. ; particular care has been devoted to choosing for mention only those passages which are genuinely relevant. The index includes, besides proper names, all those words whose discussion in the notes might conceivably be of use to others. Under the abbreviations I have gathered together all the modern literature known to me which makes the *Buddhacarita* its main subject.

Finally the introduction makes the first attempt to present a complete picture of Aśvaghoṣa based on all the sources open to us. As a first attempt its deficiencies are as patent to me as they will be to everyone else, and difficulties of finance have led me in many cases to allot only a few words or lines to problems which would have required many pages for comprehensive discussion. On the question of the poet's handling of legend my treatment is utterly inadequate ; on most traditional details of the Buddha's life it will remain impossible to make confident assertions, till the Chinese sources are made available to us on the lines which Professor Przyluski has adopted for the First Council and for the Aśoka legend. The thread is formed by two main ideas, neither of which has so far been fully accepted. Firstly, I can attribute but small value to the traditions preserved in Chinese literature about the poet's life. And secondly, I look on him as a very learned and conscientious man, who was perfectly aware of what he was doing and who never knowingly made a wrong or fantastic statement about religion, philosophy or legend. If we cannot always explain his sayings, we should ascribe this rather to our own ignorance of the literature with which he was familiar, and it is absurd to expect from him either the attitude of modern higher criticism or a historical knowledge of events in the sixth and fifth centuries B.C., which is not to be found even in the oldest parts of the Pali canon. Let it at least be counted to me for merit, if despite many shortcomings I have been able by years of work to bring into clearer relief one of the greatest figures of Indian civilisation.[1]

ADDERBURY, E. H. JOHNSTON.
August, 1935.

---

[1] As the introduction and notes contain a number of references to Cantos xv-xxviii of the *Buddhacarita*, known to us only from the Tibetan and Chinese translations, I would add that I hope to publish shortly an English version of them in a European journal.

ABBREVIATIONS

A. Books and articles dealing wholly or largely with the *Buddhacarita*.

B.	.. The *Buddhacarita*.
Bhandari	.. Madhava Shastri Bhandari, *Kāvyasārasaṁgraha*, pp. 227–261 (*Buddhacarita*, Cantos II and III). Bombay, 1929.
Böhtlingk	.. O. von Böhtlingk, *Kritische Bemerkungen zu Açvaghoṣa's Buddhacarita*, BSGW, 1894, 160.
———	T. Byōdō, *Aśvaghosha's Acquaintance with the Mokshadharma of the Mahābhārata*, Proc. of the Imp. Ac. of Japan, IV, pp. 322–325.
C.	.. Chinese translation of the *Buddhacarita*, TI, IV, no. 192.
Cappeller	.. C. Cappeller, *Noch einige Bemerkungen zu Aśvaghoṣa's Buddhacarita*, ZII, 1922, 1.
do.	.. C. Cappeller, *Buddha's Wandel*. Religiöse Stimmen der Völker, Jena, 1922.
Co.	.. E. B. Cowell, *The Buddha*-karita *of Asvaghosha*, Anecdota Oxoniensia, 1893.
do.	.. E. B. Cowell, *The Buddha*-karita *of Asvaghosha*, in SBE, XLIX.
Finot	.. L. Finot, *Notes sur le Buddhacarita*, JA, 1898, ii, 542.
do.	.. L. Finot, Review of Joglekar and Formichi, JA, 1913, i, 685.
Formichi	.. C. Formichi, *Açvaghoṣa poeta del buddhismo*. Bari, 1912.
Gawroński	.. A. Gawroński, *Gleanings from Aśvaghoṣa's Buddhacarita*, Rocznik Orientalistyczny, 1914-15, 1.
do.	.. A. Gawroński, *Studies about the Sanskrit Buddhist Literature*, pp. 1–55. Cracow, 1919.
———	C. W. Gurner, *The word* vasthānam *in Aśvaghoṣa*, JRAS, 1927, 322.
———	C. W. Gurner, *Some textual notes on Aśvaghoṣa's Buddhacarita*, JASB, 1926, 1.
Hopkins	.. E. W. Hopkins, *Buddhacarita, v. 72 ; x. 34 ; xii. 22*, JAOS, 1901, ii, 387.
Hultzsch	.. E. Hultzsch, *Zu Aśvaghoṣa's Buddhacarita*, ZDMG, 1918, 145.

Joglekar	..	K. M. Joglekar, *Aśvaghoṣa's Buddhacarita, Cantos I–V, Notes and Translation.* Bombay, 1912.
Kern	..	H. Kern, see *Nachträge* to article quoted under Böhtlingk.
Kielhorn	..	F. Kielhorn, *Zu Açvaghoṣa's Buddhacarita,* NGGW, 1894, 364.
———		T. Kimura and T. Byōdō, *Butsden bungaku no kenkyo,* pp. 1–548. Tokyo, 1930.
Leumann	..	E. Leumann, *Zu Açvaghoṣa's Buddhacarita,* NGGW, 1896, 83.
do.	..	E. Leumann, *Some notes on Aśvaghosha's Buddhacarita,* WZKM, 7, 193.
Lévi	..	S. Lévi, *Le Buddhacarita d'Açvaghoṣa,* JA, 1892, i, 201.
Lokur	..	N. S. Lokur, *Buddhaçaritam, Cantos I–V, with translation and notes.* Belgaum, 1912.
Lüders	..	H. Lüders, *Zu Açvaghoṣa's Buddhacarita,* NGGW, 1896, 1.
Nandargikar	..	G. R. Nandargikar, *The Buddha-caritam of Aśvaghoṣa, Cantos I–V.* Poona, 1911.
———		L. de la Vallée Poussin, *On Buddhacarîta, i. 30,* JRAS, 1913, 417.
Prasada	..	Pandeya Jagannatha Prasada, *Aśvaghosha's Buddha Charitam, Canto VIII.* Bankipur, 1920.
Schmidt	..	R. Schmidt, *Buddha's Leben, Aśvaghoṣa's Buddhacaritam.* Kulturen der Erde, Hagen i/W, 1923.
Schrader	..	F. O. Schrader, *Nachlese zu Aśvaghoṣa's Buddhacarita,* Journal of the Taisho University, 1930.
———		Hara Prasad Shastri, *A new MS. of Buddha Carita,* JASB, 1909, 47.
———		Sukumar Sen, *On the 'Buddhacarita' of Aśvaghoṣa,* IHQ, 1926, 657.
Sovani	..	V. V. Sovani, *Buddhacaritam by Shri Ashvaghosha, Cantos I–V,* with Sanskrit commentary by Shri Appashastri Rashivadekar and translation by V. V. Sovani. Part II, Notes by V. V. Sovani. Poona, 1911.
Speyer	..	J. S. Speyer, *Kritische Nachlese zu Açvaghoṣa's Buddhacarita,* Proc. of Amsterdam Ac., 1895, 340.
do.	..	J. S. Speyer, *Some critical Notes on Aśvaghoṣa's Buddhacarita,* JRAS, 1914, 105.
Strauss	..	O. Strauss, *Zur Geschichte des Sāṁkhya,* WZKM, 27, 257.
T	..	The Tibetan translation of the *Buddhacarita,* Bstan-Ḥgyur, Mdo 94.

W	..	F. Weller, *Das Leben des Buddha von Aśvaghoṣa* (Tibetan text and German translation). Part I (Cantos I–VIII), 1926. Part II (Cantos IX–XVII), 1928.
Windisch, i	..	E. Windisch, *Māra und Buddha.* Leipzig, 1895.
Windisch, ii	..	E. Windisch, *Buddha's Geburt und die Lehre von der Seelenwanderung.* Leipzig, 1908.
Wohlgemuth	..	Else Wohlgemuth, *Ueber die chinesische Version von Aśvaghoṣa's Buddhacarita.* Berlin, 1916.

Not seen—A translation of the first canto by P. Peterson, and the translations into Russian by Balmont and into Japanese by T. Byōdō.

B. General.

AAA.	..	*Abhisamayālaṁkārāloka*, by Haribhadra ; ed. G. Tucci, Gaekwad's Or. S. no. LXII.
AK.	..	L. de la Vallée Poussin, *L'Abhidharmakośa de Vasubandhu* (quoted by volume and page number).
AKV., i	..	*Abhidharmakośavyākhyā*, Bibl. Buddh. XXI.
AKV., iii	..	do., Mém. de l'Ac. royale de Belgique, Tome VI, fasc. ii, 1919.
ASPP.	..	*Aṣṭasāhasrikāprajñāpāramitā*, ed. Bibl. Ind.
BhNŚ.	..	*Bhāratīyanāṭyaśāstra*, Cantos I–XIV, ed. J. Grosset, Lyons, 1898 ; Cantos XV-end, Kāvyamālā no. 42.
Bṛh. Ār. Up.	..	*Bṛhad Araṇyaka Upaniṣad*, ed. Ānandāśrama S. S.
CII	..	*Corpus Inscriptionum Indicarum.*
Divy.	..	*Divyāvadāna*, ed. Cowell and Neal.
FP.	..	*Fo pen hsing chi ching*, TI III, no. 190.
HC.	..	*Harṣacarita*, ed. P. V. Kane, Bombay, 1918.
Jāt.	..	*Jātakamālā*, ed. H. Kern, Harvard O. S. no. 1.
KA.	..	*The Arthaśāstra of Kauṭilya*, ed. Jolly and Schmidt.
Kād.	..	*Kādambarī*, ed. P. Peterson, Bombay S. S., 1883.
KS.	..	*Kāmasūtra*, ed. Kashi S. S. no. 29.
LV.	..	*Lalitavistara*, ed. Lefmann.
MBh.	..	*Mahābhārata*, Calcutta edition.
Mhv.	..	*Mahāvastu*, ed. Senart.
Pāṇ.	..	Pāṇini.
Pargiter	..	F. E. Pargiter, *Ancient Indian Historical Tradition*, Oxford, 1922.
PW	..	Böhtlingk und Roth, *Sanskrit-Wörterbuch.*
PWK	..	Böhtlingk, *Sanskrit-Wörterbuch in kürzerer Fassung.*
R.	..	*Raghuvaṁśa*, ed. S. P. Pandit, Bombay S. S.

Rām.	..	*Rāmāyaṇa*, ed. Gorresio.
RL	..	S. Beal, *Romantic Legend of Śākya Buddha*, 1875.
RV	..	Rigveda.
S.	..	E. H. Johnston, *The Saundarananda of Aśvaghoṣa* (Sanskrit text), 1928, and *The Saundarananda, or Nanda the Fair* (translation), 1932.
SP.	..	*Saddharmapuṇḍarīka*, ed. Bibl. Buddh.
SS.	..	J. S. Speyer, *Sanskrit Syntax*, 1886.
Śvet. Up.	..	*Śvetāśvatara Upaniṣad*, ed. Hauschild.
TI	..	Taishō Issaikyō edition of the Chinese Tripiṭaka, ed. by Takakusu and Watanabe.
YS.	..	*The Yogasūtras of Patañjali*, ed. Bombay S. S., 1892.

CONTENTS

INTRODUCTION

AŚVAGHOṢA

i. Life and Works

One phenomenon recurs again and again in the history of Sanskrit literature, namely that we know nothing certain of the lives of its greatest figures beyond what they themselves choose to tell us and what is stated in the colophons of their works. Aśvaghoṣa is no exception to the rule. While he is silent about himself, the colophons of the three works which we know to be his agree in describing him as Sāketaka, a native of Sāketa, and as the son of Suvarṇākṣī.[1] Before discussing the bearing of these facts, it is best to determine his date with such accuracy as is possible. The lower limit given by the Chinese translation of the *Buddhacarita* made early in the fifth century A.D. can be set back by three hundred years; for Professor Lüders holds that the handwriting of the MS. fragments which contain all that is left to us of the *Śāriputraprakaraṇa* must belong to the times of the Kushan kings, probably to the reign of Kaniṣka or Huviṣka.[2] Dating by palæography does not always give as assured results as is sometimes supposed, but the margin of error in the present case cannot be large; for the MS. was corrected by a Central Asian hand, which equally on palæographical grounds may be as early as the end of the Kushan era,[3] and it shows signs of having been long in use before the overwriting took place, so that to impugn the first date means impugning the second

---

[1] The *Śāriputraprakaraṇa* (*SBPAW*, 1911, 392) has *Suvarṇākṣiputra*, shortening the *i* under *Pāṇ.*, vi. 3, 63 ; the name can only be that of his mother, i.e. Suvarṇākṣī.

[2] H. Lüders, *Bruchstücke buddhistischer Dramen* (Berlin, 1911), 11.

[3] Lüders, *op. cit.*, 15.

one also and it is hardly probable that both should be misleading.

Two other points afford some indication, though of lesser probative value, that the reign of Kaniṣka should be taken as the lower limit. At *B.*, xii. 115, Aśvaghoṣa writes :—

Vyavasāyadvitīyo 'tha . . . so 'śvatthamūlaṁ prayayau.

Now the commentary on the *Nāmasaṁgīti*[1] has preserved a line of Mātṛceṭa running :—

Vyavasāyadvitīyena prāptaṁ padam anuttaram.

The connexion between the two is obvious, and the expression, *vyavasāyadvitīya*, is apt in Aśvaghoṣa, because the Buddha has just been deserted by the five bhikṣus and has nothing but his resolution to accompany him on the march to the *bodhi* tree; but Mātṛceṭa's version spoils the point, because a Buddha can have no companions in the process of obtaining Enlightenment. This view is enforced by *B.*, xiv. 99, where Indra and Brahmā more appropriately find the Buddha with the *dharma* he had seen as his best companion. Is it not clear then that Mātṛceṭa has borrowed a phrase from Aśvaghoṣa and turned it into a cliché ? That the former is somewhat later in date seems to follow also from the style of the *Śatapañcāśatka*[2]; thus note the fanciful verbs, *jaladāya*, *Vainateyāya*, *madhyaṁdināya*, *Śakrāyudhāya*, of verses 74 and 75, which suggest some advance on Aśvaghoṣa in verbal tricks. He is moreover the author of an epistle to Kaniṣka, and if we accept the latter's name as authentic, it would follow that Mātṛceṭa lived in his reign and Aśvaghoṣa before it. I would not press this piece of evidence, but, so far as it goes, it suggests that Lüders' dating of the MS. of the dramas is at any rate not at odds with the probabilities.

Our other evidence derives from Chinese tradition, which

---

[1] *AK.*, VI, 144, *ad* ch. ii, 205, n. 2 ; the line is partially preserved in verse no. 26 in Hoernle, *Manuscript Remains*, I, 61, the first line running :—*Iti tribhir asaṁkhyeyair evam udyacchatā tvayā.*

[2] *JRAS*, 1911, 764–769.

associates Aśvaghoṣa both with Kaniṣka and with the composition of the *Vibhāṣā*, the great Sarvāstivādin commentary on the Abhidharma, said to be the outcome of a general council held in the reign of the Kushan king [1]. For a later Buddhist writer such information would be of value, seeing that the Chinese with their more practical minds are intensely interested in the collection of historical and personal detail, and that the regular intercourse of pilgrims and monks between India and China provided sufficient opportunity for obtaining contemporary information. But in this case the traditions are far from contemporary and cannot at present be traced further back than the end of the fourth century A.D. ; they are at hopeless variance among themselves regarding the poet's actual date and present him as a figure of romance, not as a sober historical personage. In considering the association with Kaniṣka we must allow for the tendency to couple the names of great writers with great kings. One Indian scholar, it is true, has seen in the mention of Ātreya at *B.*, i. 43, a reference and compliment to Caraka, the legendary physician of Kaniṣka ; but little weight attaches to so problematic a suggestion. Moreover the internal evidence of the extant works makes it somewhat doubtful whether they could have been written in the Kushan kingdom. For while Brahmanical literature represents that dynasty as hostile to the Brahmans [2], Aśvaghoṣa writes for a circle in which Brahmanical learning and ideas are supreme ; his references to Brahmans personally and to their institutions are always worded with the greatest respect, and his many mythological parallels are all drawn

---

[1] The Chinese traditions have been discussed in a series of important papers by S. Lévi in the *JA* spread over many years, of which the chief are 1896, ii, 444 : 1908, ii, 57 : and 1928, ii, 193. References to incidental mentions by other scholars will be found in these papers. For a list of the Chinese authorities on the Aśvaghoṣa legend see *JA*, 1908, ii, 65, n. 2.

[2] For this see K. P. Jayaswal in *JBORS*, 1933, 41ff. ; though he does not allow sufficiently for Brahman bias in his appreciation of the passages, the evidence is too strong to be discounted altogether.

from Brahmanical sources[1]. Further we know nothing with certainty about the date of the *Vibhāṣā*, even if we could say that it was all composed at one time; and the story of the council in Kaniṣka's reign at which it was drawn up is open to the grave suspicion of having been invented to secure authority for Sarvāstivādin views. Nor, as I shall show in the next section, does the poet appear to know the doctrines of the great commentary. In valuing this evidence we shall do well to bear in mind Professor Demiéville's verdict that Chinese tradition, for all the mass of documents on which it rests, hardly affords, at least for the early period, more positive historical information than Indian tradition with its complete absence (*carence*) of documents[2]. All we are entitled to say is that these traditions prove Aśvaghoṣa to have lived long before the time at which they first appear in the fourth century A.D.; the forms the legends took may have been determined by the popularity of the plays in the Kushan kingdom, as shown by the dilapidated state of the MS.[3]

The evidence then leads to the conclusion that the poet lived not later than the time of Kaniṣka and may have preceded him, and is thus consonant with what, as I show later, we know of his relation to classical Sanskrit literature. His style proves him to have lived several centuries before Kālidāsa, he is imitated by Bhāsa, and his vocabulary suggests a date not far removed from that of the *Arthaśāstra* of Kauṭilya. The problem would have been much more complicated if the *Kalpanāmaṇḍitikā*[4] were really by Aśvaghoṣa, since it is posterior

---

[1] The only exceptions are the two verses, *S.*, xi. 56-57, which would be suspicious on that score alone, but their clumsy style and the impossibility of fitting them logically into the argument of the canto are decisive against their genuineness.

[2] *Bulletin de la Maison franco-japonaise*, II, p. 76 of offset.

[3] And by confusion with the personality of Mātṛceṭa, if he really lived under Kaniṣka?

[4] H. Lüders, *Bruchstücke der Kalpanāmaṇḍitikā des Kumāralāta*, Leipzig, 1926.

to Kaniṣka and alludes also to the *Vaiśeṣikasūtras*, a system unknown to the genuine extant works. But as I reject the attribution to him of this collection of tales, I need not try to reconcile the irreconcilable. The further question remains of the date of Kaniṣka, and if agreement is not yet reached on this thorny point, the limits of variation are no longer large, most scholars accepting a date in the last quarter of the first century A.D. and none placing him later than the second quarter of the second century.

As the poet may have been earlier, though not much earlier, than Kaniṣka, it should be noted that the upper limit for his date is determined by the mention of the Aśoka legend in the final canto of the *Buddhacarita*, a passage not discussed by Professor Przyluski in his well-known book on the subject. According to that scholar the *Aśokāvadāna*, some early form of which was evidently known to Aśvaghoṣa, took shape between 150 and 100 B.C.[1] Allowing a certain period for it to obtain recognition, we might set the upper limit at approximately 50 B.C., and can therefore not be much in error if we say that the poet flourished between 50 B.C. and 100 A.D., with a preference for the first half of the first century A.D.

Turning back now to the colophons we can obtain a few hints of value. As belonging to Sāketa, Aśvaghoṣa is an Easterner, and his origin has left its traces in his work. While the absence of relevant texts prevents us from ascertaining if the divergencies of his grammar from the Paninean system are to be accounted for by his having studied one of the *prācya* treatises, the sect of Buddhism, to which he seems to have belonged according to the views set out in the next section, was the one most prevalent in Eastern India at this period, and the lasting impression which the historical associations of Sāketa made on him is apparent both in the influence of the *Rāmāyaṇa* displayed by his works and also in the emphasis which he lays from the very start of both poems on the descent

---

[1] *La légende de l'Empéreur Açoka*, 166.

of the Śākyas from the Ikṣvāku dynasty. The style Suvarṇākṣīputra is significant; for, though that type of nomenclature was not confined to Brahmans, it was used by them more than by any other class. As I show in detail later, he had an acquaintance, so wide that no parallel can be found to it among other Buddhist writers, with all departments of Brahmanical learning, including some knowledge of the Veda and ritual literature as well as mastery of all the sciences a *kavi* was expected to have studied. The deduction is inescapable that he was born a Brahman and given a Brahman's education, and as Chinese tradition is insistent to the same effect, we can for once accept its testimony without reserve as in accord with the evidence of the works. As to how he became a Buddhist nothing can be said beyond the fact that the choice of theme for his three works indicates much preoccupation with the phenomena of conversion. The story told in the Chinese sources is legendary in character and at variance with the evidence I adduce below to determine the question to what sect he gave his adherence. Nor do we know anything definite of his later life, though the general outline of his character and mental endowments will emerge with some degree of clearness in the subsequent discussions.

Next let us consider the works he wrote; those known for certain to be his are three in number, the *Buddhacarita*, the *Saundarananda* and the *Śāriputraprakaraṇa*. The first, the subject of the present edition, is a life of the Buddha in 28 cantos, of which only numbers two to thirteen are extant in their entirety in Sanskrit, together with three quarters of the first canto and the first quarter of the fourteenth. It begins with the conception of the Buddha and, after narrating his life and Parinirvāṇa, closes with an account of the war over the relics, the first council and the reign of Aśoka. The textual tradition of the extant portion is bad and a sound edition is only made possible by comparison with the Tibetan and Chinese translations. The *Saundarananda* has for its subject the conversion of the Buddha's half-brother, Nanda, in the course of which the opportunity is taken to set out at length the author's view of the Path to Enlightenment. It consists of 18 cantos, preserved in full, and the text tradition for the two thirds of the work found in the older MS. is far superior to that of the other poem, but the remainder, dependent on one incorrect modern MS. only, requires much conjectural emendation to restore it to something like the original. When first studying these poems, I naturally took the ordinary view that the last-mentioned is the earlier one, seeing that the other is the more interesting to read as a whole and that its verses have a richer content. But these advantages are due to the subject, not to greater experience in authorship ; for the handling of the *Saundarananda* is altogether more mature and assured than that of the *Buddhacarita,* whose effect is often marred by repetitions of the same words or phrases, or even of a whole *pāda,* in a way that the *kavis* of the classical age sedulously avoided, and the poet's technique reaches its high-water mark in passages such as *S.*, iv. 1–11, or x. 8–13, while the latter's metrical system is more elaborate and includes faultless manipulation of such difficult schemes as Upasthitapracupita and Udgatā. The third work is a nine-act play, with the conversion of Śāriputra and Maudgalyāyana for its theme ; only a few passages are extant, restored by the acumen of Professor Lüders from the Central Asian finds.

These three works are bound together in a way that would be convincing proof of the identity of their authorship, if the colophons left us in any doubt of it. Thus the play uses again *B.*, xii. 75, and the preceding passage contains reminiscences of the argument *ib.*, 72[1]. The celebrated verse, *S.*, xi. 50, is to be found again in the Tibetan of *B.*, xiv. 41. The same ideas and expressions recur with such constancy in the two poems that I was unable to edit the *Buddhacarita* till I had determined as accurately as I could the readings of the *Saundarananda.* Thus compare *B.*, xi. 10, 12, with *S.*, xi. 32, 37,

[1] *SBPAW*, 1911, 392 and 393 K IV.

or the use of the simile of the *kāraṇḍava* bird standing on a lotus, *B.*, v. 53, and *S.*, iv. 23; or notice how two different twists are given to the same three ideas in the description of a hermitage at *B.*, vii. 33, and *S.*, i. 11. So *B.*, xxviii. 63, in describing Aśoka, has the same play on words as *S.*, vii. 5, and more appropriately. If I insist here on this tendency, it is because I regard it as the point to which most attention should be paid in considering Aśvaghoṣa's authorship of other works.

The Chinese and Tibetan translations attribute to him a number of works [1], about which certainty is impossible in the absence of the Sanskrit texts; but it is improbable that any of them, which deal mainly with philosophy or belong to the fully developed Mahāyāna, are rightly given to him, seeing that he is a poet and preacher, not an original philosopher, and that his date is too early for anything but primitive Mahāyāna, even if it be admitted as a bare possibility that he may have gone over to that branch of Buddhism in later life. There are however several Sanskrit works on which an opinion must be expressed.

First come the fragments of two plays found by Professor Lüders with the remains of the *Śāriputraprakaraṇa*. One of these is a Buddhist allegory, of which nearly a whole leaf is preserved including a large part of three verses [2]. The first one contains rhymes much in Aśvaghoṣa's style, *paramam amṛtaṁ durlabham ṛtam* and *tasminn aham abhirame śānti-parame*; for the latter cp. *S.*, xii. 16, *tvaddharme parame rame*. The next verse addressed by *buddhi* to *kīrti* consists of three similar *pādas* of the form, *nityaṁ sa supta iva yasya na buddhir asti*, and the fourth supplies the contrast, ending *tiṣṭhati yasya kīrtiḥ*; the construction of the verse is like the poet's, and the idea of the first line quoted above is closely connected with

[1] Listed in F. W. Thomas, *Kavīndravacanasamuccaya* (Bibl. Ind., no. 1309), Introduction, 36ff.

[2] Fragment 1 in Lüders, *op. cit.*, 66.

S., xviii. 35, 36. The last verse describes the Buddha's display of miraculous powers on the lines of *S.*, iii. 22ff., and I would invite attention to the parallelism, which extends even to the simile, of the line,

Khe varṣaty ambudhārāṁ jvalati ca yugapat saṁdhyāmbuda [*iva* ।

with *S.*, iii. 24,

Yugapaj jvalan jvalanavac ca jalam avasṛjaṁś ca meghavat ।
Taptakanakasadṛśaprabhayā sa babhau pradīpta iva saṁdhyayā ghanaḥ ॥

Is it possible that anyone else could have imitated so closely the specialities of Aśvaghoṣa's style ?

The other play concerns a young voluptuary, probably named Somadatta, who keeps a mistress named Magadhavatī and apparently becomes a convert to Buddhism. No fragments have been put together to hold as long a consecutive piece as in the allegorical play and it is more difficult to detect similarities. The following however are worth consideration. In fragment 8 is mentioned the motif of the lover holding his mistress's mirror, which is the central point of *S.*, iv, and fragment 13, line *a*2, seems to contain the rare word *sahīyā* (*B.*, x. 26). *S.*, xiv. 15, may be compared with line *a*3 of fragment 17, but the subject is a commonplace. In fragment 59 *kulavyasanam adṛṣṭvā* recalls *S.*, vi. 43, *vyasanāny adṛṣṭvā.* Occasional words suggest that the phrases to which they belonged may have had analogies with Aśvaghoṣa's usage, but are inconclusive as they stand. Against his authorship is the fact that Professor Lüders reckons the occurrence of three verses in the Sragdharā metre, which, popular as it was with later Buddhists, especially in Kashmir, is not found in the poet's extant work. Of the two in fragment 27 the first can only be fitted into this metre by emending the MS.'s °*dveṣam* to °*doṣam*, and from the number of characters it apparently contained is far more probably a Śālinī verse, presuming the amendment to be correct. The other admittedly may be in Śikhariṇī, which Aśvaghoṣa uses several times. The third in fragment 79 may belong to the *Śāriputraprakaraṇa* and is too short for definite identification. But, if this point is open to argument, Professor Lüders also traces the occurrence of two Hariṇī and one Āryā verse in the play, which equally have not yet been found in work that certainly belongs to Aśvaghoṣa. The evidence altogether is uncertain and the prudent man will reserve his judgement about the authorship of the play.

Three other works, known to us wholly or in part in Sanskrit, have also been attributed to him. Of these the *Vajrasūcī*, a clever piece of polemics arguing against Brahman claims, shows no trace of Aśvaghoṣa's style or mentality, and the Chinese translation gives it to Dharmakīrti, who, as also a converted Brahman, would have been in possession of the Brahmanical learning displayed in the tract. I see no reason for doubting the correctness of the latter ascription and in any case would exclude it from the corpus of Aśvaghoṣa's works. Next comes the *Gaṇḍīstotra*, a collection of 29 stanzas, mostly in the Sragdharā metre, in praise of the Buddha and the monastery gong, the text of which was successfully restored from a Chinese transliteration by Baron A. von Staël-Holstein [1]. Verse 20 shows that it was written in Kashmir during one of the periods of misrule to which that land was subject ; the style has no affinities with that of Aśvaghoṣa and we have here clearly a work that is several centuries later in date. Finally I Tsing mentions a work by the poet the name of which was taken to stand for *Sūtrālaṁkāra*, and in 1908 E. Huber published under this name an admirable translation of a Chinese work, which was ascribed to Aśvaghoṣa by the Chinese translator. Subsequently fragments of a MS. of the Sanskrit original were identified among the Central Asian finds by Professor Lüders, who established that the author was there described as Kumāralāta and the name of the work as *Kalpa-*

---

[1] Bibl. Buddh. XV. For its authorship and an attempt at improving the reconstruction see *Ind. Ant.*, 1933, pp. 61–70, in which the last fourteen words of the note on verse 29 should be omitted as mistaken.

nāmaṇḍitikā. This gave rise to much controversy[1], eminent scholars maintaining that this collection of moral tales was really by Aśvaghoṣa or else a refashioning by Kumāralāta of the older writer's work. Now that the dust of warfare has settled and it is generally agreed that Aśvaghoṣa had no hand in its composition, it will be sufficient to observe that the age of the MS. is such that its evidence outweighs all other points, that the Tibetan translation supports the statement of the MS., that the Chinese translation is probably not by Kumārajīva, whose testimony would have had some value, but by a later writer[2], and that the style of the Sanskrit fragments and the internal evidence of the work itself put Aśvaghoṣa's authorship entirely out of court ; it need not be further considered here.

A few verses, not one of which occurs in his works, as brought to light so far, are also attributed to Aśvaghoṣa in the anthologies[3]; that in the *Kavīndravacanasamuccaya* is certainly not by him but shows some likeness to the *Gaṇḍīstotra,* though more elaborate than anything found there. Of the five in the *Subhāṣitāvalī* none definitely bear his sign manual or need even be by a Buddhist ; but, if the attribution is improbable, it cannot be pronounced absolutely impossible.

As is well known, late Tibetan tradition confused Aśvaghoṣa with several quite different writers, including a certain Subhūti, on which it would have been unnecessary to say anything here, if Professor S. Lévi had not recently urged that some connexion exists between the two. A verse specifically attributed to the Dhārmika Subhūti is quoted by Vasubandhu in the *AK.*, and has been found in a recently discovered MS., entitled the *Ṣaḍgatikārikāḥ,* of which a Pali version named *Pañcagatidīpanī*

---

[1] The literature on the subject is described by Tomomatsu in *JA*, 1931, ii, 135ff. ; to his references add La Vallée Poussin, *Vijñaptimātratāsiddhi*, 221–224, and Przyluski, *Bull. of the R. Ac. of Belg.*, 1930, 425–434, and *Rocznik Orientalistyczny*, VIII, 14–24.

[2] Tomomatsu, *loc. cit.*, 163.

[3] *Kavīndravacanasamuccaya*, Introduction, p. 29.

is also known[1]. The promised edition of this work has not yet appeared, but on the face of the information at present available it will be very surprising if we receive here an authentic work by Aśvaghoṣa ; among other points the latter belongs to those who recognise five *gatis* only, not six, as appears from *B.*, xiv, and *S.*, xi. 62.

ii. The Buddhist

Having stated so much as is known of the life of Aśvaghoṣa, I now proceed to discuss him from the three aspects under which his achievements naturally fall, as Buddhist, as scholar and as poet, and start with that one which he himself would have held to be alone of significance. Our first task is obviously to determine the sect or school to which he belonged. That he was a follower of the Hīnayāna is certain, and to him perhaps any further enquiry would have savoured of impertinence ; he is not a fanatical adherent of any school and avoids, as if of set purpose, all mention of those disciplinary details and philosophic subtleties which had split the community into sections, so that it is hard to detect in Vasumitra's treatise on the sects any slogan which has left definite traces on the poet's works. To modern scholars equally the question will appear otiose, since Chinese traditions, assigning him to the Sarvāstivādins and naming a *Vibhāṣā* doctor, Pārśva (or Pūrṇa or Pūrṇāśa), as having converted him, have always been held to decide the matter once for all. Yet their stories are on the face of them incredible ; for Aśvaghoṣa knows none of the *Vibhāṣā* doctrines, and, if he was a Sarvāstivādin, must have lived before its special principles were worked out. The later predominance of this sect among the Hīnayāna schools of Northern India and Central Asia is enough of itself to account for the statements of the Chinese Buddhists, who would hold that a writer of such outstanding eminence could only have belonged to the most important sect.

---

[1] S. Lévi, *JA*, 1928, ii, 204ff.

Unfortunately few Sarvāstivādin texts are available to those Sanskritists who like myself cannot find their way easily in the Chinese and Tibetan translations ; but these are sufficient to make it improbable that, despite a considerable measure of agreement in matters of general interest, Aśvaghoṣa was a member of this school. The *Divyāvadāna*, it is true, appropriates an occasional verse or phrase from his poems [1], and as a canonical work naturally does not mention his name. But the only trace of the special tenets of the Sarvāstivāda is to be found in the quotation of the rule governing the use of *asti* as a particle (*S.*, xii. 10), which may be an allusion to the famous controversy about the reality of the past and future ; it does not, however, illuminate his position in the matter. On the other hand in two points he seems to reject the standard doctrines of the school. Thus *S.*, xvii. 18*ab*, runs:—

Yasmād abhūtvā bhavatīha sarvaṁ
bhūtvā ca bhūyo na bhavaty avaśyam ।

This idea is based on canonical authority (*Majjhima*, III, 25), but was strenuously denied by the Sarvāstivādins and as strenuously upheld by the Sautrāntikas [2], to which school no one would suggest that Aśvaghoṣa belonged. The entire passage is significant, because the exegesis of the four terms, *anitya*, *duḥkha*, *śūnya* and *nirātmaka*, cannot be reconciled with any of Vasubandhu's alternative explanations and seems to be based on a scheme of *ākāras* for the supermundane path which differs from the sixteen of the Vaibhāṣika doctors [3].

Again the twelfth canto of the *Saundarananda* contains a remarkable eulogy of *śraddhā*, for which the only complete parallel is in an early Mahāyāna sūtra ; faith is not merely desire for the Buddha's *dharma* (*tvaddharme parame rame*,

---

[1] See notes on *B.*, iii. 3, 5, 23 and 26, and *S.*, xi. 50 and xviii. 1.

[2] *AK.*, I, 228-9.

[3] *AK.*, V, 30ff. Other passages (see p. xxxiv, n. 1) give dogmatic views not traceable in the Sarvāstivādin Abhidharma at present, but cannot be proved to be definitely opposed to its teachings so far as yet known.

S., xii. 16, *dharmacchanda, ib.*, 31), but personal devotion to the Buddha (*S.*, xvii. 34, 63–73, xviii. 41, 48, 50 and 51, and canto xxvii of the *Buddhacarita*), and we seem to feel blowing through these passages the breath of the *bhakti* religions, which for Buddhism reached their apogee in the Mahāyāna. It is no doubt true that, if we go through the Pali canon and the Sarvāstivādin texts and extract the passages relating to faith, they make an imposing show, but consider each passage in its context and the glowing fervour that animates Aśvaghoṣa is not to be found; there seems instead to be a subtle tendency to belittle faith, as though it were only a matter for brethren not strong enough to enter the Path under their own power. Unless the suggestion I make below is really the key to the significance of Aśvaghoṣa's views [1], it is more a matter of emphasis than of definite statement; yet till recently no one would have thought it necessary to give more than a passing word to the question of faith in any description of Hīnayāna beliefs, so little obvious is its importance in the Pali and Sarvāstivādin texts, while Aśvaghoṣa's insistence on it could not escape the most casual glance.

The attitude of Vasubandhu and his commentator Yaśomitra is also significant; when they make a quotation, one or other of them takes care to tell us who was the author, and they do this notably with regard to three writers whom later tradition confused with Aśvaghoṣa, namely Subhūti, Kumāralāta and Mātṛceṭa. Yet when Vasubandhu quotes *S.*, xiii. 18, to illustrate his explanation of a knotty dogmatic point in the *bhāṣya* on *kārikā* iv. 86, neither he nor Yaśomitra gives the author's name; and Yaśomitra makes the same omission in citing *S.*, xii. 22*d*. Surely if Aśvaghoṣa had been a leading light of the Sarvāstivādins, they would have hastened to claim the support of his authority.

[1] See p. xxxiv below. That ordinarily in the Hīnayāna *śraddhā* omits Aśvaghoṣa's leaning to *bhakti* is clear enough from such excellent statements of the general position as B. M. Barua in *Buddhistic Studies* (ed. by B. C. Law), pp. 329ff., and N. Dutt, *Some aspects of Mahāyāna Buddhism*, pp. 301–303.

In legendary matters further research by specialists must be awaited, as the only source open to me, Rockhill's summary of the *Dulva*, does not give the Sarvāstivādin tales in sufficient detail. Of obvious differences I note that at the birth of the Buddha the poet makes Māyā lie on a couch instead of grasping the bough of a tree and that after the Enlightenment Indra joins Brahmā at *B.*, xiv. 98ff., in imploring the Buddha to preach the *dharma* [1]. The *Dulva* also assigns a different name to Nanda's wife and adds a visit to hell [2].

More however can be extracted from the list of 62 chief disciples at *S.*, xvi. 87ff., all the names in which should be forthcoming in the canonical lists of the school to which the poet belonged. I have examined the two lists in the Chinese translations [3], each of which contains 100 names. Allowing for corruptions and difficulties of transliteration, I estimate that the Sarvāstivādin catalogue in the *Ekottarāgama* [4] has about 37 names in common with the *Saundarananda*, not as many as there should be, if this was the poet's authority. The other text, whose affinities are unknown, is in the *A lo han chü tê cheng* [5], which was translated by Fa Hsien in the last quarter of the tenth century A.D., and, having some 47 or more of the names given by Aśvaghoṣa, stands much closer to the authority used by him. Of the names themselves several are significant. The doubling of the epithet *mahā* before Kāśyapa's name proved that this saint was specially revered by Aśvaghoṣa's sect [6], a conclusion supported by the story

---

[1] *Life of the Buddha*, 16 and 35.

[2] *Ib.*, 55. Śāriputra took Nanda to hell according to *AAA.*, 61. To the Pali versions of the Nanda legend given in the introduction to my translation of the *Saundarananda* add the commentary on *Aṅguttara*, I, 25, which confirms my criticism of the *Udāna* sentence about the monkey.

[3] For the references I am indebted to Professor Demiéville.

[4] *TI*, no. 125, II, 557-8. I note that it gives Śīvala for the Śaivala of *S.*, xvi. 91*c*, and the latter should probably be amended accordingly, as the older MS. confuses *ai* and *ī*.

[5] *TI*, no. 126, II, 831–3.

[6] For the bearing of this see p. xxix.

of his conversion in *B.*, xvi, which is evidently intended to place him on an equality with Śāriputra and Maudgalyāyana. One of the first five bhikṣus is called Bhadrajit, a form unknown elsewhere, and Sudarśana, who is omitted by the *Ekottarāgama* but named by Fa Hsien, is otherwise only reported from the *Vinaya* of the Mahāsaṅghikas[1]. Again the Pali form of Kuṇṭhadhāna is Kuṇḍadhāna, but the *Divy.* calls him Pūrṇa Kuṇḍopadhānīyaka and the form Kuṇḍopadhāna seems to be that known to the *Ekottarāgama* and other Chinese works[2]. The list therefore seems to diverge in a number of points from the Sarvāstivādin sources.

The evidence thus consists of a number of small items, none conclusive in themselves, but their cumulative effect is definitely against the view that Aśvaghoṣa adhered to the Sarvāstivāda. Is there a more plausible case for any other sect? The extent to which the *Fo pen hsing chi ching* borrows from the *Buddhacarita* suggests a possible line of enquiry. That work quotes the canon of many sects, but never that of the Dharmaguptas, and in view of its closing statement it may therefore well belong to the latter. It can be proved however to draw material from so many unnamed sources that its frequent reliance on the *Buddhacarita* proves nothing about the affinities of the latter.

Another alternative is to investigate the position of the Mahāsaṅghikas, who, as a sect prevailing largely in Eastern India at that time[3], might well have claimed Aśvaghoṣa's allegiance. Here again we are impeded by lack of material. The *Mahāvastu*, which gives us the traditions of the Lokottaravādins, disagrees with the *Buddhacarita* about Māyā's position at the time of the Buddha's birth and about the place where Arāḍa taught, but alone of the Hīnayāna sources it makes Indra accompany Brahmā on the visit to the Buddha after his

---

[1] J. Przyluski, *Le Concile de Rājagṛha*, 206.

[2] See S. Lévi and E. Chavannes, *JA*, 1916, ii, 197ff., for a discussion of him and a translation of the *Divy.* passages.

[3] Przyluski, *op. cit.*, 311.

Enlightenment, and it alone calls Nanda by the style Sundarananda which the poet gives him [1]. The Mahāsaṅghikas also are known to share with Aśvaghoṣa a knowledge of the saint Sudarśana, a special veneration for Kāśyapa [2], and an insistence on the connexion of the asterism Puṣya with the Buddha [3], all points apparently peculiar to them.

Some light also can be obtained from the Mahāyāna. One of its two chief schools, the Vijñānavāda, is affiliated by its dogmatics to the Sarvāstivādins and the schools deriving from them, and it is precisely this school which shows hardly a trace in its works of the poet's influence and very few parallels. It is possible that Asaṅga in *Abhisamayālaṁkāra*, i. 58, is imitating *B.*, ii. 10, but even so this work belongs rather to the Mādhyamika section of the treatises attributed to that author. Again *S.*, xv, describes a group of five *vitarkas* which are not known in this form in any of the Hīnayāna sources, but which are mentioned by Asaṅga in exactly similar fashion [4]. And this is all that I can find. The Mādhyamikas on the other hand, who are an offshoot of a Mahāsaṅghika sect, have many points of connexion with the poet's works. Nāgārjuna lifts *S.*, xiii. 44*abc*, and adds a new conclusion, *bhūtadarśī vimucyate*, in which form the verse is repeatedly quoted in Mādhyamika literature [5]; and verse 26 of his recently published *Ratnāvalī* [6] may owe something to *S.*, xviii. 26. A certain Vasu, commenting on Āryadeva's *Śataśāstra*, cites *S.*, xi. 25, 30, and the former verse is paraphrased by Candrakīrti on Āryadeva's

[1] Sundarananda at *AK*, I, 227, is a mistake for Nanda, see Index s. Nanda. The Mādhyamikas use the name Sundarananda also, e.g. *SP.* and *AAA.* *LV.*, 396ff., also makes Indra accompany Brahmā, but is presumably to be treated as a Mahāyāna version.

[2] Przyluski, *op. cit.*, 302-3.

[3] Przyluski, *op. cit.*, 88, and *B.*, i. 9, and ii. 36.

[4] *Bodhisattvabhūmi*, ed. Wogihara (Tokyo, 1930), 145, against *AK.*, III, 248, and *Vibhaṅga*, 356.

[5] For references La Vallée Poussin, *Mélanges chinois et bouddhiques*, I, 394. The term *bhūtadarśin* also occurs in Aśvaghoṣa (*B.*, xxiii. 43).

[6] *JRAS*, 1934, 313.

Catuḥśataka[1]. The remarkable parallel between an early Mādhyamika sūtra quoted in the *Śikṣāsamuccaya* and the eulogy of *śraddhā* in *S.*, xii, has already been mentioned, and there is another curious little sūtra[2], apparently of Mādhyamika origin, which was translated by Kumārajīva, and which seems to have been put together out of Aśvaghoṣa's verses on the subject of subduing the passions; it is in prose and does not quote any actual verses, as I at first supposed. There is further, as will appear from my notes on the two poems, frequent parallelisms in vocabulary and phraseology between Aśvaghoṣa and the sūtras used by the Mādhyamikas; for instance, but for the existence of his poems, we might have supposed that the words *āmukha* and *ājavaṁjava* were first introduced by the Mahāyāna and subsequently adopted by the Hīnayāna. This common use of rare words extends to non-canonical literature and non-technical terms. Thus the remarkable *abhiniṣic* at *B.*, xii. 37, has its only parallels in the occurrence of *niṣic* once in the *MBh.* and once in the *Mūlamadhyamakakārikās*, xxvi. 2, and similarly Candrakīrti's use of *nirbhukta*, *ib.*, 318, 3, is our only means of explaining the same word at *B.*, iv. 47. The influence can also be seen in Mādhyamika art; for at their headquarters, Nagarjunikonda, a series of bas-reliefs have been recently discovered, which give the fullest sculptural representation extant of the story of Nanda and which seem to be based on the *Saundarananda*, though in view of the following this might be accounted for by the presence of Bahuśrutikas at that spot, as shown by the inscriptions[3].

---

[1] *Mem. As. Soc. of Bengal*, III, 471, l. 19.

[2] The *Pu sa ho sê yu fa ching* (*Bodhisattvakāmavighātanasūtra* ?), *TI*, no. 611. My attention was first drawn to it by an extract in one of the Lung Men cave inscriptions, quoted by Dr. Spruyt in *Mélanges chinois et bouddhiques*, I. He very kindly supplied me with a translation of the text.

[3] See *Ann. Bibl. of Ind. Archæology*, 1930, Pl. IIa; Professor Vogel kindly gave me photographs of them. The first, partly destroyed, seems to show the Buddha in conversation with Nanda and Sundarī. The next depicts Nanda having his head shaved with apparently Ānanda in the background

It appears then that, if we take Aśvaghoṣa to have been a Mahāsaṅghika, we are in a position to understand certain otherwise inexplicable points in his poems as well as his relationship to one section of the Mahāyāna. But more is required for cogent proof and this I would look for in a recent discovery. The Chinese Tripiṭaka has a work by one Harivarman on the subject of the four Truths and their *ākāras*, which is usually called the *Satyasiddhi*, but to which Professor de la Vallée Poussin would give the in some ways more appropriate title of *Tattvasiddhi*[1]. Little is known of this treatise, which at one time rivalled the *Abhidharmakośa* as an authority on Buddhist dogmatics and was followed by a school of its own in Japan. Professor Demiéville has however lately discovered fragments of Paramārtha's lost commentary on Vasumitra's treatise on the Buddhist sects, in which the *Satyasiddhi* is said

---

holding his headdress. The third represents the visit to Indra's Paradise; the Buddha and Nanda's robes are so disposed as to recall the simile *S.*, x. 4, *saraḥprakīrṇāv iva cakravākau*, and the two Apsarases in the trees are perhaps due to a misunderstanding of *vanāntarebhyaḥ* at *ib.*, 38. The final scene seems to show Nanda as an Arhat going forth to preach as in *S.*, xviii. 58, 62; the street is indicated by children playing and by adoring people in the background. The *garuḍa* brackets below the reliefs show their date to be not earlier than the second half of the second century A.D. Of about this date also is a jamb from Amaravati (best illustration, Bachhofer, *Early Indian Sculpture*, Pl. 128), showing in the bottom panel Nanda and Sundarī, and Nanda following the Buddha with his almsbowl. The next panel above has the Buddha giving orders for Nanda's forcible admission to the order, and above that appears the visit to Indra's Paradise. Of the fourth panel there are only scanty remains which suggest a street scene like that in the last of the other series. These reliefs too are probably intended to illustrate Aśvaghoṣa's poem, but that the Gāndhāra relief, fig. 234 in Foucher, *L'Art gréco-bouddhique du Gandhara*, I, is based on it is proved by the solitary maidservant at the side spying the Buddha's arrival (*S.*, iv. 28). The Nanda legend was so modern that naturally sculptors took the *Saundarananda* as their source for details, at least in the schools which held him to be a standard authority; but this would not apply to the Buddha-legend with its wealth of canonical description available and I cannot trace with certainty Aśvaghoṣa's influence on the details of any extant sculptures dealing with it.

[1] *Vijñaptimātratāsiddhi*, 223.

to be a work of the Bahuśrutika section of the Mahāsaṅghikas[1]. Now while Paramārtha's statements on matters of history are justly open to doubt, it seems to me incredible that he should be mistaken about the dogmatic tendencies of a work well-known and much studied in his day; surely therefore his evidence on this point should be accepted[2]. This book quotes *S.*, xvi. 15*cd* and 14 in the following way: "As the *gāthā* of the Bodhisattva Aśvaghoṣa runs, 'As one sees fire to be hot in the present, so it has been hot in the past and will be in the future; similarly, as one sees the five *skandhas* to be suffering in the present, so they have been suffering in the past and will be so in the future'"[3]. The terms of this passage prove that, unlike Vasubandhu, Harivarman treats Aśvaghoṣa as a great authority, whose words add weight to any argument. While in the absence of a translation of the work into a European language I cannot say how far its views agree with the poet's dogmatic position, two passages at least are closely related to certain statements of Aśvaghoṣa, for which I can find no parallel in the *AK.* In chapter 173 dealing with *anitya*, it points out that the *dharmas* are transitory because their causes are subject to decay; this corresponds exactly to the argument of *S.*, xvii. 18*cd*, for which previously I had been doubtful both of the reading and of my translation, feeling that it was worded in a way hardly compatible with the *Kośa's* views on causality[4]. Again in chapter 14 it says, 'There are only the

---

[1] *Mélanges chinois et bouddhiques*, I, 49.

[2] There had previously been much discussion in China and Japan, which is not accessible to me, about the tendencies of this work. That it was abortive in the absence of Paramārtha's commentary is not surprising, as Vasumitra's account of the Bahuśrutikas mentioned below shows how hard it would be to identify any work on internal evidence as belonging to that school.

[3] *TI*, XXXII, 372, *a*15-16; I am indebted to Professor Demiéville for the reference. The form of the quotation suggests that possibly we have a verse taken from a lost work by Aśvaghoṣa and modelled on the passage in *S.*

[4] Cp. also *Ratnāvalī*, 46, which I understand somewhat differently to Tucci, *JRAS*, 1934, 318, so as to be based on this argument.

skandhas, the *dhātus* and the *āyatanas*, and the complex of causes (*hetupratyayasāmagrī*), but there is no person who acts or who experiences sensations ', thus putting in a single sentence the three arguments similarly brought together in *S.*, xvii. 20*abc*[1].

As the natural inference is that Aśvaghoṣa was either a Bahuśrutika or an adherent of the school from which the Bahuśrutikas issued, we must examine the little that is known of that sect. For the present our only authority is Vasumitra's treatise[2], which states that the Bahuśrutikas followed Sarvāstivādin doctrines generally except on two points[3]. Firstly they held that the Buddha's teaching on the subject of *anitya, duḥkha, śūnya, anātmaka* and *śānta* (Nirvāṇa) is supermundane, because it leads to the way of escape (*niḥsaraṇamārga*)[4]. Is it merely a coincidence that in *S.*, xvii, verse 17 describes Nanda as shaking the tree of the *kleśas* by the mundane path with regard to the first four of these terms, that the next four verses give an exegesis of them, which departs from all the alternative Sarvāstivādin explanations but is, so far as is known, in accord with the *Satyasiddhi*'s views, and that the following verse records that by examination of these points Nanda attained the supermundane path? Further the word *niḥsaraṇa* occurs in verse 15 at the beginning of the passage. This is the most

---

[1] I am much indebted to Mr. Lin Li-Kouang, who kindly examined this work for me and brought these important passages to my notice. The references are *TI*, XXXII, 346, *c*27, and 248, *b*6. In my translation of *S.*, xvii. 20, 'knower' for *vedaka* is not accurate; it means 'one who experiences sensations'.

[2] Translated by Masuda, *Origin and Doctrines of early Indian Buddhist Schools*, in *Asia Major*, 1925, 1ff. For Paramārtha's commentary see *Mélanges chinois et bouddhiques*, I, and for recent discussions, Przyluski, *Concile de Rājagṛha*, 310ff., and Demiéville, *BEFEO*, 1924, 48ff.

[3] This fact no doubt accounts for the *Mahāvyutpatti* (275) reckoning the Bāhuśrutīyas among the sects connected with the Sarvāstivāda; no other authority supports this classification.

[4] Masuda, *loc. cit.*, 35.

important of the four places[1], in which Aśvaghoṣa gives me the impression of setting out the dogmas of some special school of Abhidharma teaching, and its correct valuation has long been a puzzle to me ; I would suggest that the proper interpretation is to see in it the raising of the banner of his school by the poet, in which case the coincidence with Vasumitra's statement should surely lead us to the conclusion that the school in question was the Bahuśrutika.

Besides this doctrine, the Bahuśrutikas, as a section of the Mahāsaṅghikas, accepted the five points of Mahādeva[2]. It is unfortunately hard to say how these tenets should be understood and probably interpretation varied from school to school and from age to age. The third point regarding 'doubt' is of uncertain meaning and may or may not be in accord with Aśvaghoṣa's teaching[3]. The fourth however lays down that Arhats gain spiritual perception by the help of others. The meaning of this is made clear by *S.*, v. 16ff., which divides religious aspirants into two classes, those who obtain salvation of themselves by virtue of the *hetu* (see p. xlii) working within them, and those who can only act in reliance on others (*parapratyaya*) ; the Buddha is an instance of the former category (*B.*, ii. 56), Nanda of the latter, but it is nowhere explicitly stated that all Arhats fall into the second class as held by Mahādeva, though perhaps hinted at in *S.*, xviii. 51. Evidently however for a man who is *parapratyaya* a firm hold on faith is an absolute prerequisite to salvation ; in the terms of the *Kośa* he is *śraddhānusārin*, because he needs the help of others[4].

---

[1] The other three are *S.*, xvi. 20–24, and 38, and xvii. 28-29.

[2] For these besides the preceding references see La Vallée Poussin, *JRAS*, 1910, 413ff.

[3] Contrast Demiéville, *Mélanges chinois et bouddhiques, I*, p. 35, with p. 32 and 39. The latter seem to me consistent with Aśvaghoṣa's views at *S.*, xvii. 28-29, the former hardly so.

[4] *AK*, IV, 194 ; the passage is important as illuminating the exact nature of the difference between the views of the Sarvāstivāda and those of Mahādeva in this matter. The same difference, corresponding to their different attitude

Here I would suggest we have the explanation of the poet's insistence on faith; for, if he accepted Mahādeva's fourth point, he could not do otherwise, and his position is certainly more intelligible, if we take the view that he did so accept it. Farther we cannot go at present in discussing whether the poet believed in the five points in some form or other, but it is worth noting that one of the three original sections of the Mahāsaṅghikas, the Kaukulikas, are recorded by Paramārtha as stressing the necessity of *vīrya*[1] and that the closing passage of the Buddha's instructions to Nanda, *S.*, xvi. 92–98, is devoted to this very matter, its position suggesting its extreme importance in the struggle for salvation.

To sum up a difficult enquiry, I would hold, till further light is shed on the dark places, that the best opinion is to consider Aśvaghoṣa as having been either a Bahuśrutika or an adherent of the school (the Kaukulikas ?) from which the Bahuśrutikas issued.

The foregoing discussion has had the incidental advantage of explaining in some degree the nature of the reputation which Aśvaghoṣa enjoyed among his co-religionists; he was revered not as an original teacher nor as a philosopher of distinction, but as a writer with an unequalled power for stating the details of the Buddhist faith. In later times he ranked as a great saint, but the emphasis lay, if we can trust Chinese tradition, on the greatness of his magical powers, which was held by ordinary persons to be convincing proof of sanctity. Thus all that Hiuan Tsang, himself steeped in the works of the Sarvāstivāda and the Vijñānavāda and consequently perhaps a little cold towards the great men of other schools, considers worthy of mention about him is a story of his prowess in dealing with evil spirits at Pāṭaliputra. But if the greatest of Chinese pilgrims did not value his poems, another saw more justly; I Tsing's judgement has often been quoted, but is too important

to religion, appears to persist between the tenets of the Yogācāra school and those of the Mādhyamikas.

[1] Demieville, *loc. cit.*, 47.

not to be given in his actual words. The *Buddhacarita*, he says, 'is widely read or sung throughout the five divisions of India and the countries of the Southern Sea. He (i.e. Aśvaghoṣa) clothes manifold meanings and ideas in a few words, which rejoice the heart of the reader, so that he never feels tired from reading the poem. Besides it should be counted as meritorious for one to read this book, inasmuch as it contains the noble doctrine given in a concise form'[1]. This surely gets the emphasis exactly right; Aśvaghoṣa's popularity in India was as a poet and as explaining the doctrine in simple terms. In the former aspect he exercised a determining influence on later *kāvya* work by Buddhists; while Mātṛceṭa has already been mentioned, every page of Śūra's *Jātakamālā* bears witness to prolonged study of his predecessor's writings. Similarly in a fragment of another *kāvya* life of the Buddha, which has been discovered in Central Asia, the passage preserved, dealing with the subject of the second half of *B.*, vii, is clearly modelled on it both in general scheme and in detail[2], while another metrical life, only extant in Chinese, the *Fo pen hsing ching* (*TI* no. 193), which I have not been able to examine in detail, certainly shows at times a definite connexion with the *Buddhacarita*[3].

---

[1] Tr. Takakusu, 166. I Tsing's notice of the poet is curious in some respects. He is unaware that this poem had been translated into Chinese two centuries previously, and besides a passing allusion to minor works he only names in addition a work whose title is given by Takakusu as *Sūtrālaṁkāraśāstra*, which has usually been understood to refer to the work now known to be the *Kalpanāmaṇḍitikā* of Kumāralāta, an author whom he does not mention. The omission of the *Saundarananda* is so curious that it seems permissible to speculate whether, in view of the frequent corruptness of Chinese works where Indian proper names are concerned, the original name that stood in this passage was not that of this poem.

[2] See *JRAS*, 1911, 770ff. Verse 84 is in the *puṣpitāgrā* metre and wrongly described there.

[3] See notes on *B.*, i. 10 and 31; the general scheme of the work (Wohlgemuth, p. 62) is also obviously affected by the *Buddhacarita*, and note Ebbe Tuneld, *Recherches sur les traditions bouddhiques* (Lund, 1915), p. 15.

Yet learned monks did not concur whole-heartedly in the popular verdict, and so it happened that of the known works only the *Buddhacarita* was translated into Chinese and Tibetan and that no commentary was ever written either on it or on the *Saundarananda*, whereas two exist for the *Jātakamālā*, which offers far fewer difficulties of interpretation. Aśvaghoṣa in fact, by writing for the general public and by introducing so much Hindu learning, offended against the Puritan moment in Buddhism, which finds expression in Pali at *Aṅguttara*, III, 107, and *Saṁyutta*, II, 267, opposing the Buddha's sūtras to *suttantā kavikatā kāveyyā cittakkharā bāhirakā sāvakabhāsitā*[1]. The poet proves himself to be conscious that his methods required justification; for the final verse of the *Buddhacarita* states that, in his devotion to the Buddha, he studied the scriptures and wrote the work, not to display his learning or his skill in *kāvya*, but for the benefit and happiness of the world. This did not go far enough to obviate criticism, and in the last two verses of the later epic he sets up a reasoned defence of his procedure, explaining that his object was to hold the attention of the worldly-minded and the non-believer (*anyamanas* covers both these), for whose benefit he had coated the medicinal powder of sound doctrine with the jam of *kāvya* method and that his hearers were to reject the superficially attractive dross and to pick out the grains of pure gold from his poem.

These points govern our attitude in determining Aśvaghoṣa's position as a Buddhist; that is, we are to expect statements which make no innovation in legend or doctrine, but which reproduce in a manner intelligible to the ordinary man of some education, whether Buddhist or Hindu, the principles of the Buddhist religion as understood in his day. His works therefore are invaluable to us, not for their originality of thought, but as giving us a complete and coherent picture of the faith of a typical Buddhist at a particular epoch. If I call it invaluable, it is because the earlier Buddhist documents have undergone

---

[1] Cp. also *ASPP.*, 328, on *kavikṛtaṁ kāvyam*.

interpolation and manipulation to such an extent that the exact state of belief at any given moment till we reach the works of well-defined personalities such as Nāgārjuna, Asaṅga, Vasubandhu or Buddhaghosa, who are all later than Aśvaghoṣa, is more a matter of subjective deduction than of objective fact.

Three sides of his religion in particular merit examination, his devotion to the Buddha, his handling of legend and his exposition of doctrine. Of the first I have already said something in treating of *śraddhā* and need only add that, if the earlier accounts have left us many striking records of the Buddha's gracious personality, in none do we find such glowing fervour, such ardent faith as in these poems, and it is a grievous loss that we do not possess the Sanskrit text of the noble eulogy in *B.*, xxvii. In sincerity and depth of religious feeling Aśvaghoṣa stands closer to the author of the *Bhagavadgītā* than to the great poets of the classical period, just as in Italian painting we find truer manifestations of religion in the productions of the Trecento and Quattrocento with their imperfect strivings after power of expression than in the technically incomparable pictures of the Cinquecento.

But devotional feeling is not always, or even often, accompanied by the historical sense and in any case we have no right to expect in a writer of the first century A.D. an account of the Buddha as he really lived. It is not yet possible however to discuss critically his handling of legend, which must wait for the full exploitation of the Chinese and Tibetan sources. Still we can see that his claim to have studied the scriptures for the story is justified. Except for one or two minor points, no incidents or details are included for which, few as our means of knowledge are, we cannot find authority elsewhere, and his additions are limited to descriptions in the *kāvya* style, such as of Śuddhodana in canto ii of both poems, of the progress through the streets of Kapilavāstu in *B.*, iii, or of the women's temptations in *B.*, iv, and to the speeches put into the mouths of his characters. When the Buddha speaks, the matter is sometimes taken from his sermons such as *B.*, xi. 22–31, an embroidery on a frequently recurring series of similes, or the still untranslated sermon to Prasenajit, *B.*, xx. 12–51, into which the chief themes of the *Kosalasaṁyutta* are worked, or sometimes from current Buddhist apologetic against Brahmanical doctrines. If the speaker is not a Buddhist, he is represented as setting out the arguments of the learned men of the day, e.g. the minister in *B.*, ix, or Arāḍa describing a prevalent form of Sāṁkhya-Yoga teaching. In some cases he seems to have used sūtras in a more original form than we have them in to-day, as for instance in his versions of the Aśoka legend and of the first council. In the latter he omits the two regular later interpolations, the humiliating treatment meted out to Ānanda and the promulgation of the Vinaya by Upāli, and follows the account of our oldest source, the verses of the *Chia yeh chieh ching* [1], omitting the legend of Gavāṁpati's end. In general the miraculous element is not stressed, and many well-known marvels, such as the removal of the elephant's body, the shade of the *jambu* tree that did not move, etc., are absent; Aśvaghoṣa wishes all through to display the moral and spiritual grandeur of the Buddha, an aim which would have been impeded by the thaumaturgy of the later legends. On the other hand he frequently hints at the existence of legends which he does not tell in detail; a demonstrable instance occurs at *B.*, i. 11, where the phrase *cyutaḥ khād iva* suggests a reference to the descent from the Tuṣita heavens, not otherwise mentioned, but which he is proved to know by *S.*, ii. 48. Similar suggestions are *vratasaṁskṛtā* of Māyā at *B.*, i. 9, the hint that the Buddha was born free of the impurities of the womb at *ib.*, 16, *vayasyavat* of Kanthaka, vi. 54, and Bimbisāra's *svavayaḥ*, x. 22, all explained in the notes; and of the same order is the insinuation at *S.*, ii. 32, of what is never explicitly stated, that Śuddhodana was a cakravartin monarch. Perhaps we should infer that the Buddha legend had already developed a good deal beyond the form it takes in the *Buddhacarita*, but that

[1] Translated Przyluski, *Le Concile de Rājagṛha*, pp. 3ff.

Aśvaghoṣa considered the innovations to be lacking in authority and therefore not fit for specific mention. Occasionally on the other hand he takes a point from an earlier work and elaborates it, as in the description of Māra's army in the guise of Hindu ascetics at *B.*, xiii. 21–24, suggested by the *Padhāna-sutta,* but dropped from the later versions of the story.

Altogether the impression left on my mind is that the poet was careful to use the most authoritative sources open to him and that the *Buddhacarita* gives us the Buddha-story in the shape which a pious Buddhist of the first century A.D., actuated more by devotion to the Buddha and respect for scripture than by love for the marvellous, would have accepted. The general framework of the plot is apparently dependent on two sources. Cantos i–xx give a continuous narrative of the Buddha's life and mission up to the dedication of the Jetavana vihāra and thus cover the exact period of the story of the 'present' in the Pali *Nidānakathā* ; the latter, as now extant, is late and the poet may be presumed to have used an earlier version, no longer in existence. Canto xxi contains a *digvijaya* of the Buddha, recounting his conversions of beings of every kind all over northern India and not probably taken from any one source, and ends with the story of Devadatta and the elephant. Cantos xxii–xxviii reproduce the full extent of the *Mahāparinirvāṇa-sūtra,* including the story of the First Council, which in the Pali canon has been severed from the version in the *Dīgha* and inserted in the *Vinaya.* In the *Saundarananda* also much of the teaching can be traced back to specific sūtras still extant in one form or another, as can be seen from the notes to my translation or from cantos xiii and xiv, whose framework seems to be modelled on the sūtra at *Aṅguttara,* IV, 166–168, though the version of the story, on which the poem is based, has still to be discovered.

The conclusion that Aśvaghoṣa had a preference for, or at least mainly used, the earlier sources, is strengthened by an examination of his doctrinal position. We are now able to grasp the Abhidharma system as a whole and to estimate how far it had travelled from the earlier dogmatism, thanks to Professor de la Vallée Poussin's richly annotated translation of Vasubandhu's *Abhidharmakośa.* Even though the *Vibhāṣā* is almost certainly substantially later in the main than the poet, its special views must have been taking shape in his day. The new school arose out of a new angle of vision, the philosophical approach replacing the moral standpoint from which the earlier teachers developed their system. The mechanism of the act, *karman,* is worked out in connexion with an elaborate theory of causation and the older dissection of the individual into *skandhas, āyatanas* and *dhātus* is politely put on one side for the conception of an individual flux of consciousness (*saṁtāna*), the elements of which consist of ultimates called *dharmas* of a fixed number of varieties ; the momentary appearance of the latter in the individual sequence is explained by the special forces *prāpti* and the *saṁskṛtalakṣaṇas,* which determine what *dharmas* can appear in any given *saṁtāna* at any given moment and how they appear and disappear. By the *kṣaṇikavāda* the individual is seen as a series of moments and this analysis of time into its minutest possible division inevitably brings in its train the atomic conception of matter (*rūpa*). In correspondence with these changes the path to enlightenment undergoes a metamorphosis which makes it almost unrecognisable to those accustomed to the older terminology. Definite traces of even the beginnings of these theories are hard to find in Aśvaghoṣa, except that it is not impossible to read the *kṣaṇikavāda* into one or two phrases (such as *samajanmaniṣṭha,* which I may have rendered wrongly at *S.*, xviii. 17). He knows nothing of the atomic system, of the *saṁtāna,* or of the new form of the Path, and his standpoint remains purely moral, free from any attempt at metaphysical speculation.

To give a full outline of his beliefs would involve going over much ground well known to us from other schools of the Hīnayāna, and I limit myself therefore to a few outstanding points. He accepts the orthodox Buddhist conception of the individual as consisting of the five *skandhas* and as being without a 'soul', and the individual existence is inevitably and always bound up with suffering (*duḥkha*) by reason of its being subject to the power of the act (*S.*, xvii. 19); how then does the act work? The answer seems to be, by reason of the *hetu*, the cause. This *hetu* is primarily made up of three factors, *rāga*, *dveṣa* and *moha*, and according as the individual's acts cause these three factors to increase or dwindle, so are the nature of his rebirths determined, just as in early Sāṁkhya the sphere of rebirth is determined by the relative proportion of the three *guṇas*; and he is only released from rebirth by their disappearance (*S.*, xvi. 20–24). These three factors are called the *akuśalamūlāni*, the roots of evil, and are recognised in the Pali Abhidhamma as the *hetu par excellence.* Schematism requires to correspond to them a group of their opposites, the *kuśalamūlāni*, and though Aśvaghoṣa never mentions such a trio, its existence is perhaps to be inferred from the fact that the *hetu* can work for good as well as for evil (*B.*, ii. 56, and xii. 68, and *S.*, v. 17). The above theory is in fact that of the Pali Nikāyas, which habitually describe Nirvāṇa as attained by the disappearance (*khaya*) of the roots of evil. In the later Abhidharma the belief in the roots of good and evil persists, but has been allotted so subordinate a position in the analysis of the causal system which governs the individual that it has lost its fundamental significance [1].

Since to obtain salvation the individual must bring about the disappearance of the three factors, through which *karman* works, he is first, we are told, to train his body by the discipline of *śīla* and next his mind by *smṛti*, constant awareness of the process of his thoughts, and then to give himself up to yoga, selecting for meditation according to *S.*, xvi. 53ff., those subjects which are specially adapted for overcoming that one of the three factors which is most active in him. Thus he rids himself

---

[1] The *gotra* theory of the Mahāyāna, however, appears to owe something to this doctrine.

of them and obtains Nirvāṇa, the deathless state. It is generally acknowledged now that Buddhism teaches salvation by means of yoga, but there is no extant treatise till we reach the Yogācāra school which lays so much stress on it as the *Saundarananda* ; it is not clear, however, whether this was a speciality of the sect to which its author belonged[1], or whether, in the desire to appeal to non-Buddhists, he was striving to show how similar in respect of yoga Buddhism was to the corresponding Brahmanical doctrine.

The evolutionary process of yogic practice in Buddhism is not yet clear to us. The original term was *samādhi*, which perhaps did not indicate any of the phenomena associated with the trances of yoga but merely some kind of mental concentration. That the interrelated terms of *dhyāna*, trance, and *prajñā*, the form of knowledge obtained by trance, came into use later, is shown by their omission from the eightfold path and the consequent difficulty of finding a place for them in that scheme[2]. *Bhāvanā*, which is closely connected with *prajñā*, is possibly of still later origin and suggests the gradual elaboration of transic methods, such as we find in the *Saundarananda.* Aśvaghoṣa's account is not easy to follow, because we have to reconcile the descriptions of method in cantos xv and xvi with those of the application in xvii. He makes three important distinctions, the first between *pratisaṁkhyāna* and *bhāvanā* at *S.*, xv. 4-5 ; the former corresponds more or less to the *darśanamārga* of the Abhidharma, but whether it is produced by yoga or not is not specifically stated. The other distinctions are between *smṛti* and *samādhi* in xv and *bhāvanā* in xvi, and between the mundane and supermundane paths in xvii. For the last the mundane path consists in preparation of the mind (*cetaḥparikarman*, xvii. 5) by means of yoga (xvii. 10, 11) and is transformed into the supermundane path by a thoroughgoing

---

[1] See Demiéville, *op. cit.*, 47, a passage which suggests that the Kaukulikas laid great stress on yogic practices.

[2] See note in translation on *S.*, xvi. 31–33.

examination of the phenomenal world (*ib.*, 15–21). In practice the three may perhaps coincide, the first of each pair being devoted to suppressing the outward manifestations of the *kleśas* and the second to rooting out the *anuśayas*, the latent tendencies to the *kleśas*. The last pair may also explain a puzzle, which has defeated wiser heads than mine. In canto xvii, after the aspirant has reached the supermundane path, he acquires successively the three stages of *srotaāpanna*, *sakṛdāgāmin* and *anāgāmin*, and it is only thereafter that the four trances are described and they are said to be the immediate precursors of Arhatship. But xvi. 1, in accordance with the view generally prevailing in the schools, shows that the trances are mastered in a preliminary stage before the process of *bhāvanā* begins; and that they are even accessible to non-Buddhists is the regular belief, which *B.*, xii, shows Aśvaghoṣa to share. Now *B.*, v. 10, proves the poet to know the distinction between *sāsrava* and *anāsrava* (=in practice *laukika* and *lokottara*) trances, and it may be therefore that Nanda was unable to obtain the *anāsrava* trances necessary to Arhatship till he became an Anāgāmin. But the point remains obscure.

To sum up, we may say that Aśvaghoṣa took his stand on the older dogmatism and was very little affected by the developments of the fullblown Abhidharma, and that to him the kernel of Buddhism lay in personal devotion to the Buddha and in the practice of yoga.

iii. The Scholar.

The traditions of Indian literature require that a poet should have mastered the general principles of all sciences and should display his knowledge of them with accuracy; *sarvatodikkā hi kavayaḥ*. Aśvaghoṣa observed this rule fervently, not to say pedantically. It is accuracy, not original thought, that is prescribed, and any lapse from correctitude evoked without fail the censure of the critics; we are therefore bound to assume that his learned references are strictly in accordance with the authorities he used. Since too these authorities are for the most part no longer extant, enquiry into the nature of his knowledge is of considerable interest for the light it throws on the history of Indian thought.

To start with the literature known to the poet, as a Brahman he was presumably taught some portion at least of the Veda, and, leaving aside for the moment the question whether he was influenced by the poetic methods of the Vedic writers, we observe occasionally in his vocabulary unmistakeable signs of his knowledge, such as *dvija* for Agni at *B.*, xi. 71, or *śri* in the sense of 'emit (heat)' at *S.*, i. 2. The phrase *randhrair nācūcudad bhṛtyān*, *S.*, ii. 27, seems to be a reminiscence of the Rigvedic epithet *radhracodana*, and very ingenious is the hint in *B.*, xiii. 68, of the application of *nābhi* to Agni and Soma by using the word *dhāman* with its Vedic sense to be understood secondarily. An allusion to a Vedic legend that was forgotten by the classic age is provided by the name Aurvaśeya, *B.*, ix. 9, for Vasiṣṭha. Similarly acquaintance with the ritual literature is shown at a few places. The ceremony of measuring out soma is referred to at *S.*, i. 15, and ii. 36, at the latter of which the occurrence of the plain root *mā*, instead of compounded with *vi* or *ud*, suggests the possibility that he knew the *Śatapathabrāhmaṇa*, which is apparently alone in using the verb thus. A knowledge of the finer points of ritual can be inferred from the employment of *prokṣaṇa* and *abhyukṣaṇa* at *B.*, xii. 30, for the latter of which in this sense *PW* and *PWK* can only quote two Śrautasūtras. The words *nivarta*, *S.*, xv. 44, and *vimad*, 'grow sober', *S.*, ix. 30, are only elsewhere substantiated by the *Brāhmaṇas*, to which stratum of literature *samāruh* at *B.*, iv. 24, seems also to belong; and the reference to Prajāpati's act of creation by *tapas* at *B.*, ii. 51, may be to any one of a hundred passages in the same class of literature. For the Upaniṣads, besides a number of possible parallels, the chief piece of evidence is *S.*, xvi. 17, whose resemblance to *Śvet. Up.*, i. 2, can hardly be fortuitous; and, taking into account the remarkable coincidence between

B., xii. 21, and *Śvet. Up.*, v. 2, I think it probable that the poet was well acquainted with this work.

When we come to the epics, the wealth of the material is overwhelming and yet uncertain in its bearing; for, if my notes are crammed with references to them for explaining difficulties or giving parallels, we cannot as a rule say that the poet must have known the particular passage quoted and that he might not have taken the phrase from literature no longer available to us. This applies with especial force to the *Mahābhārata*; thus I have shown in the notes to *B.* xii, that much of Arāḍa's exposition of the Sāṁkhya system has close parallels in the *Mokṣadharma*, the connexion in one case extending over several verses of the same passage. But it is more natural to suppose that the common matter goes back to a single original, possibly a textbook of the Vārṣagaṇya school. The two portions of the epic of which we might most surely expect the poet to show knowledge are the story of Nala, which is told in a primitive *kāvya* style, and the *Bhagavadgītā*. In the former the most striking parallels are i. 30, to *S.*, iv. 5, x. 26-7, to *S.*, iv. 42–4 (extending even to the common use of the verb *kṛṣ*), and xxi. 3, 6 and 7, to *B.*, viii. 18-9; but similar motifs may have occurred in poems intermediate between the two writers and we cannot presume direct influence. As regards the latter I am not among those who attribute a great age to it, but see no conclusive reason why, at least as regards the older parts, it should not have been in existence in Aśvaghoṣa's day. In any case it is not far apart from him in thought and phraseology, and sometimes the parallelism is close, as between *S.*, xvi. 38, and *Gītā*, xiii. 10. In one passage, *Gītā*, ii. 66, has a verse built up just like *S.*, xi. 33, one of the *pādas* being almost identical; but unfortunately the former verse is omitted in the Kashmiri recension and may be an interpolation, so that no conclusion can safely be drawn from it. We cannot therefore either assert or deny that the poet was acquainted with this work.

As for proper names, allusions to the main characters

are very few, namely to the entire destruction of the Kurus at *B.*, xi. 31, and *S.*, ix. 20, to Arjuna once only and that for the sake of alliteration at *B.*, x. 17, to Bhīṣma for a story known to the *Harivaṁśa* but not to the epic, at *B.*, xi. 18, and *S.*, vii. 44, and to Pāṇḍu as an illustration of fatal attachment to women at *B.*, iv. 79, and *S.*, vii. 45. Many legends are cited, which are to be found in the *MBh.*, but not always in quite the same form. Thus Aśvaghoṣa is fond of the story of Śantanu's love for Gaṅgā (*B.*, xiii. 12, *S.*, vii. 41, and x. 56) which is told in the *Ādiparvan*, but it is apparent that he knew a version which enlarged on Śantanu's grief when Gaṅgā left him, a point not dwelt on in the epic. Many of the stories he alludes to are not to be found in the *MBh.* and despite the many parallels we cannot establish that Aśvaghoṣa knew any portion of the epic in the form in which we now have it. But it does seem certain that he knew much literature dealing with the legends he quotes, possibly often in *kāvya* form, which is now irretrievably lost to us; besides a poem on Śantanu, which has perhaps left its impress on the *MBh.* version, and another on the love-story of Śūrpaka, the fisherman, and the princess Kumudvatī, discussed in the note on *B.*, xiii. 11, I surmise also the existence of a poem or cycle dealing with the legends of Kṛṣṇa and Balarāma, and there is some reason to think he used sources also exploited by the *Harivaṁśa*, presumably a collection of legends such as we have in a later form in the still unedited Bengali recension of the *Padmapurāṇa*, *Svargakhaṇḍa*.

The case is entirely different with the *Rāmāyaṇa*, for which an inhabitant of Sāketa, the scene of its most poignant episodes and the capital of its dynasty, could not but keep a warm place in his heart, however his religious beliefs had changed. Aśvaghoṣa never wearies of reminding us that the Buddha belonged to the dynasty of his home and strikes this note in the very first verse of the *Buddhacarita*. He acknowledges Vālmīki as the *ādikavi* (*B.*, i. 43) and calls him 'inspired' (*dhīmān*, *S.*, i. 26). We may therefore expect to find, and we do find, that he has been strongly influenced by it. In so far as this affects his poetic style, I reserve consideration for the next section, but here it is in place to enquire to what extent he knew the poem in its present form [1].

The late Professor Gawroński proved, conclusively as I hold, that Aśvaghoṣa knew certain portions of the second book, the *Ayodhyākāṇḍa*, in very much the condition that we have them in to-day and that he took pleasure in drawing a comparison between the Buddha quitting his home and Rāma leaving for the forest. That he knew the continuation of the story appears from a reference in *B.*, xxviii. 31, but whether in the present form or not is not clear to me from the wording [2]. It certainly does seem that there are many fewer passages in the later books likely to have influenced the Buddhist poet and those mostly of a commonplace order, which might have been found elsewhere. The question really turns on whether Aśvaghoṣa knew some or all of the three passages in the *Rām.*, describing how Hanumān visited Rāvaṇa's palace and saw the women asleep [3], and, till the epic is critically edited from the best surviving MSS. of all recensions, I would refrain from giving a definite answer.

More definite statements can be made on other points. Jacobi took the view that the original epic started with a passage descriptive of Ayodhyā and of Daśaratha and his court, which survives with additions in the first book [4]. That Aśva-

---

[1] Cowell raised the question of the relation of the *Buddhacarita* to the *Rām.* in the introduction to his edition. For later handling of it see especially Walter, *Uebereinstimmungen bei den indischen Kunstdichtern*, Leipzig, 1905; Gawroński, *Studies about the Sanskrit Buddhist Literature*, pp. 27–40; Gurner, *JASB*, 1927, 347–368; Diwekar, *Les Fleurs de Rhètorique dans l'Inde*, Paris, 1930.

[2] The passage ran in Sanskrit more or less thus:—

Sītābhidhānaṁ parigṛhya mṛtyum
atyutkaṭo 'pi praṇanāśa Daityaḥ |

[3] See Gurner, *loc. cit.*, 352.

[4] H. Jacobi, *Das Rāmāyaṇa* (Bonn, 1893), 50ff.

ghoṣa knew such a description and in a more extended form than Jacobi allowed in his reconstruction seems probable from the many echoes of it in his poems, and it is to be inferred from *S.*, i. 26, that the story of Vālmīki's having taught the poem to Kuśa and Lava was familiar to him. But there is a curious proof that he did not know the *Bālakāṇḍa* as we now have it. At *B.*, iv. 20, and *S.*, vii. 35, he quotes the tale of the disturbance of Viśvāmitra's austerities by the Apsaras, Ghṛtācī; our only other authority for this is a verse in almost identical terms at *Rām.*, iv. 35, 7, where it has every appearance of being an interpolation[1]. The story is told at length in the *Bālakāṇḍa*, substituting Menakā for Ghṛtācī and betraying its late date by the unusual agreement between the versions of the different recensions. But the *Fo pen hsing chi ching* (*TI*, III, 726*b*) takes up in its prose the various comparisons of the *Buddhacarita* passage, replacing Ghṛtācī by Mekayā. As the Chinese characters transliterating *yă* and *nă* are easily confused, we have evidently a case of corruption combined with transposition and should read Menakā. Why then should the compiler of this work substitute Menakā for Ghṛtācī, unless he knew the *Bālakāṇḍa*, which contains the standard version of the tale? Hence we should presumably infer that the story of Viśvāmitra and Menakā was introduced into the *Rāmāyaṇa* between the time of Aśvaghoṣa and that of the compiler of the FP. As regards the *Uttarakāṇḍa*, I can find no reason to suppose that the poet knew any portion of it.

Finally there is another point from which we may deduce an important inference. At *B.*, ix. 9, the poet compares the visit of Śuddhodana's purohita and minister to the future Buddha with the visit of Vasiṣṭha and Vāmadeva, Daśaratha's purohita and minister, to Rāma in the forest. The epic contains no such episode, but tells at length of Bharata's visit to his

[1] Interpolations in the epic may easily be later than Aśvaghoṣa and show his influence; thus iii. 1, 35, with its application of *nisvana* and *śūnya* to a hermitage, is probably inspired by *S.*, i. 10, 11, the omission of the verse from the Bombay edition suggesting that it is not authentic.

brother. Vāmadeva's name occurs very rarely in the epic as we have it, but he is mentioned coupled with Vasiṣṭha precisely in connexion with Bharata's journey to the forest in the *MBh.* version, iii. 15981. It is incredible that Aśvaghoṣa should invent such an incident, when he shows knowledge of the existing text of the *Ayodhyākāṇḍa*, and only one explanation holds water, namely that the entire passage recounting Bharata's visit to Rāma was not in the text the poet knew, that it had in its place an account of a mission headed by Vasiṣṭha and Vāmadeva with the object of inducing Rāma to return to Ayodhyā, and that in the process of gradual sentimentalising, to which the epic was subject for many generations, this passage was deliberately replaced by one which it was thought would do more honour to Bharata's character, leaving as its sole trace the *MBh.*'s mention of the purohita and minister.

Next we may consider what knowledge Aśvaghoṣa had of the various sciences, bearing in mind that, as he used treatises no longer in existence, we cannot hope to be able always to explain his statements or to trace their source.

References to secular law are rare in *kāvya* generally and none are to be found in these poems, so far as I can see, except at *B.*, xxii. 47, to the principle that women are always under guardianship. Of the ecclesiastical law, if I may call it so, governing the relation of guru and pupil, Aśvaghoṣa alludes at *S.*, i. 22-23, to the rule that a pupil of kṣatriya descent assumes the *gotra* of his guru, and the argument of canto xviii of the same poem, as we may see particularly from verses 1–3 and 48, is based on the principle that a pupil on the successful completion of his studies should give his guru a present. The rules of polity for kings, which were originally a branch of the same science, are repeatedly mentioned, mostly in similes [1]. At *B.*, i. 41, he treats as the standard authorities the works of Uśanas, or Śukra, and Bṛhaspati, which, though not extant, are equally called the fundamental treatises in the *MBh.* He

---

[1] Briefly discussed by me at *JRAS*, 1929, 77–81.

uses the term *rājaśāstra* for the science of politics, while *nīti* at *B.*, iv. 62, means the principles of worldly conduct, and *daṇḍanīti* at *S.*, ii. 28, the preservation of order ; the classifications of treasure and horses at *B.*, ii. 2*ab* and 4*d*, presumably derive from the categories of some work on *vārtā*. The details contain little worth mention and the one point of general interest is the question whether he was acquainted with the *Arthaśāstra* of Kauṭilya. The latter presupposes that the formal study of political science must have been in progress for centuries previously, and it is marked by the use of special terms whose occurrence in the *rājadharma* section of the *MBh.* is very rare. Its attitude is realistic in contrast to the idealistic, often impractical, views of the *dharmaśāstra*, but the only trace of such a standpoint in these poems is to be found in *B.*, ii. 55, which is capable of a sinister interpretation in the light of the *Arthaśāstra* ; it is improbable however that Kauṭilya was the first writer to stress the necessity for kings of keeping their sons under guard. The political riddle at *B.*, ii. 42, though soluble under the teaching of the *MBh.*, cannot be plausibly interpreted from the *Arthaśāstra*, and the use of *anaya* at *B.*, ii. 42, is contrary to Kauṭilya's vocabulary, who pronounces for *apanaya* in this sense (*KA.*, vi. 2, 6ff.) ; the technical terms introduced by Kauṭilya, such as *vijigīṣu*, *upajāpa* and *atisaṁdhā*, are missing in the poems, though regularly taken up by later writers. It seems hardly possible then that Aśvaghoṣa knew this work. On the other hand he uses several terms, not of a technical nature but unknown to the classical language, in the same way that Kauṭilya does, such as *viguṇa*, 'faithless' (*S.*, ii. 18), *rātrisattra* (*ib.*, 28)[1], and *śakyasāmanta* (*ib.*, 45) etc. To suppose that no great interval separates the two writers seems therefore natural.

Subsidiary to the science of politics according to the *Śukranīti* was the knowledge of the points of a horse, and, as we have nothing early at all on this subject, the description

[1] For this word see Charpentier, *JRAS*, 1934, 113.

of an ideal horse according to Indian views at *B.*, v. 73, is of great interest. Unfortunately the readings of the verse are uncertain and could not be settled, though I consulted the only known MS. of the *Śālihotraśāstra*, the best treatise on the subject; the tradition that Śālihotra was the standard authority for horses goes back at least to the story of Nala, but the extant work is apparently much later. So far as I can see, later writers show no advance on Aśvaghoṣa's day in the judgement of horses, except in the irrelevant matter of lucky signs (curtly referred to at *B.*, ii. 4). On the kindred subject of elephants the poet is well acquainted with the methods of catching, training and riding them, but I can identify no technical terms such as would prove the existence of a formal *hastividyā*.

I have referred above to the statement at *B.*, iv. 64, that Udāyin was learned in *nīti*, the science of worldly conduct, which may indicate some collection of sayings or a manual of etiquette, prescribing the rules for behaviour in society and for conducting affairs of gallantry. In this connexion I observe that the poet seems to know the principles laid down in the first book of the *Kāmasūtra*, for which the original authority is there said to be Cārāyaṇa. The passages in question are detailed in the notes to *S.*, iv and vi, in my translation. Whether he knew the original authorities for other sections of that work is open to question, but the *savilāsarata* of *B.*, v. 56, certainly suggests the *citraratāni* of the *Kāmasūtra*, though I would hesitate to see a technical term of erotics in *kaṇṭhasūtra* at *ib.*, 58.

Of all the sciences medicine was the one most studied by Buddhists, and Aśvaghoṣa repeatedly refers to it in similes, notably to the three humours and their special treatment (*S.*, xvi. 59ff., *B.*, xi. 40). But the allusions are too general in wording to add to our knowledge or to be capable of attribution to any known source. Magic is mentioned a few times, thus with reference to snakebite (*S.*, v. 31, and ix. 13), to the discovery of treasure (*S.*, i. 39), and to *indrajāla* (*S.*, v. 45). The only aspect of astronomy or astrology with which the poet shows acquaintance is that relating to the lunar asterisms and their regents (*B.*, ii. 36, xvi. 2, xvii. 41; see also note on ix. 11). But I find no allusions to the minor sciences, such as the *śilpa-śāstras* (except for the technique of goldsmiths, *S.*, xv. 66–69, and xvi. 65-66), the testing of jewels, the methods of theft etc.

The poems reflect at times the high level to which contemporary art had reached; several references (*B.*, viii. 25, *S.*, vii. 48 and xv. 39) imply the existence of painters with great representational powers, and occasional descriptions are based either explicitly (*B.*, v. 52) or implicitly (*B.*, iii. 19–22) on the sculpture of the day, while a standardised architectural practice, *vāstuvidyā*, is guaranteed by *S.*, i. 41ff. Chinese tradition has also a legend suggesting that Aśvaghoṣa was a great musician [1] but this is not borne out by the poems which, unlike later *kāvya* works, contain no technical terms of music and suggest only a general knowledge of the subject, such as of the four kinds of musical instruments (*S.*, x. 25).

Not much light is thrown by these works on the state of contemporary religion. For the older forms of worship we have repeated mention of oblations to Agni, and references to the soma ceremonial (*B.*, ii. 37, *S.*, i. 15, ii. 36) and to animal sacrifices (*B.*, x. 39, xi. 64–67). Brahmanical asceticism is described in general terms at *S.*, i. 1–16, and in detail in *B.*, vii, and the existence of Śaiva ascetics is to be inferred from *B.*, vii. 51, and xiii. 21, and possibly of Vaiṣṇavas, if *cakradhara* at *B.*, vii. 3, is to be understood as 'bearing the imprint of Viṣṇu's discus'. Of the more popular forms of religion *S.*, iv. 2, takes it as natural that the chief gods for a kṣatriya to worship were Indra and Kubera, and besides numerous references to the former, attention has been drawn by many scholars from Cowell onwards to the allusions to his flag festival (*B.*, i. 58, viii. 73, xxvii. 56, *S.*, iv. 46). The Maruts are his attendants (*B.*, v. 27, *S.*, i. 62), and Jayanta his son (*B.*, ix. 5), for whom *B.*, v. 27, seems to indicate Sanatkumāra as an alternative

---

[1] S. Lévi, *JA*, 1928, ii, 199.

name. We also find Śuddhodana worshipping the lunar asterism Puṣya (*B.*, ii. 36). Of the newer religions the references to Kṛṣṇa and Balarāma contain no hint that they were treated as gods, though the inscriptions prove the cult in Western India for a couple of centuries previously; and besides *B.*, xxvii. 79, where C has 'the mighty golden-winged bird' and T 'Viṣṇu's Garuḍa', the only mention of Viṣṇu is under the name of Upendra as a satellite of Indra (*S.*, xi. 49). Śiva on the other hand, to whose worship according to Chinese tradition, which on this point receives some support from the knowledge these poems show of the *Śvet. Up.*, Aśvaghoṣa was addicted before his conversion, is referred to several times in the *Buddhacarita*, but not at all in the *Saundarananda*. The verse *B.*, x. 3, implies a knowledge of his ascetic practices and xiii. 16 quotes the story immortalised by Kālidāsa in the *Kumārasaṁbhava*, but in a variant form, by which Kāma succeeds in his mission and was not burnt up by the fire of the god's eye [1]. At *B.*, i. 88, we have an allusion to the birth of Skanda, who is possibly also the Senāpati of *S.*, vii. 43. Perhaps also the belief in a Creator (*B.*, ix. 63) should come under the head of Śaivism. Altogether it is very much the picture to be expected except for omission of the newer forms of worship.

Turning next to philosophy, we note that, like most Buddhist writers, he refers to the heterodox systems, for which our knowledge is confined to casual remarks scattered over Sanskrit literature; he alludes incidentally to the fatalists, whether believers in Time or Destiny (*S.*, xvi. 17), but more fully to the materialists (*B.*, ix. 56-57) and to the Svabhāvavādins (*ib.*, 58–62), the latter being one of the fullest statements of their position that we have. Jainism is ignored [2], but the

---

[1] For the significance of this see Sten Konow on the name Anaṅga in *Festschrift Wackernagel*, pp. 1–8, in which he does not refer to this verse. I was wrong in suggesting in my translation that the crux at *S.*, x. 53, could be solved by seeing in it an allusion to the burning up of Kāma.

[2] The only allusions are to the conversion of Jains by the Buddha at Vaiśālī and Śrāvastī, *B.*, xxi. 16, 28.

īśvaravāda is also given a verse (*B.*, ix. 63). None of these however can be discussed in detail, till the important but difficult passage at *B.*, xviii. 20–56, refuting these heretical systems is disentangled, though it may be remarked in passing that the nature of the arguments there argues philosophy to have been still at a primitive stage. Of the orthodox systems, while there is no specific reference to the *Pūrvamīmāṁsāsūtras*, unless Yaśodharā's arguments at *B.*, viii. 61ff., are held to refer to vi. 1, 6–21, of Jaimini's sūtras, *vidhi* is used in the technical sense of this school at *B.*, ix. 66, and the Vedic scheme of worship is referred to several times and formally rejected at *B.*, xi. 64ff., as regards the efficacy of animal sacrifice. Nor could we expect any suggestion of the Uttaramīmāṁsā, but more important is the fact that the Vaiśeṣika system, whose outstanding position is freely recognised in later Buddhist literature, was entirely unknown to Aśvaghoṣa. The argument *ex silentio* for once has cogent force, because in later Buddhist lists corresponding to *S.*, xvi. 17 (e.g. *Laṅkāvatāra* and *Visuddhimagga*), reference to the Vaiśeṣikas is included by the addition of the word *aṇu*[1]. With regard to the *Nyāyasūtras*, my view may not be found acceptable; for I hold that after deduction of certain interpolations the first *adhyāya* is much older than the rest of the sūtras and that, unlike them, it is unaffected by Vaiśeṣika tenets and could not have originated in a milieu subject to their influence. And it is precisely this section of the sūtras, of which Aśvaghoṣa to my mind has knowledge, though in that case he may have known it in a form more primitive than that which has reached us. He seems at times to delight in expressing Buddhist views in a way that would remind Hindu readers of their own authorities, and I still can find no reason for resiling from the opinion that the wording of *S.*, xvi. 18, *lokasya doṣebhya iti pravṛttiḥ*, is deliberately taken from *Nyāyasūtra*, i. 1, 18, *pravartanālakṣaṇā doṣāḥ*, all the more so that the preceding verses 14 and 15 suggest an early theory

---

[1] Cp. also the table in Liebenthal, *Satkārya*, 31.

of *anumāna*. There is also a clear reference to Nyāya principles at *S.*, i. 14, however we explain the verse.

I have kept to the last the most important case, the Sāṁkhya as set out by Arāḍa in canto xii of the *Buddhacarita*. The standard treatise on this philosophy, Īśvarakṛṣṇa's *Sāṁkhyakārikās*, is several centuries later than this poem; and, though it was so successful in imposing its views on later generations that we have no authoritative statement of any diverging system, there were according to Chinese sources eighteen Sāṁkhya schools, one of which, the best known apparently, passed under the name of Vārṣagaṇya[1]. It is therefore hardly reasonable to suppose that Īśvarakṛṣṇa's explanations of the twentyfive *tattvas* would hold good for preceding periods, and I was able some years ago to point to some important matters in which his views are fairly recent innovations[2]. Much reflection since then and repeated examination of the relevant passages in the *MBh.*, which are our chief, almost our sole, source for early Sāṁkhya, have brought me to views on its nature, which differ in several respects from those generally held. This is not the place to set them out in detail with the necessary proofs, but I must explain them briefly in the course of discussing Aśvaghoṣa's statements.

In the first place the notes to my translation show that, except for the eight reasons which bring the motive causes of the *saṁsāra* into action, only found elsewhere in Caraka, and also to some extent for the definition of the *sattva*, the exposition of the system is closely related to certain passages of the *MBh.*, so closely in fact that a common authority must have been used. Further xii. 33 quotes a sūtra, which is as old as the *Śvet. Up.* and which we know from Vācaspati Miśra's commentary on the *kārikās* to belong to the Vārṣagaṇyas;

---

[1] Takakusu, *BEFEO*, 1904, 58.

[2] *JRAS*, 1930, 855ff. See also W. Liebenthal, *Satkārya in der Darstellung seiner buddhistischen Gegner* (Stuttgart, 1934), where the doctrine of *satkārya* is shown to be unknown to Nāgārjuna; I would not however accept all the author's conclusions about the development of early Sāṁkhya.

it is not improbable then that we have here a resumé of the teachings of that school. The first point of Arāḍa's exposition is the division of the 24 material *tattvas* into two groups, one of eight called *prakṛti*, and one of sixteen derived from the first and called *vikāra*. The *MBh.* affords ample proof of the prevalence of a school which made this division, and the classical age preserved traces of it in the explanation of *prakṛtilaya* in the *bhāṣyas* on the *kārikās* and the *Yogasūtras*. Moreover its predominance at one period over alternative schemes may be deduced from the fact that, if we add *ātman* to the *prakṛti* group, we have in essence the nine Vaiśeṣika *dravyas*, *diś* and *kāla* being included in the *prakṛti* of classical Sāṁkhya, and *buddhi* and *ahaṁkāra* coalescing into *manas*.

Further the object of investigation in early Sāṁkhya, as in early Buddhism, is the individual, not the cosmos, which is treated in the *MBh.*, as in *B.*, xii. 21, on mythical rather than philosophical lines. If then the system analyses the individual into eight primary constituents, what view does it take of the nature of the first one, to which alone Īśvarakṛṣṇa allowed the name of *prakṛti* ? In his teaching the universe consisted in the last resort of a single 'stuff' in a state of perpetual flux under the mutual interaction of three *guṇas*, which are more forces than qualities and which, entering in different proportions into all the evolutes of *prakṛti*, determined their various natures. In fact just as Buddhist philosophy in its later stages posited the existence of qualities without subjects, an idea to be seen in germ, but not yet fully developed, in *B.*, xii. 78-79, so classical Sāṁkhya posits the existence of subjects without qualities. This conception is not at all primitive and consorts ill with such crude ideas as are incorporated, for instance, in the group of the organs of action. Seeing that Īśvarakṛṣṇa finds the essence of *prakṛti* to lie in the action of the *guṇas*, it seems best to put the question asked above in a different form ; why does canto xii of the *Buddhacarita* make no mention of the *guṇas* ? Not merely do the works extant in Sanskrit prove Aśvaghoṣa's knowledge of them (*S.*, iii. 39, note in translation, and *B.*, vii. 53), but in the still untranslated portion of the *Buddhacarita* at xxvi. 10–14, the doctrine of the *guṇas* is formally refuted. The answer is to be found in the epic, which uses *guṇa* in its Sāṁkhya passages in a variety of meanings, sometimes as 'quality' generally, sometimes for the objects of the senses, sometimes for anything evolved which is described as a *guṇa* of that from which it is evolved, sometimes for the qualities which serve to distinguish the varieties of the three *guṇas* of *prakṛti*, sometimes, mainly in later passages, for the *guṇas* themselves. While it is thus often difficult to determine the exact meaning in pre-classical passages, the principle, so far as I can see, holds good in practice that the use of the word begins to be restricted to the classical sense at the time when *prakṛti* begins to denote the first of the 24 *tattvas* only, that is, when the movement of thought to which Īśvarakṛṣṇa gave final expression is taking shape. In earlier passages the three *guṇas* do not enter into the composition of the evolutes of the first principle, as in Īśvarakṛṣṇa's system; they are often called the three *bhāvas*, 'states of being', each subdivided into a number of varieties according to the possession of particular moral attributes, and, as we are often told, the form of rebirth is determined by these attributes. Here then we have a very close parallel to the action of the Buddhist roots of evil as described above (p. xlii) and this doctrine enables us to explain the original idea of the first *tattva*; for like Aśvaghoṣa, all the early authorities call it *avyakta*, which should be understood, not as the 'unmanifested', but as the 'unseen'. *Avyakta* was in reality the early Sāṁkhya equivalent of the unseen force, attaching the individual to the wheel of the *saṁsāra* and operating in accordance with the way in which the three 'states of being' were intermingled in him, that is, in accordance with the state of his moral character. That this conception is of a purely moral order is shown by the view taken of the nature of salvation; for at *B.*, xxvi. 10–14, it is described as being effected by the growth of *sattva* and the annihilation of *rajas* and *tamas*, not by the transcendence of all three, as in classical Sāṁkhya. This, the older view, is to be found also, for instance, in Caraka, and *MBh.*, xii. 7737, 12288 and 12913, and xiv. 1449, and has left traces on the older theories. Thus we see that the exponents of earlier Sāṁkhya, like the earlier Buddhist dogmatists, are more concerned with the moral, than the philosophic, side of religion, and the answer to the question put above is that the *guṇas* or *bhāvas* merely explain the mechanism of the unseen force, so that the poet, like the authors of many other early Sāṁkhya passages, did not consider it necessary to describe them.

It is further to be noted that Aśvaghoṣa, like Caraka and other authorities, uses *prakṛti* in the singular to denote the group of the eight primary material (corporeal would express the idea more correctly) constituents; that is, he sees a unity underlying the group, just as the Vaiśeṣikas similarly endeavoured to avoid the difficulties of pluralism by bringing their categories under the single head of *sattā.* The nature of this unity is fortunately explained in *B.*, xviii. 29–40, a passage refuting the false views, which argues that Nature (*raṅ-bzhin,* which translates both *prakṛti* and *svabhāva,* and stands for *svabhāva* in this passage) cannot be the cause of the world. This *svabhāva,* which represents the principle of *prakṛti* as a cosmic force, is known to the epic, whose references I cannot discuss here, and a relic of the theory is to be found in Gauḍapāda's odd statement in his *bhāṣya* on *Sāṁkhyakārikā,* 27, that the Sāṁkhyas postulate a principle called *svabhāva.* Its characteristics according to Aśvaghoṣa are that it is a single entity, all-pervading, having the quality of producing things, without attribute, eternal, unmanifested, and unconscious (*sems-med, acetana*). When we compare this with classical Sāṁkhya, particularly with the description of *prakṛti* in *Sāṁkhyakārikā,* 10-11, we see that the school which culminated in Īśvarakṛṣṇa transferred the conception of *prakṛti* as thus defined together with the name to the first *tattva,* the *avyakta,* and in doing so, gave it an entirely new content by a transformation of the *guṇa* theory; they then handed over the functions of the original *avyakta* as determining rebirth to a new group, the eightfold *buddhi,* and used the principle of *svabhāva* to explain the connection between the soul and the 24 *tattvas* (as opposed to the *naimittika* theory of the *YS.*).

This teaching about *avyakta* and *prakṛti* is the fundamental position of early Sāṁkhya, but certain other points of Arāḍa's exposition require brief notice. That in place of the *tanmātras* and gross elements of the classical period he should reckon the elements and the objects of the senses respectively among the 24 principles is normal, and the reason for it has been explained by me elsewhere [1]. The explanation of the *saṁsāra* is involved and hard to follow ; xii. 23 gives as its causes *karman, tṛṣṇā* and *ajñāna,* and the passage goes on to enumerate eight factors by which these causes work. Then it proceeds to attribute the implication of the individual in the cycle of existence to the fivefold *avidyā* (xii. 37), and ends by putting the cause down as the identification of the person with the corporeal individual (xii. 38). At present I am unable exactly to correlate these statements, which suggest that Sāṁkhya thinking was in a muddled state, due to the imperfect assimilation of new ideas. On the nature of the soul Aśvaghoṣa tells us nothing that we ought not already to know from other sources. Obviously he regards it as an individual, not a universal, soul, and he distinguishes, following the views taken in the epic, between the *ātman* which is *ajña* and the *kṣetrajña* which is *jña.* In emphasising the difficulties of this doctrine he hits upon the point which Sāṁkhya thought of every age failed to explain, and which Īśvarakṛṣṇa tried to evade by taking the soul as neither precisely one nor the other, but it is not necessary to my purpose to trace the development of thought in this respect.

This discussion does not exhaust the value of canto xii to us ; for to the *jñānamārga* of the Sāṁkhya is appended an

---

[1] *JRAS,* 1930, 864ff.

alternative method of action by yoga. In itself there is nothing strange in this, the *Yogasūtras* being based on the Sāṁkhya philosophy, and traces of the use of yoga being still visible in the *kārikās*. The system set out is said to be that which was followed by Pañcaśikha, who is treated as the great authority on the philosophic side of Yoga in Vyāsa's *bhāṣya*, together with Jaigīṣavya, also known as a teacher of Yoga, and Janaka. But actually it is a description of the first seven *dhyānas* of Buddhist dogma, substituting *ātman* for *vijñāna* in the second *ārūpya*. I have already pointed out (p. xliii) that the *dhyānas* and *prajñā* do not belong to the original Buddhism, and, as many scholars have observed, there is an extraordinary parallelism between the *Yogasūtras* and the Buddhist doctrine of trance[1], so marked in both phraseology and ideas that the two can hardly have arisen independently but must have had a common origin. Now a prominent feature of the Buddhist teaching is that each trance is connected with certain divine spheres, and Aśvaghoṣa mentions these same spheres as gained by the trances of his Yoga system. The corresponding scheme for the classical Yoga is set forth by Vyāsa on *YS.*, iii. 25; this statement is separated by five or more centuries from that we are considering, yet the two coincide in such a remarkable way that, unexpected as it may seem, the poet's description may be accepted as accurate for the Yoga of his day. This conclusion may appear less surprising, if we reflect that no parallels to Vyāsa's cosmology are to be found in Brahmanical sources outside the Yoga school, and it is fortified by the fact that in two points analogies can be found in canto xii to the older Yoga teaching. Firstly, the passage starts in verses 46 and 47 with a description of the *śīla* required of the aspirant, which might well be a summary of the teaching on the subject attributed to Jaigīṣavya at *MBh.*, xii. 8431ff. Secondly, the

[1] The relations between Buddhism and the Yoga system call for a fresh full-length study in the light of the Buddhist materials made available of recent years; for a preliminary sketch of the important points see La Vallée Poussin, *Notes Bouddhiques*, III.

expression *nigṛhṇann indriyagrāmam* in 48 is significant; for the *bhāṣya* on *YS.*, ii. 55, quotes a sutra of Jaigīṣavya to the effect that in yoga the functioning of the senses is altogether suppressed. Not only is this doctrine to be read into this passage and to be found in various passages of the *Śāntiparvan* and the *Gītā*, but we have a reference to it in the Pali canon at *Majjhima*, III, 298, where the Buddha refutes the similar views held by a Pārāsariya Brahman (i.e. a follower of Pañcaśikha)[1]; the Hīnayāna at least took the view that in yoga the senses were under control (*indriyasaṁvara*), not suppressed. The poet's description of the Yoga system of his day should therefore be treated, like the preceding account of Sāṁkhya, as fully authoritative.

Lastly, this sketch of Aśvaghoṣa's scholarship would be incomplete, if it omitted to describe to what extent his works illuminate the development of the poetic profession from the technical side in his day. For the theatre the fragments of the plays prove that the principles of dramatic technique then observed did not differ materially from those of the classical drama, but the matter has been so thoroughly explored by Professor Lüders that I am exempted from entering into details. The *Buddhacarita* several times uses terms of the theatre, *rasāntara*, iii. 51, and the dramatic forms of address, *āyuṣmat*, iii. 33, *tatrabhavat*, ix. 37, and *ārya*, xiii. 63, and of words whose use later was practically confined to the stage we find *sādhaya* in the sense of *gam* in the *Śāriputraprakaraṇa*[2]. Curious is the parallel between *S.*, iv. 39, and the description of *śūnyā dṛṣṭi* at *BhNŚ.*, viii. 63; for, while much of that work is old, we have no reason to think any of it as old as these poems. Though with the exception of a brief notice of a few rhetorical

[1] The corresponding passage in the Sarvāstivādin canon is taken up in the *Vibhāṣā*, *TI*, XXVII, 729, *a*29ff. (see *AK.*, VI, 121, s. Parāśāri), where the view is attributed to a Pārāśari *tīrthika*. For the references and a translation of the *Vibhāṣā* passage I am indebted to Professor de la Vallée Poussin.

[2] *SBPAW*, 1911, 405.

figures in the same treatise we have nothing earlier than Daṇḍin and Bhāmaha for the laws of *kāvya* poetry, the reference to *kāvyadharma* in the closing verses of the *Saundarananda* proves the poet to have known and used some regular work on poetics, and it is interesting therefore to observe how the contents of the two poems correspond almost exactly to Daṇḍin's definition of a typical *kāvya* in *Kāvyādarśa*, i. 14–19. For the *Buddhacarita* the battle and the hero's victory are to be found in canto xiii, and we should no doubt see the same motif at work in *S.*, xvii, in which the illusion of a combat is maintained by constant comparisons with a king on a campaign and with a battle against enemies. Aśvaghoṣa's use of rhetorical figures was presumably determined by his authorities, but does not conform to the strictest classical standards in respect of *upamā*. The gender fails to correspond in *B.*, ii. 45, v. 62, and vi. 26, *S.*, ii. 6, ix. 17, 18, and 43, x. 9, xiv. 15, 39 etc., and both gender and number at *B.*, viii. 26, and *S.*, xi. 29. Not all of these cases would have been considered faulty by Daṇḍin under the ruling of *Kāvyādarśa*, ii. 51, and that the poet knew the rule prescribing identity of genders appears from the otherwise pointless insertion of *prabhā* at *S.*, x. 39 (contrast the wording of the same simile at *B.*, iii. 45), and xii. 29. His handling of rhetoric generally is best reserved to the subsequent discussion on style.

Closely connected with these points is the poet's knowledge of prosody, and the following list enumerates all the metres used by him in the two poems so far as preserved to us :—

i. Samavṛttas :—

Anuṣṭubh (679). *B.*, iv. 1–96; vi. 1–55; xii. 1–115; xiv. 1–31. *S.*, i. 1–58; ii. 1–62; xi. 1–58; xii. 1–42; xiii. 1–54; xiv. 1–45; xv. 1–65.

Upajāti (936). *B.*, i. 8–24, and 40–79; ii. 1–55; iii. 1–62; vi. 56–65; vii. 1–57; ix. 1–71; x. 1–39; xi. 1–57; xii. 1–69. *S.*, i. 59–60; ii. 63; iv. 1–44; v. 1–52; vi. 1–48; vii. 1–47; x. 1–53; xi. 59; xiv. 46–49; xvi. 1–94; xvii. 1–70; xviii. 1–43.

Vaṁśastha (201). *B.*, iii. 63; iv. 97–102; vi. 66–68; viii. 1–80; ix. 72–80; x. 40; xi. 58–73; xii. 116–120; xiii. 70-71. *S.*, iv. 45; ix. 1–49; x. 54–63; xv. 66-67; xviii. 44–59.

Rucirā (4). *B.*, iii. 64-65; xii. 121. *S.*, x. 64.

Praharṣiṇī (7). *B.*, ix. 81-82; x. 41. *S.*, i. 61; xvii. 71–73.

Vasantatilakā (10). *S.*, i. 62; v. 53; vii. 48–51; viii. 58-59; ix. 51; xviii. 61.

Śarabhā (2). *S.*, xii. 43; xiii. 72.

Mālinī (2). *B.*, ii. 56; xiii. 72.

Śikhariṇī (11). *B.*, iv. 103. *S.*, viii. 60-61; xiv. 50–52; xv. 68-69; xvi. 95–97.

Kusumalatāvellitā (1). *S.*, vii. 52.

Śārdūlavikrīḍita (6). *S.*, viii. 62; xi. 60-61; xvi. 98; xviii. 62-63.

Suvadanā (2). *S.*, xi. 62; xviii. 64.

ii. Ardhasamavṛttas :—

Viyoginī or Sundarī (56). *S.*, viii. 1–56.

Aupacchandasika (78). *B.*, v. 1–78.

Aparavaktra or Vaitālīya (2). *B.*, vii. 58. *S.*, viii. 57.

Puṣpitāgrā (31). *B.*, i. 80–89; v. 79–87; viii. 81–87. *S.*, iii. 42; iv. 46; vi. 49; ix. 50; xviii. 60.

iii. Viṣamavṛttas :—

Udgatā (41). *S.*, iii. 1–41.

Upasthitapracupita, variety vardhamāna (2). *S.*, ii. 64-65.

Considering that the continuity of narration in epics does not allow as many varieties of metre as in plays or prose stories interspersed with verse, this is an imposing list, to which must be added an example of Śālinī in the *Śāriputraprakaraṇa*, and, if the third play belongs to Aśvaghoṣa, verses in the Hariṇī and possibly in the Sragdharā and Āryā metres. It should also be noted that *S.*, xiii. 55, which I hold to be spurious, is in an unknown *ardhasamavṛtta* of very curious type, the first and third *pādas* consisting of seven trochees and a long syllable each and the second and fourth of eight iambi each. The metre Śarabhā is otherwise unknown except for its description in the *BhNŚ.*, and according to Sukumar Sen [1] this is the only occurrence in literature of Kusumalatāvellitā (called Citralekhā in the *BhNŚ.*); it gave way perhaps, as he suggests, to Mandākrāntā, from which it differs only by the addition of a long syllable at the beginning. The poet's use of Udgatā and Upasthitapracupita proves great skill in the handling of difficult metres.

The *vipulās* employed in the ślokas deserve some attention, and the following table gives the number of their occurrences :—

a. *Buddhacarita.*

Vipulā	iv	vi	xii	xiv	Total
1. ⏓ ⏑ – – ⏑ ⏑ ⏑ –	12	7	6	1	26
2. ⏓ – – – ⏑ ⏑ ⏑ –	5	4	8	4	21
3. ⏓ – ⏑ – ⏑ ⏑ ⏑ –	0	1	2	0	3
4. ⏓ – ⏑ – – ⏑ ⏑ –	2	2	1	2	7
5. ⏓ – ⏑ – –, – – ⏓	0	0	7	0	7
Total ..	19	14	24	7	64

b. *Saundarananda.*

Vipulā	i	ii	xi	xii	xiii	xiv	xv	Total
1. ⏓ ⏑ – – ⏑ ⏑ ⏑ – ..	10	7	6	3	1	0	5	32
2. ⏓ – – – ⏑ ⏑ ⏑ – ..	4	6	2	7	10	5	6	40
3. ⏓ – ⏑ – ⏑ ⏑ ⏑ – ..	1	1	0	0	1	1	2	6
4. ⏓ – ⏑ – – ⏑ ⏑ – ..	1	1	1	3	0	1	1	8
5. ⏓ – ⏑ – –, – – ⏓ ..	3	1	2	0	0	2	1	9
Total ..	19	16	11	13	12	9	15	95

[1] *JASB*, 1930, 205.

The second of these, though common enough in epic verse, is apparently not used in classical *kāvya*, and the proportion of *vipulās* to *pathyās*, about 11·7 per cent, is much lower than in the *Nala* and slightly less than the general average of the *MBh.* as calculated by Professor Hopkins[1], and more than half as much again as the corresponding figure for the *Raghuvaṁśa.* In the first four forms the *pāda* is never allowed to close on a brevis and so strongly does the poet's ear demand support for the phrase after two or three short syllables that it is quite exceptional when at *S.*, xii. 37, the ending consists of a short vowel (*iti*) lengthened by the next word beginning with a compound character.

For the other metres, the striking fact is the preponderance of Upajāti, particularly in the *Buddhacarita.* The monotonous effect of its trochaic cadence makes it difficult to handle for continuous narrative, and that Aśvaghoṣa was alive to this danger is shown by the way he rings the changes on the possible variations of rhythm. The scheme of the verse having no fixed cæsura, the break occurs most often at the fifth syllable, but division at the fourth is also frequent and in a certain proportion of cases a break is found at the third syllable with a secondary one at the sixth or seventh. Words of course are not allowed to straddle the *pāda*, except for one faulty verse, *S.*, iv. 7, where the first syllable of *d* includes by *saṁdhi* the last syllable of the word at the end of *c*, *na śobhetānyonyahīnāv* ; but this could be cured by amending in accordance with epic practice to *na śobhed anyonyahīnāv.* Vaṁśastha is handled in the same manner, and for the longer metres the classical rules of cæsura are observed. For Vasantatilakā, as in the treatise of Piṅgala[2], there is no fixed cæsura ; Professor Hopkins gives as the rule for the *MBh.* a cæsura at the fourth and again at the seventh syllable[3], but this does not hold good for the classical

---

[1] *Great Epic of India*, 223-224. [2] *Indische Studien*, VIII, 387.

[3] *Great Epic of India*, 193. The metrical scheme at the end of Apte's dictionary gives a cæsura for Vasantatilakā at the eighth syllable, but Kālidāsa does not follow this rule.

period. In the metres which require a long syllable at the end other than Upajāti, the poet does not hesitate to use occasionally a short syllable at the end of the even-numbered *pādas*, but for *pādas a* and *c* the only instance is *S.*, vii. 48*c*, a Vasanta-tilakā verse; in Upajāti verses, however, a short syllable occurs frequently at the end of any *pāda*. It appears then that, while the prosodical system of *kāvya* was fully developed in Aśvaghoṣa's day, it was still capable of growth, and that a certain licence was allowed in minor matters which was to be absolutely barred in later practice.

From this point I pass to the grammar of the poems, a detailed study of which is necessary, seeing that its exact comprehension determines the handling of many textual problems and that in the absence of any other *kāvya* works of equal age it is our only means of estimating what usages were considered by strict writers of this epoch to be permissible[1]. Buddhism, we now know, had its own special grammars, though the earliest one of which any fragments are extant[2] is later in date than these poems. But assuming, as I do, that Aśvaghoṣa was born a Brahman, he would naturally not have been taught from one of them in his schooldays. We do not know on what grammar he relied, but if it is not surprising to find that as an Easterner he does not adhere strictly to the principles of Pāṇini, different grammars can only differ in minor matters, such as whether certain variant forms or constructions are allowable or not, and consequently when he parades his knowledge of abstruse rules of grammar, we can often find them in the *Aṣṭādhyāyī*. Thus *S.*, vii. 8, *śliṣṭa* with the accusative is based on *Pāṇ.*, iii. 4, 72, and *abhāginī*, *B.*, viii. 54, in a future sense with the same case, is covered by ii. 3, 70, and iii. 3, 3, though not included in the Paninean

---

[1] The grammatical material has been analysed by Sukumar Sen, for the *Buddhacarita* in *IHQ*, 1926, 657ff., and for the *Saundarananda* in *JASB*, 1930, 181ff.; see also his *Outline Syntax of Buddhistic Sanskrit*, Calcutta, 1928. His collections are useful, if sometimes open to criticism in detail.

[2] H. Lüders, *Kātantra und Kaumāralāta*, *SBPAW*, 1930, 482ff.

gaṇa in question (*gamyādayaḥ*, no. 70). Similarly iii. 2, 135, accounts for the agental form, *praveṣṭṛ*, at *B.*, v. 84, to indicate habitual action, while *B.*, ii. 34, with its contrast between *vijigye* and *jigāya*, illustrates i. 3, 19, prescribing the Ātmanepada for *ji* compounded with *vi*. The most illuminating case is that of *S.*, xii. 9-10; the former not only refers to the rule in vi. 1, 89, which lays down that the root *edh* takes *vṛddhi* in exception to the general rule, but seems also to allude to the *Dhātupāṭhas* which explain this root as used in the meaning *vṛddhau*[1]. That the poet knew a *Dhātupāṭha* is rendered probable by *B.*, xi. 70, illustrating nine senses of the root *av*, and by *B.*, v. 81, where T shows *cak* to be used in a meaning known only to those works. The following verse on the other hand refers to the threefold use of *asti* as a particle for the past, present and future; this rule played a part in the famous Buddhist controversy over the reality of the past and future, but is not to be found in Pāṇini or the orthodox grammars.

Where Pāṇini's rules are not complied with, we can usually find parallels to odd forms or constructions in the epics, but a few usages, which are peculiar to Buddhism, so far as we know at present, may conveniently be grouped together here. The method of comparison by relatives, *S.*, xi. 54, *sukham utpadyate yac ca . . yac ca duḥkham . . duḥkham eva viśiṣyate*, occurs not infrequently in the Mahāyāna sūtras. The construction of *vijugupsa* with the accusative, *B.*, v. 12, is known only to Pali, and the use of *pṛṣṭha* at the end of compounds with the force only of a preposition, *B.*, ii. 32, v. 7, and x. 39, is common in that language also. Similarly *udīkṣyamāṇarūpa*, *B.*, i. 80, is a form of compound of which Pali has several examples and which occurs also in the *ASPP*. *Sacet*, *S.*, x. 60, xv. 3, and xvi. 70, and *prāg eva*, equivalent to *kiṁ punar*, at *B.*, iv. 10, and xi. 7, and *S.*, ii. 24, are also primarily Buddhist, though the latter occurs several times in Vācaspati Miśra's commentary on the *Yogasūtras*. But there is only one instance

[1] Professor Sten Konow kindly brought this point to my notice.

of a form of expression much beloved of Buddhist canonical authors in *yenāśramas tena* at *B.*, vi. 65. With these exceptions Aśvaghoṣa's departures from classical usage are almost always either archaisms or to be found in the epics.

In going into details, it must be borne in mind that the textual tradition of both poems is bad and that a single occurrence of an abnormal usage, if not guaranteed by the metre, should be regarded as uncertain and possibly a copyist's mistake.

In the accidence of nouns the only points for comment are the genders ; *varṣa*, n., *B.*, xiii. 45, 72, and *S.*, ii. 53, *gavākṣa*, n., *B.*, viii. 14, *prakoṣṭha*, n., *S.*, vi. 27, *kaluṣa*, m., *B.*, ii. 16, and *ratha*, n., *B.*, iii. 62, may all be due to errors in the MSS., and so may *mitra*, m., at *S.*, xvii. 56, where *maitra* seems indicated by *S.*, ii. 18, though instances of this last do occur sporadically. In the comparison of adjectives the form *anuttama*, *B.*, v. 51, 83, and *S.*, xviii. 49, which is recorded elsewhere, should be classed with the use of the superlative for the comparative, dealt with below under the syntax of the ablative. The curious *pūrvatama*, *B.*, xiii. 10, may be a mistake for *pūrvatana.* For the pronouns the use of *asmi* for *aham*, *B.*, i. 67, and of *svaḥ* for *nau*, *ib.*, viii. 43, the latter unparalleled, should be noted. The enclitics, *me* and *te*, are undoubtedly used occasionally as instrumentals, a practice known to the epics but not generally sanctioned ; cp. *S.*, xiv. 22, *te* agreeing with *bādhyamānena*, for an absolutely certain case. Unusually large use is also made of the pronominal adverbs instead of the corresponding cases of the pronouns, sometimes in agreement with a noun.

Both works are peculiarly rich in verbal forms. The distinction of voice is in accord with general usage and at *S.*, ii. 26, and *B.*, ii. 33, 34, we have verses illustrating the different employment of certain verbs in the Parasmaipada and Ātmanepada, being references perhaps to rules in the grammar used by the poet. *Prārthayanti*, *B.*, ii. 10, though occurring elsewhere, and *saṁrarañja*, *S.*, ii. 63, are probably to be accounted for by faulty copying. For past tenses the use of the perfect predominates except in the second canto of each poem, which deliberately illustrate the rules governing the formation of aorists. In the conjugation of the former the strong stem occurs in three cases, which, though not allowable in classical Sanskrit, can be paralleled in the *MBh.*, viz., *B.*, i. 41, *sasarjatuḥ*, and viii. 26, *siṣiñcire*, and *S.*, x. 39, *vivepe*; *niṣīdatuḥ* at *B.*, ix. 11, and xii. 3, is probably a copyist's error, and *B.*, xiii. 44, *nirjigiluḥ* is formed from the rare present stem *gil* of the root *gṝ*. For the periphrastic perfect the verb is separated from its auxiliary by an intervening word at *B.*, ii. 19, vi. 58, and vii. 9, a practice authorised by Kālidāsa. *Viśvaset* at *B.*, xi. 16, and *S.*, xv. 59, belongs to the language of the epics, and whatever we read at *B.*, iv. 59, *śayed*, *svaped* or *suped*, we have a formation not recognised in classic literature. The periphrastic future has a passive sense at *B.*, i. 64, the earliest known instance of this use. The rules for the formation of feminine present participles would not allow, outside the epics, *rudantī*, *B.*, ix. 26, and *S.*, vi. 5, 35, and *sravatīm*, *S.*, viii. 52. Of the past participles *āroṣita*, *S.*, vi. 25, is a solecism, as are the gerundives *gṛhya*, *S.*, i. 28, and *vivardhayitvā* and *paripālayitvā* at *B.*, xi. 30; this latter irregularity occurs elsewhere, but only as here with the compounds of causative verbs. Aśvaghoṣa is peculiarly fond of desiderative formations, and unusual are *cikrīṣanti*, *S.*, xi. 26, the desiderative of this verb not being known except for *vicikrīṣu* quoted in Schmidt's *Nachträge* from the *Yaśastilaka*, and *bhikṣu*, *B.*, iv. 17, if I am right in taking it as a desiderative of *bhaj*. Of the various intensives used, that of *hrī*, *S.*, vii. 1, and x. 41, seems only known to Buddhists, and the *PW* quotes for that of *bhid*, *B.*, ii. 40, only the *Bhaṭṭikāvya*, and for that of *chid*, *ib.*, the grammarians.

So far as we can tell, the ordinary rules of *saṁdhi* are observed. The reading *gato 'ryaputro* at *B.*, viii. 34, shows that we have here the word *ăryaputra*, not *ārya°*, and at ix. 21, A is corrupt and the correct reading cannot be determined.

The syntax offers much of interest and some usages that are new. In the matter of concord a singular noun is several times employed where the sense requires a plural; thus *B.*, i. 66, *snehaṁ sute vetsi hi bāndhavānām,* and like cases at *ib.*, viii. 11, ix. 31, xiii. 7. A singular verb is occasionally used with two subjects joined by *ca* or *ca* . . *ca,* thus participles at *B.*, vi. 47 (a copyist's error ?), and viii. 32, a finite verb at *B.*, v. 87, and *S.*, ix. 28, and so of two subjects not fitting together at *B.*, viii. 33, and *S.*, viii. 2. At *B.*, ii. 13, the dual verb after two subjects disjoined by *vā* is questionable.

The use of the nominative is regular enough, but the idioms with *śakya* and the like deserve a word as sometimes affecting the reading adopted. Ordinarily *śakya* agrees with the grammatical subject in gender and number, when followed by an infinitive in a passive sense, but twice the neuter singular is used, *B.*, ii. 3, and xii. 102, once *metri causa* and once to avoid a hiatus. This latter construction is observed with *kṣamam* (only in *B.*), *sādhu*, *B.*, xiii. 63, and *sukham*, *S.*, xviii. 2; but *kṣamam* is also coupled with an intransitive infinitive, *B.*, vii. 41, or with an infinitive understood actively and governing the accusative, *B.*, xi. 20, and in that case the logical subject or agent is placed in the instrumental, or else in the genitive, *B.*, ix. 39, like the genitive after *sādhu* and *sukha* in the above quoted cases with an infinitive understood passively.

Aśvaghoṣa's fondness for the cognate accusative, which belongs more properly to the earlier and epic stages of the language, is repeatedly displayed, particularly after verbs of speaking, also after *nad*, *B.*, v. 84, and *pranad*, *B.*, xiii. 52, and *tap*. The idioms with verbs of speaking are also pre-classical in the main; in the sense of 'address' they take the accusative of the person spoken to as well as the accusative of the object spoken, and the latter remains in the accusative when the verb goes into the passive. But if the sense is 'explain', the person addressed is invariably put into the dative, and a further extension of this construction with a second accusative in apposition is at *B.*, ix. 77, *yac ca me bhavān uvāca Rāmaprabhṛtīn nidarśanam.* The accusatives after *abhāgin, śliṣṭa* and *vijugupsa* have already been referred to, and I may note one example after *abhimukha, B.*, viii. 4. The verb *smṛ* governs this case only, but unusual are accusatives after *vigrah* (*S.*, ii. 10, cp. *MBh.*, xv. 220) and *vinirgam* (*B.*, v. 67, identical phrase *MBh.*, ii. 32). *Bhūmiṁ gam, B.*, viii. 55, is natural enough but has apparently no analogies elsewhere; and for the accusative after desiderative nouns, *prayiyāsā, S.*, viii. 13, and *vivakṣā, S.*, xi. 18, see *SS.*, §52, Rem. 3. Hard to explain is a kind of accusative absolute of the time up to which an action took place, *aruṇaparuṣatāram antarīkṣam, B.*, v. 87.

The solitary instance of the Buddhist idiom *yena . . . tena* has already been mentioned and the instrumental of the direction taken is employed at *B.*, ix. 7, and x. 4, 35; but otherwise this case is not used in any way for which there is not ample authority. Aśvaghoṣa does not seem to have any decided preference for either the accusative or the instrumental of the active agent after the causative of a transitive verb, but for impersonal instruments he uses the latter case only. The dative with verbs of speaking has already been explained under the accusative. Its use with *alam, B.*, ix. 77, and *S.*, i. 40, is common in the Brāhmaṇas but survived into the classical language, and the dative regularly employed with *spṛh* and *spṛhā* is also an older use in the main. But this case with the rare verb *viruc, S.*, ii. 14, and with *utsuka, S.*, xii. 21, seems to have no parallels, and *yāvad eva vimuktaye, S.*, xiii. 16, is hard to comprehend (or is the text corrupt and should we read *tāvad* and understand a dative of aim ?), while the explanation of the curious *bhaktaye, S.*, xiv. 19, coupled with an instrumental, depends on the meaning to be given to *bhakti*, which is uncertain. The dative in *tasmai gadām udyamayāṁcakāra, B.*, xiii. 37, is by analogy with the construction of *druh* (*ib.*, 56).

For the next case the most remarkable point is the ablative of comparison after superlatives or their equivalents, *śreṣṭha-*

tama and *duḥkhatama*, *S.*, v. 24, also *pravara*, *ib.*, 25, and *parama*, *ib.* and iii. 32, *niḥsāratama*, ix. 11, *para*, xvii. 51. *Parebhyaḥ saṁsargam*, *S.*, xiv. 50, is probably a MS. corruption, and there are a number of cases in which an ablative of cause is joined with a similar instrumental, e.g. *B.*, ix. 46. As in all Buddhist writers the poet's addiction to the case-ending *taḥ* in place of the ablative or instrumental is marked; e.g. as ablative joined with an ordinary ablative at *S.*, xvii. 15, but more commonly equivalent to an instrumental, thus *manastaḥ* at *B.*, i. 47, or joined with instrumentals, *B.*, iii. 11, and *S.*, xvi. 48. A frequent use is with a verb meaning directly or metaphorically 'understand', *śubhato gacchasi*, *S.*, viii. 48, *rūkṣato naiti*, *ib.*, xi. 15, *draṣṭavyaṁ bhūtataḥ*, *ib.*, xiii. 44, etc. *doṣato gam*, *B.*, viii. 49, and *doṣato gā*, *S.*, vi. 22.

The employment of the genitive after verbs is mostly normal, such as after *anukṛ*, *S.*, i. 36, and xviii. 59, *nihan*, *S.*, iv. 14, and *śraddhā*, *S.*, vi. 19, and similarly after gerundives, *mānya*, *S.*, vi. 38, *darśanīya*, *S.*, xviii. 33; less usual is the objective genitive after *vañcayitavya*, *B.*, iv. 94, and after *rājyaṁ kṛ*, *S.*, xi. 44. While the propriety of an objective genitive after the dative of aim of a transitive verbal noun is well established, those after *smṛtaye*, *B.*, v. 20, and *bhayāya*, *B.*, xiii. 34, are odd and hard to explain. The genitives at *B.*, ii. 7, and in *darśayantyo 'sya*, *B.*, iv. 34, and *mama dhārayitvā*, *S.*, vi. 18 (this last might be a genitive absolute), come under the dative-like genitive explained *SS.*, § 131. The objective genitives after *didṛkṣā* at *B.*, i. 58, and xi. 69, and *S.*, iv. 40, are remarkable, all the more so in view of the alternative construction noted under the locative below. The only certain instances of a genitive absolute are at *B.*, v. 20, and xiv. 22.

The case which receives the greatest extension in these poems is the locative, but most of them can be classed under the sphere in which, or under the object (very often a person) in respect of which, an action takes place, frequently in lieu of a dative. Thus for instance, *kṛtvā mayi tāṁ pratijñām* *S.*, vi. 13 (see *SS.*, § 145), and similar uses *ib.*, 16 and 17; so too after *utsṛj*, *B.*, xi. 33, and after *vimuc*, *B.*, xiii. 38 (contrast the dative in the previous verse). It can also be substituted for a dative of aim after verbs of striving, determining etc., an option taken much advantage of and extended rather far in the phrase, *prītikṣaye yogam upāruroha*, *S.*, xvii. 49. The alternative is clearly put with *pratibhū* at *B.*, v. 34, and *S.*, x. 63, as compared with *S.*, xii. 13. Similarly the locative of the person addressed after *vācya*, *B.*, vi. 24, and *S.*, viii. 6, after *vivakṣā*, *B.*, iv. 63, *pravivakṣā*, *S.*, viii. 11, and *vivakṣita*, *ib.*, xviii. 53. The extreme case is perhaps the locative after *nam*, *S.*, iii. 7, and v. 1, and *praṇāma*, *ib.*, iv. 32 ; the dative is used in other passages and the accusative in *S.*, xvii. 73, Sanskrit normally allowing these two cases and the genitive. It is frequently employed after substantives, adjectives and verbs, but the only further instances worth noting are after desideratives to denote the object, *jighāṁsā*, *B.*, xiii. 66, *ārurukṣā*, *S.*, v. 40, and *didṛkṣā*, *ib.*, xviii. 2, 33 [1]. In the last two cases the subject is in the genitive, though elsewhere, as already pointed out, *didṛkṣā* takes the genitive of the object. The locative after *pramad*, 'enjoy', *S.*, ii. 63, is a Vedic use, and the same sense can be read into *ib.*, v. 41.

In the comparison of adjectives I have already drawn attention to the use of superlatives as comparatives ; the latter similarly are employed to express, not comparison, but simply enhancement of the simple adjective, thus *sphītatara*, *B.*, iii. 10, 'very widely opened', *udbhāsitara*, *S.*, iv. 17, 'shining very brightly'. Among the pronouns a curious use is that of the indefinite *kaścit* in the plural with a negative to express 'none', *B.*, iii. 52, and *S.*, iv. 27, which is apparently unknown elsewhere and should be noted for its bearing on the interpretation of *B.*, xi. 36. Nor have I anywhere else, except for a passage in the *Rāmāyaṇa* quoted by Gawroński [2] and

---

[1] My translation of *S.*, xviii, *2d*, is wrong and should run, 'and therefore he was desirous of seeing the Seer'.

[2] *Studies about the Sanskrit Buddhist Literature*, 13.

perhaps *Pratijñāyaugandharāyaṇa*, iv. 17, come across the practice of using a relative absolutely without postcedent to express the idea ' as for ' ; it occurs *B.*, v. 69, vii. 57, and xiii. 59, and *S.*, vi. 47. The relative is also used pleonastically in the way that the Avesta shows was found in the original Aryan language, e.g. *B.*, ii. 35, 38, *S.*, v. 46, xi. 43, and xiv. 41.

The employment of the tenses is normal in general, and no distinction is made between the perfect, imperfect and aorist, though the first is by far the commonest for narrative. The particle *ha* is used three times, *B.*, viii. 79, and xii. 68, 83, but only with the perfect, not with the imperfect as allowed by Pāṇini. The periphrastic future at *S.*, v. 50, *kartāsmi*, does not imply action in the remoter future (*Pāṇ.*, iii. 3, 15) as it ought to, and probably retains a good deal of the sense of the agental noun. The use of the gerunds is lax according to classical principles, agreeing with an oblique case in at least 20 instances, and in one case, *S.*, xvi. 52, with the subject understood, not expressed ; Kālidāsa does the same occasionally to the confusion of his commentators and translators, though the construction is logical and free from ambiguity. Gerunds seem to be joined with *yā* as an auxiliary at *B.*, vi. 48, ix. 54, and xiii. 5, and *S.*, v. 43, in order to indicate an action which may take place in the natural course of events or habitually does so, but that *yā* is to be so treated as an auxiliary is certain only of *B.*, xiii. 5 of these passages. Very curious is the apparently similar construction at *S.*, vii. 15, where the only satisfactory explanation is to take *yā* with the gerund as indicating a passive, like the infinitive with the same verb in the cases quoted in the note to the translation, but admittedly I can quote no parallels except the so-called passives of the modern Indo-Aryan vernaculars. At *B.*, ix. 6, we have apparently an example of *asti* used as a particle with a past participle, and the agental noun, *praveṣṭṛ*, at *B.*, v. 84, has already been mentioned. The desideratives, which occur so frequently in these poems, have often lost all sense of intention or desire and indicate merely what is about to happen, e.g. *mumūrṣu*, 'at the point of death'; and the same remark applies at times to infinitives compounded with *kāma*.

Of the prepositions *prati* is used repeatedly with the accusative in the sense of 'with respect to', 'concerning', 'towards', but others are very rare. Possibly *anu* is to be understood as governing *tām* at *S.*, vi. 36, and there is only one occurrence of *ā*, namely at *B.*, ii. 1, with the ablative. The latter is used in compounds to express 'somewhat' with *piṅgala* at *B.*, vii. 51, and with *lakṣya*, *ib.*, iv. 33, the latter ambiguous word being imitated by Daṇḍin. A point of style which is not to be commended is the fusion of *ā* with the augment in verbal compounds in *ādhārayan*, *B.*, i. 18, *nārukṣat*, *S.*, ii. 20, and possibly *nādidasīt*, *ib.*, 18, and I have already alluded to *yāvat* with the dative at *S.*, xiii. 16.

Much that is interesting is to be found in the conjunctions and interjections. The odd habit of placing *ca* and *hi* towards the end of a sentence has been frequently commented on; it then often emphasises by its position an important word or else shows the predicate in cases of ambiguity, for instance *hi* in *S.*, xv. 8, distinguishing the predicate from the epithets in the verse. A favourite use is the doubling of *ca*, which invariably denotes simultaneity (the translation of *S.*, xvi. 45*cd*, being therefore wrong), and an excellent instance, which previous translators have not fully appreciated, is at *B.*, xiii. 18, where it brings out the point that Māra has only to think of his army for it to appear. *Yataḥ* is used several times to introduce a clause in the last *pāda* of a verse, giving the action whose motive has been stated in the previous *pādas*; it is thus really equivalent to *tataś ca* and means 'and accordingly'. Twice oratio recta is not marked by an *iti* or its equivalent at the beginning or end, *B.*, iv. 29, and *S.*, iv. 37. *Sacet* and *prāg eva* have already been mentioned, and the use of *nāma* in the sense of 'as if', 'pretending to be', at *B.*, iv. 29, and *S.*, iv. 15, 17, is found in the *Kāmasūtra* and elsewhere. At *S.*, vi. 9, and *B.*, vi. 64, *āśu* is used as an expletive entirely devoid of any suggestion of quickness, a practice not unknown to

Brahmanical works of the epic period. *Iva* is wrongly placed at *B.*, iii. 64, and at *S.*, vii. 17 [1]. It is further curious that in the one instance that *yadi* is followed by *na ca*, *B.*, viii. 41, the verb is in the conditional; for this is the case with the only parallel quoted by the *PW*, viz., *MBh.*, xiii. 4797. Finally I am inclined to think that *kiṁ vā* is used in an unrecorded fashion with *astu*, 'just let there be', 'why should there not be', at *B.*, iv. 71.

The works of Aśvaghoṣa are pleasantly free from overgrown compounds, and of few other Sanskrit poets can it be said as of him that the compounds are never filled out with padding, such as the insertion of *vara* and the like. Some of them nevertheless are not quite regular. For dvandvas the MSS. show a curious variance about number, *udakāgnyoḥ* at *B.*, ix. 49, against *jalāgneḥ* at *S.*, xi. 5, and *kāyavacasoḥ* at *S.*, xiii. 11, against *kāyamanasaḥ* at *S.*, xiii. 24; in all four cases according to Pāṇini the dual is the proper form. The order of the members is hardly correct in *ugradhṛtāyudha*, *B.*, xi. 18, and *bodhyaṅgaśitāttaśastra*, *S.*, xvii. 24, which offend also against *SS.*, § 224, Rem. 3. Desiderative substantives are twice compounded with their objects in a way that is not strictly according to rule, though occurring elsewhere, *vanabhūmididṛkṣayā*, *B.*, v. 2, and *pauraprīticikīrṣayā*, *S.*, i. 49, and the compound *brahmavidbrahmavid* at *B.*, i. 50, is of a kind found only in the ritual literature. According to C and T we have an instance of the rare compounds with *na* in *nānyakārya*, *B.*, xi. 17, and I have already referred to the example of the Buddhist practice of compounding a present participle with *rūpa* at *B.*, i. 80 (an extension of *Pāṇ.*, v. 3, 66 ?). At *B.*, iv. 89, and v. 12, A shows *dharma* instead of *dharman* at the end of a bahuvrīhi, but I have corrected both passages in view of the proper form being found elsewhere in the *Buddhacarita* protected by the

---

[1] Cp. the *Rāmāyaṇa*'s *pakṣirād iva parvataḥ*, quoted by Diwekar, *op. cit.*, p. 50; the earlier Upaniṣads also occasionally make *iva* precede the object of comparison.

metre. Two examples of the rare adjective compounds with *alam* occur at *S.*, i. 48, 55, and reduplicated adjectives are used to express (1) a high degree, *śūnyaśūnya*, *S.*, i. 10, and *utsukotsuka*, *ib.*, viii. 1, (2) 'rather', 'somewhat', *bhītabhīta*, *B.*, iv. 25. At *B.*, xii. 116, *mahāmuner āgatabodhiniścayaḥ*, we have a genitive dependent on a compound, a use found sporadically in Kālidāsa and other standard writers, and in several cases the last member of a compound is understood to apply also to another word contrasted with the first member, viz., *B.*, vii. 48, *bhinnaḥ pravṛttyā* (for *pravṛttidharmād*) *hi nivṛttidharmaḥ*, *S.*, xviii. 8, *tvacchāsanāt . . sudeśikasyeva* (sc. *śāsanāt*), and *ib.*, ix. 51, *bhāvam . . gṛhasukhābhimukhaṁ na dharme* (for *dharmābhimukham*), which last is puzzling. For *abhimukha* elsewhere in these poems only takes the accusative or the genitive, not the locative, following normal practice; the locative is perhaps due to the fact that the genitive would not fit in and that the accusative would be ambiguous.

These grammatical details may seem dry, but are indispensable to those who would attempt textual criticism of the two poems. They also show how far afield Aśvaghoṣa extended his search for material, and this remark applies with even greater force to the poet's vocabulary, whose range surpasses that of any writer known to us, not excluding the most assiduous student of the lexica. My notes bear such abundant witness to the fact that I need not inflict detailed proof on the reader. Aśvaghoṣa has not overlooked the Veda and the ritual literature as sources for rare words, and a number of others such as *praveraya*, *yoktraya*, *rātrisattra* etc., are only known to us from occasional use in contemporary works. Naturally he employs many Buddhist technical terms, but in addition to these we find many words peculiar to Buddhism, so far as we know at present, *sahīyā*, *anuśaṁsa*, *āmukha*, *kṛṣṭādaka*, *pāriśuddhi*, *moṣadharman*, *upanī*, *saṁgrāhaka* etc. Many words again are not recorded from other literature and are only to be found, if at all, in the lexica, among proper names Saṁkrandana, Lekharṣabha, Māyā and Ambara[1], and among ordinary words *avi* ('mountain'), *avasaṅga, arthavat* ('man'), *upakara, dṛpti, vallarī* ('feather') etc., while of words only demonstrable otherwise for a much later date I may note *rasā* and *cak* (*tṛptau*). Finally the special *kāvya* vocabulary, which is so strongly apparent in Kālidāsa and reached its zenith with the later poets, can be seen in these poems in its early stages with the use of words such as *prasnigdha, pratiyātanā, karāla, nighna* (in the sense of *avaśa*)[2] etc.

iv. The Poet.

To estimate the æsthetic quality of poetry, written in a language which is not the critic's own and which has not been a spoken language in common use for many generations, is a precarious venture at best, and yet the improbability of much success is no excuse for evading a plain duty. First we may see if we can gain any idea of what Indians themselves thought of him, and, as no formal judgements on his performance by other Sanskrit writers are available, we can only infer their views by an examination of the passages quoting his works or betraying their influence by imitation. For the *Buddhacarita*, Rājaśekhara cites viii. 25, at *Kāvyamīmāṁsā*, p. 18, the sole quotation from the poet in works on rhetoric. The *Bhojaprabandha* takes over iv. 59, wholesale, and the *Cāṇakyarājanītiśāstra* in the Bhojarāja recension, besides some reminiscences, makes up its verse vi. 81, out of iv. 86*ab*, and an altered version of 87*cd*, and borrows ix. 62*abc*, for its viii. 136. This last verse is quoted in full in the commentary on the *Ṣaḍdarśanasamuccaya*, p. 13, and may be the source of

---

[1] *S.*, x. 9. I think we ought to accept the MS. reading here; Ambara is defined as *nāgabhid*, which should mean either Kṛṣṇa or Garuḍa, preferably the former as he is *pītavāsas*. It also applies to the lion under the *kāvya* convention that lions kill elephants, for whose occurrence in the poems see below p. lxxxviii, n. 2.

[2] Besides the *Raghuvaṁśa* passage quoted in the translation on *S.*, xiii. 33, I have since found a similar use at *Mattavilāsa*, verse 5.

Nyāyasūtra, iv. 1, 22. Verse 13 of canto viii is cited in the *Durghaṭavṛtti* and by Ujjvaladatta on the *Uṇādisūtras* and by Rāyamukuṭa on the *Amarakośa*[1]. From the *Saundarananda* Rāyamukuṭa and Sarvānanda quote i. 24, and the latter and Ujjvaladatta viii. 53, while Bhartṛhari borrowed the second line of viii. 35, altering *hālahala* (a form used by Śūra also, *Jāt.*, xxxi. 67) to *hālāhala*, his version recurring several times in literature, while Kṣīrasvāmin quotes it in its original shape, as does Pūrṇabhadra in *Pañcatantra* (H.O.S., XI), i. 145. None of these verses are in Aśvaghoṣa's more elaborate style, which, it may be inferred, ceased to appeal to later generations.

The question of imitation is important, because in the earlier writers especially borrowing was often intended as criticism of some weakness in the passage so appropriated. But it is more difficult to deal with than direct citation; on the one hand it was the regular practice of Indian poets to lift an idea or a phrase from a predecessor, it being notorious that *nāsty acauraḥ kavijanaḥ* (*Kāvyamīmāṁsā*, p. 61), and this was considered permissible as long as a new twist was given to the matter borrowed. On the other hand almost all the *kāvya* literature between Aśvaghoṣa and Kālidāsa has disappeared and we cannot be sure that an apparent loan from the Buddhist poet is not really taken from some unknown intermediate work, unless there is a marked individuality in the common features. Moreover imitation is not always conscious; an echo of a passage once read and long forgotten may rise to the mind in the course of composition and lead to appropriation of another's ideas without the borrower's being aware of his indebtedness. Bearing these considerations in mind, we may nevertheless say that for Bhāsa, whom I hold to be the author of the *Svapnavāsavadatta* and the *Pratijñāyaugandharāyaṇa* and who cannot be much later in date than Aśvaghoṣa, four passages mark themselves out at once as

---

[1] For the quotations from Aśvaghoṣa by the mediæval Bengali school of grammarians see Zachariæ, *ZII*, 1932, 1ff.

borrowing from *B.*, i. 74, xiii. 60, and xxviii. 15, and *S.*, x. 8. The last of these is interesting as implying that the dramatist considered the verse imitated to be an artificial conceit[1]. The next considerable work of *kāvya* to my mind is the *Ṛtusaṁhāra*; for, though eminent scholars still attribute it to Kālidāsa[2], few students of the niceties of style are likely to accept the verdict, but will rather see in it a halfway house between him and Aśvaghoṣa, some of whose peculiarities and weaknesses it shares, notably the tendency to repeat words and phrases. Despite the difference of subject, the influence of the Buddhist writer is possible in a number of passages, and probable in iii. 8, *kāraṇḍavānanavighaṭṭitavīcimālāḥ*, and iv. 9, *śarārikādambavighaṭṭitāni* (*B.*, v. 53, and *S.*, x. 38, where note MS. reading), and vi. 24 (or 23), *cittaṁ muner api haranti nivṛttarāgam* (*B.*, iv. 11), the idea being repeated at vi. 31 (or 30).

That there was a relationship between Aśvaghoṣa and Kālidāsa did not escape Professor Cowell in editing the *Buddhacarita*, but if a long list of parallel passages can be drawn up, for few of them can a direct loan be proved to be necessary[3]. An interesting case is the relationship between *B.*, viii. 25, and *R.*, iii. 15, in which the epithets applied by Aśvaghoṣa to women are used of lamps by Kālidāsa, as though he were criti-

---

[1] For detailed discussion see *Ind. Ant.*, pp. 95–99 and 113-114. *B.*, xxviii. 15, describes the Mallas as rushing furiously out to fight 'like snakes who have been confined in a pot'; we have the same comparison in identical circumstance at *Pratijñāyaugandharāyaṇa*, iv, p. 62 (T.S.S. edn.; cp. *loc. cit.*, p. 113).

[2] The argument that it might belong to Kālidāsa's juvenilia does not impress me; the artistic conscience of Sanskrit poets has combined with absence of printing facilities to save us from the painful immaturities of genius. Nor does the work bear any of the obvious stigmata of the novice.

[3] There has been no critical consideration in adequate detail of Kālidāsa's debt to Aśvaghoṣa, though many writers have touched on the subject. A useful collection of passages in the *Buddhacarita* which have parallels in Kālidāsa will be found in Nandargikar's *Raghuvaṁśa* (3rd edition, 1897), Intr., 161–196; see also Gawroński, *Rocznik Orientalistyczny*, 1914, Diwekar, *op. cit.*, 49 and 88ff., and Sukumar Sen, *JASB*, 1930, 185, and *Haraprasād Saṁvarddhan Lekhamālā* (Calcutta, 1932), 172ff.

cising his predecessor's *hatatviṣaḥ* as improperly said of women. The parallels at times assist in the correct interpretation of Aśvaghoṣa's text, but throw little light on his methods or on Kālidāsa's attitude to him in general, though they do show the much greater technical skill of the later poet. Of his successors Bhāravi and Māgha may be occasionally suspected of referring to the Buddhist writer, but the cases are too indefinite to be susceptible of proof. That Bhartṛhari knew him we have already seen, and many passages in Bāṇa's two prose works suggest that he had ransacked these poems to obtain material for similes, some of them being quoted in my notes, but later *kāvya* writers appear to have no acquaintance with them. Of the rhetoricians I have noted that Rājaśekhara quotes him directly, and I am satisfied that Daṇḍin has *B.*, iv. 33, in mind in his phrase *ālakṣyakeśara, Kāvyādarśa*, ii. 44, and *B.*, xi. 71, for *ib.*, iii. 120. Bhāmaha may also be referring to him, when he criticises the cacophony of *ajihladat* (*S.*, ii. 30), but the form also occurs in the *Bhaṭṭikāvya* and in the fragments of the life of the Buddha referred to above at p. xxxvi. These facts indicate that Aśvaghoṣa exercised only a minor influence on writers subsequent to Kālidāsa, and we may safely assign as the reasons for the comparative neglect of his works not only the decline of Buddhism and the prejudice against his religion, but also a change of taste and a liking for other methods of writing.

If then his style was considered out of date in the classic period, it is best to start its examination by a comparison with older models of *kāvya* writing, that is, inevitably with the *Rāmāyaṇa*. We have to treat the epic, in the shape in which it has come down to us, not as the work of a single poet, but as the production of a school, all whose members are inspired by the same ideal. Their most obvious characteristic arises from the fact that the epic was meant for continuous recitation and had to be so planned as to hold the audience without imposing too great a strain on their receptiveness[1]. It is almost entirely composed therefore in a metre, which flows evenly without obvious division, but which avoids monotony by the endless variations of rhythm of which it is capable; the verses are treated not as units in themselves, but as parts of a whole, and the tension of listening is mitigated by frequent repetitions and recurrences of the same stock phrases and by the slow movement of the story, so that anyone whose attention had wandered for a moment could pick up the threads again without embarrassment. Aśvaghoṣa follows an exactly opposite method. Each verse is a separate unit in itself both grammatically and in sense and is made up of four clearly articulated *pādas*, in which cross reference and similarity of framework serve equally to bind the whole together and to delimit it from the contiguous verses. He has chosen to point out this difference to us by occasionally taking an epic tag and demonstrating how a verse should be constructed on it. Thus at *S.*, i. 35, a recurrent epic expression is made the basis of a verse with three similar compounds :—

Baddhagodhāṅgulitrāṇā hastaviṣṭhitakārmukāḥ ।
Śarādhmātamahātūṇā vyāyatābaddhavāsasaḥ ॥

Or he takes *ib.*, 43, the common phrase *suvibhaktāntarāpaṇa* and builds round it a complicated play on words. When therefore he uses another similar compound *hastyaśvaratha-saṁkīrṇam* at *ib.*, 52, and the second line consists of two contrasted words starting with *nigūḍha* and *anigūḍha*, we see that *pāda b*, which our MSS. give in the form *asaṁkīrṇam anākulam*, must read as a single compound, that is, I should have amended to *asaṁkīrṇajanākulam*. The treatment of each verse as a separate whole is properly a reversion to the practice of the *Rigveda*, and it is remarkable in how many respects Aśvaghoṣa's methods

[1] The same motive explains the simplicity of Kālidāsa's verse in his dramas as compared with their complicated structure in his poems.

hark back to those of the more advanced poets of that collection, notably in regard to rhyme, assonance, repetition of the same words in a verse, the use of refrains[1] etc. I do not wish to suggest that he consciously modelled his work on the older poetry, but that his technique derives from a school of *kāvya* writers, which had possibly been long in existence and whose style had more affinities with the *Rigveda* than with the *Rāmāyaṇa*, and that the latter's influence should rather be sought in language, ideas, similes and other rhetorical figures.

When we come to the classical *kāvya*, we find this method much developed. The principle that each verse is a separate unit is still more strongly held and, though Kālidāsa occasionally constructs a verse on parallel or contrasted *pādas*[2], ordinarily his rhythm is based on the verse as a whole and not on the individual *pādas*. His practice was followed with more enthusiasm than discretion by later poets, so that ultimately a *kāvya* epic became little more than a collection of miniature poems loosely strung on the thread of the story. Though Aśvaghoṣa had not travelled to the end of the road, he found that the creation of a poem out of a number of stanzas, each sharply demarcated from its neighbours, brought certain difficulties in its train. Whether it was an inner compulsion of his nature or the fashion of the day that led him to seek expression in the form of poetry, he had a very definite object in his works, a message to deliver of whose supreme importance he was firmly convinced, and effective narration was therefore

[1] Refrains, which are typical of ballad literature, occur also in the *Rāmāyaṇa*, but only apparently in the later passages.

[2] A curious instance of this may be quoted. Aśvaghoṣa sometimes makes a verse with three comparisons, putting the main sentence into *c* and the last comparison into *d* and so producing the effect of the final *pāda* being an afterthought, thus *B.*, ii. 20, vii. 8, and xii. 13, against *S.*, viii. 31, xvii. 22, and xviii. 1, where the main sentence closes the verse. This procedure, to which a parallel can be found in the *Rigveda*, is followed by Kālidāsa, *Vikramorvaśīya*, i. 7, which has a further likeness to *B.*, ii. 20, in that each describes a gradual process.

to him a prime necessity, since by dispersion of interest he might fail to keep his readers' minds directed to the real issue. Further as a dramatist he had no doubt learnt in his plays how to maintain in some form or other that unity, without which the attention of the audience cannot be held, but a *kāvya* epic provided a medium less suited to the object he had in view. To the classical writers this difficulty did not present itself; they had no message to deliver beyond the appeal of their art and only a secondary interest attaches to their stories, whose unfolding could be and in most cases was neglected. In order then to obtain the unity vital to his purpose, he adopted the procedure of articulating his poems as clearly as each verse. The proportion of space allotted to each episode was calculated with care, and verses were grouped together by various devices, as it were into paragraphs, each with a single subject. The simplest way of doing this is by change of metre, an excellent instance of which is to be found in the passing from Upajāti to Vaṁśastha at *B.*, xi. 57-58, as the Buddha takes up a new point in his argument; but the possibilities of this were limited. Another expedient is the employment of *yamaka* to mark the end of a period; thus the description of Kapilavāstu is rounded off with such a verse, *S.*, i. 56, and similarly the speech of the disciple, *ib.*, ix. 49. Nanda's speech, *S.*, x. 50–57, ends with two verses which have *yamaka* at the end of each *pāda*, but the aim here is also to indicate strong emotion. Or a whole series of verses are constructed on a similar scheme, with a refrain as at *B.*, xi. 23–33, or with a set of parallel similes, *B.*, vi. 31–34, and xiii. 46–51. More simply *S.*, x. 7, ends with the words *vibhūṣaṇaṁ rakṣaṇam eva cādreḥ*, and the next four verses describe the *vibhūṣaṇa* and the two following the *rakṣaṇa*, while the purple patch is separated from the sequel by a rhyming verse. Less obvious perhaps is *S.*, xviii. 23–32, where each first line contains *adya* and describes an achievement of Nanda's and each second line contains *hi* and supports the first with the enunciation of a general principle. The twelve verses, *S.*, xvi. 53–64, are of a more intricate pattern.

Primarily there are six pairs of verses, each consisting of a statement of the wrong and right procedure in a particular case ; the first six verses form a whole, as do the last six, while the first four are interlocked by each having a simile derived from fire and the last six each have a medical simile. The carefully wrought paragraph describing Kapilavāstu in *S.*, i, is interesting as different in method from similar set pieces in later poems and as very much on the lines followed by Bāṇa in his overgrown descriptive sentences, and should be compared with the cruder procedure adopted for the character of Śuddhodana in the succeeding canto.

If I have laboured this point, it is because the methods employed by the poet to secure unity of effect with a consecutive flow of thought out of a series of clear-cut stanzas, each cast in the same mould, are partly responsible for the odd exterior which his poems too often present to us. The problem he tackled is in reality insoluble ; not even all Spenser's metrical skill and ear for rhythm can make the elaborate stanza of the *Faerie Queene* anything but monotonous in the mass, and Aśvaghoṣa was not endowed with the same subtlety of art. But though this artificial framework might advantageously have been modified or made less obvious, nevertheless he does achieve his aim, but by his narrative powers, not by these means ; for the great enjoyment which his works give us is due in large measure to their readability as wholes, which again arises from his skill in ordering his matter and in handling the individual episodes. As an instance of the latter, is there anything in Sanskrit literature equal in its own line to the scene between Nanda and Sundarī at *S.*, iv. 12–23 ? Each verse presents a perfect little picture but is subordinated to its place in the whole, and the tempo is exactly right, neither too hasty nor too long drawn out. Equally it would be hard to beat for vivid and moving presentation the still untranslated episode of the elephant loosed by Devadatta against the Buddha at *B.*, xxi. 40–65. Closely connected with his narrative skill is a remarkable capacity for setting out an argument or explaining a doctrine in clear and convincing fashion. I Tsing's appreciation of this quality has already been quoted, and it seems to have been his gnomic verse which survived longest in the memories of his non-Buddhist fellowcountrymen.

Unfortunately these virtues sometimes fail of their effect; for Aśvaghoṣa is a writer of baffling contrasts, on the one hand the literary artist as story-teller, preacher and poet, on the other the scholar anxious to conform with all the rules and to parade his knowledge. The possession of good qualities implies a liability to the corresponding defects, and among a people who treasured intelligence and learning it is not surprising to find some who lapsed at times, like the Buddhist poet, into pedantry. For if his matter is excellent, his manner is often disconcerting. Take as an example the character of Śuddhodana in *S.*, ii; read in translation, we see it to be an admirable picture of an ideal king, free from gross hyperbole and attractive in details, and often reminding us of the account that Aśoka gives of himself in his edicts [1], but our enjoyment of the original is obstructed by its unhappy resemblance to the section of a grammar which sets out the rules for the formation of the various aorists. Or take the formal descriptions in *S.*, vii. 4–11, and x. 8–13; well worked out in detail, they are deficient in inspiration and leave us with the impression of verses made merely to show how well the poet could manufacture this kind of thing.

We can trace the same tendency also in details of technique, especially in his handling of comparisons, which constitute in his case the main ingredient of the rhetoric essential for the execution of long narrative poems. For a bare statement of fact, however well worded, usually fails to convey the emotional content which the author wishes to communicate, and he can obtain his object best by stimulating the reader's imagination, that is, by suggesting more than he says. This he does

---

[1] See my remarks in the *Journal of the Society for Promoting the Study of Religions*, May 1933, 15-16.

ordinarily by indirect expression[1], which again consists almost necessarily of comparison in some form or other, the very incompleteness of the parallel being a powerful aid to suggestiveness. In a written language in close touch with the spoken word the comparison is often effected by metaphor, which has the advantage of combining economy of phrasing with vividness of language. But the Sanskrit of Aśvaghoṣa's day was already too remote from conversational speech for him to be able to employ that method to any extent and he is thrown back, like other *kāvya* writers, on the many varieties of simile. No other Sanskrit poet perhaps is so fond of simile and none certainly draws them from so wide a range, though some of those most familiar in later literature, such as the lotuses that open with the rising of the sun or moon, or the lion that kills the elephant[2], are sparingly introduced. To classify them exactly is not possible, but in general they can be divided, following the convenient arrangement of Indian writers on poetics, into those cases where the similarity is purely verbal and those where the comparison is of substance. Those in the former category appeal entirely to the intellect and are devoid of poetic emotion; so far as they are witty and neat and not used too frequently, they are free from objection and capable of giving pleasure. But too often the poet is oblivious to the necessity of fitting his comparison to the emotional situation; some are unmitigatedly pedantic, such as the grammatical similes at *S.*, xii. 9, and 10, others far-fetched conceits as at *S.*, x. 8, 9, 10, or an academical aura envelops them as in the

---

[1] This is what Bhāmaha meant by *vakrokti*; as he says, *Kāvyālaṁkāra*, ii. 85 :—

Saiṣā sarvaiva vakroktir anayārtho vibhāvyate |
Yatno 'syāṁ kavinā kāryaḥ ko 'laṁkāro 'nayā vinā ||

[2] The only instances of the former are *B.*, v. 57, and xii. 98, and of the latter, explicitly, *B.*, xxvii. 9, and, implicitly, *B.*, xxi. 46, where heroic men, following behind the maddened elephant about to charge the Buddha, utter lion-roars to induce him to turn round under the impression that he is being attacked by a lion, and also *S.*, x. 9, if correctly interpreted p. lxxix, n. 1.

type that has been called psychological[1]. The other class are often drawn from ordinary life, the regular similes of a preacher, and are brought in with telling effect for moral or didactic purposes, such as the crushed sugarcane dried for burning at *S.*, ix. 31, or the Brahminy bull that cannot be driven out of the corn, *ib.*, xiv. 43. Another favourite type is the complete *rūpaka*, which is common in the epics and contemporary literature but went out of fashion for the higher class of poetry in later ages; it may reach a certain majestic eloquence as at *B.*, i. 70, but more often its artificial nature becomes too apparent as at *S.*, iii. 14. In general the simplest comparisons are often the best, such as *rājyaṁ dīkṣām iva vahan*, *S.*, ii. 6, on which Kālidāsa for once hardly improves, *R.*, iv. 5. Some are taken from nature; thus commonplace perhaps but singularly appropriate the simile of the trembling Sundarī clinging to Nanda like a wind-blown creeper to a *sāl* tree. Though sometimes used pedantically, they often show a real freshness of observation and recall the familiar sights of north-Gangetic India, the water-birds scuttering over the leaves of a *jhil* (*S.*, x. 38), or the Brahminy ducks rising and falling on a lake as the west wind of March lashes its surface into waves (*B.*, viii. 29). Thus we find in his similes a strange mixture, the poet sometimes, the preacher often, but too frequently the pedant or the academician, and if their variety is refreshing in contrast with the restricted list of subjects for comparison in classical *kāvya*, Indian poetry has a long road to travel before it reaches the perfect fusion of matter and manner in Kālidāsa.

Besides the various methods of comparison, we find in these poems many other rhetorical figures, whose poetical value is at times open to doubt. Aśvaghoṣa is much given to distributive phrases, thus zeugma of one verb with two nouns, *S.*, ii. 15*cd*, 16*cd*, 28 *ab*, 39*ab*, or one verb with two pairs of nouns, *B.*, ii. 37, or two verbs with one noun, *B.*, x. 2, or one adjective

---

[1] See C. W. Gurner, *The psychological simile in Aśvaghoṣa*, *JASB*, 1930, 175–180.

with two dependent nouns, *S.*, ii. 5. The distributive compounds (*Kāvyādarśa*, ii. 278) are represented several times, *B.*, v. 26, and 42, and ix. 16, *S.*, xvii. 59, and numerical riddles are found four times, *B.*, ii. 41, and xxvii, 11, 26, and *S.*, xvii. 60, and the *parihārikā* once, *B.*, xi. 71. The other figures, whose descriptions fill the pages of the treatises on poetics, hardly need notice, as their identification is of no aid in estimating the quality of his poetry, beyond the remark that *arthāntaranyāsa*, almost Kālidāsa's favourite figure, occurs rarely (a good example at *B.*, x. 26, and a whole string of them at *S.*, xviii. 23ff.).

Of a different order is his fondness for repetition of the same sound in a verse; unlike the later poets, who employ *yamaka* to prove their knowledge of its varieties as catalogued by the rhetoricians and to show their skill in handling them, the emphatic positions in which, as shown above, he often places them argue that he attributed to them a definite æsthetic value, nor does he always trouble to give a different meaning to the repeated sound. An ordinary form of *yamaka* is the repetition of two syllables at the end of a *pāda*, *S.*, i. 56, ix. 49, x. 56, 57, xvii. 16. Approaching rhyme is the repetition of the same syllables at the end of *pādas b* and *d*, *°ām iva gantukāmāḥ*, *B.*, iii. 22, *°kṣā iva bhānti vṛksāḥ*, *S.*, x. 21, or of a whole *pāda*, *gām adhukṣad Vasiṣṭhavat*, *S.*, i. 3, or to enforce a comparison a verse is repeated almost without alteration, *S.*, xvi. 28 and 29, xvii. 33 and 34, or less exactly at S., xiii. 4, 5 and 6. The number of cases in which the same syllables are repeated in a verse, usually with difference of meaning but not in emphatic positions, is countless, such as *śivikāṁ śivāya*, *B.*, i. 86, *Merugurur gurum*, *ib.*, v. 37, *darīm* three times in *S.*, iv. 41*ab*, and *darī* similarly *ib.*, vi. 33. So Yaśodharā's name can never be mentioned without adding one or more compounds ending in *°dharā*. This phenomenon raises a curious question, how did Aśvaghoṣa pronounce the compound letters? As is well known, the Chinese translators in transliterating names reduce the compound letters to their Prakrit equivalents, *stha* to *ttha* etc., though the works they translated were mostly written in Sanskrit; but the latest translators, such as Fa Hsien, end of the tenth century A.D., often transliterate all the letters. The Chinese translator of the *Buddhacarita* was an Indian and must have known how Sanskrit was ordinarily pronounced by learned Buddhists, yet we find him quite clearly at xiii. 7, trying to translate a play of words on *'śvattha* and *svāsthya*, as if in the original they sounded alike. If we accept this hint, it is natural to suppose in a number of passages that the poet intended the compound letters to be resolved to the Prakrit forms; thus *B.*, x. 1, *sa rājavatsaḥ pṛthupīnavakṣāḥ*, where *vatsa* and *vakṣas* both become *vaccha* in Prakrit, an equivalence of which the Jain canonical authors took advantage [1]. Similarly the play on words at *S.*, ii. 45, is only complete if *śakya*, Śākya and Śakra are all pronounced *sakka* alike. Not to multiply instances, I only adduce one other case, *S.*, ii. 8, *śāstra*, *astra*, *artha*. After all the same principle is applied to some extent in the pronunciation of tatsamas in the modern vernaculars, and if, as I think it should be, it is admitted as proved that Aśvaghoṣa intended his poems to be so pronounced, some important consequences may be deduced. For one thing the reduction of the heavy consonant combinations would make his lines flow much more lightly in recitation. Also we have presumably the origin here of the later rule which allows the equivalence of long and short vowels and of the various sibilants in plays on words. Further does this explain how it came about that the Prakrits and Sanskrit are combined in the Indian drama? If the pronunciation of the latter was assimilated to that of the former, the plays would have been intelligible to far wider audiences and not necessarily confined to those who had a good knowledge of Sanskrit.

Let us return from this digression to other ways in which the poet's love of recurring sounds finds an outlet. One favourite practice is to take the leading word in a sentence and

---

[1] See *JRAS*, 1932, 396.

form a vocative compound of which this word is the base, of the type *niḥsaṁśaya saṁśayo me*, *S.*, xviii. 8. That he saw something formal or hieratic in this turn of speech appears from its being reserved almost entirely for the Buddha, the only instances to the contrary being once to Nanda after he was converted, *S.*, xii. 31, and once to Bimbisāra, *B.*, xi. 2; in both cases the epithets are particularly appropriate to the occasion. It is further natural that a leaning to repetitions of sounds should lead to experiments in rhyme, of which there are several in the *Saundarananda*. For the *Buddhacarita* I may note ii. 40, and the imperfect rhyme at iv. 30, at the end of *b* and *d*. The other poem has a rhyme inside the *pāda* at vi. 35, and xvii. 6, a more complicated one covering two *pādas* at x. 11, and also at vii. 5 and 42, and rhymes at the end of all the *pādas* at iv. 46, v. 20, vi. 25, x. 5 (three *pādas* only), x. 13 (the most elaborate one), and xvii. 13. Of a different type is viii. 32*ab*, where of the six words four end with *madā* and two with *pradāḥ*, a not wholly successful effort. But the recurrent beat of rhyme is in little accord with the mood of epic poetry, and all the more so that the long inflexional endings of Sanskrit require the repetition of more than one syllable for the rhyme to become plain to the ear and that therefore monotony is hard to avoid. It is not surprising then that Aśvaghoṣa's experiments in the *Saundarananda* were not seriously continued in later poetry till we reach the lyrical outbursts of the *Gītāgovinda*.

So far I have only touched the fringe of the main question, the nature of Aśvaghoṣa's poetic ear. The classical poets of India have a sensitiveness to variations of sound, to which the literatures of other countries afford few parallels, and their delicate combinations are a source of never-failing joy. Some of them, however, are inclined to attempt to match the sense with the sound in a way that is decidedly lacking in subtlety, and they have perpetrated real atrocities in the manufacture of verses with a limited number of consonants or even only one.

This last trick was fortunately unknown to Aśvaghoṣa, whose nearest approach to it is *B.*, xii. 96 :—

Apārapārasaṁsārapāraṁ prepsur apārayat ।

which has only *p*, *s*, and *r* except in the last syllable. The cruder efforts to express the sense by the sound are also missing; otherwise *B.*, xiii, would have been cast in a very different mould, perhaps on the lines of the *Gaṇḍīstotra*, or think how Māgha would have revelled in such an opportunity. The poet's mastery of the intricacies of rhythm is sufficiently proved by his success in carrying off such long stretches of Upajāti without wearying the reader, and, so far as I can see, his verse is melodious in general, if not reaching the subtleties of later *kāvya*. Occasional lines are particularly happy in their collocation of consonants; thus *S.*, x. 64*cd* :—

Tato muniḥ pavana ivāmbarāt patan
pragṛhya taṁ punar agaman mahītalam ॥

derives its success from the heaping up of labial sounds. Or take x. 17*cd* :—

Kva cottamastrī bhagavan vadhūs te
mṛgī nagakleśakarī kva caiṣā ॥

where the effect of protest depends on the use of the gutturals and sibilants, and consider how the line would be spoilt if we substituted *taru* for *naga*. On the other hand he seldom hesitates to subordinate agreeableness of sound to the display of learning and will use a word such as *ajihladat*, whose cacophony offended the ear of that excellent critic, Bhāmaha. Till we know with more certainty how he intended his poems to be read, it is wiser to defer a final judgement on this point, and best of all perhaps to leave it to his fellowcountrymen.

Reference should also be made to his habit of using words in more meanings than one, sometimes in a recondite fashion that baffles the reader; the notes to my editions are so full of examples that I need hardly quote any here. Interesting and unusual is the ironical application of this method, after the way of Indian drama, to the unconscious foreshadowing of future events unknown to the speaker but not to the reader; the passages in question are *B.*, iii. 4, viii. 34 and 40, x. 25, and xiii. 63. Occasionally also he seems to avail himself of the ambiguity of a negative *a* disappearing by elision or *saṁdhi* to enable a statement to be understood according to either Brahmanical or Buddhist ideas, *B.*, iii. 25, and xii. 82. I Tsing was unquestionably right in saying that he clothes manifold ideas in few words; for, besides this habitual use of words in two or more meanings, every single word almost in his poems is pregnant and should be given its full value in translation. In no other Sanskrit poet, it seems to me, is the construction of the sentence so packed and tight, and continually we come across compounds which in later poets would have further members added to them for ease of understanding and lightness of effect. But if he habitually eschews the *cheville,* to use a convenient French term, in two respects his handling of language falls below the standard of the classical writers. His inordinate use of conjunctions is often wearisome, in particular the perpetual recurrence of *tataḥ* at, for instance, *B.*, iii. 1–9, and *S.*, i. 30–41, and iv. 12–35. His motive perhaps was to make clear the articulation of his argument, but the obviousness of the artifice gives some passages the semblance of a formally stated proposition of Euclid. He is also wont to repeat the same word in successive verses or continually to bring in certain phrases. As examples I may quote *vayo'nurūpa*, *B.*, ii. 22 and 23, *nāthahīna*, *ib.*, ix. 24 and 27, *saṁkuc* and *praṇāda*, *ib.*, xiii. 52 and 54, °*vāhanastha*, *S.*, xvii. 23 and 24, *pṛṣatka*, *ib.*, 38 and 39, and for phrases *saṁparivārya tasthuḥ*, *B.*, i. 17, iv. 3, vii. 37, and xiii. 27, and *manasīva codyamānaḥ*, *ib.*, v. 71 and 87. I have already noted that the *Ṛtusaṁhāra* has the same trick of speech, evidence of its relatively early date; for to the later poets repetition is anathema and argues poverty of diction and imagination.

This analysis of Aśvaghoṣa's technique suggests that, if we call him rough, the Ennius to Kalidasa's Vergil, we do not quite find the centre of the target; if an analogy must be found in European poetry, I would rather seek it in Milton, equally a scholar and equally fond of displaying his learning, who similarly sought to express his religion within the limits of an epic. For where Aśvaghoṣa's text survives undamaged, he is polished enough and his work is usually highly wrought and well finished. But his intricacy and elaboration are those of the primitive, not of the sophisticated writer; not for him the subtle relations of Kālidāsa's verse or its exact harmonies of tone, still less the 'slickness' of later *kāvya*. He reminds me often of some Italian painter of the fifteenth century, who in his excitement over the new possibilities of representation will upset the balance of his picture to direct our attention to his skill in depicting the musculature of a man drawing a bow or in foreshortening an upturned head. Or, to take an Indian parallel, the Muhammadan architecture of Ahmedabad, seen in bulk, leaves on the visitor's mind the impression of singularly elaborate decoration, while the Taj Mahal, in reality far more adorned, seems simple in comparison; it is only a question of the extent to which the decoration is not merely applied ornament but has been subordinated in function to the general scheme of the structure. Similarly Aśvaghoṣa's insistence on symmetry, his exposure of the framework and his non-functional decoration are characteristic of early work, not of a time when the greatest art is so to conceal the art that the reader is unconscious of its presence pervading the whole poem. The correct view, I would maintain then, is that Aśvaghoṣa is a primitive in his art, just as he is in religion and philosophy.

But there is nothing wrong in being primitive; our enjoyment of primitive work is merely different in kind from that which more advanced art affords us, and we shall fall into grievous error if we insist on looking in these poems for what we find in classical *kāvya*, instead of concentrating on that which the author himself intends us to see. For it is not only in technique but also in feeling that the difference is seen between a primitive and a mature writer. The latter is like some well-

-bred person in a highly civilised society, who prides himself on knowing everything and being able to do everything without either parading his knowledge or appearing to make any effort. He must conceal the labour with which he achieves his results, as if his perfect skill were inborn and his work produced without toil. Above all enthusiasm is taboo and good taste his god, so that he seems almost to show a certain lack of feeling, an air of disillusionment, to insinuate, as it were, that such studied perfection is hardly worth while. But in the early stages of an art the opposite prevails. Just as the primitive artist delights to experiment with new forms and test their possibilities, so he gives his depth of feeling free rein in his work, and enthusiasm excuses an occasional lapse of taste or failure of technique. It is this freshness, this zest, which casts an abiding charm over early work, and here surely is the secret of the hold Aśvaghoṣa's poems take on us. In his verses we catch glimpses of a man of artistic temperament and strong passions, delighting in everything that appeals to the senses, yet finding no sure foothold anywhere till he seeks refuge in Buddhism. The zeal of the convert informs every word he writes, and by his intense conviction of the importance of his message he still carries away readers of different faith and alien civilisation, however inadequate to them his philosophy of life may seem. His skill in narration keeps us interested, but the real appeal derives from the spontaneous emotion which overflows in his poetry.

This emotion may be traced to two sources, the first being his ardent devotion to the person of the Buddha. Though the noble panegyric in canto xxvii of the *Buddhacarita* is no longer available to us in the original, the bright flame of his faith shines through every line of the two poems and redeems the driest passages. Equally insistent throughout is his sense of the impermanence of all mundane phenomena, however delightful they be, and the strength of this feeling is the measure of the pull which the world exerted on him ; for the passion with which he denounces the ordinary joys of life draws its force not merely from a revulsion of feeling, but also from the necessity of convincing himself. When he comes to deal with that which lies at the core of his being, he sheds his learning and drops all play with rhetorical and pedantic tricks, to speak straight from the heart. Though those who are affected by the feminist tendency of the day may not find the subject of canto viii of the *Saundarananda* to their taste, yet even they will recognize that Aśvaghoṣa there shows himself to have no superior among Sanskrit poets as a writer of satire. He has all the gifts for the purpose, a command of balance and antithesis, economy and pointedness of phrasing, and above all a furious indignation, a *saeva ira*, at heart. Listen to these lines, clear-cut and hard as a diamond, but searing like vitriol :—

Vacanena haranti valgunā niśitena praharanti cetasā |
Madhu tiṣṭhati vāci yoṣitāṁ hṛdaye hālahalaṁ mahad viṣaṁ ||
Adadatsu bhavanti narmadāḥ pradadatsu praviśanti vibhramam |
Praṇateṣu bhavanti garvitāḥ pramadās tṛptatarās ca māniṣu ||
Guṇavatsu caranti bhartṛvad guṇahīneṣu caranti putravat |
Dhanavatsu caranti tṛṣṇayā dhanahīneṣu caranty avajñayā ||

S., viii. 35, 39, 40.

These are not sparks from the anvil of some wit or courtly epigrammatist, but the outburst of a man in bitter earnest, who has himself suffered from the desires he flagellates. But if the world grips our vitals with longings which we must tear out by the roots, it is also transient, ephemeral, and the poet's spirit rises, as he surveys with noble courage man's brief glory in this existence, his restless flittings from life to life, and contrasts them with the eternal peace to be found in his religion. Again the same simplicity, the same economy of phrase, but now how elevated and majestic :—

Ṛtur vyatītaḥ parivartate punaḥ
kṣayaṁ prayātaḥ punar eti candramāḥ |
Gataṁ gataṁ naiva tu saṁnivartate
jalaṁ nadīnāṁ ca nṛṇāṁ ca yauvanam ||

S., ix. 28.

Irresistibly Catullus' famous lines, beginning *Soles occidere ac redire possunt*, rise to the mind. Or again :—

Vihagānāṁ yathā sāyaṁ tatra tatra samāgamaḥ ।
Jātau jātau tathāśleṣo janasya svajanasya ca ॥
Pratiśrayaṁ bahuvidhaṁ saṁśrayanti yathādhvagāḥ ।
Pratiyānti punas tyaktvā tadvaj jñātisamāgamaḥ ॥

S., xv. 33, 34.

Or the motif of ' Où sont les neiges d'antan ? '

Balaṁ Kurūṇāṁ kva ca tat tadābhavat
yudhi jvalitvā tarasaujasā ca ye ।
Samitsamiddhā jvalanā ivādhvare
hatāsavo bhasmani paryavasthitāḥ ॥ S., ix. 20.

On this note let me take leave of Aśvaghoṣa, a Buddhist, a scholar, above all a poet, who sought other ends and struck other strings than the poets of the classical epoch, and let us enjoy what he has to give us without attempting to assign him a precise place in that galaxy.

THE ACTS OF THE BUDDHA

CANTO I

Birth of the Holy One.

1. There was a king of the unconquerable Śākyas, Śuddhodana by name, of the race of Ikṣvāku and the peer of Ikṣvāku in might. Pure he was in conduct and beloved of his people as the moon in autumn.

2. That counterpart of Indra had a queen, a very Śacī, whose splendour corresponded to his might. In beauty like Padmā, in steadfastness like the earth, she was called Mahāmāyā, from her resemblance to the incomparable Māyā.

1. T and C leave it uncertain whether 'unconquerable' (*aśakya*) is an epithet of the king or the Śākyas; in either case there is a play of words on Śākya and *aśakya* as in *S.*, ii. 45. In *c* T's *ḥphrog-byed zla-ba* is equivalent to *hariś°* or *haric-candra*, which may either be the famous king not mentioned elsewhere in Aśvaghoṣa or mean 'the moon of the asterism Śravaṇa'; but C has 'the first-born moon' (?='the moon at the beginning of the year'). As it is the moon of autumn that gives joy to men and is the subject of comparison (e.g., *S.*, ii. 14), I conjecture an original *śaraccandra*. The verse may be tentatively restored as follows :—

Aikṣvāka Ikṣvākusamaprabhāvaḥ
Śākyeṣv aśakyeṣu viśuddhavṛttaḥ ।
Priyaḥ śaraccandra iva prajābhyaḥ
Śuddhodano nāma babhūva rājā ॥

2. The translation is not quite certain. The comparison with Māyā the goddess recurs *S.*, ii. 49; C has, 'borrowing the simile, she was called Māyā, but in reality there was no comparison between them'. *Pādas a*, *c* and *d* may have run :—

Tasyendrakalpasya babhūva patnī
. . . . ।
Padmeva lakṣmīḥ pṛthivīva dhīrā
Māyeti nāmnānupameva Māyā ॥

3. This ruler of men, dallying with his queen, enjoyed, as it were, the sovereign glory of Vaiśravaṇa. Then without defilement she received the fruit of the womb, just as knowledge united with mental concentration bears fruit.

4. Before she conceived, she saw in her sleep a white lord of elephants entering her body, yet she felt thereby no pain.

5. Māyā, the queen of that god-like king, bore in her womb the glory of her race and, being in her purity free from weariness, sorrow and illusion, she set her mind on the sin-free forest.

6. In her longing for the lonely forest as suited to trance, she asked the king to go and stay in the grove called Lumbinī, which was gay like the garden of Caitraratha with trees of every kind.

7. The lord of the earth, full of wonder and joy, recognised

3. W's translation of *b* is impossible, as Śrī was not the wife of Vaiśravaṇa; and *c* might mean 'like the knowledge of one who possesses *samādhi*'. The second line might have been :—

Tataś ca vidyeva samādhiyuktā
garbhaṁ dadhe pāpavivarjitā sā ॥

4. I reconstruct *d* : *na tannimittaṁ samavāpa tāpam.*

5. The first line ran more or less :—

Sā tasya devapratimasya devī
garbheṇa vaṁśaśriyam udvahantī ।

And the second line had probably *vītaśramaśokamāyā*, for which cp. *S.*, ii. 49, but it is not clear if *gtsaṅ-la*, 'in purity', refers to Māyā or the forest.

6. The comparison of Lumbinī to the Caitraratha garden recurs *S.*, ii. 53, and is a stock simile in these accounts; cp. *Mhv.*, I, 149, 14, and 217, 2, and II, 19, 16, and *Jātaka*, I, 52, where *cittalatāvanasadisaṁ* should probably read *cittaratha°*. The first line may have been :—

Sā Lumbiniṁ nāma vanāntabhūmiṁ
citradrumāṁ Caitrarathābhirāmām ।

7. This verse was somewhat as follows :—

Aryāśayāṁ tāṁ . . . .
Vijñāya kautūhalaharṣapūrṇaḥ ।
Śivāt purād bhūmipatir jagāma
tatprītaye nāpi vihārahetoḥ ॥

that her disposition was noble from her possession of piety, and left the fortunate city, in order to gratify her, not for a pleasure excursion.

8. In that glorious grove the queen perceived that the time of her delivery was at hand and, amidst the welcome of thousands of waiting-women, proceeded to a couch overspread with an awning.

9. Then as soon as Puṣya became propitious, from the side of the queen, who was hallowed by her vows, a son was born for the weal of the world, without her suffering either pain or illness.

10. As was the birth of Aurva from the thigh, of Pṛthu from the hand, of Māndhātṛ, the peer of Indra, from the head, of Kakṣīvat from the armpit, on such wise was his birth.

11. When in due course he had issued from the womb, he appeared as if he had descended from the sky, for he did not come into the world through the portal of life; and, since he had purified his being through many æons, he was born not ignorant but fully conscious.

9. C gives the precise date, 'the eighth day of the fourth month', for which cp. Przyluski, *Concile de Rājagṛha*, 88. For the vows that Māyā took see Windisch, ii. 113ff.

10. For Aurva see *MBh.*, i. 6802ff., and for Pṛthu, *ib.*, xii. 2219ff. Māndhātṛ's legend is given at length *Divy.*, 210ff., but Brahmanical legend differs, saying he was born from the side. He is the peer of Indra as occupying half his seat. Nothing is known of Kakṣīvat's birth. The *Fo pen hsing ching* (*TI*, IV, 59, *c*25ff.) puts the comparisons, omitting Pṛthu, into the mouths of the Brahman soothsayers; FP has all four at 690, *a*3ff.

11. This and the next verse are relative sentences depending on *tasya* in 10, and explain why the birth was miraculous. *Krama* means 'the ordinary course of events' (cp. v. 36, 37), Buddhas naturally being born in a supernatural way. *Pāda b* implies that the Buddha was born free from the ordinary defilements of birth (cp. 16 below), and *cyuta* is deliberately ambiguous, being regularly used of divine beings descending to earth for rebirth. For *samprajānan*, see *AK.*, II, 54, Oltremare, *Théosophie bouddhique*, 129, n. 4, and Windisch, ii, 88, 110, 128; probably it means 'remembering his previous births' in this connexion.

12. With his lustre and steadfastness he appeared like the young sun come down to earth, and despite this his dazzling brilliance, when gazed at, he held all eyes like the moon.

13. For with the glowing radiance of his limbs he eclipsed, like the sun, the radiance of the lamps, and, beauteous with the hue of precious gold, he illumined all the quarters of space.

14. He who was like the constellation of the Seven Seers walked seven steps with such firmness that the feet were lifted up unwavering and straight and that the strides were long and set down firmly.

15. And looking to the four quarters with the bearing of a lion, he uttered a speech proclaiming the truth: "I am born for Enlightenment for the good of the world; this is my last birth in the world of phenomena."

12. A's gap in *a* is due to a recent gash, and it may have originally had *yo*. Co's *śriyā* is unmetrical and, despite Wohlgemuth, probably not supported by C. *Dīpti* is the quality of the sun, and *dhairya* of the earth.

13. The first line refers to the illumination of birth-chambers; cp. Penzer, *Ocean of Story*, II, 168-9, and *Padyacūḍāmaṇi*, iii. 26. As he was born out of doors, not in a *sūtikāgṛha*, is it suggested that the sun took the place of the usual lights ? For the golden colour in the second line see Windisch, ii, 136.

14. C is uncertain for this verse and may have rendered *a* by 'upright, straight, with unflustered mind'. Many suggestions, none really plausible except Schrader's *anākulānyubjasamuddhṛtāni* (read as one word), have been made for emending or explaining the first *pāda*, which T may have read as in the text or else had something like *anākulo nyubjamalojjhitāni*. I accept A's original reading and treat it as a single compound, as the non-occurrence of *ubja* elsewhere is against dividing *anākulāny ubja°*; this requires us under the poet's principle of balance to read *b* also as a single compound, so reconciling A and T. For the sense I give to *samudgata* (C's 'upright'), cp. viii. 52 below. T has a word too much in *c*, but suggests that *eva* is doubtful.

15. As *c* refers to the *siṁhāvalokita* (*LV.*, 84), *gati* is hardly 'gait' here, possibly 'lionwise'. I translate *bhavya* according to C's 'piercing through to the true meaning', the sense being known to the lexica but not recorded in literature. T's equivalent, *snod-ldan-rnams-kyi* (W reads *stod-ldan*, = *ślāghya*) is unintelligible and presumably corrupt.

16. Two streams of water, clear as the rays of the moon and having the virtue, one of heat, one of cold, poured forth from the sky and fell on his gracious head to give his body refreshment by their contact.

17. He lay on a couch with a gorgeous canopy, feet of beryl and framework glistening with gold, and round him the Yakṣa lords stood reverently on guard with golden lotuses in their hands.

18. The dwellers in heaven, themselves remaining invisible, held up in the sky a white umbrella and, bowing their heads in obeisance before his majesty, muttered the highest blessings that he might obtain Enlightenment.

19. The mighty snakes in their thirst for the most excellent Law fanned him and, with eyes shining with devotion, bestrewed him with *mandāra* flowers, offices they had performed for the Buddhas of the past.

16. T renders *śubhre* 'white' and C 'pure'. In *c* perhaps *saṁparka* for *saṁsparśa*. This use of *antara*, though close to the classic use defined as *tādarthya* (e.g. *R.*, xvi. 82, and *Slokavārttika*, *Arthāpattipariccheda*, 7), is only found in Buddhist works, and then only in the phrase *kim antaram* (*Mhv.*, I, 360, 11, and II, 66, 15, and *Saṁyutta*, I, 201, and Childers s.v.). The point is that the Buddha at birth is not covered with the impurities of the womb and does not need the usual bath for cleansing purposes. The connexion of this idea with miraculous birth goes back to *RV.*, v. 11, 3, of Agni.

17. T's reading in *a* may be correct; cp. *Kād.*, 127, *avanipālaśayanair iva siṁhapādāṅkitatalair . . . pādapaiḥ*, and *Mudrārākṣasa*, ii. 11, *hemāṅkam . . siṁhāsanam*. Note also *Yasht*, 17, 9, of a couch *zaranyapakhštapad*. In *c* Lüders' amendment may be right, the difference from A being only an easily omitted dot.

18. The restoration of the first five syllables in *a* cannot be exactly determined, *adṛśya*, *avyakta* or *nigūḍha* being compounded with *bhūtāḥ* or *bhāvāḥ*. Cp. *Suttanipāta*, 688 (of Asita's visit), *marū . . . na dissare cāmara-chattagāhakā*, *Mahāvaṁsa*, xxxi. 89–90, *Jātaka*, VI, 331 (of Indra), *HC.*, ch. i, 9, 18, *adṛśyamānavanadevatāvidhṛtair bālapallavaiḥ*, and *MBh.*, ii. 1406. In *c vyadhārayan* would be best, but T's *kun-nas* supports the text.

19. *Bhaktiviśiṣṭanetrāḥ* has been much criticized, but is certified by C's *chuan* (Giles, 2702). The sense of 'characterized by' is natural and satisfactory, and contrasts with *viśeṣa* in the first line. But there may be a secondary

20. And gladdened by the virtue of his birth in this fashion, the Śuddhādhivāsa deities rejoiced in their pure natures, though passion was extinct in them, for the sake of the world drowned in suffering.

21. At his birth the earth, nailed down as it was with the king of mountains, trembled like a ship struck by the wind; and from the cloudless sky there fell a shower perfumed with sandalwood and bringing blue and pink lotuses.

22. Delightful breezes blew, soft to the touch and wafting down heavenly raiment; the very sun shone more brightly and the fire, unstirred, blazed with gracious flames.

23. In the north-eastern corner of the royal quarters a well of clear water appeared of itself, at which the household in amazement carried out their rites as at a holy bathing-place.

meaning. For T translates *gzir*, which properly means 'troubled', and it uses *mi-gzir* (*prasanna* ?) of the Buddha's eyes at 38 below; in view of the latter passage it cannot mean 'wide-open' (so W) here. Bacot's Tibetan-Sanskrit dictionary however shows *gzir* to have meanings not recorded by S. C. Das and Jäschke, but seems to be corrupt here unfortunately. *Divy.*, 518, has *yathaiva stimite jale 'sya netraṁ viśiṣṭe vadane virājate*, where *viśiṣṭa* corresponds to *stimita* and ought to mean 'untroubled', 'clear'; also *SP.*, xxiv. 20, *prajñājñānaviśiṣṭalocanā*. In the circumstances I translate freely. C translates *avyajan* as if *ayajan*.

20. *Tathāgata* cannot mean primarily the Buddha here, as Aśvaghoṣa does not apply such terms to him till he reached *bodhi*; it must be taken as an adjective to *utpāda*, the use being presumably intended to suggest the derivation of the name. By this construction a relative *yasya* can be understood through *ca* to connect the verse with the preceding and following ones. The Śuddhādhivāsa deities are incapable of going elsewhere (*AK.*, II, 216), and their presence on earth on this occasion is possibly not suggested therefore here; the Mahāyāna however does not accept this limitation on their powers.

21. Gawroński compares *CII*, III, 75, 13; note also *Kād.*, 113, *calita-kulaśailakīlitā . . . ācakampe medinī*. This probably explains Vasubandhu's *kīṭādri* (*AK.*, II, 147), i.e. *kīlādri* misread by the Chinese and Tibetan translators as *kālādri*.

22. Cp. *R.*, iii. 14.

24. And troops of heavenly beings, petitioners for the Law, thronged the grove to wait on him, and in their wonderment they cast flowers from the trees, though out of season.

25. At that time the noxious creatures consorted together and did each other no hurt. Whatever diseases there were among mankind were cured too without effort.

26. The birds and deer did not call aloud and the rivers flowed with calm waters. The quarters became clear and the sky shone cloudless; the drums of the gods resounded in the air.

27. When the Guru was born for the salvation of all creatures, the world became exceeding peaceful, as though, being in a state of disorder, it had obtained a ruler. Kāmadeva alone did not rejoice.

28. On seeing the miraculous birth of his son, the king, steadfast though he was, was much disturbed, and from his affection a double stream of tears flowed, born of delight and apprehension.

29. The queen was filled with fear and joy, like a stream of hot and cold water mixed, because the power of her son was other than human on the one hand, and because she had a mother's natural weakness on the other.

24. *Darśana* implies a formal visit to an idol or a ruler and is still so used in Hindi. A and T are against Gawroński's *kautūhaleneva* in *c*, and, as the word cannot be applied to the trees without *iva*, T must be translated as above. Whether C so understood it is not clear. The last word is a verb compounded with *ni*, equivalent to *sraṁs* or *vyadh*, possibly *nipātitāni*.

26. In *c* T's *phyog-rnams rab-snaṅ=diśaḥ praseduḥ*, and *dge-ba*, the epithet of the sky, probably stands for *śuci* as in xii. 119; C has 'in the sky was no cloud-screen'.

27. The translation of the third *pāda* follows C, on whose authority I amend T's improbable *thar-paḥi* to *thar-phyir*, equivalent to *jagadvimokṣāya guruprasūtau*.

29. C has for *a*, 'the queen saw her son born not by the ordinary way', and this probably is the sense underlying T's ambiguous phrase.

30. The pious old women failed in penetration, seeing only the reasons for alarm ; so, purifying themselves and performing luck-bringing rites, they prayed to the gods for good fortune.

31. When the Brahmans, famed for conduct, learning and eloquence, had heard about these omens and considered them, then with beaming faces full of wonder and exultation they said to the king, who was both fearful and joyful :—

32. " On earth men desire for their peace no excellence at all other than a son. As this lamp of yours is the lamp of your race, rejoice and make a feast to-day.

33. Therefore in all steadfastness renounce anxiety and be merry ; for your race will certainly flourish. He who has been born here as your son is the leader for those who are overcome by the suffering of the world.

34. According to the signs found on this excellent one, the brilliance of gold and the radiance of a lamp, he will certainly become either an enlightened seer or a Cakravartin monarch on earth among men.

35. Should he desire earthly sovereignty, then by his might and law he will stand on earth at the head of all kings, as the light of the sun at the head of all constellations.

36. Should he desire salvation and go to the forest, then by his knowledge and truth he will overcome all creeds and stand on the earth, like Meru king of mountains among all the heights.

30. Some details are uncertain, but the general sense is clear. ' Pious ', *lhag-ma spaṅs-te*, *adhimuktāḥ* or *adhimucyamānāḥ*.

31. Wohlgemuth quotes a parallel to this passage from the *Fo pen hsing ching* (*TI*, IV, 59, c15, the last quartet, etc.).

32. In Hindustan a house without a son is still said to be without a lamp.

33. ' Be merry ', lit. ' dance ' ; W translates otherwise.

34. T's text in *d* is doubtful and hard to translate ; C has the better sense, ' should he practise enjoyment in the world, certainly he will become a cakravartin '.

37. As pure gold is the best of metals, Meru of mountains, the ocean of waters, the moon of planets and the sun of fires, so your son is the best of men.

38. His eyes gaze unwinkingly and are limpid and wide, blazing and yet mild, steady and with very long black eyelashes. How can he not have eyes that see everything ?"

39. Then the king said to the twice-born : "What is the cause that these excellent characteristics should be seen, as you say, in him, when they were not seen in previous great-souled kings ?" Then the Brahmans said to him :—

40. "In respect of the wisdom, renowned deeds and fame of kings there is no question of former and latter. And, since in the nature of things there is a cause here for the effect, listen to our parallels thereto.

41. The science of royal policy, which neither of those seers, Bhṛgu and Aṅgiras, the founders of families, made, was created, Sire, in the course of time by their sons, Śukra and Bṛhaspati.

42. The son of Sarasvatī promulgated again the lost Veda, which the men of old had not seen, and Vyāsa arranged

37. 'Fires', *dud-byed*, *dhūmakara*. 'Men', *rkaṅ-gñis*, *dvipad* ; C's literal translation is misunderstood by Wohlgemuth.

39. I take *zhes* in *c* as=*kila* ; so C, 'if it is as you say'.

40. C makes *c* clear, 'every product by the nature of things arises from a cause'. In *d nidarśanāni* is an uncertain restoration, but T shows a plural word which, whatever it is, cannot be fitted in with A's *atraiva* ; the latter therefore must be wrong.

41. In *a* read *Aṅgirāś ca* ? There is no need to take the irregular *sasarjatuḥ* to the *Dhātupāṭha* root, *sarj*, since the epic has such forms sporadically (*MBh.*, iii. 11005, 12540, and vi. 3695) ; moreover *Mahābhāṣya*, I, 48, 9-10, says some grammarians allow them. Śukra and Bṛhaspati are regularly coupled together as the authors of the first treatises on political science.

42. These stories are discussed at length by Dahlmann, *Das Mahābhārata als Epos u. Rechtsbuch*, 144ff., and are referred to at *S.*, vii. 29 and 31. At the latter Vyāsa is called *vedavibhāgakartṛ*, which is to be understood of the Vedas, not of the *MBh.* For the double meaning in *d* Vasiṣṭha had a son, Śakti, and so was *saśakti*, though *aśakta* in respect of the Veda ; cp. *MBh.*, i. 6640, *putra*-

it in many sections, which Vasiṣṭha for lack of capacity had not done.

43. And Vālmīki was the first to create the verse, which the great seer, Cyavana, did not put together, and the science of healing which Atri did not discover was later proclaimed by the seer Ātreya.

44. And the Brahmanhood which Kuśika did not win was obtained by the son of Gādhin, O king. And Sagara set a limit for the ocean which the previous descendants of Ikṣvāku had not fixed.

45. Janaka reached the position, attained by none other, of instructing the twice-born in the methods of Yoga; and Śūra and his kin were incapable of the famous deeds of Śauri.

46. Therefore neither age nor family decides. Anyone may attain pre-eminence anywhere in the world; for in the case of the kings and seers the sons accomplished the various deeds their ancestors failed to do."

47. Thus was the king cheered and congratulated by the trustworthy twice-born, and, discharging his mind of unwelcome suspicions, he rose to a still higher degree of joy.

vyasanasaṁtaptaḥ śaktimān apy aśaktavat. C did not understand *pūrve* (for which *Pāṇ.*, i. 1, 34) and transliterated it as a proper name.

43. The reference in the first line has been correctly explained by Leumann; Cyavana, on an occasion similar to that which caused Vālmīki to make the first *śloka*, failed to make his outcry in the metre. Sovani observes that the *Ātreya Saṁhitā* now extant was composed by Agniveśa and re-edited by Caraka, who was, according to Chinese tradition, physician to Kaniṣka; he thinks the verse may be intended as a compliment to the latter.

44. Lüders' *rājā* in *b* may well be right.

45. Śauri as the name of Kṛṣṇa appears also in *Laṅkāvatāra*, x. 785, under the corruption of Maurī (the MSS. have Saurī). C seems to have read *te svabalā* in *d*.

46. In *a* A's *kālaḥ* could easily be a corruption from *vaṁśaḥ*.

47. I should have preferred to accept *pratyayito* in *a* in the sense of 'convinced', but there is no real authority for this meaning and *pratyāyito* breaks the metre.

48. And in his gratification he gave with full courtesy rich gifts to the best of the twice-born, wishing that his son might become lord of the earth as prophesied and that he should not retire to the forest before reaching old age.

49. Then by reason of the signs and through the power of his austerities the great seer Asita learned of the birth of him who was to put an end to birth, and came to the palace of the Śākya king, thirsting for the holy Law.

50. He was the chief among the knowers of the Absolute and shone with the majesty of priestly power and with the majesty of asceticism. Accordingly the king's spiritual director brought him into the regal palace with reverence and honour.

51. He entered the precincts of the royal women's dwelling and the rush of joy that he felt was occasioned only by the birth of the prince; for from the intensity of his austerities and the support afforded by old age he remained otherwise unmoved, deeming himself to be, as it were, in a forest.

52. Then the king rightly honoured the sage, when seated, with water for the feet and the proper offerings, and then addressed him with due courtesy, as Antideva of old did Vasiṣṭha :—

48. C expands the second line and makes the king desire to go to the forest, while his son rules, i.e. it read *yāyāñ jarām*.

50. In *a* I accept T's reading and interpretation and compare *Bṛhaddevatā*, iii. 133, *mantravinmantravittamaḥ*, also *Pañcaviṁśabrāhmaṇa*, xiii. 3, 24, *mantrakṛtāṁ mantrakṛd āsīt*. *Jāt.*, i. 5, is not a parallel, though perhaps influenced by this passage. The first line gives the reason why it was possible to admit him to the women's quarters and C expatiates on this.

51. This use of *saṁjñayā* is common in Buddhist writings, e.g. *Mhv.*, III, 153, 12, *Bodhicaryāvatāra*, vi. 6, and *Majjhima*, III, 104. For the sense cp. *S.*, iii. 17, and *Bodhicaryāvatāra*, v. 21, *pramadājanamadhye 'pi yatir dhīro na khaṇḍyate*.

52. Antideva is usually called Rantideva in Brahmanical works; the confusion is probably due to the expression *Sāṁkṛtir Antidevaḥ* being taken as a single word *Sāṁkṛti-Rantidevaḥ*, similar cases occurring in the Purāṇas (Pargiter, 129). For the comparison see *MBh.*, xii. 8591, and xiii. 6250.

53. "Fortunate am I and honoured this house that Your Holiness should deign to visit me. Be pleased to command what I should do, O benign one: I am your disciple and you should show confidence in me."

54. When the sage was invited in this befitting fashion by the king with all cordiality, his large eyes opened wide in admiration and he spoke these profound and solemn words :—

55. "It indeed accords with your great soul, your hospitality, your generosity, your piety, that you should thus show to me a kindly disposition, so worthy of your nature, family, wisdom and age.

56. And this is the course by which those royal seers, acquiring wealth by the subtile Law, ever continued giving it away according to rule, thus being rich in austerities and poor in worldly goods.

57. But hear the reason for my visit and be rejoiced.

53. In *a* T seems to have read *dhanyam* to agree with *kulam* ; its last word in this *pāda* I read as *des*, not *ṅes*.

54. T takes *a* as one word, but it might be better to divide *sa vismaya°*, comparing *S.*, x. 35.

55. Lévi and Formichi take *c* as applied by Asita to himself, on the ground that *jñāna* and *vayaḥ* could not apply to Śuddhodana. This seems to me very difficult in every way ; *vayaḥ* means 'age', not necessarily 'old age', but equally 'youth', and the implication here is that the king shows Asita the respect due from a younger man to the older one. C also takes it as referring to the king.

56. Formichi takes *te* as=*tava*, which can hardly be right, but points out, correctly probably, that *nṛparṣayaḥ* refers to Śuddhodana's ancestors. For *sūkṣma dharma* see note in my translation on *S.*, ii. 37 ; it is equivalent to 'the highest', 'most recondite'. Schrader takes it to mean 'hidden (=pre-natal) merit', which is indicated by C and may also be intended. T's *yajanto* in *c* may be correct, but *tyaj* is common enough in the sense 'give away' ; *Śiśupālavadha*, xiv. 20, combines both, *yājyayā yajanakarmiṇo 'tyajan dravyajātam apadiśya devatām*. I construe *babhūvuḥ* with *tyajantaḥ* (*SS.*, § 378). For *d* cp. *MBh.*, v. 1613, *anāḍhyā mānuṣe vitte āḍhyā daive tathā kratau*.

57. The voice was addressed to the king, though not heard by him, and was only understood by Asita, when he went into yoga.

In the path of the sun I heard a divine voice saying, "To thee is born a son for Enlightenment."

58. As soon as I heard the voice, I put my mind into trance and understood the matter through the signs. Then I came here to see the lofty banner of the Śākya race uplifted like the banner of Indra."

59. When the king heard him speak thus, his bearing was disordered with delight, and he took the prince, as he lay on his nurse's lap, and showed him to the ascetic.

60. Then the great seer wonderingly beheld the prince, the soles of his feet marked with a wheel, the fingers and toes joined by a web, the circle of hair growing between his eyebrows and the testicles withdrawn like an elephant's.

61. And when he saw him resting on the nurse's lap, like the son of Agni on Devī's lap, the tears flickered on his eyelashes and, sighing, he looked up to heaven.

62. But when the king saw Asita's eyes swimming with tears, he trembled from affection for his son, and sobbing with his throat choked with weeping, he clasped his hands and bowed his body, asking him :—

58. For Indra's banner, see *MBh.* (new Poona edition), i. 57, and Hopkins, *Epic Mythology*, § 69 ; later descriptions in the *Bṛhatsaṁhitā* and *Bhaviṣyottarapurāṇa*.

59. Lokur suggests that the *dhātri* is Māyā, which corresponds to T's reading ; at 61 T has *dhātrī*.

60. It is still disputed whether the *jāla* on the fingers and toes means webbing or meshed lines ; latest discussion, *Acta Or.*, VII, 232, and X, 298, but *AAA.*, 526, 8, read with 529, 23, shows later Buddhist writers to have understood webbing. Nandargikar points out that the last mark mentioned is still considered a sign of great strength in India ; cp. *Mahāvaṁsa*, xxiii. 5, *kosohitavatthaguyho*, of a particularly strong child.

61. Devī may mean Svāhā or Pārvatī or be taken as a plural for the divine mothers who nursed Skanda. Nandargikar remarks on *c* that to have let the tears fall would have been a bad omen. The root *cañc*, hitherto only known, except for Pāṇini, in the later classical literature, has not been recorded compounded with *vi*.

63. "Why are you, who are so steadfast, tearful on seeing him who differs little in form from the gods, whose brilliant birth has been attended by many miracles and whose future lot you say is to be the highest?

64. Will the prince be long-lived, Holy One? Surely he is not born for my sorrow? Shall the two handfuls of water have been obtained by me with such difficulty, only for Death to come and drink them up?

65. Is the treasure of my fame inexhaustible? Is the dominion to last for ever in the hands of my family? Shall I win bliss in the next world, even in the sleep of death having one eye open in the shape of my son?

66. Is this young shoot of my family, just sprung up,

64. The meaning of the second line is that the king wishes to know if his son will survive him to offer the handfuls of water to the dead. *Labdhā*, periphrastic future used in a passive sense, the earliest recorded instance; see *SS.*, § 340, Rem. 2, and *ZDMG*, 64, 316, and Renou, *Grammaire sanscrite*, 493. It occurs sporadically, usually from *labh*, in later literature, twice possibly in Kāḷidāsa (*Meghadūta*, 24, see Mallinātha thereon and Trivandrum S.S., LXIV, 20, and at *Mālavikāgnimitra*, i. 7, according to Kāṭayavema's reading), *Kirātārjunīya*, ii. 17, and iii. 22, *Śiśupālavadha*, ii. 116, *Bhaṭṭikāvya*, xxii. 4, 20, several times in the *Bṛhatkathāślokasaṁgraha* (xx. 109 and note thereon), etc.

65. The last *pāda* is an unsolved crux. The possible readings are as in the text, as in A, or as in Co. (*supte 'pi putre*). C has, 'When I die, shall I with happy mind be born peacefully and happily in the other world, like the two eyes of a man, the one closed and the other open?' This seems to imply *supto* and to take it in the sense of sleep=death; that is, the king will die, but his life on earth will continue by means of his son, and with much reserve I translate accordingly. The straightforward meaning that the king is so fond of his son that he keeps one eye open on him even in sleep is inconsistent with his being in the other world, and *animiṣa* suggests that he is a *deva* in heaven. But the passage undoubtedly hints at the common statement that kings should be awake even when asleep, e.g. *Rām.*, iii. 37, 21, *nayanair yaḥ prasupto 'pi jāgarti nayacakṣuṣā* (cp. *ib.*, v. 34, 19), *R.*, xxii. 51, *Kāmandakīyanītisāra*, vii. 58, and xiii. 29. To take a commonplace and give it a new twist is typical of *kāvya* procedure, though the number of demonstrable instances in Aśvaghoṣa is few.

66. See the Introduction for the combination of singular and plural in *d*.

fated to wither without flowering? Tell me quickly, Lord, I am all uneasy; for you know the love of fathers for their sons."

67. The seer understood how the king was troubled by the thought of misfortune and said: "Let not your mind, O king, be disturbed; what I have said is not open to doubt.

68. My agitation is not over aught untoward for him, but I am distressed for my own disappointment. For my time to depart has come, just when he is born who shall understand the means, so hard to find, of destroying birth.

69. For he will give up the kingdom in his indifference to worldly pleasures, and, through bitter struggles grasping the final truth, he will shine forth as a sun of knowledge in the world to dispel the darkness of delusion.

70. With the mighty boat of knowledge he will bring the world, which is being carried away in affliction, up from the ocean of suffering, which is overspread with the foam of disease and which has old age for its waves and death for its fearsome flood.

71. The world of the living, oppressed with the thirst of desires, will drink the flowing stream of his most excellent Law, which is cooled by concentration of thought and has mystic wisdom for the current of its water, firm discipline for its banks and vows for its Brahminy ducks.

72. For to those who, finding themselves on the desert-tracks of the cycle of existence, are harassed by suffering and obstructed by the objects of sense, he will proclaim the way of salvation, as to travellers who have lost their road.

73. Like a mighty cloud with its rain at the close of the summer heat, he will give relief with the rain of the Law to men burnt up in the world with the fire of the passions, whose fuel is the objects of sense.

67. *Asmi* for *aham* is well established, e.g., *Kirātārjunīya*, iii. 6, and *Bodhicaryāvatāra*, iii. 7.

69. The Peking edition supports W's *rnam* for *rnams* in *c*.

71. The first line covers the eightfold path (*S.*, xvi. 31–33).

74. With the most excellent irresistible key of the good Law he will throw open for the escape of living beings the door whose bolt is the thirst of desire and whose leaves are delusion and the darkness of ignorance.

75. And, as king of the Law, he will reach Enlightenment and release from prison the world which is entangled in its own snares of delusion and which is overwhelmed by suffering and destitute of refuge.

76. Therefore be not grieved for him; in this living world that man is to be deplored who through delusion by reason of the sensual pleasures or through intoxication of mind refuses to hear his, the final, Law.

77. Therefore, though I have obtained the trances, I have not won through to the goal, in that I have fallen short

74. This verse was imitated in the verse quoted from the *Svapnavāsavadatta* by Abhinavagupta; and both have a parallel difficulty in the meaning here of *tāḍa* (which can be read as *tāla*), there of *taḍana*. Primarily it must refer to some part of the door. *Tālaka* properly is the lock of a door, Hindi *tālā*, cp. *Divy.*, 577, and *HC.*, ch. vii, 54; similarly *tāla* at *KA.*, xiv. 3, 65, and defined as *dvārasyodghāṭanayantraka* by *Kalpadrukośa* (Gaekwad's O.S., XLIV), p. 17, 84. But this is impossible here. *Avadānaśataka*, II, 56, has however *tāḍa* undoubtedly in the sense of 'key', and I think it best to accept this meaning. C is no help, and T takes it in the sense of *śabda*, given by the *PW* for *tāḍa* from the lexica; or else it read °*tālena*, 'handclap', or °*nādena*. Probably a secondary sense of °*tālena* is intended. A has a marginal gloss of *vighāṭayiṣyati* in *c*; this would be distinctly better according to the above interpretations and suggests the opening of the two leaves. *Vipāṭayiṣyati* should mean 'break down' and requires *tāḍa* in the sense of 'blow'. Lokur says Peterson suggested 'hammer' for *tāḍa*.

75. Does *svaiḥ* in *a* imply delusion about the self? *Dharmarāja* is also to be understood in the technical sense of ideal ruler.

76. The readings in *b* are uncertain. I take T's *gnas* to stand for *asti*, and the restoration suggested is palæographically sound. The second letter of the hidden character in A might be *va*, which from C would indicate *śocasva*, but T shows *śocyaḥ* definitely; or A might have had originally *śocyas sa*. *Kāmasukha* refers to the pleasures derived through the five senses (see *S.*, iii. 34, note in translation, and ix. 43).

of this merit. For, since I shall not hear his Law, I hold even rebirth in the triple heaven to be a disaster."

78. Hearing this explanation, the king with his queen and friends was quit of his dejection and rejoiced; for he deemed it to be his own good fortune that his son should be such.

79. But his heart busied itself anxiously with the thought that his son would follow the path of the sages. It was most certainly not that he was opposed to the side of the Law, but that he saw the danger arising from failure of issue.

80. Then when the seer, Asita, had made known the truth about his son to the king who was troubled about him, he departed, as he had come, by the path of the wind, while they looked up at him with all reverence.

81. Then the saint, who had attained right knowledge, saw his younger sister's son and straitly charged him in his compassion, as if he were his own dear son, to listen to the words of the Sage and to follow his teaching.

82. The king too, delighted at the birth of a son, threw open all the prisons in his realm and in his affection for his

79. I follow C against A and T in *a*, as *ṣa* and *ya* are easily confused in mediæval Nepali scripts. Cp. *Theragāthā*, 1102, *isippayātamhi pathe vajantaṁ*, of an Arhat. Strictly *ārṣa* applies to what is done by an Arhat, not by a Buddha (*AKV*., i, 10, l. 20).

80. In *c rūpa* is pleonastic to heighten the honorific effect of the preposition *ud* (*Pāṇ*., v. 3, 66). This usage with present participles is not uncommon in Pali, e.g., *Dīgha*, II, 202, and *Udāna*, 61; cp. also *ASPP*., 449.

81. This verse is almost certainly spurious, since C would hardly omit a point of such purely Buddhistic interest. *Miti* is a rare word, meaning 'right knowledge', and T's reading is more probable; in the latter case all *pāda b* should be construed as governed by *kṛtamatim*.

82. *Pāda b*, which I translate according to C, has a second sense, 'loosening the bonds of the objects of sense'. For the translation cp. *KA*., ii. 36, 60, *putrajanmani vā mokṣo bandhanasya vidhīyate*, *R*., iii. 20, trumping this verse, and *Mhv*., III, 175, 13. C's 'according to the śāstras and sūtras' may imply *śrutisadṛśam* in *c*, but cp. *S*., i. 25, *svavaṁśasadṛśīḥ kriyāḥ*; perhaps therefore, 'according to the use current in his family'.

son caused the birth ceremony to be properly performed for him in the manner that befitted his family.

83. And, when the ten days were fulfilled, in the piety of his mind and the excess of his joy, he offered for the supreme welfare of his son sacrifices to the gods together with incantations, oblations and other auspicious rites.

84. Moreover for the prosperity of his son he bestowed of himself cows full of milk, in the prime of their age, with gilded horns and healthy sturdy calves, to the full number of a hundred thousand, on the twice-born.

85. Thereon, self-controlled, he prescribed the performance of ceremonies directed to many ends which delighted his heart, and when a fortunate, auspicious day had been determined, he gladly decided to enter the city.

86. Then the queen, taking the babe, did obeisance to the gods and entered for good fortune a costly ivory litter, bedecked with white *sitapuṣpa* flowers and lit by precious stones.

87. The king then made the queen, attended by aged women and accompanied by her child, enter the city in front of him, and himself also advanced, saluted by hosts of citizens,

84. For *vṛddhi*, see note on 89 below.

85. The European translations omit *viṣaya* in *a* as pleonastic. Lokur and Nandargikar translate 'religious observance', a sense given by Apte but fo which there appears to be no authority. The definition quoted by Lokur (as=*niyama*, *niyāmaka*) implies rather 'limited to'. Joglekar renders 'subject matter', 'details'. The literal meaning is either 'having many kinds of scope', or 'having many kinds of objects' (sacrificial victims ?).

86. *Sitapuṣpa* is the name of various flowering trees ; all the translators, however, follow Co. in taking the compound to mean 'filled with all kinds of white flowers'. Similarly *śivāya* has always been construed with *praṇipatya* ; not only does its place in the sentence make my translation necessary, but a *śivikā* was recognized as a lucky object. Thus it was included among the lucky things sent by Aśoka to Devānaṁpiya of Ceylon for his coronation, *Dīpavaṁsa*, xi. 32, and *Mahāvaṁsa*, xi. 31. The collocation shows that Aśvaghoṣa wrote *śivikāṁ*, not *śibikāṁ*.

87. I follow C and T in taking *sthavirajanam* as feminine.

like Indra, when on entering heaven he was saluted by the immortals.

88. The Śākya king thereon proceeded into his palace in good heart, like Bhava on the birth of his six-faced son, and, with countenance beaming with joy, directed every arrangement to be made which would lead to many kinds of prosperity and renown.

89. Thus the town named after Kapila rejoiced with its surrounding territory at the prosperous birth of the prince, just as the town of the Wealth-giver, which was thronged with Apsarases, rejoiced at the birth of Nalakūbara.

88. For the second line I accept C's rendering.

89. There is a play on words in °*vṛddhyā*, which means technically 'the impurity caused by childbirth', *jananāśauca*. Ceremonial impurity is not ordinarily a cause of pleasure, but in this case it was so.

CANTO II

Life in the Palace.

1. Day by day from the birth of his son, the masterer of self, who had come to the end of birth and old age, the king waxed mightier in riches, elephants, horses and allies, as a river waxes with the inflow of waters.

2. For then he obtained many treasures of wealth and jewels of every kind and of gold, wrought and unwrought, so as to overload even that chariot of the mind, desire.

3. And rut-maddened elephants from the Himalayas, such as even lords of elephants like Padma could not have brought to his stables in this world, served him, and that too without any effort on his part.

1. I can find no parallel to Co.'s °*antakasya* in *a*, and so prefer T's reading, for which cp., e.g., *Suttanipāta*, 401, *Buddhena dukkhantagunā*. Verses 2–4 and 6 develop *c* in detail. The reference in *d* is to a river growing with the accession of tributaries, and T may be right in taking *sindhu* to mean the Indus here.

2. *Vinaya*, III, 239, gives the definition of wrought and unwrought gold; cp. also *Majjhima*, II, 71, and *MBh.*, i. 4438 and 8012, and xiii. 2794 and 3261.

3. The meaning of *maṇḍala* is uncertain; but we must exclude 'kheddah', for which the Sanskrit is *vārī* and which does not seem to have been known in Northern India till a late period (not in Nepal till 1913). The choice lies between 'elephant stables', 'picketing ground', as at v. 23 below, and the common technical use for the turning movements which elephants and horses were, and still are, taught to execute (e.g., Meyer's translation of *KA.*, 732, Zusatz on 214). For the latter note *PW's* reference to *MBh.*, vi. 1765, for *abhinī* of training elephants. Another difficulty lies in *iha*, omitted in the European translations; possibly 'ordinarily' (Lokur), or else by contrast with Padma, the elephant of the southern quarter (*Rām.*, i. 42, 16, and *MBh.*, vi. 2866), who does not tame earthly elephants. T may have read *maṇḍale* (also proposed by Böhtlingk) and took *iha*=*asmin*, i.e. 'in his domain', corresponding to *asya* of the next two verses.

4. And his city shook with the tread of horses, adorned with the various marks and decked with trappings of fresh gold, or laden with ornaments and having flowing manes, which he acquired either by his military power, from his allies, or by purchase.

5. And so too there were in his kingdom many excellent cows, contented and well-nourished, unspotted, giving pure and abundant milk, and accompanied by well-grown calves.

6. His enemies became neutrals, neutrality turned into alliance, allies were united to him with peculiar firmness. He had only two parties; but the third, enemies, did not exist.

7. So too for him heaven rained in due time and place, with gentle winds and rumbling clouds, and with the sky adorned with rings of lightning, but without the evils of showers of thunderbolts or falls of meteoric stones.

8. At that time fruitful grain grew according to season, even without the labour of tilling; and the very herbs for him became still more abounding in juice and substance.

9. Though that hour brings as much danger to the body as the clash of armies, yet women were delivered in due time safely, easily and without disease.

10. Except for those who had taken vows of mendicancy, no one begged from others, however wretched his means might

4. T does not give the preposition for °*bhūsitaiḥ*, but it can hardly be anything else than *vi*.

5. *Arajaska* could mean 'docile'; but C translates 'of unmixed colour', i.e. white, not spotted so as to appear grey. White is considered the best colour for a cow (Grierson, *Bihar Peasant Life*, § 1113).

7. Co. divides the compound in *a* so as to apply *śabda* to the winds also. As between Co. and T in *b*, *aṅga* does not fit in well with *kuṇḍala*.

8. The three *evas* in Co.'s second line are hardly possible. T substitutes *asya* for the second one apparently, but *tā eva* is none too easy; for it should mean 'the same', whereas there is a contrast between corn and herbs.

9. The difference between Co. and T is so great in *d*, that I think A must have been partly illegible, causing Amṛtānanda to insert a guess of his own.

10. Many conjectures, none satisfactory, have been made for the amendment of *a* from Co.'s text. The restoration of T is certain, and in palæography

be; and at that time no man of position, poverty-stricken though he were, turned his face away when solicited.

11. At that time in his realm, as in that of king Yayāti the son of Nahuṣa, no one was disrespectful to his elders, or lacking in generosity, or irreligious, or deceitful, or given to hurt.

12. And by constructing there gardens, temples, hermitages, wells, water-halls, lotus-ponds and groves, they showed their devotion to *dharma*, as if they had seen Paradise before their eyes.

13. And in the joy of deliverance from famine, peril and disease, the people were as happy as in Paradise. Husband did not transgress against wife, nor wife against husband.

14. None pursued love for sensual pleasure; none withheld wealth from others to gratify his own desires; none practised religion for the sake of riches; none did hurt on the plea of religion.

15. Theft and the like and enmity disappeared. His

and sense is sound. C has, 'except for those who took on themselves the four holy seeds (?, or kinds of plants ?)'; the verb *shou*, 'receive', 'take on oneself', is several times used by it in compounds to translate *vrata*, and, allowing for the corruption or unrecorded sense of the last word, we may justifiably conclude that it had the same text. *Prārthayanti* is unusual but not without precedent; for a certain use of the active instead of the middle, besides those given in the *PW*, see *Pratijñāyaugandharāyaṇa*, iv. 8. For the second line cp. *Abhisamayālaṁkāra* (Bibl. Buddh., XXIII), i. 58, *kṛśo 'pi nārthināṁ kṣeptā*.

12. T cannot be reconstructed for *b* and may be corrupt. I understand the verse somewhat differently to the European translators, and would not take *kriyāḥ* to mean 'ceremonies', the point being that, as people follow *dharma* to gain Paradise (*S.*, ii. 37, and Aśoka Pillar Edicts *passim*), such devotion as theirs could only arise, one would think, from an actual vision of Paradise.

13. Lokur and Sovani object to the dual verb in the second line as not in accord with the use of *vā*; the same objection applies to the text of i. 41*ab*, where however the defect can easily be removed by amendment.

14. For *b* cp. *S.*, i. 52*c*, and note thereon in text.

15. This verse, which is not in C, is probably spurious. It is clearly related to *Rām.*, ii. 119, 10, which shows Anaraṇya (cp. *MBh.*, xiii. 5661,

kingdom was at ease and independent, free from foreign rule, peaceful and prosperous, like the kingdom of Anaraṇya of old.

16. For then at the prince's birth in the realm of that king, as in that of Manu, son of the Sun, joy prevailed, evil perished, *dharma* blazed forth, sin was quenched.

17. Since the prosperity of the royal race and the accomplishment of all objects had been thus brought to pass, the king named his son accordingly, saying "He is Sarvārthasiddha".

18. But when queen Māyā saw the vast power of her son, like that of a divine seer, she was unable to bear the joy it caused her ; then she went to Heaven to dwell there.

19. Then the queen's sister, who equalled her in majesty and did not fall below her in affection and tenderness, brought up the prince, who was like a scion of the gods, as if he were her own son.

20. Then the prince gradually grew up in all due perfection, like the young sun on the Eastern mountain, or the flame fanned by the wind, or the lord of the stars in the bright fortnight.

21, 22. Then they brought to him from the houses of his friends priceless unguents of sandalwood and strings of jewels, filled with magic herbs, and little golden carts to which deer were harnessed, and ornaments suited to his age and little elephants, deer and horses of gold, and chariots yoked with little oxen, and dolls gay with gold and silver.

7684, and *Maitrī Up.*, i. 4) to be the king referred to. I should prefer to read *rāṣṭram* as the last word of *d*, with T's *rājñaḥ* as an alternative though inferior.

16. Co. was probably right in conjecturing *kaluṣaṁ* in *d*.

17. Co.'s text in *a* is so weak and differs so much from T that evidently A was partly illegible here. I accordingly accept T's reading, which is implied by FP and explains how A was misread ; C is no help.

18. W thinks T may have read *jātapraharṣā* in *c* ; I doubt this.

20. All three similes exemplify the ordered growth of brightness.

21. For the magic powers of certain herbs, see Formichi's note on this verse and *S.*, v. 31, with note thereon in my translation.

22. The words in this verse must be in the same case as in 21, so I have put them all into the accusative. But *ācakrire* might be passive and then all

23. Though but a child and attended in this fashion by the various kinds of sensory pleasure suitable to his age, yet in gravity, purity, thoughtfulness and dignity he was unlike a child.

24. He passed through infancy and in course of time duly underwent the ceremony of initiation. And it took him but a few days to learn the sciences suitable to his race, the mastery of which ordinarily requires many years.

25. But, as the king of the Śākyas had heard from the great seer, Asita, that the prince's future goal would be the supreme beatitude, he feared lest he should go to the forests and therefore he turned him to sensual pleasures.

26. Then from a family possessed of long-standing good conduct he summoned for him the goddess of Fortune in the

should go into the nominative. In *d* I think *putrīḥ*, though not authenticated in this sense, is certain for T's 'little figures of men' and better than Co.'s dubious *gantrīḥ*; but the restoration of *c* is somewhat speculative. I take *phyuṅ-ṅus* as=*chuṅ-ṅus* (both being pronounced alike), comparing *phyed-du* for *ched-du* in 18*d*; and *saṁprayukta* is indicated by *T* instead of *prayukta*. For 'little oxen' the alternative to *goputraka* is *gorūpaka* (so Pali *assa*°, *hatthirūpaka*), or even possibly *govarṇaka* (cp. *vatsavarṇa*, *S.*, xviii. 11, and note in translation). Co.'s text is too much at variance with T to be authentic and W's *byuṅ-dus*, though supported by the Peking edition, is surely a wrong reading.

23. In *d* T reads *dpal* (*śrī*) twice; W conjectures *dpaḥ* for the first, i.e. *śauryeṇa* for *śaucena*.

24. Comparison of Co.'s MSS. with T shows that A here had the first three syllables of *b* correctly and the next two partially, the rest of the *pāda* being obliterated. T's *ḥdu-byed* properly=*saṁskāra*, of which *pratipatti* is a synonym. Cp. *Jāt.*, 225, 23, *kālakramād avāptasaṁskārakarmā*, and for the Buddha's initiation *S.*, ii. 63. In *d* T omits *kula* and is probably corrupt (read *raṅ rigs rjes-su* for *raṅ daṅ rjes-su* ?).

25. The last *pāda* was evidently illegible in A except for the last two syllables, but the restoration of T is not quite certain, apparently *vanaṁ* for *vanāni*. C is no help and I should prefer *vanaṁ na yāyād iti*.

26. The wording of *d* suggests invocations to Śrī (*Sir'avhāyana*, *Dīgha*, I, 11), of which Buddhists did not approve. For *abhidhāna*, see note on iii. 3.

shape of a maiden, Yaśodharā by name, of widespread renown, virtuous and endowed with beauty, modesty and gentle bearing.

27. The prince, radiant with wondrous beauty like Sanatkumāra, took his delight with the Śākya king's daughter-in-law, as the Thousand-eyed with Śacī.

28. The monarch, reflecting that the prince must see nothing untoward that might agitate his mind, assigned him a dwelling in the upper storeys of the palace and did not allow him access to the ground.

29. Then in the pavilions, white as the clouds of autumn, with apartments suited to each season and resembling heavenly mansions come down to earth, he passed the time with the noble music of singing-women.

30. For the palace was glorious as Kailāsa, with tambourines whose frames were bound with gold and which sounded softly beneath the strokes of women's fingers, and with dances that rivalled those of the beautiful Apsarases.

27. The restoration of *a* is certain, cp. *Jāt.*, xix. 19, *vidyotamānaṁ vapuṣā śriyā ca*, and *Rām.*, vi. 35, 1; *Mhv.*, II, 197, 5, has *Sanatkumārapratimo kumāro dyutimān ayam*.

28. The *harmya* is properly the upper part of the palace. For T's *vyādiśati sma* cp. iii. 51.

29. In *b* for *rañjiteṣu* T has *spyod-pa*, which translates *car* and *vṛt*. This is evidently the right sense, as is shown by *bhūmau*. For the *vimānas* are the heavenly mansions in which the *devas* live, and are always *ākāśastha* (e.g. *Mahāvaṁsa*, xxvii. 13), not on earth. So at *B.*, xviii. 87, the *vihāra* built by Anāthapiṇḍada is compared to 'the palace of the Lord of Wealth descended (to earth)', and similar comparisons occur elsewhere, e.g. *MBh.*, v. 5180, *vimānānīva niviṣṭāni mahītale*, *Kād.*, 50, *ambaratalāvatīrṇābhir divyavimānapaṅktibhir ivālaṁkṛtā*, and *Kathāsaritsāgara*, xxxiv. 143. It is very doubtful what the Sanskrit word should be; if the text is correct, we can only get the sense by referring to the Naighaṇṭuka's gloss of *raj* by *gatikarman* cited in the *PW*, and this is far from satisfactory. In *c* T translates *āśraya* by *gzhi*, which is used for *ālaya*, and my translation is corroborated by C ('suited in warmth and cold to the four seasons; according to the time of year they chose a good dwelling') and by many parallels.

31. There the women delighted him with their soft voices, charming blandishments, playful intoxications, sweet laughter, curvings of eyebrows and sidelong glances.

32. Then, a captive to the women, who were skilled in the accessories of love and indefatigable in sexual pleasure, he did not descend from the palace to the ground, just as one who has won Paradise by his merit does not descend to earth from the heavenly mansion.

33. But the king, for the sake of his son's prosperity and spurred on by the goal predicted for him, abode in holy peace, desisted from sin, practised self-restraint and rewarded the good.

34. He did not, like one wanting in self-control, indulge in the pleasures of the senses, he cherished no improper passion for women, with firmness he overcame the rebellious horses of the senses, and conquered his kinsmen and subjects by his virtues.

31. For the second part of *a* T is two syllables short and has only *rnam ḥgyur-rnams-kyis kyaṅ* (=*vikārais ca*). If we read *rnam-par rnam* etc., the lacuna would be explained and the reading would be *vividhaiś ca bhāvair*. In *d bhrūvañcitair* has intrigued some scholars; but it is quite correct and the phrase recurs *HC*., ch. vii, 57, 1, where Cowell and Thomas translate 'raised eyebrows'. T translates by *bskyod-pa*, 'agitate', 'move', and we have to do with the root *vac*, *vañc*, which originally meant 'move crookedly', 'in curves', then 'move', used in the *RV* of horses galloping; cp. *Cariyāpiṭaka*, iii. 9, 10, *pādā avañcanā*, *Bhaṭṭikāvya*, xiv. 74, and other references in *PW*.

32. *Karkaśa* properly 'firm', 'hard', often of a woman's body or breasts, and then 'experienced', 'indefatigable', as in *raṇakarkaśa*, *Ram*., v. 44, 5 (=*raṇakarmaviśārada*, *ib*., 44, 8). Cp. *BhNŚ*., xxiii. 59, *ratikalahasaṁprahāreṣu karkaśaḥ*, and the definition of *ratikārkaśya* at *Dhūrtaviṭasaṁvāda* (ed. Caturbhāṇī), 21, 16. For *puṇyakarman* cp. *S*., x. 52, and vi. 3.

34. T shows Co.'s reading in the much discussed *pāda b* to be correct, and takes *viṣamam* to mean 'improperly' (*ma-ruṅs*). *Jananī* I understand as a synonym for *mātṛgrāma*, the regular Buddhist designation for the female sex; cp. *MBh*., xii. 11141. The contrast between *jigāya* and *vijigye* is presumably a hint at the rule embodied in *Pāṇ*., i. 3, 19.

35. He did not learn science to cause suffering to others, but studied only the knowledge that was beneficent; for he wished well to all people as much as to his own subjects.

36. And for the long life of his son he worshipped the shining constellation, whose regent is Bṛhaspati, and he offered oblations in a huge fire and presented the twice-born with gold and cattle.

37. He bathed to purify his body with the waters of the sacred bathing-places and his mind with the waters of the virtues, and at the same time he drank *soma* as enjoined by the Vedas and observed in his heart the self-produced bliss of religious tranquillity.

38. He spoke what was pleasant and not unprofitable; he stated what was true and not disagreeable; for self-respect made him unable to say even to himself a pleasant falsehood or a harsh truth.

39. He gave no opening to feelings of partiality or the reverse, according as he liked or disliked his petitioners, and

35. Presumably *vidyā* in *a* implies magic practices and the other forms of knowledge deprecated by Buddhists.

36. Syllables 5 to 7 of *a* are hard to read in A but corroborated by T. The star meant is Puṣya, whose divinity is Bṛhaspati, cp. *Divy.*, 639, *Puṣya-nakṣatraṁ . . . Bṛhaspatidaivatam*, and *Bṛhatsaṁhitā*, xcviii. For the importance of Puṣya in the Buddha legend see the text, associated with the Mahāsaṅghikas, which is translated by Przyluski, *Concile de Rājagṛha*, 88. The word Āṅgirasa, sometimes applied to the Buddha, also hints at the connexion between him and Puṣya. T takes *kṛśana* to mean 'gold', a meaning only known from the Naighaṇṭuka; in the *RV* it is usually translated 'pearl'.

37. I take *papau* in *d* from *pā*, 'drink', and from *pā*, 'guard'; cp. *S.* i. 59.

39. For *doṣa*=*dveṣa* in *b* cp. v. 18 below and note on *S.*, xvi. 22 in text; for the idea *MBh.*, xii. 2456, and *Jāt.*, xxiii. 73. The sense of *c* and *d*, unlike the text, is certain. In *c* I follow T, the confusion between *śuddha* and *labdha* appearing also in Sthiramati's commentary on the *Madhyāntavibhāga* (Calcutta O.S.), note 655; for *śuddha* as applied to *vyavahāra*, see *MBh.*, xii. 3195. The conjecture in *d* is supported by C, which translates *c* twice to bring out the double meaning; it runs, 'He determined to live in solitary retirement and

observed purity of justice as being holy; for he did not esteem sacrifice to be so in the same degree.

40. He ever quenched straightway with the water of gifts the thirst of expectant suppliants, and with the battle-axe of good conduct, instead of by fighting, he broke down the swollen pride of his foes.

41. He disciplined the one; he protected the seven; seven too he abandoned and he observed five; he won the set of three; he understood the set of three; he knew the set of two and gave up the set of two.

42. He did not have the guilty executed, although he adjudged them worthy of death, nor did he even regard them with anger. And he inflicted mild punishments on them, since their release too was looked on as bad policy.

43. He carried out the most difficult vows of the ancient seers; he gave up long-cherished feuds, and he obtained renown, made fragrant by virtue; he swept away the dust of defiling passions.

decided litigation with fairness. He deemed better fortune to lie in deciding cases than in vast numbers of sacrifices.'

40. As Co. observes, the poet hints at the water poured out in giving gifts. For the second line cp. *S.*, ii. 33, and 36. The reference is firstly to the vices, peculiar to kings and subdued by his good conduct, and secondly to his external foes who submit without fighting, just as a cakravartin conquers by *dharma*, not by military might.

41. This riddle has been variously explained; I understand it as follows. One is his self. The sevens are the contituents of a kingdom and the seven vices of kings (cp. xi. 31, 32 below). Five refers to the five *upāyas* (*S.*, xv. 61, and note thereon in my translation, and also *MBh.*, iii. 11306). The threes are *dharma*, *artha* and *kāma*, and either the three *śaktis* (note *prabhāva*, *S.*, i. 45), or the three parties of verse 6 above, or the three conditions, *sthāna*, *vṛddhi* and *kṣaya*. The twos seem to be good and bad policy (*naya* and *anaya* or *apanaya*), and *kāma* and *krodha* (*MBh.*, v. 1160, and xii. 2720; for a Pali reference, see *Jātaka*, V, 112, 24-5, where the avoidance of *kodha* and *hāsa* (=*harṣa*) constitutes the *khattiya vata*).

43. For *c* cp. *S.*, i. 59. In *d* there is a play on words, *rajoharaṇa* meaning 'duster' (or 'broom'?).

44. He did not desire to exact revenue beyond the amount due, he had no wish to covet the goods of others. And he did not desire to expose the wickedness of his adversaries, nor did he wish to bear wrath in his heart.

45. Since the monarch behaved thus, his servants and the citizens followed the same course, just as, when the mind of a man in mystic trance has become wholly calm and is compact of tranquillity, his senses become so likewise.

46. Then in the course of time the fair-bosomed Yaśodharā, bearing her own fame, bore to the son of Śuddhodana a son, Rāhula by name, with the face of Rāhu's adversary.

47. Then the ruler of the earth, in possession of the son he had longed for and fully assured of the prosperity of his race, rejoiced at the birth of a grandson as much as he had rejoiced at the birth of a son.

48. Overjoyed at the thought that his son would feel paternal affection, just as he himself felt it, he attended to the various ceremonies at the proper season, as if in his love for his son he were on the point of mounting to Paradise.

44. *Bali* means land revenue ; the king takes his one-sixth without adding illegal cesses. For *apravṛtta* in the sense of 'illegal', 'not customary', see *KA.*, ii. 26, 3, and *MBh.*, v. 7534. The verb in *d* is uncertain, but *avivākṣīt* from *vah* corresponds fairly with T and is the soundest palæographically. Is it merely a coincidence that *Mahābhāṣya*, III, 279, 10, gives *acikīrṣīt* and *ajihīrṣīt* next to each other as examples of this aorist ?

45. Cp. *KA.*, viii. 1, 16, *svayaṁ yacchīlas tacchīlāḥ prakṛtayo bhavanti.*

46. As Leumann points out, Aśvaghoṣa derives Rāhula from Rāhu and *lā*, 'take' (='kill'), so that Rāhula has not merely a face like the moon, but his face is that of Rāhu's foe. When Yaśodharā carries her own fame, the reference is presumably to her carrying the Buddha's son in her womb. C has for this word, 'when Yaśodharā grew up gradually in age' ; did it read *svavayodharāyām* ?

47. *Paramapratīta* could also mean 'highly delighted'.

48. The precise point of the comparison in *d* escapes me ; Formichi holds that he wanted to go to Paradise, now that he was sure of funeral offerings, and translates *putrapriyaḥ*, 'beloved of his sons'.

49. Abiding in the path of the great kings of the golden age, he practised austerities without even doffing the white garments of ordinary life and worshipped with sacrifices that brought no injury to living creatures.

50. Then by his good merit he shone forth gloriously with the splendour of sovereignty and of asceticism alike and was illumined by his family, conduct and wisdom, wishing to diffuse brightness like the thousand-rayed sun.

51. And he, whose sovereignty was established, honoured and intoned the holy chants of Svayaṁbhū and performed works of great difficulty, like Ka in the primeval age when he wished to produce creatures.

52. He laid aside weapons, he pondered on the *Śāstra*, he pursued holy calm, he undertook the law of restraint; like one who is self-controlled, he was not a slave to any object of sense; he looked like a father on all his domains.

53. For he maintained the kingdom for the sake of his son, his son for his family and his family for his renown, his fame for heaven, heaven for the sake of his self; he only desired the continuance of his self for the sake of *dharma*.

54. Thus he performed the manifold *dharma*, which is

49. For *prāthamakalpika* cp. *AK.*, II, 172.

50. I question if this, the usual rendering of *d*, brings out the force of the simile; it can hardly be so jejune. Perhaps *teja utsisṛkṣuḥ*, as applied to the king, 'about to abandon sovereignty', or 'martial behaviour' (foreshadowing *tatyāja śastram* in 52); or else can *c* be construed to apply to the sun?

51. The first line is not clear; *ārcika*, properly part of the *Sāmaveda*. *Svāyaṁbhuva* is difficult; perhaps 'revealed by Svayaṁbhū' (so T), or else read *svayaṁbhuvam*. There seems to be a veiled reference to the Buddha, who is called Svayaṁbhū at *AK.*, II, 56, and repeatedly in the *LV* and Mahāyāna works. The second line means that he performed austerities, the Brāhmaṇas often saying of Prajāpati, when about to create, that *tapo 'tapta*. Aśvaghoṣa applies *duṣkara* to *tapas* below, xii. 94, and at *S.*, iii. 4.

52. As Formichi observes, *vaśī* in *c* could mean 'one who bears rule', suggesting the absurdity, 'like a king he possessed no kingdom'. Similarly in *d*, taking *viṣayān* as 'objects of the senses'.

54. For *nipāta*, a Vedic word, cp. *S.*, xviii. 31.

observed by the religious and is established through revelation, ever hoping that, now that the prince had seen the face of his son, he would not go to the forest.

55. Kings who in this world desire to preserve their personal sovereignty guard their sons, but this *dharma*-loving lord of men by letting his son loose among the objects of sense kept him from *dharma*.

56. But all the Bodhisattvas, those beings of incomparable natures, first tasted the flavour of worldly pleasures and then, when a son was born to them, left for the forest. Hence, though the motive cause was fully developed in him by the accumulation of past acts, he enjoyed sensual pleasure till he reached Illumination.

55. In *d* I do not follow Co.'s reading, because the collocation of perfect and imperfect is awkward; subscript *va* and *u* are easily confused in A. C and the modern translators take the first line to mean that kings who desire to keep the sovereignty in their families guard their sons from evil ways. But *KA.*, i. 17, and 18, suggests a more sinister interpretation. The most dangerous enemy of a king is his son; if he wishes to keep the rule in his own hands (*ātmasaṁsthāṁ*, cp. *KA.*, viii. 2, 5), he holds him under guard and does not let him go free in his domains (*viṣayeṣv amuñcan*).

56. *Anupamasattva* implies that the Bodhisattvas were not to be criticized for tasting sensual joys; cp. the discussion and verses quoted *AAA.*, 540 (*acintyā hi jinātmajāḥ*). *Hetu* in *c* refers to the three *kuśalamūlāni*; cp. xii. 68 below, and *S.*, v. 16, and remarks on the subject in the Introduction.

CANTO III

The Prince's Perturbation.

1. Then upon a time he listened to songs celebrating the forests, with their soft grass, with their trees resounding with koïls' calls, and with their adornment of lotusponds.

2. Then hearing of the entrancing character of the city groves, beloved of the womenfolk, he set his heart on an expedition outside, like an elephant confined inside a house.

3. Then the king learnt of the state of mind of that heart's desire, styled his son, and directed a pleasure excursion to be prepared worthy of his love and majesty and of his son's youth.

4. And, reflecting that the prince's tender mind might be perturbed thereby, he forbade the appearance of afflicted common folk on the royal road.

5. Then with the greatest gentleness they cleared away

1. C has 'singing girls told the prince (sc. of the forests) with beating their instruments and singing to the sound of lutes' which supports T's reading adopted in the text and also my interpretation of *nibaddhāni*. For the tradition, see *RL*, 107. C is mostly very free throughout this canto, especially in the description of the prince's progress.

3. The verse recurs in a corrupt form, *Divy.*, 408. Co., followed by all the translators except W, Sovani and Nandargikar, takes *putrābhidhānasya* as=*putreṇābhihitasya*, which, though possible, is somewhat difficult and requires a poorer meaning for *bhāvam* ; cp. ii. 26, and *S.*, ix. 34, x. 3.

4. *Saṁvega* as a religious term denotes the first step towards conversion, when perturbation of mind is produced by something and leads to consideration of the inherent rottenness of the world and so to the adoption of the religious life. Thus a phrase is put into the king's mouth, that means more than he intends.

5. For the usual rough way of clearing the road for royal personages, see the opening scene of the *Svapnavāsavadatta*. There is a reminiscence of this verse in the passage of the *Divy.* referred to under verse 3 above.

on all sides those whose limbs were maimed or senses defective, the aged, sick and the like, and the wretched, and made the royal highway supremely magnificent.

6. Then, when the road had been made beautiful, the prince, after receiving permission, descended at the proper time in full splendour with well-trained attendants from the top of the palace, and approached the king.

7. Thereon the ruler of men, with tears in his eyes, gazed long at his son and kissed him on the head; and with his voice he bade him set forth, but out of affection he did not let him go in his mind.

8. Then the prince mounted a golden chariot, to which were harnessed four well-broken horses with golden gear, and with a driver who was manly, skilful and reliable.

9. Then, like the moon with the constellations mounting to the sky, he proceeded with a suitable retinue towards the road which was bestrewn with heaps of brilliant flowers and made gay with hanging wreaths and fluttering banners.

10. And very slowly he entered the royal highway, which was carpeted with the halves of blue lotuses in the shape of

8. For the description of the charioteer, cp. *Jāt.*, 226, 12.

9. In *a* the Sanskrit of T's *ḥbras-spos* is uncertain; the natural meaning is 'perfumed rice'. The Peking edition's *ḥbras-sbos* suggests *ḥbras-so-ba* = *lāja*, but the metre does not allow the extra syllable in T. Possibly *ḥbras-spos* should have this sense, for there are countless passages in both epics, the *Jātakas*, *Kathāsaritsāgara* and elsewhere showing the use of flowers and *lāja* at triumphal entries. C however only refers to flowers and I have therefore retained the colourless °*jālaṁ* in the text.

10. A's *kīryamāṇaḥ* in *b* is difficult and ought to be *avakīryamāṇaḥ*, as conjectured by Böhtlingk; T does not show the case-ending, though its *bkram-pa* implies 'filled with', which could only apply to the road, and not 'beshowered with', the meaning required if the prince is meant. C is no help. For my conjecture cp. verse 25 below, *kīrṇaṁ . . . rājapathaṁ . . . pauraiḥ*, and xiii. 32. An exact parallel is *Kathāsaritsāgara*, xliv, 73, 74; but A's text can be supported by *ib.*, xxxiv. 126, and *Rām.*, vi. 44, 31 (*avakṝ* in both cases), and *Rām.*, vi. 39, 2 (*kṝ*). A's reading makes *abhivīkṣyamāṇaḥ* in *d* poor, as the idea is already fully expressed by its first line, so that one would have to

eyes open to their widest in excitement, as all around the citizens gazed at him.

11. Some praised him for his gracious bearing, others worshipped him for his glorious appearance, but for his benignity others wished him sovereignty and length of days.

12. From the great houses humpbacks and swarms of dwarfs and Kirātas poured forth, and from the meaner houses women; and all bowed down as to the flag in the procession of the god.

13. Hearing the news from their servants, "the prince, they say, is going out", the women obtained leave from their elders and went out on to the balconies in their desire to see him.

14. They gathered together in uncontrollable excitement, obstructed by the slipping of their girdle-strings, as they put their ornaments on at the report, and with their eyes still dazed by sudden awakening from sleep.

15. They frightened the flocks of birds on the houses with the jingling of zones, the tinkling of anklets and the clatter

accept T's variant there. Note the comparative *sphītatara* to show a high degree. *Ardha* is unusual in these comparisons; the stock word is *dala* (e.g., *S.*, vi. 26). Compare *R.*, xi. 5, *pauradṛṣṭikṛtamārgatoraṇau*, where by *toraṇas* are meant strings of lotuses hung along the sides of the road.

12. Humpbacks, Kirātas and dwarfs are regularly mentioned in Buddhist and Jain works and in Sanskrit literature, at least from *KA.* onwards, as inhabiting the harems. The reference in *d* is to Indra's banner; *S.*, iv. 46, shows the sense to be that the people bowed down to the Buddha as to the flag, not that their bowing was like the flag's.

13. The frequent representations of such scenes in contemporary sculpture shows that 'balconies' best renders the idea of *harmyatalāni.* The *mānya jana* are more likely to be the older women of the family than the male head of the household.

14. *Vinyasta* in *c* can only mean 'put in order', 'arranged', not 'put on awry', as has been suggested. T supports A's reading, and I do not think we should amend (e.g., Speyer's *vṛthātta°*, 'taken up at random').

15. For *a* cp. *S.*, vi. 6 and 7, and for *c ib.*, 8, and *Rām.*, ii. 101, 42. The reading and sense of *d* are uncertain. Either as above (so Co. and Formichi),

of their steps on the stairs, and reproached each other for jostling.

16. But some of these magnificent women, though longing made them try to rush, were delayed in their movements by the weight of their chariot-like hips and full breasts.

17. But another, though well able to move with speed, checked her steps and went slowly, modestly shrinking as she covered up the ornaments worn in intimacy.

18. Unquiet reigned in the windows then, as the women were crowded together in the mutual press, with their earrings ever agitated by collisions and their ornaments jingling.

19. But the lotus-faces of the women, emerging from the windows and mutually setting their earrings in perpetual commotion, seemed like lotuses stuck on to the pavilions.

20. Then with its palaces full to bursting with young women, who threw the lattices open in their excitement, the

though *samākṣip* in this sense is very rare, or 'colliding with each other in their haste' (so Schmidt and others, i.e. °*vegāc* or °*vegaiś* ?). For the latter idea cp. *R.*, xvi. 56, and *SP.*, 74, 10.

16. The more usual comparison of the hips is to a chariot-wheel, already referred to apparently at *RV.*, x. 10, 7. But cp. *Vikramorvaśīya*, i. 11, *rathopamaśroṇyāḥ*. The Indian editors suggest taking *ratha* in the sense of *avayava* known to the lexica, which is not so good. The comparison presumably is of roundness, the reference being to the two sides of a chariot with rounded tops, as shown in contemporary monuments. *PW* has no occurrence of *sotsuka* as early as this.

17. T apparently divided *hriyā pragalbhā,* but is not clear; cp. *lajjāpragalbham, Jāt.*, 116, 16. *Rahaḥ* here=*surata,* as in *R.*, viii. 57; cp. *rahaḥsaṁyoga* at *Bṛhaddevatā*, iv. 57. Contemporary statuary, e.g. at Sanchi, shows naked women with a girdle round the hips, which left the private parts visible; as proved by numerous references in literature, it was not taken off even *rahaḥ*. Note also iv. 33.

19. The verse recalls the fragment of a Buddhist *toraṇa,* illustrated Vogel, *La Sculpture de Mathurā*, pl. VIII. The suggestion is that the windows are ponds and the earrings birds among the lotuses.

20. In *b* Kern's amendment should probably be accepted. The context shows that *vātāyana* and *vātayāna* are not the same. The latter is unknown except for *Mhv.*, III, 122, 5, where the MSS. also read *vātapāna*; this last in

city appeared as magnificent on all sides as Paradise with its heavenly mansions full of Apsarases.

21. From the narrowness of the windows the faces of these glorious women, with their earrings resting on each other's cheeks, seemed like bunches of lotus-flowers tied to the windows.

22. The women, looking down at the prince in the street, seemed as if wishing to descend to earth, while the men, gazing up at him with upraised faces, seemed as if wishing to rise to heaven.

23. Beholding the king's son in the full glory of his beauty and majesty, the women murmured low, "Blessed is his wife", with pure minds and from no baser motive;

24. For they held him in reverent awe, reflecting that he with the long stout arms, in form like the visible presence of the god whose symbols are flowers, would, it was said, resign his royal pomp and follow the religious law.

25. Thus the first time that the prince saw the royal

Pali=Sk. *vātāyana* in sense and its latticework shutter (Coomaraswamy, *Eastern Art,* III, 196) is mentioned. I take it that Aśvaghoṣa understands by *vātāyana* a kind of oriel window projecting from the wall in which to take the air, and by *vātayāna* or *vātapāna* some kind of shutter, possibly lattice-work, which acted as protection against too strong a wind. The use of *karāla* here is an extension from compounds like *daṁṣṭrākarāla*, and, though not fully recognized in the dictionaries, is to be found thus or in the form *karālita* in the works of Bāṇa, Daṇḍin, Mayūra, Budhasvāmin, Māgha, etc.; in view of Pali having the word in the form *kaḷāra,* it seems that the earliest use in this sense is in the Hathigumpha inscription of Khāravela in the expression *sirikaḷārasarīravatā* (*Ep. Ind.*, XX, line 2 of inscription, which Konow, *Acta Or.*, I, 39, takes otherwise). See also Charpentier, *Monde Oriental,* xxvi-xxvii, pp. 135-136.

21. This verse with its repetition of previous ideas and words can hardly be authentic.

23. The last *pāda* recurs almost verbatim *Divy.*, 318, 14.

24. *Puṣpaketu* as a name for Kāmadeva is rare (only one reference in *PW*, also *Gaṇḍīstotra*, 8); it could also mean 'flower-bannered'.

25. The question is whether we should understand *punarbhāvam* or *'punarbhāvam* in *d*, on which T is not clear (*JRAS*, 1929, 539) and C not to

highway, it was thronged with respectful citizens, clad in cleanly sober guise; and he rejoiced and felt in some degree as if he were being re-created.

26. But when the Śuddhādhivāsa gods saw that city as joyful as Paradise itself, they created the illusion of an old man in order to incite the king's son to leave his home.

27. Then the prince saw him overcome with senility and different in form to other men. His interest was excited and, with gaze steadily directed on the man, he asked the charioteer:—

28. "Good charioteer, who is this man with white hair, supporting himself on the staff in his hand, with his eyes veiled by the brows, and limbs relaxed and bent? Is this some transformation in him, or his original state, or mere chance?"

29. When the chariot-driver was thus spoken to, those very same gods confounded his understanding, so that, without seeing his error, he told the prince the matter he should have withheld:—

30. "Old age it is called, that which has broken him down,—the murderer of beauty, the ruin of vigour, the birth-place of sorrow, the grave of pleasure, the destroyer of memory, the enemy of the senses.

be used safely. I think the poet meant the former to be understood primarily, with the latter as a hidden meaning hinting at the prince's future Enlightenment; but I know no other occurrence of *punarbhāva* without *a*. I follow T in taking *kiṁcit* with *d*.

26. *Divy.*, 408, 18, copies *a*. The infinitive *prayātuṁ*, as Bhandari rightly sees, can only be governed by *saṁcodana*, the root *cud* taking the infinitive. In order to apply to the old man, the reading would have to be *prayāntaṁ*, which is how T takes it.

28. T seems to have understood in *d*, 'is this change in him natural or chance?' So Schmidt, but I prefer to follow Co. and retain the opposition between *vikriyā* and *prakṛti*; a partial parallel at *R.*, viii. 86, and Mallinātha thereon. C accepts the same opposition, but omits *yadṛcchā*.

30. Cp. *S.*, ix. 33, and *Mhv.*, II, 152, 20.

31. For he too sucked milk in his infancy, and later in course of time he crawled on the ground ; in the natural order he became a handsome youth and in the same natural order he has now reached old age."

32. At these words the king's son started a little and addressed the charioteer thus, "Will this evil come upon me also ?" Then the charioteer said to him :—

33. "Inevitably by force of time my long-lived lord will know this length of his days. Men are aware that old age thus destroys beauty and yet they seek it."

34. Then, since his mind was purified by his intentions in the past and his good merit had been accumulated through countless epochs, he was perturbed in his lofty soul at hearing of old age, like a bull on hearing the crash of a thunderbolt near by.

35. Fixing his eye on the old man, he sighed deeply and shook his head ; and looking on the festive multitude he uttered these words in his perturbation :—

36. "Thus old age strikes down indiscriminately memory and beauty and valour, and yet with such a sight before its eyes the world is not perturbed.

37. This being so, turn back the horses, charioteer ; go quickly home again. For how can I take my pleasure in the garden, when the fear of old age rules in my mind ?"

31. *Kālena bhūyaḥ* is clumsy in *b* and there is much to be said for amending to *bālena*, to balance *śiśutve* and *yuvā* ; C perhaps had this, 'then a boy playing at games', the idea then being of *pāṁsukrīḍita*, playing in the dust, not of crawling.

32. I do not think T's *ḥdar*, 'tremble', necessarily supports Speyer's *cakitaḥ* for *calitaḥ* in *a*.

33. As the Indian editors observe, *āyuṣmat* is the form of address to be used by a charioteer to his *rathin* ; the poet intends it not only thus but also in its full sense.

34. *Āśaya* (for which see *AK.*, index s.v.) means the disposition or attitude taken towards the religious life, not intentions in general. It may imply here the Buddha's resolve in past lives ultimately to become a Buddha, something like the *bodhicitta* of the Mahāyāna.

38. So at the bidding of his master's son the driver turned back the chariot. Then the prince returned to the same palace, but so lost in anxiety that it seemed to him empty.

39. But even there he found no relief, as he ever dwelt on the subject of old age; therefore once more with the permission of the king he went out, all being ordered as before.

40. Thereupon the same gods created a man with body afflicted by disease, and the son of Śuddhodana saw him, and, keeping his gaze fixed on him, he said to the charioteer:—

41. "Who is this man with swollen belly and body that heaves with his panting? His shoulders and arms are fallen in, his limbs emaciated and pale. He calls out piteously, "mother", as he leans on another for support."

42. Then the charioteer replied to him, "Good Sir, it is the mighty misfortune called disease, developed in full force from the disorder of the humours, that has made this man, once so competent, no longer master of himself".

43. Thereupon the king's son looked at the man compassionately and spoke, "Is this evil peculiar to him, or is the danger of disease common to all men?"

44. Then the chariot-driver said, "Prince, this evil is shared by all. For men feast and yet they are thus oppressed by disease and racked by pain".

45. Hearing this truth, he was perturbed in mind and trembled like the reflection of the moon on rippling water; and in his pity he uttered these words in a somewhat low tone:—

40. T may have read *dṛṣṭvaiva* at the beginning of *c*, but is not clear.

41. For *samāśritya* cp. *Rām.*, iv. 24, 2, *tvāṁ samāśritya Tārā vasatu*, and *MBh.*, v. 5633, *paravīryaṁ samāśritya*.

44. T's reading in *d* is not good, but is connected with its reading in 46*d*. In neither case has C any hint of it (in 44, 'Who has a body necessarily has pain, yet the stupid contentedly go on rejoicing', and in 46, 'Disease the robber arrives unexpectedly, and yet they feast and rejoice'). The connexion in sense of the two lines is not obvious at first, but the charioteer has in mind the festal crowds around and explains how they too are subject to disease.

46. "This is the calamity of disease for mankind and yet the world sees it and feels no alarm. Vast, alas, is the ignorance of men, who sport under the very shadow of disease.

47. Turn back the chariot, charioteer, from going outside; let it go straight to the palace of the chief of men. And on hearing of the danger of disease, my mind is repelled from pleasures and shrinks, as it were, into itself."

48. Then he turned back with all feeling of joy gone and entered the palace, given over to brooding; and seeing him thus returned a second time, the lord of the earth made enquiry.

49. But when he learnt the reason for his return, he felt himself already abandoned by him. And he merely reprimanded the officer in charge of clearing the road, and angry though he was, imposed no severe punishment on him.

50. And he further arranged for his son the application of sensual attractions in the highest degree, hoping, "Perhaps he will be held by the restlessness of the senses and not desert us".

51. But when in the women's apartments his son took no pleasure in the objects of sense, sounds and the rest, then he directed another excursion outside with the thought that it might cause a change of mood.

46. Note *ca . . . ca* in the first line denoting simultaneity; *paśyan* therefore should not be taken as governing *a*, cp. the similar construction in 61*ab*. T's *svasthaś ca* is good and may be right. In *d* (see preceding note) read in T *bzhad-gad-byed* (=*hasanti*); W's note 2, p. 27, is based on the misreading *gaṅ*.

47. In *c ca* which T omits is difficult; query *śrutvaiva*, 'immediately on hearing', or Gawroński's *śrutvā hi*?

48. W's note 3, p. 27, is to be explained by a confusion of *ḥgro* and *gros* (for which see S. C. Das, *Tibetan Dictionary*, 253*a*).

49. The construction of the second line is difficult as it stands; for *nogradaṇḍaḥ* should mean 'averse from severe punishment', not as above. Simplest would be to amend *ca* to *hi* in *d*. Or take *ca . . . ca* as making the first clause dependent on the second, i.e. 'if he merely reprimanded etc., it was that, even when angry, he was averse from severe punishment'.

50. For *viṣayapracāra* which is much better than °*prakāra*, cp. *S.*, xiv. 48, and note *ib.*, xvii. 25.

52. And as out of his affection he understood his son's state of mind and took no account of the dangers of passion, he ordered suitable courtesans to be present there, as skilled in the arts.

53. Then the royal highway was decorated and guarded with especial care; and the king changed the charioteer and chariot and sent the prince off outside.

54. Then as the king's son was going along, those same gods fashioned a lifeless man, so that only the charioteer and the prince, and none other, saw the corpse being borne along.

55. Thereon the king's son asked the charioteer, "Who is being carried along yonder by four men and followed by a dejected company? He is dressed out gorgeously and yet they bewail him".

56. Then the driver's mind was overcome by the pure--natured Śuddhādhivāsa gods and, though it should not have been told, he explained this matter to the lord of mankind:—

52. The question of the readings in *b* is difficult. A's *saṁvegadoṣān* is odd; either it implies that there was something wrong in *saṁvega*, the first step to salvation, which is absurd, or *doṣa* must mean 'danger', a not uncommon meaning (cp. *Ind. Ant.*, 1933, 113), but ambiguous in the context. Combining A and T, *saṁrāgadoṣān* and the text adopted are the most plausible and better than the reading of either of them, *rāga* being preferable to *saṁrāga*. *KS.*, i. 3, 16, enumerates 64 *kalās*.

55. A's reading in *d* involves taking *hriyate* as well as *avarudyate* in the relative clause, which is difficult. T omits the relative and translates *eṣaḥ* by *pha-gi*, 'yonder', so that both verbs are taken in the principal sentence. Like C it employs a phrase meaning 'highly adorned', and *vibhūṣita* is not strong enough; possibly the intensive *bobhūṣita*? As I cannot determine the syllable, I leave a gap. There are many references in literature to the decking out of corpses at funerals, especially for kings, such as *Avadānaśataka*, II, 134, 5, *LV.*, ch. 14, 190, 10, *Divy.*, 28, 1, and 562, 3 (=*Majjhima*, II, 73), *MBh.*, xii. 5740, and *antyamaṇḍana* at *Kumārasaṁbhava*, iv. 22, and *R.*, viii. 70; an explanation of sorts at *Chāndogya Up.*, viii. 8, 5.

56. *Sya* in *a* is hardly possible, probably derived from a misread *tatas sa* in the original. *Arthavat* in the sense of 'man' is known to the lexica

57. "This is someone or other, lying bereft of intellect, senses, breath and qualities, unconscious and become like a mere log or bundle of grass. He was brought up and cherished most lovingly with every care and now he is being abandoned."

58. Hearing the driver's reply, he was slightly startled and said, "Is this law of being peculiar to this man, or is such the end of all creatures?"

59. Then the driver said to him, "This is the last act for all creatures. Destruction is inevitable for all in the world, be he of low or middle or high degree".

60. Then, steadfast-minded though he was, the king's son suddenly became faint on hearing of death, and, leaning with his shoulder against the top of the chariot rail, he said in a melodious voice :—

61. "This is the end appointed for all creatures, and yet the world throws off fear and takes no heed. Hardened, I ween, are men's hearts; for they are in good cheer, as they fare along the road.

only, but is probably to be recognized at *MBh.*, xiii. 5903, and *Jāt.*, xii. 21 (divide *tavārthavatsu carita°*, the wording recalling *S.*, xviii. 25). It is used here for the play on words.

57. In *a guṇa* is ambiguous, 'attributes of *buddhi*, etc.', or 'objects of sense', or 'qualities' generally. I take the original reading in *d* to have been *priya* doubled to express intensity of feeling, a common enough use. T less probably could be read as *priyaḥ priyais*; FP has 'then, much loved, he is abandoned for ever'.

58. T omits *ayam* in *d* and may have had Cappeller's *athavā*; it is not certain, as it sometimes inserts similar conjunctions, which are to be understood, though not expressed in the Sanskrit.

60. The *kūbara* is the curved rail on the top of the breastwork on each side of the chariot (*JRAS*, 1931, 577). The exact sense of *nihrāda* or *nirhrāda* seems to be uncertain, but I doubt if it ever means 'loud'. I follow T in translating it, and probably in those passages where it looks as if it might mean 'loud', it means 'thrilling', which would do here. Loudness of voice is obviously out of the question.

61. *Adhvan*, the road to the next life.

62. Therefore, charioteer, let our chariot be turned back; for it is not the time or place for pleasure-resorts. For how could a man of intelligence be heedless here in the hour of calamity, when once he knows of destruction?"

63. Though the king's son spoke to him thus, he not merely did not turn back but in accordance with the king's command went on to the Padmaṣaṇḍa grove, which had been provided with special attractions.

64. There the prince saw that lovely grove like the grove of Nandana, with young trees in full bloom, with intoxicated koïls flitting joyously about, and with pavilions and tanks beautiful with lotuses.

65. Then the king's son was carried off by force to that grove, crowded with troops of beautiful women, and was afraid of obstacles to the religious life like some anchorite novice conveyed by force to the palace of the monarch of Alakā, filled with glorious Apsarases.

62. A's *rathaṁ* must be an error. In *b* it is not clear if T read °*bhūmir* with A or °*bhūmer*; but the construction of the former seems impossible.

63. Böhtlingk conjectured °*yuktāt tu*, and it would be possible to understand T thus or as taking it as an adverb, as Co. does; but either expression seems to me odd and it is better to take *viśeṣa* in the sense of 'excellence', often found in Aśvaghoṣa, and to understand it as referring to verse 52 above.

64. *Vimānavat* also applies perhaps to Nandana, 'having heavenly mansions'; for *vimānas* in pleasure groves see *Jāt.*, xxviii. 6, xxxi. 4, and p. 192, 23. In *c* I follow Sovani in dividing *sa kamala*°; otherwise the compound is clumsy and a word is wanted to mark the change of subject from 63. For the misplacement of *iva* in *d* see the Introduction.

65. This verse is of doubtful authenticity. That it is not in C is only a minor point, but it comes in clumsily after the preceding verse. The comparison in the second line is weak and unlike Aśvaghoṣa, and the application of *vighnakātara* to the prince at variance with the next canto. *Kalila* and Alakā do not occur elsewhere in the poet's works, and *varāpsarovṛtam* is a faulty expression, cribbed perhaps from iv. 28, where it is used correctly. For Alakā, see W. Wüst in *Studia Indo-Iranica*, 181-212.

CANTO IV

The Women rejected.

1. Then the women went forth from the city garden, their eyes dancing with excitement, to meet the king's son, as if he were a bridegroom arriving.

2. And, as they approached him, their eyes opened wide in wonder and they welcomed him respectfully with hands folded like lotus-buds.

3. And they stood around him, their minds absorbed in love, and seemed to drink him in with eyes that were moveless and blossomed wide in ecstasy.

4. For the glory of the brilliant signs on his person, as of ornaments born on him, made the women deem him to be the god of love in bodily form.

5. Some opined from his benignity and gravity that the moon had come down to earth in person with his rays veiled.

6. Enthralled by his beauty, they writhed suppressedly, and, smiting each other with their glances, softly sighed.

7. Thus the women did no more than gaze at him with their eyes and were so constrained by his power, that they neither uttered anything nor laughed.

4. There are many Buddhist tales of people being born with ornaments on them ; cp. *Kād.*, 72, *sahajabhūṣaṇair iva mahāpuruṣalakṣaṇair*.

5. T in the second line has *gsaṅ*, not *gsar* as in W's text. *Iti* in *d* was conjectured by Böhtlingk and is confirmed by C.

6. I translate *jajṛmbhire* in the *Dhātupāṭha's* sense of *gātravināma* on the strength of T's *lus ni rnams* (for *rnam*) *ḥgyur-zhiṅ* ; cp. *S.*, vii. 3, and my notes thereon, and the gloss at *AAA.*, 316, *kāyaparāvartanād vijṛmbhamāṇāḥ*. *Jṛmbhaṇa* is a sign of love.

7. Laughter is a regular method of attracting love ; hence T's *jahṛṣuḥ* is inferior.

8. But the purohita's son, the sagacious Udāyin, seeing them to be so embarrassed by love as to be attempting nothing, addressed these words to them :—

9. "You are all of you skilled in all the arts, adepts at captivating the feelings, possessed of beauty and charm, and pre-eminent in your endowments.

10. With these gifts you would even grace the Northern Kurus and the pleasaunce of Kubera, much more then this earth.

11. You could make even lust-free seers waver, and captivate even gods who are accustomed to the Apsarases.

12. And by your knowledge of the sentiments, your blandishments, your wealth of charm and beauty, you have power over women, how much more then over men in respect of passion ?

13. When with such qualities you are lax, each of you, in your own special accomplishment, and exhibit such conduct, I am displeased with your simplicity.

10. *Śobhayata* and *śobhayatha* are unmetrical; metre and sense alike require *śobhayeta*. The Northern Kurus are famous for their love enjoyments; cp. *AKV.*, iii, 213, 15, and *AK.*, III, 183.

11. The missing syllable in *c* cannot be *ścā*, as this would be unmetrical. T translates *kalitān* by *śes-pa* (*jñā*), and this is the regular meaning given in commentaries (e.g. Mallinātha on *Śiśupālavadha*, ix. 83), also in Prakrit (e.g. *Saptaśataka*, 225). That it thence passes to the meaning given above is shown by *Jāt.*, xiii. 8, *antaḥpurasundarīṇāṁ vapurvilāsaiḥ kalitekṣaṇo 'pi*, 'though his eyes were accustomed to, etc.'

12. T shows clearly that *b* is a single compound; the reading *cāturyād rūpa°* of Co.'s MSS. is clumsy and *cāturyarūpa°*, indicated by A, against the metre. Evidently therefore we must amend on the lines of 9*c* above.

13. Neither Co.'s conjecture nor T's reading give a good sense in *b*. Each courtesan has her own special accomplishment as recounted later, and none of them are showing them off. *Viyukta* is no doubt difficult and the meaning suggested rare (Finot, 'paresseuses'); but it is the only way to get a good sense out of the verse. The sense of *ārjava*, 'naiveté', is made clear by the next verse and Udāyin's subsequent recommendation of *anṛta*.

14. Conduct such as this of yours would be more proper in brides who narrow their eyes in shame, or even in the wives of cowherds.

15. As for the argument that he is steadfast and exalted by the power of his majesty, after all the might of women is great ; therefore show determination in this matter.

16. Of old time, for instance, the great seer, Vyāsa, whom even the gods could hardly contend with, was kicked with her foot by the harlot, Kāśisundarī.

17. Manthāla Gautama, desirous of intercourse with the courtesan, Jaṅghā, and wishful of pleasing her, of old carried forth dead bodies with that end in view.

14. *Kuc* compounded with *ni* is very rare (*saṁnikuc* only in *PWK*, instances in Schmidt's *Nachträge* from late *kāvya*, and a variant at *BhNŚ*., vi. 57).

15. *Yad api* followed by *iti* is a regular way of introducing an argument to be rebutted; cp. vi. 21. T's *vīraḥ* in *a* may be right; A has *ayan dhīraḥ* (the change of *m* to *n* in the first word necessitates *dh* and resolves the ambiguity of the character) and C may have had either, 'now though the prince restrains his mind with great firmness'. In *d iti* is poor ; T so mixes *de* and *ḥdi* up in adverbial formations that it may be taken to read *itaḥ* here, though *ataḥ* would be slightly better.

16. The story is unidentified and it is uncertain if Kāśisundarī is a proper name or not. Cp. *S*., vii. 30.

17. This verse is most probably not authentic. All the other names in this speech are mentioned by C and are referred to elsewhere by the poet, while FP in its parallel prose passage (p. 726*b*) also omits it. The story is unknown ; I can trace no such name as Manthāla or Mānthala (which latter breaks the metre), and Jaṅghā I can only connect with Jaṅghāri of *MBh*., xiii. 256, and Jaṅghābandhu, *ib*., ii. 111. The readings are difficult ; *bhikṣu* is not likely to be used by Aśvaghoṣa of a mendicant other than a Buddhist and has to be taken therefore as a desiderative of *bhaj*, as is corroborated by its being co-ordinated with *piprīṣu* by *ca*. *Tadarthārtham* is suspicious ; T may take it as 'for the sake of her wealth', which does not accord with the rest of the verse, and Formichi ingeniously suggests 'to procure money for her'.

18. A young woman, low in caste and standing, gratified the heart of the great seer, Dīrghatapas Gautama, when he was old in years.

19. Similarly the sage's son, Ṛṣyaśṛṅga, who had no knowledge of women, was entrapped and borne off by Śāntā with various wiles.

20. And the great seer, Viśvāmitra, though he had entered on mighty austerities, was captivated by the Apsaras, Ghṛtācī, and deemed ten years with her but a day.

21. To many such seers as these have women brought emotion; how much more then can they to the innocent son of a king in the flower of his youth?

22. This being so, exert yourselves boldly, so that the good fortune of the king's family may not turn away from here.

23. For ordinary women captivate lovers of the same class as themselves; but they only are truly women who ensnare the feelings of high and low alike."

24. On hearing these words of Udāyin, the damsels were so to speak cut to the heart and set themselves to the task of capturing the prince.

25. As if somewhat frightened, the women made gestures designed to cause rapture with brows, looks and blandishments, with laughter, frolicking and movements.

18. In Brahmanical works the form of the name is usually Dīrghatamas; for the story *MBh.*, i. 4209ff. (Poona ed., i. 98).

19. Cp. *S.*, vii. 34. For Ṛṣyaśṛṅga's ignorance of women cp. *Rām.*, i. 9, 3, and *Mhv.*, III, 143ff.

20. Cp. *S.*, vii. 35, and *Rām.*, iv. 35, 7. The story is told in full, *Rām.*, i. 65, substituting Menakā for Ghṛtācī, verses 12-13 recalling this verse.

24. *Pāda c* is difficult. Rashivadekar in Sovani's edition takes *ātman* in the sense of *yatna* as given by the lexica (v. *PW*, s.v. 9). A better alternative is to take *samāruh* as used in *Kauṣītakī Up.*, iii. 6, *prajñayā manaḥ samāruhya*, 'setting the mind to work by *prajñā*'; this develops from the sense 'mount', 'take one's stand on', and goes back to passages such as *Jaiminīya Upaniṣad Brāhmaṇa*, ii. 3 (*JAOS*, 16, 144).

25. The root *laḍ* is so rare and uncertain in meaning, that T's *lalitaiḥ* in *b* may be right. Co. translates *ākṣepikāḥ* 'significant', which may be right

26. But what with the king's command, and the prince's gentleness and the power of intoxication and love, they soon abandoned timidity.

27. Then surrounded by the women, the prince wandered through the garden, like an elephant through the Himalayan forest, accompanied by a herd of females.

28. In that lovely grove he shone with the women in attendance on him, like Vivasvat surrounded by Apsarases in the pleasaunce of Vibhrāja.

29. Then some of the young women there, pretending to be under the influence of intoxication, touched him with their firm, rounded, close-set, charming breasts.

30. One made a false stumble and clasped him by force with her tender arm-creepers, which hung down loosely from her drooping shoulders.

31. Another, whose mouth with copper-coloured lower

in view of verse 40 below. The context makes it necessary to take *bhītabhīta* in the sense of 'rather frightened', not 'utterly terrified'; cp. *Pāṇ.*, viii. 1, 12, and *SS.*, § 252, 1. The occurrences in literature are mostly ambiguous, but Cowell and Thomas translate the same word 'timidly' at *HC.*, ch. vi, 44, 26 (p. 180 of translation).

28. T inserts *kumāraḥ* in *a* for which there is no room. Vibhrāja is more commonly called Vaibhrāja, but I can find no trace of any connexion of it with Sūrya, except that *vibhrāj* is an epithet of the sun in *RV.*, x. 170. Equally the connexion of Sūrya with Apsarases is unusual; but cp. the *praveśaka* of *Vikramorvaśīya*, iv, and S. P. Pandit's discussion of the Puranic passages in support (3rd ed., Bomb. S.S., p. 101). Possibly C is right in either reading *Marutvān* or in taking Vivasvat as a name of Indra.

29. The restoration of T in *ab* is hard; it omits *tatra* and *nāma*, and a possibility, too uncertain to be usable, is *madenānāyatās tāsāṁ taṁ kāścin narma-yoṣitaḥ*. For *nāma*, 'in pretence', cp. *S.*, iv. 15, 17. The conjecture in *d* seems best; *saṁhata* is a regular epithet of breasts, but *sahita* is also used in the same sense, cp. viii. 29 below and *MBh.*, iii. 16183 with iv. 392.

31. T's reading in *d* means, 'let us talk together in secret'. For the implication of *rahasyam*, see note on iii. 17. With the idea cp. *Gītagovinda*, i. 5, 5, and *Amaruśataka* (ed. Simon), 41, *bhrāntyāliṅgya mayā rahasyam uditaṁ tatsaṁgamākāṅkṣayā*.

lip smelt of spirituous liquor, whispered in his ear, "Listen to a secret".

32. Another, who was all wet with unguents, said as if commanding him, "Make a line here", in the hope of winning the touch of his hand.

33. Another repeatedly let her blue garments slip down under the pretext of intoxication, and with her girdle partly seen she seemed like the night with the lightning flashing.

34. Some walked up and down so as to make their golden zones tinkle and displayed to him their hips veiled by diaphanous robes.

35. Others grasped mango-boughs in full flower and leaned so as to display bosoms like golden jars.

36. Another lotus-eyed damsel came from a lotus-bed with a lotus and stood by the side of the lotus-faced prince as if she were Padmaśrī.

37. Another sang a sweet song with gesticulations to bring out the sense, reproving his indifference, as it were, with looks that said, "You deceive yourself".

32. The point, as appears from *S.*, iv, is that the body is first moistened with unguents and the decorative paint is then put on. *Bhakti* has a double sense, enforced, as Gawroński points out, by *ājñāpayantīva*, 'as if commanding him to be devoted to her'. The conjecture in *d* combines A and T and explains the reason for her action.

33. This may be the earliest occurrence in literature of *aṁśuka*, but *PW* s.v. omits the references to *MBh.*, iii. 11093 and x. 25. I cannot restore T in *c*, except that it had *raśanā*. For *ālakṣyaraśanā* cp. *Kāvyādarśa*, ii. 44, where *ālakṣyakesara* is equivalent to *asamagralakṣyakesara* of *Mālavikāgnimitra*, ii. 10, *ā* being used in the sense of 'somewhat', not as a preposition. The note on iii. 17, will explain the point of the verse. It seems to have been an accepted method of attraction with loose women, cp. *LV*, ch. xxi, 321, of Māra's daughters, *kāścid guhyaprakāśāni sarvābharaṇāny upadarśayanti sma*, *Jātaka*, V, 434, *guyhabhaṇḍakaṁ saṁcāleti*, and *R.*, xiii. 42, *vyājārdhasaṁdarśitamekhalāni*. In T's text of *d* for *phred* (or *phreṅ*) we should probably read *ḥphro*=*sphur*. It changes round the order of 33 and 34.

36. Cp. *S.*, vi. 36, and note in translation.

37. *Anvartham* can also mean 'suitable to the matter in hand' or 'easily understood', but I prefer to combine it with *sābhinayam*. The root

38. Another imitated him by drawing the bow of her brows on her fair countenance and making gestures in mimicry of his solemnity.

39. A damsel with fine rounded breasts and earrings shaking with her laughter mocked him out loud, saying, "Finish it, Sir".

40. Similarly, as he was retreating, some bound him with ropes of garlands, and others restrained him with words that were like ankuses but were softened with innuendoes.

41. Another in order to bring about an argument seized a mango-spray and asked, stuttering with intoxication, "Whose flower now is this?"

vañc in the passive often means 'be disappointed' and so 'miss a good opportunity'; cp. *LV.*, ch. xxi, 323, *yadi necchasi kāmasulālasikāṁ suṣṭhu suvañcitako 'si*, and Candrakīrti on *Catuḥśataka*, 72, *yo nāma yuvā bhūtvā . . . yuvatijanaṁ tuṣṭyā nopabhuṅkte sa jīvaloke paramavañcito bhavati.*

38. I cannot solve the difficulties of this verse. A and T agree in their readings, unless W is right in thinking T had *anucacāra* (cp. *Jāt.*, vi. 1, *cacāra mṛgalīlayā*). *Anukṛ* takes the genitive of the person imitated (*S.*, i. 36, and xviii. 59, and examples in *PW*) or accusative of the action imitated (*Jāt.*, 233, 13-14, *Yamasya līlām anucakāra*), so that *anucakāra* here governs either *asya* or *ceṣṭitam*. *Prāvṛtya* may come from *vṛ* in the regular sense of 'put on' clothes, but then we ought to read *veṣṭitam* in the sense of *veṣṭanam*, 'putting on a royal headdress', and there is no authority for this. So I prefer to take it to *vṛt*, for which some of the Indian editors give the sense, 'coming forward'. The above translation is based on taking it as equivalent to *pravṛtya* in the transitive sense (*PW*, *vart*, *pra+*, 14), known only to the epics and always governing an accusative of action.

39. Following a suggestion of Sovani's, I take *samāpnotu* in its plain sense to mean, 'Cap that, if you can', 'Improve on my joke', and as also to be divided *sa mā=āpnotu*, 'Catch me'.

40. Both lines refer to elephants.

41. For quarrels in the technique of love, see *KS.*, ii. 3, 18, and 5, 38, and *pratiyoga* might be translated 'quarrel' here, the literal meaning being 'opposition'. The mango blossom is specifically the flower of Kāma, and the answer to the question is therefore 'Kāma'. Formichi translates *pratiyoga* 'antithesis', and thinks *puṣpa* refers to the prince. This seems far-fetched, but there may be a secondary meaning underlying the principal one, obscene perhaps, as Rashivadekar suggests in the commentary to Sovani's edition.

42. One of them, modelling her gait and outward appearance on those of a man, said to him, "Sir, you have been conquered by women, conquer this earth now!"

43. Then another with rolling eyes sniffed at a blue lotus and addressed the prince with words that were slightly indistinct in her excitement:—

44. "See, my lord, this mango loaded with honey-scented flowers, in which the koïl calls, looking as if imprisoned in a golden cage.

45. Look at this *aśoka* tree, the increaser of lovers' sorrows, in which the bees murmur as if scorched by fire.

46. Behold this *tilaka* tree, embraced by a mango branch, like a man in white garments embraced by a woman with yellow body-paint.

47. See the *kurubaka* in full bloom, shining like lac just squeezed out, which bends over as if dazzled by the brilliance of the women's nails.

48. And look at this young *aśoka* tree, all covered with young shoots, which stands as if abashed by the glitter of our hands.

42. Query *pṛthivīm iti* in *d*? The earth is female and the woman is referring by innuendo to herself.

43. Rashivadekar observes that she smells the blue lotus to indicate that it is proper to enjoy brunettes, impregnated with the perfume of youth, and that her eyes are rolling to spur the prince on.

45. The last *pāda* (1) refers to the colour of the flowers, (2) suggests the fire of love, by which even the bees seem to be burnt.

47. The word ordinarily used for squeezing lac is *niṣpīḍ*. *Nirbhuj* properly means 'press with the teeth', *KS.*, vi. 3, 41, and *Kumārasaṁbhava*, viii. 49. *Mūlamadhyamakakārikās*, 318, 3, uses the word of a deed attesting a debt, which is *nirbhukta*, 'valueless' (Tib. *ror-gyur-pa*, 'become sediment'?) 'with the juice squeezed out', after the debt has been repaid. T, misunderstanding, translates *ma-zos-pa*, 'not eaten'. It omits the relative in *c* and translates *nirbhartsita* by *rma-phab gyur-te*, 'wounded'.

48. I do not think it necessary to hold with W that T shows *khacita* by *spras-pa*. The genuineness of the verse is open to doubt; the *aśoka* has already been mentioned, and the second line is a weak paraphrase of 47*cd*.

49. See the pond enveloped by the *sinduvāra* bushes growing on its bank, like a woman lying down and clothed in white silk.

50. Consider the mighty power of women; for instance, the sheldrake in the water there follows obediently behind his mate like a servant.

51. Listen to the sound of the impassioned cuckoo's cry; another koïl calls at once like an echo.

52. Can it be that spring brings passion to the birds, but not to the wiseacre who reflects on what he should not reflect on?"

53. Thus these young women, to whose minds love had given free rein, assailed the prince with wiles of every kind.

54. But despite such allurements the prince firmly guarded his senses, and in his perturbation over the inevitability of death, was neither rejoiced nor distressed.

55. He, the supreme man, saw that they had no firm footing in the real truth, and with mind that was at the same time both perturbed and steadfast he thus meditated:—

56. "Do these women then not understand the transitoriness of youth, that they are so inebriated with their own beauty, which old age will destroy?

50. T is definitely against reading *anuvṛtya* in *d*.

51. A's *anutkaḥ* is surely impossible in *c*. Apte gives 'visible' as a meaning of *anvakṣa*, which accounts for T's translation of it. For the sense 'directly afterwards', see *S.*, xv. 57, and *Yājñavalkya*, iii. 21, with the *Mitākṣarā's* gloss of *sadyaḥ*.

52. I can make no sense out of A's reading in *c*.

54. In *d* A's *sismiye* seems impossible. *Vivyathe* covers both T's *ḥjigs-pa*, 'was afraid', and C's 'grieved'. Cp. *S.*, xi. 7.

55. Co.'s conjecture, *asaṁvignena*, is at complete variance with the context.

56. In *c saṁmattā* would be easier, but is farther from A, while T indicates a substantive, not a participle. I take *saṁmattam* to be the former, a use common in Aśvaghoṣa; similarly *nirudvignāḥ* in 58 below, for which Co.'s MSS. substituted *nirudvegāḥ*.

57. Surely they do not perceive anyone overwhelmed by illness, that they are so full of mirth, so void of fear in a world in which disease is a law of nature.

58. And quite clearly they sport and laugh so much at ease and unperturbed, because they are ignorant of death who carries all away.

59. For what rational being would stand or sit or lie at ease, still less laugh, when he knows of old age, disease and death ?

60. But he is just like a being without reason, who, on seeing another aged or ill or even dead, remains indifferent and unmoved.

61. For when one tree is shorn both of its flowers and its fruit and falls or is cut down, another tree is not distressed thereby."

62. Then Udāyin, who was expert in worldly conduct and the *śāstras*, seeing him to be absorbed in brooding and to have lost all desire for sensual objects, addressed him thus out of friendship :—

63. "The king appointed me to be your companion because he considered me competent ; therefore I wish to speak to you to justify the confidence he reposed in me.

59. T uses *ñal* for *śī* only, hence I prefer *śayed* to *svaped*, both being irregular. The use of the former in the active goes back to *Aitareyabrāhmaṇa*, iii. 15, 1 ; cp. *LV.*, ch. xiii, 369, 1. *AK.*, V, 170, n. 2, quotes *AKV* as using *svapet*, and *svap* is used in a parallel passage at *Śatapathabrāhmaṇa*, xii. 3, 2, 7. The verse recurs with variations at *Bhojaprabandha*, 36, quoted by Gawroński.

60. *Acetas* does not mean an imbecile, but something that, unlike a man, has no reasoning faculty ('then he is a man of clay and wood', C), as the supporting instance in the next verse shows ; it is the opposite of *sacetana* in 59.

62. Or *nītiśāstra* can be taken as 'the science of worldly conduct'; for the poet's use of *nīti* cp. *S.*, ii. 28, and xvii. 11.

63. The addition of *tayā* shows that *praṇayavattayā* cannot mean 'affectionately' or 'unreservedly'; it refers the feeling indicated by it to the king.

64. The threefold characteristic of friendship is to restrain a man from what is unprofitable, to encourage him to what is profitable and to stand by him in adversity.

65. If, after having promised friendship, I should resile from the duty of a man and neglect your interests, there would be no friendship in me.

66. Therefore, having become your friend, I say that such lack of courtesy to women ill befits one who is as young in years and beautiful in person as you are.

67. The gratification of women, even by the use of falsity, is right, for the sake both of countering their bashfulness and of one's own enjoyment.

68. It is humility and compliance that bind women's hearts; for good qualities are the birthplace of affection and women like respect.

69. Therefore, O large-eyed prince, however averse your heart be, you should gratify them with a courtesy that corresponds to this beauty of yours.

65. C seems quite clearly to have read *parāṅmukhaḥ*, and T probably did so. Either reading makes good sense, but with the text reading *puruṣa* implies 'attendant'.

67. The translation of *c* is uncertain; *parihāra* properly means 'avoidance', but C understands it to mean 'taking away'. I take a hint from the use of *pariharati* in philosophical works, 'counters' an objection. To take it in the Buddhist sense of 'guarding', 'looking after' (cp. P.T.S. *Pali Dictionary* s. *pariharati* and *parihāra*) is difficult to reconcile with *vrīḍā*, which means 'embarrassment', not 'modesty' (cp. *S.*, xii. 1, 2). T's reading is inferior. *Anṛta* is no sin in dealing with women, *MBh.*, vii. 8741, viii. 3436, etc., and a Mīmāṁsaka verse quoted in *Ṣaḍdarśanasamuccaya* (ed. Bibl. Ind.), 262, 5. But here it seems to mean little more than 'insincerity'. For *dākṣiṇya* cp. its contrast with *sadbhāva* at *Saptaśataka*, 353 (note also *ib.*, 85), and there is an amusing discussion of the relative advantages of *dākṣiṇya* and *rūpa* in a courtesan in *Dhūrtaviṭasaṁvāda* (ed. *Caturbhāṇī*), 23, 10ff.; one argument is *anuvṛttir hi kāme mūlam, sā ca dākṣiṇyāt saṁbhavati*. See also note, p. 43, on *Vikramorvaśīya* (B.S.S., 3rd ed.), ii. 4.

68. *Mānakāma* is deliberately ambiguous; for *māna*, 'pride', is the regular attribute of women in love.

70. Courtesy is the balm of women, courtesy is the best ornament; beauty without courtesy is like a grove without flowers.

71. What is the good of courtesy only? Accept them with genuine feeling. For when you have obtained such rare pleasures of the senses, you should not contemn them.

72. Knowing that love is the highest good, even the god, Puraṁdara, for instance, of olden time fell in love with Ahalyā, the wife of Gautama.

73. And according to tradition Agastya asked for Rohiṇī, wife of Soma, and thereby obtained Lopamudrā who resembled her.

74. And Bṛhaspati of the great austerities begot Bharadvāja on Mamatā, the Mārutī, wife of Utathya.

71. I am doubtful of the correctness of the translation of the first line, though all the translators understand it so. But there is nothing in the rest of Udāyin's speech to develop the idea and the translators find it necessary to insert a 'but', which is not to be read out of *vā*, to justify the harsh transition. The prince in his reply makes no reference to the suggestion, though Aśvaghoṣa is very careful in all the discussions in this work to see that every point of an argument is answered. T seems to take *a* and *b* together, though I am not quite sure about this; and C certainly did not understand the passage as translated above, 'Ought you not therefore to be courteous? You should fully experience these things therefore'. I can find no authority for taking *bhāvena* as 'fully', and I should prefer to read the line as a single sentence, 'Just try accepting them with a feeling that does not go beyond courtesy'. But this use of *kiṁ vā* seems to have no analogies elsewhere and I therefore defer to my predecessors in my rendering.

72. Cp. *S.*, vii. 25. A well-known story.

73. The story of Agastya's asking for Rohiṇī is unknown; the best known version of his marriage to Lopamudrā is in the *Agastyopākhyāna*, *MBh.*, iii.

74. The Vedic form of the name is Ucathya; later Utathya is usual. It is uncertain whether we should read *saṁmatāyāṁ* with T (cp. *MBh.* (Poona ed.), i. 98, 6, *Mamatā nāma tasyāsīd bhāryā paramasaṁmatā*, the readings being doubtful) and whether Mārutī means 'daughter of the Maruts' or 'daughter of Āvikṣita Marutta'. The legends are very confused, cp. Pargiter, 157-8, and note *MBh.*, xii. 8602, where Marutta gives his daughter to Aṅgiras

75. And the Moon, the best of sacrificers, begot Budha of the god-like deeds on Bṛhaspati's wife, as she was making oblations.

76. And of old too Parāśara, with his passions inflamed, approached Kālī, the daughter of a fish, on the bank of the Yamunā.

77. The sage Vasiṣṭha through lust begot a son, Kapiñjalāda, on a despised low-caste woman, Akṣamālā.

78. And the royal seer, Yayāti, even when his term of life had run out, dallied with the Apsaras, Viśvācī, in the Caitraratha grove.

79. And though the Kaurava king, Pāṇḍu, knew that intercourse with a woman must end in his death, yet, allured by Mādrī's entrancing beauty, he gave himself up to the pleasures of love.

80. And Karālajanaka too carried off a Brahman's daughter, and, though he thus incurred ruin, he still adhered to his love.

81. Men of lofty position such as these for the sake of sexual pleasure enjoyed the objects of the senses, even contemp-

(Bṛhaspati as Āṅgirasa is at times called Aṅgiras). One of Dr. Sukthankar's MSS. in the above passage regularly reads Maratā for Mamatā, perhaps due to some recollection of Mārutī; or did Mamatā originate from a misreading of Mārutī?

75. The story is not known to the *MBh.*, and in the Purāṇas Bṛhaspati's wife is called Tārā. Co. however takes *juhvatī* as a proper name, for which there is no authority; if it is a participle, it implies a different version of the tale to that known to us. For *vibudhakarmāṇam*, cp. *S.*, i. 36.

76. A well-known story; cp. *S.*, vii. 29. What I believe to be T's reading in *c* is supported by *MBh.*, xii. 13639, and (Poona ed.) i. 54, 2, and 57, 69.

77. Cp. *S.*, vii. 28.

78. *Pāda b* refers to the extension of life that Yayāti got to enable him to enjoy the Apsarases.

79. A well-known story; cp. *S.*, vii. 45. T quaintly divides *vinā śāntam.*

80. For Karālajanaka, see Charpentier, *WZKM*, 28, 211ff., and Pargiter, 96, n. 11. The ruin of the kingdom is referred to at xiii. 5 below.

81. Both C and T, like Co.'s MSS., seem to read *evamādyā.*

tible ones, and all the more so when they were conjoined with excellence.

82. You, however, who possess vigour, beauty and youth, despise the pleasures which have come to you of right, and to which the world is attached."

83. The prince listened to his specious words, supported by scriptural tradition, and replied to him in a voice like the thundering of a cloud :—

84. "Your words make plain your friendship for me and befit you; and I shall satisfy you on the points wherein you misjudge me.

85. It is not that I despise the objects of sense and I know that the world is devoted to them; but my mind does not delight in them, because I hold them to be transitory.

86. If the triad of old age, disease and death did not exist, I too should take my pleasure in the ravishing objects of sense.

87. For if indeed this beauty of women could have been rendered everlasting, my mind would certainly have taken pleasure in the passions, full of evils though they are.

82. I understand C to explain *nyāyataḥ prāptān* as meaning that the prince had acquired these things as the result of virtue practised in former lives.

87. The close agreement of C and T shows that A's second line with the remarkable *sasaṁvitka* is a late falsification of the original, which was evidently felt not to be in keeping with the Buddha's character. The restoration of *c* is certain; in *d* the difficulty lies in *phyogs* (=*diś*). Now *Cāṇakyarājanīti-śāstra* (Calcutta O.S. no. 2, 1926), vi. 81, is made up out of the first line of verse 86 above and of a line that gives the sense of the second line of this verse, running *tadā saṁsārabhoge 'smin kāmaṁ rājatu me manaḥ*. *Rājatu* is odd here and a form from *raj* is indicated. T sometimes writes *phya* for *cha* (see note on ii. 22), and I conjecture it originally had *chags* (=*raj*) which was written *phyags*; this was not understood and was corrected to *phyogs*. It is justifiable to quote this anthology in support of my restoration, as it also has ix. 62 in part. The result is not absolutely certain, but is very probable. T apparently misunderstood *kāmam*, which is to be taken adverbially.

88. But seeing that, when their beauty has been drunk up by old age, it will be abhorrent even to them, delight in it could only arise from delusion.

89. For a man who, himself subject to death, disease and old age, sports unperturbed with those who are subject to death, disease and old age, is on a level with the birds and beasts.

90. As for your argument that those men of might were addicted to passion, that rather must cause perturbation of mind, seeing that they too perished.

91. And I do not hold that to be true greatness, which has the generic characteristic of perishing, and in which either there is attachment to the objects of sense, or self-control is not attained.

92. As for your saying that one should associate with women, even by the use of falsity, I cannot reconcile falsity with courtesy by any means at all.

93. Nor does that compliance please me, from which straightforwardness is absent. Fie upon that union, which is not made wholeheartedly!

94. For ought one to deceive a soul inflamed with passion, which is lacking in steadfastness, trusting, attached, and blind to the dangers incurred?

90. It is not quite certain what should be supplied in *c*.

91. I follow Co. in taking the second line as a continuation of *b*; for, while *vā . . . vā* seems to demand an independent sentence, it is difficult to make a satisfactory sense except as above.

92. C and T seem to have had a version of this verse, in which *d* was part of the quotation of Udāyin's argument; but I cannot reconstruct it. C runs, 'As for what you said, "Practise association by devices of pretence in accordance with courtesy", then the practice is truly defilement. Can this be called a device?' In *d dākṣiṇyena* can be understood either 'as associated with courtesy', or 'by the measure of it'; I translate a little freely to get the sense. In T's last line *de-min* is probably corrupt for *bden-min*.

94. T's reading in *b* is against the metre. For the construction cp. *Hitopadeśa* (ed. Peterson), *Mitralābha*, 57, which traces its ultimate origin perhaps to this verse.

95. And surely it is not fit for women to look at men or men at women, when the victims of passion one for the other, if they practise deceit in this way.

96. Such being the case, you should not lead me astray to the ignoble passions, when I am afflicted with suffering and my lot is old age and death.

97. Ah! Your mind must be very firm and strong, when you find substance in the fleeting passions. While observing creation on the road of death, you remain attached to the objects of sense in the midst of the most terrible danger.

98. I on the other hand am fearful and exceeding distressed, as I meditate on the terrors of old age, death and disease. I find no peace or contentment, much less pleasure, as I perceive the world blazing as it were with fire.

99. If desire arises in the heart of a man who knows that death is inevitable, I consider that his soul is made of iron, in that instead of weeping he delights in the great danger."

100. Then, as the prince uttered this discourse which was full of resolution and controverted recourse to the passions, the lord of day passed to the Western Mountain, with his orb such that men could gaze at it.

101. Then their garlands and ornaments worn in vain, their excellent arts and endearments all fruitless, the women

99. There have been many attempts to amend A's reading in *d* on the lines of the word being a participle to agree with *mahābhaye*; T is against this, and the only possible word, *tiṣṭhati*, is bad palæographically. Moreover, the argument runs incoherently. The word indicated by T is from *raj* or *sajj* (the form *sajjati* being permissible in epic and Buddhist Sanskrit), and the parallelism with *rāga* in the first line suggests that *rajyati* is the correct solution.

100. *Ca . . . ca* denoting simultaneity. The point that men's eyes can look at the sun as it sets without being dazzled recurs in language reminiscent of this verse at *Kumārasaṁbhava*, viii. 29, and *Kirātārjunīya*, iv. 4.

101. The difficulty lies in *c*. The emphatic position of *eva* shows that the translation of *sva eva bhāve* by 'in their hearts' is too commonplace. T takes *manmatha* as=Kāmadeva; he is *manasija, cittodbhava,* to which the word is clearly intended to allude here. Therefore *sve* refers to him primarily and

suppressed the god of love in his birthplace, their hearts, and returned to the city with their hopes frustrated.

102. Then the son of earth's guardian saw the glory of the women in the city garden withdrawn again in the evening and, meditating on the transitoriness of everything, he entered his dwelling.

103. But when the king heard that his son was averse from the objects of sense, then like an elephant with a dart in its heart, he did not lie down that night. Thereon wearing himself out with all kinds of counsels with his ministers, he found no means, other than the passions, for restraining his son's purpose.

we must translate literally 'in his being', which is equivalent to 'in their hearts'. To make the thought clear, I translate *bhāva* 'birthplace', and in actual fact the later lexica give this as a meaning of the word. In these circumstances T's *vinigarhya* (*garh* with *vini* not recorded elsewhere) makes no sense and A's *viniguhya* is hardly strong enough. I therefore conjecture *vinigṛhya*, which is palæographically the halfway house between the two forms.

102. T's reading is perhaps preferable in *d*, as *punaḥ* seems required by the sense.

103. T's reading is excluded in *c*, because *śrānta* takes the locative (*S.*, i. 1).

CANTO V.

FLIGHT.

1. Though the son of the Śākya king was thus tempted by priceless objects of sense, he felt no contentment, he obtained no relief, like a lion pierced deeply in the heart by a poisoned arrow.

2. Then longing for spiritual peace, he set forth outside with the king's permission in order to see the forest, and for companions he had a retinue of ministers' sons, chosen for their reliability and skill in converse.

3. He went out, mounted on the good horse Kanthaka, the bells of whose bit were of fresh gold and whose golden

1. For the reading adopted in *c* cp. *S.*, ix. 50, and *Jāt.*, v. 16. In *d* I follow Co. in taking *ati* as an adverb applying to the whole compound in preference to taking *atidigdha* as 'a highly poisoned arrow' (so Schmidt).

2. The compound *vanabhūmididṛkṣayā* would only be permissible in the classical language, if *vanabhūmi* could be taken as accusative, but Aśvaghoṣa uses an objective genitive or locative after *didṛkṣā*. Such compounds do occur however, *S.*, i. 49, *MBh.*, i. 385, and xii. 9320.

3. Probably the earliest occurrence in literature of *khalīna*, believed to be a Greek loan-word. In the second line I am doubtful of A's reading in *c*; Kanthaka is specially described later and would hardly be brought in casually here. T's *sakambalam* may be right, *mbba* and *ntha* being palæographically close, and blankets are used for saddles; but I would not accept it till its application to the simile can be explained. C does not help except that it does not give the name Kanthaka, and I can make nothing out of reading A as *sakanthakam*. For *d* I follow Schrader and Sovani in taking *drumābja* as =*drumotpala*, *karṇikāra*. This tree is compared to human beings, verse 51 below and *S.*, xviii. 5. The question is what meaning to attribute to this. There is perhaps a hint at a comparison with Abhimanyu, who had an emblem of *karṇikāra* flowers on his banners according to the *MBh.* and is therefore *drumābjaketu*, *ketu* meaning primarily the emblem at the top of the flagstaff and only secondarily a flag as a whole (cp. Hopkins, *JAOS*, 1889, 244-5). But

trappings were beautified with waving chowries, and so he resembled a *karṇikāra* emblem mounted on a flagpole.

4. Desire for the forest as well as the excellence of the land led him on to the more distant jungle-land, and he saw the soil being ploughed, with its surface broken with the tracks of the furrows like waves of water.

5. When he saw the ground in this state, with the young grass torn up and scattered by the ploughs and littered with dead worms, insects and other creatures, he mourned deeply as at the slaughter of his own kindred.

6. And as he observed the ploughmen with their bodies discoloured by wind, dust and the sun's rays, and the oxen in

of itself this does not explain *ketum*. Buddha is compared *S.*, iii. 25, to a *hemamaṇijālavalayinaṁ dhvajam*, but, if we take *ketuḥ* as 'banner', no suitable meaning again is left for *ketum*. For the sense 'comet' seems to me quite unacceptable, unless we go to the length of taking *drumābja* as='born of wood or water', i.e. Agni, the *ketu* of Agni being smoke as in xi. 71 ; this is not only far-fetched but gives no suitable application of the first line to *ketum*. Further S. C. Das's meaning 'column' for T's *tog-can* cannot be authenticated in Sanskrit for *ketu*. Nor do I see how to apply to the simile the fact that the Barhut sculptures show flagpoles with human figures for their flags, the flag-bearers being mounted. I can find no alternative therefore to the somewhat unconvincing rendering given above, except to take *drumābjaketuḥ* as 'the brilliance of *karṇikāra* flowers'; flowers were actually carried on flagpoles, cp. *Ūrubhaṅga*, 9, *mālyair dhvajāgrapatitaiḥ*. The epithets in the first line can easily apply to a banner (divide *kha-līna* and note *AAA.*, 180, for the association of bells and flags).

4. *Vanānta* could mean 'on the edge of the forest', but probably *anta* is purely collective in sense to distinguish the jungle from the city-groves. For *vikṛṣṭa=viprakṛṣṭa*, cp. *Madhyamavyāyoga* (T.S.S.), p. 6, and *BhNŚ.*, xiv. 23. The jungle is naturally further from the city than the gardens. In *c* T possibly read *vikāra* and took it to *kṝ*.

5. The Indian editors quote the *Medinikośa* for the form *krimi* ; cp. Lüders, *Bruchstücke buddhistischer Dramen*, fragment 18, and *AKV.*, iii, 149, 16. *Kṛmikīṭa* is a common combination, e.g. *Manu*, i. 40, and *SP.*, iii. 44.

6. In *b* T's reading may be correct. C's 'their bodies covered with dust' suggests that *varṇa* should perhaps be taken here as=*rūpa*, a common Pali usage.

distress with the labour of drawing, the most noble one felt extreme compassion.

7. Then alighting from his horse, he walked slowly over the ground, overcome with grief. And as he considered the coming into being and the passing away of creation, he cried in his affliction, "How wretched this is."

8. And desiring to reach perfect clearness with his mind, he stopped his friends who were following him, and proceeded himself to a solitary spot at the root of a *jambū*-tree, whose beautiful leaves were waving in all directions.

9. And there he sat down on the clean ground, with grass bright like beryl; and reflecting on the origin and destruction of creation he took the path of mental stillness.

10. And his mind at once came to a stand and at the same time he was freed from mental troubles such as desire for the objects of sense etc. And he entered into the first trance of calmness which is accompanied by gross and subtle cogitation and which is supermundane in quality.

11. Then he obtained possession of concentration of mind, which springs from discernment and yields extreme ecstasy and bliss, and thereafter, rightly perceiving in his mind the course of the world, he meditated on this same matter.

8. *Viviktatā* has also here the sense of 'solitude'. It is impossible to decide between *nivārya* and *nivartya* in *d*; many passages could be cited in support of each.

9. In *a* I combine A and T. The prince enters on the meditation known as *dharmapravicaya* in the Abhidharma. There may be a hint in *ālalambe* of the technical meaning of *ālambana*, which is to the mind what *viṣaya* is to the senses.

10. *Āsrava* cannot be satisfactorily translated; for my rendering, see note on *S.*, xvi. 3, in my translation. The phrase does not usually occur in descriptions of the first trance, but *Divy.*, 391, calls it *anāsravasadṛśa* on this very occasion, and according to Hīnayāna dogmatics this trance can be either *sāsrava* or *anāsrava*. T is possibly corrupt and may originally have had *rab-spyod-pa*, i.e. *anāsravapracāram*, which would be quite good.

12. "A wretched thing it is indeed that man, who is himself helpless and subject to the law of old age, disease and destruction, should in his ignorance and the blindness of his conceit, pay no heed to another who is the victim of old age, disease or death.

13. For if I, who am myself such, should pay no heed to another whose nature is equally such, it would not be right or fitting in me, who have knowledge of this, the ultimate law."

14. As he thus gained correct insight into the evils of disease, old age and death, the mental intoxication relating to the self, which arises from belief in one's strength, youth and life, left him in a moment.

15. He did not rejoice nor yet was he downcast; doubt came not over him, nor sloth, nor drowsiness. And he felt no longing for sensual pleasures, no hatred or contempt for others.

16. While this pure passionless state of mind grew within his lofty soul, there came up to him a man in mendicant's clothes, unseen of other men.

17. The king's son asked him, "Tell me, who are you?" On this he explained to him, "O bull among men, I am a *śramaṇa*, who in fear of birth and death have left the home life for the sake of salvation.

12. *Vijugupsa* is recorded by the *PW* only in a single verse from the older Upaniṣads and then only with the ablative in the sense of 'feel disgust for'. Pali however has *vijugucchati* with the accusative (see P.T.S. *Dict.* s.v.) in the sense of literally 'despising' and so 'thinking nothing of', 'taking no heed of'. Here it really means 'fail to draw the moral from'. The construction of *jugupsa* in Sanskrit with the accusative is parallel, and to translate here 'despise' misses the point.

13. *Hi* perhaps merely expletive to emphasize the predicate.

14. For *mada* and the second line cp. *S.*, ix. 1–34.

15. The *kāmaguṇas* are the five *guṇas* or objects of the senses in that aspect in which *kāma* is felt for them.

16. *Rajas* in *nīrajaska* means *rāga* and *dveṣa* as described in the preceding verse; cp. note in translation on *S.*, iii. 39.

18. Since the world is subject to destruction, I desire salvation and seek the blessed incorruptible stage. I look with equal mind on kinsman and stranger, and longing for and hatred of the objects of sense have passed from me.

19. I dwell wherever I happen to be, at the root of a tree or in a deserted temple, on a hill or in the forest, and I wander without ties or expectations in search of the highest good, accepting any alms I may receive."

20. After saying this, he flew up to the sky before the prince's very eyes; for he was a heavenly being who in that form had seen other Buddhas and had encountered him to rouse his attention.

21. When that being went like a bird to heaven, the best of men was thrilled and amazed. And then he gained awareness of *dharma* and set his mind on the way to leave his home.

22. Then he, who was Indra's peer and had conquered the horses of the senses, mounted his horse with the intention of

18. There are many parallels to c, e.g. *Kāśyapaparivarta*, 29, p. 56, *putre ca śatrumhi ca tulyamānaso*. *Doṣa* for *dveṣa* again (see note on ii. 39).

19. I translate *āyatana* 'temple', as Indian tales so often mention wandering mendicants as living in deserted temples.

20. The difficulty in the second line lies in *tadvapuḥ*, which T takes as nominative ; but the order of its words is such that *kyis* may, as often, be a mistake for *kyi*, which would make it compounded with *anyabuddhadarśī*, hardly a good reading. C is not clear. Formichi ingeniously takes it as accusative, 'assumed that form', much the best sense, if authority for such a use of *i* with *samā* were available. For *anyabuddhadarśin* cp. *pūrvabuddhadarśin*, *LV.*, ch. xxii, 350, 16, and *Śikṣāsamuccaya*, 13, 1, and 189, 13 ; *darśin* properly 'who was in the habit of seeing'. For *smṛtaye*, see the Introduction.

21. The use of *upalabh*, which is specially used of perception by the senses, shows that *saṁjñā* has the technical sense of the action of the mind in forming ideas or conceptions, based on the perceptions presented to it by the senses. As Speyer notes, the expression, *dharmasaṁjñā*, is common in *Jāt.*, though I take it in a somewhat different way to him.

22. For the horses of the senses cp. *S.*, x. 41, and note in translation. I do not agree with W that T reads *parivārajane 'py abhīkṣamāṇe* and I believe it indicates the text (read *mthoṅ-ba* for *ḥdod-pa* ?). In *S.*, *īkṣ* with *ava* is used

entering the city; but out of regard for his following he did not go straight to the longed for forest.

23. Though he entered the city again, it was not out of any wish to do so, since he desired to make an end of old age and death and had fixed his mind in all attention on the forest life; his feelings were those of an elephant returning to the picketing-ground from the jungle.

24. A nobleman's daughter, looking up at him, as he entered along the road, folded her hands and said, "Happy indeed and blessed is that woman, whose husband is such in this world, O long-eyed one!"

25. Thereon he, whose voice was like that of a mighty thunder-cloud, heard this announcement and was filled with supreme calm. For on hearing the word "blessed", he set his mind on the means of winning final beatitude.

26. In stature like the peak of the golden mountain, in arm, voice and eye resembling an elephant, a thunder-cloud and a bull respectively, in countenance and step like the moon and a lion respectively, he next proceeded to the palace with yearning aroused for the imperishable *dharma*.

27. Then with the gait of the king of beasts he approached his father in the midst of his corps of ministers, like Sanatkumāra in the third heaven approaching Maghavat, as he shines in the assembly of the Maruts.

several times where one would expect *apa*, and I construe it thus here. The natural rendering of the second line in C is given in Beal, but probably it really intended what I believe the Sanskrit to mean. The point is that the retinue would have got into trouble with the king, if they did not bring the prince back with them; and this would be brought out more clearly by reading *hy* for *tv* in *c*.

26. The first line of 27 shows that *vikrama* means primarily 'gait' here; it may mean 'prowess' secondarily. The poet plays again on *kṣaya* at *S.*, x. 57.

27. For the simile to be exact Sanatkumāra should be the son of Indra and C has 'the son of Śakra'; does Sanatkumāra stand for Jayanta, just as at *Chāndogya Up.*, vii. 26, 2, Sanatkumāra and Skanda are identified ?

28. And prostrating himself with folded hands, he said "O king, graciously grant me permission. I wish to become a mendicant to seek salvation; for separation is inevitable for me."

29. Hearing his words, the king shook like a tree struck by an elephant and, grasping him by his hands folded like a lotusbud, he spoke to him thus in a voice choking with sobs :—

30. "Refrain, dear one, from this intention. For it is not yet the time for you to give yourself up to *dharma*. For they say the practice of *dharma* in the first flush of youth, when the intelligence is still unbalanced, is full of dangers.

31. When a man is young with senses liable to excitement over the objects of sense and with resolution unfit to cope with the hardships of the life governed by vows, his mind shrinks back from the forest, especially so when he has had no experience of solitude.

32. But, O lover of *dharma*, it is now my time for *dharma*, after I have devolved the sovereignty on you, the cynosure of all eyes; but if you were forcibly to quit your father, O firmly courageous one, your *dharma* would become non-*dharma*.

33. Therefore give up this your resolve. Devote yourself for the present to the duties of a householder. For entry to the penance grove is agreeable to a man, after he has enjoyed the delights of youth."

30. *Mati* seems to be used here for *prajñā* (*AK.*, I, 154); it is so used at *S.*, iii. 11, where correct translation accordingly.

31. *Kutūhala* as an adjective is odd; query *kutūhalīndriyasya*? *Viveka* in its usual double sense.

32. It is uncertain whether in *b* we should read *lakṣa*, *lakṣya* or *lakṣma*; I prefer the last as closest in sound to *lakṣmī*. *Lakṣmabhūta* (*lakṣya*° wrongly in text) recurs *S.*, iv. 8. Cp. *Tantrākhyāyikā*, iii. 126, *lakṣmabhūto vanānāṁ . . . pādapendraḥ*. The meaning is doubtful here, perhaps 'the apple of my eye'. I follow T in taking the last line as a single sentence, not with Co. as two, which makes *vikrameṇa* difficult. Like ix. 66, and x. 25, this passage suggests the poet to understand by *vikrama* 'the wrong course of action', as opposed to *krama* 'the right course'.

34. Hearing these words of the king, he replied in a voice like the *kalaviṅka* bird's: "I will refrain from entering the penance grove, O king, if you will be my surety on four points.

35. My life is not to be subject to death. Disease is not to injure my health. Old age is not to impair my youth. Disaster is not to take away this my worldly fortune."

36. To his son, who had propounded a matter so hard of fulfilment, the king of the Śākyas made reply: "Give up this idea which goes too far. An extravagant wish is ridiculous and unfitting."

37. Then he, who was as grave as Meru is weighty, said to his father: "If this is not possible, then I am not to be stopped; for it is not right to hold back a man who wishes to escape from a house, that is being consumed by fire.

38. And seeing that separation is the fixed rule of the world, is it not better to make the separation myself for the

36. Read *atipravṛddhām* in *c* ? The text in *d* is doubtful and C not definite enough to help. *Krama* means 'the proper, natural order of things' (common in *Jāt.*, e.g. p. 85, 21 ; xvii. 9 ; xix. 1 ; xxxii. 42 ; and of the due order of the Buddha's life at *Mahāyānasūtrālaṁkāra*, xix. 79). *Akrama* could therefore mean 'impossible' as contrary to the natural order of things ('widernatürlich', *PWK*), but the more normal sense seems to be 'unfitting', e.g. *LV.*, ch. xxvi, 416, 16, *Śṛṅgāraśataka*, 51 (where coupled with *anucita*), *Abhiṣekanāṭaka*, i. 17. T's reading is clearly wrong and Co.'s difficult to translate.

37. As Speyer pointed out, *niścikramiṣuḥ* alone is grammatically possible.

38. In *a* T's *yadā* is typical of the poet's style. One can read either *nanu* or *na tu* in *b* and *c*, and *varaṁ svayaṁ* or *varaṁ tv ayaṁ* in *b* without affecting the general sense. C and FP are hard to translate ; the former has, 'Separation is the permanent law to which everyone is subject. It is better to go away in accordance with *dharma* than undergo destruction oneself in the future. If one does not go away in accordance with *dharma*, who can grasp (*dharma*), when death comes ?' This suggests *dharmeṇa* and *svayam* in *b*. FP is free, 'Since one sees all things to be definitely impermanent, the law of all that exists is separation ultimately. It is better to bear separation from one's earthly relations ; since death is about to come, the business must be accomplished'. In *c na tu* would be difficult, since Aśvaghoṣa only contrasts two nouns, not a noun and a verb, in the construction *varam . . . na*, and else-

sake of *dharma*? Will not death sever me helplessly, still unsatisfied before I attain my goal?"

39. When the lord of the earth heard this resolve of his son who was longing for salvation, he said "He shall not go", and arranged for an increased guard on him and for the choicest pleasures.

40. But after the ministers had duly instructed the prince according to the *śāstras* with respect and candour and his father with floods of tears had stopped him from going, then he entered his dwelling in grief.

41. The women looked up at him with restless eyes, like young hinds, as their earrings, swinging to and fro, kissed their faces, and their bosoms heaved with uninterrupted sighs.

42. For, bright as the golden mountain, he bewitched the hearts of the best of women, and captivated their ears, limbs, eyes and beings with his voice, touch, beauty and qualities respectively.

43. As the day departed then, he mounted, blazing like the sun with his beauty, to his palace, even as the rising sun climbs Meru, in order to dispel the darkness with the splendour of his self.

44. Going up to a chamber which was filled with incense of the finest black aloe and had lighted candelabra glittering

where he only uses *na* or *na ca*, not *na tu*, after *varam*. *Atṛpta* is probably equivalent here to *avītarāga*.

39. T takes *bhūyaḥ* with *d*, C apparently both with *d* and with the preceding words.

40. *Nidarśita* implies that they enlivened their discourses with illustrations from the Itihāsas and Purāṇas.

42. For *ātmabhāva*, see *attabhāva* 2 in Andersen and Smith's *Pali Dictionary*; the usage is common in Buddhist Sanskrit. Cp. *S.*, iii. 16, for the simile. *Timira* in the double sense of *tamas*.

44. I follow W who understands T as above. *Abhiruhya* requires an object, which can only be *garbham*, unless alternatively *vimānam* is supplied from the previous verse. To take this compound as referring to the couch makes nonsense; for its interior would not be filled with incense, and we should

with gold, he repaired to a splendid golden couch inlaid with streaks of diamond.

45. Then the noblest of women waited with musical instruments on him, the noblest of men, the peer of Indra, just as the troops of Apsarases wait on the son of the Lord of Wealth on the moon-white summit of Himavat.

46. But even those splendid instruments, like though they were to the music of the gods, failed to delight or thrill him ; the one desire of the saintly prince was to leave his house in search of the bliss of the highest good, and therefore he did not rejoice.

47. Thereon the Akaniṣṭha deities, supreme in austerities, taking cognisance of his resolve, all at once brought sleep there over the women and distorted the gestures of their limbs.

48. So one, as she lay there, supported her cheek on an unsteady hand, and, as if angry, abandoned the flute in her lap, dear though it was to her, with its decoration of gold leaf.

49. Another, lying with her bamboo pipe in her hands and her white robe slipping off her breasts, resembled a river with lotuses being enjoyed by a straight row of bees and with banks laughing with the foam of the water.

have to read something like °*gandhim* suggested by C's ' a seven-jewelled couch, fragrant with the best sandalwood '. *Garbha* in the sense of ' room ' seems unknown in classical Sanskrit except in compounds such as *prāsādagarbha*, but occurs in Pali (see P.T.S. *Pali Dict.* s. *gabbha*, Coomaraswamy, *Eastern Art*, III, 191, and also *Mhv.*, II, 316, 8).

46. The alternative of taking the second line as one sentence governed by *yataḥ* with *reme* in the sense of ' stopped ' is difficult. How T understood it is not clear, but it translates *reme* ' rejoiced ', as apparently did C. Aśvaghoṣa uses *yataḥ* elsewhere to introduce a final clause at the end of a verse, e.g. *S.*, v. 15, and xviii. 2.

47. The Akaniṣṭhas are the supreme deities of the Rūpadhātu, the highest of the five Śuddhāvāsa classes.

49. The bees are the flute, the lotuses the hands, the banks the breasts and the foam the white robe. Laughter is white in comparisons.

50. Similarly a third was sleeping, clasping her drum, as if it were her lover, with arms tender as the hearts of young blue lotuses, so that the bright golden armlets had met together.

51. So others, decked with ornaments of fresh gold, and wearing peerless yellow garments, fell down helpless with deep sleep, like *karṇikāra* boughs broken by an elephant.

52. Another lay, leaning against the side of a window with her beautiful necklaces dangling, and seemed with her slender body bent like a bow as if turned into the statue of a *śāla*-plucker on a gateway.

53. Another again had her lotus-face bowed down, thereby causing the jewelled earrings to eat into the lines of paint, so that it took the likeness of a lotus with its stalk half-curved, as it is shaken by a *kāraṇḍava* bird standing on it.

54. Others lay in the position in which they had sat down, and, embracing each other with intertwined arms decorated

50. For the idea cp. *Rām.*, v. 13, 44. I take *saṁgata*, which T omits, to mean that the arms were clasped so tight as to bring the armlets on both of them together. In *a* I follow T for *garbha* ; cp. the gloss *madhya* for *garbha* at *AAA.*, 182, 20.

51. A's reading in *c* seems to me hopeless. My text is sound palæographically and legitimately deducible from T. *Navahāṭaka* is presumably gold of a very light colour to resemble the whitish flowers of the *karṇikāra ;* the *pīta* clothes stand for the rubescent shoots.

52. The verse is an exact description of the statues below the crossbars on the Sanchi gateways, cp. Vogel, *Acta Or.*, VII, 208. This seems to be the only occurrence in literature of *bhuj* with *vi*.

53. It is difficult to choose between °*pattralekham* and °*gaṇḍalekham* ; many parallels to both. I have opted for A's probable reading, because at *S.*, iv. 23, *viśeṣakānta* replaces this word in a similar compound. *Gaṇḍa* is specially suitable too, because it means 'stalk' in Buddhist works (*Avadānaśataka*, II, 133, n. 4, *Mhv.*, I, 21, 9, and *Bodhisattvabhūmi*, 99), and among parallels I note *Aupapātikasūtra*, § 12, *kuṇḍal'ullihiyagaṇḍalehā*. In *c* perhaps *ivāgravakranāḍam*, comparing *S.*, v. 52 ; and in *d* there is much to be said for T's *cakampe*, *pa* in A being not unlike *śa*. The face is the lotus, the earring the bird, the neck the bent stalk.

54. If the verbs in this and the preceding verses mean 'appear beautiful', as the negatives show them to do in 57, 60 and 61, we should have the con-

with golden bracelets, appeared to have their bodies bent down under the load of their breasts.

55. Yet another clasped her mighty *parivādinī*, as if it were her friend, and rolled about in her sleep, so that her golden threads shook and her face had the pendent strings on her ears all disordered.

56. Another young woman lay, bringing her *paṇava*, whose beautiful netting had slipped from her armpit, between her thighs, like a lover exhausted at the end of his sport.

57. Others, though really large-eyed and fair-browed, showed no beauty with their eyes shut, like lotus-beds with their flowerbuds closed at the setting of the sun.

58. Another too had her hair loose and dishevelled, and with the ornaments and clothes fallen from her hips and her necklaces scattered she lay like an image of a woman broken by an elephant.

59. But others, helplessly lost to shame despite their natural decorum and endowment of excellent beauty, lay in immodest attitudes, snoring, and stretched their limbs, all distorted and tossing their arms about.

tradiction that the women were attractive in these attitudes. The last line of T has two syllables in excess ; *gnas-te* is clearly an interpolation.

55. T translates *yoktraka* by *śog-dril*, 'roll of paper', which W understands to be the palmleaf rolls worn in the ears, quoting Grünwedel, *Buddhistische Kunst in Indien* (1920), 187, n. 16. I know no authority in Sanskrit for this and it does not fit the use of the word at viii. 22 below, or *S.*, vi. 3.

56. The exact meaning and reading of the compound in *b* is uncertain, but °*pāśam* fits the simile better than °*pārśvam*.

58. The reference perhaps is to the dummies used to train elephants in killing, implied by *KA.*, ii. 32, and alluded to in the *HC.* (Cowell and Thomas's translation, 190 and 220, where understood rather differently). One Indian editor gives *kaṇṭhasūtra* the meaning it has in erotics. For *pratiyātanā* cp. *R.*, xvi. 17.

59. T is not clear in the second line, because *gya-gyu*, 'twisting', 'crooked', may correspond to *jajṛmbhire* in the sense *gātravināma* (cp. iv. 6) or to *ulbaṇam* ; in the latter case *gsal-bar* must be corrected to *glal-bar* with W. *Anulbaṇa* is common in the sense of 'modest', 'decent', of dress or behaviour. and *ulbaṇam* is to be understood accordingly.

60. Others looked ugly, lying unconscious like corpses, with their ornaments and garlands cast aside, the fastening knots of their dresses undone, and eyes moveless with the whites showing.

61. Another lay as if sprawling in intoxication, with her mouth gaping wide, so that the saliva oozed forth, and with her limbs spread out so as to show what should have been hid. Her beauty was gone, her form distorted.

62. Thus these womenfolk, lying in various attitudes according to their natures, family and breeding, presented the appearance of a lotus-pond whose lotuses have been blown down and broken by the wind.

63. When the king's son saw the young women lying in these different ways and looking so loathsome with their uncontrolled movements, though ordinarily their forms were beautiful, their speech agreeable, he was moved to disgust:—

64. "Such is the real nature of woman in the world of the living, impure and loathsome; yet man, deceived by dress and ornaments, succumbs to passion for women.

65. If man were to consider the natural form of woman and such a transformation produced in her by sleep, most certainly

60. Co. divides in *b* *visṛta-agranthana*; I follow T in dividing *visṛta-* *-āgranthana*, but the latter word does not seem to occur elsewhere. *Visṛta*, lit. 'come apart', very apt for a cloth knotted round the waist. In *c* *śukla*, as the mention of corpses shows, must mean 'the white of the eyes'; *animīlita*, lit. 'not disappeared'.

61. *Vivṛddhagātrī* is difficult; I translate according to T, which gives what is evidently the proper sense. The only analogous use of *vivṛddha* that I have noted is at *Avadānaśataka*, I, 265, 4, perhaps not quite on all fours.

62. My conjecture in *a* accounts by the likeness of *nva* and *nu* for A's omission of two syllables. *Anvaya* may mean 'training' here.

63. A and T agree in *valgubhāṣā* in *a* and are supported by C's 'their laughing words'; otherwise Speyer's *phalgubhāso* might have been preferable.

64. Cp. *S.*, viii. 48, and ix. 26.

65. The authenticity of this verse is a problem; for it is unlike C to omit so moral a statement and the repetition of the ending is clumsy. On the other hand the language and thought of *abc* at least are not unlike Aśvaghoṣa's.

his heedlessness in respect of her would not increase; yet, overcome by his impressions of her excellence, he succumbs to passion."

66. Thus he recognised the difference and there arose in him a desire to escape that night. Then the gods, understanding his purpose, caused the doors of the palace to fly open.

67. Thereon he descended from the palace roof, contemning the women lying there, and, having descended thence, he went out unhesitatingly to the first courtyard.

68. He awoke the groom, the swift-footed Chandaka, and addressed him thus: "Quickly bring the horse Kanthaka; I desire to depart hence to-day to reach deathlessness.

69. Since contentment arises in my heart to-day, and since

That FP should quote this verse and 64 together is in its favour, but its differing version of *d* is more appropriate and may represent the original of which the present text is a corruption. Notice the play on Sāṁkhya phraseology, *prakṛti*, *vikāra*, and *guṇa*. *Svapnavikāra* also means 'a transformation as unreal as a dream'. *Pramāda* is a term occurring frequently in *S.*, and implies heedlessness to the considerations that turn a man to the religious life. The distinction between *saṁkalpa* and *parikalpa* is a fine one; the latter is the conception formed by the mind about an object, impressions of which are presented to it by the senses. The former seems particularly to mean the impressions produced on the senses by an object; thus *S.*, xii. 5, *saṁkalpāśvo manorathaḥ* (the usual word being *indriyāśva*), and xiii. 35, *saṁkalpaviṣadigdhā hi pañcendriyamayāḥ śarāḥ*. *Guṇa* therefore is employed here in the secondary sense of 'object of the senses', as in a certain stage of Sāṁkhya development and in the word *kāmaguṇa*.

66. *Antara* also means 'opportunity' here, as well as the difference between *svabhāva* and outer adornment.

67. The accusative after *vinirgam* is odd. The first courtyard is the outermost one where the stables would be.

68. C expands and has equivalents for both *yiyāsā* and *pipāsā*; it may have had the latter, understanding it literally for *amṛta*, 'nectar', and metaphorically for *amṛta*, 'the deathless country'. The metaphorical use is unusual, not occurring in classical Sanskrit and employed only by Buddhists in compounds in a bad sense (=*tṛṣṇā*); so with some hesitation I keep A's reading.

69. For the construction of the relative cp. vii. 57, and *S.*, vi. 47, and remarks in the Introduction.

my resolve is fixed in my mind and since I have as it were a guide even in loneliness, most certainly the longed for goal has come into my view.

70. Since these women lay in my presence without regard to their own modesty or to respect for me, and since the doors opened of themselves, most certainly it is the time to-day for me to depart hence."

71. Then the groom accepted his lord's bidding, though he was aware of the purport of the king's orders, and, as if spurred on by another in his mind, he decided to bring the horse.

72. Then he brought for his master that noble steed, who was endowed with strength, mettle, speed and breeding. A golden bit filled his mouth and a light stall-blanket covered his back.

73. His chine and rump and fetlocks were long, while his hair, tail and ears were short and kept still; his back and flanks

70. In *d ito* perhaps is better, but *ato* corresponds more closely to A palæographically.

71. *Pareṇa* in *c* implies not only Co.'s 'higher power', but also 'as if incited by a foe' to do a deed that would damage the king, his master.

72. I follow Hopkins, who quotes the *MBh.*, in translating *śayyāstaraṇa*, but it may mean 'a blanket for riding on'.

73. It is difficult to determine the readings of this verse, as our authorities for the points of a horse are all much later and cannot be exactly reconciled. I have consulted *Bṛhatsaṁhitā* (*Br.*), lxvi, Jayadatta's *Aśvavaidyaka* (*J.*), ii. and iii. and Nakula's *Aśvacikitsā* (*N.*), vi, both in the Bibl. Ind., *Śukranīti* (*ŚN.*), iv. 7, ed. J. S. Desau, Bombay, 1912, and the *Śālihotraśāstra* (*ŚŚ.*), *sthāna* i, *adhyāya* 8, in I.O. MS. 2536 (=Eggeling 2762), ff. 41–48. The last is full and the best authority, but corrupt in reading. C has, 'With high . . . (? kingfisher ?), long mane and tail, short hair and ears, belly like a deer, neck like a *rājahaṁsa*, forehead broad, nose round like a gourd, throat like a dragon, kneecaps and breast square, true and sufficient marks of high breeding', which cannot be made to square exactly with the Sanskrit.

Each *pāda* for balance must consist of a single compound, therefore I accept in *b nibhṛtahrasva°*, which may have been T's reading. Further the text of *d* agrees with all authorities; note that the horses chosen by Nala for

were depressed and raised, and the point of his nose, forehead, haunches and chest were broad.

Ṛtuparṇa were *pṛthuprotha*, *MBh.*, iii. 2784. In *b* the Indian editors object to *pṛṣṭha* on the ground that a short back is not a good point in India. The only mention of the length of back is *J.*, iii. 25, *nātidīrgham* ; but I agree with them, partly because *nibhṛta* could not apply to the back, and partly because it is adequately dealt with in *c*. Their proposal to substitute *kukṣi* (*ŚN.*, iv. 7, 75, *hrasvakukṣikhuraśrutiḥ*) will not do, because *nibhṛta* does not apply, and no one else supports *ŚN.* in this point except a quotation from a certain Parāśara in the commentary (Viz. S.S. edn.) on *Bṛ.* ; *ŚŚ.*, 46*b*, and *N.*, vi. 16, do not give it in their lists of members that should be short. The former's list is *protha*, the ears, *puccha*, *daṣaṇau* (probably for *vṛṣaṇau*), the *kuṣṭikās*, the hoofs, *guda* and *meḍhra*. The obvious one to which *nibhṛta* applies and which is good palæographically is *puccha*, the bony part of the tail. *Bṛ.* also requires it to be short, but the hair of the tail should be long according to *ŚŚ.*, 45*b*, *puccham na* (corrupt for *ca*, as appears from the list of short points) *hrasvaṁ . . . dīrghavālam*. By *nibhṛta* I understand that the tail does not swish or the ears twitch (*acalitau*, *ŚŚ.*, 44*a*, and *nibhṛtordhvakarṇa*, *Śākuntala*, i. 8, quoted by Gawroński). The length of the hairs of the tail would account for C's divergence.

The other two compounds have several knotty points. The *trika*, the lower part of the backbone with the pelvic bones that join it, to which perhaps the corrupt word in C corresponds, should be *pṛthu* (*Bṛ.* and *ŚŚ.*), near enough to *pratata*, perhaps. *Pucchamūla* is defined *J.*, ii. 28, and in the commentary on *Bṛ.* (Viz. S.S. edn., 817), but not described anywhere ; C suggests that a word for neck should stand here, and *Bṛ.* and *ŚŚ.* require that member to be long. T may have read *pūrvamūla*, but it is difficult to see a word for ' neck ' in that and I have let A's text stand. *Pārṣṇi* is defined *J.*, ii. 2, as *khurasya pārśve*, but is nowhere described. T's reading of *pārśva* agrees with *ŚŚ.*, 46*b*, giving it as one of the eight long limbs. As this word occurs again in *c* and C gives no help, I have kept *pārṣṇi* and understand ' fetlock '. In *c* T is at fault in reading *vitatonnata*, for *ŚŚ.*, 45*a*, has *pṛṣṭhaṁ ca suvinītaṁ ca m īṣadbaddham samunnataṁ vinataṁ ca praśastaṁ syāt*, and *J.* and *ŚN.* also support *vinata*. It is quite uncertain if *kukṣipārśva* is to be taken as one word or two ; the application of *vinatonnata* in either case is difficult and it is not clear whether *kukṣi* stood at all in T, which understood only one thing to be mentioned in the *pāda*. C's ' belly like a deer ' has a curious parallel in *ŚŚ.*, 45*a* and *b*, where the two *pārśvas* are described as *mṛgavat* and the *kukṣi* as *mṛgasyopacitaṁ yathā*. In this uncertain state the verse must be left, till better MSS. of the *ŚŚ.* are forthcoming and critically edited.

74. The broadchested prince embraced him and patted him with a lotus-like hand, and ordered him in a gentle-toned voice, as if he were about to plunge into the middle of a hostile array.

75. "Oftentimes, I have been told, has the king, after mounting you, overthrown his enemies in battle. So act, O best of steeds, that I too may obtain the deathless stage.

76. Easy it is to find companions for battle, for the pleasure of acquiring the objects of sense and for the accumulation of wealth ; but hard it is for a man to find companions, when he has fallen into distress or attaches himself to *dharma*.

77. Moreover as for those who are companions in this world whether in action that brings defilement or in resort to *dharma*, undoubtedly they too, as my inner soul realises, take their share of the fruit.

78. Understand therefore, O best of steeds, this my departure from here to be connected with *dharma* for the benefit of the world, and strive with speed and courage in a matter which concerns your own good and the good of the world alike."

74. *S.*, viii. 34, *praviśanti ca yac camūmukham*, suggests on the strength of T the reading *dhvajinīmukhyam*.

75. The first line recalls Varāhamihira's remark in the passage quoted on 73 that a horse with these points is *nṛpateḥ śatrunāśāya*. In the second line *yathāvat* is difficult, but supported by T. As it stands, one ought to take *api* as initiating a wish, 'Would that I might, etc. ! Do that'; but this does not seem probable. The correct construction would be *yathā . . . tathā*, but *S.*, x. 57, has *yathā . . . tat*. If one must amend, Gawroński's *yathā tat* is better than Speyer's *yathā yat*. In *c* C's 'ford of *amṛta*' suggests *amṛtaṁ taram*, but *padam* is Aśvaghoṣa's regular word in this connexion.

76. *Avāpta* in *b* is best taken as a noun ; Gawroński compares *atyārūḍha* at *R.*, x. 42. For the sentiment, see *Jāt.*, xx. 31.

77. I cannot determine T's reading in *b*, and I do not agree with W that it read °*bhāgāḥ* in *d*.

78. For *parigam*, 'understand', cp. *S.*, v. 32, xvi. 42, and xviii. 43. The verse refers to the legend of Kanthaka's being reborn as a god.

79. Thus the best of men, beautiful in form and shining like black-tracked Agni, instructed the white horse, the best of steeds, in his duty as though he were a friend, and mounted him to go to the forest, just as the sun, blazing like fire, mounts a white autumnal cloud.

80. Thereon the good horse suppressed all noise, that would seem terrifying in the night-time or might awaken the attendants; his jaws were soundless and he silenced his neighing, as he went forth with steady steps.

81. Then the Yakṣas bowed down their bodies and bore up his hoofs off the ground with the tips of their hands, that thrilled with joy; their forearms were adorned with golden bands and their hands were like lotuses, so that they seemed to be throwing lotuses beneath him.

82. The city gatehouses, which were closed with gates furnished with heavy bars and which could not easily have been forced even by elephants, opened noiselessly of their own accord as the king's son passed along.

80. *Cakitavimukta*, lit. 'devoid of trepidation', so 'steady', explained by C 'did not rush impetuously'. T takes *cakita* to mean 'a frightening noise', which gives the correct effect but is not literal. A's correction in *d* may indicate °*kramair*.

81. A's reading in *b* seems correct, T being uncertain (*kamalān viprakṛtya*, or *viprakīrya* ?); the forearms presumably represent the stalks of the lotuses. In *d cakita* is difficult, and T takes it in the sense *tṛptau* of the *Dhātupāṭha*. The root significance is 'tremble', and one can tremble with joy as well as with fear, hence the extension of meaning. There are a few other passages where the same meaning is possible, *Padyacūḍāmaṇi*, ix. 65, *Vāsavadattā*, 287, where the commentator glosses *cakitā* with *tṛptāḥ saṁśayitā vā*, and the Khalimpur copperplate inscription, verse 11, *Ep. Ind.*, IV, 248. *Cakitagati* occurs at *Daridracārudatta*, iv. 6, in an uncertain sense.

82. T renders *pratolī* 'gatehouse', obviously right here and adequately authenticated. In *KA*. the word is used of constructions along the wall between towers for providing access from inside to the wall. References in P. K. Acharya's *Dictionary of Hindu Architecture*, s.v.; see particularly Vogel, *JRAS*., 1906, 539.

83. Then he went forth out of his father's city, in the firmness of his resolve quitting without concern his father, who was devoted to him, his young son, his affectionate people and his unequalled magnificence.

84. Thereon he, whose eyes were long like stainless lotuses born of the mud, looked back at the city and uttered a lion--roar: "I shall not be entering the city named after Kapila, till I have seen the further shore of life and death."

85. Hearing his words, the troops of the court of the Lord of Wealth rejoiced, and the hosts of gods with joyful minds foretold the fulfilment of his resolve.

86. Other heavenly beings of fiery forms recognised his purpose to be of the greatest difficulty and, like moon-beams piercing a rift in a cloud, produced a bright light on his frosty path.

84. In *a* it is perhaps not easy to reconcile palæographically the *vimala* indicated by C with A's *vikaja*, but it gives much the best sense. The word *paṅkaja* suggests that the poet is referring to the well-known comparison between the Buddha, who lives in the world but is not stained by the *lokadharmas* (such as the feelings detailed in 83), with the lotus, which springs from the mud but is unstained by the water. *Vimala* brings this out; cp. *S.*, xiii. 5 and 6. I do not think we should understand *praveṣṭā* as for *praveṣṭāsmi*. Though it is convenient here to translate it by the future, the agental form implies habitual action (*Pāṇ.*, iii. 2, 135) and therefore with a negative is more forcible than the future.

85. *Āśaṁs* in the sense 'foretell', which the context indicates as better than 'wish', is rare and only found in the active. Therefore *āśaśaṁsur asmai* ?

86. The heavenly beings with fiery forms recall the *aggikhaṁdhāni*, which Aśoka's practice of *dharma* caused his people to see (Fourth Rock Edict); cp. also *AK.*, III, 229, n. 3, and *AAA.*, 116, 19. Hence the epithet *svayaṁprabha* of the heavenly inhabitants at *S.*, x. 32, and cp. *MBh.*, xii. 6789ff. for the deities who live above the sun and moon and are *svayaṁprabha* and *agnivarcas*. A's *akuruta* is difficult; it can hardly be held that the poet is illustrating an unknown grammatical rule allowing the use of a singular verb with a plural subject. *Adadhata* will not do, because T shows *kṛ* and it is the fiery bodies of the deities that cause the light. Joglekar takes *akṛṣata* to *kṝ*, 'scatter', but the form is known to the grammarians from *kṛ* also; and I take it to the latter.

87. But that steed, like a steed of the Sun, speeding on as if spurred in mind, and the prince travelled very many leagues, before the stars in the sky grew discoloured with the dawn.

87. That T is right in taking *harituraga* to mean the sun, not Indra, is shown by the mention of Aruṇa in the second line. T's reading in *b* means 'as if speeding on (or, considering) as if transformed by mind', for which I cannot find the Sanskrit. A's reading is not good and is a reminiscence of 71 above. The construction in the second line is unusual; *pāda c* seems to be a kind of accusative absolute of time covered. For the combination of *paruṣa* and *aruṇa* cp. *Bṛhatsaṁhitā*, iii. 38, *paruṣarajo'ruṇīkṛtatanu* of the sun; also the curious use of *paruṣa* at *Vikramorvaśīya*, v. 4. The verb with two subjects and attracted into the singular by the nearer has parallels, viii. 33 below, *S.*, viii. 2, *Manu*, ix. 23, and *Daridracārudatta*, i. 18.

CANTO VI

The Dismissal of Chandaka.

1. Then the world's eye, the sun, rose in a moment, and the best of men saw the hermitage of the descendant of Bhṛgu.

2. When he saw it with the deer sleeping in perfect trust and the birds sitting at peace, he felt, as it were, rested and as if the goal were attained.

3. In order to eschew arrogance and to show honour to asceticism, and in accordance with his politeness he dismounted from the horse.

4. And alighting, he patted his steed, saying, "Your task is accomplished", and well-pleased he said to Chandaka, bedewing him as it were with his eye :—

5. "In following this horse, whose speed is like that of Tārkṣya, you have shown, good friend, both loyalty to me and your own prowess.

6. Although I am entirely given up to other matters, I am gripped to the heart by you, who possess equally this devotion to your master in such a degree and also capability.

3. C and T agree in giving *vismaya* the sense of 'arrogance', which the context demands. C has in *c*, 'keeping his deportment'.

5. Tārkṣya is a name for Garuḍa, to whom speedy horses are often compared, e.g. *Divy.*, 444, *MBh.*, viii. 687, *Karṇabhāra*, 13, *Vikramorvaśīya*, i, p. 9.

6. W understands *hṛdi* to refer to Chandaka's heart, but T does not require this and *grah* takes the locative of the place caught hold of. The conjecture in *d* is almost certain. Gawroński's *īdṛśī* would do but is not so close to A. I suspect T of having read *īdṛśasya eva,* two syllables short, corrupted from an original *īdṛśas sa* or *īdṛśaś śa*, *ssa* and *śśa* being liable to misreading with a *ya* as second member.

7. A man, though not devoted, may be capable, or though not capable, may be devoted; but it is hard to find in the world a man like you who is at the same time loyal and capable.

8. Therefore I am well-pleased with this your noble action in displaying towards me this feeling, which takes no count even of possible rewards.

9. Who would not be favourably disposed to a man in a position to reward him? In the opposite case even kinsfolk for the most part become strangers.

10. The son is cherished to continue the family; the father is honoured to obtain maintenance. The attachment of the world is always due to some motive. No feeling that this or that person is one's kin subsists without a cause.

11. Why speak many words? In short, you have done me a very great kindness. Return with the horse. I have arrived at the desired spot."

12. With these words the mighty prince unloosed his ornaments and gave them to Chandaka, whose mind smarted with sorrow, in order to do him a benefit.

8. C and T's *parāṅmukhaḥ* in *d* is essential for the sense; in fact Chandaka was more likely to be punished than rewarded for his action. If we read *dṛśyate* in *c* with A, *'pi* in *d* perhaps should be amended to *hi*, but I do not like the omission of *te* or its equivalent in the line.

9. For *janībhavati*, against which A has an old marginal gloss *apara*, cp. the use of *jana* at *S.*, xv. 31.

10. There seems to be no parallel to this use of *svatā*; Co. understands *asvatā*, 'unselfishness', but T divides as in the text. Gawroński takes *svatā* =*mamatva* of 48 below. The literal meaning seems to be the feeling that something is one's own, and here the context demands that the something should be one's relation to others. For W's translation of this verse, see his note on the Tibetan of ix. 10.

11. If it were not for C, I should have supposed T's *gnas* in *d* to be a mistake for *nags*, the equivalent of A's reading.

12. *Anuśaṁsa*, the regular form, is indicated by T, but *ānuśaṁsa* and *ānuśaṁsā* also occur in Buddhist Sanskrit; the Pali form *ānisaṁsa* supports A's spelling. For the meaning cp. the use in the *Divy.* (see index s.v.); C

13. Taking from his diadem the blazing jewel, which performed the function of a light, he stood like mount Mandara with the sun on it, and uttered these words :—

14. "With this jewel, Chanda, you must make repeated obeisance to the king, and in order to abate his grief you must in full confidence give him this message from me :—

15. "I have entered the penance grove to put an end to birth and death, and not forsooth out of yearning for Paradise, or out of lack of affection or out of anger.

16. Therefore you should not grieve for me, since I have left my home for this purpose. For a union, however long it has lasted, in time will cease to be.

17. And since separation is inevitable, therefore my thoughts turn to salvation, in order that there may be no more severing from my kindred.

18. You should not grieve for me, who have gone forth to leave grief behind. It is rather the slaves of passion, enthralled by those sources of grief, the loves, for whom grief should be felt.

19. And since this, they say, was the firm determination of our ancestors, grief should not be felt for me who am travelling along the hereditary road.

20. For when a man passes away, there are heirs to his wealth ; but heirs to *dharma* are hard to find on earth or do not exist at all.

renders 'comfort'. As appears from the opening scene of the *Śākuntala*, it was not proper to enter a hermitage wearing ornaments.

14. Co. takes *amuktaviśrambham* to refer to the king, but T rightly applies it to Chandaka, who has every reason to be afraid of delivering the message.

15. A's *jarā*° for *janma*° is a natural corruption ; at xii. 17, *janma* is almost indistinguishable from *janā*. For the second line *Jāt.*, xxxii. 41.

17. My conjecture in *d* is palæographically sound and necessitated by the sense ; A's °*ādibhiḥ* is improbable.

19. Formichi's defence of *dāyādabhūta*, 'divenuto dell' erede' and so 'ereditario', is contrary to Aśvaghoṣa's use of *bhūta* in compounds.

21. Should it be argued that this person has gone forth to the forest at the wrong time, I reply that there is no such thing as a wrong time for *dharma*, seeing how uncertain life is.

22. Therefore my determination is that the supreme good must be sought by me this very day. For when death is present as our adversary, what reliance can be placed on life ?"

23. In such wise, my good friend, should you speak to earth's guardian and also strive that he should not even think on me.

24. You should also tell the king that I am lacking in virtue. Lack of virtue causes the disappearance of affection ; when affection has vanished, there is no sorrowing."

25. On hearing these words Chanda was overcome with anguish and, folding his hands, replied with a voice strangled with sobs :—

26. "At this disposition of yours, O my lord, which must cause distress to your kinsfolk, my mind sinks down like an elephant in the mud of a river.

27. To whom would not such a determination as this of yours cause tears, even if his heart were of iron, how much more when it is faltering with love ?

28. For this delicacy of limb, fitted only for lying in a palace, is not compatible with the ground of the penance grove, covered by sharp blades of *darbha*-grass.

29. But as for my bringing this horse to you after hearing your resolve, it was some divine power, O my lord, that forcibly caused me to do it.

30. For if I had been in command of myself, how could I, on knowing this your resolve, have brought you the horse, the bale of Kapilavāstu ?

26. T's *chu-boḥi ḥgram-na* (*nadītīre*) is so obviously a mistaken spelling for *ḥdam-na* (°*paṅke*), that I have not included it among the variants. Similarly *ḥgyur-ba* (*bhavati*) may be a mistake for *rgud-pa* (*sīdati*), or, as it is preceded by an unnecessary *ḥdi* (*idam*) not in the Sanskrit, *ḥdi ḥgyur* may be a corruption of *yi-mug*, which would give the metaphorical sense of *sīdati*.

31. Therefore, O mighty prince, you should not desert, as a nihilist the good Law, your loving aged father, who yearns so for his son.

32. Nor should you forget, like an ingrate kind treatment, the queen, your second mother, who exhausted herself in bringing you up.

33. You should not abandon, like a coward the sovereignty he has obtained, the virtuous princess, mother of a young son, devotedly faithful to her husband and of illustrious lineage.

34. You should not abandon, like a vicious man his excellent repute, the young son of Yaśodharā, worthy of praise and best of the cherishers of fame and *dharma*.

35. Or if, O my master, you are determined to abandon your father and your kingdom, you should not abandon me. For your feet are my sole refuge.

36. I cannot leave you in the forest, as Sumantra did Rāghava, and go to the city with burning heart.

37. For what will the king say to me, if I return to the capital without you? Or what shall I say to the women of your household, since I am in the habit of seeing what is proper.

34. In *b* T is ambiguous; I think it agrees with C in reading *varam*, whereas W takes it to indicate *vara*. The former is the better, as Chandaka usually calls the prince by some formal title of respect such as *bhartṛ* or *nātha*.

35. I follow Gawroński in taking *bandhu* as 'father' here, a meaning occurring several times in canto ix.

36. C is undoubtedly right in keeping the traditional form of Sumantra's name. The simile foreshadows the poet's imitation in canto viii of the account of Sumantra's return to Ayodhyā.

37. The meaning of *ucitadarśitvāt* is uncertain and the renderings of my predecessors unconvincing. *Darśin* means a person who sees or is in the habit of seeing, physically or mentally, as in *dīrgha°* and *doṣa°*, and *ucita* can only signify 'what is proper' or 'what is wonted'. The word may be applied either to Chandaka, in which case, as Böhtlingk pointed out, it signifies knowledge of the proprieties, or to the palace women, when we might understand it similarly or else take it as expressing Chandaka's not being accustomed to appear before the ladies except in attendance on the prince. T, despite W's

38. As for your saying that I am also to tell the king of your lack of virtue, am I to say what is untrue about you, as about a sinless sage ?

39. Or if with halting tongue and shame in my heart I should so speak, who would believe it ?

40. For only the man who would tell of, or believe in, the scorching power of the moon, would tell of, or believe in, the existence of faults in you, who know the faults.

41. To desert the affectionate ill befits him who is always compassionate and ever feels pity. Turn back and have pity on me."

42. The best of speakers heard these words of the grief-stricken Chanda and spoke to him, self-possessed and with the utmost firmness :—

43. " Quit this affliction, Chanda, over parting from me ; separation is the fixed law among corporeal beings, in that they are subject to different births.

44. Should affection lead me not to quit my kinsfolk of myself, still death would part us one from the other against our wills.

45. My mother bore me in her womb with pains and great longing. Her efforts have been fruitless. What am I to her now or she to me ?

translation, is ambiguous, but C possibly took the last view, ' Or, if all the palace people reproach me, with what words can I reply to them ? ' Or had it a different reading ?

40. Possibly we should read *doṣajñaḥ* in *c* ; T is ambiguous, and A often omits *visarga*. The propriety of a groom so addressing his master is open to question and is not supported by the formal use the poet makes of this style of address elsewhere.

43. *Niyataḥ* is perhaps better in c. The idea is that expressed in *S.*, xv. 32 ; those who are kinsfolk in one birth are separated from each other in the next birth. For *nānābhāva* cp. *Majjhima*, III, 242 (=*Saṁyutta*, II, 97).

44. If C's text had had *mumukṣayā*, it is not likely he would have omitted it ; and T's text with the opposition of *svayam* and *avaśān* is stronger than A's.

46. As birds collect on the roosting tree and then go their separate ways again, so inevitably the union of beings ends in their parting.

47. And as the clouds come together and depart asunder again, so I deem the meeting and severance of creatures that draw breath.

48. And since this world is in a state of continuous separating, therefore the feeling that 'this is mine' is improper with regard to a coming together that is transitory as a dream.

49. Trees are parted from the colouring of their leaves, though it is connate with them. How much more then must there be a severance of one thing from another that is separate from it?

46. For the first line cp. *S.*, xv. 33, and for *vāsavṛkṣa* note in translation on *S.*, i. 54.

47. Gawroński would read *matau* in *d* as more in accord with Aśvaghoṣa's syntax. I doubt this; he uses a singular verb with a double subject several times.

48. A difficult verse. *Vipralabhya* is used in the sense of *vipralambha*, the 'parting' of lovers, an extension from 'deception', 'disappointment'. T gives the literal sense of 'deceive' and also the derived sense of 'separate'; and C renders by *kuai* (Giles 6326), used in this text for 'separate', e.g. vii. 47. *Yāti* with the gerundive implies continuous or habitual action, possibly here in a passive sense, 'is being continually separated', as is apparently the construction at *S.*, vii. 15. A's *paṛasparam* is difficult and T's curious *phyir-na*, while apparently indicating the text reading, would perhaps be better amended to *phyi-ma*. C translates 'separating of their own accord'. For *mamatva*, see note on *svatā* on verse 10 above; C, as I understand it, has 'It is not proper to reckon relatives as mine'. I follow Schmidt in taking *samāgame* as dependent on *mamatvam*. It should be noted that FP quotes this and the two preceding verses and follows them with seven more verses on the same subject, which are not in our text, though the simile of verse 49 is included in them. This is the only case where in a quotation by FP of a passage from this poem verses not to be found in our text are added, and it is hard to account for them. A, T and C agree in the extent of the text, but verse 49 is laconic in argument, as C evidently felt, and perhaps the author of the original of the FP or someone else expanded the passage to make it clear, without the addition being received in the standard text.

50. Since such is the case then, my good friend, be not afflicted; go your way. But if your affection tarries, still go and then return again.

51. And you should say to the folk in Kapilavāstu, who keep regard for me, "Quit your love for him and hear his resolve.

52. Either, he says, he will quickly come back, after destroying birth and death; or, lacking in right effort and failing to reach the goal, he will perish." "

53. On hearing his speech, Kanthaka, the finest of steeds, licked his feet and shed scalding tears.

54. With his webbed hand, which was marked with svastikas and bore the wheel sign on the palm, the prince stroked Kanthaka and spoke to him as if he were his comrade of like age:—

55. "Do not shed tears, Kanthaka; you have displayed the qualities of a good horse. Be patient; this your toil will soon bring forth its fruit."

56. Then he resolutely took from Chanda's hand the sharp sword which had a jewelled hilt and was decorated with gold inlay, and drew it from the scabbard, as if he were drawing a snake from a hole.

51. A's reading in *a* is nonsense, and T and C are clearly right in indicating that °*kṣepaṁ* is an inversion of °*pekṣaṁ*; cp. the similar variant in Co.'s ix. 71. It would be closer palæographically to A, if we amended *byas* to *bcas* in T, i.e. *cāsmāsu sāpekṣaṁ*. Kapilavāstu is preferable to °vastu; cp. verse 30 above and the MSS. of *S*.

52. I accept C's reading in *b* as the best; cp. note on verse 15 above. For *ārambha*, see *S*., xiv. 22.

53. Cp. *Mhv.*, II, 166, and, for the next verse as well, the description in *Vimānavatthu*, 81.

54. According to tradition Kanthaka was born on the same day as the Buddha, hence *vayasyavat* is significant.

55. The absence of *iti* is unusual; *bhaved iti* or *bhavatv iti* ?

56. How did Co.'s MSS. come to have T's reading, not A's, in *b* ? C has 'the prince', but cannot be relied on in such matters. The practice of letting down a bait on a line into a snake's hole and drawing the snake out by it is said still to persist in India.

57. Having unsheathed it with its blade dark blue as a blue lotus petal, he cut off his decorated headdress with the hair enclosed in it and tossed it with the muslin trailing from it into the air, as though tossing a goose into a lake.

58. And the inhabitants of Heaven caught it reverently, as it was thrown, with the intention of worshipping it, and the divine hosts paid it due adoration in Heaven with celestial honours.

59. But when he had divorced his ornaments and sheared off the royal splendour of his head, he looked at his garments with their embroidery of golden geese, and in his steadfastness longed for a hermit's robe.

60. Then an inhabitant of Heaven of purified nature, knowing his thoughts, took on the form of a hunter of deer and

57. C's 'dark hair' implies that he construed *utpalapattranīlam* with °*keśam*, but it is better to take it with T to the sword and it thus gives point to the unusual *niṣkāsya*, i.e. he causes as it were the bud of the lotus to open out to show the blue petal. On the verse generally, see Coomaraswamy, *JRAS.*, 1928, 822. The difficulty lies in *aṁśuka*, which may mean silk cloth or may, as T takes it, be equivalent to *aṁśu*; parallel ambiguities occur elsewhere, but only when *aṁśuka* is at the end of a compound. By itself it is probably not equivalent to *aṁśu*, as Apte gives it, but is *aṁśu* with *ka* added for the purpose of ending a compound. Cp. *R.*, x. 9, *Śiśupālavadha*, v. 52, vi. 27, etc. *Vāsavadattā*, 92, *Kād.*, 72. If it is from *aṁśu*, it cannot refer to the actual threads of the cloth, for they were not cut. The Buddha's hair was bound up in the headdress and he cuts through the hair below it. *Aṁśuka* is therefore to be understood as (1) 'cloth', i.e. the muslin wrapped round the framework of the headdress like a modern pagṛī, and (2) *aṁśu* in the sense of rays of light only.

59. Compare *b* with the more elaborate imagery of *S.*, v. 51-52. *Vipravāsa* comes primarily from *vas*, 'cut', as *pravāsyamāna* does in that passage (see notes in text and in addenda of translation), and secondarily implies 'banishment', the sense T gives it; for the latter cp. *Vinaya*, III, 198, 263. The implication of *śrī* is too obvious to need explaining. For the embroidery of geese Leumann compares a Jain passage, and Gawroński *Kumārasaṁbhava*, v. 67; see also *SP.*, iii. 82, *HC.*, ch. vii, p. 53, l. 12, *R.*, xvii. 25.

60. *Viśuddhabhāvaḥ*, i.e. a Śuddhāvāsa deity, as C expressly states.

approached him, wearing ochre-coloured clothes. To him the scion of the Śākya king spake :—

61. "Your holy ochre-coloured robe, the mark of a seer, does not go with this murderous bow. Therefore, good sir, if you are not attached to it, hand it over to me and accept this one of mine."

62. "O giver of desires", the hunter said, "although by this garment I cause the deer to trust me near them and then kill them, yet if, O Śakra-like prince, you have any use for it, take it then and give me the white one."

63. Then with the greatest joy he took the hermit's dress and gave up the silk raiment. But the hunter, assuming his heavenly form again, went to heaven with the white clothes.

64. Then, when he departed thus, the prince and the groom marvelled greatly and straight entertained all the more reverence for the forest dress.

65. Then he dismissed the weeping Chandaka and, wearing the ochre robe and bearing the fame of his steadfastness,

62. T indicates *nihanmi* in *b*, not *nihanyām* ('I can kill'), which is perhaps closer to A palæographically. *Ārāt* apparently must mean 'near' here, a well authenticated meaning, but its use with *viśvāsya* is a little difficult and perhaps it should be taken with *nihanmi* ; or could it mean 'giving them confidence from far off'? Its signification at *S.*, v. 13, is also doubtful. The point is that, as countless authors down to Rudyard Kipling tell us, deer are not afraid of holy men and associate with them ; the robe is intended to deceive them into thinking the hunter a ṛṣi. *Aupapātikasūtra,* §74, oddly enough mentions a class of ascetic known as *migaluddhaga*. T's *kāmasārāt* seems hopeless.

64. *Āśu* expletive ; cp. *S.*, vi. 9, and note in text.

65. The reading in *b* is uncertain, though T and C show clearly that A's *saṁvid* stands for a word meaning 'wearing'. *Saṁvid* can hardly have this sense, and *saṁvṛt*, better palæographically, seems more forced, if to be taken as equal to *kāṣāyasaṁvṛta* of *LV.*, ch. xxiv, 382, than the *saṁbhṛt* which I have preferred. *Dhṛtikīrtibhṛt* is apparently C's authority for his 'carefully considering and scanning his steps', that is, *dhṛti* is equivalent to *śīla*, which prescribes this method of walking ; *dhṛti* corresponds in fact to *śīla* at *S.*, iii. 11. In *d uḍurāja* should stand for the moon (cp. *Kād.*, 72), not for the sun,

moved majestically to where the hermitage was, resembling the monarch of the stars enveloped in a sunset cloud.

66. Then when his master went thence to the penance grove in his discoloured clothes and free from desire for rule, the groom flung up his arms and, wailing bitterly, fell to the ground.

67. Looking back once more, he wept aloud and clasped the horse, Kanthaka, with his arms. Then in despair he lamented again and again and started for the city with his body, but not with his mind.

68. Sometimes he brooded and sometimes he lamented, sometimes he stumbled and sometimes he fell. So journeying in grief under the force of his devotion, he performed many actions on the road in complete abandon.

as the word *saṁdhyā* would lead one to expect ; C mentions both and so does not commit himself.

66. Did T take °*vāsasi* to *vas*, ' shine ' ? *Vivarṇa* should not be translated ' mean ' ; it refers to the *kāṣāya* colour, cp. *S.*, v. 53, and *Jāt.*, xii. 19, and 122, 9.

CANTO VII

Entry into the Penance Grove.

1. Then since his state of longing for the forest had freed him from all attachments, Sarvārthasiddha left the weeping tear-faced Chanda and proceeded to the hermitage, overpowering it with his beauty, as if he were a Siddha.

2. With the gait of the king of beasts the prince entered that arena of deer, himself like a deer, and, though he had given up his royal trappings, the majesty of his person was such as to hold the eyes of the anchorites.

3. For the wheel-bearers, accompanied by their wives and standing with their yoke-poles in their hands, gazed, just as they were, in their excitement on him who was like

1. *Sarvārthasiddha* is probably to be understood in its actual sense as well as a proper name, and *siddha* in *d* means not only the mythical ṛṣis referred to also at *S.*, x. 6, but a man who has reached enlightenment.

2. T may understand *mṛgarāja* as 'king of the deer', but C translates 'lion'. The point of *mṛgavat* in *b* is not obvious; perhaps it refers to the colour of the prince's dress as being like that of a deerskin (or of a lion ?), so accounting for FP's substituting for *b* that he was 'clad in a *kāṣāya* robe only'.

3. For the following description, see Eggers, *Das Dharmasūtra der Vaikhānasas* (Göttingen, 1929), pp. 18ff., but it is difficult to determine the class referred to in this verse, as they cannot be definitely identified with any of the various kinds of ascetics who are accompanied by their wives. It is natural to take *cakradhara* as meaning those who are branded with the discus of Viṣṇu and to understand *yuga* as a 'carrying-pole', which wandering ascetics carried (*Dīgha*, I, 101, and Eggers, *op. cit.*, 88, note on iii. 8) and which explains the comparison to oxen with heads bowed down under the yoke; the practice of branding is called *cakradhāraṇa* at *Sarvadarśanasaṁgraha* (ed. A.S.S.), 53. The word *cakradhara* occurs for a kind of ascetic at *MBh.*, xiv. 429, and Utpala on *Bṛhajjātaka*, xv. 1, gives it as a synonym of *caraka* (cp. *Bṛh. Ār. Up.*, iii. 3, 1). So *cakradhara* may be the same as *cakracara* mentioned at *MBh.*,

Indra, and did not stir, like beasts of burden with half-bowed heads.

4. And though the Brahmans, who had gone out to fetch fuel and had returned with their arms full of wood, flowers and *kuśa* grass, were pre-eminent in austerities and had their minds fully trained, yet they went to see him and did not go to their huts.

5. And the peacocks rose up in delight and uttered cries as at the sight of a black rain-cloud; and the restless-eyed deer and the ascetics who grazed like deer let their grass fall and stood facing him.

6. And although the cows, that gave milk for the oblations, had already been milked, yet such was the joy produced in them at the sight of him, the lamp of the Ikṣvāku race, shining like the rising sun, that their teats flowed again.

7. "Is he the eighth Vasu or one of the Aśvins come down to earth?" Such were the voices raised loud by the sages there in their amazement on seeing him.

xiii. 6493–6497, and perhaps also the same as *cākrika* of *ib.*, xii. 2646. The commentary on the latter glosses *cākrika* with *śākaṭika*. The *KA*. also alludes to *cakracaras* at iv. 4 (see Meyer's translation, 330, n. 3, and additional note, p. 816) and vii. 17, 63, at the latter of which their *śakaṭas* are mentioned. *Pañcarātra*, i. 9, *cakradharasya dharmaśakaṭīm*, has probably something else in mind. These passages suggest that Co. may have been right in taking *yuga* literally as 'yokes', but if so, in view of C's 'making the weights carried on their shoulders to be held by their hands' and of the fact that yokes are not ordinarily held in the hand, the reference may be to ascetics who drew carts like oxen. As I am not certain of the sense, I leave the translation ambiguous. *Tathaiva* seems pointless, and the translation 'just as they were' open to doubt; read *tatraiva*?

4. T's reading in *a* may well be correct. In *b* it takes *pavitra* in the sense of 'pure' and I may be wrong in following Co.'s rendering. With the reading *havir* in *a*, *pavitra* should perhaps be translated 'clarified butter', a meaning so far known only to the later lexica.

5. *Unnam* is often used of clouds, but C and T are both agreed against A's reading.

6. T is two syllables short in *c*, omitting the word for 'cows'.

8. For like a second form of the chief of the gods, or like the magnificence of the world of moving and stationary beings, he illumined the entire grove, as if he were the sun come down of his own accord.

9. Then, when those hermits duly honoured and invited him, he in return did honour to the supporters of *dharma* with a voice like a cloud full of rain.

10. Then he, who desired liberation, traversed the hermitage which was crowded with folk, desirous of Paradise and working to accumulate merit, and steadfastly he viewed their various austerities.

11. And when the benign one had viewed the various austerities of the ascetics in that penance grove, he thus addressed a certain anchorite who was following him, in order to ascertain the truth :—

12. "As I have never seen a hermitage till to-day, I am unacquainted with this method of *dharma*. Will you therefore kindly explain to me what is your resolve and to what point it is directed ?"

13. Then the twice-born, who took delight in austerities, described in due order to the bull of the Śākyas, a very bull in prowess, the particularities of the austerities and the fruit thereof :—

14. "Uncultivated food, that which grows in the water, leaves, water, fruit and also roots, this is what the sages live

8. This seems to be the only occurrence in literature of Lekharṣabha as a name for Indra, though appearing in the lexica as early as the *Amarakośa*.

9. I have preferred *sāmbho'mbu°* in *d*, because it is closer to A and because repetitive expressions such as *sajalajalada* seem to occur more in less stylish work.

11. *Vikāra* in *a* may imply 'extravagances'.

13. Or *ṛṣabhavikramāya*, 'stepping like a bull'. Though C and T agree against A in *d*, I do not consider their reading usable.

14. *Salile prarūḍham* refers to *śaivāla* (Eggers, *op. cit.*, 22). C has for *b*, 'Some eat roots, stalks and leaves ; others again eat flowers and fruit', omitting *toya*.

on in accordance with the scriptures; but there are various separate alternatives.

15. Some live like the birds by what they can pick up from the ground, others graze on grass like the deer, and others pass their time with the snakes, turned into anthills by the forest wind.

16. Some gain their subsistence by laborious pounding with stones, others eat only what has been husked by their own teeth, and some again cook for others and meet their needs on anything that may be left over.

17. Some with their coils of matted hair soaked with water twice offer oblations to Agni with sacred texts; others plunge into the water and dwell with the fishes, their bodies scored by turtles.

18. With such austerities accumulated for the due time, they win by the higher to Paradise, by the lower to the world of men. For bliss is obtained by the path of suffering; for bliss, they say, is the ultimate end of *dharma*."

15. The second line implies no doubt that they lived on air, C's 'air-inhaling snake-ṛṣis', and one could construe *vartayanti vanamārutena* as 'feed on the forest-wind'. But as I understand it, the wind piles up earth round the motionless ascetics lying on the ground, turning them into anthills, and thus giving them an additional resemblance to snakes who are often mentioned as living in anthills. For *vanamāruta*, *Bodhicaryāvatāra*, viii. 86.

16. The *aśmakuṭṭas* are described in *a* and the *dantolūkhalikas* in *b*. C's version of *a* and T's 'what they pick up with their teeth' in *b* are therefore inferior.

17. The exact point of the first line escapes me; is the reference to those who live in wet clothes in winter? But a parallel passage at xxiii. 22, suggests a reference only to bathing three times and making oblations twice a day. The reading in *d* is doubtful and T may be preferable. C is no help ('fish-ṛṣis practising water-dwelling').

18. For *c* cp. *Majjhima*, I, 93, and II, 93, and *Milindapañha*, 243. Whether one should read *duḥkham* as suggested by A or T's *sukham* in *d* depends on the meaning given to *mūlam*. The point is settled by *Manu*, xi. 235, *tapomūlam idaṁ sarvaṁ daivamānuṣakaṁ sukham*; so the commentary on *KS*., i. 2, 47,

19. The child of the lord of men listened to these and the like statements of the anchorites; though he had not yet reached the perception of reality, he was not satisfied and said these words in an undertone to himself :—

20. "Seeing that asceticism in its varied kinds is suffering by nature, and that the reward of asceticism is Paradise at the highest, and that all the worlds are subject to change, truly this labour of the hermitages is to small effect.

21. Those who forsake their dear kindred and worldly pleasures to practise restraint for the sake of Paradise, truly they, when parted from its delights, will travel again to far greater bondage.

22. And he, who by the bodily toils known as austerities strives for the continuance of being in order to indulge passion, does not perceive the evils of the cycle of existence and seeks by suffering nothing but suffering.

23. Living creatures are ever in fear of death and yet they aim by their efforts at a fresh birth; and with the persistence of active being death is inevitable. Therefore they drown in that very thing of which they are afraid.

24. Some enter into labour for the sake of this world, others undergo toil for the sake of Paradise. Truly living beings, making themselves miserable in their hopes of bliss, miss their goal and fall into calamity.

25. It is not indeed that I blame the effort, which leaves aside the base and is directed to a higher object, but rather the wise with a like toil should do that in which the need for further effort ceases.

dharmamūlaḥ smṛtaḥ svargaḥ, and cp. *BhNŚ.*, xxii. 142, and a quaint skit *Mattavilāsa*, verse 8. FP's 'therefore suffering is the cause of all pleasure' leaves its reading uncertain.

19. *S.*, viii. 14, repeats *d* almost verbatim in a different metre.

21. *Viprayuktāḥ* I take to mean 'when parted' from the joys of Paradise, cp. *RL.*, 156. *Gantukāma* merely expresses the future.

26. But if mortification of the body in this world is *dharma*, then the body's pleasure is contrary to *dharma*; if pleasure is obtained in the hereafter by means of *dharma*, then *dharma* in this world bears as its fruit what is contrary to *dharma*.

27. Inasmuch as it is under the direction of the mind that the body acts and ceases to act, therefore it is the taming of the mind only that is required. Apart from the mind the body is nothing but a log.

28. If merit is held to derive from purity of food, then merit accrues also to the deer and even to those men who are excluded from the rewards of *dharma* and on whom by some fault of their destiny wealth has turned its back.

29. But again, if it is the intention that is the cause of acquiring merit in the case of suffering, should not the same intention be applied in the case of pleasure? Or if the intention is no criterion in the case of pleasure, is not the intention no criterion in the case of suffering?

30. Similarly for those who sprinkle water on themselves to purify their deeds, acting on the assumption that it is a *tīrtha*, in that case too their satisfaction is restricted to the feelings; for water will not make a sinner pure.

31. For if whatever water has been touched by the virtuous is claimed as a *tīrtha* on earth, then it is only the virtues that I regard as the *tīrtha*, but beyond all doubt the water is just water."

26. *Sukha* is defined by the Abhidharma as 'bodily pleasure' in contrast to *saumanasya*, 'mental happiness'

27. *Manas, cetas* and *citta* are synonyms in this verse.

28. I take the reference in *c* to be to those who under the rules of caste could not practise the higher forms of Brahmanical religion. The implication, explicitly stated by C, is that they are too poor to afford anything but food such as hermits live on.

30. The heart is the seat of the feelings; hence the translation in *c*. If T's *'sya* is right in *c*, we must amend in *ab* to *yaḥ . . . spṛśaty . . . pravṛttaḥ*.

31. Cp. the play on the meanings of *tīrtha* in *S.*, i. 8.

32. As he thus discussed various points with provision of many arguments, the sun went to its setting. Then he entered the grove, where was the holy quiet of austerities and where the trees were discoloured by the smoke of the oblations.

33. It was in full activity, a workshop as it were of *dharma*, with the transference elsewhere of the blazing sacrificial fires, with its throngs of seers who had completed their ablutions and with the shrines of the gods humming with the din of prayers.

34. And there he, who resembled the night-making orb, passed several nights, examining the austerities, and after considering them all and forming a judgement on them, he departed from that place of austerities.

35. Then the hermits followed him, their minds drawn to his beauty and majesty, just as great seers follow *Dharma*, as it withdraws from a land overrun by infidels.

36. Then he saw the ascetics with their fluttering coils

32. *Tapaḥpraśānta* was translated by Co. as if *praśāntatapaḥ*, which has been generally rejected except by Speyer. The point is settled by the use of *śānta* at *S.*, i. 27.

33. The same points are selected for the description of a hermitage in *S.*, i. 11. Gawroński was the first to see the real sense of the verse, but *karmānta* is not exactly a 'forge', but a 'workshop', a sense common in *KA.*; Medhātithi on *Manu*, vii. 62, defines it as including sugar mills, distilleries and the like. It is an extension of meaning from the sense common in Buddhist Sanskrit and Pali of 'business', 'occupation', to the place where the business is carried on. The reference here is to a place where gold or other metal is worked by heating it, quenching it with water and hammering it (cp. *S.*, xv. 66–69, and xvi. 65-66). *Agnihotra* in the sense of 'sacrificial fire' is very rare. For *koṣṭha* cp. *koṣṭhaka* in *KA.*, ii. 4.

34. The third *pāda* is hopelessly corrupt. I translate T which cannot be put back into Sanskrit (*paricchidya* the most probable), but C is perhaps nearer the original reading. For the context requires something approaching the adverse judgement on austerities in *S.*, iii. 2. Possibilities are *sarvaṁ pratikṣipya tapaś ca matyā* and *sarvaṁ pratikṣepyam ataś ca matvā*, but it is not a case for putting a conjecture into the text.

36. I have retained the difficult °*khelān* in *a*, as T has it also, but should prefer Hultzsch's °*celān*. It may however be merely a way of writing °*kheḍān*,

of hair and clothes of bark, and in deference to their austerities he stopped by a beautiful auspicious tree on the roadside.

37. Thereon the hermits approached the best of men and stood round him, and the oldest of them addressed him respectfully with soft conciliatory words:—

38. "When you arrived, the hermitage became as it were full, with your departure it turns as it were into a desert. Therefore, my son, you should not quit us, as the loved life should not quit the body of one who wishes to live.

39. For in front stands the holy mountain Himavat, frequented by Brahman seers, royal seers and celestial seers; and by its neighbourhood these very austerities of the ascetics become multiplied in efficacy.

40. So too all round are holy pilgrimage places, very stairways to the sky and frequented by the celestial seers and the great seers who are self-controlled and whose beings are compact of *dharma*.

41. And from here again it is proper to pursue only the northern direction for the sake of the highest *dharma*, but it would not be fitting for the wise man to move even a single step towards the south.

'clothes', unfortunately not adequately authenticated. T in fact inserts another word *zur-phud* (=*śikhā*) into the compound and may thereby indicate the Sanskrit word *khela* by *rol-pa* and the meaning by the other. Aśvaghoṣa uses *anurodha* for 'liking', 'having a friendly feeling for', *S.*, xiii. 48; hence the translation. To render *anurudhyamāna* 'considering' or 'approving' would go against the context.

37. T appears to be corrupt in *d*, having *ḥdi rab-tu ḥdi* for the text's *iti*.

40. For *b* cp. *CII*, III, 44, *svargasopānarūpam*. In the last line of T *chen-po-rnams* is probably copied from the previous line in place of *daṅ-ldan-rnams*, which would give the text. Here again Co.'s MSS. have T's reading against A.

41. The idea of the north being auspicious and the south inauspicious is so frequently mentioned in the Upaniṣads and elsewhere that references are unnecessary.

42. But if you do not wish to live in the penance grove, because you have seen here one who neglects the rites or is impure from having fallen into an adulterated *dharma*, mention it and just be pleased to dwell here.

43. For we here desire to have you, who are as it were a depositary of asceticism, for our companion in asceticism. For to abide in company with you who are like Indra would bring success to Bṛhaspati."

44. When the chief of the ascetics had thus spoken in the midst of the ascetics, he, the chief of the wise, declared his inward feelings, inasmuch as he had made a vow for the annihilation of existence :—

45. " At such a display of their feelings towards me on the part of the upright-souled sages, the supporters of religion, whose delight in hospitality makes them like one's own kindred, my joy is extreme and I feel highly honoured.

46. To put it in a word, I am as it were bathed by these affectionate words, which touch my heart, and, as I am a novice in *dharma*, my pleasure now shows itself doubled.

47. When I reflect that I am about to go away, leaving you thus engaged, who are so hospitable and have shown me

42. T divides *saṁkīrṇadharmā=apatito*. I understand *yāvat* as=*tāvac ca*, this use of the relative being not uncommon in Aśvaghoṣa.

43. *Nidhāna* means ritually the ' putting down ' of the sacred fires, and *tapaḥ* is perhaps to be understood therefore as the ' heat ' of a fire. In *d* Lüders' reading is better than the text, but not adequately substantiated by T.

46. Co., followed by the other translators, understands that the joy felt by the Buddha when he first grasped the idea of *dharma* is redoubled ; but I do not see how this can be extracted from the Sanskrit, which as it stands means that the Buddha as a novice in *dharma* (Gawroński first pointed this out as the meaning of *navagraha*) is particularly gratified at his treatment, as if he were already a leader of ascetics. I am not quite sure however that the text is in order and should like to amend *saṁprati* to *taṁ prati* (i.e. towards *dharma*), which would be clearer and agree more closely with C's ' Hearing what you say, still more I take pleasure in reverence for *dharma* '.

such very great kindness, I feel indeed as much grief as I did when quitting my kinsfolk.

48. But your *dharma* aims at Paradise, while my desire is for release from rebirth and leads me not to wish to dwell in this grove. For the *dharma* of cessation from activity is apart from the continuance of active being.

49. It is not for dissatisfaction on my part or for an offence committed by anyone else that I am going forth from this grove; for you are all like the great seers, in that you take your stand on a *dharma* that conforms with the primeval ages."

50. Thus the prince spoke words, gracious and full of meaning, very gentle yet determined and dignified; and the ascetics then felt the highest degree of reverence for him.

51. But a certain twice-born there, who was in the habit of lying in the ashes, tall and with his hair in a tuft, clothed in tree-bark, with reddish eyes and a long thin nose, and carrying a waterpot in one hand, spoke to him thus:—

52. "Wise sir, noble in sooth is your resolve, in that, young as you are, you have seen the dangers of birth; for he who, on a right consideration of Paradise and final salvation, decides for final salvation, only he truly exists in reality.

53. For those who are possessed by passion desire to go to Paradise by means of all those sacrifices, austerities and

48. I follow Co. in *d*; alternatively, 'the *dharma* of *nivṛtti* is destroyed by *pravṛtti*'.

50. I know of no suitable sense for T's *garbhitam*. *Garvitam*, if the original reading, would seem to be treated as a formation from *guru*; but I can find no exact parallel for the meaning I give it, except viii. 57 below.

51. *Bhasmaśāyin* shows that he was a Śaiva ascetic. In the second line A is much rubbed and of the third letter of *d* only the loop of *ka* is visible.

52. The exact meaning of *so 'sti*, which, though rewritten and difficult to read in A, is corroborated by T, is uncertain in *d*; C omits the *pāda*.

53. There can be no doubt that the phraseology here is deliberately Sāṁkhya; *rāga* is for *rajas*, and *sattva* for the first *guṇa*. Arāḍa is a Sāṁkhya teacher of *mokṣa* according to canto xii, and it is to be remembered that Buddhism had its counterpart to the theory of the *guṇas*, as elaborated by pre-

restrictions ; but those who have absolute goodness battle with passion as with an enemy and desire to attain liberation.

54. If therefore this is your settled purpose, go speedily to Vindhyakoṣṭha. There dwells the sage Arāḍa, who has gained insight into final beatitude.

55. From him you will learn the path of the *tattvas*, and, if it pleases you, you will follow it. But since your resolution, I see, is such, you will depart, rejecting his theory also.

56. For this face of yours has a straight high nose, large long eyes, a red lower lip with white sharp teeth, and a thin red tongue ; and as such, it is sure to drink up to the very last drop the ocean of what is to be known.

classical Sāṁkhya, in its doctrines of the three roots of good, *kuśalamūlāni*, which correspond to *sattva*, and of the three roots of evil, *akuśalamūlāni*, which correspond to *rajas* and *tamas*. The last finds no place here, because the verse deals only with those who use effort for some good purpose. This interpretation is borne out by *B.*, xxvi. 10, which describes as the Sāṁkhya view that *rajas* plus *tamas* leads to evil, and *rajas* plus *sattva* to good.

54. Did Sāṁkhya teachers specially frequent the Vindhyas ? There was a Sāṁkhya teacher known as Vindhyavāsin, and the Sāṁkhya system, or a special school of it, is called *Vindhyavāsitā* at *Tattvasaṁgraha*, pp. 22, 27.

55. *Tattvamārga* could also mean the 'path to truth', but the reference must surely be to the twenty-five Sāṁkhya *tattvas*, enumerated xii. 18–20. The construction of the second line is obscure. *Tavaiṣā* is impossible, because of *bhavān* and the verbs in the third person. But if we read as in the text, *eṣā matiḥ* means presumably the Buddha's *mati*, and this corresponds to C, which Takakusu translated (*NGGW*, 1896, 2), '(but according as) I perceive thy inclination, I fear that thou wilt (or, it will) not be at rest'. It would perhaps be better to understand, 'As I see your resolution, so you will fear that it (sc. Arāḍa's doctrine) is not *śānta*'. It is best to take *paśyāmi* as an interjection, in which case, if it were not for the order of the words, one would naturally construe *matis tathaiṣā yathā yāsyati*. But we have a similar odd construction in viii. 19, of *yathā* without a correlative in the sense of 'since', 'in view of the fact that', and I translate accordingly. The alternatives are to understand a concealed conditional, 'But if your decision (or, wisdom) is such as I see it, then you will depart, etc.' or to take *matiḥ* as the subject of *yāsyati* ; for this last may be a simple auxiliary here, as Cappeller takes it, the one certain instance of this use in the poet being at xiii. 5.

57. But it is clear from your unfathomable depth, from your brilliance and from your bodily signs, that you will obtain on earth a position as teacher, such as was not won even by the seers of the golden age."

58. Then the king's son replied, "Very well", and, saluting the seers, proceeded on his way; and the hermits too, after showing him due honour, entered the penance grove.

57. For this use of the relative without a correlative in the sense of 'in view of', 'having regard to', see the Introduction.

58. There does not seem to be any exact parallel to this use of *anuvidhā*; C understands *pradakṣiṇīkṛtya*.

CANTO VIII

Lamentations in the Palace.

1. Then, when his master had gone to the forest in self-renouncement, the dejected groom did his utmost to repress his grief on the road; nevertheless his tears did not cease to flow.

2. But he now took eight days to traverse the same road, which by his lord's command he had covered in a single night with the horse; for he was ever thinking of the separation from his master.

3. And the horse Kanthaka, powerful as he was, travelled onward with flagging feelings and all his fire lost; and though decked with ornaments as before, yet without his master he seemed to have lost his beauty.

4. And turning back towards the penance grove, he

1. For *d* cp. *Jāt.*, viii. 42, where Gawroński would amend *saṁcikṣipe* to *saṁcikṣiye*, but *saṁcikṣipe* would do there, 'grew less'. *Cikṣipe* cannot have this meaning, and *cikṣiye* must be taken to be certain on the basis of C and T.

3. The text of the first line is uncertain. I would have accepted T's reading in *a* as giving the best sense, if C did not seem to postulate some such text as that I have adopted with slight modification from A. In *b* T evidently read *taṭāma bhāvena* as a single compound of which the second part was *abhāvena*; therefore the first part cannot end in *a*, which makes it hard to restore. *Tena* in *d* seems to require a specific mention of the prince in the first line and *bhāvena* by itself is difficult; C gives no help. One possibility, too speculative for insertion in the text without further support, is *svabhartra-bhāvena*, palæographically sound and which might have been deliberately altered on the ground of *bhartṛ* appearing three times in the two preceding verses.

4. For the accusative after *abhimukha*, to which Prasada objects, see the instances quoted in the *PW*.

neighed loudly and often, in a mournful tone. And, though overcome with hunger, he took no pleasure on the road in grass or water as before and would not take either.

5. Then in due course they approached the city named after Kapila, which seemed empty like the sky without the sun, now that it was deserted by the magnanimous prince, whose being was concentrated on the weal of the world.

6. That very same city-grove, though still gay with lotus-covered waters and adorned with trees in full bloom, was now like a forest and no longer brilliant with citizens; for all their happiness had gone.

7. Then those two came slowly to the city as if going to a funeral bathing rite, while melancholy men wandered round them, depressed and with eyes struggling with tears, and seemed to stop them from proceeding.

8. And when the townsfolk saw the arrival of the pair without the bull of the Śākya race and that they were walking with drooping bodies, they shed tears in the road, as happened of old when the chariot of Daśaratha's son returned.

9. Thereon the folk burst into tears and followed behind Chandaka along the road, saying in the access of their grief,

5. W thinks verses 5 and 6 interpolations, the matter being covered by 7. But verses 4 and 7 do not join well, and verse 6, describing the grove outside the city, which, as Formichi points out, is the same as that of canto iv (*tasya* referring to *puram* in verse 5), shows that *upajagmatuḥ* means 'approached', not 'arrived at'; I see no adequate ground for doubting the verses. At first sight T seems to read in *d* as in the text plus *ḥbras-med* (*vṛthā*, *aphala*) and might therefore have had the nonsensical *vinā vṛthā*; but as the same locution appears in 37*c* below, it is probably only a roundabout way of distinguishing *vinākṛta* from *vinā*.

7. For *apasnātam* cp. *Rām.*, ii. 41, 20; see also *Therīgāthā*, 469 (misunderstood in *Psalms of the Sisters*). The simile recurs at *B.*, xxiv. 63.

8. T reads *ṛṣi* for *ṛṣabha* again at xii. 11. Note *vinā* separated from the word it governs.

9. *Manyu* may mean 'wrath' here (so Co.) or 'sorrow' (so T). The people's words can be understood as a single sentence, as T construes it, but the position of *asau* speaks for Co.'s division, which I follow.

"Where is the king's son, the delight of the town and kingdom? You have carried him off."

10. Then he said to those devoted people, "It is not I who am deserting the king's son. On the contrary, it was by him in the uninhabited forest that for all my tears I and the householder's garb were dismissed together."

11. When the people heard those words of his, they came to the conclusion that it was in truth a superhuman deed; for they did not restrain the tears that fell from their eyes and blamed the state of mind which arises from the fruit of the self.

12. Thereon again they said, "This very day let us go to the forest, where he, whose stride is as that of the king of elephants, has gone. Without him we have no wish to live, like embodied beings, when the senses have decayed.

13. This city without him is the forest, and that forest

11. The significant word in the text is *patad*; for, while A might read *patad vijahruḥ* with T, to talk of shedding falling tears is pleonastic and bad style. Therefore one must read *patad dhi*, and the particle *hi* shows the second line to be an explanation of or a statement in support of the first. This leads me to reject Lüders' conjecture in *b*; I do not think C really supports it and the sentiment of *vismaya* according to verse 50 below is inconsistent with tears. The first line implies that they thought the prince's deed too difficult to imitate, and the second gives the reason; they could not stop weeping and their minds were still dominated by the idea of self, the prince being *nirmama* (verse 1; cp. notes on vi. 10, 48). *Atha* in the next verse implies a change of mind on further thought. T, who had a MS. which, as other passages prove, did not distinguish between *dva* and *ddha*, seems to have been a syllable short in *c* and not to have understood *d* at all. My explanation is, subject to the different readings adopted, on all fours with that of Formichi, who saw the right sense but could not extract it satisfactorily from the text before him.

12. Query *mṛgarājavikramaḥ* in *b*? The translation of the second line follows Prasada; Co. construes *vigame* as governing *śarīriṇām*. C may have possibly understood by *indriya* the Abhidharma term *jīvitendriya*, but is not clear.

13. Windisch, i, 301, n. 2, points out that, besides the quotation of this verse by Ujjvaladatta, Rāyamukuṭa on the *Amarakośa* attributes it to the

possessed of him the city. For without him our city has no beauty, like Heaven without the lord of the Maruts when Vṛtra was slain."

14. Next the women betook themselves to the rows of windows, thinking that the prince had come back again, and when they perceived that the horse's back was empty, they shut the windows again and wailed aloud.

15. But the lord of men, who had undertaken religious observances for the recovery of his son and whose mind was afflicted by the vow and by grief, muttered prayers in the temples and performed various rites suitable to his intention.

16. Then the groom, leading the horse, entered the palace, with the tears welling from his eyes and overcome with grief, as if his master had been carried off by an enemy warrior.

17. And Kanthaka, penetrating into the royal dwelling and looking round him with tear-streaming eye, cried out with a loud voice as if proclaiming his suffering to the people.

18. Then the birds which lived in the palace and the favourite horses which were tethered near by gave back the charger's cry, supposing the prince to have returned.

Buddhacarita. Ujjvaladatta's text is not an improvement, *tat* in *b* being required to correspond to *idam* in *a*. It is also quoted by the *Durghaṭavṛtti* (*ZII*, 1932, 6), substituting *visarjitam* in *a* and *praśobhate* in *c*. The verse is cited to illustrate *diva* as a separate stem, an epic use. The separation of *vinā* from its object occurs also at 7 and 12 above (cp. *Ślokavārttika*, i. 2, 142). *Rām.*, ii. 33, 23-24, for the sentiment. The killing of Vṛtra being equal to the murder of a Brahman, Indra hid himself after it in the waters, *MBh.*, v. 299ff.

16. According to the *PW*, *yudh*, 'warrior', is confined to the *MBh.* and the *Harivaṁśa*.

17. *Puṣṭena* in *c* is odd but seems to be supported by C and 40*b* against T's *dīptena*, which means the shrill sound of an animal that is inauspicious and is so used at *MBh.*, v. 5307 (for the origin of this sense, see *ib.*, iv. 1290, and v. 4699). T's *bsal* is for *gsal*, used in the *Gaṇḍīstotra* for *paṭu* of a sound. *Pūrṇena* is not possible, as it implies an auspicious sound.

18. I have accepted Kern's emendation in *b*, because the only authority given by the *PW* for *śaṅkita* in this sense is *Rājataraṅgiṇī*, iii. 288, where the correct meaning is 'fearing'.

19. And the people who frequented the precincts of the queens' apartments were deceived by superabundant joy and thought from the way the horse Kanthaka neighed that the prince must be entering the palace.

20. The women rushed hopefully out of the buildings, like lightning flashing from an autumn cloud; they had been fainting with grief and now from the excess of their delight their eyes darted this way and that to see the prince.

21. Their hair was hanging down, their silk attire filthy, their faces without collyrium and their eyes struggling with tears; thus the women no more shone with their toilet unperformed than do the stars paling at night's close.

22. Their feet were without anklets and not stained red, their faces were without earrings and their necks unadorned, their hips, full by nature, were held in by no girdle, their breasts without their ropes of pearls looked as if they had been robbed.

23. The women's eyes flooded with tears, as they saw only Chandaka and the horse without their master; with downcast faces they wept, like cows lowing in the midst of the jungle when deserted by the herd-bull.

24. Then the lord of the earth's chief queen, Gautamī,

19. The wording of *a* is unexpected, but I would not accept Gawroński's ingenious conjecture without some authority for it. A's reading seems impossible (it should be *cañcantaḥ*) and it writes *ca* and *va* so much alike that it may have meant *vañcitā*.

20. The autumn cloud and the palace are both white; hence the comparison.

22. I can make nothing out of A's *ārjavakarṇikaiḥ*, unless it could mean 'with the tips of their ears unadorned', i.e. without the usual flowers placed in them. In *d* T divides *ahāra-yoktraiḥ*, not *a-hārayoktraiḥ*; if *yoktra* means a 'string', this is not good sense.

23. My translation of *nirāśrayam* may be thought surprising; but the master is the *āśraya* of his servants and we get the same use of the word at xiii. 71, certified by T and C. Cp. my remarks on *Jāt.*, xxiii. 21, at *JRAS*, 1929, 84.

24. C translates *d* 'like a golden plantain-tree blown down by a violent wind', which suggests a different reading and a simile that fits with *nipapāta*.

as affectionate for the son she had lost as a fond she-buffalo who has lost her calf, flung up her arms like a golden plantain--tree with leaves tossing about, and fell weeping to the ground.

25. Some of the other women, bereft of their brightness and with drooping arms and shoulders, seemed to become unconscious through despondency; they wailed not, they dropped no tears, they sighed not, they moved not, there they stood like figures in a picture.

26. Other women, losing self-control, swooned from grief for their lord, and with streams pouring down their faces their eyes watered their breasts from which the sandalwood was banished, as a mountain waters the rocks with its streams.

27. Then with the women's faces whipped by the water from their eyes the royal dwelling resembled a pond with dripping lotuses whipped by rain from the clouds at the time of the first rains.

28. As creepers waving in the wind strike themselves with their own tendrils, so these noble women beat their breasts with jewelless lotuslike hands, whose veins were hidden and whose fingers were plump and well-rounded so as to leave no interstices.

29. And thus, as their close-set upstanding breasts shook under the blows of their hands, those women looked like rivers

25. This verse was utilized by Kālidāsa for *R.*, iii. 15, and is quoted at *Kāvyamīmāṁsā*, p. 18.

26. It is not certain what verb T had in *c*, perhaps the unauthenticated *vyasikṣata*; the correct form of the perfect in earlier Sanskrit is *sisicire*, in later *siṣicire*. The comparison is against the rules, as *dharādharaḥ* should be nom. pl. f. to correspond with *striyaḥ*. T may have had *dharādharāt*, or, if *nas* is corrupt for *rnams*, *dharādharāḥ*.

27. For the simile cp. *S.*, v. 52, and vi. 36.

28. Co. and Schmidt understand *nirantaraiḥ* 'falling incessantly', which would require the reading *nirantaram* against T as well as A.

29. For *sahita*, which Kern rightly equated with *saṁhita*, see T's reading in iv. 29, and note there; both it and *unnata* apply to the ducks, though this is not brought out in the translation. In the simile the rivers are the women,

with pairs of Brahminy ducks, which are made to tremble by the lotuses when blown about by the forest wind.

30. And as they hurt their breasts with their hands, so they hurt their hands with their breasts. There the women, all feelings of pity dulled, made their hands and breasts inflict mutual pains on each other.

31. But then up spoke Yaśodharā, her eyes reddened with anger, her voice choking with the bitterness born of despair, her bosom heaving with sighs, and tears streaming down with the grief she was enduring :—

32. " Where, Chandaka, has he gone, my heart's desire, after deserting me at night against my will while I slept ? My mind trembles, when both you and Kanthaka have returned, while three went forth together.

33. Why do you weep here to-day, you brute, after doing me an ignoble, unkind, unfriendly deed ? Hold back

and the Brahminy ducks the breasts ; these birds are too big to sit on lotuses, as Co. and Schmidt translate. The lotuses are the hands which do the beating, a stock comparison ; the wind blows the heads of the lotus-flowers about so that they hit the ducks. The verse would have given no trouble but for the use of the ambiguous *kampita,* which implies here ' made to shake ' when beaten ; T spoils the point by translating ' trembling like lotuses when blown about by the wind '. I see no ground for amending *vanānilā°* (*navānilā°*, Böhtlingk, *ghanānilā°*, Kern). Bhartṛhari uses the comparison in part in the description of a woman as a river, *Śṛṅgāraśataka*, 81, *prottuṅgapīnastanadvan-dvenodyatacakravākamithunākārāmbujodbhāsinī . . . nadīyam* ; cp. also *R.*, xvi. 63.

30. Tasteless hyperbole to show the firmness of the breasts ; cp. *S.*, iv. 35. In *d* T's *le-lo-can-ma brtse-med stobs-med-ma-yis* seems to indicate a double saṁdhi, *abalādayālasāḥ*, both unnecessary and improbable.

31. I cannot solve the puzzle of T's reading in *b* ; *sbrel,* literally *saṁsyūta,* may stand for *saṁnaddha.* There is nothing to choose between *saṁbandhi* and *saṁbaddha.* It looks as if *vigāḍha* here and in verse 76 means ' grievous ' ; T translates *brtan-pa* (*sthira*) here and *tshabs-che,* ' very great ', ' dangerous ' at the other.

32. Note *upāgate* in the singular with two subjects.

your tears, be contented in mind. Tears go ill with that deed of yours.

34. For through you, his loving obedient faithful good companion, always doing what is proper, my lord has gone never to return. Rejoice, by good fortune your toil is rewarded with success.

35. Better is it for a man to have a wise enemy than a silly friend, who is skilful only in the wrong way. For your imprudence and so-called friendship have wrought great ruin for this family.

36. For these princesses with their ornaments laid aside and their eyes reddened and stained by incessant tears are sorely to be pitied like widows whose splendour has departed, though their lord is still in existence as much as are the Himalayas or the earth.

34. Yaśodharā means the verse ironically, but it is literally true to a Buddhist. Chandaka merits praise for his work, and the prince has gone to obtain final *nivṛtti*, cessation from *pravṛtti*.

35. In *a* T would naturally be understood as reading *narendrasya* and omitting *vicakṣaṇa*, but probably *dbaṅ-po* should be taken to represent the latter. *Ayogapeśala* is divided by Co. and Schmidt *a-yogapeśala* ; I prefer with T and Formichi to divide *ayoga-peśala*, 'skilful in impropriety', 'in the wrong means', with the hint of the second meaning 'skilled in disunion', 'in parting people'. For *c* C is against T's reading ; the lexica know *dhruva* in the sense of *pāpa*, but the only instance in literature is *Bṛhatkathāślokasaṁgraha*, xx. 392, *suhṛddhruvaḥ* (wrongly divided in text *suhṛd dhruvaḥ*). As the MSS. of that work come from Nepal, the correct reading there however may be *suhṛdbruvaḥ*.

36. In *a* *Himavanmahīsame* has several meanings, primarily as in the translation ; Kapilavāstu being in the foothills, one is at liberty to imagine Yaśodharā enforcing the point with a gesture towards the snowpeaks, whose visibility to all present would back up her assertion. Secondarily it implies, as C has it, 'as reliable as the snowy mountain, as steadfast as the great earth'. It may also mean, as Formichi takes it, 'on the plain (i.e. the upland) of the Himalayas', Chandaka having left the prince in the terai under the mountains (see vii. 39).

37. And these rows of pavilions seem to weep together with the women, on separation from him, casting up their pinnacles for arms and heaving long sighs with their enamoured doves.

38. This horse Kanthaka too must have been desirous of my ruin in every way ; for, when everyone was asleep at night, he thus carried off my treasure from here, like a jewel-thief.

39. Seeing that he is certainly able to stand up even to the strokes of the arrows that fall on him, not to speak of the whip, how was it he went off under fear of the fall of the whip, taking with him my good fortune and my heart together ?

40. To-day the base creature neighs loudly, filling as it were the royal abode ; but when he was carrying away my beloved, it was then that the wretched horse was dumb.

37. *Viṭaṅka* means not only a ' dovecot ', which would be dubious here with one mention of pigeons already in *b*, but also an excrescence from a building shaped like one ; see references s.v. and s. *kapotapālikā* in Acharya's *Dictionary of Hindu Architecture.* In *b* T translates *prasakta* ' incessant ' as an epithet of *nisvana*, so too Co. and Formichi ; this makes a very uncomfortable, though not absolutely unparalleled, compound, and it is better to take it as an epithet of *pārāvata*. Schmidt, who does so, understands it as the pigeons who live in the pavilions from the sense ' fixed ', which is difficult. My translation explains the reason for the long sighs. The verse is intended to overtrump *Rām.*, ii. 43, 33, and iii. 58, 40.

38. W holds that T read *eva* for *eṣa* in *b* ; I am not convinced, for this would leave *de* without equivalent in the text.

39. In *a* T suggests *hayaḥ samarthaḥ kila* as possible ; *ha* and *da* being liable to confusion, A's *yadā* could have arisen from a misunderstood transposition of the characters of *hayaḥ*. Kern's amendment in *c* is probable in itself and apparently supported by T ; one could translate also ' did he then go off under fear, etc.' *Śrī* may mean the ' royal fortune ', not merely Yaśodharā's ' good fortune '.

40. *Nirvāhayati* in *c* is difficult, as there is no authority for *nirvahati* in the sense of ' go out ' ; but the context forces the translation on us. The verb is used for its double significance, *nirvahana* meaning *mokṣa* ; therefore unconsciously Yaśodharā says, ' when he caused him to obtain *mokṣa* ' ; cp. ix. 38, and note thereon.

41. For if he had neighed and so woken up the people, or if he had made a noise with his hoofs, or if he had made the loudest sound he could with his jaws, such suffering would not have come on me."

42. When Chandaka heard the princess's words, with their undercurrent of lament and with their syllables strangled with sobs, he looked downwards and, folding his hands, he muttered this answer in a low voice, hardly intelligible through his tears.

43. "Princess, you should not disparage Kanthaka nor should you be angry with me. Know us to be entirely guiltless. For the god among men, Princess, departed like a god.

44. For, although I knew the king's command, I was compelled as it were by certain divine beings and speedily brought him this horse. Thus too I felt no weariness in following him along the road.

45. This best of steeds too, as he went along the road, did not touch the ground with the tips of his hoofs, as if he were held up off from it in the air ; similarly his mouth was restrained as if through divine power, so that he did not make any noise with his jaws or neigh.

46. Seeing that, when the king's son went forth, the gate was thrown open at that time of itself and the darkness of night was broken through by what seemed to be the sun, this therefore too must be understood to have been of divine ordering.

47. Seeing that the people by thousands in the palace and city, observant though they were of the king's command, did

42. Böhtlingk objected to *itīha* ; it is certified by T and recurs xii. 26. *Paridevanā*° is also possible in *a*. In *c* C seems to understand °*kalaḥ* as from the verb *kal*.

43. In *c* *samavehi* demands an object, so that we must take *svaḥ* as equivalent to *nau*, presumably to avoid the ugly combination *anāgasau nau* ; I know no parallel, but cp. the use of *asmi*, i. 67.

45. This and the next verse imply that the deities were invisible to Chandaka.

47. This verse and 48 are not in C, which does not usually omit such matter. The only reference to the guard, evidently alluded to here, is the

not awake at that time but were overcome by sleep, this therefore too must be understood to have been of divine ordering.

48. And seeing that a garment, suitable for forest wear, was handed over to him at the time by a denizen of Heaven, and that his headdress was borne off, when thrown into the sky, this therefore too must be understood to have been of divine ordering.

49. Therefore with regard to his departure you should not, Princess, consider us two to be at fault. Neither I nor the horse acted of our own will; for he went forth with the gods in attendance."

50. When those women heard thus of his wondrous departure with its accompaniment of many gods, they were lost in amazement as if their grief had gone, but they became the prey of mental fever because of his taking up the mendicant's life.

51. Then Gautamī, with eyes restless with despair, lost her self-control and wailed aloud in her suffering, like an osprey that has lost its nestlings; she swooned and with tearstrewn face exclaimed :—

---

bare mention in v. 39 ; late legend pleased itself with retailing their numbers in an exaggerated fashion foreign to Aśvaghoṣa. If Chandaka had spoken the next verse, could Gautamī four verses later have suggested that the prince's hair, when cut off, was cast on the ground ? Both verses should be regarded with suspicion.

48. *Samaye*, 'by agreement', i.e. in exchange for the prince's clothes ?

49. 'To consider some one to be at fault' is either *doṣeṇa gam* (*Rām.*, iv. 21, 3, *MBh.*, i. 7455, vi. 3645, and xi. 743 ; cp. *Mudrārākṣasa* (ed. Hillebrandt), 95, l. 4, where we should read with the MSS. *doṣeṇāvagantum*) or *doṣato gam* (*Rām.*, ii. 23, 24, and vi. 89, 12, and *MBh.*, i. 4322 ; cp. *Dūtavākya*, p. 38, l. 13) with the accusative of the person.

51. *Pāriplava* applied to the eyes apparently cannot mean 'swimming with tears', as taken by Co. here and by me at *S.*, vii. 19 ; cp. Mallinātha on *R.*, iii. 11, and the use at *S.*, ix. 51, and xii. 42. Any one to whom the mournful cry of the fishing eagle is familiar will realize that the simile here applies to *virurāva* ; the comparison is not uncommon, e.g. *Rām.*, ii. 39, 45, *Pratijñāyaugandharāyaṇa*, iv. 24.

52. "Have those hairs of his which are worthy of being encircled by a royal diadem, been cast to the ground, hairs which were soft, black and glossy, in great locks and curling upwards with each hair growing separately from its own orifice?

53. His arms are long, his gait that of the king of beasts, his eyes like a mighty bull's, his chest broad, his voice like the drum of the gods, and he shines with the brilliance of gold. Ought such a one to live in a hermitage?

54. Is this earth then not to have its portion of that peerless, noble-doing lord? He has gone from here; for it is only through the good fortune and virtues of the subjects that such a virtuous ruler of men is born.

55. His feet are soft with a beautiful network spread over the toes, tender as the fibre of a lotus or a flower, with the

52. All but two of the verses given to Gautamī are formally put as rhetorical questions, and it is better to construe both the others in the same way. *Samudgata* is difficult, the verb being rare according to the *PW* but occurring i. 14 above; I accept T's rendering (*gyen-du ḥkhyil*), though it may have had a different reading (*samuddhṛtāḥ* ?). C's 'curling to the right' (lit. *dakṣiṇāvarta*) possibly represents this word. For the exact sense of *praverita* note the use at *S.*, xviii. 20.

53. The drum of the clouds is thunder, cp. *Jāt.*, xv. 13, *payodatūryasvanalabdhaharṣā vidyullatā*, and *Theragāthā*, 522, *gajjati meghadundubhi.*

54. This verse is partially in C, as well as being quoted by FP, but it intrudes so oddly into the sequence of verses, that it may well be an early interpolation. For *abhāginī*, verbal adjectives in °*in* govern the accusative under *Pāṇ.*, ii. 3, 70, read with iii. 3, 3, when they have a future sense; the use is, strictly speaking, limited to the *gaṇa gamyādayaḥ*, which does not include *bhāgin.* It governs the infinitive verse 67 below. Note Speyer's remarks, *JRAS*, 1914, 114-5. The earth is metaphorically the king's wife, and the second line means that the prince has gone because of his subjects' lack of merit. In *c gataḥ* is evidently Amṛtānanda's conjecture; C and FP throw no light on it, but it seems probable. *Āryakarmāṇam* is chosen to hint at the prince's becoming an *ārya* in the religious sense.

55. The *viṣapuṣpa* according to the *PW* is the name of a plant *Vangueria spinosa*, also called *piṇḍītaka*, which cannot possibly be meant here; the sense 'blue lotus' is not well authenticated, though C has 'coloured like the pure

anklebones concealed and wheels in the middle of the soles. Shall they tread on the hard ground of the jungle ?

56. His powerful body is accustomed to sitting or lying on the palace roof and has been adorned with priceless clothes, aloes and sandalwood. How will it fare in the forest in the heat, the cold and the rains ?

57. He is ennobled by race, goodness, strength, beauty, learning, majesty and youth, and so fitted to give, not to ask. Is he to practise begging alms from others ?

58. He has been sleeping on a spotless golden bed and awakened at night by the strains of musical instruments. How then shall he lie in accordance with his vows on the ground with only a piece of cloth interposed ? "

59. Hearing these piteous ravings, the women clasped one another with their arms and let fall tears from their eyes, as shaken creepers drop honey from their flowers.

60. Then Yaśodharā fell upon the ground, like a Brahminy duck without its mate, and in her distress she uttered all sorts of laments with a voice that was repeatedly held back by sobs :—

61. ' If he wishes to carry out *dharma* and yet casts me off, his lawful partner in the duties of religion and now husband-

lotus '. I have combined A's and T's readings ; the fibres of the lotus root are often referred to for their softness. *Vanānta*, ' the jungle ' in a general sense, not ' the edge of the forest '.

56. *Vimānapṛṣṭhe*, perhaps simply ' in a pavilion ', like Pali *piṭṭhe*. I follow T in taking *arcita* as ' bedecked ', cp. *Rām.*, i. 2, 27, or one could read *°ācitam*. In *c jalāgama* means the rainy season (inaccurately translated at *S.*, v. 3).

57. For *garvita* cp. vii. 50. Gawroński aptly compares *Kirātārjunīya*, iii. 23, for *abhyucita*.

58. In *b niśi* is curious, as it is at dawn that kings are woken by drums and the songs of bards. I take *me* in *c* as merely expletive.

61. Formichi and W take the second line as a general proposition ; this requires the reading *kva tasya* and misses the point of the argument which lies in the contrast between the ordinary religious rites, in which the wife has

less, in what respect is there *dharma* for him who wishes to follow austerities separated from his lawful partner ?

62. Surely he has not heard of our ancestors, Mahāsudarśa and the other kings of old, who took their wives with them to the forest, since he thus intends to carry out *dharma* without me.

63. Or else he does not see that in the sacrifices it is both husband and wife who are consecrated and purified by the precepts of the Veda and who will enjoy together in the hereafter too the recompense of the rites ; therefore he has become miserly of *dharma* towards me.

64. Being distinguished for *dharma*, he must have held my mind to be secretly and repeatedly given to jealousy and quarrelling ; so lightly and without fear deserting me as being

always to share, and austerities, in which she did not necessarily do so. The next verse gives an illustration in support of her contention, that there is no distinction between the two cases. For the whole passage cp. *Pūrvamīmāṁsāsūtras*, vi. 1, 6–21.

62. *Hi* seems the only word capable of giving the required sense in *d*. Mahāsudarśa is presumably the Mahāsudassana of the genealogies of the *Dīpavaṁsa* and *Mahāvaṁsa*.

63. Lüders' amendment in *b* is unnecessary, as *vā* carries on the construction from the previous verse, so allowing *sa* to be understood. *Parataḥ* for *paratra* is due to metrical exigencies ; or else read *ca paratra*. The argument is that he thinks (wrongly) that the husband can get the reward of the sacrifice, if he sacrifices without his wife, so that he can safely exclude her from sharing his austerities, whereas by doing so he will miss the reward of them.

64. The exact significance of the first line is not clear to me. *Vallabha* can only mean 'beloved of', not 'fond of'. Therefore *dharmavallabha* is 'the favourite of *dharma*', and so 'distinguished for it'; *PW* gives one reference, *samastaguṇavallabha*, for this use. Can *muhur* have the Vedic sense of 'for a moment', 'suddenly' ? T's construction cannot be squared with the Sanskrit, though it evidently had the same text. C gives the correct general sense but throws no light on the difficulties. In the second line *sukham* has been found puzzling ; for T takes it as the object of *jighṛkṣati* and *Apsarasaḥ* as the ablative singular, while Sukumar Sen (*Outline Syntax of Buddhistic Sanskrit*, 12), takes

of a wrathful nature, he wishes to obtain the Apsarases in great Indra's heaven.

65. But I am anxious on this point, namely, what kind of excellent beauty is possessed by the women in that world, for whose sake he gave up sovereign glory and my devotion too and is practising austerities.

66. It is not in truth that I envy him the delights of Paradise ; their acquisition is not difficult even for an ordinary person like me. But my one desire is to secure that my beloved shall not leave me either in this life or in the hereafter.

67. If it is not to be my lot to look up at the sweetly-smiling long-eyed face of my lord, still is this poor Rāhula never to be dandled in his father's lap ?

68. Alas ! If my lord is tender in body and high in spirit, how cruel and exceeding hard is his mind, when in sooth he abandons such an infant son with his babbling talk, who would charm even an enemy.

it as accusative after *vibhīḥ* 'afraid of pleasure' (but see *PW* s. *vibhī*). Neither alternative seems possible.

66. There has been much discussion on *b*. *Tat* refers to *sukham*, but the translation depends on the meaning given to *spṛhā* in *a*. It seems to me more natural that the delights of Paradise should refer to the prince than to Yaśodharā, and so we must accept for it the rare sense 'envy', which recurs verse 79 below. I take *ātmavato* primarily as equal to *madvato*, though I can only cite the adverb *ātmavat* in support of this ; secondarily it means either, as T has it (*sems-ldan*), 'prudent', 'resolute', or else 'self-controlled'. In both cases *api*, 'even', or *hi* would do. T always translates *api*, but often omits *hi*, so that it may have had the latter, not *asti* as W supposes. The sense is that she is not jealous of the prince going to Paradise, so long as he does not deny her the opportunity of obtaining rebirth with him there ; she is explaining the momentary jealousy of the previous verse.

68. T renders *varcas* 'body' ; it is used as equivalent to *rūpa*, 'form', several times in the *Rām*., e.g. i. 3, 72, *devavarcas* corresponding to *devarūpin*, i. 29, 14, and vi. 92, 27. So on *Dīgha*, I, 114, Buddhaghosa explains *brahmavaccasī* as 'having a body like Brahmā'. C may have read *kulapradīpaṁ* in *c*, 'the pride and glory of his splendid race, reverenced even by his foes'.

69. My heart too is certainly exceeding hard, made of stone or even of iron, in that it does not break in its orphaned state, when my lord, accustomed to all pleasures, has departed to the forest without his royal glory."

70. In such terms the princess, fainting with grief for her husband, wept and brooded and lamented repeatedly. For, though steadfast by nature, she forgot the rules of decorum and felt no shame.

71. When the women saw Yaśodharā lying there on the ground, undone by grief and lamentation, they mourned aloud and their faces with the tears on them looked like mighty lotuses whipped by the rain.

72. But, his prayers ended and the auspicious oblations completed, the king came out of the temple and, smitten by the distressed wail of the people, trembled like an elephant at the roar of a thunderbolt.

73. And perceiving the two of them, Chandaka and Kanthaka, and hearing of his son's firm resolve, the lord of the earth was overwhelmed with grief and fell down like the banner of Śacī's lord when the festival is over.

74. Then for a moment he swooned with grief for his son and was held up by persons of birth equal to his own; and still on the ground he fixed the horse with tearful gaze and thus lamented :—

69. I follow T in taking *anāthavat* to agree with *hṛdayam* ; it might refer to the prince ('like an orphan', Co.), but should it not then mean 'without Śrī, like one who is not a ruler'? Śrī is compared to Yaśodharā at ii. 26; so we get the antithesis, she is without her *nātha*, he in a double sense without his Śrī.

73. The last *pāda* is almost identical with *Rām.*, ii. 76, 32 ; which is the original? For *vṛttotsava* cp. *ib.*, iii. 68, 27, and *MBh.*, xii. 8405.

74. It would have been improper for any one of lower birth to raise the king up.

75. "Many, Kanthaka, are the services you have rendered me in battle; one great disservice you have done me in that, though you do love him, you have thrown off in the jungle my loved one, who is so fond of virtue, as if you did not love him.

76. Therefore either take me at once there where he is, or go quickly and bring him back again. For without him no more is there life for me than for a man fallen ill who lacks the right medicine.

77. Saṁjaya achieved the impossible by not dying when Suvarṇaniṣṭhīvin was carried off by death; I however, now that my *dharma*-loving son has departed, wish to yield up my soul like one who has no self-control.

78. For would not the mind even of Manu have been distracted, if parted from a dear virtuous son, Manu, the son of Vivasvat, the knower of the former and the latter things, the mighty lord of creation, from whom issued ten races of kings?

75. Schmidt alone understands *d* as I do; the others take *priyo 'pi sann* as 'although he is dear to me', thus repeating *me priyaḥ* of *c* without point. *Apriyavat* however could also mean 'as if he were not dear to me', somewhat spoiling the antithesis.

76. In *b* T may have had *vrajan*, or, as it construes it with *yatra sa*, it may have read *yatra so 'vrajad*, with an improbable avagraha at the beginning of the *pāda*. C and T make *enam* certain in *b*. For the line cp. *Vikramorvaśīya*, iv. 11.

77. The name is Sṛñjaya in the *MBh.*, which tells the story twice, vii. 2138ff., and xii. 1088ff. In both the son is brought to life again, and the reference here suggests that the poet knew only a version to which the happy ending had not been added. Co.'s *'mumukṣur* in *d* is against C and T and seems *a priori* improbable.

78. I can find no reference to Manu's grief for a lost son and presume from the optative that the case stated is purely suppositious. Manu's ten sons, or nine sons and a daughter, founded ten lines of kings, cp. especially *Harivaṁśa*, 633, also 433. In the second line T is not at all clear but, as it stands, omits *Manor api*. Possibly there is a corruption due to the number of times *yid* occurred in the line, Manu being translated *yid-śes* in Tibetan. A

79. I envy the king, the friend of Indra, the wise son of king Aja, who when his son departed to the forest, went to Heaven instead of continuing to live in misery with futile tears.

80. Point out to me, good steed, that hermitage-place to which you carried off him who is to give me the funeral water. For these my vital airs are about to travel the way of the departed and long for him in the desire to drink the draught."

81. Thus the king grieved over the separation from his son and lost his steadfastness, though it was innate like the solidity of the earth; and as if in delirium, he uttered many laments, like Daśaratha dominated by grief for Rāma.

82. Then the counsellor, who was endowed with learning, decorum and virtue, and the aged purohita addressed him thus as was proper in a well-balanced manner, neither distressed in face nor yet untouched by sorrow:—

83. "Cease grieving, O best of men, return to firmness; you should not, O steadfast one, shed tears like a man without self-control. For many kings on earth have cast aside their sovereignty like a crushed wreath and entered the forests.

might read *vimano* instead of *dhi mano*, and to read *vimano mano manoḥ* would enable us to divide *vinā kṛtam*, the text reading being difficult. But T does not definitely justify the conjecture and C is no help.

79. The son of Aja is Daśaratha, father of Rāma.

80. C translates the verse at such length as to suggest that a verse may have dropped out here. It takes *pretagatim* in the Buddhist sense, birth as a Preta, which is no doubt hinted at by the word *pipāsavaḥ*, the Pretas suffering from a thirst that can never be satisfied.

81. The reference is to the element earth, which in Buddhist philosophy provides the qualities of firmness and solidity in all things, defined as *kaṭhinatva* at *S.*, xvi. 12.

82. *Matisaciva* is a synonym for *mantrin*, a *saciva* employed for giving counsel, as against those whose duties were executive. It is curious that both C and T mention the purohita first, as if disapproving the order in which they appear here. For *samadhṛta*, *Manu*, viii. 135.

83. T translates *kudhṛti* by *mya-ṅan*, 'suffering', either corrupt for *brtan-ṅan* or else taking *dhṛti* as 'pleasure'. *Atīyuḥ* is certified by T; cp.

84. Moreover this his state of mind was predestined; call to mind the words of the seer Asita of old. For it is not possible to make him stay happily even for a moment in Paradise or in a Cakravartin's rulership.

85. But if, O best of men, the effort can be carried out at all, quickly give the word and we will go there at once. Just let there be a struggle of many kinds on this point between your son and the various prescriptions of scripture."

86. Thereon the king ordered them, "Therefore do you two set out speedily from this very spot. For my heart, like that of a forest bird hankering after its young, finds no peace."

87. "Very well", said the minister and purohita and at the king's command they left for the forest. The king too, considering the matter to have been successfully disposed of, performed the remaining rites in company with his wives and daughters-in-law.

Mallinātha on *Kirātārjunīya*, xiv. 54, and Jacobi, *Ausgewählte Erzählungen*, 37, l. 30.

84. Leumann took *vāsayitum* to be the verb from which *vāsanā*, 'impression of the past', is derived; its use in the sense 'impregnate' is well authenticated in Jain and Buddhist literature, but I do not see that it fits in here.

85. The text and general sense are certain, the exact construction doubtful. Speyer's *eṣa* for *eva* in *a* is not supported by T, and *kārya*, when emphasized by *eva*, must mean more than 'to be done'; the alternatives are 'to be carried out at all' and 'to be carried out successfully', the latter being perhaps corroborated by *kṛtam* in 87. *Yāvat* in *b* I take as equivalent to *tāvac ca*, and *tāvat* in *c* refers back in sense to *kārya eva*. I give *vidhi* the sense of 'scriptural injunction' in view of the arguments employed in the next canto, especially verses 65–67. The sentiment is, 'We shall do the best we can, but we do not hope for much success'. For an alternative view see Formichi's note.

CANTO IX

The Deputation to the Prince.

1. Then at that time the counsellor and the purohita, spurred on by the king with the goad of words, set out for the forest with the speed of devotion and made every effort like noble steeds when pricked.

2. In due course and accompanied by a suitable retinue, they reached the hermitage, wearied out by their exertions. Discarding their official pomp and assuming a sober demeanour, they proceeded straight to the abode of the descendant of Bhṛgu.

3. They did reverence to the Brahman in accordance with propriety and were duly honoured by him. When they had been given seats and the Bhārgava had taken his, they entered on their tale and stated their business :—

4. " Know us two to be charged with the preservation of the sacred traditions and with the practice of counsel respectively for the royal scion of Ikṣvāku's line, who is pure in his might, pure in his widespreading fame.

2. Böhtlingk's *vinītaveṣāv* in *c* is against C and T. T translates Bhārgava here and in 3 by ' son of Aṅgiras '.

3. T, which I would amend as W suggests, takes *kathām* with *ūcatuḥ* and *ātmakṛtyam* with *chittvā*. The exact meaning of *kathāṁ chid* does not seem to go beyond that given above, cp. *Mhv.*, III, 388, 1, *Dūtavākya*, verse 30, and *Dhūrtaviṭasaṁvāda*, p. 6, l. 19. Alternatively it may mean ' putting the matter briefly ', a sense in which the same phrase appears to be used at xxiv. 48.

4. The word in *c* for which A has *adhīram* corresponds to *adhikṛta* in x. 1, and I would therefore amend T's *nag-por*, ' black ', to *bdag-por*, which is used there. Properly *adhītam*, which seems the only possible word, should mean ' learned ', and I know of no precise parallel for its use, etymologically quite possible, in the sense of ' set over ', ' employed in '.

5. He who resembles Indra has a son resembling Jayanta, who, we hear, has come to this place in his desire to pass beyond the dangers of old age and death. Your Holiness should know that we have come on his account."

6. He answered them, "The long-armed prince did come here, a boy in years but of fully developed intelligence. But, understanding that our rule of life leads to rebirth, he went on to seek Arāḍa in his desire for salvation."

7. Then on learning the true state of affairs from him, they immediately bade farewell to the sage, and started off in the direction the prince had taken, wearied indeed but in their devotion to the king as if unwearied.

8. Then as they went along, they saw him sitting on the road at the foot of a tree, not adorned with the artifices of the toilet but blazing with his form, like the sun when it has entered a circle of cloud.

9. Then leaving the chariot, the purohita, accompanied by the counsellor, went up to him, as the seer, the son of Urvaśī, accompanied by Vāmadeva, approached Rāma when he was in the forest.

6. *Asti* is here used as a particle and its exact force is rendered by the English idiom with 'did', implying that there has been a subsequent change in the position. There have been several plausible attempts to amend the last words of *b* and it would be easy to add to them, but the MS. reading, which is also certified by T, is quite satisfactory, if *kumāraḥ* is taken in the double sense of 'prince' and 'boy', and the full force is given to the doubled negative.

9. The son of Urvaśī has hitherto been taken to be Agastya, but to make the comparison correct, as Vāmadeva was minister to Daśaratha, the seer must have been his purohita, namely Vasiṣṭha. This is confirmed by C's transliteration which gives Vasiṭṭha, and by the fact that in the very rare references to Vāmadeva in the *Rām.* and *MBh.*, in the latter of which he is confused with a ṛṣi of the same name, he is usually coupled with Vasiṣṭha. T's equivalent, *slar-gnas,* is uncertain, but, if *slar* is from *sla-ṅa*, 'pot', it may mean Kumbhayoni, which would be either Agastya or Vasiṣṭha (*Bṛhaddevatā*, v. 150). The legend of Vasiṣṭha's descent from Urvaśī is alluded to in the Rigveda, but had apparently already been lost sight of by the time of the

10. They paid him due honour, as Śukra and the son of Aṅgiras did to the mighty Indra in heaven, and he paid them due honour in return, as the mighty Indra did to Śukra and the son of Aṅgiras in heaven.

11. Then obtaining his permission, they sat down on either side of the banner of the Śākya race and, thus close to him, they resembled the twin stars of Punarvasu in conjunction with the moon.

12. The purohita addressed the king's son as he sat, shining gloriously, at the foot of the tree, just as Bṛhaspati addressed Indra's son Jayanta, as he sat in Paradise by the *pārijāta* tree :—

13. " Listen, Prince, to this that the king said to you, with his eyes raining tears, when he was stupefied for a moment on the ground with the dart of grief for you plunged into his heart :—

14. " I know of your fixed resolve with regard to *dharma* and I realise that this will be your future goal. But by reason of your proceeding to the forest at the wrong time I am burnt up with the fire of grief as with a real fire.

epics. This passage therefore suggests the poet's knowledge of Vedic literature. The epics know of no such visit to Rāma, and the significance of this reference is dealt with in the Introduction.

10. T correctly divides in *b* and *d* Śukra and Āṅgirasa (Bṛhaspati). These two are always mentioned together as the gurus of the gods and as authors of the first political treatises ; cp. i. 41 above and *S.*, i. 4. The comparison suggests that the poet looked on Śukra as the minister of the gods. I can find no exact parallel ; the *MBh.* knows of Indra's honourable treatment of Bṛhaspati, but Śukra does not seem to be joined with him in that.

11. Nepali MSS. show a good deal of confusion between *ī* and *e*, *ai*, so that I have no hesitation in correcting *niṣīdatuḥ*. The simile occurs *Rām.*, vi. 51, 22. In the *Śāriputraprakaraṇa* (*SBPAW*, 1911, 397) the Buddha with three disciples is compared to the moon in conjunction with some three-starred asterism whose name is lost ; so also at *B.*, xvii. 41, while at *B.*, xvi. 2, the comparison, misunderstood by W, is to the moon and the five stars of Hastā, whose regent is the sun.

14. For *b* cp. ii. 33*b*, in T as well as in the Sanskrit.

15. Therefore come, lover of *dharma*, to do me a favour, and give up this purpose for the very sake of *dharma*. For the current of my grief has swollen and is afflicting me, as the swollen current of a river cuts away the bank.

16. For the actions, which the wind, the sun, fire and the thunderbolt exercise on a cloud, water, dry grass and a mountain respectively, are being exercised on me by grief with its dispersing, drying up, burning and shattering.

17. Therefore enjoy lordship for the present over the earth and you shall go to the forest at the time approved by the Scriptures. Have regard for me, your unlucky father; for *dharma* consists in compassion for all creatures.

18. Nor is it only in the forest that this *dharma* is achieved; its achievement is certain for the self-controlled in a city too. Purpose and effort are the means in this matter; for the forest and the badges of mendicancy are the mark of the faint-hearted.

19. The *dharma* of salvation has been attained by kings, even though they remained at home, wearing the royal tiara, with strings of pearls hanging over their shoulders and their arms fortified by rings, as they lay cradled in the lap of imperial Fortune.

20. The two younger brothers of Dhruva, Bali and Vajrabāhu, Vaibhrāja, Aṣāḍha and Antideva, Janaka the Videha king, . . . Druma and the Senajit kings,

16. Cp. *S.*, xvii. 59.

18. *Liṅga* is the shaven head, robe etc.; cp. xii. 46, *S.*, vii. 49, and *JRAS*, 1930, 863.

19. C alters the arrangement of the verses here, not at all to their advantage, reading in the order 22, 20, 19, 21. T takes *viṣakta* in *a* as 'earring', so that *viṣaktahārā*=*karṇayoktraka* of v. 55; for this sense of *viṣakta* cp. *S.*, xvi. 76. For *b* cp. *LV.*, 41, 8, and 49, 2, and *Mhv.*, I, 201, 8. A's *mokṣadharmaḥ* in *d* would ordinarily be inferior to T's *mokṣamārgaḥ*, but is more in accord with the king's repeated use of the word *dharma*.

20. Of the names in this verse Janaka is well-known, Druma is referred to elsewhere by the poet (see note on verse 70 below), the *MBh.* praises various

21. All these lords of men, you must know, were versed in the method of practising the *dharma* that leads to final beatitude, while still remaining in their homes. Therefore resort even to both at once, lordship over knowledge and royal sovereignty.

Senajit kings, and Antideva is the same as Rantideva (see note on i. 52); Dhruva I take to be Brahmā, Bali the Asura and Vajrabāhu Indra, the latter being called the *anuja* god in xvii. 41, a verse misunderstood by W. The rest I cannot trace. In *d* C is corrupt; it runs, filling up the gaps in brackets, 'Druma, Sena(jit) king(s), Anuja, Āṣā(ḍha), Vajra, Bāhu, Vaibhrā(ja), Anti(deva), Videhajana(ka), Naraśavara(?)'. Owing to Druma and Dhruva starting with the same two characters in Chinese, the final line has taken the place of the first one; for the missing name in *d* we have the enigmatic last column of five characters. FP reproduces the names in its prose portion, but is also not clear for *d*. It names (749, *a*17 bottom to 19 bottom) Dhruvānuja (Sui-chang), Balivajra, Băhu, Vaibhrāja(?), Aḍhya, Antideva and Videharāja Janaka. Column 20 mentions Yayāti and Rāma with a group of characters following each, which may originally have been other names. These two versions agree against T and Co. in dividing Balivajra and Bāhu, not Bali and Vajrabāhu. A's *yāṅge* or *yāṅgi* in *d* might stand palæographically for Padmi. On the two other occasions that the poet names Druma, he calls him Śālvādhipati, probably because otherwise Buddhists would have taken him for Druma, king of the Kinnaras. Now while nothing can be made out of T's *ḥgro-ba*, we should, if we correct to *do-ba*, have Śālva as translated below at verse 70; this would explain the puzzling *can* (=*sa*°, or 'having') at the end of the name, and apparently *ḥgro* and *do* are pronounced in practically the same way. The best conjecture therefore would be *Śālvadrumaṁ*; though it does not fully explain A's reading, it corresponds to C's last three characters by transposing the last two.

21. The reading in *c* is insoluble; A's *ubho* indicates the impossible *ubhau*, the *ubhe 'pi* of Co.'s MSS. is also bad, and to read *ubhe hi* with Böhtlingk will not do, as *hi* is not wanted and *api* after *ubha* is a regular use to signify totality (*PW* s. *api*, 9). A and T both read *vittādhipatyam*, which disposes of the *cittādhipatyam* of Co.'s MSS., but to translate it as 'lordship over wealth' makes very poor sense, though *Jāt.*, ii. 3, probably uses it thus. Similarly at *MBh.*, xii. 784, *dharmam anye vittam anye dhanam īhanti cāpare*, the meaning 'wealth' will not do (if the verse refers to the *trivarga*, then *vitta* is *kāma* here). C has, 'You can now return home and reverently practise both duties; prepare your mind for the highest *dharma* and become the highest ruler on

22. For it is my wish to embrace you closely while you are still wet with the coronations waters, to behold you beneath the imperial umbrella, and with the selfsame joy to proceed to the forest."

23. So spoke the king to you with a speech whose utterance was strangled by tears. You should listen and, to do him pleasure, you should follow after his love with love.

24. The Śākya king is drowning in the unplumbed ocean of suffering, which originates from you and whose waters are grief. Therefore rescue him who is without a protector or support, as a ship rescues a man drowning without support in the ocean.

25. Hearing of the deeds done by Bhīṣma, who sprang from the womb of Gaṅgā, Rāma, and Rāma the descendant of Bhṛgu, to please their fathers, you also should do what your father wants.

26. Know that the queen, who brought you up, weeps piteously and incessantly in distress like a fond cow who has lost her calf, and has almost gone to the region over which Agastya presides.

27. You should save by the sight of yourself your wretched wife, who, though not a widow, is husbandless and resembles a goose separated from her mate or a cow-elephant abandoned in the forest by the bull-elephant.

earth', on the strength of which I put in 'knowledge' as a stopgap, till the correct solution is found.

23. Perhaps better to divide *tatsneham anu prayātum* in *d*.

25. The deeds referred to are too well known to need specification.

26. Each verse from here to 37, except 30, 33 and 36, have gaps in A of varying length caused by the destruction of the end of leaf 37; the lacunæ can be filled up with certainty from T. In *a samehi* cannot mean 'consider' or 'know', and T undoubtedly had the better *samavehi*. The second *pāda*, by saying that she has not died, implies that she is on the point of doing so; C seems also to have understood it thus. In *c* T translates *vatsalām* by *gñen-bśes*, which would stand more naturally for *bāndhavām*. *Rudantī*, though grammatically incorrect, is the form used by Aśvaghoṣa.

demon who eats the moon during eclipse

28.   Deliver Rāhula from grief for his parent as the full moon from eclipse by Rāhu ; he is your only son, an infant unfitted for suffering, yet bearing the smart of sorrow in his heart.

29.   The palace and the entire city are being burnt up with the fire of grief, whose fuel is separation from you, whose smoke is sighs and whose flames sorrow, and they long for the water of a sight of you." *— certain level of understanding*

30.   The Bodhisattva, fulfilled in resolution, listened to the words of the purohita, and after a moment's meditation, in his knowledge of all qualities, he thus made an excellent and courteous reply :—

31.   "I am fully aware of the feelings fathers have for their sons, more especially that which the king has for me ; but though I know it, I am afraid of disease, old age and death and have no alternative but to quit my kindred.

32.   For, if in the end there were not parting from one's dear ones, who would not wish to see his dear kinsfolk ? But since, however long delayed, separation does take place, I quit even my affectionate father.

33.   As for your mention of the king's grief on my behalf, it does not please me that he should feel distress, since unions are fleeting as dreams and parting is certain.

28.   *PW's* references for *udvah* in this sense are all much later ; cp. *Jāt.*, xix. 20, and *Śiśupālavadha*, xiv. 17.

29.   The missing character in *c* was wrongly restored by me at *JRAS*, 1929, 541.

30.   *Paripūrṇasattva* means not only that his resolution was unshaken but, as in ii. 56, that he was ripe for enlightenment. *Guṇavadguṇajñaḥ* is capable of several interpretations, all probably meant by the poet. I follow C ; Co. and Schmidt take it as a compound, 'knowing all the virtues of the virtuous', while Formichi, relying on *Manu*, ii. 30 (still more to the point *guṇavati muhūrte* at i. 85 above), takes *guṇavat* as agreeing with *muhūrtam*.

31.   The construction of *c* is curious and parallel passages (*Bodhicaryā-vatāra*, vi. 56, *Vairāgyaśataka*, 12, *Jāt.*, xix. 1, *Jātaka*, V, 180 and 186) put it rather differently.

33.   It is better in the second line to take the locatives as absolute, not as depending on *saṁtapyate*.

9

this distress is a
nature of world is transitory; problem is ignorance
can't hold on to anybody; attachment — father has tied him down

34. And, perceiving the mutable course of the world, your mind should come thus to this conclusion that the cause of affliction is neither the son nor the father; this distress is the outcome of ignorance.

35. The separation of creatures who have come together in this world, as of wayfarers, is inevitable in the course of time. What wise man then would cherish grief, when forsaken by those who are only his kindred in name?

36. A man comes hither, abandoning his kindred in the previous existence; and he gives them the slip in this life and journeys on again; after going to the next existence too, he goes to a further one. How can there be attachment to folk who are ever deserting others?

37. And since from the womb onwards in all circumstances Death is ready to strike, why does His Majesty in his love for his son describe my departure to the forest as being at the wrong time?

34. But for T, which perhaps we should amend with W to *ḥchir-ba* (=*kheda*, *tāpa*), I would have accepted Gawroński's amendment in *d*. One could understand with W its *ñid* as for *eva* (i.e. *evaiṣa*), but more probably it represents the ending °*ika* of the previous compound.

35. In *a* I have only preferred T to A after some hesitation; *yadā* requires a correlative in the main sentence, and in view of the Buddhist use of *adhvan* for the three divisions of time, past, present and future, *adhvagānām* might be ambiguous without *iha* as implying those who are travelling from birth to birth. Cp. *S.*, xv. 34, for further development of the simile, in which this meaning of *adhvaga* may be hinted at. *Pratijñāta* in *d* as in the philosophical term *pratijñā*; cp. *Jāt.*, xx. 23, *suhṛtpratijñaiḥ*.

36. The repetition of *api* in *c* is suspicious; *gatvā ca* would be better. T translates *anuródha* 'consideration', as in vii. 36; cp. *S.*, xiii. 48, for the meaning I give it. The difference between *yogini* and *tyāgini* palæographically is minute and I see no reason for not accepting T's reading.

37. For the restoration of *ab* cp. *S.*, v. 22, and xv. 54. W holds T did not have *akāle* in *c*, but I am not certain. The reading would have to be *akālaṁ vanasaṁśraye*, as Aśvaghoṣa does not use *akāla* as an adjective, the usual Buddhist form being *ăkālika*; and I therefore prefer the locative.

38. There is a wrong time for giving oneself up to the objects of the senses; similarly a time is prescribed for the means to wealth. At all seasons Time constrains the world; Time does not exist in the highest good which leads to salvation.

39. And as for the king's desire to hand the kingdom over to me, that too is noble and worthy of a father, but it would not be right for me to accept it, like a sick man greedily accepting unwholesome food.

40. In what way could it be right for a wise man to take sovereignty on himself? It is the abode of delusion in which are to be found fearfulness, the intoxication of pride, weariness and loss of *dharma* by the mishandling of others.

38. A difficult stanza. The reading of the first line is curious, and Cappeller ingeniously takes both *akālaḥ* and *kālaḥ* with each locative, 'there is a wrong time and a right time similarly, etc.', but I do not think this is really possible nor do I like T's *praviṣṭaḥ* (in Nepali MSS. a bit earlier than A *va* and *da* are sometimes hard to distinguish). C translates, 'Wait (Giles' 9915 taken in the sense of 10569) for the time to experience the five pleasures, in seeking wealth there is time also'. In the second line *kāla* in *c* primarily means Time as Death; cp. xi. 61, *antako jagad vikarṣati*. For *d nirvāhaka* only occurs *ASPP.*, 203 and 439 (=*AAA.*, 283 and 477), but cp. the use of *nirvāhaya* at viii. 40, and C and T both seem to indicate it, while palæographically it is the best solution of A's reading. In Pali *nibbāhana* occurs several times, but only in the *Milindapañha*, a work which originated in a still unidentified Hīnayāna school. The use of *nirvahana* for *mokṣa* and for the 'catastrophe' of a drama at *Śiśupālavadha*, xiv. 63, should also be noted. The *pāda* has more than one meaning; time is *saṁskṛta* and therefore finds no place in the summum bonum which is *asaṁskṛta*. Similarly death finds no place there, for it is *amṛta*.

40. It would be natural to take *parāpacāreṇa* as meaning 'by the ill-doing of others', the reference being to the king's having to take his share of the wrongdoing of his subjects. But *AK.*, III, 91, says that kings with their *adhikaraṇasthas* and *daṇḍanetṛkas* are incapable of *saṁvara*, because the maintenance of order requires them to use personal violence to others which is fatal to the religious life, and this must be the primary sense here in view of 48 below. For *dharmapīḍā* cp. *MBh.*, xiii. 4556, *KS.*, i. 5, 6, *Svapnavāsavadatta*, i. 6, and *S.*, iv. 34.

41. For kingship is at the same time full of delights and the vehicle of calamity, like a golden palace all on fire, like dainty food mixed with poison, or like a lotus-pond infested with crocodiles.

42. And thus kingship is neither pleasure nor *dharma*, so that the kings of old, when age came on with its unavoidable suffering, felt disgust and, giving up their kingdoms, betook themselves to the forest.

43. For it is better to eat herbs in the forest, embracing the highest contentment as if one were concealing a jewel, than to live with the dangers to which sovereignty is exposed, as if with loathsome black snakes.

44. For it is praiseworthy for kings to leave their kingdoms and enter the forest in the desire for *dharma*, but it is not fitting to break one's vow and forsaking the forest to go to one's home.

45. For what man of resolution and good family, having once gone to the forest in the desire for *dharma*, would cast off the robe and, dead to shame, proceed to the city even of Puraṁdara ?

46. For only the man, who from greed, delusion or fear, would take again the food he has vomited up, would from greed, delusion or fear, abandon the lusts of the flesh and then return to them.

47. And the man, who, after escaping with difficulty from a burning house, would enter that very house again, only he, after giving up the state of a householder, because he sees its dangers, would desire out of delusion to assume it again.

43. For *adṛśya*, which applies also to *doṣa*, see reference in *PWK*.

46. A like T could read *lobhād vimohād* in *a*, but the reading in *c* settles the matter. For the simile cp. *MBh.*, xii. 3038.

47. The verse I omit after this verse cannot be genuine ; it is unlike the rest of the passage or the poet's style, and repeats the simile of verse 49. Nor would C omit so moral a verse, if he had had it in his text.

48. As for the tradition that kings obtained final emancipation while remaining in their homes, this is not the case. How can the *dharma* of salvation in which quietude predominates be reconciled with the *dharma* of kings in which severity of action predominates ?

49. If a king delights in quietude, his kingdom collapses ; if his mind turns to his kingdom, his quietude is ruined. For quietude and severity are incompatible, like the union of water which is cold with fire which is hot.

50. Either therefore those lords of the earth resolutely cast aside their kingdoms and obtained quietude, or stained by kingship, they claimed to have attained liberation on the ground that their senses were under control, but in fact only reached a state that was not final.

51. Or let it be conceded they duly attained quietude while holding kingship, still I have not gone to the forest with an undecided mind ; for having cut through the net known as home and kindred I am freed and have no intention of re-entering the net."

52. Thus spoke the king's son with vigour, freed from all ambition in accordance with his virtues and self-knowledge, and adducing good arguments. The counsellor too, hearing him, thus made reply :—

48. For *daṇḍa* as the supreme duty of a king, see *Manu*, vii. 17–55, and *MBh.*, xii. 425ff., and for the sentiment note *MBh.*, iii. 1396, and *Kād.*, 37, l. 17, *sāmaprayogaparo 'pi satatāvalambitadaṇḍaḥ*, of a hermit. For *śamapradhāna*, *Śākuntala*, ii. 7.

50. I cannot square any possible reconstruction of T in c with A palæographically. *Rājyāṅgitā* is a stopgap, adopted because in A *ṅga* and *dma* are almost identical, but *rājyānvitā* or *rājyāśritā* would be better sense. It is also possible to divide *vā=anibhṛt°* and take the compound with the preceding word. T's *abhimāna*, as appears from *AK.*, IV, 27, is peculiarly suitable here ; for it is the claim of a man who has certain good qualities that they are higher qualities than they really are.

52. With regard to W's note on the first line, I would make A and T correspond by amending the latter's *de-ḥdod* to *re-ḥdod* (=*spṛhā*, translated sometimes by *ḥdod-pa*, sometimes by *re-ba*).

53. "It is not that your resolution for the practice of *dharma* is unfitting in itself, but only that the present is not the time for it. For it could not be your *dharma*, delighting in *dharma* as you do, to deliver up your father in his old age to grief.

54. And surely your intellect is not subtle or else is short--sighted in the matter of *dharma*, wealth and pleasure, that you should despise the object before your eyes in favour of an unseen result and so depart.

55. And some say there is rebirth, others confidently assert that there is not. Since this matter is thus in doubt, it is proper to enjoy the sovereignty that offers itself to you.

56. If there is any continuance of activity hereafter, we shall enjoy ourselves in it according to the birth we obtain; but if there is no continuance of activity in another existence, this world accomplishes liberation without any effort on its part.

57. Some say there is a future life but do not explain the means of liberation. They teach that there is an essential force of nature at work in the continuance of activity, like the essential heat of fire and the essential liquidity of water.

54. Perhaps *yāsi* here should be taken as simply an auxiliary to the gerundive.

55. Cp. *Kaṭha Up.*, i. 20; also see *MBh.*, xiv. 1348ff., for a much longer list of alternatives. Could *niyatapratijñāḥ* mean 'those who assert that the world is ruled by *niyati*'?

56. I take *upapatti* here in its Buddhist sense; cp. the definition *AK.*, II, 5, and P.T.S. *Pali Dictionary* s.v. But it would do to translate 'according to what we obtain there', the general sense remaining the same.

57. Co. translated *b*, 'but they do not allow the possibility of liberation', free but perhaps right. C and T render *prakṛti* and *svabhāva* by the same words, and the identity here is apparent by comparing the second line with *S.*, xvi. 12; and the former is not to be understood therefore in the classical Sāṁkhya sense. Gawroński's conjecture requires that *pravṛtti* should be to *prakṛti* what *auṣṇya* is to *agni*, and is more in accord with Sāṁkhya views; but the school described here is certainly not Sāṁkhya, but some variety of materialism.

58. Some explain that good and evil and existence and non-existence originate by natural development; and since all this world originates by natural development, again therefore effort is vain.

59. That the action of each sense is limited to its own class of object, that the qualities of being agreeable or disagreeable is to be found in the objects of the senses, and that we are affected by old age and afflictions, in all that what room is there for effort? Is it not purely a natural development?

60. The oblation-devouring fire is stilled by water, and the flames cause water to dry up. The elements, separate by nature, group themselves together into bodies and, coalescing, constitute the world.

61. That, when the individual enters the womb, he develops hands, feet, belly, back and head, and that his soul unites with that body, all this the doctors of this school attribute to natural development.

62. Who fashions the sharpness of the thorn or the varied nature of beast and bird? All this takes place by natural

59. I take *viṣayeṣu* with *a* as well as *b* the latter implies that the quality of being agreeable or the reverse is to be found in the object, not in the attitude we bring to it. Perhaps it is also intended to deny the Buddhist doctrine of *adhipatiphala*, according to which our surroundings in the world are the fruit of our actions in previous existences. In *d* T construes *nanu* with the preceding words.

60. The argument seems to be that the elements play a double part, first by destroying each other by mutual opposition, secondly by coalescing to form the world; C states this definitely. In *d* T's reading may indicate *gatvā*.

61. T's °*mūrdhnāṁ* was conjectured by Kern, and this is apparently also the reading in I.O.MS. Hodgson 31/5 (vol. 29), fol. 21, where verses 60–64 and 66-67 are quoted; these excerpts seem to have been made by Amṛtānanda and probably reproduce the original state of A's text. In *c* T divides *yadā* =*ātmanaḥ*.

62. This verse is quoted in full (with the variant *kāmacāro* in *d*) in *Ṣaḍdarśanasamuccaya*, p. 13, and the first three *pādas* (substituting *hi siddhaṁ* for *pravṛttaṁ* in *c*) in *Cāṇakyarājanītiśāstra*, viii. 136; it is also perhaps referred to at *Nyāyasūtra*, iv. 1, 22. For a similar sentiment cp. *Jāt.*, xxiii. 17, and

development. There is no such thing in this respect as action of our own will, *a fortiori* no possibility of effort.

63. So others say that creation proceeds from Īśvara. What is the need in that case for action by man? The very same being, who is the cause in the continuing activity of the world, is certainly also the cause in its ceasing to be active.

64. There are others who assert that the coming into being and the passing away from being is solely on account of the soul. But they explain coming into being as taking place without effort, and declare the attainment of liberation to be by effort.

65. On the ground that a man discharges his debt to his ancestors by the procreation of offspring, to the seers by the Vedas, to the gods by sacrifices, that he is born with these three debts on him, and that whoever obtains release from them obtains that which alone can be called liberation,

66. The doctors declare that liberation is for him only who strives thus in accordance with these Vedic injunctions; for those, who desire liberation by means of their individual energy, however much they exert themselves, reap nothing but weariness.

Gauḍapāda on *Sāṁkhyakārikā*, 61. For *d* cp. *Jātaka*, V, 242, *y'āhu n'atthi viriyan ti*, in describing the tenets of this school, and for a few references for the *svabhāvavāda* generally, see *JRAS*, 1931, 566–8, and notes in text and translation on *S.*, xvi. 17.

64. This verse refers to the Sāṁkhya; that *ātman* stands for the Sāṁkhya soul appears from xii. 20, and *ayatnāt* is equivalent to *svabhāvāt*, which is the principle underlying the action of the eightfold *prakṛti*. Possibly the sense of *nimitta* here is connected with its use in similar circumstances at *Śvet. Up.*, i. 4, and vi. 5, where it means 'characteristic' or *liṅga* (cp. *JRAS*, 1930, 860); T's *mtshan-ma* would support its being so rendered, but all previous translators, including C, understand the first line to mean that the *ātman* alone causes the coming into being, etc.

65. This verse is the statement of the *tajjñāḥ* in 66. See note on verse 76.

66. *Vidhi* in the technical sense here. The readings of the second line are corroborated by T and the general sense is certain, but would be more

67. So, my good sir, if you are attached to liberation, follow in due form the injunctions I have just described. Thus you will obtain liberation and the king's grief will be brought to an end.

68. As for your idea that it is wrong to go back to the palace from the penance groves, be not disturbed, my son, on that score either; those of old went to their own families from the forests.

69. Although he was living in the penance grove surrounded by his subjects, Ambarīṣa went back to his city; so too Rāma left the penance grove and protected the earth, when it was oppressed by the infidel.

70. Similarly the king of the Śālvas called Druma with his son entered the city from the forest, and Antideva, the Sāṁkṛti, who was a Brahman seer, accepted the royal dignity from the sage, Vasiṣṭha.

clearly expressed by taking *vikrama* to mean 'wrong course of action' (cp v. 32, and x. 25). C has, 'If one uses other means (or, efforts), it is vain toil and no truth', but I do not think this really supports Speyer's conjecture.

69. The reference in the first line is uncertain, as there were several Ambarīṣas, of whom the most important was the son of Nābhāga; it is also another name of Hariścandra (Pargiter, 92). No apposite story is preserved, but both are related to have gone to heaven with their people; hence my rendering of *prajābhiḥ*, instead of 'children' with T. The second line can hardly refer to Rāma, son of Daśaratha, unless Aśvaghoṣa knew an entirely different legend to that we have, and it is natural to see an allusion to Paraśurāma and his delivery of the earth from Arjuna Kārtavīrya; *S.*, vii. 51, which has the same four names as this and the next verse, has *Rāmo 'ndhra,* which I took to be for *Rāmo 'ndha* and to mean Balarāma. Possibly one should take Andhra there to refer to the domains of the Andhra kings with the western portion of which Paraśurāma is associated by legend.

70. The king of the Śālvas who returned from the forest with his son can only be Dyumatsena, father-in-law of Sāvitrī; but here, as in verse 20 above and *S.*, vii. 51, the form Druma is certain. In the second line *brahmarṣibhūta* refers to the fact that the Sāṁkṛtis were Kṣatriyan Brahmans, but I cannot trace the legend referred to here, though Antideva's connexion with Vasiṣṭha is known from the *MBh.* and i. 52 above.

71. Such as these, who blazed with the fame of *dharma*, gave up the forest and proceeded to their palaces. Therefore there is nothing wrong in going home from the penance grove, when it is for the sake of *dharma*."

72. The prince listened to the affectionate words, meant for his good, of the counsellor, the king's eye, and then taking his stand on steadfastness, gave him a reply, which met every point without being over-discursive and was devoid of attachment as well as measured in tone :—

73. " As for this disputed question of existence and non-existence in this universe, no decision is possible for me on the strength of another's words. I will arrive at the truth for myself by asceticism and quietude and will accept what is determined accordingly in this matter.

74. For it would not be proper for me to accept a doctrinal system, which is born of doubt and is obscure and mutually contradictory. For what wise man would go forward in dependence on another, like a blind man with a blind leader in the dark ?

71. For *atīyuḥ* cp. viii. 83, and *S.*, vii. 50. C perhaps supports Gawroński in *a*, ' declared to have a good name for their excellent *dharma* . . . just as lamps shine in the world '.

72. With much hesitation I have retained A's readings in *b* and *d*. For *b* Gawroński cites *CII*, III, 75, *rājñas tṛtīyam iva cakṣuḥ*. The epithets *hita* and *priya* apply better to the minister's action for the king (so T) than to his words to the prince (so C). *Adruta* is a very rare word, only known from the *Taittirīya Prātiśākhya* according to *PWK*, *druta* being one of the three ways of speaking known to the Vedic schools.

74. C does not make clear what text it had in *b*, possibly *avyaktaparamparāgatam* or °*parasparā*° ; for the reading adopted cp. *avyavasthita āgama* of verse 76 and *viruddheṣv āgameṣu* of *S.*, i. 14. The prince's rejection of *parapratyaya* has doctrinal significance. It is only the man of feeble faculties, in whom the roots of good are weak, who depends on others ; those like the prince, in whom the force working for enlightenment is strong (note ii. 56, *rūḍhamūle 'pi hetau*), act of themselves, as clearly put at *S.*, v. 15–18.

75. But although I have not yet seen the final truth, still if the reality of good and evil is in dispute, my decision is for the good. For better is the toil, though vainly, of the man who devotes himself to the good than the bliss, even though in the real truth, of the man who gives himself up to what is contemptible.

76. But seeing that the scriptural tradition is uncertain, understand that to be good which is spoken by the authorities, and understand that the only basis for authority is the expulsion of sin. For he who has expelled sin will not speak what is false.

77. And as for your quoting the instances of Rāma and the others to justify my return, they do not prove your case; for those who have broken their vows are not competent authorities in deciding matters of *dharma*.

78. Such being the case, the sun may fall to the earth, Mount Himavat may lose its firmness, but I will not return to

75. The exact text of the second line is doubtful, the general sense clear. The reference is to verse 58, which lays down that *śubha* and *aśubha* are spontaneous and that effort is of no avail; *tattva* here means this doctrine. T, as W points out, though corrupt, must have read *vṛthā hi khede 'pi*, by which we must take *sukham* with *śubhātmanaḥ* as well as *vigarhitātmanaḥ*, and *vṛthā khede* balances *tattve*.

76. I doubt if this, the standard, rendering is correct; should not *iti* govern all the first line, 'And as for your statement, "But seeing that the sacred traditions (i.e. as described in 55–64) are uncertain, you should accept the views of the authorities", (I reply that) you should know, etc.'? This would imply that the hiatus in argument between 64 and 65 is due to a verse having dropped out which suggested that in view of the uncertainty of the philosophical systems the only thing to do was to trust the *tajjñāḥ*; *RL* has in fact such a statement. For the second line cp. the verse quoted by Gauḍapāda on *Sāṁkhyakārikā*, 4:—

Āgamo hy āptavacanam āptaṁ doṣakṣayād viduḥ |
Kṣīṇadoṣo 'nṛtaṁ vākyaṁ na brūyād dhetvasaṁbhavāt ||

Note also *Mūlamadhyamakakārikās*, 268, 2, and *Nyāyabindu*, 90, 15.

78. Cp. *LV.*, ch. xix, 284, 3. The exact scope of the word *pṛthagjana* was a matter of dispute in the schools. The ordinary view was that a man

my family as a worldly man who has not seen the final truth and whose senses are drawn towards the objects of pleasure.

79. I would enter a blazing fire, but I would not enter my home with my goal unattained." Thus he proudly made his asseveration and, rising in accordance with his declaration, he departed in all selflessness.

80. Then the minister and the Brahman, perceiving his resolution to be unshakable, tearfully followed him, grieving and with faces downcast, then slowly for lack of other resource wended their way to the city.

81. Then out of affection for him and devotion to the king, they turned back full of cares and stood still; for, as he blazed with his own brightness, as unapproachable as the sun, they could neither look on him on the road nor yet quit him.

82. And they deputed trustworthy spies in disguise in order to know the way taken by him whose way was the highest, and with much difficulty they set off, thinking how they were to go and see the king who was thirsting for his dear son.

remained a *pṛthagjana* till he entered on the Path, when he became an *ārya*; the Buddha thus remained one till the moment of receiving *bodhi*. See La Vallée Poussin, *Vijñaptimātratāsiddhi*, 639.

79. The doctrinal sense of *ālaya* is also hinted at, as at *S.*, v. 39.

81. For *sāpekṣam*, 'anxiously', cp. *Aṅguttara*, III, 296. In *c* A's *durdharṣaṁ* is practically identical in content with T's *durdarśaṁ*, but stronger; cp. *Rām.*, ii. 1, 16, *durdharṣaḥ samare 'rīṇāṁ śaradbhānur ivāmalaḥ*.

CANTO X

ŚREṆYA'S VISIT

1. So the prince of the broad stout chest dismissed the officers who were in charge of the king's sacrifices and his council chamber, and passing over the tossing waves of the Ganges, he came to Rājagṛha of the lordly palaces.

2. As peacefully as Svayaṁbhū proceeding to the highest heaven, he entered the city distinguished by its five hills, which is guarded and adorned by mountains and supported and purified by auspicious hot springs.

3. The people there at that time, perceiving his gravity and might and his glorious form surpassing that of mankind, as of him who has taken the pillar vow and has the bull for his sign, were lost in amazement.

4. On seeing him, whoever was going in another direction stood still; whoever was standing in the road followed him; whoever was going quickly went slowly, and whoever was sitting down sprang up.

5. Some worshipped him with joined hands, others honoured him by saluting him with their heads, others greeted him with kindly words; none passed on without doing him reverence.

2. The hot springs, called *tapoda* and still in use at Rajgir, are referred to at *Majjhima*, III, 192, as well as in the Jain sources given by Leumann. The form of the first line suggests the probability of a second meaning applying to *nākapṛṣṭha* for *śaila* (adjective of *śila* ?), *tapoda* (ascetic ? heatgiver ? or are we to infer from verse 3 the special worship of Śiva as an ascetic at Rājagṛha ?), and *pañcācalāṅka*. *Aṅguttara*, III, 44, seems to play on *sīla* and *sela* in the same way. For Svayaṁbhū as a name of Buddha see note on ii. 51.

6. On seeing him, the gaudily-dressed felt ashamed and the chatterers on the roadside fell silent ; as in the presence of Dharma incarnate none think thoughts not directed to the way of salvation, so no one indulged in improper thoughts.

7. The gaze of the women or men on the royal highroad, busied though they were with other affairs, was not satiated with looking most reverently on the godlike son of the human god.

8. His brows, his forehead, his mouth or his eyes, his form or his hands, his feet or his gait, whatever part of him anyone looked at, to that part his eyes were riveted.

9. And Rājagṛha's Goddess of Fortune was perturbed on seeing him, who was worthy of ruling the earth and was yet in a bhikṣu's robe, with the circle of hair between his brows, with the long eyes, radiant body and hands beautifully webbed.

10. Then Śrenya, lord of the Magadha land, saw from an outer pavilion the mighty concourse of people and enquired the reason thereof. Then an officer explained it to him :—

11. "This is the son of the Śākya monarch, of whom the Brahmans said he would attain either supreme knowledge or lordship over the whole earth. He has become a wandering mendicant and the people are gazing at him."

12. Then the king, on hearing the reason, was excited in mind and said to the same officer, "Find out where he is stopping". "Very well", he replied and followed the prince.

6. In relation to *dharma*, *nyāya* is used as in *S.*, xiv. 43, xv. 26, etc., of the plan, course of action, by which salvation is obtained ; for the Sarvāstivādin use of it see *AK.*, V, 32ff. *Vicitraveṣāḥ*, because modest apparel is alone proper to seeing or worshipping great saints.

7. The last *pāda* is a sentiment often repeated, *e.g.*, *R.*, ii. 73, *Rām.*, ii. 2, 15, *LV.*, 114, l. 12, and 240, l. 14, *Mhv.*, II, 201, 3. To read *nirīkṣya* with T in *d* would be better, but there is no clue in that case to the next two syllables.

8. Cp. *Nala*, v. 9, and *Rām.*, v. 22, 15.

10. The exact meaning of *ajira* here is uncertain.

13. But with moveless eyes looking only a yoke's length ahead, voice stilled and walk slow and restrained, he, the best of mendicants, kept his limbs and active mind under control and begged his food.

14. And accepting the alms without distinction, he proceeded to a lonely rivulet of the mountain, and after taking his meal there in due form he climbed Mount Pāṇḍava.

15. On that mountain, fledged with groves of *lodhra* trees and with its glades resounding with peacocks' calls, he, the sun of mankind, appeared in his ochre-coloured robe like the sun in the early morning above the eastern mountain.

16. The royal officer, seeing him there, informed king Śreṇya, and the king, on hearing the news, set off, but only with a modest retinue from his feeling of veneration.

17. In heroism the peer of Pāṇḍu's son, in stature like a mountain, he ascended Pāṇḍava the best of mountains; this lion-man, with the gait of a lion and wearing a royal tiara, resembled a lion with shaking mane.

18. Then he saw the Bodhisattva, sitting cross-legged with tranquil senses, being as it were a peak of the mountain and shining like the moon rising out of a bower of clouds.

13. For *a* cp. *BhNŚ.*, xiii. 79. T seems faulty in *b*. For *nidhāya* cp. *S.*, vii. 48.

14. T again seems faulty in *b*.

15. *Avi*, 'mountain', is known to the Indian lexica and occurs at *S.*, i. 48, in the expression *avibhrānta*, 'wandering on the mountain'. It is the only word that enables A and T to be fitted together and may be taken to be a certain reading.

16. It is more proper for a king to visit a saint with a small retinue, e.g. *HC.*, ch. viii, p. 72, l. 33; but some versions of this legend make Bimbisāra go out with a large following and C here gives him 100,000 followers and may have read *pratasthe 'nibhṛtānuyātraḥ*, if it did not wilfully alter the sense.

17. The second line is probably suggested by Bimbisāra's lineage; for Aśvaghoṣa apparently took the dynasty to descend from the Bṛhadrathas (see note on xi. 2), who, it may be inferred from *S.*, viii. 44, were fabled to descend from a lion.

19. As he sat there in the majesty of his beauty and in holy tranquillity, like some being magically projected by Dharma, the lord of men drew near him with amazement and deference, as Śakra drew near Svayaṁbhū.

20. And as he came in fitting manner up to him, who was the best of those who know the Plan, he enquired about his health, and he too with equal courtesy spoke to the king about his peace of mind and freedom from illness.

21. Then the king sat down on a clean piece of rock, dark blue as an elephant's ear, and being seated beside him with his permission spoke to him, desiring to ascertain his state of mind :—

22. "I have a strong friendship for your family, which has come down by inheritance and has been well tested ; hence, my friend, my desire to speak with you. So listen to these words of affection.

23. Your family is mighty, originating from the Sun, your age the prime of youth, this your beauty radiant. Why then this decision of yours, out of all due order, to delight in alms-seeking instead of in kingship ?

24. For your limbs are worthy of red sandalwood, not meant for contact with the ochre robe. That hand is fitted for protecting subjects and does not deserve to take food given by another.

25. Therefore, my friend, if out of love for your father you do not wish for your hereditary kingdom by force and if you

22. The word *svavayaḥ* in *c* refers presumably to the legend that Bimbisāra was of exactly the same age as the Buddha ; some schools (e.g. *Dīpavaṁsa*, iii. 58) made him a few years younger.

23. One would have expected *bhaikṣākya* rather than *bhaikṣāka* here and in xiii. 10 ; at xii. 46, the word is used adjectivally.

24. Windisch takes *kāṣāyasaṁśleṣam* as agreeing with *gātram* ; it seems better to take it as accusative after *anarha*, though *PW* records the accusative only after *arha*, not *anarha*.

25. A typical case of Indian irony. Bimbisāra, who sees nothing unreasonable in the Buddha turning his father out of his kingdom and killing

do not care to wait for the succession in due course, accept straightway the half of my realm.

26. For thus there will be no need to oppress your kinsfolk, and in course of time sovereignty will come to you peacefully. Therefore do me this kindness; for association with the good makes for the prosperity of the good.

27. Or if now from pride of race you cannot show your trust in me, with me as your comrade plunge into the arrayed battle-lines with arrows and conquer your foes.

28. Choose therefore one or other of these alternatives, and in all propriety devote yourself to *dharma*, wealth and pleasure; for by confusing these three objects in this world out of passion, men go to ruin in the next world as well as in this.

29. For if the entire goal is desired, you must give up that pleasure which is obtained by suppressing *dharma* and wealth, and that wealth which is obtained by overpowering *dharma* and pleasure, and that *dharma* which is obtained by the cessation of wealth and pleasure.

30. Therefore by pursuit of the triple end of life make this beauty of yours bear fruit; for they say that the complete attainment of *dharma*, wealth and pleasure is for mankind the complete object of the individual.

31. Therefore you should not let these two stout arms, fitted for drawing the bow, lie useless; for like Māndhātṛ's, they

him in the process, was himself to experience that treatment at the hands of his son. *Vikrameṇa*, as at ix. 66, 'by a wrong course of action'?

26. The text of *b* is undoubtedly corrupt and neither T nor C are any help in its reconstruction; conjecture in the absence of further light is hopeless. *Sahīyā* is a curious word only known to Buddhism, viz., *Divy.*, 312, 5, and 446, 3–5, *Avadānaśataka*, I, 365, 15, and 366, 2 and 6, and Lüders, *Bruchstücke buddhistischer Dramen*, leaf 13 *a*2.

27. For *vyūḍhāny anīkāni* cp. *Jāt.*, xx. 27, *Bhag. Gītā*, i. 2, and *MBh.*, ii. 682, ix. 467, and xvi. 54. This use of *vigāh* is also common in the epic.

29. Cp. *R.*, xvii. 57, *Rām.*, v. 84, 5-6, *MBh.*, iii. 1285–1305, and *KS.*, i. 2, 1, and 52.

31. I follow T in taking *iha* with *kiṁ punar gām*; this brings the verse into order.

10

are capable of conquering even the three worlds, how much more this earth here ?

32. Truly I say this to you out of affection, not out of love of dominion or arrogance ; for, seeing this bhikṣu's robe of yours, I am moved to compassion and tears come to my eyes.

33. Therefore, lover of the mendicant's stage of life, enjoy the pleasures, before old age comes again on you, the pattern of your race, and confounds your beauty ; in due time, lover of *dharma*, you will perform *dharma*.

34. The aged truly can obtain *dharma* and age has no capacity for enjoying the pleasures. And therefore they attribute the pleasures to youth, wealth to middle age, *dharma* to the old.

35. For, in the world of the living, youth is naturally opposed to *dharma* and wealth, and, however tightly checked, it is hard to hold, so that the pleasures carry it off by that path.

36. Old age is given to reflection, grave and intent on stability ; with little labour it acquires holy tranquillity, partly from incapacity for anything else, partly from shame.

37. Therefore when men have passed through the restless, deceptive period of youth, which is given up to the objects of the senses, heedless, intolerant, and short-sighted, they breathe again as if they had safely crossed a desert.

33. I have accepted T's order of the two lines, because the clause governed by *yāvat* obviously refers only to the enjoyment of the pleasures. With this order the reference to *dharma* in *d* connects with the next verse. C throws no light on this point.

34. Hopkins aptly quotes for the second line *MBh.*, iii. 1304.

35. In view of Aśvaghoṣa's syntax *yataḥ* in the final *pāda* cannot mean 'because', but indicates the consequence ; so it would make better sense in *d* to take *haranti* as intransitive or to read *hriyante*, as Gawroński suggested and T may do, so that youth would be the subject of the verb and *tena pathā* would correspond to *yataḥ*. Note that *ḥphrogs-par-byed* stands for *hriyate* at xii. 50. Alternatively Windisch's *svena pathā*.

38. Therefore just let this unbalanced time of youth pass away with its heedlessness and rebelliousness; for the flush of youth is a target for the God of Love and cannot be protected from the senses.

39. Or if *dharma* is really your intention, offer sacrifices; that is the *dharma* of your family. For taking possession of the highest heaven by means of sacrifices, Marutvat also went to the highest heaven.

40. For with their arms marked by rings of gold and their headdresses bright with the glitter of radiant jewels, the royal seers travelled through sacrifices the very same path that the great seers reached by their austerities."

41. Such was the speech of the king of Magadha, who in speaking rightly resembled Valabhid. The king's son heard it,

38. The argument is that it is useless to struggle against the domination of the passions in youth; old age will gradually come on and rectify the matter.

39. The second line is a puzzle. If C's reading of *nāgapṛṣṭham* in *c* is correct, *adhiṣṭhāya* means 'mounting' as in xii. 9, and *yajñaiḥ* must be construed with *d*. But this reading may well be due to the translator's misunderstanding, and A and T both read *nākapṛṣṭham*, which ought presumably to have a meaning different from the one it bears in *d*. No other sense however seems possible and the question is of the exact purport of *adhiṣṭhāya*, which T takes to mean 'blessing with magic practices'; for the Buddhist use of this word see *AK.*, II, 31, n. 2, and V, 119, n. 2, and *Vijñaptimātratāsiddhi*, 771. This use cannot be proved for as early a period as Aśvaghoṣa, but he might have known the sense of 'stabilise', 'cause to endure'. I have thought it best to take a more ordinary sense for the translation. The reference is not certain; Indra's sacrifices are mentioned more than once in the *MBh.* and possibly we have an allusion here to some version of the story (ix. 2434ff.) by which Indra, after the slaughter of Namuci, freed himself by sacrifice from the guilt of Brahman murder and so returned to heaven.

41. The use of the name Valabhid for Indra, when comparing Bimbisāra to him, suggests that it is to be understood as Balabhid, 'the router of armies', in relation to the king. Alternatively, if we read as is perhaps better, *dhruvaṁ babhāṣe* with A, I would take *dhruva* as a proper name, 'who spoke rightly to him, as Valabhid to Dhruva'. In that case Dhruva means Brahmā,

but wavered no more than the mountain of Kailāsa shakes with its many sparkling peaks.

repeating the comparison of x. 2, and 17; cp. my interpretation of ix. 20 and we should no doubt see a suggestion that Bimbisāra ranked as an *anuja* of the Buddha (see note on verse 22 above). *Naikacitrasānu* should have an application to the prince; query *sānu* in the sense of *kovida* given to it by the lexica ?

CANTO XI

The Passions Spurned

1. Thereon, when the Magadha king spoke to him with friendly face but with matter that was repugnant to him, the son of Śuddhodana, who was purified by the spotlessness of his race, remained calm and unmoved and addressed this reply to him :—

2. "There is nothing for wonderment . . . , that you should behave thus towards your friends, when you spring from the illustrious family of Haryaṅka and from the purity of your conduct are so devoted to your friends.

2. A very difficult verse, for which I do not fully understand C. In *a* I have followed T in the text, because it is not clear if A meant *abhidhātum* or *abhidhātur*, but T also is probably corrupt, as C's *so-shuo*, 'what was said', implies a form from *abhidhā*. The conjunction of *bhavataḥ* in *a* and *tava* in *c* is open to suspicion, nor should *āścaryam etat* have as predicate both a noun and a dependent clause beginning with *yat*. The latter must be right, and, as the verse stands, one can only construe by taking *bhavato vidhānam* in apposition to *vṛttir eṣā*, which is very harsh. The six syllables may be a corruption for an epithet of *āścaryam* or for a complementary phrase of the type *na ca nānurūpam* (I do not suggest this as possible, but only as illustrative of the required form). In *b* I take Haryaṅka to be the same as Haryaṅga, a Bṛhadratha king, whose greatness is described at *Harivaṁśa*, 1700. The name suggests the lion-legend of the Bṛhadrathas referred to at *S.*, viii. 44; and in the fragments of the Buddhist dramas (Lüders, *Bruchstücke*, leaf 7, read with *SBPAW*, 1911, 409) we have what is clearly a description of Rājagṛha, in which its foundation by Bṛhadratha is mentioned (cp. *Harivaṁśa*, 6598). I infer that the poet considered the Śaiśunāgas to be of Bṛhadratha descent. C has 'the family called Hari'. Benares is similarly associated with Bhīmaratha at xiv. 107, and Śrāvastī with Haryaśva at xviii. 58. In *d* I understand T to read *pariśuddhavṛtteḥ* (rather than °*vṛttiḥ*, as W holds), and to take it as a substantive, not as an adjective agreeing with *tava*. A's reading, rejected also by Co., is out of the question.

3. Like sovereignty among cowards, friendship, inherited in their families, does not stand firm among the vicious; but the virtuous increase the same friendship, originated by their ancestors, with an uninterrupted succession of friendly acts.

4. And those men in the world I hold to be truly friends, who share in the enterprises of their friends when in straits. For who in this world would not be a friend to a man who is at ease in the enjoyment of prosperity?

5. And thus those who, gaining riches in the world, employ them on behalf of their friends or of *dharma*, obtain the full value of their wealth, and, if it is lost, it causes them no pain at the end.

6. Certainly this resolution of yours regarding me, O king, proceeds from friendship and nobility of heart. I shall content you about it with similar friendship; I would not answer you in any other wise in this matter.

7. Because I recognise the danger of old age and death, I have betaken myself to this *dharma* out of longing for salvation and have quitted my tearstained relations, and still more therefore the passions, the causes of evil.

8. For I am not so afraid of venomous snakes or of thunderbolts that fall from the sky or of fire allied with the wind, as I fear the objects of the senses.

9. For the passions are ephemeral, robbers of the treasury of good, empty, like will-o'-the-wisps in the world. The mere expectation of them deludes men's minds, how much more then their actual possession?

3. T certainly did not read *svakulānurūpā*, which does not make good sense.

4. W thinks T's *raṅ-gnas-dag ni ḥphel-bar* in *d* is equivalent to *svastheṣu vṛddhiṣv iha*; I doubt this, but T may be out of order here. I see no need to amend with Böhtlingk and Speyer.

6. A's reading in *b* is taken from the following verse and the restoration is almost certain. *Anunī* means 'pacify', 'conciliate' 'convince', a use occurring several times in *Jāt*. *Atra* refers to *niścaya*.

10. For the victims of the passions find no relief in the triple heaven, still less in the world of mortals. For the lustful man can no more win satiety from the passions, than a fire companioned by the wind can from fuel.

11. There is no calamity in the world equal to the passions, and it is to them that mankind in their delusions are attached. What wise man, afraid of calamity and recognising the truth to be thus, would of himself yearn for calamity ?

12. Even when they have won the earth, girdled by the sea, they wish to extend their conquests beyond the great ocean. There is no satiety for man with the passions, as for the ocean with the waters that fall into it.

13. Though the heavens rained gold for him and though he conquered the whole of the four continents and won half the seat of Śakra, yet Māndhātṛ's longing for the objects of sense remained unappeased.

14. Although he enjoyed sovereignty over the gods in heaven, when Śatakratu hid himself for fear of Vṛtra, and though out of wanton pride he made the great ṛṣis carry him, yet Nahuṣa fell, being still unsatisfied with the passions.

10. For the second line and for the second line of 12 below cp. *S.*, xi. 32, and 37.

12. This verse is clumsy with its omission of the subject in the first line and its repetition of the third *pāda* of 10 in *c*. But C has it, and it is required to introduce the string of instances that follows and is presumably genuine. The first line is a rendering of *Theragāthā*, 777 (=*Jātaka*, IV, 172), and the third *pāda*, of 778. Lüders' conjecture in *c* may be right, as the *pāda* occurs in the form he proposed at *S.*, v. 23 ; but time has proved his reasoning wrong, as *vitṛpti* occurs in a similar passage at *S.*, xv. 9 (cp. *ib.*, xii. 15).

13. For Māndhātṛ, see note on i. 10.

14. The references in this and the next verse are well known from the *MBh.* versions. The form Naghuṣa should perhaps have been retained, as T's *sgra-med* indicates it too and it is occasionally found in classical Sanskrit, e.g. *Pañcatantra* (H.O.S., XI), 227, 20. For *b*, see note on viii. 13, or does it indicate an occasion before Vṛtra's death ?

15. Although the royal son of Iḍā penetrated the triple heaven and brought the goddess Urvaśī into his power, he was still unsatisfied with the objects of sense and came to destruction in his greedy desire to seize gold from the ṛṣis.

16. Who would trust in those objects of sense, which are subject to disturbance by all sorts of fate, either in heaven or on earth, seeing that they passed from Bali to great Indra, from great Indra to Nahuṣa and from Nahuṣa back again to great Indra ?

17. Who would seek after the enemies known as the passions, by whom even sages were undone, despite their bark-dresses, their diet of roots and water, their coils of hair long as snakes, and their lack of worldly interests.

18. For their sake Ugrāyudha, armed though he was with a terrible weapon, met death at the hands of Bhīṣma. The

16. For the passing of Śrī from Bali to Indra cp. the *Balivāsavasaṁvāda* of *MBh.*, xii, particularly 8145-6. *Viṣaya* in *d* has, as in verses 13 and 15, the secondary sense of 'kingdom', but refers primarily to the objects of sense that kings gain control over by extending their sovereignty.

17. With much hesitation I have adopted T's *nānyakāryā*, as it is apparently supported by C. Compounds with *na* are rare, though commoner perhaps than admitted by the grammarians (*Pāṇ.*, vi. 3, 73, 75, and Wackernagel, II, i. 77 ; cp. *Bṛhaddevatā*, iii. 9). Besides the stock examples, *naciram* etc., I note in *kāvya Pratijñāyaugandharāyaṇa*, iv. 5, *Kirātārjunīya*, i. 19, and iii. 8, *Śiśupālavadha*, xiv. 84 ; *MBh.*, viii. 185, has *nasukara*, and iii. 13664, *nānyacintā* (for °*cittā ?*), and *Gaṇḍīstotra*, 12, Nāṅga for Anaṅga. *Catuḥśataka* (Mem. A.S.B., III), 497, 13, explains *netara* by *utkṛṣṭa*, and this perhaps is the meaning to be given to *nānya* here. *Manu*, vi. 96, says an ascetic should be *svakāryaparama* (cp. *ekakāryam anantaram* of a Brahman's conduct at *MBh.*, iii. 13997), and *Kād.*, 43, describes sages as *apagatānyavyāpāra*, where the primary sense is so as to gaze uninterruptedly on Jābāli, but where the secondary sense is probably as in *nānyakārya* here. Cp. also *ananyakarmaṇā* at *AAA.*, 95, 20.

18. For Ugrāyudha, *Harivaṁśa*, 1082ff., and *S.*, vii. 44 (see note in translation). For the irregular compound *ugradhṛtāyudha* cp. *bodhyaṅgaśitāttaśastra* at *S.*, xvii. 24. The reference defeated C, who substituted an allusion, better known to the Buddhists, to the legend of Arjuna Kārtavīrya and

mere thought of them is unlucky and fatal to the well-conducted, still more so therefore to those not restrained by vows.

19. Who would swallow the poison known as the passions, when he knows how paltry is the flavour of the objects of sense, how great the bondage, how incomplete the satisfaction, how much despised by the good, and how certain the sin ?

20. It is right for the self-controlled to cast aside the passions, when they hear of the suffering of the passion-ridden, afflicted as they are by pursuits such as agriculture, etc., and of the well-being of those whom the passions fail to excite.

21. Success in the passions is to be recognised as a misfortune for the passionate man ; for he becomes intoxicated by achievement of the passions, and because of intoxication he does what he should not, not what he should, and wounded thereby, he obtains rebirth in a lower sphere.

22. What wise man in this world would delight in those passions, which are only won and retained by labour and which, cheating men, depart again, as though they were loans borrowed for a time ?

Paraśurāma. As regards W's note 11, p. 101, T can be understood to read either Bhīṣma or Bhīma. In the second line T was either corrupt or is trying to explain A's reading ; the latter makes no good sense nor does Windisch's amendment meet the case, as it deprives *avratānām* of all point. My conjecture is palæographically sound and provides the right counterweight to the closing words.

19. I take *saṁyojana* in the Buddhist sense of ' bond ', ' fetter ' ; *kāmarāga* is one of the ten *saṁyojanas*. Co., followed by Windisch and Formichi, takes *b* as a single clause, but Schmidt separates the two words, while W translates T according to the rules of Tibetan grammar with a very different result. All give to *saṁyojana* one or other of the classical Sanskrit meanings.

20. For *a* cp. *S.*, xviii. 37, which corroborates T's reading. Query *niśāmya* in *b* ? In *d kāmā* would be better grammar.

22. This and the similes in the following verses form a series which recurs frequently in the Pali canon, e.g., *Majjhima*, I, 130, 364, *Aṅguttara*, III, 97, *Therīgāthā*, 488ff.

23. What self-controlled man in the world would delight in those passions, which are like a torch of grass ? When men seek and hold them, they excite desire, and if they do not let them go, they undergo suffering.

24. What man of self-control would delight in those passions, which are like fierce raging serpents ? The uncontrolled, when bitten by them in the heart, go to destruction and obtain no relief.

25. What self-controlled man would delight in those passions, which are like skeletons of dry bones ? Even if they enjoy them, like famished dogs eating a bone, men are not satisfied.

26. What self-controlled man would delight in those passions, which are like an exposed bait ? Since they are held in joint tenancy with kings, thieves, fire and water, they originate suffering.

27. What self-controlled man would delight in those passions, which are like dangerous haunts ? By abiding in

23. The point is that a lighted torch, if held in the hand, may burn it, and the first line should be translated so as to bring this out.

26. Kings etc. hold the passions jointly with the owners in the sense that they may take away the objects of enjoyment at any time. This idea and the use of *sādhāraṇa* to express it are both common. The group consists sometimes of these four (*KA.*, iii. 15, 4, Vācaspati Miśra on *Sāṁkhyakārikā*, 50, *Mhv.*, II, 366, 12), sometimes of five, adding kinsfolk (*Majjhima*, I, 86, *Aṅguttara*, III, 259, *Therīgāthā*, 505, *Bodhisattvabhūmi* (ed. Wogihara), 5, and *MBh.*, iii. 85), sometimes of six, adding foes (*Aṅguttara*, II, 68, *Jāt.*, p. 122, 6–8), or of eight (*Saṁyutta*, IV, 324). The exact connexion of *praviddhāmiṣa* with the first line is not clear to me, presumably bait or prey which attracts robbers etc.

27. Cp. *S.*, xvi. 79, for the use of *api* to co-ordinate two substantives opposed in sense. There is a suggestion here that *āyatana* refers to the twelve *āyatanas*, the six external ones of which are compared to thieves at *Saṁyutta*, IV, 175. T in fact renders it so. But the main sense is as above, in which I see no difficulty ; compare the use of *āyatana*, particularly *araññāyatana*, in Pali (P.T.S. *Pali Dict.*, s. *āyatana* 1). Kinsfolk are a real danger in India, as in the note on the preceding verse. C's translation, if I understand it right,

them there is misfortune on all sides at the hands of one's enemy and of one's relations as well.

28. What self-controlled man would delight in those passions, which are like fruit hanging on the topmost boughs of a tree? On the mountains, in the forest, on the rivers, on the sea, men precipitate themselves after them and thereby come to ruin.

29. What self-controlled man would delight in those passions, which are like the enjoyments of a dream? Acquired at the price of many bitter efforts, they are lost in this world in a moment.

30. What self-controlled man would delight in those passions, which are like trenches full of red-hot charcoal? Though men procure them, increase them, guard them, yet they find no comfort in them.

31. What self-controlled man would delight in those passions, which are like the knives and fuel-wood of slaughter-

is purely fanciful. T takes *abhitaḥ* to mean 'quickly', as in the *Amarakośa*, which is possible.

28. In *b* A's *yadbhraṁśam* is untranslateable, and to divide *yad bhraṁśam* is contrary to the scheme of this set of verses. T does not show the plural but can only have read *yān*, the reading conjectured by Cappeller. *Laṅgh* with *abhi* is only known in the causative; for it with *vi* cp. *Śiśupālavadha*, xvii. 55 (reading *vyalaṅghiṣuḥ*), the proper meaning being 'climb up to'. A free rendering meets the case better here, as one cannot climb up to a thing on the sea.

30. C takes the simile to refer to walking over a fire-pit falsely covered over, and T translates *aṅgāra* 'cow-dung', which is perhaps better than 'charcoal'. I understand the simile to mean that red-hot charcoal in a trench (such as is sometimes used for cooking still) gives out no heat to those sitting by it and soon dies down, however much looked after. *Aṅgārakarṣū* is a regular simile for *kāma*; besides the lists referred to under 22 above and Windisch's quotation of *Mhv.*, II, 327, 331, 332, note *LV.*, ch. xxi, 329, 9, *Śikṣāsamuccaya*, 79, 5, *Suttanipāta*, 396, as typical instances.

31. The reading *sūnāsi*° in *c* is certain. The corresponding Pali passages and the *Divy.* use the curious phrase *asisūnā* instead. The association of *asi* with *sūnā* goes back to *RV.*, x. 86, 18, and is found as late as *Pādatāḍitaka*,

-houses? For their sake the Kurus, the Vṛṣṇi-Andhakas and the Mekhala-Daṇḍakas went to destruction.

verses 22 and 29. *Kāṣṭha* refers presumably to the fires on which the butchers cook the meat, and for the first line to the funeral fires; cp. *LV.*, ch. xv, 207, 9-10, and my remarks, *JRAS*, 1929, 546. Of the seven vices peculiar to kings four are known as *kāmaja*, dicing, wine, hunting and women, and these four are illustrated in this and the next verse (cp. *Kāmandakīyanītisāra*, i. 56, for a similar set of examples, of which the Vrṣṇi-Andhakas are the only one in common with this verse), the Kurus for dicing, the Vrṣṇi-Andhakas for drink (cp. *MBh.*, xvi, with *Jāt.*, xvii. 18, and *Divy.*, 560, 20, where *Vṛṣṇyandhakāḥ* should be read for *tṛṣṇāndhakāḥ*), Sunda and Upasunda for women. The other therefore relates to hunting and is not to be treated as two separate instances (contra *WZKM*, 28, 230, n. 4). The question then arises of the form of the first part of the name. A's *Maithila°* is clearly wrong, and the difficulty of C lies in the middle character, Giles' 4059, *hsi* but only used in the pronunciation *ch'ih*; and it is not given by St. Julien, Eitel or Karlgren. It belongs to a group of characters, Giles' 1003, 1119 and 1130, which are used interchangeably for each other. The only one of them known to me in transliteration is Eitel's example of 1119 for *kha*, and I therefore take it that C had *Mekhali* here. The correct form can only be determined by a consideration of the Daṇḍaka legend. The Hindu versions are at *KA.*, i. 6, *Rām.*, vii. 88, and commentaries on *KS.*, i. 2, 44, and *Kāmandakīyanītisāra*, i. 58 (cp. also *MBh.*, xiii. 7178, 7213), and agree that, when out hunting, Daṇḍaka saw a Brahman girl and outraged her, whence his kingdom was destroyed. None of these references are probably as old as the present passage. The Buddhist accounts go back to *Majjhima*, I, 378 (cp. *Milindapañha*, 130), where the ṛsis destroy the forests of Daṇḍaka, Kaliṅga, Mātaṅga and Mejjha, but the last name is doubtful; for the Sanskrit version of the sūtra treats *medhya* as an adjective (S. Lévi, *JA*, 1925, i, 29), and the only allusion outside Pali literature to a forest of this name is a doubtful one in the Sāvitrī tale, *MBh.*, iii. 16693. The *Jātakas* tell the same tale both of the Daṇḍaka forest (V, 135, cp. *Mhv.*, III, 363, and *LV.*, ch. xvi, 316, 2) and of the Mejjha forest (IV, 389), and mention both with the Vṛṣṇi-Andhakas at V, 267. On the other hand the *Saddharmasmṛtyupasthāna-sūtra* (S. Lévi, *JA*, 1918, i, 18, 27, 76) knows a Mekala (Chinese, Mekhala) forest and associates it with Kaliṅga and Daṇḍaka (*ib.*, 97). It looks therefore as if Mejjha was taken in Pali to be a proper name by confusion with Mekala. The latter survives in the name of the Maikal range, the source of the Narmadā, and the people of this district are associated with the Utkalas of the Orissa highlands in the *Rām.* This area formed part of the original Daṇḍaka forest which stretched between the Godāvarī and the upper waters

source of conflict among friends

32. What self-controlled man would delight in those passions, which dissolve friendship? On their account the Asuras, Sunda and Upāsunda, were involved in a mutual feud and perished.

33. What self-controlled man would delight in those passions, inauspicious and ever inimical as they are? For their sake men deliver their bodies up to water and fire and wild beasts in this world.

34. For the passions' sake the ignorant man behaves wretchedly and incurs the suffering of death, bonds and the like. For the passions' sake the living world, made wretched by expectation and tormented, goes to toil and death.

35. For deer are lured to their destruction by songs, moths fly into the fire for its brightness, the fish greedy for the bait swallows the hook; therefore the objects of sense breed calamity.

36. But as for the idea that the passions are enjoyments, none of them are reckoned to be enjoyments; for the

of the Narmadā (or over a wider area, *JRAS*, 1894, 242). There is some confusion in the sources between Mekala and Mekhala, but I can find no authority for C's Mekhali. Reviewing the evidence, the reading indicated is clearly Mekhala and it appears that in the form of the story known to the poet the offence rose out of addiction to hunting.

32. See *MBh.*, i. 7619ff.

33. In A the first seven syllables of *a* are taken from 34 by error. W reconstructs T with *yadartham evāpsu ca*, but it does not show *eva*, usually translated by it, and it indicates the plural of the relative.

35. A's readings suggest in *c matsyā giranty āyasam āmiṣārtham*, the plural corresponding better with *ab*, and FP may have had this too, but C and T seem to have read *āmiṣārthī*, which requires *matsyo giraty*. For the comparisons, Pavolini, *GSAI*, 1900, 101ff., and Zachariæ, *WZKM*, 28, 182ff.

36. In *b*, if T read *parivartyamānāḥ*, it may be taken as meaning 'falsely represented as'; if it is right in omitting *na*, was *parikalpyamānāḥ* the original reading, comparing the use of *parikalpa* at *S.*, xiii. 49, 51? I follow Co. in taking *na* with *kecit*, 'none of them'; cp. *B.*, iii. 52, and *S.*, iv. 27. In the second line for *guṇa* in the meaning 'object of sense', see *JRAS*, 1930, 867ff., and cp. the Buddhist use of *kāmaguṇa*.

material objects of sense such as clothes and the like are to be held as merely remedies against suffering in the world.

37. For water is desired for allaying thirst ; food similarly for destroying hunger, a house for protection against wind, sun and rain, and clothing for a covering of the privy parts or against cold.

38. Similarly a bed is for riddance of drowsiness ; thus too a carriage for avoidance of road-fatigue ; thus too a seat for relief from standing, and bathing as a means of cleanliness, health and strength.

39. Therefore the objects of sense are means for remedying people's suffering, not enjoyments ; what wise man engaged in a remedial process would assume that he is partaking of enjoyments ?

40. For he who, burning with a bilious fever, should decide that cold treatment was enjoyment, even he, when engaged in a remedial process, would have the idea that the passions were enjoyment.

41. And since there is nothing absolute in the pleasures, therefore I do not entertain with regard to them the idea of enjoyment ; for the very states which show pleasure bring in their turn suffering also.

42. For warm clothes and aloewood are pleasant in the cold and unpleasant in the heat ; the rays of the moon and sandalwood are pleasant in the heat and unpleasant in the cold.

43. Since the pairs, gain and loss, etc., are attached to everything in the world, therefore there is no man on earth who is absolutely happy or absolutely miserable.

37. Cp. *Majjhima*, I, 10.

39. In *d* T probably read *pravṛttaḥ*, which is made certain by *c* of the next verse.

40. For this use of *saṁjñā*, see note on i. 51.

43. As C makes clear, the pairs are the eight *lokadharmas* ; cp. *S.*, xiv. 51, and *Dīgha*, III, 260. For a Brahmanical parallel *MBh.*, xiv. 535-6.

44. When I see how intermingled are the natures of pleasure and suffering, I deem kingship and slavery to be alike; for a king is not ever happy, nor a slave always in distress.

45. As for the argument that in sovereignty there is great authority, it is from this very fact that a king has great suffering; for a king, like a carrying-pole, endures toil for the sake of the world.

46. For if a ruler relies on his sovereignty, which is transitory and has many enemies, he is ruined; or if he does not trust in it, what then is the happiness of a king, who is always trembling with fright?

47. And seeing that, even after conquering the whole earth, only one city can serve him as a residence, and in that too only one palace be occupied, surely kingship is but weariness for others' sake.

48. A king too can only wear one pair of garments and similarly take only a certain measure of food to still his hunger; so he can only use one bed, only one seat. The other luxuries of a king lead only to the intoxication of pride.

49. And if you seek to justify this enjoyment on the ground of contentment, I am content without a kingdom and, when a man is contented in the world, are not all luxuries indifferent to him?

50. Therefore I, who have set out on the auspicious, peaceful road, am not to be led away towards the passions. But if you bear our friendship in mind, say to me again and again, "Most certainly hold to your vow".

45. The meaning of *āsaṅgakāṣṭha* is uncertain; my translation follows C. For the sentiment see *Therīgāthā*, 464, *Catuḥśataka*, 472, 24, *MBh.*, xii. 11992, and *Śākuntala*, v. 6.

47. For this and the next verse cp. *MBh.*, xii. 513, 11986, and *Jātaka*, II, 215.

49. *Iṣṭam* in *c* is used in the same sense as in philosophical works, of a principle that is asserted or accepted. For *phala* cp. verse 51 below.

51. For I have not entered the forest because of anger nor have I cast aside my diadem because of enemy arrows, nor have I set my ambitions on loftier enjoyments, that I decline this proposal of yours.

52. For he, who, after letting go a malignant snake, whose nature it is to bite, or a blazing grass torch, whose nature it is to scorch, would decide to catch hold of it again, only he would, after giving up the passions, resort to them again.

53. Only such a man as having eyesight would envy the blind, or being free the prisoner, or being wealthy the destitute, or being sound in mind the maniac, only he would envy the man given up to the objects of sense.

54. And it is not right, just because he subsists on alms, to pity the wise man who desires to pass beyond the danger of old age and death, who has the supreme pleasure of religious peace in this life and for whom suffering in the life beyond is abolished.

55. But pity should be felt for him who, though placed in the height of sovereignty, is overcome by desire, and who does not win the pleasure of religious peace in this life and is subjected to suffering in the life beyond.

56. But it was worthy of your character, conduct and family to make such a proposal, and so too it befits my character, conduct and family, that I should keep my vow.

57. For I have been transfixed by the arrow of the cycle of existence and have left my home in order to obtain tranquil-

51. *Amarṣeṇa* is perhaps a reference to *marṣayitum* at x. 25, and, if so, means 'because I have not the patience to wait for my succession'. Similarly *b* refers to the offer in x. 27; it could also be translated, 'nor have enemy arrows ripped off my diadem'. The reference in *c*, as Co. pointed out and as C translates, is to the joys of Paradise etc.

54. *Bhaikṣopabhogin* is an unusual expression, intended to imply that for the wise man *bhaikṣa* takes the place of *kāma*.

57. This verse is omitted by C and comes in rather uncomfortably here; it would fit the run of the argument better if inserted after 51, but is not quite

lity. I would not wish to win a kingdom free from all drawbacks even in the triple heaven, how much less then one in the world of men ?

58. But as for what you said to me, O king, about the pursuit of the three objects of life in their entirety, that they are the supreme end of man, my doctrine on this point is that they are calamity too ; for the three objects are transitory and fail also to satisfy.

59. But I deem the highest goal of a man to be the stage in which there is neither old age, nor fear, nor disease, nor birth, nor death, nor anxieties, and in which there is not continuous renewal of activity.

60. As for your saying that old age should be awaited and that youth is liable to alteration of mind, this is not a fixed rule ; for in practice it is seen to be uncertain, old age too may be volatile and youth constant.

61. But seeing that Death drags the world away against its will at all stages of life, ought the wise man, who desires religious peace, to wait for old age, when the hour of his destruction is not certain ?

62. Seeing that Death stands like an ill-omened hunter, with old age for his weapon, and scattering the arrows of disease, as he strikes down like deer the people, who dwell in the forests of fate, what illusion can there be about the prolongation of one's days ?

at home there either. The FP quotes it as a *gāthā*, and possibly it is an interpolation.

59. The first part of *a* is corrupt in T and the order wrong ; *ḥgro* for *pada*, usually rendered by *go-ḥphaṅ*, is odd and should probably be *go*.

60. *Capalam* in *c* is doubtful, but I see no reasonably probable conjecture ; *bahuśo hi dṛśyate* would be preferable to Kern's *bahulam* in sense, but is too remote palæographically.

61. Cp. ix. 38, for *jagad vikarṣati*, and for *avaśam S.*, v. 27, and *Vairāgyaśataka*, 30, *vivaśaṁ mṛtyuḥ karoty ātmasāt*.

62. The context makes it necessary to take *manoratha* in this very rare sense (reference in *PWK*).

63. Therefore whether a man be in the prime of life or old or a child, he should haste so to act that, purified in soul and endowed with *dharma*, he may come into possession of the desired continuance or cessation of activity.

64. And as for your saying that for the sake of *dharma* I should carry out the sacrificial ceremonies which are customary in my family and which bring the desired fruit, I do not approve of sacrifices; for I do not care for happiness which is sought at the price of others' suffering.

65. For it does not befit the man of compassionate heart to kill another being, who is helpless, out of a desire for a profitable outcome, even though the fruit of the sacrifice should be permanent; how much less should one act thus, when the fruit is transitory?

66. And if the true *dharma* were not a different rule of life to be carried out by vows, moral restraint, or quietude, nevertheless it would still be wrong to practise sacrifice, in which the fruit is described as attained by killing another.

63. The previous translations miss the point of *pravṛtti* and *vinivṛtti* by taking *iṣṭa* in the second line as predicate; men follow *dharma* either for *pravṛtti* by birth in Paradise or for *vinivṛtti* by complete *mokṣa*, and it is not a question of activity or inactivity in the present life.

64. In *d* for *yad iṣyate* see note on 49 above; perhaps therefore 'which is asserted as being'.

65. The sense is obvious enough and for once clearly expressed by C, but the construction of the second line is difficult. Formichi takes it separately from the first, understanding *tathāpi kṛtvā na yuktarūpam, kim u yat kṣayātmakam*; this may well be right. Windisch also separates the two lines but understands *tathāpi na yuktarūpam, kṛtvā kim u* etc., taking *kim u kṛtvā* as equivalent to *kiṁ kṛtvā*, 'what is the good of doing it?'; but I do not think *kim u* can be so used with the gerundive. The above translation follows Co., Cappeller and Schmidt more or less, but is dubious as not giving *tathāpi* its proper sense of 'nevertheless', as in the next verse.

66. Previous translators took *param* with *phalam* in *d*; my translation follows T and was first suggested by Gawroński.

67. That happiness even, which accrues to a man, while still existing in the world, through hurt to another, is not agreeable to a wise compassionate man; how much more so that which is beyond his sight in another existence?

68. And I am not to be seduced into continuance of activity for future reward. My mind, O king, takes no joy in the spheres of existence; for continuance of activity extends to all forms of rebirth and is uncertain in its effects, just as creepers, struck by rain from a cloud, wave unsteadily in all directions.

69. And therefore I have come here because I wish to see the sage Arāḍa, who teaches salvation; and I am starting this very day. Good fortune be yours, O king, and bear patiently with my words, which sound harsh in their truth.

70. Be happy like Indra, shine ever like the sun, flourish with your virtues, understand the highest good in this world, rule the earth, obtain long life, protect the sons of the good

67. 'Compassionate' is an incomplete rendering of *saghṛṇa*, which also implies *nirveda*; cp. *S.*, viii. 52, xiii. 52, and xv. 15.

68. The sense of *sarvagata* is uncertain; it might mean 'directed to *sarva*', i.e. the twelve *āyatanas* (references at *AK*, V, 248, n. 1). I take it as equivalent to *sarvatragāmin*, 'penetrating all the *gatis*'; *pravṛtti* is as likely to take a man to hell as to existence among the gods, and in fact rebirth in hell according to Buddhist dogmatics is the usual sequel to life as a god.

69. *Ato* in *a*, first suggested by Böhtlingk, is better than *ito* and may be right.

70. According to the grammarians (*Dhātupāṭha*, i. 631, etc.) the root *av* has eighteen senses, many of them probably assumed for etymological purposes, and, though T translates it throughout by *bsruṅs*, 'protect', there can be no doubt that Aśvaghoṣa intends it to be understood in nine different ways here. C took it so, but it is not easy to follow the exact meaning attributed in each case, except that it took the second one to mean 'shine'. The translation is therefore necessarily tentative. For *av* in the sense of *avagam*, 'understand', cp. *AK.*, I, 117. In *c* I do not comprehend *āryair ava satsutān* where C seems to take *āryair* with *avāyur* and to translate 'with upright mind', and in *d* should one read *śriyaṁ ca*, 'embrace Śrī'? T does not show the plural.

with the Āryas, and enter into the glories of sovereignty, O king, observe your own *dharma*.

71. Just as when rain is produced from the clouds which originate from the smoke, the sign of fire, which is the enemy of cold, then the twice-born fire is freed from its external appearance, so do you liberate your mind on the occasion of the slaughter of the enemies of the destruction of *tamas*, which is the opponent of the sun, the foe of cold."

72. The king clasped his hands and spoke with eager longing, "May you succeed without hindrance in accordance with your desires! And when you have in due course obtained the accomplishment of your task, be pleased to show me too your favour."

71. This is a riddle of the type called *parihārikā* by Daṇḍin, whose simpler example at *Kāvyādarśa*, iii. 120, was evidently influenced by it. The translation of *a* follows C, which runs, 'Fire is the enemy of *hima*, from fire the banner of smoke arises. The smoke-banner brings about the floating cloud; the floating cloud brings forth great rain'. Cp. *Śatapathabrāhmaṇa*, v. 3, 5, 17, *agner vai dhūmo jāyate, dhūmād abhram, abhrād vṛṣṭiḥ*. For the interpretation of *b* the use of *tanu* limits the possible senses of *dvija*. It might possibly refer to a snake sloughing its skin; but I do not know if a snake does that, when it rains. This would go well with the second line, for *Śatapathabrāhmaṇa*, xi. 2. 6, 13, tells us that a man is released from sin as a snake from its skin; *tanu*, however, in this sense is difficult. I prefer the alternative of taking *dvija* as Agni, a Vedic use; for Agni is several times called *dvijanman* in the Vedas (Macdonell, *Vedic Mythology*, 94) and once *dvijā* at *RV.*, x. 61, 19. The poet elsewhere shows knowledge of Vedic expressions and the explanation suits very well. *Tanu* is the word regularly used in the Vedas for the visible forms of Agni, and the use can be traced down to *HC.*, ch. iv, 17, 24, *nakhamayūkhadhavalitatanur . . . vibhāvasuḥ*. The idea is that, when a fire is extinguished, it has not perished for good and all, but has merely lost its visible form (e.g., *MBh.*, xii. 6902-3), and it is thus the standard analogy for Nirvāṇa (e.g., *S.*, xvi. 28-9). The amendment in *c* is, I think, certain, as it must be parallel in form to *a*; the point made is that the king is to destroy all hindrances to the extirpation of *tamas*, the use of the latter in a double sense being very common. The translation endeavours to show how I arrive at the solution.

72. FP's version of this and the next verse transliterates Bimbisāra's as Bindu, a curious confusion with the Maurya Bindusāra.

73. He made a firm promise to the king accordingly and then set out for the Vaiśvaṁtara hermitage. The king also looked up at him with amaze, as he wandered on, and then returned to the city of Girivraja.

73. I can find no other references to the Vaiśvaṁtara hermitage, unless the scene of the Viśvaṁtara Jātaka is meant, about whose situation the authorities differ. The *LV*. and the *Mhv*. place Arāḍa in Vaiśālī, substituting perhaps a better known name for an obscure one.

CANTO XII

Visit to Arāḍa

1. Then the moon of the Ikṣvāku race proceeded to the hermitage of Arāḍa, the sage who dwelt in holy peace; and he filled it, as it were, with his beauty.

2. As soon as the sage of the Kālāma *gotra* saw him from afar, he called out aloud "Welcome"; and the prince came up to him.

3. In accordance with propriety each enquired after the other's health, and then they sat down on pure wooden seats.

4. The best of sages, drinking in, as it were, the seated prince with eyes opened wide in reverence, said to him :—

5. "It is known to me, fair sir, how you have come forth from the palace, riving asunder the bonds of family affection, as a savage elephant rives his hobbles.

6. In every way your mind is steadfast and wise, in that you have abandoned sovereignty, as if it were a creeper with poisonous fruit, and have come here.

7. No cause for wonder is it that kings, grown old in years, have gone to the forest, giving their children the sovereignty, like a garland that has been worn and is left lying as useless.

8. But this I deem a wonder that you, who are in the flush of youth and are placed in the pasture-ground of sensory pleasures, should have come here without even enjoying sovereignty.

9. Therefore you are a fit vessel to grasp this, the highest *dharma*. Go up into the boat of knowledge and quickly pass over the ocean of suffering.

9. Cp. *MBh.*, viii. 3551.

10. Although the doctrine is only taught after an interval of time, when the student has been well tested, your depth of character and your resolution are such that I need not put you to an examination."

11. The bull of men, on hearing this speech of Arāḍa, was highly gratified and said to him in reply :—

12. "The extreme graciousness, which you show me in spite of your freedom from passion, makes me feel as if I had already reached the goal, though it is yet unattained by me.

13. For I look on your system, as one who wants to see looks on a light, one who wants to travel on a guide or one who wants to cross a river on a boat.

14. Therefore you should explain it to me, if you think it right to do so, that this person may be released from old age, death and disease."

15. Arāḍa, spurred on through the prince's loftiness of soul, described briefly the conclusions of his doctrine thus :—

16. "Listen, best of listeners, to our tenets, as to how the cycle of life develops and how it ceases to be.

17. Do you, whose being is steadfast, grasp this : primary matter, secondary matter, birth, death and old age, these, and no more, are called "the being".

10. Though the equivalence is not perfect, W is almost certainly right in holding that T read *na parīkṣyo* ; the context makes the reading imperative. For *vijñāte* cp. *avijñāte* in *S.*, xiv. 10, where the sense given in the note should be adopted in preference to that in the translation in view of this passage.

13. *Darśana*, primarily 'system' here, as is shown by *tat* in the next verse, means also that the prince looks on the sight of Arāḍa as lucky ; for the sight of a holy man or of a king (cp. *S.*, ii. 8, and the epithet *piyadassana* given to cakravartin kings in the Pali canon) is deemed to bring good luck in India.

15. Query *māhātmyād iva coditaḥ* ? Cp. v. 71, 87.

16. A's reading in *d* is faulty and *vai* is suspicious ; for the Sāṁkhya use of *parivartate* cp. *MBh.*, xii. 7667 (*saṁparivartate*) and *Bhag. Gītā*, ix. 10 (*viparivartate*). The corruption is easily explained palæographically.

17. This use of *parā* with *i* is not recorded outside this poem ; cp. iv. 99, vii. 31, ix. 14, and xi. 4, which make T's *tat* more probable here. For the

18. But in that group know, O knower of the nature of things, that primary matter consists of the five elements, the ego-principle, intellect and the unseen power.

19. Understand that by secondary matter is meant the objects of the senses, the senses, the hands and feet, the voice, the organs of generation and excretion, and also the mind.

following exposition of the Sāṁkhya doctrines see the discussion in the Introduction. *Sattva* here means the individual corporeal being as opposed to the *kṣetrajña*, and this usage is common enough in early expositions, *MBh.*, xii. 7103 (=9020 and 10517), and 10518. Similarly xii. 8678 (a passage with several parallels to this description), runs, *Sattvaṁ kṣetrajñam ity etad dvayam apy anudarśitam | Dvāv ātmānau ca vedeṣu siddhānteṣv apy udāhṛtau*, the two *ātmans* being the *śarīrātman* and *antarātman* of *Mahābhāṣya*, I, 292, 14, and II, 68, 20. Similarly *MBh.*, xiv. 1372ff. ; and that we are dealing with a regular early Sāṁkhya term appears from its use by Pañcaśikha (quoted by Vyāsa on *YS.*, ii. 5), *vyaktam avyaktaṁ vā sattvam ātmatvenābhipratītya*, and by Vyāsa frequently in the *bhāṣya* on the *YS.* (e.g. on ii. 26, *sattvapuruṣānyatāpratyayo vivekakhyātiḥ*). The three constituents of the *sattva*, birth, old age and death, are properly the characteristics of the corporeal aspect of the individual which keep him in a perpetual state of change ; they are described as four (adding disease) at *MBh.*, xii. 8677, and we may compare in Buddhist dogmatics the three *lakṣaṇas* of the *saṁskṛta dharmas*, which equally account for the perpetual flux of the *saṁtāna* (full discussion *AK.*, I, 222, the Vaibhāṣikas dividing them into four). Note also the application of *sthiti*, *utpatti* and *pralaya* to the three *guṇas* at *Tattvasaṁgraha*, p. 59, verses 97–100. This verse perhaps explains the mysterious *pañcāśadbhedām* of *Śvet. Up.*, i. 5 (inconclusively discussed *JRAS*, 1930, 873-4), where I would now read the palæographically sound *pañcasadbhedām*, understanding *sat* as equivalent to *sattva* and interpreting on the lines of this definition.

18. It is not clear if T read *prakṛtiṁ* or *prakṛtir*. For the early Sāṁkhya division of the 24 material *tattvas* into a group of eight called *prakṛti* and a group of sixteen called *vikāra*, see the Introduction and *JRAS*, 1930, 863–872. The five elements here are not the *tanmātras*, and C rightly has *mahābhūtas*. For *prakṛtikovida* cp. *S.*, xvii. 73, *prakṛtiguṇajñam*, where *jña* also has secondarily a Sāṁkhya sense as a synonym of the soul *kṣetrajna*.

19. Can *vāda* really mean 'voice'? C and T's translations would go better with *vācam*, but I have left A's reading, as certainty is not possible.

20. And that which is conscious is called the knower of the field, because it knows this field. And those who meditate on the *ātman* say that the *ātman* is the knower of the field.

21. And awareness is intellection, that is, Kapila and his pupil in this world. But that which is without intellect is called Prajāpati with his sons in this world.

20. Co. translates the first line, 'there is also a something which bears the name *kṣetrajña* etc.', and T corroborates this; but the above version gives the standard doctrine better. Cp. *MBh.*, xii. 6921, *Atmā kṣetrajña ity uktaḥ saṁyuktaḥ prākṛtair guṇaiḥ* । *Tair eva tu vinirmuktaḥ paramātmety udāhṛtaḥ*. C regularly translates *kṣetrajña* 'knower of the cause', i.e. *hetujña*; cp. *MBh.*, xii. 7667.

21. As this enigmatic verse precedes a verse, defining two opposed principles, it too should presumably define two such principles. Further, verses 29 and 40 couple as opposed *pratibuddha* and *aprabuddha*. The meaning of these is apparent from the *MBh.*'s parallel to 40 at xii. 8677, *Caturlakṣaṇajaṁ tv ādyaṁ caturvargaṁ pracakṣate* । *Vyaktam avyaktaṁ caiva tathā buddham acetanam*. Despite C and T's readings the conclusion seems to me unescapable that this verse refers to *pratibuddha* and *apratibuddha* (=*aprabuddha*), and A in my opinion preserves relics of the original verse in *pratibuddhi* in *b* and in *tu* in *c*, which implies an opposition between the two lines; if T's *daṅ* were a corruption for *yaṅ*, it too would read *tu*. If we read *pratibuddha* with Co., then probably *smṛtiḥ* should be corrected to *smṛtaḥ*, but the *Māṭharavṛtti* on *Sāṁkhyakārikā*, 22, gives among the synonyms of *buddhi* the following, *smṛtir āsurī hariḥ haraḥ hiraṇyagarbhaḥ*; Kapila further is identified with Viṣṇu several times in the *MBh.* and Āsuri is a pupil of his. Similarly *MBh.*, xiv. 1085, names *smṛti*, Viṣṇu and Śambhu among the synonyms for *buddhi*. Therefore I take it that A's reading in *b* stands for an original *pratibuddhir* and that Kapila and Āsuri are names for the *buddhi* in the sphere of the 24 *tattvas* (*iha*); *iha* is not easy to explain in the two lines except by my version. There is a remarkable parallel in *Śvet. Up.*, v. 2, where, as pointed out by Keith, *Sāṁkhya System*, 9, Kapila stands for *buddhi*; note also the association of *pradhāna* and Kapila at *Laṅkāvatāra*, 192.

If then the second line refers to *apratibuddha*, one can only amend against C, T and A to my text, taking A's *tu* to justify the conjecture in part. Prajāpati is a name for the *bhūtātman*, here taken as equivalent to *ahaṁkāra*, for which I cite *MBh.*, xii. 11601, *Mano grasati bhūtātmā so 'haṁkāraḥ Prajāpatiḥ*, and 11234, *Ahaṁkāraṁ . . . Prajāpatim ahaṁkṛtam*; cp. also 11578, *Parameṣṭhī tv ahaṁkāraḥ sṛjan bhūtāni pancadhā* । *Pṛthivī* etc., as well as *ib.*,

22. The "seen" is to be recognised as that which is born, grows old, suffers from disease and dies, and the unseen is to be recognised by the contrary.

23. Wrong knowledge, the power of the act and desire are to be known as the causes of the cycle of existence. The individual person, which abides in these three, does not pass beyond that "being",

24. By reason of misunderstanding, of wrong attribution of personality, of confusion of thought, of wrong conjunction, of

6781, and xiv. 1445. The sons of Prajāpati are the five elements, an idea that can be traced back to the Brāhmaṇas. This nomenclature shows parallelism of idea with the four forms of Vāsudeva in the Pañcarātra system at *MBh.*, xii. 12899ff., where Aniruddha is *ahaṁkāra* ; this becomes more apparent at *ib.*, 13037, where Aniruddha produces *ahaṁkāra* as *pitāmaha*, the Creator, and at 13469 Brahmā is *ahaṁkāra*.

In support of C and T's text I can only quote *MBh.*, xii. 7889, where Kapila and Prajāpati are joined as names of Pañcaśikha. This seems to be the only occurrence of the identification and hardly justifies giving the verse in a form which is in discord with the context.

22. Hopkins and Strauss compare this verse with *MBh.*, xii. 8675-6, *Proktaṁ tad vyaktam ity eva jāyate vardhate ca yat* ı *Jīryate mriyate caiva caturbhir lakṣaṇair yutam* ‖ *Viparītam ato yat tu tad avyaktam udāhṛtam*.

23. These three causes of the *saṁsāra* recur at *MBh.*, xii. 7695 read with 7698, and again at iii. 117 ; the *Carakaśaṁhitā*, *Śarīrasthāna*, which expounds a Sāṁkhya system closely allied to that known to Aśvaghoṣa, gives the causes as *moha*, *icchā*, *dveṣa* and *karman* (Jibananda Vidyasagar's edition, pp. 330 and 360 ; note the parallel at the latter place, *yair abhibhūto na sattām ativartate*). Pañcaśikha's system, *MBh.*, xii. 7913-4, controverts these causes, substituting *avidyā* for *ajñāna* or *moha*, but the explanation is so different from what follows here that Hopkins, *Great Epic of India*, p. 147, may have been right in thinking the passage to be anti-Buddhist.

24. This group of eight reasons, for which the soul fails to free itself, is found elsewhere only in the *Carakasaṁhitā*, *Śarīrasthāna*, v. p. 360, but there is some similarity of idea at *MBh.*, xii. 7505-6. The first five apparently cause *ajñāna*, the sixth *karman*, and the last two *tṛṣṇā*. Co. conjectured *viparyaya* for the first word, and apparently T read so ; but C clearly has *vipratyaya*, as has the *Carakasaṁhitā*, and the group known to classical Sāṁkhya as *viparyaya* is described in 33ff. *Ahaṁkāra* as part of the eightfold *prakṛti* should presumably be understood differently from this *ahaṁkāra* as defined in 26 ;

lack of discrimination, of wrong means, of attachment, of falling away.

25. Now of these misunderstanding acts topsy-turvily. It does wrongly what has to be done, it thinks wrongly what it has to think.

26. But, O prince free from all egoism, wrong attribution of personality shows itself in this world thus, by thinking, " It is I who speak, I who know, I who go, I who stand ".

27. But, O prince free from doubt, that is called in this world confusion of thought which sees as one, like a lump of clay, things which are not mixed up together.

28. Wrong conjunction means thinking that the ego is identical with this, namely mind, intellect and act, and that this group is identical with the ego.

29. That is said to be lack of discrimination, which does not know, O knower of the distinctions, the distinction between the intelligent and the unintelligent or between the primary constituents.

Caraka explains it as the idea that " I am endowed with birth, beauty, wealth etc. ", that is, the quality for which Aśvaghoṣa uses the term *mada*. *Abhisaṁplava* is only known to me from the *bhāṣya* on *Nyāyasūtra*, i. i, 3, *pramātuḥ pramāṇānāṁ saṁbhavo 'bhisaṁplavaḥ, asaṁbhavo vyavasthā*, where *saṁbhava* means ' cooperation ', ' mixture ' (Randle, *Indian Logic in the Early Schools*, 164, n. 3). A's *abhisaṁbhavāt* is therefore not impossible, with *abhi* giving as often the sense of wrongness to the rest of the word ; but C, T and verse 28 all support Co.'s correction. C translates ' excess ' here and ' excess-grasping ' in 28. Caraka defines it, *sarvāvastham ananyo 'ham ahaṁ sraṣṭā svabhāvasaṁsiddho 'haṁ śarīrendriyabuddhiviśeṣarāśir iti grahaṇam.* The last word, *abhyavapāta*, is difficult ; C has here ' being inextricably bound up with what is I ' (i.e., as always in C, with the idea of *mama*, that the corporeal person belongs to the self), and in 32 ' union-receiving ' (i.e., wrongly uniting things together). T's translation is mechanical and no help.

26. *Iha* here and in 27 better perhaps ' in this group '.

27. The use of *asaṁdigdha* coupled with *mṛtpiṇḍa* recalls *saṁdegha*, ' a mere lump of bodily matter ', at *Śatapathabrāhmaṇa*, iii. 1, 3, 3.

28. *Idam* in *a* suggests that A's reading in *c* derives from *eṣa*.

29. See note on verse 21.

30. Wrong means, O knower of the right means, are declared by the wise to be the use of the invocations *namas* and *vaṣaṭ*, the various kinds of ritual sprinkling, etc.

31. O prince free from attachment, attachment is recorded as that through which the fool is attached to the objects of sense by mind, voice, intellect and action.

32. Falling away is to be understood as wrong imagination about suffering that " this is mine ", " I belong to this ", and thereby a man is caused to fall away in the cycle of transmigration.

33. For thus that wise teacher declares ignorance to be five-jointed, namely torpor, delusion, great delusion and the two kinds of darkness.

34. Of these know torpor to be indolence, and delusion to be birth and death, but great delusion, O prince free from delusion, is to be understood as passion.

30. Co. translates *b*, ' sprinkling water upon the sacrifices etc. with or without the recital of Vedic hymns ', and C, ' cleansing by fire and water '. Strauss compares *MBh.*, xii. 11290 ; note also *ib.*, xiv. 1032.

31. Or in *b*, ' by the actions of the mind, voice and intellect '.

32. The construction and sense are uncertain ; Co. has, ' Falling away is to be understood as the suffering which etc. ', not quite as good sense. *Abhimanyate* evidently has the significance of *abhimāna* as applied in Sāṁkhya to *ahaṁkāra*.

33. Did T read *vidvāṁsaḥ . . . pratīyate* ? The teacher referred to is Vārṣaganya according to Vācaspati Miśra on *Sāṁkhyakārikā*, 47 ; the sūtra is *Tattvasamāsa*, 14, and is alluded to in the *Yogasūtrabhāṣya* and the Purāṇas, but not specifically in the *MBh.* (for discussion, see *JRAS*, 1930, 861-2). *Samīhate*, ' desire ', ' wish ', is equivalent to *iṣ* as used in philosophical works of asserting a principle.

34. The explanations in these three verses equate the five-fold ignorance to the five *doṣas*, which appear in varying form in the *MBh.* and later became the five *kleśas* (for references *JRAS*, 1930, 862 and 873). The explanation of the last three agrees with that of Vācaspati Miśra in his commentaries on the *Sāṁkhyakārikās* and the *YS.*; the first two differ. The passage mentioning the five at *MBh.*, xiv. 1018-9, appears to be corrupt, but explains *mahāmoha* and *tāmisra* as here. The first verse suggests a common origin with 35, running,

35. And because even mighty beings become deluded over this passion, therefore, O hero, it is recorded as great delusion.

36. And darkness they refer to, O angerless one, as anger, and blind darkness they proclaim, O undesponding one, to be despondency.

37. The fool, conjoined with this five-jointed ignorance, passes on from birth to birth through the cycle of transmigration which for the greatest part is suffering.

38. Thus believing that he is the sëer and the hearer and the thinker and the instrument of the effect, he wanders in the cycle of transmigration.

39. Through the action of these causes, O wise one, the stream of birth flows in this world. You should recognise that, when the cause does not come into being, the result does not come into being.

40. In that matter, O prince desiring salvation, the man of right knowledge should know the group of four, the intelligent, that which lacks intelligence, the seen and the unseen.

Abhiṣvaṅgas tu kāmeṣu mahāmoha iti smṛtaḥ । *Ṛṣayo munayo devā muhyanty atra sukhepsavaḥ.*

36. T's *ajñatāmisram* is contrary to all the Sanskrit authorities.

37. For *abhiniṣicyate* cp. *Mūlamadhyamakakārikās*, xxvi. 2, *saṁniviṣṭe 'tha vijñāne nāmarūpaṁ niṣicyate*, the commentary having *niṣicyate kṣarati prādurbhavatīty arthaḥ.* Cp. also *MBh.*, xii. 10706-7, *Daśārdhapravibhaktānāṁ bhūtānāṁ bahudhā gatiḥ* । *Sauvarṇaṁ rajataṁ cāpi yathā bhāṇḍaṁ niṣicyate* ‖ *Tathā niṣicyate jantuḥ pūrvakarmavaśānugaḥ.* T's *abhinipātyate* is good palæographically and agrees with 32 above; for *abhinipāta*, 'activity', see *AK.*, II, 65, n. 4.

38. The reading in *b* is uncertain, but C seems to support A which gives the best sense. In *c* for *āgamya* cp. *S.*, xvi. 42, where it can only mean 'understand'; the use is unusual but recurs at 116 below. Böhtlingk's *ity evāvagamya* is against the metre.

39. Co.'s *hetvabhāve* is as good as T's *hetvabhāvāt* and it is not clear which C read.

40. See note on verse 21.

41. For when the knower of the field properly discriminates these four, it abandons the rushing torrent of birth and death, and obtains the everlasting sphere.

42. For this purpose the Brahmans in the world, who follow the doctrine of the supreme Absolute, practise here the *brahman*-course and instruct the Brahmans in it."

43. The king's son, on hearing this speech of the sage, questioned him both about the means to be adopted and about the sphere of final beatitude :—

44. " Deign to explain to me how this *brahman*-course is to be practised, for how long and where, and also where this *dharma* ends."

45. Arāḍa explained to him concisely by another method the same *dharma* in clear language and according to the *śāstra* :—

46. " The aspirant, after first leaving his family and assuming the mendicant's badges, takes on himself a rule of discipline which covers all proper behaviour.

47. Displaying entire contentment with whatever he gets from whatever source, he favours a lonely dwelling and, free from the pairs of worldly life, he studies the *śāstra* diligently.

48. Then, seeing the danger that arises from passion and

41. For *ājavaṁjavatā*, see *JRAS*, 1931, 569-70, and add to the references there *LV*., ch. xv, 205. The second line is equivalent to *MBh*., xii. 8767, *Tad vidvān akṣaraṁ prāpya jahāti prāṇajanmanī*.

42. This use of *vāsaya* goes back to the old phrase *brahmacaryaṁ vas* with the locative of the person under whom the study takes place ; cp. *Bṛh. Ār. Up*., vi. 2, 4, and *Chāndogya Up*., iv. 4, 3, and 10, 1 with *Majjhima*, I, 147. Later use prefers *car*, e.g. *Dīgha*, I, 155, and III, 57.

46. For *liṅga*, see note on ix. 18.

47. *Nirdvandva* refers to the eight *lokadharmas* (xi. 43, note). For the Brahmanical use see references in *PW* under *nirdvandva*, 1) ; *nirdvandvatā*, *MBh*., xii. 11882, seems to mean the state of being soul alone, disjoined from *prakṛti*. The sense of *kṛtin* is not certain ; I take C's translation, T's being purely mechanical.

48. See the mention of the Yoga system in the Introduction for the significance of *c*.

the supreme happiness derived from passionlessness, he arrests his senses and exerts himself in the matter of mental quietude.

49. Then he wins the first trance, which is dissociated from the loves, malevolence and the like, which is born of discrimination and which includes thought.

50. And when the fool obtains that transic bliss and reflects on it repeatedly, he is carried away by the gain of previously unexperienced bliss.

51. Deceived by the feeling of content, he wins to the world of Brahmā by means of quietude of this kind, which rejects love and hatred.

52. But the wise man, knowing that the thoughts cause agitation of mind, obtains the trance, which is disjoined from it and which possesses ectasy and bliss.

53. He, who is carried away by that ecstasy and does not see any stage superior to it, obtains a station of light among the Ābhāsvara deities.

54. But he, who dissociates his mind from the joy of that ecstasy, gains the third trance which is blissful but void of ecstasy.

49. *Vitarka* here includes *vicāra,* and T renders it by the equivalent for the latter.

50. *Tat tat* should mean 'various matters', which is not good sense, and the addition of *eva* seems to justify the above translation.

51. T's *vāsitaḥ* may be the correct reading, C giving no help; it means both 'caused to dwell there' and 'impregnated with'. The canonical accounts of the Brahmā deities emphasise their feeling of self-satisfaction (*AK.*, I, 169).

52. Cp. *S.*, xvii. 45, and *AK.*, V, 158. T translates 'possessed of the bliss of ecstasy' in accordance with its faulty version of 54, but *prīti* and *sukha* are always treated as separate qualities in these trances.

53. This use of *viśeṣa* is common in the *AK.*; and the same sense is probably to be inferred at *MBh.*, xii. 11874, where Janaka talks of the *vaiśeṣika jñāna* in connexion with *mokṣa* and the doctrine of Pañcaśikha, the Sāṁkhya seer.

55.   But he who, immersed in this bliss, does not strive for progress, attains bliss in common with the Śubhakṛtsna deities.

56.   He who, on attaining such bliss, is indifferent and feels no desire for it, wins the fourth trance, which is void of bliss and suffering.

no -   *making distinctions, unity of things*

57.   Some in that trance through vain imagination conclude that it is liberation, because bliss and suffering are abandoned and the mind ceases to function.

58.   But those who investigate the transic knowledge of the Absolute describe its fruit as enduring for many ages with the Bṛhatphala deities.

59.   On emerging from that concentrated meditation, the wise man sees the evils that exist for those who have a body and betakes himself to knowledge for the cessation of the body.

no material reality   60.   Then, abandoning the practice of that trance, the wise man sets his mind on progress and turns away from all desire for material form even, as previously from the passions.

nothingness   61.   First he forms a mental conception of the empty spaces which exist in this body and then he obtains a clear idea

physics   of space with regard to its solid matter also.

non - matl of body + everything

E = mc²

55.   The word *sāmānya* is possibly significant, as the Śubhakṛtsna deities are all alike in body and mentality (*saṃjñā*) according to *AK.*, II, 20.

56.   The alternative reading in *b*, which is consistent with T, is *yo virajyann upekṣate ; upekṣakaḥ* is the expression commonly used in these formulas, e.g., *S.*, xvii. 50, and *LV.*, ch. xi, 129, l. 6ff.

57.   *Pāda d* recurs in verse 75 below.

58.   The reading in *c* and the construction are uncertain. A's *bṛhatphalaṃ* is opposed to C and T, and gives an irregular metre ; it is not clear however whether T read °*kālaṃ* or °*kāle*. I take *bṛhat* in *d* to be a synonym of *brahman* (neuter), according to *MBh.*, xii. 12753, and *PW's* reference from the *Bhāg. Pur.*, but possibly it should be taken separately as an epithet of *phalam*. C suggests the possibility in that case of reading *bṛhatkālād* in *c*.

59.   The verb *sthā* with *vyut* is the technical term for emerging from trance and is so used in the *YS.* also, where it has taken on a slightly pejorative twist. Quite possibly T had *charīriṇām* in *b*.

61.   The readings and construction of the first line are uncertain. A's *asya* referring to the subject of the sentence is uncomfortable ; so I accept T's

62. But another wise man, contracting his self which has extended over space, looks on that very thing as unlimited and reaches a higher stage.

63. But another, skilled in regard to the inner self, causes his self to cease by his self and, since he sees that there is nothing, he is declared to be one for whom nothing exists.

64. Then like the *muñja* stalk from its sheath or the bird from its cage, the knower of the field, escaped from the body, is declared tc be liberated.

65. This is that supreme Absolute, without attribute, everlasting and immutable, which the learned men who know the principles call liberation.

asmin. T's version implies taking *ākāśam* as the object of *parikalpayan*, for which there is something to be said; but then it would be better to read *khāni yāny asmin teṣv ādau*. The sense anyhow is clear, the object of the trance being to suppress all sensation of matter with regard to the body and to substitute for it the sensation of unoccupied space. *Adhimucyate* is a troublesome word, for which I would refer to the employment of *adhimukti* and *adhimokṣa* in the *AK*., and to the discussions there (see Index s.v.). The general idea is of an act of mental attention which leads a man to approve a particular object or course of action, so that he makes up his mind to attain or do it, as the case may be. C translates, 'he completely achieves looking on it (i.e. the solid parts) as space', and I paraphrase this above. W similarly has 'wird er sich klar', though T seems hardly to mean this with *lhag-par mos-par byed*.

62. The difficulty lies in *ātmānam*, which I translate mechanically. From the Buddhist descriptions of this trance *vijñāna* is apparently meant and the original reading might have been *ākāśagatavijñānam*. Vasubandhu, *AK*., I, 74, however, defends the use of *ātman* for *citta*, and in Arāḍa's mouth it might stand for the *mahān ātmā*, the *buddhi* (so *Kaṭha Up*., iii. 3, *buddhi*= *ib*., iii. 9, *vijñāna*). Should not the reading be *tam eva* in *c* ?

63. *Ākiṁcanya* is suspicious, being properly the name of this trance; query *akiṁcana* ?

64. For the *muñja*-stalk comparison, besides *Kaṭha Up*., vi. 17, cp. *Śatapathabrāhmaṇa*, v. 1. 2, 18, and xii. 9, 2, 7, *MBh*., v. 1690, and xiv. 553-4, *Dīgha*, I, 77, and *Visuddhimagga*, 406.

65. I take *tattva* in the Sāṁkhya sense. Strauss aptly quotes *MBh*., xii. 8136.

66. Thus I have fully shown to you the means and the liberation; if you have understood it and if it pleases you, undertake it properly.

67. For Jaigīṣavya and Janaka and Vṛddha Parāśara and other seekers after liberation have been liberated by following this path."

68. But the prince, marking these words and pondering on them, thus made reply, since he was filled with the force of the motives perfected in previous births:—

69. "I have listened to this doctrine of yours, which grows more subtile and auspicious in its successive stages, but I consider it not to lead to final beatitude, since the field-knower is not abandoned.

70. For I am of opinion that the field-knower, although liberated from the primary and secondary constituents, still possesses the quality of giving birth and also of being a seed.

66. *Ruci*, neuter, in *c* does not seem possible.

67. Jaigīṣavya is quoted by Vyāsa on *YS.*, ii. 55, and his colloquy with Avāṭya reported by the same on iii. 18; *MBh.*, xii. 8431ff., records his conversation with Asita about *śīla* in the Sāṁkhya system, and he is mentioned in a list of Sāṁkhya seers, *ib.*, 11782, which includes Vārṣagaṇya, Kapila and Pañcaśikha. Vṛddha Parāśara is proved to be Pañcaśikha by *ib.*, 11875, where Janaka says, *Parāśarasagotrasya vṛddhasya sumahātmanaḥ | Bhikṣoḥ Pañcaśikhasyāhaṁ śiṣyaḥ paramasattamaḥ.* Other references to Parāśara in the *Śāntiparvan* show confusion between the Śāṁkhya teacher and the father of Vyāsa. The *Vibhāṣā*'s reference to *Pārāśari tīrthika* (*AK.*, Index, 121, cp. *Majjhima*, III, 298) is therefore to a follower of Pañcaśikha's system.

68. *Hetu* refers to the three *kuśalamūlāni*, as in ii. 56.

69. *Parataḥ parataḥ* could mean 'pre-eminently' (so Co., etc.), but cp. verse 82 and *hitvā hitvā* in verse 74.

70. For *prasavadharman* cp. *prasavadharmin* in *Sāṁkhyakārikā*, 11, where it is explained as the capacity to give birth, as *buddhi* gives birth to *ahaṁkāra*. *Bījadharman* is practically co-extensive in meaning; so *MBh.*, xii. 11662, of *avyakta*, *Kartṛtvāc cāpi bījānāṁ bījadharmā tathocyate.* At *ib.*, xiv. 1401, the eight *prakṛtis* are each described as *bījadharman* and *prasava*, because they give birth to the subsequent *tattvas*.

71. For although the soul by reason of its purity is conceived as being liberated, it will again become bound from the continued existence of the causal conditions.

72. Just as a seed does not grow for want of the proper season, soil or water, but does grow when these causal conditions are present, such I deem to be the case of the soul.

73. And as for the statement that liberation is deemed to come by severance from the power of the act, from ignorance and from desire, there is no complete severance from them so long as the soul persists.

74. It is true that advance is obtained by the progressive abandonment of these three, but where the soul still remains, there these three remain in a subtile state.

75. But such liberation is a creation of the imagination based on the subtility of the faults, the inactivity of the mind and the length of life in that state.

76. And as for this imagined abandonment of the ego-principle, so long as the soul persists, there is no abandonment of that principle.

77. And as the soul is not released from the activity of reason and the like, it is not devoid of attribute; therefore, as it is not devoid of attribute, it is not admitted to be liberated.

72. In *a* °*vihārāt* is metrically impossible and °*viharāt* makes no sense; for the authority for it in the meaning of 'separation' appears, as *PW* points out, to be due to a corruption.

73. *Kalpyate* properly 'is brought about', but cp. 71.

74. The argument recalls the Buddhist theory of the *anuśayas*.

75. The verse is used again in the *Śāriputraprakaraṇa*, where the entire passage is reminiscent of the preceding verses, there being a clear allusion to the argument of 72 (*SBPAW*, 1911, 392, C 4 *a*5, and K iv *a*2-3). Life in the *arūpa* spheres is measured by thousands of *kalpas*.

77. The exact meaning of *saṁkhyā* here is uncertain; if it could be solved, we should perhaps know how the name Sāṁkhya arose. The use in Pali of *saṁkhā* is also enigmatical and not fully explained yet; see *Saṁyutta*, I, 12, and Geiger's note thereon in his translation. At *Suttanipāta*, 1074, *saṁkhaṁ upeti* is opposed to *atthaṁ paleti*, and *ib.*, 209, and 749, the same

78. For no distinction exists between the attributes and the possessor of the attributes; for instance, fire is not perceived, when devoid of outward appearance and heat.

79. Before a conglomerate mass exists, there cannot be a possessor of the mass; so, before attributes exist, there cannot be a possessor of the attributes. Therefore the soul, as possessor of the body, being first released, is subsequently bound to it again.

80. And the knower of the field, when without a body, must be either knowing or unknowing. If it is knowing, there is something for it to know, and if there is something for it to know, it is not liberated.

phrase is used negatively in contrast to *saṁkhāya*, which latter apparently should be equated with the later *pratisaṁkhyā* (cp. Stcherbatsky, *Central Conception of Buddhism*, 51, n. 1). The meaning in these passages is equivalent to 'phenomenal existence', but this is not the exact sense. Here I take the reference to be to *sampaśyan* of verse 63, showing that the intelligence is still active, and I translate tentatively accordingly. What attributes are indicated by *ādi* also escapes me. It would be wrong to understand a secondary sense in the second line with reference to the *guṇas* of classical Sāṁkhya, for the word *guṇa* in Aśvaghoṣa's day was ordinarily used in Sāṁkhya discussions of anything rather than the three factors of *prakṛti*, and in the Sāṁkhya known to the poet salvation was attained by the destruction of *rajas* and *tamas* only, *sattva* remaining alone in an enhanced state.

79. Co.'s conjecture in *c* is negatived by C and T as well as A and is not too easy in sense either. T's *lus-bzhin* for *śarīrin* is surely a corruption (*lus-ḥdzin* ?). The argument apparently is that the fact that the *kṣetrajña* is called *śarīrin* shows that it did not exist before there was a body for it to inhabit (the bond therefore being *anādi*); if it thereafter attains liberation, the fact of its being by nature a *śarīrin* involves the consequence that it will be bound up again with a body.

80. The opposition between *kṣetrajña* in this verse and *ātman* in the next is intentional. According to the *MBh.*, the *kṣetrajña* is *jña* (*cetanāvān*, xii. 11649, *jñānalakṣaṇaḥ*, xiv. 1250), and the *ātman ajña* (*ajñaḥ svabhāvataḥ*, xii. 11658); and the *puruṣa* is hence described as both *jña* and *ajña* at xii. 11763.

81. Or if your teaching is that it is unknowing, what then is the use of inventing the existence of a soul? For even without a soul the existence of the quality of not-knowing is well established as in the case of a log or a wall.

82. But since this successive abandonment is declared to be meritorious, therefore I deem complete success in reaching the goal to derive from the abandonment of everything."

83. Thus he was not satisfied on learning the doctrine of Arāḍa, and, discerning that it was incomplete, he turned away from there.

84. Thereon in his desire to hear something higher he proceeded to the hermitage of Udraka, but he did not accept his system, because it too involved the tenet of the soul's existence.

85. For the sage Udraka, knowing the defects of consciousness and unconsciousness, found beyond the way of nothingness a way which was characterised by neither consciousness nor unconsciousness.

81. I have not thought it necessary to follow C and T in the second line, as it is a question, not of reading, but of division of words, and the first line makes *ajnānam* certain in the second. The Buddhist, however, would naturally read the line as C and T; for to him the existence of knowledge without a soul is as obvious as the existence of a wall. For the simile, cp. *MBh.*, xii. 11184, of the senses, *Ātmanā viprahīṇāni kāṣṭhakuḍyasamāni tu* ǀ *Vinaśyanti*.

83. The use of *pratijagāma* in this sense is unusual, but certified by T. Hultzsch's correction may be right, as *dharma* is masc.

84. *Grāha* is regularly used in Buddhism of holding to a wrong doctrine; cp. the expression *antagrāhadṛṣṭi*, and the P.T.S. *Pali Dict.* s. *gāha*. Cappeller's conjecture in *c* is probably sound.

85. This and the next two verses are very summarily treated by C. The definitions of the two previous *ārūpya* states in 62 and 63 above show that *saṁjñā* here has not the technical Buddhist sense, the 'naming' faculty of the mind, but means something like 'cognition' or 'consciousness', *vijñāna*, as appears from the use of *buddhi* as a synonym in 87 and from *saṁjñin* in 20 (cp. *S.*, ix. 1). *Saññā* is often used in Pali where classical Sanskrit would have *buddhi* (note i. 51 above). Cp. also the four kinds of *saṁjñā* in the *YS.* (Vācaspati Miśra on i. 15) and the equation of *saṁjñā* and *vijñāna* by Śabarasvāmin in quoting a Buddhist's views (on *Mīmāṁsāsūtra* i. 1, 5, see O. Strauss, *SBPAW*, 1932, 58 (524), n. 1), and also *Bṛh. Ār. Up.*, ii. 4, 12.

86. And since the conscious and unconscious states have each an object in a subtile condition, therefore he thought that beyond them was the state of neither unconsciousness nor consciousness and fixed his desires thereon.

87. And since the intellect remains in the same condition, without moving elsewhere, subtile and inert, therefore in that state there is neither consciousness nor unconsciousness.

88. And since a man returns again to the world, even after reaching that point, therefore the Bodhisattva, desiring to obtain the highest stage, left Udraka.

89. Then with his mind made up in the search for the supreme good, he departed from that hermitage and betook himself to the hermitage, Nagarī by name, of the royal seer Gaya.

90. Thereon the sage, whose every effort was pure and who delighted in a lonely habitation, took up his dwelling on the pure bank of the Nairañjanā river.

91. Then he saw five mendicants, who had come there before him; they had taken vows on themselves and practised austerities, vaunting themselves of control of the five senses.

86. The verse is too compressed for clear construction. *Ālambane* I take to be dual, in the technical sense of the object of mental or psychical action, as opposed to the subject. 'Though' should be supplied with *sūkṣme*. *Saṁjñāsaṁjñe*, presumably locative singular of a neuter dvandva compound. If it were not for *iti* in *c*, it would have been better to take *ālambane* as locative, understanding *sati*, and to treat *yasmāt* as governing *a*, *b* and *c*. Co. and T's division in *d* involves taking *tatra* as applying to consciousness and unconsciousness, not to the state that is neither. But *tatraiva* in the next verse implies division as in the text, and *spṛh* is always used in these poems with the dative, so that the text should have run *tasmai gataspṛhaḥ*.

87. The amendment in *c* is certain; of the many available passages in proof note especially *AK.*, V, 144, and 208.

91. I have given in the text so much of this verse as seemed to me capable of certain reconstruction. That C and T both have it shows that its omission by A is a mistake.

92. The mendicants saw him there and, desiring liberation, approached him, as the objects of sense come to a lordly man, whose good merit has earned him wealth and freedom from disease.

93. Thereon they served him reverently, abiding as pupils under his orders, and were humble and compliant because of their good training, just as the restless senses serve the mind ;

94. While he undertook extraordinary austerities by starvation, thinking that that might be the method for ending death and birth.

95. Carrying out many kinds of fasting that are difficult for a man to perform, for six years in his desire for quietude he made his body emaciated.

96. Yearning to reach the further shore of the cycle of transmigration whose further shore is unbounded, he lived by taking at mealtimes a single jujube fruit, sesamum seed and grain of rice.

97. Whatever his body lost by reason of these austerities, just so much was made good again through his psychic power.

98. Emaciated as he was, yet with his glory and majesty unimpaired, he was a source of joy to the eyes of others, as the moon in autumn at the beginning of the bright fortnight is to the night lotuses.

99. Though he had wasted away, so that only skin and bone remained, with fat, flesh and blood all gone, yet with

93. *Lolaiḥ* should also be understood of the five mendicants, implying that they had not yet acquired proper self-control. For the type of simile in this and the preceding verse cp. *Śiśupālavadha*, xiii. 28, and *MBh.*, iii. 398, 402, vii. 3553-4, and viii. 4196 and 4201.

95. T's *karmaprepsur* in *c* breaks the metre, because the Vipulā, ⏓ – ⏑ – – – – ⏓ requires a caesura after the fifth syllable.

96. T's *pha mthaḥ-med-pa* in *c* indicates literally *anantapāra°*, but is probably intended to give the correct meaning of *apāra* as ' boundless '.

97. It is not clear to me whether *tejas* in *d* means ' outward brilliance ' or ' internal vigour ', both perhaps. Kern conjectured *tejaso 'sya* in *d*, which is easier, but *tejasā* is wanted to correspond to *tapasā* in the first line.

undiminished depth of soul he shone like the ocean, whose depth never diminishes.

100. Thereon dreading existence the sage, whose body was clearly tormented to no purpose by pernicious austerities, thus resolved in his longing for Buddhahood :—

101. "This is not the way of life for passionlessness, for enlightenment, for liberation. That is the sure procedure which I won that time beneath the *jambu* tree.

102. Nor can that be obtained by one who is weak." So in all seriousness he pondered further on this point in order to increase his bodily strength.

103. How can the result to be attained by the mind be reached by a man, who is not calmly at ease and who is so worn out with the exhaustion of hunger and thirst that his mind is unbalanced with the exhaustion ?

104. Inward tranquillity is rightly gained by constant appeasement of the senses, and from the full appeasement of the senses the mind becomes well-balanced.

105. The man whose mind is well-balanced and serene develops concentrated meditation ; when the mind is possessed of concentrated meditation, the practice of trance begins.

106. By the practice of trance those *dharmas* are obtained, through which is won that highest, peaceful stage, so hard to reach, which is ageless and deathless.

102. *Āgatādara* has been variously understood, 'resuming his care for his body' (Co.), 'so reflecting' (Formichi), 'who has gained respect for himself' (W).

103. T is surely wrong in omitting *śrama* in *a*, for the repetition of the word makes the second *pāda* the sequel of the first.

104. The first line is undoubtedly corrupt both in A and T, as the reading should be °*tarpaṇam* with the first word of *a* in the ablative ; C has preserved the right sense, 'Eating and drinking satisfy the senses', but I cannot determine the opening word from this, *vihṛteḥ* being perhaps the best.

105. Read *raṅ-bzhin* for the first words of T, not *raṅ-zhiṅ* ?

106. The reference is to the *bodhipakṣika dharmas*.

107. Accordingly the steadfast seer of unbounded wisdom concluded that this method was based on the eating of food and made up his mind to take food.

108. He bathed and, as in his emaciation he came painfully up the bank of the Nairañjanā, the trees growing on the slope bent low the tips of their branches in adoration to give him a helping hand.

109. At that time on divine instigation Nandabalā, the daughter of the cowherd chief, went there, joy bursting from her heart.

110. She was wearing a dark-blue cloth and her arms were brilliant with white shells, so that she seemed like Yamunā, best of rivers, when its dark-blue water is wreathed with foam.

111. Her delight was enhanced by faith, and her blue-lotus eyes opened wide, as, doing obeisance with her head, she caused him to accept milk rice.

112. By partaking of it he secured for her the full reward of her birth and himself through the satisfaction of the six sense faculties became capable of obtaining enlightenment.

113. Then the sage's form together with his fame reached full roundness and he bore united in his single person the loveliness of the moon and the steadfastness of the ocean.

114. The five mendicants, holding that he had renounced the holy life, left him, as the five elements leave the thinking soul when it is liberated.

107. Constructionally this verse is joined to the next, which contains the main verb.

108. In the variants I have not given T's *draṅs* for *uttarāra*, but it might stand for *ujjagrāha* (cp. verse 111), and, if so, T should be understood to read *taṭadrumam* in *d*, no case-sign being given; this is inferior to the text in style. C does not indicate either reading clearly; it runs, 'After bathing, he wanted to come out of the pool; owing to the weakness of emaciation he could not rise up. A heavenly spirit pressed down a tree-branch; raising his hand, he grasped it and came out'.

113. The verse illustrates T's faithfulness to his text; he found *śaśākā*° in *d* and refused to make the obvious amendment to *śaśāṅkā*°.

115. On this with his resolution for sole companion, he made up his mind for enlightenment and proceeded to the root of a *pipal* tree, where the ground was carpeted with green grass.

116. Then at that moment Kāla, the best of serpents, whose might was as that of the king of elephants, was awakened by the incomparable sound of his feet, and, realising that the great sage had determined on enlightenment, he uttered this eulogy :—

117. " Since, O sage, the earth thunders, as it were, again and again, as it is pressed by your feet, and since your splendour shines forth as of the sun, certainly you will to-day enjoy the desired result.

118. Since, O lotus-eyed one, the flocks of blue jays, circling in the air, proceed round you right-handed, and since gentle breezes blow in the sky, to-day without doubt you will become a Buddha."

119. Then, after the lordliest of serpents had thus extolled him, he took clean grass from a grass-cutter, and, betaking himself to the foot of the great pure tree, he made a vow for enlightenment and seated himself.

120. Then he took up the supreme, immoveable cross--legged posture with his limbs massed together like the coils of a sleeping serpent, saying, " I will not rise from this position on the ground till I achieve the completion of my task ".

115. For the imitation of the first *pāda* by Mātṛceṭa see the Introduction.

116. Apparently both C and T read *gajarājavikramapada*°, but the poet never elsewhere runs a compound over the division between two *pādas* of so long a metre, and in Vaṁśastha he always ends *pādas a* and *c* on a long syllable. For *āgata*, which T also takes in this sense, see note on 38 above.

119. For the use of grass as a seat in yoga see *MBh.*, xii. 7164, and *Bhag. Gītā*, vi. 11.

120. W holds that T had the compound in *b* in the locative case (i.e. °*piṇḍane* ?) ; but I think it more probable it took it as an adverb.

121. Then when the Holy One took his seat with determined soul, the denizens of the heavens felt unequalled joy, and the birds and the companies of wild beasts refrained from noise nor did the forest trees, when struck by the wind, rustle at all.

121. For *niścitātman* cp. xiii. 11, and *Jāt.*, xx. 38.

CANTO XIII

Defeat of Māra

1. When the great sage, the scion of a line of royal seers, sat down there, after making his vow for liberation, the world rejoiced, but Māra, the enemy of the good Law, trembled.

2. Him whom in the world they call the God of Love, him of the bright weapon and also the flower-arrowed, that same one, as the monarch of the activities of the passions and as the enemy of liberation, they style Māra.

3. His three sons, Caprice, Gaiety and Wantonness, and his three daughters, Discontent, Delight and Thirst, asked him why he was depressed in mind, and he answered them thus :—

3. The verse is puzzling because no other version mentions three sons of Māra ; the *LV* knows of Māra having many sons, but none of the names correspond. All mention of them is omitted by C too, as if their presence were contrary to the legend in the form he knew. The three daughters according to *LV* are called Rati, Arati, and Tṛṣṇā, according to *Mhv.*, Tandrī (a corruption ?), Rati and Arati, and in the Pali canon Ragā, Arati and Taṇhā. The equivalents of the names in the various Chinese versions I am unable to determine with precision, but, as the one point in which the Sanskrit and Pali versions agree is that one of the daughters was called Arati and as Rati is known to Aśvaghoṣa as the wife of Kandarpa (*S.*, iv. 8), it is best to assume that the name of the first daughter should be read here as Arati and to insert an avagraha accordingly. It is remarkable that the sons and daughters play no part in the actual fight except for bare mentions in verses 7 and 14. In the oldest version of the tale (*Padhānasutta*, *Suttanipāta*, 425ff.,=*LV*., ch. xviii, 261–3), the daughters are not mentioned at all, but among the armies of Māra are named Kāmāḥ, Arati, Kṣutpipāsā and Tṛṣṇā. It looks as if the group of three daughters arose from a misunderstanding of this verse. In later legend (e.g., *LV*., ch. xxi and xxiv, and the FP) they play a great part, and it is perhaps to be inferred that this development was just beginning in the poet's time.

4. "The sage, wearing the armour of his vow and drawing the bow of resolution with the arrow of wisdom, sits yonder, desiring to conquer my realm; hence this despondency of my mind.

5. For if he succeeds in overcoming me and expounds to the world the path of final release, then is my realm to-day empty, like that of the Videha king, when he fell from good conduct.

6. While therefore he has not yet attained spiritual eyesight and is still within my sphere, I shall go to break his vow, like the swollen current of a river breaking an embankment."

7. Then, seizing his flower-made bow and his five world-deluding arrows, he, the causer of unrest to mortal minds, approached the *aśvattha* tree accompanied by his children.

8. Next Māra placed his left hand on the tip of the bow and, fingering the arrow, thus addressed the sage, who was tranquilly seated in his desire to cross to the further shore of the ocean of existence :—

9. "Up, up, Sir Kṣatriya, afraid of death. Follow your own *dharma*, give up the *dharma* of liberation. Subdue the

4. I follow C and Formichi in the translation of *āyudha* as 'bow'; T has 'sword' and Co. 'barb'.

5. In *a yāti* seems to be purely an auxiliary to the gerundive. For *c* cp. *LV.*, ch. xxi, 303, 9, and *Mhv.*, II, 408, 9. The Videha king is presumably Karālajanaka, mentioned in iv. 80 ; Co. considers it a reference to Nimi Videha, who according to the *MBh.* gave his kingdom to the Brahmans.

7. T is apparently corrupt in *b*, as shown by the repetition of *gṛhītvā*. C assumes a play of words on *'śvattha* and *asvāsthya*.

8. There is little to choose between A and T's readings in *a*, C giving no lead.

9. The use of *mṛtyubhīta* is typical of the poet ; it implies (1) ordinary cowardice, (2) a reference to the Buddha's statements such as at xi. 7, *ahaṁ jarāmṛtyubhayaṁ viditvā*, (3) an allusion to the etymology of Māra, i.e. 'afraid of Māra', just as at xxvii. 38, the word *māra* is used for "death". For the second line I follow T except for reading *vinīya*, certified by C ; but *d* can hardly

world both with arrows and with sacrifices, and from the world obtain the world of Vāsava.

10. For this is the path to issue forth by, the famous one travelled by kings of olden time. It is ignominious for one born in a renowned family of royal seers to practise this mendicancy.

11. Or if, O firm in purpose, you do not rise up to-day, be steadfast, do not give up your vow. For this arrow that I have ready is the very one I discharged at Śūrpaka, the fishes' foe.

12. And at the mere touch of it the son of Iḍā, though he was the grandson of the moon, fell into a frenzy, and Santanu lost his self-control. How much more then would anyone else do so, who is weak with the decadence of the present age?

13. So rise up quickly and recover your senses; for this ever-destructive arrow stands ready. I do not discharge it at

be in order as it stands. Taking the indications of C, I surmise an original *lokāt paraṁ prāpnuhi vāsavaryam.*

10. The only occurrence of *pūrvatama* apparently. *Bhaikṣākyam* in *d* ?

11. *Pāda b* is ironical, meaning 'you will need all your firmness not to give up your vow'. According to *S.*, viii. 44, Śūrpaka was loved by Kumudvatī; and if he is the *abjaśatru* of *ib.*, x. 53, he was burnt up by love (after being hit by Kāma's arrow ?). The name is known to the lexicographers as that of the enemy of Kāmadeva and is so used at *Padyacūḍāmaṇi*, vi. 23. The story was well known at one time and formed apparently the subject of a play, as appears from the reference at *Padmaprābhṛtaka* (ed. *Caturbhāṇī*), 25, l. 20, to the manuscript of a part in it, which was entitled *Kumudvatī-prakaraṇe Śūrpakasaktāṁ rājadārikāṁ dhātrī rahasy upālambhate.* That it dealt with an enemy to love is perhaps hinted at by the phrase *avinaya-grantha* in the following verse. I can find no trace of any existing MS. of the play, and it may be an imaginary one. The details suggest that we may have a variant version in the story of the fisherman, Suprahāra, and the princess Māyāvatī, in *Kathāsaritsāgara*, ch. cxii.

12. *Vicitta* is a very rare word, only recorded by *PW* from *Suśruta.* The reference is to Santanu's infatuation for Gaṅgā, cp. *S.*, vii. 41, and x. 56. T's equivalent for *asvatantra* is not clear.

13. For *saṁjñāṁ* C seems to transliterate *aṁjñā.* The exact correspondence of T in *b* is not clear (*yin yaṅ* for *hy ayam*), but its *byar-ḥos*

those who are given to sensual pleasures and show compliance to their mistresses, any more than I would at sheldrakes."

14. Despite these words the sage of the Śākyas showed no concern and did not change his posture; so then Māra brought forward his sons and daughters and discharged the arrow at him.

15. But even when the arrow was shot at him, he paid no heed to it and did not falter in his firmness. Māra, seeing him thus, became despondent and, full of anxiety, said softly to himself:—

16. "When Śambhu, god as he was, was pierced with this arrow, he became agitated with love towards the mountain-king's daughter. That very arrow causes this man no feeling. Is it that he has no heart or that this is not that arrow?

17. Therefore he is no fit subject for my flower-arrow or for my excitation or for the application of sexual delight; he merits threats, revilings and blows at the hands of my troops of awe-inspiring spirits."

18. Then as soon as Māra thought of his army in his desire to obstruct the tranquillity of the Śākya sage, his followers

in *c* can only indicate A's °*vidheyeṣu*, not the °*abhidheyeṣu* of Co.'s MSS. There is a double point in the simile of the Brahminy ducks; not only are they the type of true lovers, but it is generally considered improper to shoot them in India, and many castes, which will eat other wild duck, will not touch them.

16. The first line is interesting as showing that the poet knew a different version of the story of Kāma, Pārvatī and Śiva to that immortalized in the *Kumārasaṁbhava* and that, when he calls the god of love Anaṅga, he does not refer to this legend (see the Introduction). The line implies the Buddha's superiority to Śiva. I translate *d* according to T; Gawronski objected that the text should mean 'is this no arrow?', but I do not see that this is necessarily so. Formichi takes the question to be whether the sage or the arrow is *acitta*.

17. See note on verse 3, in view of which I do not take *harṣaṇa* and *rati* as names of Māra's son and daughter.

18. *Ca ... ca* to denote simultaneity, correctly rendered by C. In *c* *āśraya* in this sense is almost entirely restricted to Buddhism, but cp. Gauḍapāda on *Sāṁkhyakārikā*, 62. The exact equivalence of T in *d* is uncer-

stood round him, in various forms and carrying lances, trees, javelins, clubs and swords in their hands;

19. Having the faces of boars, fishes, horses, asses and camels, or the countenances of tigers, bears, lions and elephants, one-eyed, many-mouthed, three-headed, with pendulous bellies and speckled bellies;

20. Without knees or thighs, or with knees vast as pots, or armed with tusks or talons, or with skulls for faces, or with

tain, but *gsum-mduṅ* (=*triśūla*) stands for the word I conjecture to be *śala*, i.e. T may have had *śūla*. *Śala* is only known to the lexicographers, but the reading must be either that or *śūla* to bring A and T together. The corruption of A is perhaps due to the writing of a double sibilant (*parīyuś śala*°, or *śūla*°) in some earlier MS.

19. The last compound of the verse is uncertain. For A's reading cp. *kabarakucchi* of a Yakṣa at *Jātaka*, I, 273, but T and C agree in a word meaning 'with large bellies'; *akṛśodarāś ca* involves amending the preceding *caiva* to *cāpy*, and *mahodarāś ca* the change of two letters, while *pṛthūdarāś ca* does not agree with T and C's indications. For Windisch's conjecture cp. *MBh.*, x. 275.

This and the next five verses have parallels in *LV.*, ch. xxi, *Mhv.*, II, 338 and 410, and FP, ch. xxviii, and also in the descriptions of Śiva's and Skanda's followers, *MBh.*, ix. 2576ff., and x. 265ff. Whether Aśvaghoṣa knew any of these Buddhist passages in their extant form is not clear, but Windisch's discussion should be consulted (i, 312ff.). C translates all the verses very fully except 23, which it omits entirely, and I have little doubt that this verse is spurious. Verses 21, 22 and 24 describe Māra's host as taking the form of Brahmanical ascetics (note *kapālahasta* also at 49 below), and this verse interrupts the order and adds nothing of value to the account. The description of the fiends as ascetics is developed from a hint in the *Padhānasutta* referred to under verse 3. According to Windisch's reconstruction (i, 31), which seems well established in this point, the following verse occurs in the account of Namuci's army, *Pagāḷhā ettha dissanti eke samaṇabrāhmaṇā Tañ ca maggaṁ na jānanti yena gacchanti subbatā.* This detail was omitted in later works and suggests that the poet either is embroidering on the early tale or knew an extended version, no longer extant.

20. C appears to support T's reading in *c*, its real meaning being perhaps 'some with heads that had neither faces nor eyes'. A's *kabandhahastā* is difficult; it should mean, not 'carrying *kabandhas* in their hands', for which

many bodies, or with half their faces broken off or with huge visages;

21. Ashy-grey in colour, tricked out with red spots, carrying ascetics' staves, with hair smoke-coloured like a monkey's, hung round with garlands, with pendent ears like elephants, clad in skins or entirely naked;

22. With half their countenances white or half their bodies green; some also copper-coloured, smoke-coloured, tawny or black; some too with arms having an overgarment of snakes, or with rows of jangling bells at their girdles;

23. Tall as toddy-palms and grasping stakes, or of the stature of children with projecting tusks, or with the faces of sheep and the eyes of birds, or with cat-faces and human bodies;

24. With dishevelled hair, or with topknots and half--shaven polls, clothed in red and with disordered headdresses, with bristling faces and frowning visages, suckers of the vital essence and suckers of the mind.

Windisch cites *Mhv.*, II, 411, in the account of the attack (not of the description of the army), but 'having hands like *kabandhas*'. The exact equivalent of T is *kaṅkālavaktrā*, but I prefer *karaṅka*° as better sense, as closer to A palæographically and as apparently indicated by C.

21. The first line seems to describe Śaiva ascetics. For *bhasmāruṇa* cp. *MBh.*, xvi. 5. Did C ('some like the brightness of the dawn-star') take *lohita* as meaning Mars? For the colour of ascetics' hair note *Mhv.*, II, 195, 19, of a ṛṣi, *tāmradhūmrāruṇajaṭa*. The first word in *c* is uncertain; C's meaning is not clear, but it might have had *laṃbasphico*. The garlands, if °*srajo* is correct, may be garlands of skulls. For the next word cp. Bāṇa's description of the ascetic Jābāli, *Kād.*, 43, 3-4, *praśastavāraṇam iva pralambakarṇatālam*.

22. In *d* one can divide *ghaṇṭā-kula* as I do, or *ghaṇṭā-ākula* as T does. For the compound cp. *Gaṇḍīstotra*, 10, which I restore (*Ind. Ant.*, 1933, 65) *prakaṭapaṭutaṭābaddhaghaṇṭā*.

24. For *ardhamuṇḍa* cp. *MBh.*, vii. 3383. Apte gives *raktāmbara* as the name of a kind of ascetic, presumably the *raktapaṭas* of *Kād.*, 95, 1. I can make nothing out of A's *rajvambara*, and the confusion of *jva* and *kta* might easily occur. For *tejohara* I follow C; its apparent reading, *vayoharāś ca*, may well be right.

25. Some, as they ran, leapt wildly about, some jumped on each other; while some gambolled in the sky, others sped along among the treetops.

26. One danced about, brandishing a trident; another snorted, as he trailed a club; one roared like a bull in his excitement, another blazed fire from every hair.

27. Such were the hordes of fiends who stood encompassing the root of the *bodhi* tree on all sides, anxious to seize and to kill, and awaiting the command of their master.

28. Beholding in the beginning of the night the hour of conflict between Māra and the bull of the Śākyas, the sky lost its brightness, the earth shook and the quarters blazed and crashed.

29. The wind raged wildly in every direction, the stars did not shine, the moon was not seen, and night spread forth still thicker darkness and all the oceans were troubled.

30. And the earth-bearing Nāgas, devoted to *dharma*, did not brook obstruction to the great sage and, turning their eyes wrathfully on Māra, they hissed and unwound their coils.

31. But the divine sages of the Pure Abodes, absorbed in the fulfilment of the good Law, developed compassion for Māra in their minds, but were untouched by anger, because they were freed from all passion.

32. When those who were given to *dharma* and desired the

27. Co. takes the *bodhi* tree as the object of *pāda* c; it seems more natural to suppose that the Bodhisattva is intended. Acceptance of T's reading would have made this clear.

28. According to *Gaṇḍīstotra*, 4, the phenomena in this and the next verse were caused by Māra's followers.

30. For the eight Nāga kings who support the earth see *AK.*, II, 175, n. 4. If *dharmabhṛtaś* is correct, cp. the use at *S.*, i. 1. T takes *jṛmbh* in the sense of *gātravināma* here, which I understand as above.

32. *Dharmātman* is applied to the deities of the Buddhist heavens again at *S.*, ii. 47.

liberation of the world saw the root of the *bodhi* tree beset by Māra's cruel host, they raised cries of " Ha ! Ha ! " in the sky.

33. But when the great seer beheld Māra's army standing as a menace to that method of *dharma*, like a lion seated amidst kine he did not quail nor was he at all perturbed.

34. Then Māra gave orders to his raging army of demons for terrifying the sage. Thereon that army of his resolved to break down his steadfastness with their various powers.

35. Some stood trying to frighten him, their many tongues hanging out flickering, their teeth sharp-pointed, their eyes like the sun's orb, their mouths gaping, their ears sticking up stiff as spikes.

36. As they stood there in such guise, horrible in appearance and manner, he was no more alarmed by them or shrank before them than before over-excited infants at play.

37. Then one of them, wrathfully turning his gaze on him, raised his club ; then his arm with the club became immovable, as was Puraṁdara's of old with the thunderbolt.

38. Some lifted up rocks and trees, but were unable to hurl them at the sage. Instead they fell down with the trees and rocks, like the spurs of the Vindhyas when shattered by the levin.

33. T gives *dharmavidhi* no case-sign, but it can only have read as in the text. *Upaplava* in this sense is unusual ; perhaps there is a suggestion of ' portent ', without which the way of Buddhahood cannot be accomplished.

34. T's *draṅ-po* in the second line should be corrected to *drag-po* (*udīrṇa*). For the odd use of *bhayāya* see the Introduction.

35. For *nāma* see note on iv. 29 ; *kila nāma,* literally ' apparently pretending '.

36. T does not express *su* in °*subālebhyaḥ*.

37. C deals very scantily with the passage beginning here. The *MBh.* mentions several occasions of Indra's being paralysed ; the use of the name Puraṁdara suggests that it was the occasion of the taking of Tripura, narrated at xiii. 7490, and in the Bombay edition at the close of the *Droṇaparvan*.

39. The rocks and trees and axes, discharged by some who flew up into the sky, remained hanging in the air without falling down, like the many-hued rays of the evening clouds.

40. Another flung above him a blazing log as big as a mountain peak ; no sooner was it discharged than, as it hung in the sky, it burst into a hundred fragments through the sage's magic power.

41. Another, shining like the rising sun, let loose from the sky a vast shower of red-hot coals, just as at the close of the æon Meru in full conflagration throws out the pulverised scoriæ of his golden rifts.

42. But the shower of hot coals, scattered full of sparks at the foot of the *bodhi* tree, became a shower of red lotus petals through the exercise of universal benevolence on the part of the best of sages.

43. And the Śākya sage, embracing his resolution like a kinsman, did not waver at all from his posture in spite of these various afflictions and distresses of body and mind, which were cast at him.

44. Thereon others spat out snakes from their mouths as

39. In *d* I follow the previous translations. W objects, not unreasonably, that a cloud does not send out rays, and suggests 'the under edge', also somewhat difficult ; cp. *S.*, iii. 24.

40. *Kaḍaṅgara*, which beat T (did it read *gajaṁ varam* ?), is evidently the same as Pali *kaliṅgara*, as Kern pointed out. Schmidt's *Nachträge* quotes the same form from the *MBh.* ; cp. also *kalāṅgala*, *ib.*, iii. 642.

41. For references for the second line see *AK.*, II, 184, n. 2.

42. *Maitrīvihāra* is one of the Brahmavihāras ; cp. *LV.*, ch. xxi. 310, 4-5.

43. *Ātapa* as a substantive seems to be only known in the sense of 'heat', but as it cannot be an adjective here, I take it as a substantive in the sense of the adjective. Sukumar Sen (*Outline Syntax of Buddhistic Sanskrit*, 25) construes the instrumentals of the first line as absolute ; more probably Aśvaghoṣa feels the intransitive *cacāla* to be equivalent to a causative passive, 'was not caused to waver by'.

44. The form *nirjigiluḥ* is remarkable ; *Pāṇ.*, viii. 2, 21, allows the present stem *gil* for *gṝ* when compounded with a preposition ending in a vowel and the

from rotten treetrunks; as if bound by spells, they did not hiss or raise themselves or move in his presence.

45. Others transformed themselves into huge clouds, accompanied by lightning and the fearsome crash of thunderstones, and let loose on the tree a shower of stones, which turned into a pleasant rain of flowers.

46. One too placed an arrow on his bow; it blazed there, but did not shoot forth, like the anger of a poor ill-tempered man, when it is fanned in his heart.

47. But five arrows shot by another stood arrested in the air and did not fall on the sage, just as, when their objects are present, the five senses of a wise man who is afraid of the cycle of existence remain inactive.

48. Another rushed wrathfully against the great seer, grasping a club in order to kill him; he fell helpless without obtaining his object, as men, not obtaining their desires, fall helplessly into calamitous sins.

49. But a woman, black as a cloud, with a skull in her hand, wandered about there unrestrainedly and did not remain still, with the intention of deluding the great seer's heart, and resembling the intelligence of a man of inconstant mind wandering uncertainly among the various sacred traditions.

preceding rule authorises the intensive *jegilyate*. But a perfect formation from this stem appears to have no parallel. *Utsasṛpuḥ*, Kern's conjecture, seems certified by T, which takes it in the sense of 'going along'; the sense I propose is better, as suggesting preparation to strike.

46. The point of the simile lies in *anīśvara*, whose exact sense is uncertain; *īśvara* is used by the poet for 'rich', so I conjecture 'poor' here. Co.'s 'impotent' is as good. A man who is *anīśvara* has perforce to keep his anger in his heart, because he cannot give it effective expression.

47. There is nothing to choose between *nabhasi* and *viyati* in *b*, except that Aśvaghoṣa uses the former rather oftener.

49. C may be right in taking *meghakālī* as a proper name; he describes her as an elder sister of Māra, but otherwise she is unknown. Or the verse may be intended as a reference to some Hindu goddess or to female Śaiva ascetics. *Aniyatam* probably implies making lewd gestures, as C suggests.

50.   One, wishing to burn him up like a venomous snake with the fire of his glance, levelled a blazing eye on the seer, but failed to see him, as he sat still in the same place, just as a man absorbed in the passions fails to see the true good when it is pointed out to him.

51.   Thus another, lifting a ponderous rock, toiled in vain with his efforts baffled, like one who desires to obtain by affliction of the body the *dharma* which is the ultimate good and which is only to be reached by knowledge and concentration of mind.

52.   Others again, assuming the forms of hyenas and lions, loudly roared mighty roars, from which living beings cowered away on every side, thinking the sky had been split by the blow of a thunderbolt.

53.   The deer and the elephants, giving forth cries of distress, ran about and hid themselves, and on that night, as if it were day, the birds on all sides fluttered about, screaming in distress.

54.   But although all beings shivered at such howls of theirs, the sage, like Garuḍa at the noise of crows, neither trembled nor quailed.

55.   The less the sage was afraid of the fearsome troops of that array, the more was Māra, the enemy of the upholders of the Law, cast down with grief and wrath.

56.   Then a certain being of high station and invisible form, standing in the sky and seeing that Māra was menacing the seer and without cause of enmity was displaying wrath, addressed him with imperious voice :—

The simile is a reference to the various *āgamas*, which the poet considered to be mutually contradictory and uncertain (cp. ix. 76, and *S.*, i. 14, and iii. 2).
    55.   A's *sasāra* in *d* is hopeless, and C and FP clearly indicate *sasāda* ; T's mysterious *byer* is probably corrupt for *byiṅ* (to *ḥbyiṅ-ba*), which would stand for the same reading.
    56.   *Vaira* is not exactly 'enmity', but more like 'feud', the hostile feeling which two factions or opponents maintain to each other.   In this case

[margin note:] demons compared to various vad mind state

57. "Māra, you should not toil to no purpose, give up your murderous intent and go in peace. For this sage can no more be shaken by you than Meru, greatest of mountains, by the wind.

58. Fire might lose its nature of being hot, water its liquidity, earth its solidity, but in view of the meritorious deeds accumulated by him through many ages he cannot abandon his resolution.

59. For such is his vow, his energy, his psychic power, his compassion for creation, that he will not rise up till he has attained the truth, just as the thousand-rayed sun does not rise without dispelling the darkness.

60. For by rubbing wood long enough a man obtains fire, and by digging the earth deep enough he obtains water ; nothing is impossible of achievement to the man of perseverance. Everything that is undertaken by the proper method is thereby necessarily carried out with success.

61. Therefore since the great physician, in his pity for the world lying distressed in the diseases of passion, etc., toils for the medicine of knowledge, he should not be hindered.

62. And since the world is being carried away along wrong paths, it is no more proper to harass him, the guide who is laboriously searching for the right path, than it is to harass a good guide, when a caravan has lost its way.

the enmity was only on Māra's side, the Buddha having no similar feeling against him ; there was therefore no real *vaira* between them.

57. *Śarma*, 'home' and 'peace'. Presumably the reading should be either *hiṁsātmatām* here or *hiṁsrātmanā* in verse 32.

59. In T for *bcom gnas* read *bcom-nas.*

60. The point in *d*, as correctly seen by most translators, lies in the significance of the doubled *ca* ; *yuktam* properly 'conjoined with'. The verse, which is imitated in *Pratijñāyaugandharāyaṇa*, i. 18, contains ideas used again in *S.*, xii. 33, 34, and xvi. 97.

61. *Rāgādi*, i.e. *dveṣa* and *moha* also.

62. The collocation of *daiśika* and *sudeśika* is suspicious. The MSS. of *S.* read *daiśika* in every case and *sudaiśika* once and *sudeśika* once. Probably *sudaiśikaḥ* is right here.

63. When all beings are lost in the great darkness, he is being made into the lamp of knowledge; it is no more right for your Honour to cause his extinction than it would be to put out a lamp which has been made to shed light in the darkness.

64. But what honourable man indeed would meditate wrong towards him who, when he sees the world to be drowning in the great flood of the cycle of existence and to be unable to find the further shore, engages himself in ferrying it across?

65. For the tree of knowledge, when flourishing, should not be cut down, the tree whose fibres are forbearance, which is rooted deep in resolution, whose flowers are good conduct and whose boughs awareness and wisdom, and which yields the fruit of *dharma*.

66. His purpose is to deliver creation which is bound fast in mind by the snares of delusion. It does not befit you to try to kill him who is exerting himself to deliver mankind from their bondage.

67. For to-day is the appointed time for the ripening of those deeds which he has done in the past for the sake of illumination. Thus he is seated in this place exactly like the previous sages.

63. The application of *ārya* to Māra is curious. Properly it means either a member of one of the three *ārya* castes or one who has entered on the path to salvation and is no longer a *pṛthagjana*. I take it here primarily as equivalent to *bhavat* in accordance with dramatic usage; secondarily it may allude to the legend that Māra was ultimately converted. The verb *nirvāpayitum*, which T renders 'cause to attain Nirvāṇa', probably hints at the story of Māra's tempting the Buddha to enter Parinirvāṇa before his time.

64. The three conjunctions have bothered the critics. I take *tu* as governing the whole sentence to emphasise that it is taking up the *ārya* of the previous verse and giving it a new twist. The doubled *ca* I construe only in the relative sentence, implying the simultaneity of the two clauses, 'as soon as he saw . ., he started etc.', but properly a finite verb is wanted in the first line.

66. Aśvaghoṣa uses *śrānta* for 'wearied by strenuous activity', and so 'strenuous'; cp. iv. 103, and *S.*, i. 1.

68. For this is the navel of earth's surface, entirely possessed of the highest power; for there is no other spot on earth which can bear the force of his concentrated thought.

69. Therefore be not grieved, calm yourself, Māra, and be not over-proud of your might. Inconstant fortune should not be relied on; you display arrogance, when your very position is tottering."

70. And when Māra heard that speech of his and observed the great sage's unshakenness, then, his efforts frustrated, he went away dejectedly with the arrows by which the world is smitten in the heart.

71. Then his host fled away in all directions, its elation gone, its toil rendered fruitless, its rocks, logs and trees scattered everywhere, like a hostile army whose chief has been slain by the foe.

72. As he of the flower-banner fled away defeated with his following, and the great seer, the passion-free conqueror of

68. This idea of the navel of the earth goes back to the *Rigveda*, where the place of Agni and Soma is repeatedly called the navel of the earth. That the poet had this in mind is shown by *dhāmnā*, a word specially applied to the seat of Agni and Soma, and which should therefore possibly be understood here as also meaning the supreme 'seat', the *vajrāsana* described at *AK.*, II, 145-6. For the general idea see *Jātaka*, I, 71, and IV, 229, and *AAA.*, 178 (explaining the word *aviṣahyatvam* of Asaṅga's *kārikā*), and for the use of *nābhi Mhv.*, III, 275, 1-2, and Coomaraswamy's reference to *Mahābodhivaṁsa* 79, in *Eastern Art*, III, 217. For *d* cp. *Rām.*, v. 3, 78, and *MBh.*, v. 55.

69. C gives no help in determining the reading in *d*.

70. In *d* T takes *jagaccetasi* as a compound and *vihanyate* (if it read so) therefore as impersonal; it may have read *yasya* (i.e. *hanyate* ?). Possibly one should take *yair* as equivalent to *yasya*, 'by whose arrows', and attracted into the instrumental by the nearer noun.

71. C and T agree that *āśraya* here means 'leader'; cp. viii. 23, and note. It is a well-recognized phenomenon in Indian history and literature that, when the leader is killed in battle, his army promptly disperses.

72. *Paripakṣa* does not occur elsewhere; those who do not like it can choose between *saparirakṣe*, *saparivāre* and *saparibarhe*. The following verse, as pointed out by Lüders long ago, is undoubtedly spurious, as not in C, as

the darkness of ignorance, remained victorious, the heavens shone with the moon like a maiden with a smile, and there fell a rain of sweet-smelling flowers filled with water.

simply repeating 72 in different terms, as containing words not used elsewhere by the poet (*pāpīyas*, *yoṣā*, *vikalmaṣa*), and as following a verse in a longer metre.

CANTO XIV

Enlightenment

1. Then, after conquering Māra's host by his steadfastness and tranquillity, he, the master of trance, put himself into trance in order to obtain exact knowledge of the ultimate reality.

2. And after winning entire control over all the methods of trance, he called to mind in the first watch the succession of his previous births.

3. As though living them over again, he recalled thousands of births, that he had been so-and-so in such-and-such a place and that passing out of that life he had come hither.

4. Then after recalling his birth and death in these various existences, the compassionate one was filled with compassion for all living beings :—

5. " Truly the world, in abandoning its kinsfolk in this life and yet proceeding to activity in another existence, is without means of rescue and turns round and round like a wheel."

6. As he thus with resolute soul was mindful of the past, the conviction grew in him that the cycle of existence was as lacking in substance as the pith of a plantain-tree.

3. T's *amuko* is contrary to the usual wording, e.g. *LV.*, ch. xxii, 345, 12.

5. The words *ca kriyāḥ* are very puzzling and can only be construed by understanding *kṛtvā* from *a* ; in view of the assonance with *cakravat* in *d*, the original reading may have been *cakriyaḥ*, 'travelling onwards' (*Aitareya-brāhmaṇa*, i. 14, 4). In either case the thought is that the Buddha and the world generally both have to abandon their kindred, but the world does it to repeat the performance in the next life, while the Buddha intends never to have to do it again. But C's 'The wheel turns round in the six *gatis*, birth and death (=*saṁsāra*) are never exhausted', suggests that the reading should be *cākṣayam*, 'without ever stopping', which is palæographically sound and expresses the sense more clearly. The form *bhramati* is permissible according to *Pāṇ.*, iii. 1, 70.

7. But in the second watch he, whose energy had no peer, gained the supreme divine eyesight, being himself the highest of all who possess sight.

8. Then with that completely purified divine eyesight he beheld the entire world, as it were in a spotless mirror.

9. His compassionateness waxed greater, as he saw the passing away and rebirth of all creatures according as their acts were lower or higher.

10. Those living beings whose acts are sinful pass to the sphere of misery, those others whose deeds are good win a place in the triple heaven.

11. The former are reborn in the very dreadful fearsome hell and, alas, are woefully tormented with sufferings of many kinds.

12. Some are made to drink molten iron of the colour of fire; others are impaled howling on a redhot iron pillar.

13. Some, head downwards, are boiled like meal in iron cauldrons; others are miserably broiled on heaps of burning redhot coals.

14. Some are devoured by fierce horrid dogs with iron teeth, others by the gloating Iron-beaks as if by crows of iron.

15. Some, exhausted with the burning, long for cool shade and enter like captives the dark sword-leaved forest.

7. For the divine eyesight, see *AK.*, Index s. *divyacakṣus.*

9. Cp. *AAA.*, 130, 25, *ayaṁ hi hetuphalayor dharmo yat prakṛṣṭād dhetoḥ prakṛṣṭaṁ phalam aprakṛṣṭāc cāprakṛṣṭam.*

10. The *durgati par excellence* is hell, but the term usually includes existence as an animal or as a Preta.

12. The following description has many analogies in Buddhist literature; for another *kāvya* account see *Jāt.*, xxix, and for the classic description with references to literature *AK.*, II, 148ff.

13. Should it be *dahyante 'karuṇaṁ* in *c* ?

14. For the *ayastuṇḍas*, *AK.*, II, 151; it is wrong to take *vāyasaiḥ* with *ayastuṇḍaiḥ.*

15. The *asipattravana* figures also in Brahmanical literature, *MBh.*, xii. 12075, *Manu*, iv. 90, *R.*, xiv. 48; see also Kirfel, *Kosmographie der Inder*, Index s.v. The point of *baddhā iva* escapes me; should it be *vadhyā iva* ?

16. Some have their arms bound and like wood are chopped up with axes; even in this suffering they do not cease to exist, the power of their acts holding back their vital breaths.

17. The retribution of the act which was committed by them for the cessation of suffering in the hope of obtaining pleasure, is experienced by them against their will in the shape of this suffering.

18. These did evil for the sake of pleasure and are now exceedingly tormented. What pleasure, even the slightest, does that enjoyment of theirs cause?

19. The consequences of the foul act, mirthfully carried out by the foul-minded, are reaped by them with lamentations, when the hour of retribution has matured.

20. If sinners could thus see the fruit of their acts, they would vomit forth hot blood, as if they had been struck in a vital part.

21. By reason of their various actions arising from the activity of the mind, these other unfortunates are born among the various kinds of animals.

22. In this state they are miserably slaughtered, even before the eyes of their relatives, for the sake of their flesh, skin, fur or tusks, or out of mutual enmity or mere wantonness.

23. And powerless and helpless too, tormented by hunger, thirst and exhaustion, those who become oxen or horses are driven along, their bodies wounded with goads.

16. In T correct *bteg* to *btags* in *b*. *Vipacyante* seems better than *vipadyante*; it refers to *vipāka*, the retribution of the act, but primarily it means 'come to an end', by transition from the idea of completion on maturity. The passive of *paripac* is recorded in this sense.

20. The verse which A and T add here is so obviously out of place that there can be no doubt of the correctness of Lüders' opinion rejecting it; it is not in C.

21. For *vispanda*, see references in *Ind. Ant.*, 1933, 114.

22. I understand *vairād api* to mean the animals kill each other; as C has it, 'still more they mutually tear and kill each other'. T's *rāgād* for it is inferior.

24. And those who become elephants are ridden despite their strength by weaklings, who kick them with foot and heel or torment their heads with the ankus.

25. In this state, though there are other forms of suffering, suffering arises especially from mutual enmity and from subjection to others.

26. For catching each other mutually, the sky-dwellers are oppressed by sky-dwellers, water-dwellers by those who move in the water, and land-dwellers by land-dwellers.

27. And so those, who are obsessed by stinginess, are reborn in the dark world of the Pretas and reap their reward in wretchedness.

28. With mouths small as the eye of a needle and bellies vast as mountains, their lot is suffering and they are tortured with the sufferings of hunger and thirst.

29. For reaching the limit of longing, yet kept in existence by their own deeds, they do not succeed in swallowing even the filth thrown away by others.

30. If man knew that such was the fruit of avarice, he would always give away even the limbs of his own body, as Śibi did.

24. The mahout sits on the neck of the elephant with his feet under the ears, ordinarily controlling him with his feet, but, when he is refractory, bringing down the ankus, often with great force, on the crown of his head.

26. I do not like the reading in *d*, but see no alternative.

27. *Pitṛ* is here used for *preta*, a class of being about whom Buddhist traditions are very confused. The reference here, as is shown by *nirāloka*, is to the realm of Yama, which according to the *Saddharmasmṛtyupasthānasūtra* (S. Lévi, *JA*, 1918, i, p. 36) is 'tout assombri par l'égarement et par l'obscurcissement des esprits qui s'y trouvent.' It places the land of Yama on the surface of the earth, while *AK.*, II, 156, puts it 500 *yojanas* below.

29. C and the sense show that this and the next verse must be read in this order. The reading in *a* is not quite satisfactory; the sense clearly being that they reach the extreme limit of starvation, should it run *aśanāsamatikrāntā*? Note the idiomatic use of *labh* with the infinitive.

31. These other creatures take form again in the filthy hell-like pool called the womb and experience suffering amongst men.

32. At the first even at the moment of birth they are gripped by sharp hands, as if sharp swords were piercing them, whereat they weep bitterly.

33. They are loved and cherished and guarded by their kindred who bring them up with every care, only to be defiled by their own various deeds as they pass from suffering to greater suffering.

34. And in this state the fools, obsessed with desire, are borne along in the ever-flowing stream, thinking all the more, 'this is to be done and this is to be done'.

35. These others, who have accumulated merit, are born in heaven, and are terribly burned by the flames of sensual passion, as by a fire.

36. And from there they fall, still not satiated with the objects of sense, with eyes turned upwards, their brilliance gone, and wretched at the fading of their garlands.

37. And as their lovers fall helplessly, the Apsarases regard them pitifully and catch their clothes with their hands.

38. Some look as if they were falling to earth with their ropes of pearls swaying, as they try to hold up their lovers falling miserably from the pavilions.

39. Others, wearing ornaments and garlands of many kinds and grieved at their fall into suffering, follow them with eyes unsteady with sympathy.

40. In their love for those who are falling, the troops of Apsarases beat their breasts with their hands and, distressed, as it were, with great affliction, remain attached to them.

33. 'Defiled', *ñon-moṅs*, *kliś* or *kaluṣa*.

38. *Luṅ-ḥdod*, inexplicable by the dictionaries, I interpret through the use of *luṅ mno-ba* at *Kāśyapaparivarta*, 159, corresponding to *udgṛhṇeya dhāra*<*yeya*>. Cp. iii. 22 above and *S.*, vi. 3.

40. The sense of the main verb *brten* (*sev*, *saj*, *bhaj* etc.) is not clear to me.

41. The dwellers in Paradise fall distressed to earth, lamenting, "Alas, grove of Caitraratha! Alas, heavenly lake! Alas, Mandākinī! Alas, beloved!"

42. Seeing that Paradise, obtained by many labours, is uncertain and transitory, and that such suffering will be caused by separation from it,

43. Alas, inexorably this is in an especial degree the law of action in the world; this is the nature of the world and yet they do not see it to be such.

44. Others, who have disjoined themselves from sensual passion, conclude in their minds that their station is eternal; yet they fall miserably from heaven.

45. In the hells is excessive torture, among animals eating each other, the suffering of hunger and thirst among the pretas, among men the suffering of longings,

46. In the heavens that are free from love the suffering of rebirth is excessive. For the ever-wandering world of the living there is most certainly no peace anywhere.

47. This stream of the cycle of existence has no support and is ever subject to death. Creatures, thus beset on all sides, find no resting-place.

48. Thus with the divine eyesight he examined the five spheres of life and found nothing substantial in existence, just as no heartwood is found in a plantain-tree when it is cut open.

49. Then as the third watch of that night drew on, the best of those who understand trance meditated on the real nature of this world:—

41. This is *S.*, xi. 50.

43, 44. C shows T's order to be wrong here; my verse 43 is made up of W's 44*ab*, 45*cd*, and verse 44 of 45*ab*, 44*cd*. In the first line of 43 I read *ṅes-par* for *des las* and understand something like *lokakāryasya dharmo 'yaṁ dhruvaṁ bata viśeṣataḥ*. Verse 44 refers to the inhabitants of the Brahmā world.

50. "Alas! Living creatures obtain but toil; over and over again they are born, grow old, die, pass on and are reborn.

51. Further man's sight is veiled by passion and by the darkness of delusion, and from the excess of his blindness he does not know the way out of this great suffering."

52. After thus considering, he reflected in his mind, "What is it verily, whose existence causes the approach of old age and death?"

53. Penetrating the truth to its core, he understood that old age and death are produced, when there is birth.

54. He saw that head-ache is only possible when the head is already in existence; for when the birth of a tree has come to pass, then only can the felling of it take place.

55. Then the thought again arose in him, "What does this birth proceed from?" Then he saw rightly that birth is produced from existence due to the power of the act.

56. With his divine eyesight he saw that active being proceeds from the act, not from a Creator or from Nature or from a self or without a cause.

50. 'Pass on', *ḥpho-ba, cyu*; W takes 'die and pass on' as a compound, but there is a distinction, as *cyu* implies passing to the next life, particularly from a higher sphere to a lower.

51. 'Passion', *chags-pa, rajas*, i.e. *rāga* and *dveṣa*. 'Sight is veiled', *bsgribs-pa, āvṛta*. I read *śin-tu dgos-pa* (for *dogs-pa*) and take it as equivalent to *atyartha*.

52. The translation of the second line involves reading *rga-ba* for W's *rga-bas* and the xylographs' *sga-bas*, but the context shows it to be the only possible text. C has wrongly 'birth and death', but 'old age and death' correctly in the next column. The following description of the *pratītyasamutpāda* is on perfectly orthodox lines.

53. 'To its core', *skye-gnas-nas, yoniśaḥ*.

55. 'Existence due to the power of the act', *las-srid, karmabhava*; cp. *AK.*, II, 64.

56. 'Active being', *ḥjug-pa, pravṛtti*.

57. Just as, if the first knot in a bamboo is wisely cut, everything quickly comes into order, so his knowledge advanced in proper order.

58. Thereon the sage applied his mind to determining the origin of existence. Then he saw that the origin of existence was to be found in appropriation.

59. This act arises from appropriating the various vows and rules of life, sensual pleasure, views of self and false views, as fire arises by appropriating fuel.

60. Then the thought occurred to him, " From what cause does appropriation come ? " Thereon he recognised the causal condition of appropriation to lie in thirst.

61. Just as the forest is set ablaze by a little fire, when the wind fans it, so thirst gives birth to the vast sins of sensual passion and the rest.

62. Then he reflected, " From what does thirst arise ? " Thereon he concluded that the cause of thirst is sensation.

63. Mankind, overwhelmed by their sensations, thirst for the means of satisfying them ; for no one in the absence of thirst takes pleasure in water.

64. Then he again meditated, " What is the source of sensation ? " He, who had put an end to sensation, saw also the cause of sensation to be in contact.

57. C shows clearly that *tsheg* in T stands for *tshigs*, 'a joint'. W suggests that the simile refers to cutting holes in a bamboo flute ; I take it to splitting a bamboo, a common operation in India, in which all depends upon accurate splitting of the first knot.

58. 'Appropriation', *upādāna*.

59. The reference is to the four kinds of *upādāna* ; cp. *AK.*, II, 86.

60. 'Cause', *rgyu, hetu* ; 'causal condition', *rkyen, pratyaya*.

61. *Bus*, read *phus* ? 'Sin', *ñon-moṅs, kleśa*.

62. C adds the threefold definition of *vedanā* as *sukha, duḥkha, upekṣā*.

63. W misunderstands *gñen-por byed-la* as *gñen-byed-la*, 'marrying' ; *gñen-po* means 'remedy', 'means'. The last word of the verse should be clearly *min*, not *yin*, as *kha-cig*=*kaścit*, not *kaḥ*.

65.　Contact is to be explained as the uniting of the object, the sense and the mind, whence sensation is produced, just as fire is produced from the uniting of the two rubbing sticks and fuel.

66.　Next he considered that contact has a cause. Thereon he recognised the cause to lie in the six organs of sense. — *mel. mind*

67.　The blind man does not perceive objects, since his eye does not bring them into junction with his mind; if sight exists, the junction takes place. Therefore there is contact, when the sense-organ exists.

68.　Further he made up his mind to understand the origin of the six organs of sense. Thereon the knower of causes knew the cause to be name-and-form. — *mental and physical concepts — not Tao & undifferentiated*

69.　Just as the leaf and the stalk are only said to exist when there is a shoot in existence, so the six organs of sense only arise when name-and-form is in existence.

70.　Then the thought occurred to him, " What is the cause of name-and-form ? " Thereon he, who had passed to the further side of knowledge, saw its origin to lie in consciousness.

71.　When consciousness arises, name-and-form is produced. When the development of the seed is completed, the sprout assumes a bodily form.

72.　Next he considered, " From what does consciousness come into being ? " Then he knew that it is produced by supporting itself on name-and-form.

feed each other and give rise to rest.

73.　Then after he had understood the order of causality, he thought over it; his mind travelled over the views that he had formed and did not turn aside to other thoughts.

entire order of causality

71.　The translation of the first line is conjectural; for T's nonsensical ḥdas-pa I put an o over ḥ and read ḥoṅs-pa, and I also retain ni for W's amendment na. T inserts a single *pāda* before this verse, ' when there is knowledge by means of consciousness'; this must be an interpolation, not a fragment of an incomplete verse. For C has nothing to correspond, and the composition of the parallel passages and the sense negative the idea of a verse being missing here.

74. Consciousness is the causal condition from which name-and-form is produced. Name-and-form again is the support on which consciousness is based.

75. Just as a boat conveys a man . . . . . . , so consciousness and name-and-form are causes of each other.

76. Just as redhot iron causes grass to blaze and as blazing grass makes iron redhot, of such a kind is their mutual causality.

77. Thus he understood that from consciousness arises name-and-form, from the latter originate the senses and from the senses arises contact.

78. But of contact he knew sensation to be born, out of sensation thirst, out of thirst appropriation, and out of appropriation similarly existence.

79. From existence comes birth, from birth he knew old age and death to arise. He rightly understood that the world is produced by the causal conditions.

80. Then this conclusion came firmly on him, that from the annihilation of birth old age and death are suppressed, that from the destruction of existence birth itself is destroyed, and that existence ceases to be through the suppression of appropriation.

81. Further the latter is suppressed through the suppression of thirst; if sensation does not exist, thirst does not exist; if contact is destroyed, sensation does not come into existence; from the non-existence of the six organs of sense contact is destroyed.

82. Similarly if name-and-form is rightly suppressed, all the six organs of sense are destroyed too; and the former is

75. T has one *pāda* missing. C suggests the sense to be that a boat carries a man on the water and the man carries the boat on dry land, but one would expect to be told that a man propels a boat, as the boat conveys the man.

76. C omits this verse.

82. 'The factors', *ḥdu-byed*, *saṁskāra*, here the working of deeds done in a former life.

suppressed through the suppression of consciousness, and the latter is suppressed also through the suppression of the factors.

83. Similarly the great seer understood that the factors are suppressed by the complete absence of ignorance. Therefore he knew properly what was to be known and stood out before the world as the Buddha.

84. The best of men saw no self anywhere from the summit of existence downwards and came to tranquillity, like a fire whose fuel is burnt out, by the eightfold path of supreme insight, which starts forth and quickly reaches the desired point.

85. Then as his being was perfected, the thought arose in him, "I have obtained this perfect path which was travelled for the sake of the ultimate reality by former families of great seers, who knew the higher and the lower things".

86. At that moment of the fourth watch when the dawn came up and all that moves or moves not was stilled, the great seer reached the stage which knows no alteration, the sovereign leader the state of omniscience.

87. When, as the Buddha, he knew this truth, the earth swayed like a woman drunken with wine, the quarters shone bright with crowds of Siddhas, and mighty drums resounded in the sky.

84. The translation is uncertain as regards the first phrase and the closing relative sentence. In T's third line I take *bar-las* as *bar-la*=Sk. *ā*. C inserts the expression *kṛtaṁ karaṇīyam*, for which T has no equivalent as it stands; it omits the reference to the summit of existence, substituting 'without self at all (or, finally)'.

85. T's *mṅaḥ-ma-rnams-kyi* is sheer nonsense, the literal Sanskrit equivalent being *vadhūnāṁ paramārthahetoḥ*. An instrumental is also required, and I propose *sṅa-ma-rnams-kyis* (*pūrvaiḥ*) to agree with the words in the previous line. This in fact is the word that the context makes indispensable. *Tshogs* in view of C I take as=*kula*. *Mchog daṅ mchog-min mkhyen-pa*, *parāparajña*.

86. 'All that moves or moves not', *rgyu daṅ mi-rgyu-ḥi ḥbyuṅ-po-rnams*, *carācarāṇi bhūtāni*.

88. Pleasant breezes blew softly, the heaven rained moisture from a cloudless sky, and from the trees there dropped flowers and fruit out of due season as if to do him honour.

89. At that time, just as in Paradise, *māndārava* flowers, lotuses and water-lilies of gold and beryl fell from the sky and bestrewed the place of the Śākya sage.

90. At that moment none gave way to anger, no one was ill or experienced any discomfort, none resorted to sinful ways or indulged in intoxication of mind; the world became tranquil, as though it had reached perfection.

91. The companies of deities, who are devoted to salvation, rejoiced; even the beings in the spheres below felt joy. Through the prosperity of the party who favoured virtue the *dharma* spread abroad and the world rose above passion and the darkness of ignorance.

92. The seers of the Ikṣvāku race who had been rulers of men, the royal seers and the great seers, filled with joy and wonder at his achievement, stood in their mansions in the heavens reverencing him.

93. The great seers of the groups of invisible beings proclaimed his praises with loud utterance and the world of the living rejoiced as if flourishing. But Māra was filled with despondency, as before a great precipice.

94. Then for seven days, free from discomfort of body, he sat, looking into his own mind, his eyes never winking. The

88. The second *pāda* may have run, *payāṁsy anabhre pravavarṣa devaḥ*. Read at the end of the last *pāda* with the Peking edition *brul-par-gyur*; C confirms the reading.

91. 'The beings in the spheres below', primarily those in hell, but may include pretas and animals.

93. The last four words of the translation are conjectural, the text being uncertain both in reading and meaning (*ltuṅ-ba mchog-la*, Peking ed.; *ltuṅ-ba mtshog-la*, W).

94. C says the Buddha sat examining the *bodhi* tree, for which cp. *LV.*, ch. xxiv. 377, 5, and 385, 9, and W therefore takes *gzigs-śiṅ*, which is normally

sage fulfilled his heart's desire, reflecting that on that spot he had obtained liberation.

95. Then the sage, who had grasped the principle of causation and was firmly fixed in the system of impersonality, roused himself, and, filled with great compassion, he gazed on the world with his Buddha-eye for the sake of its tranquillity.

96. Seeing that the world was lost in false views and vain efforts and that its passions were gross, seeing too that the law of salvation was exceeding subtle, he set his mind on remaining immobile.

97. Then remembering his former promise, he formed a resolution for the preaching of tranquillity. Thereon he reflected in his mind how there are some persons with great passion and others with little passion.

98. Then when the two chiefs of the heavenly dwellings knew that the Sugata's mind had taken the decision to preach tranquillity, they were filled with a desire for the world's benefit and, shining brightly, approached him.

99. As he sat, his aim accomplished by the rejection of sin, and the excellent *dharma* he had seen as his best companion,

simply 'looking', to mean 'looking at the tree'; this is so odd a construction that I hesitate to follow.

95. 'Principle of causation', possibly *idaṁpratyayatā*.

97. C and T agree in the meaning of this verse, the second *pāda* of which may have run, *śamāvavādaṁ prati niścayaṁ yayau*. The intention evidently is to remove from the Buddha the reproach of having decided not to preach the Law for the good of the world; the heavenly visitants do not change his resolution as in the parallel accounts such as *Majjhima*, I, 168, and *Mhv.*, III, 314ff., but merely strengthen it by their encouragement.

98. That Indra accompanies Brahmā is a form of the legend current only among the Mahāsaṅghikas (*Mhv.*, III, 315), so far as we know at present, but it may well have been the original form in view of the condominium of Indra and Brahmā in the older teaching (J. Przyluski, *Le Bouddhisme*, 34). C omits all mention of Indra.

99. The translation of the second line follows W and recalls *vyavasāya-dvitīya* of xii. 115.

they lauded him in all reverence and addressed these words to him for the good of the world :—

100. "Ah ! Does not the world deserve such good fortune that your mind should feel compassion for the creatures ? In the world there exist beings of varied capacity, some with great passion, some with little passion.

101. O sage, having yourself crossed beyond the ocean of existence, rescue the world which is drowning in suffering, and, like a great merchant his wealth, bestow your excellencies on others also.

102. There are some people here who, knowing what is to their advantage in this world and the hereafter, act only for their own good. But it is hard to find in this world or in heaven one who will be active for the good of the world."

103. After thus addressing the great seer, they returned to the celestial sphere by the way they had come. After the sage also had pondered on that speech, the decision grew strong in him for the liberation of the world.

104. At the time for the alms-round the gods of the four quarters presented the seer with begging-bowls ; Gautama, accepting the four, turned them into one for the sake of his *dharma*.

105. Then at that time two merchants of a passing caravan, being instigated thereto by a friendly deity, joyfully did obeisance to the seer with exalted minds and were the first to give him alms.

100. The translation of the first hemistich is speculative, following C's line of thought.

101. 'Great merchant', *legs-kyi dbaṅ-phyug*, evidently *śreṣṭhin*. The third *pāda* is two syllables in excess ; I omit *thob-nas*, which appears to be an interpolation.

102. W translates differently, missing the antithesis ; for a more elaborate treatment of the idea see *S.*, xviii. 55-56.

105. It is not clear from T whether it is the Buddha or the merchants who were exalted in mind ; C gives no help and W takes the former alternative.

THE BUDDHACARITA

Or

ACTS OF THE BUDDHA

PART III

Cantos XV to XXVIII translated from the
Tibetan and Chinese Versions

INDEX

N.B.—References are to the page numbers of the Introduction and to the numbers of the verses in the text and translation, adding to the latter the letter n., where the occurrence is in the notes only. The colon is used to separate different meanings of the same word or different per ions of the same name.

Dharmagupta, xxviii.
dharmapīḍā, ix. 40.
dharmarāja, i. 75.
dhā, ni+, x. 13. anuvi+, vii. 58.
dhātu, iii. 42 : (pañca) xii. 114.
Dhātupāṭha, lxviii ; i. 41 n. ; iv. 6 n. ; v. 81 n.
dhāman, xlv ; xiii. 68.
dhiṣṇya, iv. 102 ; viii. 40 ; ix. 2.
dhṛti, vi. 65.
dhyāna, xliii ; i. 77 ; xii. 105, 106 ; xiv. 1, 2 : (prathama) v. 10 ; xii. 49, 50 : (dvitīya) xii. 52 : (tṛtīya) xii. 54 : (caturtha) xii. 56, 58, 60.
Dhruva, ix. 20 ; x. 41 n.
dhruva, viii. 35 n.

Nagarī, xii. 89.
Naghuṣa, xi. 14 n.
Nanda, xxvii ; xxx ; xcii. *See* Sundarananda.
Nandana, iii. 64.
Nandabalā, xii. 109.
Nalakūbara, 1. 89. *See* Draviṇendra.
navagraha, vii. 46.
Nahuṣa, xi. 14, 16.
nākapṛṣṭha, x. 39.
Nāga, xiii. 30.
Nāgārjuna, xxix-xxx ; xxxviii. *See Addenda.*
nānābhāva, vi. 43.
nānyakārya, xi. 17.
nābhi, xlv ; xiii. 68.
nāma, lxxvi ; iv. 29 ; xiii. 35.
Nāhuṣa, ii. 11.
Nidānakathā, xl.
Nimi Videha, xiii. 5 n.
nimitta, ix. 64.
niyati, liv ; ix. 55 n.
nirārambha, vi. 52.
nirāśraya, viii. 23.
nirudvigna, iv. 56 n., 58.
nirguṇa, xii. 77.
nirdvandva, xii. 47.
nirvāhaka, ix. 38.
nivṛtti, vii. 48 ; ix. 63.
niṣpeṣavat, i. 14.
nihrādavat, iii. 60.
nī, abhi+, ii. 3.
nīti, li ; lii ; iv. 62.
Nairañjanā, xii. 90, 108.
nairguṇya, xii. 77.
nyāya, *see* anyāya *and* nyāyavid.
nyāyavid, x. 20.
Nyāyasūtra, lv.

pac, vi+, xiv. 16.
Pañcagatidīpanī, xxiii.
pañcaparva, xii. 33, 37.
Pañcaśikha, lxii ; xii. 21 n., 23 n., 53 n., 67 n.
paṭu, *see* apaṭu.
pattralekha, v. 53.
Padma, ii. 3.
Padmapurāṇa, xlvii.
Padmaśrī, iv. 36.
Padmaṣaṇḍa, iii. 63.
Padmā, i. 2.
Padhānasutta, xl ; xiii. 3 n., 19 n.
parapratyaya, xxxiv ; ix. 74.
Paramārtha, xxxi ; xxxv.
parāparajña, xiv. 85 n.
Parāśara, iv. 76 : (Pañcaśikha) xii. 67.
parikalpa, v. 65 n.
parinirvāṇa, v. 25.
paripakṣa, xiii. 72.
parihāra, iv. 67.
parihārikā, xc ; xi. 71 n.
paruṣa, v. 87.
pavanapatha, i. 80.
pavitra, vii. 4.
pā, ni+, ii. 54.

Bharadvāja, iv. 74.
Bhartṛhari, lxxx ; lxxxii.
Bhava, i. 88.
bhava, i. 15 ; vii. 44 ; ix. 58, 64 ; xi. 67, 68 ; xii. 100 ; xiii. 8.
bhavya, i. 15 ; ii. 25.
Bhāmaha, lxxxii ; lxxxviii ; xciii.
Bhāratīyanāṭyaśāstra, lxii.
Bhāravi, lxxxii.
Bhārgava, vi. 1 ; ix. 2, 3 : (Paraśurāma) ix. 25.
bhāva, lviii-lix.
bhāvanā, xliii.
Bhāsa, xvi ; lxxx.
bhikṣu, des. of bhaj (?), lxx ; iv. 17 : v. 16 : (pañca) xii. 91, 92, 114 ; xiv. 106.
Bhīmaratha, xiv. 107.
Bhīṣma, xlvii ; ix. 25 ; xi. 18.
bhuj, vi+, v. 52.
bhuj, nis+, xxx ; iv. 47.
bhūta, ix. 60 ; xii. 18.
Bhūtagaṇa, i. 24.
bhūtātman, xii. 21 n.
Bhṛgu, i. 41.
bhaikṣāka, x. 23 ; xii. 46 ; xiii. 10.
bhoga, xi. 36ff.
Bhojaprabandha, lxxix ; iv. 59 n.

Magadha, x. 10, 41 ; xi. 1.
Maghavat, i. 87 ; v. 27.
maṇḍala, ii. 3 ; v. 23.
mati, v. 30.
mada, i. 76 ; v. 14.
Manu, ii. 16 ; viii. 78.
manoratha, xi. 62.
Manthāla, iv. 17.
Mandara, vi. 13.
Mandākinī, xiv. 41.
Manmatha, iv. 101.
Mamatā, iv. 74.
mamatva, vi. 48.
Marut, liii ; iv. 74 n. ; v. 27.
Marutta, iv. 74 n.
Marutvat, iv. 27 n. ; viii. 13 ; x. 3 n.
Mahādeva, xxxiv.
Mahāparinirvāṇasūtra, xl.
Mahābhārata, xlvi-xlvii.
mahāmoha, xii. 33, 34, 35.
Mahāsaṅghika, xxviii–xxxvi ; ii. 36 n. ; xiv. 98 n.
Mahāsudarśa, viii. 62.
Mahendra, viii. 64 ; ix. 10 ; xi. 16.
Māgha, lxxxii ; xciii.
Mātaṅgī, iv. 77.
Mātṛceṭa, xiv ; xxvi ; xxxvi ; xii. 115 n.
Mādrī, iv. 79.
Mādhyamika, xxix-xxx ; xxxv.
Māndhātṛ, i. 10 ; x. 31 ; xi. 13.
Māyā, xxvii ; xxviii ; xxxix ; i. 2, 5 ; ii. 18 : (*goddess*) i. 2.
Māyāvatī, xiii. 11 n.
Māra, xl ; xiii. 1, 2, 8, 14, 15, 18, 28, 30, 31, 32, 33, 34, 55, 56, 57, 69, 70 ; xiv. 1, 93. *See* Kāmadeva, Citrāyudha, Puṣpaketu, Puṣpaśara.
Mārutī, iv. 74.
miti, i. 81.
muc, adhi+, i. 30 n. ; xii. 61.
muñja, xii. 64.
mṛgacārin, vii. 5.
Mekhala, xi. 31.
Meghakālī, xiii. 49 n.
Menakā, xlix ; iv. 20 n.
Meru, i. 36, 37 ; v. 37, 43 ; xiii. 41, 57.
maitrīvihāra, xiii. 42.
Maithila, xi. 31 (v. l.).
moha, xlii ; xii. 33, 34.
Maudgalyāyana, xix ; xxviii.

Yakṣa, i. 17 ; v. 81.
yadṛcchā, iii. 28.
Yamunā, iv. 76 ; xii. 110.

Vijñānavāda, xxix ; xxxv.
viṭaṅka, viii. 37.
vitarka, v. 10 ; xii. 49, 52.
vitta, ix. 21.
Videha, ix. 20 ; xiii. 5.
vidhi, lv ; viii. 85 ; ix. 66, 67.
vinivṛtti, xi. 63.
Vindhya, xiii. 38.
Vindhyakoṣṭha, vii. 54.
Vindhyavāsin, vii. 54 n.
vipratyaya, xii. 24, 25.
vipravāsa, vi. 59.
Vibhāṣā, xv ; xxiv ; xli.
Vibhrama, xiii. 3.
Vibhrāja, iv. 28.
vimāna, ii. 29 ; iii. 64.
vivarṇa, vi. 66.
Vivasvat, iv. 28 ; vii. 32 ; viii. 78.
viveka, v. 11 ; xii. 49.
viśiṣṭa, i. 19.
viśeṣa, xii. 53, 55, 60, 62, 74, 84. *See* aviśeṣa.
Viśvācī, iv. 78.
Viśvāmitra, xlix ; iv. 20. *See* Gādhin.
viṣakta, ix. 19.
viṣama, ii. 34.
viṣaya, i. 85.
Viṣṇu, liv.
vispanda, xiv. 21.
vṛt, pari+, xii. 16 n. prā+, iv. 38.
Vṛtra, viii. 13 ; xi. 14.
vṛddhi, i. 84, 89.
vṛdh, vi+, v. 61.
Vṛṣṇi, xi. 31.
Veda, xlv ; i. 42 ; ii. 37.
vedaka, xxxiii.
vedanā, xiv. 62 n.
veraya, pra+, viii. 52.
Vaibhrāja, iv. 28 n. : ix. 20.
Vaiśālī, liv ; xi. 73 n.
Vaiśeṣika, xvii ; lv ; lvii.
Vaiśravaṇa, i. 3. *See* Kubera.
Vaiśvaṁtara āśrama, xi. 73.
vyakta, xii. 22, 40.
Vyāsa, i. 42 ; iv. 16.

śaṁs, ā+, v. 85.
Śakti, i. 42 n.
Śakra, i. 58 ; vi. 62 ; ix. 12 ; x. 19 ; xi. 13.
Śacī, i. 2 ; ii. 27.
Śacīpati, viii. 73.
Śatakratu, xi. 14.
Śatapañcāśatka, xiv.
Śatapathabrāhmaṇa, xlv.
Śantanu, xlvii ; xiii. 12.
Śambhu, xiii. 16.
śarīrin, xii. 79.
śala, xiii. 18.
Śākya, i. 1, 58 ; viii. 8 ; ix. 11.
Śākyanarendra, Śākyarāja, Śākyādhipati, Śākyeśvara, i. 49, 88 ; ii. 25 ; v. 1, 36 ; vi. 60 ; ix. 24 ; x. 11.
Śākyamuni, xiii. 14, 18, 43 ; xiv. 89.
Śākyarṣabha, vii. 13 ; xiii. 28.
Śāntanu, xiii. 12 n.
Śāntā, iv. 19.
Śāriputra, xix ; xxvii ; xxviii.
Śāriputraprakaraṇa, xiii ; xviiiff ; lxii ; lxiv ; xii. 75 n.
śālabhañjikā, v. 52.
Śālihotraśāstra, lii ; v. 73 n.
Śālva, ix. 20 n., 70.
Śikṣāsamuccaya, xxx.
Śibi, xiv. 30.
Śiva, liv ; xiv. 107 n. *See* Bhava, Śambhu, Sthāṇuvrata.
śivikā, i. 86.
śīla, xlii ; lxi ; i. 71 ; vi. 65 n. ; xi. 66 ; xii. 46.
Śivala, xxvii.

ADDENDA ET CORRIGENDA

PART I

Despite the great help rendered to me in proof-reading by Professor Raghu Vira, there are a few misprints left in the text, in addition to the usual casualties due to the breaking of type in printing. The following list is, it is hoped, complete.

i. 24*b*, variants, read ***nags-tshal*** for ***nags-tsha.***
i. 54*a*, read ***nṛpeṇopanimantritaḥ*** for °***opamantritaḥ.***
i. 89*c*, read °***āpsaro'vakīrṇaṁ*** for °***āpsaraso'vakīrṇaṁ.***
iv. 10*c*, read *Kuberasyāpi* for *Kuve*°.
iv. 23*d*, read ***tu tāḥ striyaḥ*** for ***tā tu.***
v. 37*a*, read *Merugurur* for °*garur*.
v. 61*a*, variants, read ***brgyaṅ*** for ***brgyan.***
vi. 15*a*, read *jarāmaraṇa*° for metrical reasons.
vii. 19*a*, read *dvipadendravatsaḥ* for *dvipendra*°.
vii. 37*b*, read ***manuṣyavaryaṁ*** for °***varya.***
ix. 45*d*, read ***puraṁda***° for ***puranda***°.
x. 18*d*, variants, read ***mtshan*** for ***mtuhan.***
xii. 46*d*, read °***vistīrṇaṁ*** for °*vistīrṇa*.
xii. 111*a*, read ***śraddhāvardhita***° for *śrāddhā*°.
xiii. 8*a*, variants, read °*saṁstham* for °*saṁtham*.
xiii. 18*b*, variants, read ***thub-paḥi*** for ***thub-pa-ḥ.***

PART II

Introduction, p. xvii. Mr. K. P. Jayaswal has edited and explained in *An Imperial History of India* (Lahore, 1934) the fifty third chapter of the *Aryamañjuśrīmūlakalpa*, which gives the Buddhist version of the history of India as current about the beginning of the Pāla dynasty ; he holds that the *akārākhyo yatiḥ* of the verse he numbers 940 (Trivandrum S.S. ed., p. 651) is Aśvaghoṣa and that his time is given as that of king Buddhapakṣa, whom he identifies with Kadphises I (p. 19) and whose name he would read as Buddhayakṣa. While this supports the date I think the most probable, the evidence is not in my opinion usable. The textual constitution of the passage in question remains uncertain, and, if it is accepted as it stands, I do not think it is possible to avoid the identification of Buddhapakṣa with Kaniṣka, that is, the text merely gives the Buddhist legend already current in China three centuries earlier.

p. xxii. My view of the date of the *Gaṇḍīstotra* is corroborated by the evidence of the late Professor S. Lévi's *Sanskrit Texts from Bāli* (Gaekwad's O. S. no. 67), which contains on p. 49 under the heading of *Buddhastava* verses 1 and 11 of this work. As the remaining Buddhist texts still extant in Bali are from Tantric works, it seems likely that this text also is of more or less the same epoch.

p. xxix. For Aśvaghoṣa's influence on Nāgārjuna see now *Ratnāvalī*, iv. 46–49 (*JRAS*, 1936, 249), which is closely related in argument and wording to *B.*, xi. 36–48.

p. lxx. On the question of *saṁdhi* note that the MS. at *B.*, xi. 24, 28, and xiv. 31, shows *arccha(n)ti* in place of *ārccha(n)ti* prescribed by the grammarians; this is in accord with *arti* at *S.*, x. 32, but the MSS. of the latter poem apparently indicate the use of the simple verb only (viii. 4, ix. 44, xvi. 51, xviii. 45) except at ix. 35, where the length of the vowel in the first syllable cannot be determined.

Translation, p. 83, vi. 15, line 2. For 'birth' read 'old age', in accordance with the correction in Part I above.

p. 190, note on xiii. 11. It is probable that the figure on which Kāmadeva is standing in the Kushan terracotta plaque at Mathurā, reproduced in *Ann. Bibl. Ind. Arch.*, IX, plate IV *d*, is to be identified with Śūrpaka.

Published for the University of the Panjab, Lahore, and printed by P. Knight, Baptist Mission Press, 41A, Lower Circular Road, Calcutta.

CONTENTS

The Buddha's Mission and last Journey: *Buddhacarita*, xv to xxviii.

Translated by

E. H. Johnston, Banbury.

In preparing for the Panjab University Oriental Publications an edition of the Sanskrit text and a translation of the first fourteen cantos of Aśvaghoṣa's *Buddhacarita*, which at the time of writing are passing through the press, I found it advisable to examine in detail the Tibetan and Chinese versions of the second half of that work. The contents of these fourteen cantos seem to me to be of such interest to students of Buddhism and of Sanskrit literature alike that, as Beal's translation from the Chinese gives an entirely inadequate idea of the original and as Dr. Weller's edition and translation of the Tibetan will apparently never go beyond the seventeenth canto, which they reached years ago, I am glad to be allowed space here for a complete translation of them.

The object of my version is not to give a translation of either the Tibetan or the Chinese alone, but to handle the two together critically, so as to arrive as near may be at the meaning of Aśvaghoṣa's original text. The imperfections of the authorities prevent the full realisation of this aim, though another, and more competent scholar, working afresh over the material, might well succeed in solving difficulties that have defeated me. The basis for my work is inevitably the Tibetan translation, which renders the original more or less *verbatim*, but, as we know from a comparison of it for the first fourteen cantos with the Sanskrit text, it is not capable by itself of communicating Aśvaghoṣa's intentions to us with precision. The text itself is full of corruptions and has a number of lacunae; in places it gives inferior readings or reproduces literally a corrupt original, while occasionally it makes ludicrous mistakes in the construction of the Sanskrit, and finally it is only too often ambiguous. For cantos xv to xvii I have used Dr. Weller's excellent text and have taken full advantage of his translation, on which I hope to have improved in a few passages; for the remainder I have collated the India Office copy with an admirable rotograph of the red Peking edition, kindly supplied to me from Paris. These two versions do not differ from each other as much as two good copies of the same manuscript would, but, when they vary, the Peking edition offers the best text some four times in five. If the Chinese, for which I have depended on the Taisho Issaikyo edition, does not suffer from these imperfections, it is on the other hand only a very free paraphrase, omitting to explain many phrases and difficult words, and often contracting or expanding the original for no obvious reasons. It is, however, fuller and closer to the Sanskrit text in the last seven cantos, and it is an invaluable check on the understanding of the Tibetan by its reproduction of the general sense of the original; in a certain number of cases too it enables corrupt readings in the latter to be corrected. The general method I have followed therefore is to translate the Tibetan in the light of the Chinese, but I have also at times been guided by the form in which the original Sanskrit can be reconstructed; this latter practice is dangerous and can only be followed with the greatest caution, there being few verses or even *pādas* which can be put back into Sanskrit with any degree of certainty. Very occasionally also, when the metre can be identified, I have been influenced by metrical considerations. I would maintain that the translation I have arrived at by these means gives the correct general sense of almost every verse, but is at times defective in detail, especially in the rendering of *kāvya* turns of phrase as well as of the philosophical arguments in xviii and of the references to legends in xxi. It is necessarily literal and clumsy, but not, I hope, ambiguous or untrue to Aśvaghoṣa's ways of thought and expression. For facility of comprehension I have often added in brackets the Sanskrit words which I believe to have stood in the original. I have not annotated the text as fully as that of the first fourteen cantos, contenting myself as a rule with indicating the more important corrections I would make in the Tibetan and with mentioning the passages of whose translation I am doubtful.[1]

Of the contents of these cantos it will be sufficient to remark that the account of the Buddha's mission in cantos xv to xx follows the order of the *Nidānakathā* in the main and is based probably on an earlier version of that work, and that cantos xxii to xxviii reproduce the contents of the *Mahāparinirvāṇasūtra* in its complete extended form. Canto xxi contains a kind of *digvijaya* of the Buddha, with numerous proper names, some of which I am unable to identify, and the story of Devadatta's attempts on the life of the Buddha. The philosophical passages in cantos xviii and xxvi, about the earliest specimens we possess of dialectics in a modern form, are of great interest for the history of the evolution of Indian thought; but, as in the Buddha's refutation of the Sāṃkhya in canto xii, the real import of the arguments is not always easy to understand.

CANTO XV

Turning the Wheel of the Law.

1. Having fulfilled His task, He was informed with the might of religious tranquillity (*śama*), and proceeded alone, yet as if many accompanied Him. A pious mendicant, seeing Him on the road, folded his hands and thus addressed Him:—

---

[1] The following abbreviations are used in the notes: C, the Chinese translation, Taisho Issaikyo no. 192: I.O., India Office copy of the Tanjore: P, copy of the Tanjore in the Bibliothèque Nationale, Paris: S., Saundarananda, as edited and translated by me: T, the Tibetan translation: W, Tibetan text and translation by Friedrich Weller in Das Leben des Buddha von Aśvaghoṣa, II (1928). Except in *kāvya* passages which the Chinese so abridges as to make the identification of its rendering of different verses difficult, I have marked with an asterisk all verses which are found in the Tibetan but are missing in the Chinese; some of these are undoubtedly interpolations.

2. "Inasmuch as You are devoid of attachment and have tamed the horses of the senses, while (abiding) among beings who are subject to attachment and the horses of whose senses still run wild, Your form (*ākṛti?*), like that of the moon, shows contentment through the sweet-tasting savour (*rasa*) of a new wisdom.

3. Your steadfast face glows here, You have become master of Your senses, and Your eye is that of a mighty bull; certainly You have succeeded in Your aim. Who is Your guru, Reverend Sir, from whom You have learnt this accomplishment?"

4. Thereat He replied, "No teacher have I. There is none for Me to honour, still less none for Me to contemn. I have obtained Nirvāṇa and am not the same as others. Know Me to be the Originator (*Svayaṃbhū*) in respect of the Law.

5. Since I have entirely comprehended that which should be comprehended, but which others have not comprehended, therefore I am a Buddha. And since I have overthrown the sins (*kleśa*) as if they were foes, know Me to be One Whose self is tranquillised (*śamātmaka*).

6. I, good Sir (*saumya*), am now[1] on the way to Varāṇasī to beat there the drum of the deathless Law, not for the bliss of renown, nor out of pride, but for the good of My fellowmen who are harassed by suffering.

7. Of yore, on seeing the world of the living to be in distress, I vowed thus, that, when I had crossed Myself, I would bring the world across, that, when Myself liberated, I would emancipate its inhabitants (*sattva*).

8. Some in this world, gaining wealth, hold it for themselves alone and thereby come to shame; but for the great man (*mahājana*) whose eyes are open, on acquiring pre-eminent objects (*viśeṣa*), that alone is wealth which he distributes.

9. When a man is being carried away by a stream, he who, standing on dry land, does not try to pull him out, is no hero;[2]

---

[1] Read *ḥdi riṅ, adya,* for *ḥdi yaṅ*?

[2] So C.

and the man who, finding treasure, does not share it with the poor, is no giver.[1]

10. It is proper for one in good health to doctor a man overcome by disease with the remedies he has to hand, and it is fitting for a master of the ways (*mārgapati*) to point out the road he should take to one who is on the wrong road.

11. Just as, when a lamp is lit, there is by reason of it no access of darkness,[2] so when the Buddha makes His knowledge shine, men do not become a prey to passion.

12. Just as fire must abide in the wood, wind in the air, and water in the earth, so the Enlightenment of the Sages (*muni*) must take place at Gaya and their preaching of the Law at Kāśi."

13. Thereon, expressing his admiration below his breath (*upāṃśu*),[3] he quitted the Buddha and went his way according to his desire, but given over to longing and repeatedly looking back at Him with eyes full of wonderment.

14. Then in due course the Sage saw the city of Kāśi, which resembled the interior of a treasure-house, and which the Bhāgīrathī and the Varāṇasī, meeting together, embrace like a woman friend.

15. Resplendent with power and glory, He came shining like the sun to the Deer Park, where dwelt the great seers among trees resounding with cuckoos' calls.

16. Then the five mendicants, he of the Kauṇḍinya *gotra*, Mahānāman, Vāṣpa, Aśvajit and Bhadrajit, seeing Him from afar, spoke these words among themselves:—

17. "Here approaches the mendicant Gautama, who in his fondness for ease has turned away from asceticism. He is certainly not to be met, nor to be saluted; for he who has resiled from his vow merits no reverence.

---

[1] Read *sprad-po* or *sbyin-po* for W's *spyaṅ-po*.

[2] Uncertain. Read with the xylographs *de-yi rgyu-can* in *b*, and for *dmar-por*, which makes no sense, I conjecture *dmun-par*, "darkened"; C may have had some such reading. W's translation gives a sense which does not fit the context.

[3] Read *ñe-bar ḥod-las* with the xylographs, as suggested by C; alternatively *ñe-bar hoṅs* is his name, Upaga.

18. Should he however wish to talk with us, by all means enter into conversation with him; for men of gentle blood (*ārya*) should certainly[1] do so, whoever may be the guest who arrives."

19. The Buddha moved towards the sitting mendicants, who had thus laid their plans; and according as He drew nearer to them, so they broke their agreement.

20. One of them took His mantle, and similarly another with folded hands accepted His begging-bowl. Another gave Him the proper seat, and similarly the other two presented Him with water for His feet.

21. Showing Him many attentions in such wise, they all treated Him as their Guru; but, as they did not cease calling Him by His family name, the Holy One in His compassion said to them:—

22. "O mendicants, do not speak to the venerable Arhat after the former fashion with lack of reverence; for, though I am in truth indifferent to praise and blame, I would turn you away from what has evil consequences (*apuṇya*).

23. Seeing that a Buddha obtains Enlightenment for the good of the world, He ever acts for the good of all beings; and the Law is cut off for him who maliciously calls his guru by his name, just as in the case of disrespect to parents.[2]"

24. Thus did the Great Seer, the Best of speakers, preach to them out of the compassion of His heart; but led astray by delusion and lack of ballast (*asāreṇa*), they answered Him with gently smiling faces:—

25. "You did not forsooth, Gautama, come to an understanding of the real truth by those supreme and excellent austerities, and, though the goal is only to be obtained with difficulty (*kṛcchreṇa?*), you indulge in comfort. What is your ground for saying, 'I have seen'?"

26. Since the mendicants thus displayed their scepticism regarding the truth about the Tathāgata, then the Knower of the

[1] A double negative, misunderstood by W.

[2] Read *ḥjoms-las* in *c* and *chod-do* in *d*.

Path, knowing the path to Enlightenment to be other than that, expounded the path to them:—

27. "The fool who tortures himself and equally he who is attached to the domains of the senses, both these you should regard as in fault, because they have taken paths, which do not lead to deathlessness.

28. The former, with his mind troubled and overcome (*ākrānta*?) by the bodily toils called austerities, becomes unconscious and does not know even the ordinary course (*vyavahāra*) of the world, how much less then the supersensual way of truth?

29. Just as in this world one does not pour out water to obtain a light for the destruction of darkness, so bodily torments are not the prerequisite for the destruction of the darkness of ignorance by the fire of knowledge.[1]

30. Just as a man who wants a fire does not obtain it by boring and splitting wood, but does succeed by using the proper means, so deathlessness is obtained by *yoga*, not by torments.

31. Similarly those who are attached to the calamitous lusts have their minds overwhelmed by passion (*rajas*) and ignorance (*tamas*); they do not even attain the ability to understand the doctrines (*śāstra*), still less then the passionless (*virāga*) method of suppression.

32. Just as the individual who is overcome by illness is not cured by eating unwholesome food, so how shall he, who is overcome by the disease of ignorance (*ajñāna*) and is addicted to the lusts, reach religious peace?

33. Just as a fire does not go out, when it has dry grass (*kakṣa*?) for fuel (*āśraya*) and the wind fans it, so the mind does not come to peace, when passion (*rāga*) is its companion and the lusts its support (*āśraya*).

34. Abandoning either extreme, I have won to another, the Middle Path, which brings surcease from sorrow and passes beyond bliss and ecstasy.[2]

---

[1] So C understands the verse; W construes differently.

[2] *Prīti*; read *dgaḥ-ba* for *dge-ba*?

35. The sun of right views illumines it, the chariot of pure right thought fares along it, the rest-houses (*vihāra*) are right words rightly spoken, and it is gay with a hundred groves of good conduct.

36. It enjoys the great prosperity (*subhikṣa*) of noble livelihood, and has the army and retinue of right effort; it is guarded on all sides by the fortifications of right awareness and is provided with the bed and seat of concentrated thought.

37. Such in this world is this most excellent eightfold path, by which comes release from death, old age and disease; by passing along it, all is done that has to be done, and there is no further travelling in this world or the next.

38. 'This is nothing but suffering, this is the cause, this is the suppression and this the path to it (sc. suppression)': thus for salvation's sake I developed eyesight for an unprecedented method of the Law, which had been hitherto unheard of.

39. Birth, old age, disease and eke death, separation from what is desired, union with what is not desired, failure to attain the longed for end, these are the varied sufferings that men undergo.

40. In whatever state a man be existing, whether he is subject to the lusts or has conquered self, whether he has or has not a body, whatever quality (*guṇa*) is lacking to him, know that in short to be suffering.

41. It is My settled doctrine that, just as a fire, when its flames die down, does not lose its inborn nature of being hot, however small it be, so the idea of self, subtle though it may become through quietude and the like, has still the nature of suffering.

42. Recognise that, just as the soil, water, seed and the season are the causes of the shoot (*aṃkura*), so the various sins (*doṣa*), passion (*kāmarāga*) and the like, as well as the deeds that spring from the sins, are the causes of suffering.

43. The cause for the stream of existence, whether in heaven or below, is the group of sins, passion and the like; and the root of the distinction here and there into base, middling and high, is the deeds.

44. From the destruction of the sins the cause of the cycle of existence ceases to be, and from the destruction of the Act that suffering ceases to be; for, since all things come into being from the existence of something else, with the disappearance of that something else they cease to be.

45. Know suppression to be that in which there is not either birth, or old age, or death, or fire, or earth, or water, or space, or wind, which is without beginning or end, noble and not to be taken away (*ahārya*), blissful and immutable.

46. The path is that which is described as eightfold, and outside it there are no means for success (*adhigama*). Because they do not see this path, men ever revolve (*paribhram*) in the various paths.[1]

47. Thus I came to the conclusion in this matter, that suffering is to be recognised, the cause to be abandoned, the suppression to be realised and the path to be cultivated.

48. Thus insight (*cakṣus*) developed in me that this suffering has been recognised and the cause abandoned, similarly that the suppression has been realised, similarly that this path has been cultivated.

49. I did not claim to be emancipated in this world and did not see too in Myself the attainment of the goal, so long as I had not seen these four stages of the noble right truth.

50. But when I had mastered the noble Truths, and, having mastered them, had done the task that was to be done, then I claimed to be emancipated in this matter and saw that I had attained the goal."

51. When the Great Seer, full of compassion, thus preached the Law there in these words, he of the Kauṇḍinya clan and a hundred deities obtained the insight that is pure and free from passion (*rajas*).

52. When he had completed all that was to be done, the Omniscient said to him with a voice loud as a bull's, "Is the

---

[1] So C; T is evidently corrupt.

knowledge yours?" That great-souled[1] one replied, "Truly (*paramam*); I know Your excellent thought."

53. Then by saying "Truly, I know," Kauṇḍinya ⟨was the first⟩ in the world[2] to grasp the knowledge of that stage and came into possession of the Law at the head of the mendicants of the holy Guru, the Tathāgata.

54. When the Yakṣas, who lived on the earth, heard that cry, they proclaimed with resounding voices, "Most certainly the Wheel of the Law has been well turned by the Best of those who see, for the deathless tranquillity of all beings.

55. Its spokes are the discipline (*śīla*), its felloes tranquillity (*śama*) and the Rule (*Vinaya*), wide in understanding (*buddhi?*) and firm with awareness (*smṛti*) and wisdom (*mati*),[3] its pin is self-respect (*hrī*). By reason of its profundity, of its freedom from falsehood, and of the excellence of its preaching, it is not overturned by other doctrines when taught in the triple world."

56. Hearing the shouts of the mountain Yakṣas, the troops of deities in the sky took up the cry, and so it mounted loudly from heaven to heaven up to the world of Brahmā.

57. Certain self-controlled (*ātmavat*) dwellers in the heavens, on hearing from the Great Seer that the triple world is transitory, desisted from attachment to the various objects of sense, and through their perturbation of mind (*saṃvega*) reached a state of tranquillity with respect to the three spheres of existence.

58. At the moment[4] when the Wheel of the Law was thus turned in heaven and earth for the best tranquillity of the three worlds, a shower of rain, laden with flowers, fell from the cloudless sky, and the inhabitants of the three spheres of existence caused mighty drums to resound.

---

1 Read *chen-po* in *c*?

2 Read *ḥjig-rten-na*? I supply the two missing syllables as above.

3 According to C the feloes are six in number, and T is probably corrupt.

4 Read *tsam-na* for *tsam-nas* in *b*.

CANTO XVI

Many Conversions.[1]

1. Then the Omniscient established in the Law of Salvation Aśvajit and the other mendicants who had become well-disposed (*prayata*) in mind.

2. He appeared surrounded by that group of five, who had subdued the group of five (senses), like the moon in the sky conjoined with the five stars of the asterism (Hastā) whose regent is the sun.

3. Now at that time a noble's[2] son named Yaśas saw certain women carelessly asleep and thereby became perturbed in mind.

4. Uttering the words, "How wretched all this is," he went just as he was, retaining all the glory of his magnificent ornaments, to where the Buddha was.

5. The Tathāgata, Who knew men's dispositions and sins, on seeing him said, "There is no fixed[3] time for Nirvāṇa, come hither and obtain the state of blessedness."

6. Hearing these far-famed[4] words, he came, like one entering a river when afflicted with heat, to extreme contentment of mind.

7. Then by reason of the force of the previous cause, but with his body as it was (i.e. in the householder's garb), he realised Arhatship with body and mind.

8. As the dye is absorbed by a cloth which has been bleached with salted[5] water, so he, whose mind was white, fully understood the good Law as soon as he heard of it.

9. The Best of speakers, He who had fulfilled His task and knew the good goal, saw him standing there ashamed of his clothes and said:—

---

[1] Lit. "Having (or, Who has) many disciples."

[2] *chen-po*; if the original had had *śreṣṭhin,* one would have expected a compound with *legs-pa.*

[3] Read *ñid* for *ñer*?

[4] Or, "of Him, Whose fame was widespread."

[5] T has *ston-ka,* "autumn," but the context requires *kṣāra* or the like; perhaps *śo-ra* (v. Jaeschke) or *lan-tshva.*

10. "The mendicant's badges (*liṅga*) are not the cause[1] of the Law; he who looks with equal mind on all beings and has restrained his senses by quietude and the Rule, though he wears ornaments, yet walks in the Law.

11. He who leaves his home with his body, but not with his mind, and who is still subject to passion, is to be known as a householder, though he live in the forest.

12. He who goes forth with his mind, but not with his body, and who is selfless, is to be known as a forest-dweller, though he abide in his home.

13. He is said to be emancipated, who has reached this attainment, whether he abide in his home or whether he has become a wandering mendicant.

14. Just as one who would conquer puts on his armour to overcome a hostile army, a man wears the badges to overcome the hostile army[2] of the sins."

15. Then the Tathāgata said to him, "Come hither, mendicant"; and at these words he appeared[3] wearing the mendicant's badges.

16. Then out of attachment to him his friends, to the number of fifty and three and one, gained the Law.

17. As garments, covered with potash (*kṣāra*), quickly become clean on contact with water, so they quickly became pure, in virtue of their acts having been purified in former ages.

18. Then at that time sixty in all was the first company of the disciples, who were also Arhats; and the Arhat, fittingly revered by the Arhats, spoke to them as follows:—

19. "O mendicants, you have passed beyond suffering and fulfilled your great task. It is proper now to help others who are still suffering.

20. Therefore do all of you, each by himself, traverse this earth and impart the Law to mankind out of compassion for their affliction.

---

[1] Read *rgyu*.

[2] Read *dgra-sde* for *dgra de* in *c*, as in *a*?

[3] Read *gsal-to, babhau,* for the pointless *grol-to,* "was emancipated."

21. I for my part am proceeding to Gaya, the abode of royal seers, in order to convert the Kāśyapa seers, who through their attainments[1] are possessed of supernatural powers."

22. Then they, who had seen the real truth, departed on His orders in all directions, while the Great Seer, the Blessed One (*Sugata*), Who was freed from the pairs (*dvandva*),[2] went to Gaya.

23. Then in due course He arrived there, and, approaching the forest of the Law, saw Kāśyapa, abiding there like Asceticism in person.

24. Although there were dwellings in the mountains and the groves, the Lord of the Ten Powers, desirous of converting him, asked him for a lodging.

25, 26. . . . . .[3]

27. Then in order to destroy the Saint (*siddha*),[4] in his evil disposition (*viṣamastha*) he gave Him a fire-house, ⟨infested⟩ by a great snake . . .

28. At night the snake, whose gaze was poisonous, saw the Great Sage calm and fearless there looking at him, and in his fury he hissed at Him.

29. The fire-house was set alight by his wrath, but the fire, as if afraid, did not touch the Great Seer's body.

30. Just as at the end of the great aeon Brahmā shines sitting when the conflagration dies down, so Gautama remained unperturbed, though the fire-house was all blazing.

31. On the Buddha sitting there, unharmed and moveless, the snake was filled with wonderment and did obeisance to the Best of seers.

32. The folk in the deer-park thought of the Seer sitting there, and deeply distressed(?) were overcome with pity that such a mendicant should have been burnt.

---

[1] A reference to the *siddhis* of the Yoga?

[2] The eight *lokadharmas*.

[3] There seems to be a lacuna of uncertain length here, C giving a long account of the conversation. The line which W takes as the last of 26, I take to 24, understanding *rab-tu-brten* as *pratiśraya*.

[4] Or less probably, with W, "to test his saintliness."

33. On the night passing away, the Teacher (*Vināyaka*) took up the snake quietly in His alms-bowl and showed it to Kāśyapa.

34. On perceiving[1] the might of the Buddha, he was amazed, yet he still believed himself to have no superior in power.

35. Then, as He knew those thoughts of his, the tranquil Sage purified his heart by assuming various shapes suited to the occasion.

36. Thereon, as he deemed the Buddha to be greater than him in magic power, he determined to win His Law.

37. The company of Auruvilva Kāśyapa's five hundred followers, seeing his sudden change of heart, adhered also to the Law.

38. When their brother and his pupils had passed to the further shore (*pāraga*) and cast aside their bark garments, the two who were called Gaya and Nadī (Kāśyapa) arrived there and betook themselves to the path.[2]

39. On the Gayaśīrṣa mountain the Sage then preached the sermon of salvation[3] to the three Kāśyapa brothers with their followers:—

40. "The entire world is helplessly burnt up by the fire of love and hate (*rāgadveṣa*), which is overspread with the smoke of delusion (*moha*) and originates in the thoughts (*vitarka*).

41. Thus scorched by the fire of the sins, without peace or leadership, it is unceasingly consumed again and again by the fires of old age, disease and death.

42. On seeing this world without refuge and burnt up by manifold fires, the wise man is perturbed over his body with its accompaniment of mind and sense-organs.

43. From perturbation he proceeds to passionlessness and from that to liberation; thereon being liberated, he knows that he is liberated in all respects.

---

[1] T seems to have had *niśamya*, "hearing," for *niśāmya*, "perceiving."

[2] There may be a lacuna of one or more verses here between the two hemistiches, as C tells the story at much greater length.

[3] *nirvāhaka*? Cp. ix. 38 in my edition and note in translation.

44. Having fully examined[1] the stream of birth, he takes his stand on the ascetic life and completes his task; for him there is no further existence."

45. When the thousand mendicants heard this sermon of the Holy One, by reason of non-appropriation (*anupādāna*) their minds were immediately released from the infections (*āsrava*).

46. Then the Buddha appeared with the three Kāśyapas, whose wisdom (*prajñā*) was great, like the Law incarnate surrounded by Charity (*dāna*), Discipline and the Rule.

47. The penance grove, deprived of those excellent . . .,[2] was no longer brilliant, like the life of a sick man (*sattva*), who is without religion (*dharma*), wealth or pleasure.

48. Then remembering His former promise to the Magadha king, the Sage, surrounded by all of them, took His way to Rājagṛha.

49. Then when the king heard of the Tathāgata's arrival at the domain of the Veṇuvana, he went to visit Him, with his ministers in attendance on him.

50. Then the common folk, with their eyes opened wide in wonderment, came out along the mountain road, on foot or in vehicles[3] according to their station in life.

51. On seeing the excellent Sage from afar, the Magadha sovereign hastily alighted from his chariot in order to show Him reverence.

52. The king left behind him his yaks' tails, his fans and his retinue, and approached the Sage, as Indra approached Brahmā.

53. He did obeisance to the Great Seer with his head so that his headdress shook, and with His permission sat down on the ground on the soft grass.

---

[1] So C; perhaps *yoṅs mthoṅ* (for *mdzad*) *nas* in T.

[2] T has *bgres* (*vṛddha?*), for which W conjectures *bkris* (*maṅgala*). Perhaps *bgros* in the sense of "disputants" or "enquirers."

[3] Keep the xylographs' *bzhon-pas*; I find no support in C for W's *gzhon-pas* and translation.

54. The thought occurred to the people there, "Oh! The might of the Śākya Sage. Has the seer, His Holiness Kāśyapa, become His pupil?"[1]

55. Then the Buddha, knowing their minds, said to Kāśyapa, "Kāśyapa, what was the quality you saw that you abandoned fire-worship?"

56. When the Guru thus incited him with a voice like that of a mighty raincloud, he folded his hands and said aloud in the crowded assembly:—

57. "I have given up the fires, because the fruit of worshipping them and of making oblations in them is continuance in the cycle of existence and association with the various mental ills.

58. I have given up the fires, because by muttering prayers, offering oblations and the like out of thirst for the objects of sense the thirst for them merely grows stronger.[2]

59. I have given up the fires, because by muttered prayers and fire-oblations there is no cessation from birth, and because the suffering of birth is great.

60. I have given up the fires, because the belief that the supreme good comes from rites of worship and from austerities is false.

61. I have given up the fires, because, as I affirm (?), I know the blissful immutable stage, which is delivered from birth and death."

62. On hearing the converted Kāśyapa thus speak words, so productive of faith[3] and so full of matter, the Master of the Rule (*Vinaya*) said to him:—

63. "Hail to you, most noble one (*mahābhāga*); this is most certainly the good work that you have done, in that among the various Laws you have attained that which is the best.

---

[1] T shows no sign of a question here, but verse 71 seems to require this translation.

[2] So C; read *ḥphel* (*vardhate*) for *med* in *c*?

[3] Or, "born of faith."

64. Just stir up then the hearts of the assembly[1] by displaying your various magic powers, as one who has great possessions displays his various treasures."

65. Then Kāśyapa said, "Very well," and, contracting himself into himself, he flew up like a bird into the path of the wind.[2]

66. This master of the miraculous powers stood in the sky as on a treestump,[3] walked about as on the ground, sat down as on a couch and then lay down.

67. Now he blazed like a fire, now he shed water like a cloud, now he blazed and poured forth water simultaneously.

68. As he took great strides, blazing and shedding water, he appeared like a cloud pouring forth rain and brilliant with flashes of lightning.

69. The people looked up at him in amazement, with their eyes glued to him, and, as they did obeisance to him in reverence, they uttered lion-roars.

70. Then, bringing his magic display to a close, he did obeisance to the Sage with his head and said, "I am the pupil who has done his task; my master is the Holy One."

71. The inhabitants of Magadha, seeing Kāśyapa do obeisance to the Great Seer in this fashion, concluded that it was the Blessed One Who was Omniscient.

72. Then He, Who abode in the supreme good, knew that the soil was prepared and for his welfare said to Śreṇya, who was desirous of hearing the Law:—

73. "O lord of the earth, O thou who art possessed of great majesty and hast control of the senses, Form (*rūpa*) is born and decays accompanied by the mind and the senses.

74. Their birth and passing away should be known for the furtherance of virtue, and, by knowing these two matters correctly, come to a right understanding of the body.

---

[1] Keeping the xylographs' *ḥkhor* (*dkor*, W), but not quite certain.

[2] *rluṅ-gi*, for W's *kluṅ-gi* (*nāgasya*) and the xylographs' *klu-yi*.

[3] Reading *sdoṅ-dum* for the xylographs' *sdod-dum* and W's *sdod-du ḥam*

75. By knowing the body with the senses to be subject to birth and passing away, there is no appropriation at all, no coming to the idea that it is 'I' or 'mine.'

76. The body and the senses have no objectivity outside the mental conceptions; they are born as suffering, as suffering they pass away.

77. When all this is understood to be neither 'I' nor 'mine,' then the supreme unchangeable Nirvāṇa is reached.

78. Through the sins of assuming the existence of the ego and the like men are bound in the false conception of self (*ātmagrāha*), and when they see that there is no self, they are released from the passions.

79. The false view binds, the right view releases; this world, abiding in the thought that there is a self, does not grasp the truth.

80. If a self did exist, it would be either permanent or impermanent; great defects follow from either alternative.

81. Just suppose it to be impermanent, then there would be no fruit of the act; and, since there would be no rebirth, salvation would come without effort on our part.

82. Or if it were permanent and all-pervading,[1] there would be neither birth nor death;[2] for space, which is all-pervading and permanent, neither passes away nor is born.

83. If this self were all-pervading in nature, there would be no place where it is not; and when it passed away, there would simultaneously (*ca . . ca*) be salvation for everyone together.

84. As being all-pervading by nature, it would be inactive and there would be no doing of the act; and without the doing of acts, how could there be the union with the fruit of them?

85. If the self did perform deeds, it would cause no suffering to itself; for who, that is his own master, would cause suffering to himself?

---

[1] Or, reading with the xylographs *khyad* for W's *khyab*, "Or if it possesses the attribute (*viśeṣa*) of permanence."

[2] C suggests either that one *skye-ba* should be *ḥchi-ba*, or that *skye-ba med* means "death."

86. The theory of a permanent self leads to the conclusion that it undergoes no change; but, since it experiences pleasure and suffering, we see that it does incur change.

87. Salvation comes from the winning of knowledge and the abandonment of sin; and since the self is inactive and all-pervading, there would be no salvation for it.

88. One should not say this, namely that there is a self, since in reality it has no existence (*asattvabhāvāt tattvena*); moreover, as having no causal efficiency, it is incapable of any action.[1]

89. Since then it is not clear what is the work to be done nor by whom it is done, the self cannot be said to exist in such wise (i.e. as either permanent or impermanent), and therefore it has no existence.

90. Listen, best of listeners, to this teaching how the stream of the cycle of existence flows along, bearing away this body, in which there is neither one who acts, nor one who experiences sensations (*vedaka*), nor one who directs.[2]

91. A sixfold consciousness arises based on the six organs of sense and their six objects; a system of contact develops separately for each group of three, whence awareness, volitions and actions come into activity.

92. Just as, from the conjunction of a burning-glass jewel, fuel and the sun, fire is produced by virtue of the union, even so all actions dependent on the individual take place, based on the consciousness (*buddhi*), the objects of sense and the senses.

93. Just as the shoot is produced from the seed, and yet the shoot is not to be identified with the seed, nor can either of them exist without the other, on such wise is the body and the interaction (*krama*?) of the senses and the consciousness."

94. When the Magadha king heard the sermon of the Best of sages, announcing the highest goal, the supreme beatitude, then the

---

[1] I am not certain of having correctly rendered the argument of this verse.

[2] Cp. *S.*, xvii. 20–21.

eye of the Law grew in him, the eye that is without stain, without equal, and devoid of passion (*rajas*).

95. Many men who dwelt in the capital of Magadha and the inhabitants of heaven became pure in mind in that assembly, on hearing[1] the Sage's preaching, and won to the stage where death and change are not.

CANTO XVII

Conversion (*pravrajyā*) of the Great Disciples.

1. Thereon the king presented to the Sage for His abode the glorious garden of Veṇuvana, and with His permission returned to the city, entirely changed in being (*dvitīya*?) through his comprehension[2] of the truth.

2. Then holding up for salvation's sake the auspicious lamp that is produced from knowledge, the Buddha dwelt in the Vihāra in company with Brahmā, the gods and saintly beings (*ārya*) of the various spheres of existence (*vihāra*?).

3. Then Aśvajit, who had broken the horses of his senses in, entered Rājagṛha in search of alms, and held the eyes of a great crowd by his beauty, his tranquillity and his demeanour.

4. A mendicant of Kapila's sect, who had many pupils, famed (*praśasta*?) as Śāradvatīputra, saw him coming with his senses tranquillised, and, following him on the road, thus addressed him:—

5. "On seeing your fresh appearance and your tranquillity, my mind is exceedingly amazed. Just tell me therefore if you know the final truth,[3] what is the name of your teacher, what he teaches and who he is."

---

[1] So C, i.e. read *thos* for *thob* in T.

[2] So C; same expression at xix. 28 and 36 below, apparently ***avabodha*** (cp. Bacot, Dictionnaire Tibétain-Sanscrit, s. *khoṅ-du chud-pa*').

[3] According to C this is part of the question. Alternatively, reading *rigs-pa* for *rig-pa*, "if it is indeed fitting."

6. When the Brahman spoke thus with every mark of respect, Aśvajit also said to him, "My Master was born of the Ikṣvāku race and is omniscient and without peer.

7. As I am ignorant and only recently born into the Law, I am not capable of explaining the teaching to you. Hear (*nibodha*?) however a small portion of the words of the Great Sage, Who is the Best of those who know how to speak.

8. The Holy One has explained the causes of all the elements (*dharma*) which arise from causes. He has explained what is the suppression of them and what the means of their suppression."

9. When the twice-born, whose name was Upatiṣya, heard these words of Aśvajit, straightway his eyes were opened to the Law and became free from passion (*rajas*), blissful and pure.

10. Previously he had held the theory that the field-knower (*kṣetrajña*) is uncaused, inactive, and the originator (*īśvara*); on hearing that all these things take place in dependence on causes, he perceived that there is no self and saw the supreme truth.

11. He held that the Sāṃkhya consider the body to consist of parts and therefore only destroys the group of gross sins, but that under the Buddha's teaching gross and subtle are destroyed alike.

12. When one embraces the idea of the soul (*ātman*) as the origin, there is no abandonment of the ego-principle, and therefore no abandonment of the ego. When a lamp and the sun are both present, what is to be known as a cause of the destruction of light?[1]

13, 14. Just as if one cuts off the roots of a lotus, the fine fibres remain entangled with one another, so he deemed the ⟨Sāṃkhya⟩ method of salvation not to lead to finality, while the Buddha's method was like cutting a stone.[2]

---

[1] So C and T, but one would have expected, "which of the two is to be known as the cause of the dispelling of darkness (or, diffusion of light)?" As it stands, the ego is the lamp, the soul the sun.

[2] W takes this, against C and T, as the two halves of two distinct verses, with the other halves missing. In the first line following C, amend *chu-ba* to *rtsva-ba* and take *che* as for *phye*, which is identical in pronunciation. C explains the last sentence by adding that no remains are left.

15. Then the Brahman did reverence to Aśvajit and himself departed in high contentment to his dwelling, while Aśvajit, after completing his alms-round in due order, proceeded soberly and wisely to the Veṇuvana.

16. When he who was born in the Maudgala *gotra* and whose actions corresponded to his learning and knowledge saw Upatiṣya returning thus filled with the highest peace (*prasāda*), he said to him:—

17. "O mendicant, why being the same have you become like another? You have returned steadfast and rejoicing.[1] Have you to-day found the deathless state? Such calm as this is not without a cause."

18. Then he explained the truth to him, saying "Thus is it done." Then he said, "Tell me the doctrine." Thereon he repeated the same words to him, and on hearing them the right eyesight was produced in him too.

19. As their minds had been purified by their actions and dispositions (*āśaya?*), they saw the real truth as it were a lamp held in their hands, and since by reason of their knowing it their feelings towards the Teacher were unswerving, they set off at that instant to see him.

20. The Great Seer, the Holy One, saw from afar these two[2] coming with their company of disciples and said to the mendicants, "These two, coming here, are my chief disciples, the chiefs, the one of those who have wisdom, the other of those who have magic powers."

21. Then the tranquil Sage in deep and solemn tones addressed His speech to the pair, "O mendicants, who have come hither for the sake of quietude, receive this Law rightly in proper form."

22. The Brahmans were bearing the triple staff and twisted locks, but in the very moment that the Tathāgata uttered these

---

[1] T omits two syllables; C suggests "with the marks of steadfastness and rejoicing."

[2] Read *de-gñis* for *de-ñid*?

words to them, they were turned by the Buddha's might into mendicants dressed in ochre-coloured robes.

23. These two, thus habited, with their company of disciples, did obeisance to the Omniscient with their heads. Then, on the Buddha's preaching the Law to them, in due time both reached the final beatitude.

24. Then a Brahman, the lamp of the Kāśyapa clan, who was possessed of colour, beauty and riches, abandoned his wealth and his beautiful wife, and, taking on himself the ochre-coloured robe, went in search of salvation.

25. He who had given up all his possessions[1] saw by the Bahuputraka Caitya the Omniscient blazing like a sacred flag-pole (or, caitya)[2] of the finest gold; and, filled with amazement, he folded his hands and approached Him.

26. He did obeisance to the Sage from afar with his head, and, having folded his hands, spoke out loud in fitting manner, "I am the disciple, the Holy One is my Master; O Steadfast One, be my light in the darkness."

27. The Tathāgata, the Appeaser of the mind with the water of His word, recognised that the twice-born had come because desire (for knowledge) had been bred in him, and that he was pure in disposition and desirous of salvation; therefore He said to him, "Welcome."

28. With his weariness relieved, as it were, by these words, he abode there in order to search for the final beatitude. Then, as his nature was pure, the Sage took pity on him and explained the Law to him summarily.

29. Because, when the Sage merely explained the Law briefly, he arrived entirely at its purport, therefore from his penetration (*pratisaṃvid*?) and great fame[3] he was called the Arhat Mahākāśyapa.

---

[1] Possibly *bhāva* in the sense of "feelings," to contrast with the feeling of amazement.

[2] Read *mchod-sdoṅ,* and cp. *S.*, iii. 25.

[3] So C; T has "great *vayas,*" which I find unintelligible.

30. He had held the self (*ātman*) to be both "I" and "mine,"[1] as being other than the body and yet in the body. He now abandoned that view of self and looked on it as perpetual(?)[2] suffering.

31. He had sought for purity by discipline and vows (*śīla-vrata*), finding the cause in that which was not a cause; now he had arrived at the nature of suffering and the path, and held discipline and vows not to be the supreme method.

32. He had wandered on the wrong course and failed to obtain the best; now he saw the stages of the Four Truths and fully cut off doubts and hesitations.

33. Recognising the impurity and unreality of the lusts, about which the world has been deluded, is deluded and will be deluded, he abandoned the objects of sense known as the passions.

34. Thus having attained benevolence (*maitrī*?) in thought, he made no distinction between friend and foe, and, compassionating all creatures, he was freed too in mind from internal malevolence (*vyāpāda*).

35. He abandoned the ideas (*saṃjñā*), informed with manifoldness,[3] that are based on matter and the reactions (*pratigha*?) to it, and understood the evils that are active in matter; so he overcame attachment to the sphere of matter (*rūpadhātu*).

36. He recognised that the stage of the Arūpa deities, who deem in their delusion that the trances are salvation, is transitory; and becoming tranquil, he achieved the mind that is empty of object (*nimitta*) and gave up attachment to the Arūpa existence.

37. He realised that the restlessness of the mind was a source of disturbance, flowing as it does like the mighty current of a great river (*sindhu*), and abandoning indolence by the help of

---

[1] T's *b* is one syllable short; C shows *bdag grib zhes* to be for *bdag-gi rab* (for *daṅ*?) *zhes*.

[2] *ñi-tshe-ba min*, "not ephemeral"; "in less than a day," W, not supported by C.

[3] The exact scope of this phrase is not clear to me; possibly it refers to seeing things as separate entities, not as mere compounds of the five elements.

steadfastness (*dhairya*),[1] he won to quietude and came to a standstill, like a lake that is full.[2]

38. He saw the states of being (*bhāva*) to be without substance (*sāra*) or self and to be subject to passing away (*vyaya*); and seeing nothing to be inferior, equal or superior,[3] he put away false self-esteem (*abhimāna*?) and held that there was no reality (in the states of being).

39. Dispelling the darkness of ignorance (*ajñāna*) with the fire of knowledge (*jñāna*), he saw the transitory and the permanent to be different, and perfecting his science (*vidyā*) by yoga, he duly extirpated delusion (*avidyā*).

40. Conjoined with insight (*darśana*) and contemplation (*bhāvanā*), he was released from this group of ten (*saṃyojanas*), and, his task completed, his soul at rest, he stood regarding the Buddha, with folded hands.

41. The Blessed One shone with His three disciples, who had the triple knowledge (*traividya*), and who had exhausted the three (*āsravas*), and who were in full possession (*adhigama*?) of the three (*śīla, samādhi, prajñā*?), like the moon when full (lit., in the third *parvan*) and united at the fifteenth *muhūrta* with the three-starred asterism (Jyeṣṭhā), whose regent is the after-born (*anuja*) god (Indra).[4]

CANTO XVIII

The Instruction of Anāthapiṇḍada.

1. Thereafter at a certain time there came from the north out of the Kośala country a wealthy householder, who was in the habit of giving wealth to the destitute and who was known under the famous name of Sudatta.

---

[1] So C and T, but one would expect *vīrya*.

[2] *gaṅ-ba*; should it not be *dad-pa, prasanna*?

[3] So C; T is incomprehensible and probably corrupt.

[4] This verse is of great difficulty, but I think the solution to be certain. For Jyeṣṭhā see the description in *Divyāvadāna*, 640, which agrees entirely with this verse. Vajrabāhu, the *anuja* of Dhruva, at ix. 20 is to be understood in my opinion as Indra, the younger brother of Brahmā.

2. He heard that the Sage was abiding there, and having heard he desired to see Him and went to Him at night. He did obeisance to the Blessed One, Who, knowing that he had arrived[1] with his nature purified (*viśuddhasattva*), instructed him:—

3. "O wise man, since in your thirst for the law you have given up sleep[2] and come to see Me at night, let then the lamp of final beatitude be raised here at once for the man who has thus come (*tathāgata*).

4. The display of these great qualities is due to your disposition (*adhyāśaya*), to your steadfastness, to your faith on hearing tell of Me, and to the activity of your mind by virtue of the previous cause.

5. Therefore, knowing that fame in this world and the reward in the hereafter arise from giving the best, you should at the proper time with due honour and devout mind give the treasure that is won through the Law.

6. Regulate your conduct by taking on yourself the discipline (*śīla*); for discipline, when observed and adorned, removes all danger of the evil spheres of existence below and cannot but raise a man to the heavens above.

7. Observing the evil consequences, of search, &c.,[3] that are involved in the many attachments to the lusts, and realising the good consequences of the way of renunciation, devote yourself to the truth of quietude which is born of discrimination (*viveka*).

8. Rightly seeing that the world wanders under the affliction of death and the oppression of old age, strive for the quietude that is delivered from birth and that, by not being subject to birth, is devoid of old age and death.

9. Just as you know that by reason of impermanency suffering ever persists among men, so know that there is the same suffering among the gods. There is no permanence at all in the continuance of active being (*pravṛtti*).

---

[1] *rab-sleb,* I.O., omitted by P, which is two syllables short; but the reading may be corrupt, as not corresponding to C.

[2] Following C, read *sgom-pas gñid* for *bsgoms-pas ñid.*

[3] Cp. *S.*, xv. 7 and 9.

10. Where there is impermanence, there is suffering; where there is no absolute self, there also is suffering. How then can there be an 'I' or a 'mine' in that which is impermanent, suffering and without self?

11. Therefore look on this suffering as the suffering, and the origin of this as the origin, and know the suppression of suffering as the suppression (*vyupaśama*) and the auspicious path as the path.

12. Know this world to be suffering and transitory, and observing mankind to be entirely burnt up with the fire of Time as with a real fire, hold existence and annihilation alike to be undesirable.

13. Know this world to be empty, without 'I' or 'mine,' like an illusion, and considering this body as merely the product of the factors (*saṃskāra*), think of it as consisting only of the elements.[1]

14. Shake your mind free from transitory existence; and observing the various spheres of rebirth (*gati*) in the cycle of existence, educate (*bhāvaya*) your mind, so that it is devoid of thought (*vitarka*?), fixed in quietude and free from passion. Then practise the 'absence of object' (*animitta*)."

15. Then on hearing the Law of the Great Seer, he obtained the first fruit of practice of the Law; and by its attainment only one drop remained over from the great ocean of suffering for him.

16. Though still living in the house, he realised by insight the highest good, the real truth, which is not for him who has no insight, whether in the grove or in heaven, though he dwell in the forest of those who are free from desire or on the peak of incorporeal existence.

17. Since they are not released from the meshes of the various false views and from the sufferings of the cycle of existence, they are lost by not seeing the real truth and arrive at a loftier station (*viśeṣa*) merely by being rid of passion.

18. With the correct view born in him, he shed the wrong views, like an autumnal cloud shedding a shower of stones, and he

[1] C puts verse 14 before verse 13.

did not hold that the world proceeded from a wrong cause, such as a Creator[1] (*īśvara*) and the like, or that it was uncaused.

*19. For, if the cause is of a different nature (to the effect), there is no birth (*upapatti*), and (to believe in) the absence of a cause is a great mistake. Seeing these points respectively by his learning and knowledge, he was certainly free from doubt in his view of the real truth.

20. If a Creator produced the world, there would be no ordered process of activity in it, and men would not revolve in the cycle of existence; in whatever state of existence anyone was born, there would he remain.

21. Corporeal beings would not encounter what they did not desire, nor for beings of such a nature would there be any production of what they desire. Whatever good and evil should come for corporeal beings would take place in the Creator for the sake of the Creator himself.[2]

22. Men would entertain no doubts about the Creator himself and would feel affection for him as for a father. When calamities come on them, they would not speak injuriously of him, nor would the world worship various deities.

23. If there should be a purpose (*bhāva*?) in his creation, then he is not the creator here to-day, as it (sc. the creation) would be the effect of the purpose (not of the Creator); for, if this continued activity of the purpose is asserted, it is that that would be the cause of there being a Creator.[3]

24. Or if his creation is not actuated by any intention,[4] his actions are causeless like a child's, and if the Creator has no dominion over himself, what power can he have to create the world?

---

[1] I translate *īśvara* by "Creator," but the latter term covers only a portion of the functions implied by the Sanskrit word.

[2] Or, "by reason of the fact of his being the Creator."

[3] Not certain. In *a* I read *ḥdi-yi skyed-la* for *ḥdi mi-skyed-la*, which is in better accord with C. For the argument here and in 25, see *Vijñaptimātratāsiddhi*, p. 30.

[4] C has "without mind," and T *nus-pa cuṅ-zhig med*, "without any capacity," possibly misreading *śakti* for *sakti*.

25. If he causes beings in the world to feel pleasure and suffering according to his desires, then, since thereby attachment to, or aversion from, the object takes place in him, the dominion does not reside in him[1] (but in the objects).

26. Men would stand under his control without will of their own, and his would be the responsibility for their efforts. There would be nothing done by the corporeal being and no fruit of the act; junction with the act (*karmayoga*) would depend on him.

27. If it is his actions that make him the Creator, then (since his actions are shared in common with men) he would not be the Creator. Or if he is all-pervading (*vibhu*) and without cause, then the Creatorship of the whole world would be established.

28. Or if there is any action other than that of the Creator, by reason of that very fact there would be an efficient Creator other than him, and it is not agreed (*avyavasthita*) that there is any (creator) other than him; therefore there is no creator of the world.

29. He saw the many kinds of contradiction that arise from the conception of Īśvara as the Creator, and therefore also the same defects are inherent in the theory of Nature.[2]

30. The latter view denies to some extent the principles (*āśraya*) of those who proclaim theories of causality and does not admit the cause to have any efficiency with regard to the effect; but, since one sees various things such as seeds and the like which produce effects, therefore Nature is not the cause.

31. An agent which is single cannot at all be the cause of things which are manifold; therefore as Nature is described as single in essence, it is not the cause of mundane evolution (*pravṛtti*).

---

[1] So apparently C. It would be more natural to take T, "If beings in the world act according to their own will with respect to pleasure and suffering, then, since their activity proceeds from their own attachment or aversion, the dominion does not reside in him."

[2] According to C and T, "Nature" might be either *svabhāva* or *prakṛti*; here I take it to be the former as the principle underlying the eightfold *prakṛti* of xii. 18.

32. Since Nature is asserted to be all-pervading, it follows that it can produce no effect; and, since one sees no form of result (of a cause) except effects, therefore Nature is not a cause of production.

33. Since it is all-pervading, it should, by reason of its being the cause, be the universal cause of everything unceasingly; but since we see a limitation in the activity (of a cause) to its (individual) result, therefore Nature is not a cause of production.

34. Since it is established that it is without attribute (*guṇa*), there should be no attribute in its results; but since we see everything in the world to have attributes, therefore Nature is not the cause of mundane evolution.[1]

35. Since, as a perpetual cause, it can have no special characteristics (*viśeṣa*), there can never be any specific attribute in its evolutes (*vikāra*); and since specific attributes are found to be present in the evolutes, therefore there is no productivity from Nature.

36. Since Nature is productive in essence, no cause of destruction is established with respect to its results; and, since we observe the destruction of the evolutes, therefore we must hold the cause at work to be something different.

37. Since union subsists with that which has the potentiality (of causing rebirth), nothing is gained by ascetics (*yati*) desirous of absolute salvation (*sunaiṣṭhika mokṣa*); for, since the continuance of activity is the essence of man's nature, how can they be released (from this life) except to pass on (to renewed activity) in the beyond?

38. Since Nature has by hypothesis the characteristic of being productive, its evolutes must equally have the same characteristics, but this is not always the case with regard to the evolutes in this world; therefore Nature is not productive.

---

[1] Owing to the repetition of *yon-tan*, T telescopes *b* and *c* into one line, omitting seven syllables; C enables the gap to be filled with certainty.

39. The action of Nature, they say, is not perceptible (*avyakta*) to the mind,[1] yet it is said to have perceptible evolutes. Therefore Nature is not a cause of the continuance of activity; for it is established that a result in the world can only proceed from a cause which is equally manifest.

40. An inanimate (*acetana*?) Nature cannot have for its effects animate beings such as horses, oxen or mules; for nothing animate proceeds from inanimate causes.

41. Just as a garland of gold is a special form (*viśeṣa*), so the evolutes of Nature are special forms; and, since the result is a special form, while the cause is not one, therefore Nature has no productive efficiency.[2]

42. If Time is postulated as the creator of the world, then there is no liberation for seekers. For the cause of the world would be perpetually productive, so that men would have no end.

43. Some see the determining principle as the selfness in the matters (*dravya*),[3] which is one and is made manifold by the attributes (*guṇa*); though they take their stand on a single cause, yet it has separate characteristics (*bhinnaviśeṣa*).[4]

*44. The attribute-theorist sees in the variety of attributes the operation of matter, which is born from a certain maturation (*pāka*?).[5] Since the cause is held to be not different (from the effect),[6] one must conclude that the matters are ineffective (*śūnya*).

---

[1] Uncertain. C seems to put this verse after 40.

[2] T puts this verse wrongly after 46, C here. The argument is that effects show characteristics not to be found in the cause as postulated.

[3] Reading *rdzas* for I.O.'s *rdzes* and P's *rjes*, as indicated by C.

[4] I do not understand this verse. It seems to be taken by T as connected with the three following verses, which are wanting in C and probably interpolated, and which are apparently intended to refute the classical Sāṃkhya, whose main principles were only developed at a substantially later date (see the Introduction to my translation of the *Buddhacarita* for the Sāṃkhya as known to Aśvaghoṣa).

[5] Uncertain; I omit an unintelligible *sar* ("on earth," or for *sad*?) at the end of *a*.

[6] Or, "without special characteristics."

*45. Certainly the unmanifested (*avyakta*), from which matter arises, cannot be the subject of a valid inference; for by perception (*pratyakṣataḥ*?) we do not see in fact the development of a result which is manifest from that which is unmanifest.

*46. As for the result which first arises from the unmanifest and comes into activity from the pair of manifests,[1] from it (sc. the unmanifest?) which is postulated arises in this world the great one (*mahat*) which is not postulated, and there ensue the defects of the Nature-hypothesis.

47. If Man (*puruṣa*) were the cause with respect to the effect, everyone would certainly obtain whatever he wanted; yet in this world some desires remain unfulfilled, and against their will (*avaśa*) men get what they do not want.

48. If it were a matter within his own control, man would not let himself be born as an ox, horse, mule or camel; for, since men perform the acts they want and hate suffering, who would bring suffering on himself?

49. If Man were the agent in the world, he would certainly do what is agreable to himself, not what is disagreable; yet in the execution of his wishes the undesired is done as well as the desired, and who, if he were the controller of events (*maheśvara*), would carry out the undesired?

*50. Whereas man is afraid of evil (*adharma*) and strives to attain the good (*dharma*), yet the various sins carry him away against his will; therefore in this matter man falls into bondage to an outside force (*paratantra*).

*51. Man has no dominion over himself but is subject to others; for we see the effects of cold, heat, rain, thunderbolts and lightning to frustrate his efforts. Therefore Man is not master (*īśvara*) over the effects.

52. Inasmuch as corn grows from the seed with the support of soil and water and by union with the right season. and as fire

[1] Incomprehensible; should perhaps be amended to "from the second unmanifest (*puruṣa*)."

originates from the wood and blazes with the addition of ghee there is no absence of cause such as is called existence without a cause.

53. If the activity of the world proceeded without a cause, there would be no action by men. Everyone would obtain everything, and inevitably there would be universal (*sarvatragāmin*?) accomplishment in this world.[1]

*54. Seeing that,[2] if pleasure and suffering were without a cause, there would be no apportionment of pleasure and suffering to everyone, and pleasure and suffering would not be comprehensible without a cause, therefore this which is called "without a cause" is not a cause.

*55. He knew that these and the like disparate causes do not cause the activity of the world. He saw the world not to be without a cause and he comprehended these defects of causelessness.

56. The various beings too, moving and stationary, come into existence in dependence on various causes; there is nothing in the world without a cause, yet the world does not know the universal cause.

57. Then Sudatta, having been given that good gift, understood the good Law of the Great Seer, Whose Law is noble, and with mind unalterably fixed in faith, addressed these words to Him:—

58. "My dwelling stands in Śrāvastī, a city renowned for virtue and ruled by the scion of Haryaśva's race. There I wish to make a monastery for You; deign to accept that flawless excellent abode.

59. Although, O Sage, I see that You are indifferent to whether You live in a palace or a lonely forest, yet, O Arhat, out of compassion for me You should accept it for a dwelling."

60. Then He knew that he intended to give and that his mind was liberated. So He, Whose mind was free from passion and

---

[1] Reading *ḥdir* for *ḥdi*.

[2] Read *gaṅ-tshe* for *gaṅ-char*.

Who knew the intentions, uttered His intention with the greatest gentleness (or, calm):—

61. "Your resolution is firm, (though you dwell) among treasures transitory as lightning, and your being is set (*adhimuc*) on giving. It is no wonder then that you should see the truth, rejoicing as you do by nature in the Law and delighting in giving.

62. Whatever goods are taken out of a burning house are not burnt up; similarly when the world is being burnt up with the fire of death (*kāla*), a man gains whatever he gives away.

63. Therefore the liberal-minded know giving to be the real (*samyak*) enjoyment of the objects of sense. But niggardly men, seeing the danger of exhaustion (of their wealth), do not give for fear they may have nothing to enjoy.

64. Giving wealth (*artha*) at the right time to a proper recipient (*pātra*) is like fighting with heroism and pride. The man who is eminent in resolution knows this, but not others, and he alone gives and fights with determination.

65. Because he is a giver, who fares through the world delighting in giving and thereby obtains fame and a good name, good men honour him for his generosity and associate with him.

66. Thus he is at ease in the world and does not fall into sin from lack of longsuffering. Ever contented, because he claims to have done good, in the hour of death he is not affrighted.

67. The fruit[1] of the gift in this world may be some flowers, yet in the hereafter he will obtain the reward of the giver. For there is no friend like unto liberality for man who revolves on the wheel of the cycle of existence.

68. Those who are born in the world of men or in the heavens receive a station superior to their equals by reason of their charity; those too who are born as horses or elephants, will obtain the fruit by becoming chiefs (of horses or elephants).

---

[1] So T, apparently in the sense of "substance"; "recompense," C.

69. By means of the gift he will go to heaven, surrounded by enjoyments and protected by his discipline. The man who is tranquillized and conducts himself with knowledge (*jñānapūrvam*) is without support (*āśraya*) and does not go the way of number.[1]

70. He practises liberality also in order to obtain deathlessness and delights in thinking (*smṛ*) on giving; his mind by reason of that delight certainly becomes concentrated.

71. With this success (*samudaya*) in concentration of mind gradually he comes to a knowledge of birth and suppression; for by giving to others, the sins that abide in the heart of the giver of the gift are diminished.

72. First, it is said, the giver cuts off attachment to those goods which he gives away, and since he gives with an affectionate mind, he thereby abandons wrath and pride.

73. In the case of the giver who rejoices on seeing the recipients' pleasure and is therefore not niggardly, and who reflects on the fruit of the gift, scepticism (*nāstitva*) and the darkness of ignorance are destroyed.

74. Therefore giving is one of the elements of salvation, since by it are subdued the avarice to which the ignoble resort and the thirst by which the habit of giving is destroyed; for when it is present, there is salvation by destruction of the sins.

75. Just as some like trees for their shade, some for their fruit and some for their flowers, so some employ themselves in giving for the sake of quietude, others for the sake of wealth.

76. Therefore in particular householders do not store up their goods, but give according to their means; and since it is giving which alone bestows value on wealth,[2] this is the path for the good to follow.

---

[1] T has two syllables each in excess in *c* and *d*; I omit *kyaṅ ni* and *gaṅ* (or *daṅ*) *na*. The translation, guaranteed by C, is mechanical; *āśraya* perhaps "the body with its organs," and "number" recalls *na upeti saṃkhaṃ*, *Suttanipāta*, 209, &c. (see note on xii. 77, in my translation).

[2] Literally, "Giving is the pith (*sāra*) of wealth which is pithless."

77. The giver of food gives strength, the giver of clothes too beauty, but he who gives an abode for the religious gives everything in the world.

*78. The giver of a vehicle also gives comfort, and the giver of a lamp illumination. Hence he who preaches the Law of ultimate beatitude gives the deathlessness that cannot be taken away.

79. Some give gifts for the sake of the passions, others for riches, others for fame, some for heaven, others in order not to be wretched (*kṛpaṇa*?); but this gift of yours has no ulterior motive.

80. Therefore bravo to you, who have formed such a desire; and when you have brought your intention to fulfilment, be contented. You, who came here possessed of passion (*rajas*) and the darkness of ignorance (*tamas*), will go away with your mind purified by knowledge."

81. He who had come rightly to the real truth by the path, full of joy and . . .,[1] took the matter of the Vihāra much to heart and set off in due course with Upatiṣya.

82. Thereon he came to the capital of the Kośala king and wandered about in search of a site for the Vihāra. Then he saw the garden of Jeta, majestic and suitable, with trees entrancing in their beauty.

83. Then in order to buy it he visited Jeta, who was too attached to it to sell it. "Even," he said, "if you were to cover it entirely with money, still I would not let you have the land."

84. Then Sudatta said to him there, "I have need(?) of the garden[2]," and persisted in his desire for it. Then he covered it with treasure and, looking on it as a business (*vyavahāra*) of the Law, he bought it.

85. When Jeta saw that he was giving the money, he became extremely devoted to the Buddha, and gave up to the Tathāgata the rest of the grove in its entirety.

---

[1] *gzhug-pa byas-pa*, T; "with intelligence increased by conversion," C.

[2] *tshal de-la rim byas*, T; C expands and does not explain this phrase.

86. Then with Upatiṣya, the great seer, in charge of the works as Superintendent, Anāthapiṇḍada determined to do it quickly, and with mind liberated and unattached, he started to build a mighty Vihāra, glorious in beauty,

87. And the embodiment of his wealth and power and insight, even like the palace of the Lord of Wealth come down to earth, and like the Fortune of the Northern Kośala capital, and like the stage (*bhūmi*) of Tathāgatahood.

(*To be continued.*)

The Buddha's Mission and last Journey: *Buddhacarita*, xv to xxviii.

Translated by

E. H. Johnston, Oxford.

(*Continuation.*)

CANTO XIX

The Meeting of Father and Son.

1. Then the Sage, having overcome by His knowledge all the teachers of the various systems, set forth in due course from the city of the Five Mountains for that inhabited by his royal father.

2. Then the thousand disciples He had just converted went too. He arrived at his father's realm, and then, in order to do him a favour, stayed near His native city.

3. Then the purohita and the wise minister, hearing the joyful news from their trustworthy spies that the Noble One had returned with His aim accomplished,[1] respectfully informed the king.

4. Then the king, learning of His arrival, was filled with joy, and desiring to see Him, set out to meet Him with a cortege of all the citizens, forgetful in his haste of all decorum (*dhairya*).

5. He saw Him in the distance surrounded by His disciples, like Brahmā in the midst of the seers; and out of respect for the Law of the Great Seer,[2] he alighted from his chariot and approached on foot.

---

[1] T omits two syllables in *c* and I complete the translation from C.

[2] Or possibly, " in accordance with the custom regarding great seers."

6. Hastening into His presence, at the sight of the Sage he uttered no words; for he was as incapable of calling Him "Mendicant" as of calling Him "Son."

*7. Then as he looked at His mendicant's robes and contemplated the various ornaments on his own person, his sighs came fast, and shedding tears he lamented in an undertone:—

8. "Like a traveller overcome by thirst, who approaches the distant pool to find it dried up, my affliction becomes overwhelming on seeing Him sitting close by me calmly and without change of feeling.

9. As I look on that same form of His, as one might look at the pictured representation of a dear one, still remembered in mind, but abiding at the end of the world, I feel no delight just as He feels none.

10. The earth, engirdled by all the mountains, should belong to Him, as it did to Māndhātṛ in the golden age; yet He, Who should not beg even from a king, now lives by begging from others.

11. He dwells here, surpassing Meru in steadfastness, the sun in brightness, the moon in beauty, a great elephant in stride, a bull in voice; yet He eats the food of mendicancy instead of winning the earth."

12. Then the Buddha knew that His father still thought of Him in his mind as his son, and in His compassion for the monarch (*lokādhideva*) He flew up into the sky for his sake.

13. He touched the chariot of the sun with His hand and walked on foot in the path frequented by the wind; He transformed His single body into many and then made the many bodies into one.

14. Without impediment He plunged into the earth as if into water, and walked on the surface of the water as if on dry land; and He calmly (*prasanna*?) penetrated the mountain, passing through it[1] as free from obstruction as if moving through the air.

15. With one half of His body He emitted showers of rain, and with the other He blazed as if with fire. He appeared in the

---

[1] *thad-kar mdzad-pa*; *thad-ka* = *tiryak* according to Bacot, Dictionnaire Tibétain-Sanscrit. Two syllables missing in *c*.

sky shining gloriously, as brilliant as the bright herbs on the mountain.

16. Thus He produced delight in the mind of the king, who was so fond of Him, and, seated in the sky like a second sun, He expounded the Law to the ruler of men:—

17. "I know, O king, that in your compassionate nature you are overtaken by sorrow at the sight of Me. Give up that delight in having a son, and, becoming calm, accept from Me the Law in place of a son.[1]

18. What no son has ever before given to a father, what no father has ever before received from a son, that which is better than a kingdom or than Paradise, know that, O king, to be the most excellent deathlessness.

19. Guardian of the earth, recognize the nature of the act, the birthplace of the act, the vehicle (*āśraya*) of the act and the lot that comes by maturation of the act, and know the world to be under the dominion of the act; therefore practise that act which is advantageous.

20. Consider and ponder on the real truth of the world. The good act is man's friend, the bad one the reverse. You must abandon everything (when you die) and go forth alone, without support (*āśraya*), accompanied only by your acts.

21. The world of the living fares on under the impulse (*āśraya*) of the act, whether in heaven or hell, among animals or in the world of men. The cause of existence is threefold,[2] threefold the birthplace (*yoni*), and various are the deeds that men commit.

22. Therefore rightly direct yourself to the other alternative (or, the class of two, *dvivarga*) and purify the actions of your body and voice. Strive for quietude of the mind. This is your goal; there is no other.

---

[1] T is two syllables short in *d*; following C, read something like *gnas-su chos-la* for *gsar-pa*.

[2] Probably *rāga*, *dveṣa* and *moha*.

23. Knowing the world to be restless as the waves of the sea and meditating on it, you should take no joy in the spheres of existence, and should practise that act which is virtuous and leads to the highest good, in order to destroy the power of the act.

24. Know that the world ever revolves like the circle of the asterisms; even the gods pass their peak and fall from heaven, how much less then may one rely on the human state?

25. Know the bliss of salvation to be the supreme bliss, and internal (*adhyātma*) delight to be the highest of all delights. What self-controlled (*ātmavat*) man rejoices in the pleasures of splendour, seeing that it is attended by many dangers, like a house infested with snakes?

26. Look therefore on the world as encompassed with great dangers like a house on fire, and seek for that stage which is tranquil and certain, and in which there is neither birth nor death, neither toil nor suffering.

27. Crush the hostile armies of the faults, for which there is no need of wealth or territory or weapons or horses or elephants. Once they are conquered, there is nothing more to conquer.

28. Comprehend suffering, the cause of suffering, the appeasement and the means of appeasement. By thoroughly penetrating these four, the great danger and the evil births (*durgati*) are suppressed."

29. Then, since the Blessed One's display of miraculous power had previously made the king's mind a fit field for instruction, now on receiving His Law by hearing, he was thrilled and folding his hands he uttered these words:—

30. "Wise and fruitful are Your deeds, in that You have released me from great suffering. I, who formerly rejoiced in the calamitous gift of the earth for the increase of grief, now rejoice in the fruit of having a son.

31. Rightly (*sthāne*) You went away, abandoning sovereign glory. Rightly You toiled with great labour, and rightly, beloved as You were, You left Your dear relations and have had compassion on us.

32. For the good of the distressed world You have also obtained this final beatitude, which not even the divine seers or the royal seers arrived at in olden times.

33. If You had become a universal monarch (*cakravartin*), You would not have caused me such joy as I now firmly feel by the sight of these magic powers and of Your Law.

34. If You had remained bound up with life here even in this existence, You would as a Cakravartin have protected mankind, but now as a Sage, having broken down the great suffering of the cycle of existence, You preach the Law for the sake of the world.

35. By displaying these miraculous powers and deep-searching wisdom and by completely overcoming the perils of the cycle of existence, even without sovereignty You have become the Lord (*īśvara*) in the world, but even with sovereignty prospering You would not have become so, if helplessly conjoined with existence."

36. Many such things spoke the Śākya king, who had become fit ⟨to receive⟩[1] the teaching of the Compassionate One's Law, and, though he stood in the position of king and father, yet he did obeisance to his Son, because he had penetrated the truth.

37. Many persons, who had witnessed the Sage's possession of miraculous power, who had understood the doctrine (*śāstra*) that pierced through to the real truth, and who saw the king His father reverencing Him,[2] conceived a desire to leave their homes.

38. Then many princes, in possession of the fruit of their deeds,[3] adopted that method of religion (*dharmavidhi*), and, regardless of the Vedic Scriptures (*mantra*) and their great means of enjoyment, abandoned their loving weeping families.

39. Ānanda, Nanda, Kṛmila, Aniruddha, Nanda, Upananda, and also Kuṇṭhadhāna, and Devadatta, the false teacher of the disciples, after instruction by the Sage, left their homes.

---

[1] T omits two syllables in *a*.

[2] Or, "saw the king reverencing Him as his Guru."

[3] *phalastha*, referring to the fruit of their past deeds and to their present enjoyments.

40. Then the purohita's son, the great-souled Udāyin, went forth on the same path; and Upāli, the son of Atri (or, the Atreya), seeing their decision, made up his mind to the same course.

41. The king too, seeing his Son's power, entered the stream of the supreme deathlessness, and dead to attachment he handed over the realm to his brother and abode in the palace, behaving as a royal seer.

42. The Buddha, having converted these and other relations, friends and followers, entered the city at the proper time in full control of Himself amid the welcome of the weeping citizens.

43. Hearing the news that the King's Son, Sarvārthasiddha, His task accomplished, was entering the town, the women in the palaces rushed to the doors and windows.

44. When the women saw Him clad in the ochre-coloured robe, yet shining like the sun half-covered by an evening cloud, they shed tears and, folding their lotus-like hands, did obeisance to Him.

45. As the women saw Him proceeding with down-gazing face, illuminated by the Law and the beauty of His person, they manifested pity and devotion, and, their eyes turbid with tears, they thus lamented:—

46. "His beautiful body[1] is transformed by the shaving of His head and the wearing of cast off garments, yet He is enveloped in the colour of gold from His body. So He walks, directing His eyes on the ground.[2]

*47. He Who was worthy to shelter under the white umbrella, to . . ., to . . .[3] and to be a conqueror, now goes along, holding the begging-bowl.

48. He Who ought to ride on a horse under the shelter of an umbrella, white as the face of a beautiful woman, when a *tamāla* leaf has been applied to her cheek, goes on foot, holding the begging-bowl.

---

[1] Supplied conjecturally from C; two syllables missing in *b*.

[2] Two syllables missing in *d*; I supply *sa-la*, indicated by C.

[3] I can find no plausible translation for *b* and the first half of *c* of this interpolated verse.

49. He Who should be humbling enemy princes and Who, wearing a brilliant headdress, should be gazed at by troops of women and by His attendant retinue, walks along looking at only a yoke's length of ground in front of Him.

50. What is this system (*darśana*) of His, what these mendicant's badges, what goal does He seek, why has pleasure become His enemy, that He should delight in vows, not in children and wives?

51. The king's daughter-in-law, Yaśodharā, was certainly gripped by grief, yet what a difficult thing she did, that, on hearing of this her Lord's conduct, she survived the news and did not pass to destruction.

52. When too the lord of men sees his Son's form shining in accordance with His beauty but no longer adorned (*vivarṇa*), does he remain fond of his Son, or does he look on Him as a harmful enemy?[1]

53. If, on seeing His son Rāhula bathed in tears, He feels no attachment to him, what is one to think of such resolute vows that turn a man's face away from his affectionate kinsfolk?

54. Neither His lustre, nor the form of His body, nor His stride have been destroyed by the practice of pleasure; and yet, shining with these qualities, He has come to quietude and separated Himself from the objects of sense."

55. Thus the women uttered many laments, grasping at different opinions like the various teachers. The Buddha too with His mind untouched entered His native city and, obtaining alms, returned to the Nyagrodha grove.

56. With mind free from desire the Tathāgata had entered His father's town for alms; and He kept in mind His wishes to liberate the folk, whose means were small from their not having practised good (in the past) and who could give but little alms, to strengthen the brethren (*śramaṇa*), who had not gained control of their minds and who did not find contentment by such proceedings

---

[1] Translation of second hemistich uncertain; C not literal enough to help.

(i.e. alms-seeking), to be able to answer "Happiness be yours" (?) to the world, and similarly to preach the Scriptures (?).[1]

CANTO XX

Acceptance of the Jetavana.

1.[2] ⟨The Buddha⟩, having had compassion on the great multitude ⟨in Kapilavāstu⟩,[3] set forth with a mighty following for the city guarded by the arm of Prasenajit.

2. Then he arrived at the glorious Jetavana, brilliant with the outspread bloom of its *aśoka* trees, resonant with the voices of intoxicated[4] cuckoos, and having a row of lofty dwellings, white as the snow of Kailāsa.

3. Then taking an ewer of pure water, which was embossed with gold and adorned with a white wreath, Sudatta in due course presented the Jetavana to the Tathāgata.

4. Then king Prasenajit, desiring to see the Sage of the Śākyas, set off for the Jetavana. Then on his arrival he reverently did Him obeisance, and sitting down thus addressed Him:—

5. "Your desire, O Sage, to stay in this city will certainly bring good fortune to the Kośala people. For is not the country, which has not the support of such a Knower of the real truth (*tattvadarśin*), ruined or unfortunate?

6. Or rather at the sight of You and at Your acceptance of our obeisance in order to do us a favour, a satisfaction is now ours, such as is not felt by men even on meeting with the good.

7. The wind assumes the nature (i.e. scent) of whatever thing it blows upon; and birds, by gaining contact with Meru, lose their natural selves and are turned to gold.

---

[1] *yoṅs-su bris ñid*; perhaps for *yoṅs-su dris ñid*, "(to preach) on being questioned."

[2] Verses 1–19 in T are misplaced, following on verse 38.

[3] One line missing in T.

[4] Read *yaṅ-dag dmar-por* (*saṃrakta*) for *yan-lag dmar-por* (*raktāṅga*).

8. Therefore it is only by obtaining the residence in it of a saintly Being, Who is Lord of this world and of the hereafter, that my grove is glorious to see, like the palace of Triśaṅku, when it received the great sage, the son of Gādhin (Viśvāmitra).

9. The various gains that are won in the world are transitory and come to an end,[1] but for those countless things which arise from proximity to You there is no destruction.

10. O Saint (*sādhu*), no gain is known outside this, namely the sight of Your doctrine (?). O Lord, I have suffered and been harassed by passion (*rāga*) and the kingly profession (*rāja-dharma*)."

11. The Sage listened graciously to these and other such words from the Indra-like king, and knowing him to be addicted to rapacity and lust, replied thus to stir up his mind:—

12. "O king, it is no great wonder that you should speak thus or act thus towards the saintly . . .[2]

13. Those who desire to come up from below . . . to the righteous people who desire their benefit . . .

14. Since, O guardian of the earth, such is your state of mind, I desire therefore to say somewhat to you. Do you then comprehend My teaching and so act that it may be fruitful.

15. Lord of men, when Time binds and drags away the king, neither relations nor friends nor sovereignty will follow you; all will depart, afflicted and helpless. Your deeds alone will accompany you like a shadow.

16. Therefore guard your kingdom according to the Law, if you desire Paradise and a good reputation. For there is no kingdom at all in Paradise for the king who in his delusion misapplies (*ākulaya*?) the Law.

17. By guarding his kingdom in this world according to the Law Kṛśāśva gained Heaven, while the lord of men, Nikumbha,

---

[1] Reading *ḥdzad-pa-can* for *mdzad-pa-can* ("bound up with *karma*").

[2] T has telescoped two verses into one, omitting two lines of each; it is not possible to supply the missing part from C, which paraphrases freely here.

resiling from the Law in this world out of delusion, entered the earth in Kāśi.

18. I have given you this example, my friend (*saumya*), of good (*ārya*) and evil deeds. Therefore ever guard your subjects well, and with due reflection strive steadfastly for the right.

19. Thus do not harass human beings, never give free play to your senses; do not consort with the vicious or give way to anger, do not let your mind wander on evil courses,

20. Do not trouble (*muh*?) virtuous people through pride, do not oppress (*han*) ascetics who are to be treated as friends (*mitrasaṃjña*),[1] do not undertake holy vows under the influence of sin, and do not adhere at all to evil views.

21. Do not resort to the marvellous (?),[2] be not addicted to evil deeds, be not affected by arrogance (*mada*), do not listen with displeasure or intolerance, do not exhaust (?)[3] your fame or fix your mind on falsehood, do not take land revenue in excess of the share allowed by the laws (*śāstra*).

22. Keep your mind level and carry out the Law, consort with the good and . . .;[4] so act that, having obtained this eminence (as king now), you may arrive again (in the next life) at a noble position.

23. Applying energy (*vīrya*), grasping steadfastness (*dhairya*),[5] producing learning (*vidyāḥ*), overcoming the sins (*doṣa*), do the work of a religious man (*ārya*) in constant recollection of death, and winning a great position gain possession of the path.[6]

---

1 Two syllables missing, one of which must be the negative; I conjecture, as apparently indicated by C, *dkaḥ-thub-ldan-rnams* for *dkaḥ-thub-rnams* for the other, "ascetics" for "austerities."

2 *mtshar-la*; possibly for *mtshan-la*, which could be understood as *nimitta*, "omens."

3 *mi-bzad* (*kṣi*); possibly for *mi-bzaṅ*, i.e. "do not fix your mind on falsehood that brings ill fame."

4 *ri-mo khod mdzod-cig*.

5 Reading *brtan-pa* for *bstan-pa*, a very common corruption.

6 *māhātmyalābhād adhigaccha mārgam*.

24. You should, my friend, again do that work which protects[1] this fruit; for the prudent man, who has done this deed (in the past), sows the seed whose fruit he has seen.

25. In this world he who, being in a lofty position, gives way to sin, is in the light, but his mind stands in darkness; but he who is devoted (*pradhāna*) to the Law yet is not a chief among men, is in darkness, but his mind stands in the light.[2]

26. Whoever, being of high degree, practises the way of the Law, his mind becomes extremely white (*śukla?*); and whoever, being of low degree, does sinful acts, his mind becomes extremely dark.

27. Therefore, O king, knowing the existence of these four groups, exert yourself as you will; but if you wish to fare in pleasure, you will find yourself in the three lower classes, not in the first.

28. It is impossible for a man to do good (*kuśala*) for another's account, or, if he does it, it does not accrue to the other. The effect of one's own act is not destroyed, but is experienced by oneself, and the accrual of what is not done is not accepted as a fact.

29. Since what is not done has no efficacy,[3] that which is not done does not turn to good (*śreyas*) in the hereafter, and, as thereby there is not even cessation of existence (*vibhava*) in the world, therefore exert yourself in the method of good deeds.

30. The wicked man who commits sin to excess has no enjoyment in himself in the world of the living. Having committed his own sins to his own account, in the hereafter he will certainly experience the fruit himself.

31. Four great mountains, O mighty king, come together and crush the world; what is there to be done except with the support (*āśraya*) of the various deeds done in accordance with the Law to the best of one's capacity (*yathopapattau*)?[4]

---

[1] *skyoṅ-ba*; but should it not be *skyed-pa*, "produces"?

[2] Cp. *Saṃyutta*, I, 93 ff., for this and the next two verses.

[3] Reading *rgyu-la* for *brgya-la*.

[4] Cp. *Saṃyutta*, I, 100 ff.

32. Similarly when these four, birth,[1] old age, disease and eke death come together, the entire world revolves helplessly, encompassed as it were by four mountains.

33. When then this suffering comes on us against our will, and against it we have neither support nor power of resistance nor protection, there is no resource (*auṣadhi*?) for us to take except the Law, which is unfailing and inexhaustible.

34. Therefore, inasmuch as the world is impermanent and given to sensual pleasures, which are transitory as a flash of lightning, and as it stands on the fingertips of Death, man should not undergo the fruit of not following the Law.

35. Those various kings, who were like Great Indra, fought even in the divine battles and were mighty and proud(?),[2] yet in course of time suffering was their lot.

36. Even the earth that supports all beings is destroyed, and Meru is burnt up by the cosmic fire; the mighty ocean dries up, how much more then does the world of man, transitory as foam, go to destruction?

37. The wind blows violently and yet dies down, the sun scorches the world and yet goes to its setting, the fire too blazes and yet becomes extinguished; all that is, I ween, is in such case and subject to change.

38. This body, though long guarded with care and cherished with various enjoyments, yet abiding here but a few days . . .[3]

39. Know that in this state of the world men, fostering pride and arrogance (*mada*), in time lie down to sleep on lofty couches; do not lie down on them, but keep awake for the sake of the highest good.

40. The world mounts the ever-moving swing[4] of the cycle of existence, and is heedless, though its fall is certain . . .[5]

---

[1] So C; T has *rgud-pa* (*vipatti*, for *upapatti*?).

[2] *ṅes-par zum-pa-rnams*; *nismita* for *vismita*?

[3] Last line missing in T; exact sense of it apparently not given by C.

[4] T omits two syllables; supplied from C.

[5] Two lines missing in T and the sense not given in C.

41. Do not resort to that which does not have pleasant consequences (*saṃbandha?*), do not do that which has evil fruit; he is not a friend who is not conjoined with good, that is not knowledge which does not dispel suffering.

42. If you have knowledge, there is no more existence for you, or if there is existence, it is in the bodiless state; for, if you continue incarnated in a body, you are not released from the objects of sense, and the sphere of passion is ephemeral and calamitous.

43. Since even the Arūpa deities, as still subject to the power of the act, are impermanent and under the dominion of Time, therefore set your mind on the cessation of activity (*apravṛtti*); if there is no activity, there is no suffering.

44. Since the body is the root of suffering in view of its dependence on the various actions such as moving, standing and the like, therefore the debt of the body is acquitted by the existence of knowledge which is competent with regard to the bodiless state.

45. Since the world comes to birth by reason of passion and thereby undergoes much great suffering, therefore when a man can detach himself (*vivic*) from the sphere of passion (*kāmabhava*), he is no longer attached to suffering and ceases to be afflicted.[1]

46. Therefore whether among the Arūpa deities or among the Rūpa deities who are still subject to the lusts (*kāma*), the continuance of activity is not stilled because of the liability to transmigration, how much more then is it not so for those in the domain (*pracāra*) of the six lusts?

47. Seeing the three spheres of existence to be thus impermanent, suffering and without self, and to be ever on fire, there is no place of refuge for men to enter, as for birds whose roosting-tree is ablaze.

---

[1] Two syllables missing in *d* and the translation is accordingly not certain, though the general sense is right.

48. This is the best thing to be known, nothing else is to be known. This is the best wisdom (*mati*), nothing else is wisdom. This is the best task, nothing else is admitted (to be such) . . .[1]

49. It is certainly not to be thought that this Law is not for those who dwell in houses. Whether abiding in the forest or in the house, only he really exists who achieves quietude.

50. A man, when scorched with heat, enters the water, and everyone obtains relief from a cloud. He who has a lamp sees in the darkness. Yoga is the means (*pramāṇa*), not age nor family.

51. Some, though they live in the forest in their old age (*vayas*), fail to practise yoga, and, breaking their vows, descend to an evil existence (*durgati*); others, though living in their homes, purify their actions and, taking proper heed, attain to the final beatitude.

52. Among the folk struggling in the ocean of ignorance (*tamas*), whose waves are wrong views and whose water existence, only he who has the boat of mystic wisdom (*prajñā*) with the oars of awareness and energy is rescued therefrom."

53. Thus the king, who was much given to the objects of sense, received this truth (*tattva*) of the Law from the Omniscient, and, with the conviction born in him that evil kingship is impermanent and unstable, returned to Śrāvastī in sober mood like an elephant freed from *must*.

54. The other doctors of learning (*tīrthika*), knowing that the lord of the earth had bowed down to Him, challenged Him of the Ten Forces to a display of magic powers; and, when the guardian of the earth requested Him to do so, the Seer Who had conquered self consented[2] to exhibit His magic might.

55. Then the Sage shone with an orb diffusing splendour, like the rising sun outshining the stars, and He defeated the teachers

[1] Last line missing in T. C has, "By this one approaches the doctrine, separated from this one is parted from the right."

[2] Read *sdum-pas* for *sdug-pas*, as indicated by C.

of the various systems by magic powers of many kinds, giving general delight(?).

56. Then after the people of Śrāvastī had honoured and reverenced Him therefor, He departed with the extremest (*niruttara*?) majesty and mounted above the triple universe in order to preach[1] the Law for the benefit of His mother.

57. Then the Sage converted by His knowledge His mother who dwelt in Heaven; and passing the rainy season there and accepting alms in due form from the ruler of the Sky-gods, He descended from the heavenly worlds to Saṃkāśya.

58. The gods, who had acquired tranquillity, stood in their mansions and followed Him with their eyes, as if they were falling to earth,[2] and the various kings on earth, raising their faces to the sky, received Him with their heads, as they did obeisance to Him.

CANTO XXI

Progress (*srotas*) of the Mission.

1. After converting in Heaven His mother and the heavenly dwellers who were desirous of salvation, the Sage travelled over the earth, converting those who were due for conversion by Him.

2. Then in the city that lies in the midst of the five mountains, the Teacher (*Vināyaka*) converted Jyotiṣka, Jīvaka, Śūra, Śroṇa and Aṅgada.

3. He turned from their former views the king's son, Abhaya, Śrīgupta, Upāli, Nyagrodha and others, who held the (views of the two) ends (permanence and annihilation).

4. He converted the lord of Gāndhāra, Puṣkara by name, who abandoned his royal glory immediately on hearing the Law.

5. Then He, Whose energy (*parākrama*) was extensive (*vipula*), converted on Mount Vipula the Yakṣas Haimavata and Sātāgra.

---

[1] Read *gsuṅ-bar* for *bsruṅ-bar*, as indicated by C.

[2] This is apparently the meaning, but T omits two syllables in the first line and is not clear.

6. The Knower of qualities (*guṇadarśin*) brought to the faith at night in Jīvaka's mango-grove the king (Ajātaśatru) accompanied by his five hundred[1] queens.

7. Then on Mount Pāsāṇa the Brahman Pārāyaṇa, who was intent on quietude,[2] started the study of the meanings decided by subtle words.[3]

8. Then in Veṇukaṇṭaka He converted the saintly mother of Nanda, who by good awareness (*satsmṛti*) saw (hidden) treasures before her eyes.[4]

9. Then in the village of Sthāṇumatī the excellent Brahman Kūṭadatta, who wished to sacrifice with all sorts of sacrifices, was caused to enter the Law of Salvation.

10. Then on the Videha mountain Pañcaśikha and the Asurīs(?) and gods[5] entered into firm conviction.

11. Then in the city of Aṅga the Yakṣa Pūrṇabhadra and the great snakes, Śreṣṭha,[6] Daṇḍa, Śveta(?), Piṅgala(?) and Caṇḍa(?) were converted.

12. In the city of Āpaṇa the Brahmans Kenya and Śela, who were practising austerities ⟨for the sake of being reborn in heaven⟩,[7] were brought to salvation.

13. Among the Suhmas the Holy One by the might of His magic power converted Aṅgulimāla, a Brahman who was cruel like Saudāsa.[8]

---

[1] Read *lṅa-brgya* for *lta-byed*; the occasion was that of the delivery of the *Śrāmaṇyaphalasūtra*.

[2] Doubtful; T is apparently corrupt, and I understand an original *śama-parāyaṇaḥ*.

[3] Cp. the *Pārāyaṇavagga* of the *Suttanipāta*. C has, "was converted by the subtle meaning of half a *gāthā*."

[4] C puts this verse after verse 10.

[5] So T apparently; C names merely "a heavenly spirit of great majesty and virtue named Pañcaśikha."

[6] "Śroṇa," C; cp. Soṇadaṇḍa, the Brahman of Campā, *Dīgha*, I, 111 ff. C does not give the last three names.

[7] Supplied from C; T omits a line.

[8] *bran-bzaṅs*, T; cp. the *Sutasomajātaka*.

14. In Bhadra the son of a gentleman (*bhadra*), Meṇḍhaka by name, of good livelihood and a generous giver, and like Pūrṇabhadra in wealth, was caused to take the right views.[1]

15. Then in the city of Videha the Best of speakers overcame by His preaching him who was named Brahmāyus, and whose lifetime was as extensive as Brahmā's.

16. He converted the flesh-eating monster (Markaṭa) in the pool at Vaiśālī as well as the Licchavis headed by Siṃha, and Uttara(?) and Satyaka.[2]

17. Then in the city of Alakāvatī He, Whose work was good, brought to the way of the Law the Yakṣa Bhadra, who possessed a good disposition.

18. Then in a very evil forest (*aṭavī*) the Wise One instructed the Yakṣa Āṭavika and the young prince (*kumāra*) Hastaka.[3]

*19. Then in the city of . . .[4] He Who saw salvation preached salvation to the Yakṣa Nāgāyana(?),[5] while the Yakṣa king did obeisance.

20. At Gaya the Seer instructed the Ṭaṃkita(?) sages[6] and the two Yakṣas, Khara and Śūcīloma.

21. Then in the town of Varāṇasī the Possessor of the Ten Forces converted the Brahman Kātyāyana, nephew of Asita the sage.

22. Then He went by His magic powers to the city of Śūrpāraka and in due course instructed the merchant Stavakarṇin,

---

[1] C mentions after this the conversion of two Yakṣas, Bhaddāli and Bhadra, in the same village; perhaps a misunderstanding of the epithets qualifying Meṇḍhaka.

[2] For the last two C has simply "the Nirgranthaputras."

[3] Read *lag-hoṅs* for *legs-hoṅs*. "Very evil" is perhaps the name of the forest.

[4] *bde-dgaḥ*; first syllable perhaps *śam*.

[5] *sdig-med*, which stands for *nāga* verse 55 below; cp. *Suvarṇaprabhāsasūtra*, xv. 41.

[6] For "Ṭaṃkita sages" C has "the demon Ṭakana," and it describes Khara as sister's son to Śūcīloma. *Suttanipāta*, p. 47, gives the Yakṣas' dwelling as Ṭaṃkitamañca, the first member of which Professor Helmer Smith points out to me probably means "chiselled"; a reference perhaps to carved caves such as the Lomas Rishi Cave in the Barabar hills near Gaya.

23. Who, on being instructed, became so faithful that he started to build for the Best of seers a sandalwood Vihāra, which was ever odorous and touched the sky.

24. Then He converted Kapila the ascetic in Mahīvatī,[1] where the wheel-marks of the Sage's feet were seen on a stone.

25. Then in Varaṇa He instructed the Yakṣa Vāraṇa; similarly in Mathurā the fierce Gardabha was converted.

26. Then in the town of Sthūlakoṣṭhaka the Teacher converted him who was called Rāṣṭrapāla, whose wealth was equal to that of a king.

27. Then in Vairañjā a great being (or, crowd) like Viriñca[2] was converted, and similarly in Kalmāśadamya the learned Bhāradvāja (?).[3]

28. In Śrāvastī again the Sage dispelled the darkness of Sabhiya, of the Nirgrantha Naptṛīputras and of the other doctors (*tīrthika*).[4]

29. Here too the Brahman sacrificers (*yajñaka*?), Puṣkalasādin(?) and Jātiśroṇi(?),[5] as well as the king of Kośala, were brought to believe on the Buddha.

30. Then in the forest land of Śetavika[6] the Best of teachers taught a parrot and a starling (*śārikā*), birds (*dvija*) who were as learned as Brahmans.

---

[1] T takes *mahī* as *mah*, "brightness"; apparently the same place as that described in Watters, *On Yuan Chwang*, I, 233.

[2] Perhaps "He Who was like Viriñca converted, &c."

[3] The reference must be to the *Māgandiyasutta* of the *Majjhima*, and I take T's *rgya-chen skyes-bu-can* to stand for Bṛhadvājin, but the last part may represent Māgandika (*Divyāvadāna*, 515 ff.) and *mkhas-pa rgya-chen* may be another name, as C has two, Sa-vi-sa-san and Agniveśya. The latter cannot be reconciled with T or the known legends, unless Agniveśya corresponds to the Aggikabhāradvāja of the *Suttanipāta*.

[4] The correspondence of C for this and the next verse is not exact and its order may be wrong.

[5] These seem to be the names indicated by C, T perhaps having Puṣkala-ādi and Jātiśreṇi; the Pali canon associates Pokkharasāti and Jānussoṇi with Śrāvastī and Kośala.

[6] Setavya in Pali, between Śrāvastī and Kapilavāstu.

31. Then in the town of . . .[1] the savage Nāgara (?)[2] and Kālaka and Kumbhīra whose deeds were ferocious were brought to tranquillity.

32. Then among the Bhārgasas (Bhārgas?) He converted the Yakṣa Bheṣaka[3] and favoured similarly the aged parents of Nakula.

33. In Kauśāmbī the wealthy Ghoṣila, Kubjottarā and other women, and a multitude beside were converted.

34. Then in the Gāndhāra country the snake Apalāla, with his senses tamed by the Rule, passed beyond evil.

*35. Then the Wise One in due course preached sermons, after converting . . .,[4] who desired to burn up like Death.

36. By the conversion of these and other beings, whether faring on earth or in the sky, the fame of the Buddha kept on waxing like the ocean at springtide (*parvaṇi*).

37. Devadatta, seeing His greatness (*māhātmya*), became envious and, losing control over the trances, he did many improper things.

38. With his mind sullied he created a schism in the Sage's community, and by reason of the separation, instead of being devoted to Him, he endeavoured to do Him hurt.

39. Then he set a rock rolling with force on Mount Gṛdhrakūṭa; but, though aimed at the Sage, it did not fall on Him but divided into two pieces.

40. On the royal highway he set loose in the direction of the Tathāgata a lord of elephants, whose trumpeting was as the thundering of the black clouds at the dissolution of the world, and whose rushing as the wind in the sky when the moon is obscured.

41. The streets of Rājagṛha became impassable through the corpses, which he had struck with his body or taken up with his trunk or whose entrails were drawn out by his tusks and scattered in heaps.

---

[1] *ḥthob-pa*, T; C gives the names of two places, A-śu-ca and Śa-ve-ra. There was a Kālakārāma at Sāketa according to the Pali canon.

[2] *groṅ-khyer gtso*, T; "Śa-ve-ra," C.

[3] The Pali canon knows a Bhesakalāvana in the Bhagga country.

[4] *ḥbar-zhiṅ ḥjigs-paḥi las-can*, T.

42. In his thirst for flesh he dug into men's thighs, and when his trunk touched the entrails, he cast twitching wreaths of them, as though they were stones, into the air to free himself while his fearsome head, ears and tongue dripped with blood.

43. The townsfolk were panicstruck and terrified of him, as he wandered in limitless fury, stained with drops of gore and putrescent blood, and imbued with the smell of the ichor that spread over his forehead.[1]

44. As they saw the maddened elephant, like the fearsome club of Death (Yama), with his face swollen with insolence, trumpeting and rolling his eyes in wrath, cries of "Woe! Woe!" arose from Rājagṛha.

45. Some ran despairingly in all directions, some hid in places where they could not be seen, and others, so frightened as to be afraid of nothing else, entered the houses of others.

46. Some took no account of their lives in their fear that the elephant might hurt the Buddha, and valiantly shouted behind him, uttering roars like a lion about to spring.

47. Similarly others called out to the mahout; some raised their hands to him imploringly, some too threatened him then, and others appealed to his love of money.

48. The young women, looking on from the balconies, flung their arms about and wept; some in terror covered[2] their eyes with copper-coloured hands, which had golden bracelets.

49. Despite the on-coming (?)[3] elephant intent on slaughter, despite the weeping people holding up their arms (in warning), the Blessed One advanced, collected and unmoved, not breaking His step nor giving way to malevolence.

50. Quietly the Sage came on; for not even that great lord of elephants had power to touch Him, since in His benevolence (*maitrī*) He had compassion on all creatures and since the gods followed Him from devotion.

---

[1] The literal meaning and construction of the last clause is uncertain.

[2] Read *ḥgebs-pa-ḥo* for *ḥgeṅs-pa-ḥo*.

[3] *yoṅś-su ro-myaṅ* (*paryāsvadat* for *pratyāsadat*?), T.

51. The disciples who were following the Buddha fled, on seeing the great elephant from afar. Ānanda alone followed the Buddha, just as the inherent nature follows the multiform world.

52. Then, as the enraged elephant drew near, he came to his senses through the Sage's spiritual power (*prabhāva*), and, letting his body down, he placed his head on the ground, like a mountain whose wings[1] have been shattered by a thunderbolt.

53. Just as the sun touches a cloud with its rays, the Sage stroked the lord of elephants on the head with His beautiful hand, soft as a lotus and having well-formed webbed fingers.

54. As the elephant bent low at His feet, like a black raincloud overladen with water, the Sage, seeing his palmleaf-like ears to be moveless, preached to him the religious peace, which is fit for rational beings:—

55. "The slaughter of the Sinless One (*nāga*)[2] is accompanied by suffering; do no harm, O elephant, to the Sinless One. For, O elephant, the life of him who slays the Sinless does not develop from existence to existence in the eight good births.

56. The three, love, hatred and delusion, are intoxicants hard to conquer; yet the sages are free of the three intoxicants. Free yourself therefore of these fevers and pass beyond sorrow.

57. Therefore in order to abandon this love of darkness, be quit of intoxication and resume your natural self. Do not, O lord of elephants, slip back through excess of passion into the mud of the ocean of transmigration."

58. Then the elephant, hearing these words, was freed from intoxication and returned to right feeling; and he obtained the good internal (*antargata*) pleasure, like one released from illness on drinking the elixir (*amṛta*).

59. On seeing the lord of elephants straightway giving up his intoxication and doing obeisance as a pupil to the Sage, some flung

---

[1] T read *pakṣma* for *pakṣa*.

[2] *sdig-med*, T; "the great *Nāga*," C.

up arms covered with clothes, others brandishing their arms let the clothes go.

60. Then some folded hands to the Sage,[1] and others surrounded Him. Some praised the great elephant for his nobility (*āryatva*), and others, filled with wonder, stroked him.

61. Of the women in the palaces, some did Him honour with new clothes of great price, and others showered down on Him their various ornaments and fresh garlands of entrancing quality.

62. When that elephant, who was like Death (*kāla*), stood humbled, those who did not believe entered the middle state, those who were already in the middle state reached a special degree of faith, and the believers were mightily strengthened.

63. Then Ajātaśatru, standing in his palace,[2] saw the lord of elephants tamed by the Sage and was overcome with amazement; joy grew in him, and he believed in the Buddha to the highest degree.

64. Just as, when the evil age passes away and the age of ascent begins, Law and Wealth increase, in such wise waxed the Sage by His fame, His magic powers, and His difficult undertakings.

65. But Devadatta, having in his malice done many evil and sinful deeds, fell to the regions below, execrated by king and people,[3] by Brahmans and sages.

CANTO XXII

The Visit to Amrapālī's Grove.

1. Then in course of time, when the Best of speakers had favoured the world and filled the earth with His Law, His mind turned to Nirvāṇa.

2. Then in due time the Saint proceeded from Rājagṛha to Pāṭaliputra, where he stayed in the caitya known by the name of Pāṭali.

---

[1] Two syllables missing.

[2] T read *prasāda* for *prāsāda*.

[3] Reading *skye-dgu-ba* for *sten rgu-ba*; the translation of the last clause is not quite certain.

3. Now at that time Varṣākāra, the minister of the Magadha king, had made a citadel to keep the Licchavis quiet.

4. The Tathāgata saw the gods bringing their treasures there and prophesied that the city would become pre-eminent in the world.

5. The best of Doers, after being honoured in due form by Varṣākāra, proceeded with his disciples towards the chief wife of Ocean.

6. Then he (Varṣākāra) caused the gate, by which the Holy One, brilliant as the sun, emerged, to be reverenced as the Gautama Gate.[1]

7. He, Who had seen the crossing (of the ocean of transmigration), came to the bank of the Ganges, and, seeing the people with their various boats available,[2] reflected within Himself:—

8. "As it would be improper for Me to cross the river by effort, therefore I should go Myself without a boat by the force of My magic powers."

9. Thus unseen by the spectators, He with His disciples then passed to the other side in a moment, exceeding even the pace of the wind.

10. Inasmuch as the Sage knew that it is the boat of knowledge which crosses the ocean of suffering, He crossed the Ganges without again using this (i.e. a material?) boat.

11. The bank, from which the Teacher crossed to the other side of the Ganges, is famous in the world as a place of pilgrimage, known by His family name (Gautama).

*12. Then the faces of the men, who wished to cross, who were crossing and who had crossed, opened wide in wonder, as their eyes fell on Him.

13. Then from the bank of the Ganges the Buddha went on to the village of Kuṭi, and, after preaching the Law there, went on to Nādīka.

---

[1] T places this verse after 10; C rightly here.

[2] I am not sure of the exact sense and construction; C expands and, in contradiction with the next verse, makes the Buddha act out of fear of showing partiality by choosing one boat.

14. Many people had died there at that time, and the Sage explained in what world each of them had been reborn and as what.

15. After passing one night there, the Śrīghana moved on to the city of Vaiśālī and abode in a glorious grove in the domain of Amrapālī.

16. The courtesan Amrapālī, hearing the Teacher was there, mounted a modest equipage and went forth with great joy.

17. She wore diaphanous white garments and was without garlands or body-paint, like a woman of good family at the time of worshipping the gods.

*18. In the pride of her beauty,[1] she attracted by her united charms the minds and the wealth of the Licchavi nobles.

19. Self-assured in her loveliness and glory, like a forest goddess in beauty, she descended from her chariot and quickly entered the grove.

20. The Blessed One, seeing that her eyes were flashing and that she was a cause of grief to women of family, commanded His disciples with voice like a drum:—

21. "This is Amrapālī approaching, the mental fever of those whose strength is little; do you take your stand on knowledge, controlling your minds with the elixir of awareness.

22. Better is the neighbourhood of a snake or of an enemy with drawn sword, than that of woman for the man who is devoid of awareness and wisdom.

23. Whether sitting or lying down, whether walking or standing, or even when portrayed in a picture, woman carries away men's hearts.

24. Even if they be afflicted by disaster (*vyasana*), or fling their arms about weeping, or be burnt with dishevelled hair, yet women are pre-eminent in power.

25. Making use of extraneous things, they deceive by many adventitious (*āhārya*) qualities, and concealing their real qualities they delude fools.

[1] Or this may refer to the Licchavis, not to Amrapālī.

26. By seeing woman as impermanent, suffering, without self and impure, the minds of the adepts are not overcome on looking at her.

27. With minds well accustomed to these temptations (*ālaya*), like cattle to their pastures, how can men be deluded when attacked by the pleasures of the gods?

28. Therefore taking the arrows of mystic wisdom, grasping the bow of energy in your hands and girding on the armour of awareness, think well[1] on the idea of the objects of sense.

29. It is better to sear the eyes with red-hot iron pins than to look on woman's rolling eyes with misdirected awareness.

30. If at the moment of death your mind be subject to passion, it binds you helplessly and takes you to a rebirth among animals or in Hell.

31. Therefore recognize this danger and do not dwell on the external characteristics (*nimitta*); for he sees truly, who sees in the body only Matter (*rūpa*).

32. In the world it is not the sense-organs which bind the objects, nor is it the objects which bind the senses. Whoever feels passion for them (the objects of sense), to them is he bound.

33. The objects and the sense organs are[2] mutually attached, like two oxen harnessed to the same yoke.

*34. The eye grasps the form and the mind considers it, and from that consideration arise passion with regard to the object and also freedom from passion.

*35. If then great calamity ensues by not properly examining the objects of sense, activity in the domain of the senses is conjoined with all disasters.

36. Therefore not abandoning awareness, faring with the highest heedfulness, and having regard to your own good (*svārtha*), you should meditate (*bhāvaya*) energetically[3] with your minds."

---

[1] *mnos*, T, but "fight," C.

[2] Reading *yin* for *min*, as apparently C, and understanding "through passion"; otherwise a negative must be inserted.

[3] *gduṅ-med*, T, i.e. *atāpin* for *ātāpin*?

37. While He thus instructed the disciples who had not proceeded to the end of the matter, Amrapālī, seeing Him, drew near with folded hands.

38. Seeing the Seer seated with tranquil mind under a tree, she deemed herself highly favoured by His occupation (*paribhoga*) of the grove.

39. Then with great reverence, setting her eyes, restless as they were, in order, she did obeisance to the Sage with her head, which was like a *campaka* flower fully opened.

40. Then when she had seated herself in accordance with the Omniscient's directions, the Sage addressed her with words suited to her understanding:—

41. "This your intention is virtuous and your mind is steadfast by purification; yet desire for the Law is hard to find in a woman who is young and in the bloom of her beauty.[1]

42. What cause is there for wonder that the Law should attract men of intelligence (*dhīmat*?) or women who are afflicted by misfortune (*vyasana*) or are self-controlled (*ātmavat*) or ill?

43. But it is extraordinary that in the world solely devoted (*ekarasa*) to the objects of sense a young woman, by nature weak in comprehension and unsteady in mind, should entertain the idea of the Law.

44. Your mind is turned to the Law, that is your real wealth (*artha*); for since the world of the living is transitory, there are no riches outside the Law.

45. Health is borne down by illness, youth cut short by age, and life snatched away by death, but for the Law there is no such calamity (*vipat*).

46. Since in seeking (for pleasure) one obtains only separation from the pleasant and association with the unpleasant, therefore the Law is the best path.

47. Dependence on others is great suffering, self-dependence the highest bliss; yet, when born in the race of Manu, all females are dependent on others.

---

[1] *phul-gnas-pa*; or "wealthy."

48. Therefore you should come to a proper conclusion, since the suffering of women is excessive by reason equally of their dependence on others and of child-birth."

49. Young in years, but not like the young in disposition, intelligence and gravity, she listened joyfully to these words of the Great Sage.

50. Through the Tathāgata's preaching of the Law,[1] she cast aside the condition of mind that was given up to the lusts, and, despising the state of being a woman and turning aside from the objects of sense, she felt loathing for her means of livelihood.[2]

*51. Then entirely prostrating her slender body, like a mango-branch laden with blossom, she fixed her eye with devotion on the Great Sage and again stood with purified sight for the Law.

52. The woman, though modest by nature, yet ever spurred on by longing for the Law, joined her hands like a clump of lotuses (*paṅkajākara*) and spoke with gently uttered voice:—

53. "O Holy One, You have attained the goal and soothe suffering in the world. Deign in company with Your disciples to make the time of alms-seeking fruitful for me who am ripe for the fruit (?, *phalabhūta*), in order that I may receive a sermon."

54. Then the Blessed One, seeing her to be so devoted, and knowing animate beings to be dependent on food, gave His consent by silence and announced His intention to her with a gesture (*vikāra*).

55. He, Who possessed the supreme Law and an eye that discerned occasions (*kṣaṇakṛtyavat?*), rejoiced exceedingly in the vessel of the Law, . . . knowing that the best gain is by faith, He praised her.[3]

---

[1] Two syllables missing.

[2] *raṅ-gi skye-boḥi rten-la*, T; properly *svajanāśraya*.

[3] T omits one line, either *b* or *c*, and the exact sense and construction cannot be determined; Amrapālī may be the subject, not the Buddha. C is very brief and no help, but suggests the possibility that the real lacuna is in xxiii. 1, one line of this verse having been turned into two and transferred to that one to make up two missing lines in it.

(*To be continued.*)

The Buddha's Mission and last Journey: *Buddhacarita*, xv to xxviii.

Translated by

E. H. Johnston, Oxford.

(*Continuation.*)

CANTO XXIII

Fixing the Factors of Bodily Life.[1]

1. Then, understanding the Sage's intention, she did obeisance and returned to the town. The Licchavis, hearing the news, came to see the Buddha.

2. Some had white horses, chariots, umbrellas, garlands, ornaments and clothes; others again had them ruddy gold in hue.

3. Some had everything of beryl-yellow, and others of the colour of peacocks' tails. Thus gloriously apparelled, each to please himself, they came out.

4. With bodies vast as mountains and arms like golden yokes, they appeared like the glorious . . .[2] in bodily form in heaven.

5. As they stood, about to alight from their chariots, they shone like streaks of lightning across an evening cloud (*saṃdhyābhrapāda*).

6. Inclining their waving headdresses, they gravely saluted the Sage; though full of pride, yet they stood there as if become sober in their desire for the Law.

7. Their passion-free (*rajohīna*?)[3] circle shone beside the Buddha like the bow of Indra (?) opposite the cloudless sun.

---

[1] *Śarīrāyuḥsaṃskārādhiṣṭhāna.*

[2] *bod-riṅ,* I.O.; *boṅ-riṅ,* P. For *ḥod-riṅ*?

[3] This epithet should surely apply to the Buddha to make the comparison right.

8. Then Simha and the others seated themselves on lion-seats decorated with gold, having the form (*saṃsthāna*?) of lions on the ground, and the Man-lion said to them then:—

9. "This devotion of yours to the Law far exceeds in value your distinctions such as beauty of form, sovereignty and strength.

10. Neither your beauty, nor your magnificent clothes, nor your ornaments or garlands, have the same brilliance as the virtues of discipline and the like have.

11. I hold the Vṛjjis to be favoured and fortunate in that they have for lords you who are knowers of the Law and seekers of the Rule (*vinayaiṣin*).

12. O nobles (*ārya*), protectors who abide in the Law are hard to find in due course for countries not outside the pale (of Āryāvarta)[1] and are not to be found for the unfortunate.

13. This country is favoured even by the Law, in that it is guarded by majestic nobles (*mahābhāga*), who protect the knowledge of the Law.

14. Therefore, just as cattle who want to cross a stream follow the herd-bull, so people flock to the country which is held by kings.

15. This discipline should be ever present in you, so that your riches (*svārtha*?) in this world and the next cannot be snatched away by the passions.

16. Great is the reward of discipline,—a contented mind, honour, gain, renown, trust and delight, and in the hereafter bliss.

17. As the earth is the support of all beings, moving and stationary, so discipline is the best support of all the virtues.

18. Know the man who abandons discipline and yet desires final beatitude to be like one without wings who wishes to fly, or like one without a boat who wishes to cross a river.

19. The man who, having renown and beauty and wealth, resiles from the discipline, resembles a tree loaded with flowers and fruit, yet covered with thorns.

[1] The original probably had the equivalent of Āryāvarta, and T may have misunderstood part of the compound as a vocative.

not circumstance, but quality of mind

20. A man may live in a palace and wear gorgeous clothes and ornaments, but, if he have discipline, his way of life[1] is equal to that of a seer.

21. All are to be known as shams, who, though they wear dyed or bark garments and dress their hair in the various ascetic styles, have ruined their discipline.

22. Though he bathe three times a day at a sacred spot (*tīrtha*), though he pour oblations twice in the fire, though he be scorched with fiery heat, if he have not discipline, he is nothing.[2]

23. Though he deliver his body to beasts of prey, though he cast himself down a mountain, though he leap into fire or water, if he have not discipline, he is nothing.

24. Though he subsist on a modicum of fruit and roots, though he graze the grass like a deer, though he desire to live on air, if he have not discipline, he is not cleansed.

25. The man, whose discipline is vile, is like the birds and beasts; he is not a vessel of the Law, but like a leaky vessel of water.

26. In the present life he reaps fear, ill report, mistrust and discontent, and in the hereafter he will incur (lit., eat) calamity.

27. Therefore discipline, like the guide in the desert, should not be killed; discipline, which is self-dependent and hard to acquire, is the boat that conveys man to Heaven.

28. He whose mind is overcome by the sins loses everything in life. Taking your stand on discipline, destroy the sins and cherish faith.[3]

29. Therefore he who desires progress (*bubhūṣu?*) should first rid himself of the thought of self; for the thought of self obscures the virtues, as smoke obscures the fire.

30. The virtues, even when really existent, do not shine, if overcome by pride, like the stars, sun and moon when covered by a great mass of cloud.

---

[1] Possibly *gati*, and, if so, "future birth."

[2] Here and in 23 *bdaj* (*ātmā*) *ma-yin* (*nāsti*), but in 24 *dag mi-ḥgyur*, "he does not become pure."

[3] Better to amend *dad-pa* to *dam-pa*, "do what is good," having *puṇya*.

31. Arrogance (*auddhatya*?) destroys self-respect (*hrī*), grief steadfastness, and old age beauty,[1] and the thought of self destroys the roots[2] of the virtues.

32. Because of envy and pride the Asuras, being defeated by the gods, were cast down to Pātāla, and Tripura was destroyed.

33. That man is not held to be wise, who in ephemeral states of being deems himself to be the best and thinks that he is not vile.

34. What is it but lack of consideration, when a man is proud, thinking 'It is I,' while his very form is inconstant and he is transitory and by nature subject to destruction?

35. Passion (*kāmarāga*) is the violent covert connate adversary, which strikes under the guise of friendship, like an evil-doing enemy.

36. The fire of passion and an ordinary fire are alike in their nature of burning, but when the fire of passion is blazing, the night will indeed be long.

37. But a fire is said not to have the same force as the fire of passion; for a fire is quenched[3] by water, but the fire of passion not even by a whole lake.[4]

38. When the forest has been burnt by fire, in time the forest trees will grow again, but when fools are burnt by the fire of passion, there is no birth to the Law.

39. By reason of passion man seeks pleasure and for the sake of pleasure does evil; through doing evil he falls into Hell. There is no enemy equal to passion.

40. From passion arises desire, and from desire attachment to the lusts. From the lusts man comes to suffering. There is no adversary[5] equal to passion.

41. The fool takes no account of the great illness called passion, and . . .[6]

---

[1] Reading *brtan rga-bas* for *gtan dgaḥ-bas* with C.

[2] Read *rtsva-ba-rnams* for *rtsva-ba-nas*.

[3] Read *zhi-ste* for *śes-te*.

[4] *mtshos*. [5] Read *gyul* for *yul*.

[6] Two lines missing. C's version not quite clear.

42. Though a man may rid himself of passion by grasping its impermanence, its impurity, its nature as suffering and its absence of self, yet by reason of his perverted mind he becomes impassioned again.

43. Therefore he who can see a thing (*vastu*) as it really is (*yathābhūtam*), when attachment arises with regard to it, is said to be one who sees reality (*bhūtadarśin*).

44. Just as when one looks at the virtues (of an object), attachment arises, so, when one considers its demerits, anger is brought on.

45. Therefore he who wishes to suppress anger should not let himself be affected by aversion; for as smoke from fire, anger arises from aversion.[1]

46. Anger is as old age to the beautiful, as darkness to those who have eyes, the frustration of Law, Wealth and Pleasure, and the enemy of learning.

47. Anger is the chief darkness of the mind, the chief enemy of friendship, the destroyer of respect, the causer of degradation (*abhibhava*?).

48. Accordingly do not give way to anger, or if you do so, give it up. You should not follow after anger any more than you would after a snake whose nature it is to bite.

49. I deem him to be the true charioteer who steadfastly keeps anger in check with reins as though it were a chariot that had left the road; the other kind merely holds the reins.[2]

50. Whoever wishes to be angry[3] and does not wish to suppress its birth, afterwards when his anger passes away, he is burnt as if by touching fire.

---

[1] T has this the other way round, which seems nonsense; C is too free to help. C and T agree in reading "anger" in 44, where one would expect "aversion."

[2] *Dhammapada*, 222; *Udānavarga Sanskrit*, I, p. 258.

[3] One could understand "Whatever the angry man wishes," but the postcedent to the relative is *sa* in *c* and excludes this. Cp. *Udānavarga Sanskrit*, I, p. 253, where one should read *yas* for *yan* in *a* and *dahyate* or *tapyate* for *dahati* in *d*; the translation there is wrong.

51. When a man gives birth to anger, his own mind is burnt up first; afterwards, as the anger increases, others may be burnt by it or they may not.

52. What is the good of malevolence towards those of one's enemies who have bodies, seeing that the world (of embodied beings) is oppressed (already) by the calamities of disease, &c.?

53. Therefore knowing the world to be subject to suffering, you should cultivate benevolence and compassion for all beings in order to restrain anger."

54. Thus the Buddha, seeing them at that time to be full of sin, had compassion on them and reproved them with His sermon.

55. Just as, when people are ill, the doctor prescribes medicine for them according to their constitutions, in order to cure the disease,

56. So the Sage, knowing the dispositions of beings who are afflicted by the diseases[1] of passion, old age, &c., gave them the medicine of knowledge of the real truth.

57. The Licchavis were delighted with such a sermon from the Sage and did reverence to Him with their heads, so that their jewelled crests hung down.

58. Then joining the palms of their hands and slightly inclining their bodies, they requested the Buddha to visit them, just as the gods requested Bṛhaspati.

59. The Sage, informing them that Amrapālī's turn came first, explained that those of low degree[2] should not be deprived of their rights in favour of the nobles.

60. On learning that the woman had forestalled them, they did much reverence to the Tathāgata and returned to their natural frame of mind (i.e. wrathfulness).

61. But on the Omniscient's teaching them, they gained calmness of mind, just as the poison of snakes abates with the well-spoken spells of sages.

---

[1] Reading *nad* for *naṅ*.

[2] Read *sñan dman* for *sñan mnan*.

62. When the night had passed, Amrapālī entertained Him, and ⟨He went on⟩ to the village of Veṇumatī ⟨to pass the rainy season there⟩.[1]

63. After passing the rainy season there, the Great Sage returned to Vaiśālī and sat down on the bank of Markaṭa's pool.

64. He sat down by the root of a tree, and, as He shone there, Māra appeared in the grove and, approaching Him, said:—

65. "Formerly, O Sage, on the bank of the Nairañjanā when I said to You, 'You have fulfilled Your task, enter Nirvāṇa,' You made reply there:—

66. 'I shall not enter Nirvāṇa till I have given security to the afflicted and caused them to abandon the sins.[2]'

67. Now many have attained salvation, or similarly wish to do so or will do so. Therefore enter Nirvāṇa."

68. Then on hearing these words, the Best of Arhats said to him, "In three months' time I shall enter Nirvāṇa, be not then impatient."

69. Then knowing his desire to have been fulfilled by the promise, he disappeared from there, greatly exulting.

70. Then the Great Seer entered with such force of yoga into concentration of mind that He gave up the bodily life due to Him (*bhūtapūrva*?) and continued to live in an unprecedented way[3] by the might of His spiritual power.

71. At the moment that He abandoned His bodily life, the earth staggered like a drunken woman, and great firebrands fell from the quarters, like a line of stones from Meru, when it is coloured[4] with fire.

72. Similarly Indra's thunderbolts flashed unceasingly on all sides, full of fire (*agnigarbha*) and accompanied by lightning; and flames blazed everywhere, as if wishing to burn up the world at the end of the aeon.

---

[1] T omits the last line; gap supplied from C.

[2] Reading *dor-byas* for *don-byas*, as suggested by C.

[3] Or perhaps, "He Who had no equal."

[4] *tshos-pa*; perhaps for *tshig-pa*, "blazing."

73. The mountains lost their peaks and scattered abroad heaps of broken trees, while drums in the sky gave forth discordant (*viṣama*) sounds, like caverns filled with the wind.

74. Then at that moment of universal commotion in the world of men, in heaven and in the sky, the Great Sage emerged from His deep concentration and uttered these words:—

75. "My body with its age released is like a chariot whose axle has been broken, and I continue to carry it on by My own power. Together with My years I am released from the bond of existence, as a bird when hatching breaking the egg."

CANTO XXIV

Compassion for the Licchavis.

1. Thereon, when Ānanda saw the earthquake, his hair stood on end; and in his perturbation (*āgatāvega*) at what it could be, he trembled and was distressed.

2. He asked the Omniscient, the Knower of causers, what was the cause of it. The Sage then said to him with the voice of a maddened bull[1]:—

3. "The reason for this earthquake is that I have cut off My days on earth; My life is fixed (*adhiṣṭhā*) at three months from now."

4. Ānanda, hearing this, was deeply moved, and his tears flowed, as gum flows from a sandalwood-tree when a mighty elephant breaks it down.

5. He was grieved, because the Buddha was his kinsman and his Guru; and, mourning miserably, he lamented in his wretchedness:—

6. "On hearing my Master's decision, my body sinks as it were, I have lost my bearings,[2] and the teaching of the Law that I have heard is confused.

---

[1] *khyu mchog mos-pa*; perhaps for *khyu-byug mos-pa, mattakokila.*

[2] Doubtful; *bdag-gi phyogs-rnams spobs-pa-med*, possibly for *tshigs-rnams stobs-pa-med*, equivalent to "My joints are turned to water."

7. Alas! The Tathāgata, praised of men (*narāśaṃsa*), is speedily going to Nirvāṇa, like a fire quickly extinguished for men who are perished with cold and whose garments are worn out.[1]

8. The guide points out the path to embodied beings lost in the great forest of the sins and disappears all at once.

9. Men travel on a far road, overcome with thirst, and then the pool of cool water on their way suddenly dries up.

10. The Eye of the world, which is limpid and has dark-blue[2] eyelashes, which sees the past, the present and the future, and which is wide open with knowledge,[3] is about to close.

11. Verily, when the crop springs up and is withering for want of water, a cloud gives a shower and at once passes away (*majj*).

12. The lamp that shines on all sides for beings going astray on the road by reason of the darkness of ignorance, is very suddenly extinguished."

13. Then seeing Ānanda to be thus troubled in mind with grief, the Chief of comforters, the Best of those who know the truth, explained the truth to him:—

14. "Recognise, Ānanda, the real nature of the world and be not grieved. For this world is an aggregation, and therefore impermanent because its state is compound (*saṃskṛta*).

15. I have told you before that you should look on creatures who delight in the pairs (*dvandvārāma*) with compassion entirely devoid of affection.

16. Whatever is born is compound and ephemeral; being dependent on a support, it has no self-dependence.[4] It is impossible then for anyone to attain the state of permanence.

17. If beings on earth were permanent, the state of active being (*pravṛtti*) would not be subject to change; and what need then of salvation? For the end would be (the same as) the beginning.

---

[1] Last phrase doubtful.

[2] Following C, read *sño-nag* for the nonsensical *blo ni*.

[3] According to C, "which dispels the darkness by *prajñā*."

[4] So C suggests, but better perhaps "it is helplessly dependent on a support."

18. Or again what is the desire you and other beings have for Me? For you have done without Me that for which effort is made.[1]

19. I have steadfastly explained the path to you in its entirety; you, as disciples, should understand that the Buddhas withhold nothing.

20. Whether I remain or whether I pass to peace, there is only the one thing, namely that the Tathāgatas are the Body of the Law (*dharmakāya*); of what use is this mortal body to you?

21. Since at the time of My passing My lamp has been lit with full devotion (?)[2] through perturbation of mind (*saṃvega*) and heedfulness (*apramāda*), therefore the light of the Law goes on for ever.

22. You should know it as your lamp, devoting steadfast energy to it; and, freed from the pairs, recognise your goal (*svārtha*) and let not your mind be a prey to other things.

23. You should know that the lamp of the Law is the lamp of mystic wisdom (*prajñā*), with which the skilful and learned man dispels ignorance, as a lamp the darkness.

24. For obtaining the highest good, there are four spheres of action (*gocara*), to wit, the body, sensation, the mind, and absence of self.

25. There is no attachment to the body for him who sees the impurity in the body, enveloped as it is with bones, skin, blood, sinews, flesh, hair, &c.

26. The idea[3] of pleasure is overcome by him who sees that the sensations are but suffering, each arising from their respective causes.

27. For him who sees with tranquil mind the birth, duration and decay of the (mental) elements (*dharma*), the grasping of wrong views (*grāha*) is for ever rejected.

28. For him who sees that the components (*skandha*) arise from causes, the thought of self which gives rise to the belief in an ego ceases to be active.

---

[1] Doubtful; C simply "attained the aim."

[2] *dad-dam*, T. I am not sure of having hit the exact sense of the verse.

[3] T has *śes-rab, prajñā*, but C shows the correct reading to be *ḥdu-śes, saṃjñā*.

29. This is the only road to take to annihilate suffering; accordingly remain attentive on the Path with respect to these four.

30. Accordingly, when I pass to the Beyond, those who take their stand on this will obtain the excellent stage that does not pass away, the final beatitude."

31. Thus the Teacher preached to Ānanda; and the Licchavis, hearing the news, came there hurriedly out of devotion to Him.

32. Their minds were carried away by bitterness (*saṃtāpa*) by reason of their pity and of their devotion to the Seer, and at the news they speedily abandoned[1] alike the affairs on which they were engaged(?) and their usual pomp (*ṛddhi*).

33. Wishing to speak to the Master, they bowed and stood on one side, and the Master, the Sage, knowing their wish to speak, addressed them thus:—

34. "I know all that has come into your minds regarding Me; you, still the same, yet as if changed by grief, have now become self-confident(?).[2]

35. Still abiding in the company (*varga?*) of sovereignty, you now have entirely present in you both outward brilliance (*dīpti?*) and knowledge of the Law.

36. If indeed by hearing a little you have acquired knowledge from Me, calm yourselves and be not distressed at My passing.

37. Inasmuch as the states of being are impermanent and compounds, they are ephemeral, subject to change, without substance and not to be relied on; they do not remain stable in the least degree.

38. Vasiṣṭha, Atri and others, and whoever else was ascetic (*ūrdhvaretas*) came under the dominion of Time. Existence here is pernicious.

39. Māndhātṛ, the ruler of the earth, and Vasu, the peer of Vāsava, and Nābhāga, whose lot was noble (*mahābhāga*), became one with the elements.

---

[1] Reading *dor-rnams-so* for *don-rnams-so*, as suggested by C.

[2] *spobs-par-gyur*, *viśārada*?

40. Yayāti too, who walked in the path, Bhagīratha of the magnificent chariot, the Kurus who achieved blame and ill fame, Rāma, Girirajas(?),[1] Aja,

41. These majestic (*mahātman*) royal seers and many others like Great Indra went to destruction; for there is no one who is not subject to destruction.

42. The sun falls from his station, the gods of wealth came to earth, hundreds of Indras have passed away; for no one exists for ever.

43. All the other Saṃbuddhas, after illuminating the world, entered Nirvāṇa, like lamps whose oil is exhausted.

44. All the great-souled beings, who will become Tathāgatas in the future, will also enter Nirvāṇa like fires whose fuel has been consumed.

45. Therefore I too should go on, like an ascetic in the forest who seeks liberation; for there is no reason why I should drag out a useless corporeal existence (*nāmarūpa*).

46. Since it is My intention to depart from this pleasant (*ramaṇīya*) Vaiśālī, in which there are some to be converted, do ye never follow another faith (*anyamanas*?).

47. Therefore know the world to be without refuge, helpless and ephemeral; and walking in passionlessness obtain perturbation of mind (*saṃvega*).

48. Thus to put it briefly, in due course when the Tathāgata is no more seen, proceed in the direction of Kubera (i.e. the north), like the sun in the month of Jyeṣṭhā."

49. Thereon the Licchavis followed Him with eyes full of tears; and, with stout arms laden with ornaments, they joined the palms of their hands and lamented:—

50. "Alas! The Master's body, like refined gold and having the thirty-two marks, will break up. The Compassionate One is impermanent too.

---

[1] *ri-mo rdul*; name untraced, but no other reconstruction fits the metre.

51. The wretched calves, who have not yet attained reason, are thirsty[1] for lack of milk, and the milch-cow of knowledge, Alas!, too quickly deserts them.

52. The Sage is the sun whose light of knowledge has dispelled the darkness of delusion for men without a lamp,[2] and suddenly this sun will set.

53. While the stream of ignorance flows hither and thither in the world, the far-reaching embankment of the Law is breached too soon.

54. The great compassionate Physician has the medicine of excellent knowledge, yet, abandoning the world which is sick with mental diseases, He will depart.

55. The flag of Indra, garnished with the diamonds of the mind and decorated with the ornaments of mystic wisdom, will fall, while people still thirst for it[3] in the feast.

56. Seeing that[4] for the world, whose lot is suffering and which is bound with the fetters of the cycle of existence, this is the door of release, Death will close it fast."

57. Thus the Licchavis lamented, their eyes turbid with tears; and when they followed after Him, the Sage turned them back again.

58. Then knowing the Sage's decision[5] they became calm[6] and in the deepest grief determined to return.

59. As, fair as the golden mountain, they did obeisance to the Sage's feet, they resembled *karṇikāra* trees, when their flowers are being shaken by the wind.

60. With hearts attached to Him, their feet too lagged, and like waves moving against the stream, they turned back without moving onward.

---

[1] Read *sred* for *srid.*

[2] Read *sgron-ma* for *ḥgro-na.*

[3] This phrase not certain: "on which the world gazes without satiety," C

[4] T read *yadi*, which I take as mistaken for *yadā.*

[5] Uncertain; *thub-pas bcad* (*chid*) *śes-nas*, T.

[6] Reading *brtan-pa* for *bstan-pa*, as indicated by C.

*61. Without joy in that for which they had had reverence, and without reverence for that in which they had rejoiced, their joy in, and reverence for, the Sage were immovable.

*62. Like mighty bulls, when the herd-bull has gone away from the forest, they kept on stopping and gazing repeatedly at the Holder of the Ten Forces.

63. Then with their minds dwelling on the Tathāgata and with their bodies too bereft of brilliance, they went on foot in grief, as if proceeding to the final bath of a funeral ceremony (*apasnāta*).[1]

*64. The Licchavis returned to their palaces with their faces working with grief, though they had overcome their foes with bows whose arrows never missed the mark, though they were proud and strong and . . .,[2] and though they sought sovereignty in the world and had great command over the means of pleasure.

CANTO XXV

The Journey to Nirvāṇa.

1. When the Sage departed for His Nirvāṇa, Vaiśālī, like the sky overspread with darkness on the eclipse of the sun, no longer appeared brilliant.

2. Though beautiful and free from pride, though delightful (*ramaṇīya*) in all parts, it did not shine because of its burning sorrow (*saṃtāpa*), like a woman whose husband has died,

3. Like beauty without learning, like knowledge without virtue, like intelligence without power of expression, like power of expression without education (*saṃskāra*),

4. Like sovereignty (*śrī*) without good conduct, like affection without faith, like good fortune (*lakṣmī?*) without energy, like action without religion (*dharma*).

---

[1] T is corrupt apparently, but the sense given is correct; for *mya-ṅan ḥdas* we should probably read *mya-ṅan ḥoṅs*, and for *rjes-su ḥoṅs*, "followed," a verb meaning "returned," "went away."

[2] *Ḥgugs-ldan*, lit. "having *vikarṣa*," but perhaps a mistake for *gzugs-ldan*, "beautiful."

5. At that time . . .,[1] it was not brilliant because of its grief, like the earth with its dried up rice-crop, when the rain fails in the autumn.

6. There from grief no one cooked or ate his food; they all wept, as they recounted the fame of the famous Sage.

7. With others neither saying, nor doing, nor thinking anything at all, the city was given up to one single business, mourning and weeping.

8. Then the Senāpati Siṃha, distressed with grief for all his firmness and thinking on the Chief . . .,[2] uttered these laments:—

9. "He overcame the heretical systems and taught the good path, Himself proceeding on such a path. Now He has gone never to return.

10. The Lord (*nātha*) is abandoning the world which is destroyed by afflictions and is without brilliance, and is turning the people into orphans; so He goes to obtain peace (*śama*).

11. As the strength of the body (*ojas?*) with the lapse of time, so my steadfastness is destroyed, now that the excellent Guru, the Master of Yoga, is on His way to the final peace.

12. As king Nahuṣa[3] lost[4] his magic powers and fell from heaven, so the earth without Him is an object of pity, and I know not what is to be done.

13. To whom now shall people resort for the solution of their doubts, as one resorts to water when distressed by heat, or to a fire, if afflicted with cold?

14. When the Sage, the spiritual Director of the world (*lokācārya*), He Who is the Bellows of the final good, like bellows for blowing up a fire, is lost, the Law will be lost too.

---

[1] Third line missing in T. Note for the simile that the success of the rice-crop is largely dependent on a good rain early in October.

[2] *dgaḥ-ḥdun* (*saṃstava* in Bacot, *op. cit.*), perhaps for *dge-ḥdun*, "Saṅgha"; but C has "relative," suggesting *gñen-ḥdun.*

[3] *sgra-ṅan*, properly Kuru, which does not seem to apply; Nahuṣa is *sgra-med*.

[4] T has *ldan*, "possessing," but C shows *bral* to be the correct reading.

15. Who is there like Him to break the mighty revolving wheel of suffering for beings, who are subject by nature to disease and death and are fettered by lack of discipline or wrong discipline?

16. Who else is able by his word to animate men in whom passion is born with mirth, like a cloud at the end of spring animating the dried up *sinduvāra* plants?

17. When the Omniscient Guru, solid as Meru, shall pass away, who in the world will have the wisdom that will make him an object of trust?

18. The world of the living, being deluded,[1] is born but to die, as the condemned criminal is made intoxicated[2] and then led out to execution.

19. As a tree is cloven by a sharp saw, so this world is cloven by the saw of destruction.

*20. Though the excellent spiritual Director of the world has the strength of knowledge and has entirely burnt up the sins, yet He is going to destruction.

21. He Who with the mighty boat of knowledge rescues men from the ocean of existence, whose billows are desires and whose water ignorance,[3] and in which are the creatures of false views and the fish of passion (*rajas*);

22. He Who cuts down with the great weapon of knowledge the tree of existence, whose boughs are old age and whose flowers disease, whose root is death and whose shoots rebirths (*bhava*);

23. The cool water of Whose knowledge puts out the fire of the faults, which is produced from the rubbing-sticks of ignorance with the flames of passion and the fuel of the objects of sense;

24. He Who has taken the path of quietude, Who has abandoned the great darkness (of ignorance), Who, knowing the supreme knowledge of the final beatitude, has lovingly taught it;

---

[1] T has *sdug*, an ambiguous word in itself and often confused with *stug*, but C shows the original to have had *mūḍha* or the like.

[2] Read *chaṅ* for *skyaṅ*, as shown by C.

[3] Reading with C *mun-pa* and *sred-pa* for *ṅan-pa* and *srid-pa*.

25. The Omniscient, Who has gone too to the end of all the sins and looks benignly on all, Who works everyone benefit, He is going away to abandon everything.

26. If the Great Sage, Whose voice is soft and clear[1] and Whose arms long, comes to an end, who will be able to avoid coming to an end?

27. Therefore the wise man should quickly resort to the Law, as a caravan-merchant, who is lost in the wilderness, on seeing water, quickly resorts to it.

28. He who is not asleep to the Law, knowing impermanency to be an evil which makes no distinctions for the purpose of destruction, is not asleep, even though lying down."

29. Then Siṃha, the man-lion, the eater(?) of knowledge, denounced the evils of birth and praised the destruction of existence.

30. Desiring to give up the root of existence, to undertake good vows, and to control his restless mind, he desired to abide in the path of beatitude.

31. Desiring to walk in the path of quietude, to escape from the ocean of existence, and to be ever charitable, he desired to cut off rebirth.

32. At the time when the Sage wished to enter Nirvāṇa, he gave in charity and abandoned pride, he meditated on the Law and reached quietude, and thus he treated the earth as an empty stage.[2]

33. Then the Sage, turning round with His entire body like a king of elephants and looking at the city, uttered these words:—

34. "O Vaiśālī, I shall not see you again in the period of life that still remains to Me; for I am going to Nirvāṇa."

*35. Then seeing that they were following Him full of faith and desiring the Law, the Sage dismissed them, whose minds still tended to the continuance of activity.[3]

---

[1] So C, probably *viśada*; *rnam-yaṅs* (*viśāla)*, P, *rnam-mdas* (or *mṅas*, for *mṅar*), I. O.

[2] The last sentence is uncertain.

[3] This verse is clearly an interpolation.

36. Then in due course the Teacher proceeded to Bhoganagara, and, staying there, the Omniscient said to His followers:—

37. "After I have passed away to-day, you must fix your best attention on the Law. It is your highest goal; anything else is but toil.

38. Whatever is not entered in the Sūtras or does not appear in the Vinaya is contrary to My principles (*nyāya*?) and should not be accepted by any means.

39. For that is not the Law nor the Vinaya nor My words; though many people say it, it is to be rejected as the saying of darkness.

40. The preaching of the pure is to be accepted, for that is the Law, the Vinaya, My words; and not to abide in it is backsliding.

41. Therefore what is to be believed is stated succinctly in My Sūtras. Who does (i.e. follows?) them is to be trusted, and apart from this there is no authority.

42. Out of delusion there will arise doctrines of the Law, laying down what is not the Law, through uncertainty and ignorance about these subtle views of Mine,

43. Either by views associated with darkness, or from ignorance of the distinctions, just as men are cheated by brass which looks like gold.[1]

44. Accordingly that which is not the Law, but merely a counterfeit of the Law, is a deception, arising from lack of mystic wisdom or from failure to grasp the real truth.

45. Therefore you should test it in the proper form (*nyāyataḥ*) by means of the Vinaya and Sūtras, just as a goldsmith tests gold by filing, cutting and heating it.

46. Those are not wise men who do not know the doctrines (*śāstra*); they determine that as the course to be followed (*nyāya*) which is not the right course and see in the right course the wrong one.

47. Therefore it is to be accepted with the right hearing according to the meaning and the word; for he who grasps the doctrine wrongly hurts himself, as one who grasps a sword wrongly (by the blade) cuts himself.

---

[1] Still a common form of fraud in India.

48. He who construes the words wrongly finds the meaning with difficulty, as a man at night finds a house with difficulty, if he has not been there before and the way is winding.[1]

49. When the meaning is lost, the Law is lost, and when the Law is lost, capacity is lost; therefore he is intelligent whose mind abides unperverted in the meaning."

50. After the Gracious One had uttered these words, He went on in due time to the town of Pāpā, where the Mallas did him all honour.

51. Then the Holy One took His last meal in the house of the excellent Cunda, who was devoted to Him, doing so for his (Cunda's) sake, not for His own support.

52. Then, after the Tathāgata with His company of disciples had eaten, He preached the Law to Cunda and went to Kuśinagara.

53. Thus accompanied by Cunda He crossed the river Irāvatī(?)[2] and betook Himself to a grove of that city, which had a peaceful lotus-pool.

54. He Who shone like gold bathed in the Hiraṇyavatī, and then He thus ordered the mourning Ānanda, the joy of the world (*lokanandana*?):—

55. "Ānanda, prepare a place for Me to lie on between the twin *śāla* trees;[3] this day in the latter part of the night the Tathāgata will enter Nirvāṇa."

56. When Ānanda heard these words, a film of tears spread over his eyes; he prepared a place for the Buddha to lie on, and having done so, informed Him of it, lamenting.

57. Then the Best of the two-footed approached His final couch, in order never to wake again and to put an end to all suffering.

---

[1] Last four words doubtful; *ḥkhyogs maṅ-po*, may refer to the ruinous state of the house.

[2] *nor-ldan*, T, alternative forms of the name being Acirāvatī, Ajirāvatī, and Airāvatī. C has "Kuku," evidently the Pali Kakutthā.

[3] T seems to understand "twin wall," *gśiṅ-rjeḥi ra-ba*, taking the other meaning of *śāla*; C has "these two trees."

58. In the presence of His disciples He lay down on His right side, pillowing His head on His hand and crossing His legs.

59. Then at that moment there the birds uttered no cries and sat with bodies all relaxed, as if fixed in trance.

60. Then the trees, with their restless leaves unstirred by breezes, shed discoloured flowers, as if weeping.

61. Like travellers coming in sight of their resting-place, when the maker of day stands on the Sunset mountain, so, gazing at the Sage on His couch, they quickly came in sight of the good goal.

62. Then the Omniscient, lying on His last resting-place, said in His compassion to the tear-stained Ānanda:—

63. "Tell the Mallas, Ānanda, of the time of My entering Nirvāṇa; for if they do not witness the Nirvāṇa, afterwards they will deeply regret it."

64. Then Ānanda, swooning with tears, obeyed the order, and told the Mallas that the Sage was lying on His final bed.

65. Then at that time on hearing Ānanda's words, overcome by distress, they issued forth from the town, like bulls from a mountain in fear of a lion, mourning and raining down tears from their eyes.

66. In their lack of joy[1] their clothes were disordered and tumbled, and their headdresses shook with the agitation of their steps. Then they came to that grove, a prey to affliction like the dwellers in heaven when their merit is exhausted.

67. Coming there thus they saw the Sage, and on seeing Him, their faces were covered with tears, as they did obeisance; having paid their reverence, they stood there, their hearts burning within them. As they stood there, the Sage spoke to them:—

68. "It is not proper to grieve in the hour of joy. Despair is out of place, resume your composure. That remote (*atidurlabha*) goal, for which I have longed for many aeons, is now come near to Me.

69. That goal is most excellent, without the elements of earth, water, fire, wind and space, blissful and immutable, beyond the objects

[1] *zhen-pa med-pas*, meaning uncertain; possibly equivalent to *nirāsthatā*.

of sense,[1] peaceful, inviolable (*ahārya*), and in which there is neither birth nor passing away. On hearing of it, there is no room for grief.

70. Formerly at the time of Illumination in Gaya I put away from Me the causes of evil existence as if they were snakes; but this body, this dwelling house of the acts accumulated in the past, has survived till to-day.[2]

71. Is it proper to sorrow for Me that you weep, when this aggregate, the great storehouse of suffering, is passing away, when the great danger of existence is being extirpated and I am departing from the great suffering?"

72. When they heard the Sage of the Śākyas announce with a voice like a cloud that the time had come for Him to enter on peace,[3] their mouths opened with the desire to speak, and the oldest of them uttered these words:—

73. "Is sorrow fitting that you all weep? The Sage is like a man who has escaped from a house blazing with fire, and when even the chief of the gods should so look on it, how much more should men do so?

74. But this causes us grief that the Lord, the Tathāgata, on entering Nirvāṇa, will be no more seen; when in the desert the good guide dies, who will not be sorely afflicted?

75. Surely men become objects of derision, like those who come away poor from a goldmine, if, having seen the Guru, the Omniscient Great Seer, in person, they do not win to the higher path (*viśeṣa*)."

76. Thus the Mallas spoke much that was to the point, folding their hands in devotion like sons, and the Best of the high-souled replied to them with words of excellent meaning directed to the highest good and to tranquillity:—

---

[1] Two syllables missing in *b*.

[2] So C; but T may have had *adyopagamiṣyati*, which hardly fits the context.

[3] So C; T could mean, "When they heard the Sage speak with a voice like a cloud, though it was a time of calm (*praśānti*)," the last words applying to a raincloud in fine weather and to the Buddha's passing away.

77. "So indeed is it the case that salvation does not come from the mere sight of Me without strenuous practice in the methods of yoga; he who thoroughly considers this My Law is released from the net of suffering, even without the sight of Me.

78. Just as a man does not overcome disease by the mere sight of the physician without resort to medicine, so he who does not study (*bhāvaya*) this My knowledge does not overcome suffering by the mere sight of Me.

79. In this world the self-controlled man who sees my Law may live far away in point of space, yet he sees Me; while he who is not active in concentration (*parāyaṇa*) on the highest good may dwell at My side and yet be far distant.

80. Therefore be ever energetic and control your minds; with diligence practise the deeds that lead to good. For life is like the flame of a lamp in the wind,[1] flickering and subject to much suffering."

81. Thus they were instructed by the Seer, the Best of beings, and with harassed minds and tears pouring down from their eyes, they returned to Kuśinagara reluctantly and helplessly, as if crossing the middle of a river against the stream.

---

[1] So C, *pravāte*; *prabhāte*, T.

(*To be continued.*)

The Buddha's Mission and last Journey: *Buddhacarita*, xv to xxviii.

Translated by

E. H. Johnston, Oxford.

(*Concluded.*)

CANTO XXVI

The Mahāparinirvāṇa.

1. Then Subhadra, a holder of the triple staff, who was properly endowed with good virtue and did no hurt[1] to any being, desired to see the Blessed One in order to obtain salvation as a mendicant. So he said to Ānanda, the causer of universal delight:—

2. "I have heard that the Sage's hour for entering Nirvāṇa has come, and therefore I desire to see Him; for it is as hard in this world to see One Who has penetrated to the highest Law as it is to see the moon on the day it is new.

3. I desire to see your Teacher, Who is about to proceed to the end of all suffering; let Him not pass away without my seeing Him, like the sun setting in a sky veiled by clouds."

4. Then Ānanda's mind was filled with emotion,[2] for he thought the wandering ascetic (*parivrājaka*) had come in order to dispute under the pretext of a desire for the Law; and with face covered with tears, he said, "It is not the time."

5. Then He, Who shone like the moon, knowing the dispositions of men, recognized that the ascetic's eye was opening like a petal,

---

[1] Reading *mi-ḥtshe-ba* for *mi-ḥtshod-pa*; "protecting all beings," C.

[2] *la-ba*, possibly for *laṅ-ba*, which might stand for *paryavasthāna* (something like "anger" here).

and He said, " Do not hinder the twice-born, Ānanda, since I was born for the good of the world."

6. Thereat Subhadra, comforted and highly delighted, approached the Śrīghana, the Doer of the highest good; then, as befitted the occasion, in a quiet way he greeted Him and spoke these words:—

7. " It is said that You have gained a path of Salvation[1] other than that of philosophers (*parīkṣaka*) like myself; therefore explain it to me, for I wish to accept it. My desire to see You arises from affection, not from desire for disputation."

8. Then the Buddha explained the Eightfold Path to the twice-born, who had come to Him; and he listened to it, like a man who has lost his way listens to the correct directions, and he . . .[2] fully considered it.

9. Then he perceived that the final good was not obtained on the other paths he had previously followed, and winning to a path he had not seen before, he put away those other paths which are accompanied by darkness in the heart.

10. For in those paths, it is said, by obtaining darkness (*tamas*) accompanied by passion (*rajas*) evil (*akuśala*) deeds are heaped up, while by passion associated with goodness (*sattva*) good (*kuśala*) deeds are extended.[3]

11. With goodness increasing through learning, intelligence and effort, and by reason of the effect of the act being destroyed through the disappearance of darkness and passion, the effect of the act becomes exhausted; and that power of the act they postulate is said to be the product of nature.[4]

---

[1] Two syllables missing in *b*.

[2] Four syllables missing in *d*.

[3] This passage deals with that form of pre-classical Sāṃkhya, one of the earliest, in which salvation comes by the extension of *sattva* and the extirpation of *rajas* and *tamas*.

[4] A free translation. For the last words I. O. has *ḥbad-pa-min*, and I understand *ayatnatas tat kila karma teṣām*, where *ayatnatas* is equivalent to *svabhāvatas*. P reads *ḥthad-pa-min*, perhaps *tat karma teṣāṃ kila nopapannam*. C is either very free or had a different text.

12. For in the world they attribute darkness and passion, which delude the mind, to Nature.[1] Since Nature is acknowledged to be permanent, those two equally do not cease to exist, being necessarily also permanent.

13. Even if by uniting oneself with goodness those two cease to exist,[2] they will come into being again under the compulsion of time, just as water, which gradually becomes ice at night, returns to its natural state in the course of time.

14. Since goodness is permanent by nature, therefore learning, wisdom and effort have no power to increase it; and since it does not increase, the other two are not destroyed, and since they are not destroyed, there is no final peace.

15. Previously he had held birth to be by Nature, now he saw that there was no salvation in that doctrine; for since one exists by Nature, how can there be final release any more than a blazing fire can be stopped from giving out light?

16. Seeing the Buddha's path to be the real truth, he held the world to depend on desire;[3] if that is destroyed, there is religious peace (*śama*), for with the destruction of the cause the result also is destroyed.

17. Previously he had held with respect to that which is manifested (*vyakta*)[4] that the "self" is other than the body and is not subject to change; now that he had listened to the Sage's words he knew the world to be without "self" and not to be the effect of "self."

18. Realising that birth depends on the interrelation of many elements (*dharma*) and that nothing is self-dependent,[5] he saw that the continuance of active being (*pravṛtti*) is suffering and that the cessation thereof (*nivṛtti*) is freedom from suffering.[6]

---

[1] *svabhāva*, as in xviii the principle underlying the eightfold *prakṛti*.

[2] Reading *med-par* for the nonsensical *de-bar*, as indicated by C.

[3] Reading *sred-pa-las* for *srid-pa-las*, as indicated by C.

[4] The construction and place in the sentence of this phrase about the *vyakta* is not clear.

[5] Two syllables missing in T.

[6] So C understands it; T is corrupt and should presumably read *sdug-bsṅal med-du* for *sdug-bsṅal ñid-du*.

19. Since he considered that the world is a product, he gave up the doctrine of annihilation, and since he knew that the world passes away, he speedily gave up without shrinking (*dhīra*) the view of its permanence.

20. Hearing and accepting the Great Seer's teaching, he thus gave up on the spot his former views; for he had formerly prepared himself (*parikarma kṛ*), so that he quickly adhered to the good Law.

21. His mind was filled with faith and, obtaining the best, he reached the peaceful immutable stage; and therefore, as he gazed gratefully on the Sage lying there, he formed this resolution.

22. "It is not proper for me to stay and see the venerable excellent Lord enter Nirvāṇa; I shall myself go straight to the final end, before the compassionate Master passes to Nirvāṇa."

23. Then he did obeisance to the Sage, and assuming a moveless posture snakewise, he passed in a moment into the peace of Nirvāṇa, like a cloud dissipated by the wind.[1]

24. Thereon the Sage, the Knower of rites, gave orders for the rite of his cremation, saying, "He has gone to the end, the last disciple of the Great Seer Who has noble disciples."[2]

25. Then when the first part of the night had passed away,[3] and the moon had eclipsed the light of the stars, and the groves were without a sound as if asleep, He Whose compassion was great instructed His disciples:—

26. "When I have gone to the Beyond, you should treat the Prātimokṣa as your spiritual director (*ācārya*), as your lamp, as your treasure. That is your teacher, under whose dominion you should be, and you should repeat it just as you did in My lifetime.

27. In order to purify your bodily and vocal actions give up all worldly concerns (*vyavahāra*), and, as from grasping a fire, refrain from accepting lands, living beings, grain, treasure and the rest.

---

[1] Two syllables missing in *c*; "like rain putting out a little fire," C.

[2] Two syllables each missing in *b* and *c*.

[3] Two syllables missing in *a*.

28. The proper means of livelihood is to abstain from the cutting and felling of what grows on the earth, from digging and ploughing the surface of the ground, and from medicine and astrology.

29. There is neither moderation nor contentment nor life in resorting to the knowledge of go-betweens, in the practice of charms and philtres, in not being open and candid, or in the attainments not forbidden by the Law.[1]

30. In this way the Prātimokṣa is the summary of the discipline (*śīla*), the root of liberation;[2] from it arise the concentrated meditations, all forms of knowledge and the final goals.

31. For this reason he has the Law, in whom is found pure inviolable discipline, neither rent nor destroyed; and without it all these (advantages) are absent, for discipline is the support of good qualities.

32. When discipline abides undestroyed and purified, there is no activity in the spheres of the senses; for, just as cattle are kept from the crops by a stick, so the six senses should be guarded (*saṃvṛta*) with firmness.

33. But the other man who lets the horses of his senses loose among the objects of sense is carried away and obtains no satisfaction (?)[3] from them. Like one carried out of the road (*kumārga*) by runaway horses, he incurs disaster for their sake.

34. Some men in this world suffer bitterly by falling into the hands of great enemies, but those, who from delusion fall into the power of the objects of sense, become subject to suffering, whether they will or no (*avaśa*), in their future lives as well as in this.

35. Therefore recourse should no more be had to the senses than to evil (*viṣama*) enemy kings; for after taking one's pleasure of the senses in this world, one sees in the world the executioner of the senses.

---

[1] C does not explain the exact scope of the last phrase, which perhaps covers the improper use of magic powers &c.

[2] Two syllables missing in *b*.

[3] Conjectural; T has *de-tsam-ñid*, *etāvad eva* or *iyattā*, which must be corrupt, perhaps for *re-tsam ñid*. C omits the phrase.

36. One should not fear tigers or snakes or blazing fires or enemies in the world so much as one's own restless mind, which sees the honey but overlooks the danger (*śaṅkā*).[1]

37. The mind wanders in all directions as it wills, like a mad elephant unrestrained by the iron ankus or like a monkey (*śākhāmṛga*) gambolling in the trees; no occasion should be given to it for restlessness.

38. When the mind is a law unto itself, there is no quietude, but when it comes to a stand, the task is done. Therefore strive with all your might that these minds of yours may desist from restlessness.

39. Observe exact measure in eating, as you would for doses of physic, and do not feel repulsion or desire towards it, only taking so much as is necessary for satisfying hunger and for maintaining the body.

40. As in the garden the bees do not destroy the flowers in sipping their juice, so you should practise alms-begging at the proper time without ruining other believers.

41. The rule that a load must always be put on correctly applies equally to an ox and to an alms-giver. The load falls off from being wrongly attached in this world, and the giver is in the same case as the ox.[2]

42. Pass the entire day and also the first and last watches of the night in the practice of yoga, and lie down in the middle watch, full of awareness so that the time of sleep does not bring on calamity.

43. For when the world here is being burnt up by the fire of Time, is it proper to sleep for the whole night? When the sins, which strike down like enemies, abide in the heart, who would go to sleep?

44. Therefore you should sleep, after exorcizing with knowledge and the repetition of sacred texts the snakes of the sins which reside

---

[1] So C; T is corrupt and I read *yaṅ-ba* (*Gaṇḍīstotra*, 20) for *yaṅ-dag*, the reference being to the precipice (*S.*, xi. 29).

[2] So apparently T, but one would expect, as C suggests, the simile of an ox falling under too heavy a load.

in the heart, as one does black snakes in a house by magic and charms; besides it is a question of self-respect (*hrī*).

45. Self-respect is an ornament and the best clothing, the ankus for those who have strayed from the path. Such being the case, you should act with self-respect; for to be devoid of self-respect is to be devoid of the virtues.

46. A man is ⟨honoured⟩[1] to the extent to which he has self-respect, and he, who is lacking in self-respect and who is devoid of discrimination between what is and what is not his real good, is on a level with the brute beasts.

47. Even should anyone cut off your arms and limbs with a sword, you should not cherish sinful thoughts about him or speak unforgiving (*aśānta*?) words; for such action is an obstruction to you alone.

48. There are no austerities equal to forbearance, and he who has forbearance has strength and fortitude, whereas those who cannot tolerate harsh treatment from others do not follow the way of those who lay down the Law, nor are they saved.

49. Do not allow the slightest opening to anger, which ruins the Law and destroys fame, and which is the enemy of beauty and a fire to the heart; there is no enemy to the virtues like unto it.

50. While anger is contrary to the profession of religion (*pravrajyā*), like the fire of lightning to cold water, it is not contrary to the life of the householder; for the latter are full of passion and have taken no vows about it.

51. If pride arises in your heart, it must be controverted by touching your head shorn of its beautiful locks, by looking on your dyed clothes and your begging bowl, and by reflecting on the conduct and occupations (*karmānta*) of others.

52. If worldly men who are proud[2] ⟨strive⟩ to overcome pride, how much more should those do so, whose heads are shaven, who

---

[1] Two syllables missing in *b*; meaning supplied from C.

[2] Two syllables each missing in *a* and *b*.

have directed themselves to salvation, and who eat the bread of mendicancy and have proved themselves.

53. Since deceitfulness and the practice of the Law are incompatible, do not resort to crooked ways. Deceitfulness and false pretences (*māyā*) are for the sake of cheating, but for those who are given to the Law there is no such thing as cheating.

54. The suffering which comes to him whose desires are great does not come to him whose desires are small.[1] Therefore smallness of desire (*alpecchatā*) should be practised, and especially so by those who seek for the perfection of the virtues.

55. He who does not fear the rich at all is not afraid of the sight of stingy people;[2] for he obtains salvation, whose desires are small[3] and who is not cast down on hearing that there is nothing for him.

56. If you desire salvation, practise contentment; with contentment there is bliss here and it is the Law. The contented sleep peacefully even on the ground, the discontented are burnt up even in Paradise.

57. The discontented man, however rich, is always poor, and the contented man, however poor, is always rich. The discontented man, seeking the beloved objects of sense, creates suffering for himself by toiling to obtain satiety.

58. Those who desire to obtain the highest bliss of peace should not give themselves up to the pleasures in such degree. For even Indra and the other gods envy the man in the world who is solely devoted to tranquillity.

59. Attachment is the roosting-tree (*vāsavṛkṣa*) of suffering; therefore give up attachment, whether to relations or to strangers. He who has many attachments in the world is stuck fast in suffering, like a decrepit elephant in the mud.

---

[1] The exact construction of T is uncertain, but the general sense is guaranteed by C.

[2] Uncertain; there may be a corruption in T, and C treats the hemistich as referring to the giver.

[3] One syllable missing in *d* (add *ñid* after *ḥdod*), and read *yin* for *min* at the end.

60. A stream, whose waters ever flow, however softly, in time wears away the surface of the rock. Energy finds nothing impossible of attainment. Therefore be strenuous and do not put down your loads.

61. The man who stops repeatedly in drilling with fire-sticks finds it hard to get fire from wood, but by the application of energy it comes easily. Therefore where there is diligence, the task is accomplished.

62. When awareness (*smṛti*) is present, the faults do not enter into activity; there is no friend or protector equal to awareness, and if awareness is lost, all certainly is lost. Therefore do not lose hold of awareness directed towards the body.

63. The firm in mind, putting on the armour of awareness towards the body, conduct themselves in the battlefield of the objects of sense like heroes, who gird on their armour and plunge fearlessly into the ranks of their foes.

64. Therefore, keeping your feelings level and restraining your minds, know the origin and passing away of the world and practise concentration. For no mental ills touch him who has obtained concentration of mind.

65. Just as men diligently make embankments[1] for holding up water that is overflowing, so concentration is declared to be like the embankment for bringing the water of knowledge to a stand.[2]

66. The wise man (*prājña*), who abides giving away his possessions and entirely devoted to this Law in his heart, is saved; how much more then should the mendicant, who has no home, be saved?

67. Mystic wisdom is the boat on the great ocean of old age and death, a lamp, as it were, in the darkness of delusion, the medicine that smites all illnesses, the sharp axe that cuts down the trees of the sins.

68. Therefore practise learning, knowledge and meditation (*bhāvanā*) for the increase of mystic wisdom; for he who has the

---

[1] Lit., "ditches and trenches."

[2] Should not "knowledge" be "thoughts"? C apparently had this verse after 67, substituting *prajñā* for *samādhi*.

eye that is of the nature of mystic wisdom, though without ocular vision, has indeed sight.

69. Although a man has left his home, yet, if he is engaged in the varied activities[1] of the mind, he is not saved; those who desire to obtain the supreme tranquillity should know this and become free from all activities.

70. Therefore adhere to heedfulness (*apramāda*) as to a guru, and avoid heedlessness as an enemy. By heedfulness Indra obtained sovereignty, by heedlessness the arrogant Asuras came to destruction.

71. I have done all that should be done by a compassionate sympathetic Master, Who aims at others' good; do you apply yourselves (*praṇidhā?*) and bring your minds to tranquillity.

72. Then, wherever you may be, on the mountains or in empty dwellings or in the forest, ever be strenuous in religious practice (*prayoga*) and do not give way to remorse (*paścātparitāpa*).

73. It is for the physician, after full consideration of their constitutions, to explain the proper medicines to his patients, but it is the sick man, not the physician, who is responsible for attending to their administration at the proper time.

74. When the guide has pointed out the magnificent straight level road which is free from danger, and those who hear him do not proceed along it but go to destruction, there is no debt in the way of instruction still due from the guide.

75. Whoever of you has any desire about My teaching of the Four Truths, suffering and the rest, let him confidently speak out to Me at once and cut off doubt (*ativimarśa?*)."

76. When the Great Seer thus spoke aloud, they were free from doubt and said nothing. The saintly (*kṛtin*) Aniruddha, penetrating their minds with his mind, then uttered these words:—

77. " Though the wind cease from movement, the sun become cold and the moon hot, yet it is not possible to prove the four steps (of the Truths) to be false in the world.

---

[1] *spros-pa.*

78. What is declared to be suffering is not pleasure; there is no other producer of suffering than that which is its cause; liberation inevitably comes from suppression of the cause, and the path thereto is certainly the means.

79. Therefore, O Great-souled One, the disciples have no doubt about the Four Truths; but those who have not accomplished their object suffer, thinking that the Teacher is about to pass away.

80. Even he in this assembly, who from the newness of his vows had not yet seen the goal, sees it to-day in its entirety, as by a flash of lightning, through this Your sermon.

81. But even those, for whom there is nothing remaining to be done and who have crossed to the further shore of the ocean of existence, are anxious in heart on hearing that the perfect (*svalaṃkṛta*?) Lord is about to pass away."

82. At these words of the noble (*ārya*) Aniruddha, the Buddha, though He knew the matter, again took cognizance of it and addressed them affectionately, in order to strengthen the minds of the faithful:—

83. "Since a being may last for an aeon and yet must come to destruction, there is certainly no such thing as mutual union. Having completed the task both for Myself and for others, there is no gain in My further existence.

84. All those in the heavens and on earth, who were to be converted by Me, have been saved and set in the stream. Hereafter this My Law shall abide among men through the successive generations of mendicants.[1]

85. Therefore recognize the true being of the world and be not anxious; for separation must be. Knowing the world to be of this nature,[2] so strive that it may be thus no more.

86. When the darkness has been illuminated with the lamp of knowledge and the spheres of existence have been seen to be without

---

[1] Or "mendicants" may be in the vocative.

[2] Two syllables missing in c; add *rnam-par* before *śes-nas*.

substance, contentment ensues at the suppression of the life-force (*āyuḥ*), as at the cure of an illness.[1]

87. Who is not pleased at the cessation of life, as at the destruction of calamity-causing enemies, when the stream of the ocean of existence called the body, which is to be abandoned with the opposites (*dvandva*), is cut off?

88. Everything, whether moving or stationary, passes away; therefore take ye good heed. The time for My entering Nirvāṇa has arrived. Do not lament; these are My last words."

89. Then the Best of those who know the trances entered the first trance at that moment, and emerging therefrom went on to the second, and so in due order He entered all of them without omitting any (*avikala*?).

90. Thereon having passed through all the trances, the group of nine attainments (*samāpatti*), in the upward order, the Great Seer following the reverse order returned to the first trance again.

91. Emerging therefrom also, He rose in due order again to the fourth trance, and emerging from the practice of the fourth trance, He passed to realization of the eternal peace.

92. Thereon, as the Sage entered Nirvāṇa, the earth quivered like a ship struck by a squall,[2] and firebrands also fell from the sky, as if cast(?)[3] by the elephants of the quarters.

93. A fire, without fuel or smoke and unfanned by the wind, arose burning the quarters, like a forest fire arising in the sky to burn the heavenly garden of Citraratha.

94. Fearsome thunderbolts fell, vomiting fire with hundreds of sparks, as if Indra[4] was hurling them in his wrath, in order to overcome the Asuras in battle.

---

[1] T has no pronouns in this verse; C renders, "I have illumined &c., you should all rejoice etc."

[2] T read *varṣāhatā gaur iva*, evidently for *vātāhatā naur iva*.

[3] *spyad-pa*, I.O., *sbyaṅ-ba*, P; corrupt, perhaps for *spaṅ-ba* or *ḥphyaṅ-ba*.

[4] *khro-ba brgya-bas*; for *mchod-sbyin brgya-bas*, Śatakratu?

95. The winds blew violently, splintering the creepers and laden with dust, as if the peaks of the earth-bearing mountains had fallen when struck by raging tempests.[1]

96. The moon's light waned, and it shone with feeble colourless beams, like a royal goose, when it is covered with muddy water and its body is surrounded by young reeds.

97. Though the sky was cloudless and the moon was up, unholy darkness spread over the quarters, and at that moment the rivers ran with boiling water as if[2] overcome by grief.

98. Then the *śāla* trees that grew near by bent down and showered beautiful flowers, growing out of due season, on to the Buddha's body to rest on the golden column (?)[3] of His form.

99. In the sky the five-headed Nāgas stood motionless, gazing on the Sage with devotion, their eyes reddened with grief, their hoods closed and their bodies kept in restraint.

*100. In the affliction of their minds[4] they gave vent to hot sighs, but, reflecting that the world is impermanent by nature, they refrained from grief and despised it.

101. In the divine abode the virtuous assembly of king Vaiśravaṇa, which was engaged in the practice of the Law of final beatitude, did not grieve or shed[5] tears by reason of their attachment to the Law.

102. The holy (*kṛtin*) Śuddhādhivāsa deities, though they held the Great Seer in the utmost reverence, were composed and felt no agitation of mind; for they despised the nature of the world.

103. The gods, who rejoice in the good Law, the Gandharva kings, the Nāga kings and the Yakṣas, stood in the sky, mourning and absorbed in uttermost grief as if confounded (*mahākula*).

---

[1] C treats the second half of the verse as a fact, not a simile.

[2] Reading *bzhin* for *zhiṅ*.

[3] *stegs-bu*, normally equivalent to something like *aṭṭāla* or *vitarda*.

[4] Two syllables missing in *a*.

[5] Reading *chud-par* for *chuṅ-bar*, and understanding as in *Gaṇḍistotra*, 13, something like *kṣip*.

104. But the hosts of Māra, who had obtained his heart's desire, uttered loud laughs in their exultation, and showed their joy by gambols, hissing like snakes, dancing and the beating of tattoos on great drums, *mṛdaṅgas* and *paṭahas.*

105. Then on the Bull of seers passing to the Beyond, the world became like a mountain whose peak has been shattered by a thunderbolt, or a despondent elephant when his *must* has ceased, or a bull whose form is deprived of its hump.

106. From the loss of Him Who destroyed existence, the world became like the sky without the moon, or a pond whose lotuses have been withered by frost, or learning rendered futile by the absence of wealth.

CANTO XXVII

Eulogy of Nirvāṇa.

1. Then a certain mighty inhabitant of heaven, bowing his head a little from out of the palace (*vimāna*) of the . . .[1] god, looked on the Omniscient for a moment and spoke:—

2. " Alas! Since all states of being are impermanent and subject to the law of birth and the law of decay, suffering is the peculiar lot of those who are born. Thus peace comes only from the peace that leaves naught behind.

3. As water puts out fire, so the water of Time had to put out the Tathāgata's fire, whose flames are knowledge, whose smoke renown, and which has burnt up without residue the fuel of existence."

4. Then another seer, resembling the best of seers, and who, though abiding in Paradise, was not drawn to its enjoyments, gazed on the Seer, the Arhat Who had obtained tranquillity; and steadfast as the lord of mountains, he uttered these words:—

5. " There is nothing in the world that does not go to destruction, nothing too that has not gone, nothing that will not go, seeing that

---

[1] *daṅ-po stoṅ daṅ ldan-paḥi lha*, T; " thousand white palace," C.

the incomparable Master, Who had reached the highest knowledge and knew the supreme goal,[1] has gone to tranquillity.

6. The world of the living, whose eyes are inevitably blinded by delusion, is deprived of this Leader, Whose mystic wisdom was purified and Who possessed the supreme sight; and losing its senses, it abides in the evil path."

7. Then on the Sage's passing to peace Aniruddha, who was not obstructed (*viruddha*) by the world, in whom attachment (*anurodha*) was destroyed, and who had annihilated (*niruddha*) birth, saw the world to be deprived of its light,[1] and spoke thus with calmness of mind:—

8. "The wise man, who is exposed to the action of the factors (*saṃskāra*), should have no confidence at this time, when the great mountain of the Sage is struck by the fall of the thunderbolt of impermanence.

9. Alas! The world, which is without substance or self and which is subject to the law of destruction, is called the world of the living, the world in which even the unassailable Lion, the Great Sage, after destroying the elephants of the sins, Himself goes to destruction.

10. The world is ever active and involved in passion; whose hand then now will give the great security, seeing that sharing the general lot (*sādhāraṇataḥ?*) even the Tathāgata has fallen(?)[2] like a golden column?

11. The elephant, the Sage, pulled up this tree of the sins, which has six seeds, one sprout, one offering (*bali*),[3] six roots, five fruits, two boughs, three stems (?, *rāsi*) and one trunk; yet here He lies.

12. The Sage has gone to peace, after conquering all His foes like a world-monarch, without attachment like a peacock in the dry season, having completed His journey like a steed, freed from birth like fire (without fuel).

---

[1] Two syllables missing in *c*.

[2] *kun-nas chags-par-gyur*, corrupt, possibly reading *saṁsasañje* for *saṁsasāda*.

[3] "One water that is rained on it," C.

13. The Guru sent forth His teachings, like the satisfying streams which the lord of heaven, the wielder of the thunderbolt, sends forth, when his eye waxes,[1] and wandering over the earth like an ox afflicted by the glare, He pervaded the quarters with His renown; yet here He lies.

14. The Sun of men went out on His road, attended by the host of Vaiśravaṇa, the lord of wealth,[2] and full of fame and brilliancy, He streamed forth gold like a great river (*sindhu*); yet He has set.

15. To-day when the Sage has entered into peace, the world shines no more, like the quarters invested with banks (*hāra*) of fog, like the sun with its beams intercepted by masses of cloud, or like a fire without ghee, when the oblations are completed.

16. Being without crookedness (*granthi*), He took the (straight) road of truth; and being without ties (*granthi*), He obtained the Law of tranquillity. Now He has abandoned that abode of suffering known as the body, though able by His spiritual power (*ṛddhi*) to maintain its existence.

17. After overcoming ignorance as the sun dispels the darkness, after allaying passion as a shower lays the dust, the Sage has gone as . . .[3] went, never again to return to the revolving wheel of suffering.

18. He was born to destroy the suffering of birth, to Him the world resorted for the sake of tranquillity, He shone with glorious brilliancy, and He illuminated with acute (*viśiṣṭa*) intelligence.[4]

19. He sent the people towards the final good, He overspread the earth with His noble virtues, His dear shining fame waxed, and even when dwelling in the palace, He waxed in renown.[5]

---

[1] Meaning? Something like *netravṛddhau*. C apparently had an entirely different verse here.

[2] A reference to v. 85.

[3] *thub-pa skar-rgyal*, which literally would be Puṣyamuni or Tiṣyamuni.

[4] From here to verse 27, the verses are relative clauses; the relatives are omitted in the translation. The passage possibly illustrated the different uses of verbs, and is hard to understand.

[5] I do not understand the exact point of the last two lines.

20. In the extent of His learning[1] He was not downcast at blame, He spoke with pity to men who were in distress, He rejected wrong food and did not consume it, and on meeting with good food He felt no enjoyment.[2]

21. Keeping the restless senses in peace, He rightly did not abide in the objects of sense by reason of the strength of His faculties, and, obtaining the good path unobtained by others, He tasted renunciation (*naiṣkramya*?), He Who knew the tastes.

22. He gave what had never been given before ⟨by man⟩,[3] and His gifts were never prompted by desire for reward; He abandoned sovereignty with mind unmoved(?) and attracted the minds of the good with His virtues.

23. He guarded His restless eye with firmness and was accustomed to guard His mind with firm conduct. He guarded and increased the final good, and He felt no desire for any phenomenon (*dharma*) that arose.

24. He firmly abandoned evil deeds as being evil (*aśubhataḥ*?) and rid Himself of the enemies, the faults, by the highest good. He entirely extirpated the vices by His intelligence, yet He has succumbed to ignoble[4] impermanence.

25. He rightly followed the Law[5] and joyfully grasped the best resolutions; yet He, the Lord Who had the treasures of knowledge, is dead (*gatāsu*), like a fire the treasure of whose fuel (*sāra*) is consumed.

---

[1] Reading *mkhyen-zhiṅ* with P for I.O.'s *mkhyen-zhes*.

[2] The last two lines evidently contain an antithesis which I cannot solve; the verb in each is *gsol* and the meaning may be that he did not turn away from bad food or run after good food. C seems to render, "The four profits (for 'foods,' *āhāra*, here?) did not cause Him elation or the four decays grief'," but may be referring to the eight *lokadharmas*, one of which, "blame," is mentioned in the first line.

[3] Two syllables missing in *a*; supplied from C.

[4] It is doubtful if this word agrees with "impermanence"; and T may be corrupt, as C suggests something like "He, the good Physician" in its place.

[5] Two syllables missing in *a*, and I follow the lines indicated by C. T, as it stands, means, "Whom the Law rightly followed."

26. The Guru is lying here, He Who excellently subdued the group of five with regard to the eight, Who saw the three, Who brought the triple conduct to an end, Who had the triple sight, Who guarded the one, Who obtained the one, Who perpended the one, Who abandoned the seven weighty ones (*gurūṇi*?).

27. He illumined the road for the sake of quietude and graciously caused good men to believe, He cut down the ...[1] trees of the sins and delivered the faithful from the spheres of existence.

28. With the nectar of His words He fully satisfied the world, and subdued anger by His forbearance. He made the assembly of His disciples to delight in the highest good, and introduced those who sought the highest good to subtle investigations.

29. He engendered the seed of the Law in those who were good, and brought them to the Noble Path, whose essence is the cause; though He did not teach outsiders (*anārya*) by the supermundane (*lokottara*) way, He did not set them in any path other than that of the good Law.

30. In Kāśi He turned the Wheel of the Law and by His wisdom brought content to the world; He caused those who were to be converted to practise the way of the Law, and brought bliss to us for our good.

31. Others He caused to see the real truth that they had not yet seen, and He united the followers of the Law with the virtues. By refuting (*nigrah*?) the other systems and by argument He caused men to understand the meaning which is hard to grasp.

32. By teaching everything to be impermanent and without self and by denying the presence of the slightest happiness in the spheres of existence, He raised aloft the banner of His fame and overturned the lofty pillars of pride.

33. Censure never disturbed His mind, and in all matters He had no desire for worldly activities ...[2]

---

[1] *rab-tu chags-pa*, perhaps *prasakta*; possibly it does not agree with "trees.'

[2] Two lines missing; C is too brief to make the sense clear.

34. Himself crossing over, He caused the drowning to cross over too; Himself tranquillized, He brought tranquillity to those who were agitated; Himself liberated, He liberated those who were bound; Himself enlightened, He enlightened the delusion of others.

35. The Sage of sages, Who knew the right course (*nyāya*) and the wrong one, after favouring creation with right instruction, has passed away, as the Law passes away in that age of fear, when beings follow the wrong course and delight in so doing.

36. Overcoming the views[1] of the world, yet attracting the gaze of the world, He fared in His gait like a cloud full of rain, like the forest of the earth-bearing mountain, like an old man in his glory, like a young man in his brilliancy.

37. . . .,[2] He followed the path of supreme quietude, and the world, which, full of faith, saw Him obtain quietude, is to-day like a loving man without his relative (or, father).

38. Even Māra, accompanied by his hosts and raging mightily to destroy Him, was no match for the Sage; yet to-day Māra, raging mightily to destroy Him, has been able by alliance with Death (*māra*) to lay Him low.

39. All beings, for whom the dangers of the cycle of existence are still unexhausted, are assembled together with the gods and are overwhelmed with suffering; for thus they have not obtained the excellent passage beyond grief.[3]

40. Illuminating all beings He saw the world as though reflected in a mirror, and His divine hearing perceived all sounds, far and near, even up to the heavens.

41. He mounted to the starry mansions in the sky, He penetrated the earth too without obstruction, He walked on the water also without sinking and produced many transformations with His body.

---

[1] With the secondary sense of "dazzling the eyes."

[2] *dbaṅ-phyug dam-pa gaṅ-la ltuṅ-bas me reg ciṅ*, T, which is untranslateable in the context and apparently corrupt, as C has, "After destroying the heterodox views, He obtained the self-dependent (or, Īśvara) path."

[3] Perhaps a double sense, (1) they grieve, (2) they are not saved.

42. He remembered too His many births, like a traveller the various stopping-places on the road, and with His mind He understood the various mental movements of others, which are beyond the sphere of sensory perception.

43. He behaved alike to everyone and was omniscient, He cut off all the infections and completed all the task, through knowledge He abandoned all the sins and obtained the perfect knowledge (*jñānatattva*), yet here He lies.[1]

44. He converted those men whose minds were active (*paṭu*), and gradually stimulated torpid minds to activity. He made them abandon vice by understanding (*vidyā*) of the Law.[2] Who will now teach the Law for deathlessness?

45. Who will give the offering (*bali*) of the Law for the sake of tranquillity to the world, which is harassed and without hope?[3] Who, after completing his own task, will be so compassionate as to cut through the net of sin for others?

46. Who will declare the good knowledge for the tranquillity of the world, which is absorbed (*parāyaṇa*?) in the ocean of the cycle of existence? Who will declare the good knowledge for the happiness of the world, which is absorbed in ignorance (*ajñāna*)?

47. The world without Him Who knew the world is like the day-maker without his light, or a great river deprived of its current, or a king who has lost his sovereignty.

48. The world, deprived of the Best of men, exists and yet is not, like learning (*vidyā*[4]) without intelligence, like investigation without discrimination,[5] like a king without majesty, like the Law without forbearance.

---

[1] Verses 40—42 describe the five *abhijñās*, and this verse the special sixth one, the *āsravakṣayajñāna*.

[2] Reading *chos-kyi rigs-las* for *rigs-las chos-kyi*.

[3] Reading *sred* for *steṅ*, as suggested by C.

[4] C seems to have read *vaidya*.

[5] Conjectural; following the indications of C, I read *dben-pas dpyad-pa* for *bde-bas dbyaṅs-pa*.

49. The world, on losing the Blessed One, is like a chariot abandoned by the charioteer, or a boat by the steersman, or an army by the general, or a caravan by the leader, or a sick man by the physician.

50. To-day the affliction of those who desire salvation is like a cloudless sky in autumn without the moon, like the air when there is no breeze, like the suffering of those who would live (but are dying)."

51. Thus though he was an Arhat who had completed the good task, he spoke much about the evils of existence and the virtues of the Master; for he acted out of gratitude to the Guru.

52. Then those who had not put away passion shed tears, and the company of mendicants, losing their steadfastness of mind, gave way to grief; but those who had completed the cycle reflected that it is the nature of the world to pass away and did not depart from self-control.

53. Then in due course the Mallas, hearing the news, came streaming forth quickly under the stress of calamity, and, like cranes overwhelmed by the might of a hawk, cried in their affliction, " Alas! The Saviour! "

54. Because of the great darkness of their minds, when they saw the Sage lying there like the sun without its light, they wept and uttered loud lamentations in their devotion, like cattle when a lion has struck down the herd-bull.

55. Among those whose eyes were overcome by tears and who were mourning according to their faith and disposition, when the Guru of the Law passed to peace, there was a certain excellent majestic man, who delighted in the Law; he then spoke these words:—

56. " He, Who woke up the world of the living when it was asleep, now lies on His last bed. This Banner, incarnating the Law, has fallen, like Indra's banner when the feast is over.

57. The Sun of the Tathāgata, with the brilliancy of Enlightenment, the heat of energy, and the thousand rays of knowledge,

dispelled the darkness of ignorance; now at Its setting It has again brought darkness over the world.

58. Inexorably now the Eye of the world is closed, Which saw the past, the present and the future; inexorably the Embankment has been breached, Which saved us from the rolling billows of the great ocean of suffering."

59. Thus some wailed piteously there, others brooded, bowed down like chariot-horses; some uttered cries, others flung themselves on the ground. Each man behaved in accordance with his nature (*sattva*).

60. Then in due course the weeping Mallas, with arms like the trunks of mighty elephants, placed the Seer on an unused priceless bier of ivory inlaid with gold.

61. Then with ceremonial that befitted the occasion they did Him reverence with entrancing garlands of many kinds and with the most excellent perfumes, and then with affection and devotion they all took hold of the bier.

62. Then tender-bodied maidens, with tinkling anklets and copper-stained hands, held over it a priceless canopy, like a cloud white with flashes of lightning.

63. Similarly some of the men held up umbrellas with white garlands, while others waved white yaks' tails set in gold.

64. Then the Mallas, with eyes reddened like bulls, slowly bore the bier, while musical instruments (*tūrya*), pleasant to the ear, sounded in the sky like clouds in the rains.

65. Divine flowers, lotuses and every kind of bloom, fell from the sky as though shed by the trees of the garden of Citraratha(?), when shaken by the lordly elephants of the quarters.

*66. The great elephants, born of Indra's elephant, cast down lotuses with jewelled interiors and *mandārava* flowers which scattered drops of water and adhered in falling.[1]

*67. Then the Gandharva queens, whose beautiful bodies were born for the time of pleasure, removed the juice of red sandalwood

[1] Last three words doubtful; *ḥbab bcas chags-pa-rnams.*

and threw down white clothes which had been perfected without effort.

68. Holding fluttering pennons aloft and scattering all manner of garlands about,[1] they drew the bier (*śivikā*) for the sake of good fortune (*śivāya*) along the sacred (*śiva*) road to the accompaniment of music.

69. The Mallas, full of devotion, bore it along, doing obeisance hundreds of times because of the Sage's spiritual power and bewailing His decease; and so they carried it through the middle of the city.

70. Proceeding outside through the Nāga gate, they crossed the river called Hiraṇyavatī, and at the foot of the caitya known as Mukuṭa they raised a pyre ⟨corresponding to⟩[2] His fame.

71. Then they heaped on the pyre sweet-scented barks and leaves, aloewood, sandalwood and cassia (*elagaja*) and placed the Sage's body thereon, sighing with grief all the while like snakes, and with unsteady eyes.

72. Then although they applied a lighted lamp three times to it, the Great Sage's pyre would not take fire at that moment, like the sovereignty of a king of cowardly (*klība*) nature, whose never-missing bow is in disorder (*vyākula*?).[3]

73. Kāśyapa was coming along the road, meditating with purified mind, and it was by the power of his wish to see the holy remains of the dead Holy One that the fire did not burn.

74. Then at that moment the disciple came up quickly in order to see the Guru, and when he had done obeisance to the Best of sages, the fire immediately blazed up of itself.

75. The fire burnt up the skin, flesh, hair and limbs of the Sage's body, which the sins had not burnt, but, despite the quantity of ghee and fuel and despite the wind, it was unable to consume the bones.

---

[1] Two syllables missing in *b*.

[2] Two syllables missing in *d*; sense supplied conjecturally.

[3] Last clause uncertain; *bab-med ldan-pa gzhu ni rnam-par ḥkhrugs-pa-yis* (read *yi*); possibly *viklava*, "frightened despite his never-failing bow."

76. Then in due time they purified the bones of the deceased Saint (*mahātman*) with the finest water, and, placing them in golden pitchers[1] in the city of the Mallas, they chanted hymns of praise:—

77. "The jars hold the great relics, full of virtue, like the jewelled ore (*dhātu*) of a great mountain, and the relics (*dhātu*) are unharmed by fire, just as the sphere (*dhātu*) of the chief of the gods (Brahmā) in heaven (is unharmed by the fire at the end of the aeon).

78. These bones, informed (*paribhāvita*?) with universal benevolence (*maitrī*), and not liable to burning by the fire of passion, are preserved under the influence of devotion to them (or, to Him), and, even though cold, still warm our hearts.

79. The bones of Him Who overcame desire and was without peer in the world, cannot, by reason of His spiritual power, be borne even by Viṣṇu's Garuḍa; yet they are borne by us of the human race.

80. Alas! The law of the world has inexorable might, and its power has prevailed even against Him Who had power over the Law, and so these bodily remains of Him, Whose fame overspread the whole of creation, are placed in these jars.

81. His brilliancy was as the brilliancy of another sun, and He illuminated the earth therewith. His body had the hue of gold, yet the fire has left only the bones remaining.

82. The Seer shattered the vast mountains of the sins, and, when suffering came on Him, He did not lose His steadfastness; He suppressed all suffering, yet His body was consumed by the fire.

83. The Mallas are wont to cause tears to their enemies in battle, to wipe away the tears of those who take refuge with them, and to refrain from shedding tears even over a loved one, yet now they mourn,[2] shedding tears on the road."

84. Thus they lamented, despite their pride and strength of arm, and entered the city as though it were a wilderness, and after the relics had been adored by the inhabitants in the streets, they made a pavilion glorious for their worship.

---

[1] Plural; one would expect the singular.

[2] "Return," C, suggesting *bzlog* for *zlos* in T.

CANTO XXVIII

The Division of the Relics.

1. For some days they worshipped the relics in due form with excellent ceremonies; then there came for them to the town one after another (*kramena*) ambassadors from seven neighbouring kings.

2. Then at that time, after hearing them in due course, the Mallas, in their pride and by reason of their devotion to the relics, made up their minds not to surrender them, but preferred to fight instead.

3. Then on learning of their answer, the seven kings, like the seven winds, came up with great violence against the city called after Kuśa, with forces like the current of the Ganges in flood.

4. Then at the sound of the horses of those kings the townsfolk hurriedly entered the town from the jungle with terror-stricken faces . . .[1]

5. Then the kings invested the town, tethering their lordly elephants in the foremost groves, and, arrayed in the style that accorded (*anukūla*) with their lineage,[2] they acted in hostile fashion (*pratikūla*) to the excellent Mallas.

6. Then that town descended into affliction, like a woman who meets with grief, flinging up the arms of its roofs[3] and closing the eyes of its gates, with the beautiful long eyelashes of yaks' tails.

7. With the seven kings, united in intent (*ekakārya*), shining in their majesty and flashing with their impetuousness, the earth became as fearsome as the sky, when the seven planets shine together at the same time.

---

[1] I do not understand the third line, *ḥkhros-pa-las ni mgo-bo-rnams-la bzuṅ-ba bzhin* (simile or present participle); C gives no help. Literally, "as if holding their heads from anger."

[2] Uncertain. The last words *rnams-la gsos-so* are unintelligible; perhaps it should be *la-sogs-rnams-so*.

[3] Presuming *khyogs* to stand for *thog*.

8. Then the nostrils of the womenfolk even were assailed by the odour of elephants in rut, their eyes by the dust raised by the elephants' trunks, and their ears by the clamour of horses, elephants and drums.

9. Then in all directions there was fighting at the siege, with the gates half invested and surrounded by elephants and troops of horses, and with the preparation of darts and of blazing liquids in the throwing machines.[1]

10. Then the citizens abandoned[2] embarrassment out of fear and courage and collected on the ramparts, with lances, swords and arrows, glaring like hawks on their enemies.

11. Some shouted out in their excitement, so others collecting together blew conchshells. Some flung themselves about violently, similarly others brandished sharp swords.

12. Then the wives of the warriors, seeing the Mallas about to fight for victory and roaring out their names like wrestlers (*malla*), prepared at the same time their minds, medicines, and rewards (for the warriors).

13. The womenfolk of the warriors there, all trembling, bound on the armour of their sons who wished to go in the forefront of battle, and they performed magic rites for their safety (*śāntividyā?*), while their faces were despondent and their tears unrestrained.

14. Others, with downcast faces like hinds, in going to their husbands clung to the bow he wanted, and as they looked on the hero whose face was towards the battle, ⟨their steps⟩[3] were checked and they neither went forward nor stood still.

15. When the kings saw the Mallas thus arrayed and coming forth to fight, like snakes which have been confined in a jar, they made up their minds to fight.

[1] The last part is conjectural; I read *sgyogs*, any kind of machine for throwing projectiles, for *skyogs*, and, as suggested by C, *khu-ba ḥbar-ba* for *khu-ba ḥbab-pa*, and I understand *mdun-ṅu-bdar* as the same as *mduṅ-dar*.

[2] Reading *gtad-pa* for *gtaṅ-ba*; I understand *paurās tataḥ śaktiśarāsihastās trāsena śauryeṇa ca muktalajjāḥ*.

[3] Two syllables missing; meaning completed conjecturally.

16. The Brahman, Droṇa, saw the chariots, elephants, cavalry and footsoldiers all excited and fully intent on fighting, and out of his learning and lovingkindness he uttered these words:—

17. "You are able on the battlefield to overcome with your arrows the life and fury of your foes, but you cannot do so easily to those who dwell apart in forts, how much less then when your adversaries are all of one mind (*ekakārya*)?

18. Or if you conquer your enemies by investment, is it right (*dharma*) with determined minds to extirpate them and to besiege and injure the innocent townsfolk?

19. Just as when black snakes, entering a hole, meet together on the way and bite each other,[1] either there will be no complete (*ekānta*) victory from the siege, or else the besieged will obtain the victory.

20. For even men of little worth, taking fire on hearing the news of the siege in the town, will come to great worth, like a small fire heaped high with combustibles.

21. Religious men (*dharmātman*), though besieged in a town, repulsed by their austerities those who came with intent to kill them, and despite their withered arms they conquered Karandhama[2] in the city of Kuśa by the strength of religion.

22. Those kings, who acquired the whole earth, whether for fame or for obtaining territory (or, the objects of sense), had to leave it and returned to dust, as oxen, after drinking water from the pool, have to return to the pasture ground.

23. Therefore seeing rightly what religion and profit (*artha*) require, you should strive by peaceful means (*sāman*); for those who are conquered by arrows may again blaze (into enmity), but those who are conquered by peaceful means never change in feeling.

---

[1] Taking *dus-su* (*kāle*) to be a corruption for a word meaning "mutually."

[2] I cannot pick up the allusion, which may be to Karandhama's son, Avīkṣit, or his grandson, Marutta.

24. All this is not within your competence, and your forces are not[1] able to meet the enemy's forces. You should practise forbearance in accordance with the teaching of that very Śākya Sage, Whom it is your intention to honour."

25. Thus, although they were kings, did that good man instruct them with decision and tell them of the real good, with all the plainspeaking and lovingkindness of a Brahman. Then they made reply:—

26. "These words of yours are timely and wise and spoken in friendly fashion for our good;[2] learn now what is the intention of the kings, (which proceeds) from delight in the Law and reliance on their strength.[3]

27. Men as a rule undertake affairs for the sake of passion, or out of anger, or for their power, or for death;[4] but we, inspired by reverence (*sābhimāna*), have taken up our bows simply in order to do honour to the Buddha.

28. Śiśupāla and the Cedis, in taking the sacrificial gifts (*dakṣiṇā*) for the sake of pride, strove with Kṛṣṇa; why should we not risk even our lives in order to perform our adoration to Him Who abandoned pride?

29. The Vṛṣṇi-Andhakas, kings who ruled the earth, came to blows for the sake of a maiden; why should we not risk even our lives to adore Him Who overcame passion?[5]

30. The very wrathful seer, the son of Bhṛgu, took up arms to exterminate the Kṣatriyas; why should we not risk even our lives to adore Him Who overcame wrath?

---

[1] T omits a syllable in *b*, which I supply with a negative; but the sense of the line is doubtful, as one would expect, as C has it, the statement that it is not proper to fight.

[2] Two syllables missing in *b*.

[3] C seems to take this last clause to Droṇa, not to the kings.

[4] *ḥchi-ba*; should it be *ḥtshe-ba* (*hiṁs*)?

[5] According to C, a similar verse is omitted here, taking the Kurus and Pāṇḍavas as an instance.

31. The Daitya, extremely ferocious though he was, went to destruction by embracing (*parigrah*) death in the shape (*abhidhāna*) of Sītā; why should not we risk even our lives to adore Him Who abandoned all possessions (*parigraha*)?

32. Similarly Eli and Paka, with enmity increasing between them, were destroyed, . . .;[1] why should we not risk even our lives to adore Him Who was free from delusion?

33. These and many other contests that arose in the world had their origin in the faults; why should we not fight, when we are bound by devotion to the Supreme Master and it is to our advantage (*sahita*)?

34. Such then is our purpose; do you go quickly as our envoy and strive with all your might (*sarvātmanā*) that this object may be accomplished without fighting.

35. Your words, spoken in accordance with religion, have checked us, though we are ready to fight and have sharp arrows, just as spells check snakes, which drink down the poison spreading within them."

36. The Brahman accepted the kings' instructions with the words, "Thus will I do," and entered the city; in due course he saw the Mallas, and after seeing them he addressed these words to them at the proper time:—

37. "These kings of men, with bows in their hands and with shining armour glorious as the sun,[2] are at the gates of this city of yours, ready to spring like lions licking their chops.

38. Having regard to the swords set in their scabbards and to their golden-backed bows, they are not afraid of the challenge to battle, but, remembering the Sage's Law, they are afraid of trespassing against the Law.

---

[1] *rgyal-rigs bye-ba-rnams*, T, which probably is corrupt for some reference to *moha*. The allusion is not traced; C has, "Ali and Paka (or, Baka), two demons in perpetual enmity, only by reason of *moha*, widely harmed all beings," meaning possibly Alāyuddha and Baka.

[2] Two syllables wanting in *b* (*ñi-ma ji-ltar* for *ñi-ltar*?).

39. 'You should respect,' they say, 'our intention in that we have come, not for territory or wealth, nor out of pride or enmity, but because of our devotion to the Sage.

40. The Sage was Guru to you and us alike; hence this trouble. Therefore the company of brethren have assembled and come here with the sole object of adoring the relics of the Guru.

41. Miserliness about wealth is not so great a sin as miserliness in the practice of the Law. It is a sin to decide to speak in miserly fashion, and sin is indeed the enemy of the Law.

42. If your decision is against giving, then come out from the fort and wait upon your guests. Those whose strength is in their gates, not in their arrows, are not born of a Kṣatriya family.'

43. This is the message addressed to you by the lords of men, and it manifests good feeling and courage. I have also considered the matter affectionately within myself, listen then to what I am about to say.

44. Quarrelling with others makes neither for happiness nor for the Law; do not bear ill-will, but follow the way of peace. For the Sage used to preach forbearance, by which the fire of devotion will ever increase.

45. Men betake themselves to contention for one of the two, wealth or passion, but for the man who has become saintly (*ārya*) for the sake of the Law, religious peace and enmity are said to exclude each other mutually.

46. It ill accords with your principles to do hurt, while worshipping the Compassionate One,[1] Who, Himself attaining peace, with benevolent mind preached mercy to all beings.

47. Therefore by the gift of the relics share (*saṃvibhaj?*) with them fame and the body of the Law. Thereby you will be at peace with them, and they too will gain the Law and fame.

48. We, as followers of the Law, should unite to the Law, by effort even, those who have fallen away from the Law. For those who unite others with the Law cause the Law to endure.

[1] Two syllables missing in c.

49. The supreme holy Seer said that the gift of the Law is the most excellent of all gifts; anyone may give wealth, but the giver of the Law is hard to find.[1] "

50. Then, when they heard from the Brahman, who was the peer of Droṇa in knowledge, the words of the Law, which are renowned and bring pleasure, they looked at each other much abashed and said to him:—

51. "Ah! Your resolution is that of a good friend and associated with the virtues, as befits a Brahman. We are like bad horses straying down the wrong road, and you have put us on the well-worn track.

52. We should certainly do as you have said, since it is proper to accept the advice of a compassionate friend. For those who neglect the words of a friendly man afterwards fall into suffering and grieve."

53. Then the Mallas with devotion and virtue (*guṇa*)[2] divided the relics of Him Who knew the universe (*lokadhātu*) into eight parts, and then keeping one part for themselves, they handed over the remaining seven to the others, one for each of them.

54. The lords of the earth too, thus honourably treated by the Mallas, returned joyfully to their own lands, their goal attained. Then with due ceremony they set up stūpas in their cities for the relics of the Seer.

55. Then Droṇa, wishing to erect a stūpa for the Sage in his own country, took the pitcher for his share, and the people named Pisala[3] also, filled with devotion, took the ashes that were left over.

56. Then at first there were eight stūpas, like white hills, which contained the relics. The Brahman's stūpa, holding the pitcher, was the ninth, and the one which housed the ashes became the tenth.

57. The kings with their subjects and the Brahmans with their children adored on earth these various stūpas of the Sage,

---

[1] So C, involving in T the amendment of *sbyor-bar* to *sbyin-par* in *c*, and of *rnam-par bsags-pa* (*vicita*?) to *rñed-par dkaḥ-ba* in *d*.

[2] But for *yon-tan-las bgos* read *yaṅ-dag rnam bgos* (*saṃvibhaj*)?

[3] The Pippalivanika Mauryas; therefore read Pippala? C has "the men of Kuśinagara."

which had waving flags and resembled the snowy peaks of Mount Kailāsa.

58. The various lords of men paid excellent reverence to the stūpas which held the relics of the Saviour (Jina) with the chanting of hymns(?)[1] and the finest perfumes and lovely garlands and the sound of music.

59. Then in course of time the five hundred Arhats assembled in the town marked by the five mountains, and on the side of the mountain collected the Sage's sermons in order properly to establish the Law again.

60. The disciples, deciding that it was Ānanda who had heard all the sections from the Great Seer, asked the Vaideha sage with the agreement of the assembly[2] (*saṃgha*) to repeat the doctrine (*pravacana*).

61. Then he sat down in the midst of them and repeated the sermons as they had been preached by the Best of speakers, saying "Thus I heard this," and explaining the place, the reference, the time and the person addressed.

62. Thereby in union with (*anubaddha*) the Arhats he established the scriptures (*śāstra*) of the Great Sage's Law, and it is by its full acquisition with effort that men have passed, are passing and will pass beyond sorrow.

63. In course of time king Aśoka was born, who was devoted to the faith; he caused grief to proud enemies and removed the grief of people in suffering, being pleasant to look on as an *aśoka* tree, laden with blossoms and fruit.

64. The noble glory of the Maurya race, he set to work for the good of his subjects to provide the whole earth with stūpas, and so he who had been called Caṇḍāśoka became Aśoka Dharmarāja.

---

[1] *phreṅ-ba mṅon sbyar-rnams*, lit. *mālābhiyogaiḥ*; the first part is presumably corrupt, as garlands are mentioned later on in the verse. C suggests something like the translation, for which compare Pali *abhiyoga*.

[2] This seems to imply a distinction between the 500 Arhats and the Saṃgha and to attribute the authority to the latter.

65. The Maurya took the relics of the Seer from the seven stūpas in which they had been deposited, and distributed them in due course in a single day over eighty thousand majestic stūpas, which shone with the brilliancy of autumn clouds.

66. The eighth of the original stūpas, situated in Rāmapura, was guarded at that time by faithful Nāgas, and the king therefore did not obtain the relics from it; but thereby his faith in them was much increased.

67. Therefore, although the king retained the sovereignty, which is fugitive, and though he continued to abide among the enjoyments (*phala*), which are the enemies of the mind, yet, without assuming the ochre-coloured robe, he purified his mind and obtained the first fruit.

68. Thereby whoever anywhere has revered, does revere or will revere the Sage, has obtained, does obtain or will obtain the very highest fruit which is enjoyed by the good.

69. The wise know[1] the virtues of the Buddha to be such that, given equal purity of mind, the same fruit will be won either by reverencing the Seer during His worldly existence or by doing obeisance to His relics after the Parinirvāṇa.

70. Therefore one should ever pay reverence to the lofty-minded compassionate Sage, the best Object of worship, the Knower[2] of the excellent Law, which is supreme, immutable, never-failing and profitable.

71. Why should it not be right in this world for wise religious men, who know what He did, to present a thank-offering to Him Who for others' good underwent the greatest toil in His compassion and in His supreme knowledge of the dispositions of men?

72. Seeing that on earth there is no danger like that of old age and death, and in heaven like that of the fall therefrom, what good man is to be so worshipped as He Who ever recognized these two dangers of the universe?

---

[1] Or, "Know, O wise men."

[2] Reading *mkhyen-pa-po* for *mkhyen-pa-ḥo* in *a*.

73. So long as birth exists, unhappiness is produced, and there is no bliss to compare with that of freedom from new existence; what good man therefore is to be so reverenced as He Who obtained this freedom and gave it to the world?

74. Thus this poem has been composed for the good and happiness of all people in accordance with the Sage's Scriptures, out of reverence for the Bull of sages, and not to display the qualities of learning or skill in poetry.

The work of the venerable mendicant and teacher, Aśvaghoṣa of Sāketa, the son of Suvarṇākṣī, the great poet, eloquent and of universal renown.

INDEX OF PROPER NAMES

I. Sanskrit.

N.B. The colon is used to separate the references to two persons of the same name, and the letter 'n.' to denote the occurrence of the name in the footnote to the verse in question. References are given to the rarer names only of the Buddha.

Īśvara, xviii. 18–29.

Uttara(?), xxi. 16.
Udāyin, xix. 40.
Upaga, xv. 13 n.
Upatiṣya, xvii. 9, 16; xviii. 81, 86.
Upananda, xix. 39.
Upāli, xix. 40: xxi. 3.

Eli(?), xxviii. 32.

Auruvilva, xvi. 37.

Kakutthā, xxv. 53 n.
Kapila, xvii. 4: xxi. 24.
Kapilavāstu, xx. 1; xxi. 30 n.
Karandhama, xxviii. 21.
Kalmāśadamya, xxi. 27.
Kātyāyana, xxi. 21.
Kālaka, xxi. 31.
Kāśi, xv. 14; xx. 17; xxvii. 30. See under Varāṇasī.
Kāśyapa (pl.), xvi. 21, 39, 46: (Auruvilva) xvi. 23, 33, 37, 54, 55, 62, 65, 71: (Gaya) xvi. 38: (Nadī) xvi. 38: (Mahā) xvii. 24, 29; xxvii. 73.
Kuṭi, xxii. 13.
Kuṇṭhadhāna, xix. 39.
Kubera, xxiv. 48.
Kubjottarā, xxi. 33.
Kumbhīra, xxi. 31.
Kuru, xxiv. 40; xxviii. 29 n.
Kuśa, xxviii. 3: xxviii. 21.
Kuśinagara, xxv. 52, 81; xxviii. 55 n.
Kūṭadatta, xxi. 9.
Kṛmila, xix. 39.
Kṛśāśva, xx. 17.
Kṛṣṇa, xxviii. 28.
Kenya, xxi. 12.
Kośala, xviii. 1, 82, 87; xx. 5; xxi. 29.
Kailāsa, xx. 2; xxviii. 57.
Kauṇḍinya, xv. 16, 51, 53.
Kauśāmbī, xxi. 33.

Khara, xxi. 20.

Gaṅgā, xxii. 7, 10, 11; xxviii. 3. See under Bhāgīrathī.
Gandharva, xxvi. 103; xxvii. 67.
Gaya, xvi. 21, 22; xxi. 20; xxv. 70.
Gayaśīrṣa, xvi. 39.
Garuḍa, xxvii. 79.
Gardabha, xxi. 25.
Gādhin, xx. 8.
Gāndhāra, xxi. 4, 34.
Girirajas(?), xxiv. 40.
Gṛdhrakūṭa, xxi. 39.
Gautama (Buddha), xv. 17, 25; xvi. 30: (gate) xxii. 6: (ghat) xxii. 11.

Ghoṣila, xxi. 33.

Caṇḍa(?), xxi. 11.
Caṇḍāśoka, xxviii. 64.
Citraratha, xxvi. 93; xxvii. 65(?).
Cunda, xxv. 51, 52, 53.
Cedi, xxviii. 28.

Jātiśroṇi(?), xxi. 29.
Jina, xxviii. 58.
Jīvaka, xxi. 2, 6.
Jeta, xviii. 82, 83, 85.
Jetavana, xx. 2, 3, 4.
Jyeṣṭhā, xvii. 41: xxiv. 48.
Jyotiṣka, xxi. 2.

Ṭaṃkita(?), xxi. 20.
Ṭaṃkitamañca, xxi. 20 n.

Tripura, xxiii. 32.
Triśaṅku, xx. 8.

Daṇḍa, xxi. 11.
Devadatta, xix. 39; xxi. 37, 65.
Daitya, xxviii. 31.
Droṇa, xxviii. 16: xxviii. 50.
Dhruva, xvii. 41 n.

Nakula, xxi. 32.
Nanda, xix. 39: xix. 39.

Nandamātā, xxi. 8.
Naptrīputra, xxi. 28.
Nahuṣa(?), xxv. 12.
Nāga, xxvi. 99, 103; xxviii. 66: (gate) xxvii. 70.
Nāgāyana(?), xxi. 19.
Nādika, xxii. 13.
Nābhāga, xxiv. 39.
Nikumbha, xx. 17.
Nirgrantha, xxi. 28.
Nirgranthaputra, xxi. 16 n.
Nairañjanā, xxiii. 65.
Nyagrodha (grove), xix. 55: (disciple) xxi. 3.

Paka (or Baka), xxviii. 32.
Pañcaśikha, xxi. 10.
Paraśurāma, see under Bhṛgu.
Pāṭali caitya, xxii. 2.
Pāṭaliputra, xxii. 2.
Pāṇḍava, xxviii. 29 n.
Pātāla, xxiii. 32.
Pāpā, xxv. 50.
Pārāyaṇa, xxi. 7.
Pāṣāṇa, xxi. 7.
Pisala, xxviii. 55.
Puṣkara, xxi. 4.
Puṣkalasādin(?), xxi. 29.
Pūrṇabhadra, xxi. 12, 14.
Prasenajit, xx. 4.

Baka (or Paka), xxviii. 32.
Bahuputraka caitya, xvii. 25.
Bṛhaspati, xxiii. 58.
Brahman (masc.), xv. 56; xvi. 30, 52; xvii. 2, 41 n.; xix. 5; xxi. 15; xxvii. 77. See under Viriñca.
Brahmāyus, xxi. 15.

Bhagīratha, xxiv. 40.
Bhaddāli, xxi. 14 n.
Bhadra, xxi. 14: xxi. 14 n.: xxi. 17.
Bhadrajit, xv. 16.
Bhāgīrathī, xv. 14.
Bhāradvāja(?), xxi. 27.
Bhārgasa (Bhārga?), xxi. 32.
Bhṛgu, xxviii. 30.
Bheṣaka, xxi. 32.
Bhoganagara, xxv. 36.

Magadha, xvi. 48, 51, 71, 94, 95; xxii. 3.
Mathurā, xxi. 25.
Manu, xxii. 47.
Marutta, xxviii. 21 n.
Markaṭa, xxi. 16; xxiii. 63.
Malla, xxv. 50, 63, 64, 76; xxvii. 53, 60, 64, 69, 76, 83; xxviii. 2, 5, 12, 15, 36, 53, 54.
Mahānāman, xv. 16.
Mahīvatī, xxi. 24.
Māgandhika(?), xxi. 27 n.
Māndhātṛ, xix. 10; xxiv. 39.
Māra, xxiii. 64; xxvi. 104; xxvii. 38.
Mukuṭa caitya, xxvii. 70.
Meṇḍhaka, xxi. 14.
Meru, xix. 11; xx. 7, 36; xxiii. 71; xxv. 17.
Maudgala, xvii. 16.
Maurya, xxviii. 55 n., 64, 65.

Yakṣa, xv. 54, 56; xxi. 5, 11, 17, 18, 19, 20, 25, 32; xxvi. 103.
Yama, xxi. 44.
Yayāti, xxiv. 40.
Yaśas, xvi. 3.
Yaśodharā, xix. 51.

Rājagṛha, xvi. 48; xvii. 3; xxi. 41; xxii. 2.
Rāma, xxiv. 40.
Rāmapura, xxviii. 66.
Rāvaṇa, see under Daitya.
Rāṣṭrapāla, xxi. 26.
Rāhula, xix. 53.
Rūpadhātu, xvii. 35.

Licchavi, xxi. 16; xxii. 3, 18; xxiii. 1, 57; xxiv. 31, 49, 57, 64.

II. Tibetan-Sanskrit Equivalents.

N.B. Names transliterated in Tibetan are omitted, and minor errors in the xylographs have been corrected *sub silentio.*

skul-byed, Cunda.
skyes-bu-can, Māgandika (?).
kha-spu ldan-pa, Śūcīloma.
khyab-ḥjug, Viṣṇu, Kṛṣṇa.
khyu-ḥjigs (xxiii. 7), Indra (?).
mkhaḥ-ldiṅ, Garuḍa.
ḥkhyil-ba ḥdzin, Kuṇṭhadhāna.

gaṅ-ldan, Haimavata.
gaṅ-ba bzaṅ-po, Pūrṇabhadra.
Gayaḥi rtse-mo, Gayaśīrṣa.
gyad, Malla.
grags-pa, Yaśas.
grags ḥdzin-ma, Yaśodharā.
graṅs-can, Sāṃkhya.
gro-bzhin skyes, Śroṇa.
groṅ-khyer gtso, Nāgara (?).
groṅ gsum-pa, Tripura.
glaṅ-po, Vāraṇa.
glaṅ-po ldan-pa, Varaṇa.
dgaḥ-baḥi skyed-ma, Nandamātā.
dgaḥ-bo, Nanda.
dgaḥ-byed groṅ, Rāmapura.
dge-sogs, Puṣkalasādin (?).
dgra-can, Vairañjā.
mgon-med zas-sbyin, Anāthapiṇḍada.
ḥgro-mgyogs, Yayāti.
rgya-chen skyes-bu-can, Bhāradvāja (?).
rgyan-byed daṅ mtshuṅs, Alakāvatī.
rgyal poḥi khab, Rājagṛha.
rgyal-ba, Jina.
rgyal-byed, Jeta.
rgyal-byed tshal, Jetavana.
rgyun-śes, Atri.
sgur mchog, Kubjottarā.
sgra-ṅan, Kuru, Nahuṣa (?).
sgra-gcan ḥdzin, Rāhula.
brgya-byin, Vāsava.

ṅa-la nu, Māndhātṛ.
ṅan-spoṅ, Bhṛgu.
rṅo-ba, Pāṣāṇa.

cod-pan, Mukuṭa.
bcu-phyed rtse-mo, Pañcaśikha.
bcom-rlag, Mathurā.

chu-kluṅ, Nadī (Kāśyapa).
chu dbyibs, Varṣākāra.
chu srin klu, Kumbhīra.
mchog, Śreṣṭha, Uttara (?).
mchog-dbyaṅs, Ghoṣila.
ḥchar-ka, Udāyin.

ḥjigs-bcas, Sabhiya.
ḥjigs-byed, Bheṣaka.
ḥjigs-med, Abhaya.

ñe-dgaḥ-ba, Upananda.
ñe-bar ḥkhor, Upāli.
ñe-bar hoṅs (?), Upaga.
ñe-rgyal, Upatiṣya.
ñon-moṅs dul-ba, Kalmāśadamya.
mñan-yod, Śrāvastī.

ti-se, Kailāsa.
gtum-po, Caṇḍa (?), Vṛṣṇi.
gtum-po mya-ṅan med-pa, Caṇḍāśoka.
rta-ljaṅ rta, Haryaśva.
rta thul, Aśvajit.
lteṅ-rgyas, Auruvilva.
brtan-ldan, Sthāṇumatī.

thub-pa skar-rgyal (xxvii. 17), ?
ḥthob-pa, Ayodhyā.

daṅ-po stoṅ daṅ ldan-pa (xxvii. 1), ?
dus-byed, Kālaka.
don kun grub-pa, Sarvārthasiddha.
drag-po, Cedi.
drag-poḥi las-can, Khara.
dri-za, Gandharva.
dregs-pa yaṅs, Ṭaṃkita (?).
bdud, Māra.
bde-dgaḥ (xxi. 19), ?
bde-bar pha-rol ḥgro, Śūrpāraka (Supāraga).

bden-byed, Satyaka.
sdig-pa, Pāpā.
sdig-med, Nāgāyana (?).
sde-rab phams-byed, Prasenajit.

nor-ldan, Irāvatī (?).
gnas-ḥjog, Vasiṣṭha.
gnod-sbyin, Yakṣa.
rnam-rgyas, Vipula.
rnam-thos sras (or, bu), Vaiśravaṇa.
sna stod, Stavakarṇin.
sna-tshogs śiṅ-rta, Citraratha.
snron, Jyeṣṭhā.

padma, Puṣkara.
dpal sdug, Śrīghana.
dpal spas, Śrīgupta.
spoṅ-byed-pa, Vṛjji.
spos ḥdzin, Gāndhāra.
spre-ḥu, Markaṭa.

pha-rol ḥgro-ba-can, Pārāyaṇa.
phur-pa gsum-pa, Triśaṅku.
phur-bu, Bṛhaspati.
phra-mo, Suhma.

buḥi bu-mos ḥjug bu, Naptrīputra.
bu-maṅ, Bahuputraka.
bu-ram-śiṅ, Ikṣvāku.
boṅ-bu, Gardabha.
bod-riṅ, or boṅ-riṅ (xxiii. 4), ?
bya-rgod phyuṅ-po, Gṛdhrakūṭa.
byis-pa skyoṅ, Śiśupāla.
bran bzaṅ, Saudāsa.
bre-bo, Droṇa.
dbaṅ-po, Indra, Śūra.
dbaṅ-phyugs, Īśvara.
dbyigs-nor, Vasu.
dbyug-pa, Daṇḍa.
ḥbar-zhiṅ ḥjigs-paḥi las-can (xxi. 35), ?
ḥbrog gnas, Āṭavika.

ma-skyes, Aja.
ma-skyes dgra, Ajātaśatru.
ma-ḥgag-pa, Aniruddha.
mi-skyoṅ tā-la, Pātāla.
miṅ-chen, Mahānāman.
mya-ṅan med-pa, Aśoka.
dmar, Piṅgala (?).

gtsaṅ-mar lhag-par gnas-pa, Śuddhādhivāsa.
rtse-mo rgyas-pa, Sātāgra.
rtsegs sbyin, Kūṭadatta.

tshaṅs-pa, Brahman, Viriñca.
tshaṅs-paḥi tshe-ldan, Brahmāyus.
mtshams bzaṅs, Nirgrantha.
ḥtsho-byed, Jīvaka.

mdzes-dgaḥ, (Sundara) Nanda.

gzugs-kyi khams, Rūpadhātu.
gzugs-med, Arūpa.
bzaṅ rgyal, Bhadrajit.
bzaṅ-po, Bhadra.
bzaṅ sbyin, Sudatta.
bzo sbyaṅs, Śreṇya.

ḥod-ldan, Jyotiṣka.
ḥod-ma ldan-pa, Veṇumatī.
ḥod-maḥi tshal, Veṇuvana.
ḥod-maḥi tsher-ma-can, Veṇukaṇṭaka.
ḥod-zer ldan-pa, Mahīvatī.
ḥod sruṅs, Kāśyapa.

yaṅs-pa-can, Vaiśālī.
yan-lag sbyin, Aṅgada.
yul-ḥkhor skyoṅ, Rāṣṭrapāla.

rags-paḥi mdzod-ldan, Sthūlakoṣṭhaka.
raṅs-byed, Rāma.
ri-mo rdul, Girirajas (?).
rigs-med, Nakula.
rigs gtsaṅ (for gtsar?), Jātiśroṇi (Jātiśreṇi).
riṅ-min rta, Kṛśāśva.
rlaṅs-pa, Vāṣpa.

lag-pa sgra-byed, Karandhama.
lag-hoṅs, Hastaga (for Hastaka).
lug, Meṇḍhaka.
lus ṅan, Kubera.
lus ḥphags (or, ḥphags-po), Videha.
lus ḥphags thub-pa, Vaidehamuni.
legs-bzaṅ, Subhadra.
loṅ-byed, Andhaka.
loṅs-spyod groṅ, Bhoganagara.

seṅ-ge, Siṃha.
ser-skya, Kapila.
sog-ma-med, Apalāla.
sor-moḥi phreṅ-ba-can, Aṅgulimāla.
srin-po, Daitya.
gser-ldan, Hiraṇyavatī.

lha-min, Asura.
lha-min skyes-ma, Asurī (?).
lhas byin, Devadatta.
lhun-po, Meru.

amra skyoṅ-ma, Amrapālī.

ADDENDA

xxi. 31. Apparently *ḥthob-pa* here stands for *mi-thub-pa* (Ayodhyā), and C should be understood as giving corruptly the names Ayodhyā and Sāketa.

xxi. 41 ff. The representation of this scene at Amaravati (Vogel, Buddhist Art in India, Ceylon and Java, pl. 17) is evidently based on these verses.

100 YEARS

मोतीलाल बनारसीदास
सैद मिठा
बाजार
लाहौर

1903

MOTILAL B

PUBL